Macmillan
Encyclopedia of
Computers

Macmillan

Volume 2

Encyclopedia of Computers

Gary G. Bitter
Editor in Chief

Macmillan Publishing Company
New York
Maxwell Macmillan Canada
Toronto
Maxwell Macmillan International
New York · Oxford · Singapore · Sydney

Macmillan Publishing Company
A Division of Macmillan, Inc.
866 Third Avenue, New York, NY 10022

Maxwell Macmillan Canada, Inc.
1200 Eglinton Avenue East, Suite 200, Don Mills, Ontario M3C 3N1

Macmillan, Inc., is part of the Maxwell Communication Group of Companies.

Library of Congress Catalog Card Number: 91-45339

Printed in the United States of America

Printing number
   3 4 5 6 7 8 9 10

Library of Congress Cataloging-in-Publication Data

Macmillan encyclopedia of computers / Gary G. Bitter, editor in chief.
      p.   cm.
      ISBN 0-02-897045-4 (set). — ISBN 0-02-897046-2 (vol. 1). — ISBN 0-02-897047-0 (vol. 2)
      1. Computers—Encyclopedias.   I. Bitter, Gary G.
   QA76.15.M33   1992
   004'.03—dc20
                                                                91-45339
                                                                CIP

The paper used in this publication meets the minimum requirements of American National Standard for Information Sciences—Permanence of Paper for Printed Library Materials. ANSI Z39.48–1984.

(continued)

INFORMATION SYSTEMS QUALITY AND CONTROL

The accuracy and reliability of information systems processing depend on the organization's concern for and emphasis on quality. A focus on quality will influence the establishment of control standards. Various controls can be specified to achieve accurate and reliable processing of information.

QUALITY LIFE CYCLES

Quality control procedures in information systems are built around the development life cycle. The life cycle is the methodology, or process, that begins with the information systems project initiation process and continues through to production implementation of the system (see SYSTEMS DEVELOPMENT LIFE CYCLE).

The objective of the quality life cycle approach is to ensure that quality is designed into the system at every stage of development. The procedures for quality assurance in the life cycle are specified within the context of the reviews performed. An in-depth review would normally include issues such as whether time and cost budgets are being met, whether user needs are being satisfied, what problems are being encountered, and how they are being resolved.

QUALITY SYSTEMS APPROACH

Information systems quality can be achieved by a systems approach that incorporates three components: quality assurance, systems audit, and security. The responsibilities of quality assurance in the information sys-

tems area include creation of programming and systems development standards; review of systems development, programming, and documentation practices to ensure that they comply with standards; analysis of development projects for adequacy of controls; examination of data conversion procedures for adequacy; and assurance that adequate security procedures and audit trails are included in specifications and implementation of projects.

A second systems component is the information systems audit. The audit function is responsible for the independent evaluation of the effectiveness of the organization's control structure. The purpose of the structure is to prevent, detect, and correct errors.

The third systems component is the information security officer. The security function is responsible for ensuring that organizational data are protected from unauthorized access, disclosure, modification, and destruction.

CONTROL STRUCTURE

The control structure for information systems consists of general controls and application controls. General controls are pervasive and pertain to all processing performed by the system. For example, a hardware error caused by a poorly maintained computer will affect all processing performed on the system. Application controls are task specific. They pertain only to the processing performed by the programs in a specific application system. For example, failure to obtain authorization numbers on Visa or Mastercard sales by a catalog order entry application may lead to uncollectable receivables.

General Controls

General controls consist of several different categories. These include (1) organization controls, personnel practices, and standard operating procedures, (2) systems development and documentation procedures, (3) hardware and systems software controls, and (4) system security controls.

Organization controls relate to the segregation of duties within information systems and within the information systems department itself. The purpose of organization controls is to reduce the risk of error or fraud in information systems. The segregation of duties makes it more difficult for employees to make undetected errors or to make unauthorized changes in the processing of data. Sound personnel practices provide control over the quality of work by ensuring that the information systems staff are competent and honest, and they provide policies that encourage the staff to comply with management policies. Standard operating procedures identify procedures for the operation of the computer that ensure high-quality processing and limit the opportunity for errors and unauthorized use of files, programs, and reports.

Systems development and documentation controls are standard practices relating to the design, development, programming, maintenance, and documentation of application systems. They encourage the proper design of systems and increase the chances that systems will operate reliably when completed.

Hardware and systems software controls are controls provided by the manufacturer of the hardware and by the software vendor and utilized by the information system and its applications. They provide reasonable assurance that the reliability of processing will not be affected by errors resulting from equipment failure, and from system problems such as the improper handling of errors and the failure to protect files and programs from unauthorized access.

System security is the protection of computer facilities, equipment, programs, and data from destruction by environmental hazards, by equipment, software, or human error, or by computer abuse (see SECURITY, INFORMATION SYSTEMS). System security controls prevent failures in system security, detect failures in system security, and provide for recovery from failures in system security. The prevention of failures in system security is provided by limiting access to the equipment, programs, and data and by taking other steps to reduce the likelihood of security failures.

Application Controls

Application controls work together with the general controls to ensure that the control structure is satisfactory. Application controls include input controls, processing controls, and output controls.

Input Controls for Batch Processing. Input controls cover data capture, batch data preparation, and batch input for batch processing methods in which data entry is done prior to processing on batches of input data. Controls over data capture include user procedures manuals, properly designed source documents, and evidence of preparation and approval. Batch controls and reviews by the user provide assurance that data capture errors will be detected. Written and complete error correction procedures and an adequate audit trail ensure that data capture errors will be corrected.

The reliability of data preparation for batches of data is enhanced by the use of written instructions, reviews of input data, turnaround documents, and formatting. Batch controls, validation tests, and key entry verification are used to detect source or preparation errors. Common validation tests are shown in Table 1. Proper correction of data preparation errors can be ensured by the use of transmittal logs and tickets that document the flow of data from one part of the system to another. After batch preparation, the batch is input to processing. Controls over batch input focus on the detection of errors using batch controls and validation tests. Data validation tests check for inconsistent, missing, or incorrect data. Correction of errors detected during batch input must be controlled to avoid introduction of more errors. Controls include a suspense file to hold all items awaiting correction, error notices requesting correction, return of transac-

TABLE 1. Common Data Input Validation Tests

Step in Transaction Processing Cycle	Controls Objective		
	Error Prevention	Error Detection	Error Correction

Data capture	1. User procedures manual
	2. Source document design
	3. Prenumbering
	4. Forms security
	5. Separation of duties
	6. Personnel practices
	7. Identification of preparer
	8. Evidence of approval
		1. Batch controls
		  • Batch identification numbers
		  • Batch size control
		  • Control totals
		  • Control log
		  • Transmittal ticket
		2. User review
			1. Error correction procedures
			2. Audit trail
			  • Source documents
			  • Source listing
			  • Transaction identifiers

Batch data preparation	1. Written instructions
	2. Low error environment
	3. Review of input data
	4. Turnaround documents
	5. Formatting
		1. Batch controls
		  • Batch assembly control
		  • Control totals
		  • Batch header record
		  • Control log
		2. Key entry validation
		  • Classification tests
		  • Code tests
		  • Sign tests
		  • Value tests
		  • Alphanumeric condition test
		  • Field size test
		  • Limit test
		  • Check digit
		  • Balancing of control totals
		3. Key entry verification
			1. Audit trail
			  • Transmittal tickets
			  • Transmittal log
			  • Error log
			2. Reverification
			3. Control total adjustment

Batch input	1. Written procedures
	2. Field restriction on input data
		1. Batch control
		  • Review
		  • Control log
		  • Reconciliation of control totals
		2. Input validation
		  • Sequence test
		  • Anticipation control
		  • Invalid data combination test
		  • Field presence check
			1. Error correction procedures
			2. Upstream resubmission
			3. Audit trail
			  • Manual error log
			  • Error listing
			  • Validated transaction files listing
			  • Error suspense file listing

On-line entry	1. Written procedures
	2. Screen formats
	3. Computer dialogue
		1. Batch control totals
		2. Data entry validation
		  • Classification tests
		  • Code validity tests
		  • Valid character tests
		  • Valid field tests
		  • Reasonableness tests
		  • Check digit
		  • Echo check
		  • Data echo check
		  • Record confirmation check
		  • Verifying data
		  • Data approval tests
			1. Error correction procedures
			2. Audit trail
			  • Transaction identifier
			  • Transaction listings

Note: For additional information see Watne and Turney 1990, pp. 304–392.

tions to source for correction or resubmission, and an adequate audit trail of actions taken.

Input. When transactions are entered online one at a time as they are recorded, different controls are needed. On-line entry controls that prevent errors include written procedures for data entry, computer aids for the terminal operator, and general on-line access controls. Common computer aids for the terminal operator are shown in Table 2. Error detection relies on after-the-fact batch control and immediate data validation of each transaction as it is entered. The immediate validation of individual transactions is a powerful error detection device and simplifies the process of error correction. Special care must be taken, however, so the audit trail will be adequate in a terminal entry environment.

Processing and Output Controls. Processing controls that aid detection of errors during processing include reviews of processing activity output; validation tests such as file label checks and record identification tests that detect data errors, and limit and crossfooting tests that detect processing errors; and system balancing controls. The proper correction and resubmission of errors are ensured by error correction and resubmission procedures, an adequate audit trail, and processing breakpoints from which processing may be restarted.

Unauthorized individuals should not have access to output, and output should be correct and complete. Controls that prevent unauthorized access to output include output handling procedures and general terminal display controls. Controls that detect inaccurate or incomplete output, and unauthorized distributions of output, include con-

TABLE 2. Common Data Input Computer Aids

Type of Screen Controls	Description
Screen formats	Used to control the information that the operator supplies to the system. The screen format reduces errors in data entry by providing the operator with a framework within which to enter data. Formats on large systems differ from those on small systems. Large systems are often source document oriented, whereas small systems are journal oriented. Formats in a large microcomputer system usually involve the display of a document on the screen. The operator is required to enter names, addresses, part numbers, or amounts on the lines or in the spaces provided on the screen. Formats on a small microcomputer often display account titles from a journal on the screen. The operator then enters the amounts or a zero for each account shown.
Screen prompting	Closely associated with formatting. Prompting is used to control the order in which the operator supplies the information. The format may be a display of all the information needed, for example, while a blinking line, frame, or cursor will prompt the first entry of data. The first entry of data could be the name of a customer. Once the customer's name has been entered, the system will prompt the entry of the amount of the sale and then other data in proper order until all the required information has been supplied.
Screen editing	Used to control, character by character, the information submitted to the system. The user, for example, may be prompted to enter a customer name onto the format of a sales order. If only alphabetic characters are allowed, the screen editor will display an error message to the user as soon as a numeric character is entered.

trol group procedures and user department procedures. Controls that ensure proper correction and resubmission of output errors include procedures for error correction and resubmission as well as a complete audit trail.

For Further Reading

American Institute of Certified Public Accountants. 1977. *The auditor's study and evaluation of internal control in EDP systems.* New York: American Institute of Certified Public Accountants.

California CPA Society's Committee on Electronic Data Processing. 1987. *Audit implications of small business computers.* Carol Stream, Ill.: EDP Auditors Foundation, Inc.

Institute of Internal Auditors. 1984. *Quality assurance review manual for internal auditing.* Altamonte Springs, Fla.: Institute of Internal Auditors.

Institute of Internal Auditors. 1988. *Management and control of end-user computing.* Altamonte Springs, Fla.: Institute of Internal Auditors.

Watne, D. A., and P. B. B. Turney. 1990. *Auditing EDP systems.* 2nd ed. Englewood Cliffs, N.J.: Prentice-Hall.

Weber, R. 1986. *EDP auditing: Conceptual foundations and practice.* 2nd ed. New York: McGraw-Hill.

Donald A. Watne

INFORMATION THEORY AND CODING

Communication systems are designed to convey information-bearing signals from a source to a destination over a communication channel. During transmission, signals are distorted by noise and other channel disturbances that limit the communication system performance. The receiver attempts to recover the transmitted information from the received distorted signal. The goal of any communication system is to transmit information as accurately as possible.

Shannon, in 1948, presented a mathematical theory for the communication process. This theory is known as information theory. It attempts to address a number of basic issues regarding the design of information processing and transmission systems. Information theory was a remarkable breakthrough in that it provided a quantitative representation for a rather vague and qualitative notion of the amount of information contained in a message. Shannon suggested that the amount of information conveyed by the occurrence of an event is related to its uncertainty and was defined to be inversely related to the probability of occurrence of that event. Information theory also provides fundamental limits on the transmission of information, on the extraction of information from the environment, and on the representation of information. These fundamental limits are employed as benchmarks and are used to evaluate the performance of practical systems by determining how closely these systems approach the fundamental limits.

In his celebrated work, Shannon laid the foundation for the design and analysis of modern communication systems. He proved that nearly error-free information transmission over a noisy communication link is possible by encoding signals prior to transmission over the link and by decoding the received signals. He only provided an existence proof stating that such procedures exist but did not specify the approach to design the best encoders and decoders. Also, he did not discuss the implementation complexity. These results have provided the impetus for researchers to try to design encoding and decoding procedures that approach the fundamental limits given by information theory.

A communication system can be represented as in Figure 1. The data from the source are processed by the source encoder, which represents the source data in an efficient manner. The sequence of source code words generated by the source encoder is fed to the channel encoder, which yields the sequence of channel code words. The channel encoder adds redundancy to each source code word to provide error-control capabilities. In some channel encoding schemes, the input data stream is divided into blocks of

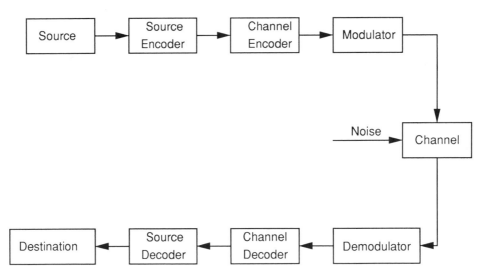

FIGURE 1. Block diagram of a communication system.

fixed length and then some additional symbols are added to each block to yield channel code words. These codes are known as block codes. In the class of codes known as tree codes, the encoding process exhibits memory in that a block of input data stream is encoded based on the past blocks also. In either case, the output of the channel encoder is a string of symbols to be transmitted. The modulator converts source code word symbols to analog waveforms suitable for transmission over the channel. The received waveforms are distorted because of noise and other interference processes present over the channel. The demodulator converts the received waveform into symbols and then furnishes received words to the channel decoder. Because of channel noise, the received word may be in error. The channel decoder exploits the redundancy introduced at the channel encoder to detect and/or correct errors in the received word. This corrected word is the best estimate of the source code word that is delivered to the destination.

Research efforts have led to the development of many efficient source and channel encoding/decoding schemes. The objective in the source encoding operation is to represent the source output in a compact form with as high fidelity as possible, that is, with as little information loss as possible. In channel encoding, redundancy is introduced to attain error correction and detection capabil-

ities. The goal is to exploit the redundancy in the most effective manner, that is, to achieve a high degree of error-control capability for a specified amount of redundancy. The error-control capability of a code is given in terms of the number of symbol errors that can be corrected or detected. The encoding and decoding operations are to be implemented with a reasonable amount of computational complexity. These systems have become increasingly important as a result of the continued growth in the volume of data handling and transmission requirements. Principles of information theory and coding have been applied in many diverse fields. One noteworthy application is in the area of cryptography and data security where information theory and coding were used as the basis for the development of the field.

For a more in-depth discussion, see COD-ING THEORY.

Reference

Shannon, C. E. 1948. A mathematical theory of communication. Parts 1, 2. *Bell System Technical Journal* 27:379–423, 623–56.

For Further Reading

Blahut, R. E. 1983. *Theory and practice of error control codes.* Reading, Mass.: Addison-Wesley.

———. 1987. *Principles and practice of information theory.* Reading, Mass.: Addison-Wesley.

Gallagher, R. G. 1968. *Information theory and reliable communication.* New York: Wiley.

Hamming, R. W. 1980. *Coding and information theory.* Englewood Cliffs, N.J.: Prentice-Hall.

IEEE Transactions on Information Theory. Journal publishing recent results in the areas of information theory and coding.

Imai, H. 1990. *Essentials of error control coding techniques.* San Diego, Calif.: Academic.

Konheim, A. G. 1981. *Cryptography: A primer.* New York: Wiley.

Lin, S., and D. J. Costello, Jr. 1983. *Error control coding: Fundamentals and applications.* Englewood Cliffs, N.J.: Prentice-Hall.

McEliece, R. J. 1977. *The theory of information theory and coding.* Reading, Mass.: Addison-Wesley.

Rao, T. R. N. 1989. *Error control coding for computer systems.* Englewood Cliffs, N.J.: Prentice-Hall.

Pramod K. Varshney

INSURANCE, COMPUTER USE IN

A basic knowledge of insurance is the first step in understanding how computers are used in insurance companies. Insurance provides protection against an unexpected financial loss. Insurance can be bought for protection against almost any kind of financial loss. However, the most common examples of financial loss are the death of a primary wage earner, property damage, unexpected medical bills, and disability.

Insurance companies provide financial protection in return for payments they receive. These payments, called premiums, are invested until a loss occurs and a claim is filed. Money to pay claims comes from investment and premium income. The insurance company is profitable if it receives more in premiums and earns more in investments than it pays in claims and expenses.

The industry is changing as a result of computers. New products offer flexibility that can meet the changing needs of the policyholder with the help of computers. Products that were once too complex to design, sell, and service are now possible. Actuaries, specially trained professionals who forecast claims and expenses and then set premiums, use complex mathematical formulas for pricing insurance products. Computers help actuaries do their job faster and more accurately.

INSURANCE ADMINISTRATION

For efficiency, insurance company administration is typically done at a central site. Centralizing data lends itself well to large database management systems, and this helps to provide quality service to customers.

To issue an insurance policy, the insurance company must receive a signed "application for insurance" and the initial payment. Both of these are sent to a central processing center. Computer entries are made to start the process of underwriting and issuing a policy. Data are captured from the application as an initial screening looks for obvious errors on the application.

Application data are stored in a centralized database management system. The computer system that stores the initial application data also creates a record for tracking an application through the application process. If further information is needed, the system requests it. A life insurance application, for example, may need additional medical information. This is electronically requested from the national Medical Information Bureau (MIB). The response from the MIB is also electronic. If further information is needed from the applicant, a letter requesting it is automatically generated.

After the record is created and all requests for further information are completed, an underwriter becomes involved. Underwriters examine the potential risk of providing insurance. Using established underwriting rules, the underwriter decides either to provide insurance or to refuse the insurance

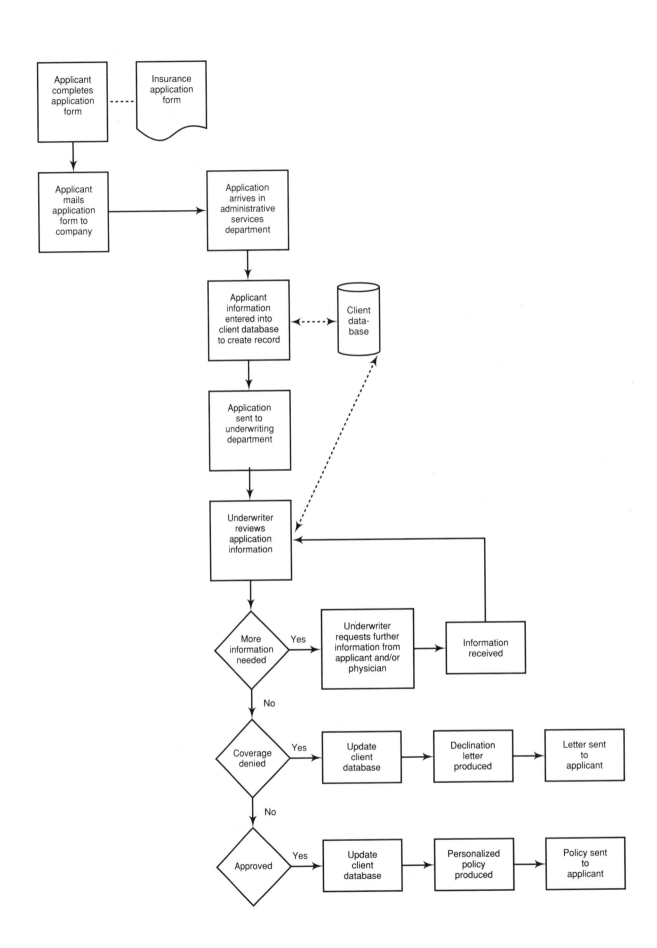

coverage requested. The underwriting process can benefit from the use of an "expert system." For simple cases, an "expert system" can imitate the underwriting process and recommend approval for applications that meet the underwriting rules. This allows the underwriters to handle more complex and challenging cases.

After the application has been approved, a policy is issued. Issuing the insurance policy is now streamlined because all of the necessary information is in the computer, which prints a policy that confirms the coverage and legally defines the insurance company's obligations.

The administration functions don't end once a policy has been sold and issued. Service to the policyowner continues as long as the policy is in force. Changes to names, addresses, and benefits have to be recorded. Premium billing and payments also must be accurately accounted. All of these administrative and accounting services are performed more efficiently with computer systems.

When a loss does occur, a claim is submitted by the customer. Payment of the claim occurs after proof of a covered loss has been verified. Computer systems aid the claim process by allowing a claims processor to view the needed policy coverages on-line. Without computers helping this process, additional costs would be incurred, along with delays in the claim payment.

MARKETING

Competition creates a fast-paced marketing environment for the insurance industry. Insurance products are continually evolving responses to changes in the marketplace. To stay ahead of the competition, knowledge of the marketplace is essential. Computer-based market research tools help a company to identify new marketing opportunities. These tools assist in defining new products and identify the type of person most likely to buy a product. By analyzing the market before creating a product, insurance companies avoid unnecessary research and development costs and improve future marketing performance. Surveys used to get information about a market are studied with the help of computers.

Computers also play a role in presenting and selling insurance to the customer. Agents, direct mail, and telephone marketing are just a few of the ways insurance is sold. All use computers to enhance the sales process. Computer use has paved the way for innovative sales techniques that result in increased sales performance.

In the past, for example, direct mailings were made with limited knowledge about target households and often resulted in very few responses. Computer systems can combine U.S. Census Bureau data, along with information from other sources, to classify households. With these new data, products can be matched with the households most likely to buy, saving mailing costs and improving the likelihood of a sale.

Marketing insurance is changing in other ways, too. Today, insurance sales are often linked to the sale of another product. Financing for a house, for example, cannot be completed without homeowner's insurance. As a result, lending companies often set up affiliated agencies to offer this insurance when the loan application is completed. Because most of the information needed for an insurance application is on the loan application, the insurance agency can electronically share the loan application data. Service to the home buyer is better, the expense of providing insurance is lower, and additional income for the lending company is higher, all as a result of computer technology.

INSURANCE AGENTS

The insurance agents who sell and service insurance typically work for an agency that

FIGURE 1 (facing page). Flowchart illustrating the steps that an insurance policy goes through. The shaded boxes indicate functions that rely on a centralized computer system. The computer system generates correspondence requesting additional information or providing information to the client, as well as the personalized insurance policy itself. Expert systems and image processing will make it possible to automate even more of the steps required to underwrite an insurance policy.

represents one or more insurance companies. Providing helpful computer systems is one way to improve the agent's performance and also will benefit the company by producing more sales.

With computers, the agents can provide the quality service that will keep good customers. Much of the information the agent needs to know is maintained in a centralized computer system. This information can be electronically retrieved by the agent's computer, where automatic functions help agents maintain, market, and service their accounts. Computers can even suggest specific insurance for specific customers.

Today's insurance products can be very complex. One way to simplify and help sell these complex products is with computer programs. Computer graphics help present complex financial information to customers in an easy-to-understand format. This not only helps the agent, it also aids the customer in deciding if a proposal meets his or her needs.

Along with the briefcase, a laptop computer is becoming a standard business aid for many agents. It can help illustrate various options that may be important to the customer and can make presentations more effective, and customer information can be readily available to agents wherever they are.

Computer technology also keeps agencies informed with electronic mail, voice mail, and the data from a central computer.

For Further Reading

DeBow, Y., and P. Meade. 1991. Technology priorities for the 1990s. *Insurance & Technology,* Feb., pp. 17–24.

Dock, V. T., and J. C. Weatherbe. 1988. *Computer information systems for business.* St. Paul, Minn.: West.

Konsynski, B. R., and F. W. McFarlan. 1990. Information partnerships—shared data, shared scale. *Harvard Business Review* 68(5): 114–20.

McLeod, R., Jr. 1985. *Information management in insurance companies.* Chicago: Science Research Associates.

QED Information Sciences. 1989. *Information systems planning for competitive advantage.* Wellesley, Mass.: QED Information Sciences.

Rook, F. W. 1991. Increasing role of expert systems in insurance industry. *RESOURCE* (Life Office Management Assoc., Atlanta, Ga.), March, pp. 28–33.

Conrad Rossow

INTERACTIVE COMPUTER SYSTEMS

The computer is an electronic machine that takes in and processes data in some way to arrive at information (Bitter 1984). Information is data that are made meaningful. Data are the raw facts, figures, or statistics. A computer, or more accurately termed *computer system,* interprets and executes commands for input, output, computation, and logic operations (comparisons) of data. A computer system is made up of four fundamental components—input, processing, output, and storage/memory (Simkin 1990, Long 1988, Bitter 1984).

Interactive is a term often used in combination with computer systems or other technology systems. When applying the term *interactive* to the term *computer systems,* we are looking at how the user and the computer system exchange data and information back and forth. Today's interactive computer systems allow the user to work directly with the machine without the need of a middle person (a computer professional) (Long 1988). This capability of direct interaction by user did not exist with the earlier machines.

TYPES OF INTERACTIVE COMPUTER SYSTEMS

There are three main types of interactive computer system in today's world. The first is the microcomputer, which is the smallest and least expensive. Next in size is the minicomputer. The third type of computer system, the mainframe, is the largest. Mainframes also have a subcategory, supercomputers, which operate with tremendous power and speed.

Microcomputer systems Microcomputers are sometimes called personal or home computers and can be used as standalone machines (Long 1988, Simkin 1990, Bitter 1984, Lockard et al. 1990). Their memory capacity as well as their storage capacity is rather small in comparison to the larger systems (typically measured in thousands of memory locations up to megabytes). Processing power is also modest when compared with minicomputers or mainframe computers.

Minicomputer systems Minicomputers have most of the operational capabilities of mainframe computers, but they perform their tasks more slowly and are also less costly than mainframes (Long 1988, Simkin 1990, Bitter 1984). As they are multiuser systems, several people can use the computer system at the same time. Several individual workstations can be connected through cables to the larger system at one time. These workstations can be "dummy" terminals (no standalone processing capabilities) or "intelligent" computer systems (microcomputers).

Mainframe computer systems Mainframe computers perform operations that allow for more input, output, and storage than the other two computer systems (Long 1988, Simkin 1990, Bitter 1984). They are known for having greater speed, more powerful processing capabilities, larger primary memory capacity (measured in millions of memory locations), and more external storage than the other two types. In addition, they can serve as a host computer to thousands of computer terminals at one time and at different locations.

Supercomputer systems Supercomputers, sometimes considered a subset of the mainframe computer system, are the most advanced. Only a few supercomputers are in operation today because few organizations can afford or need the advanced capabilities of processing and execution of program instructions. These computers have huge memories (measured in billions of memory locations) and prices can often exceed $10 million (Simkin 1990, Long 1988, Bitter 1984).

COMPONENTS OF THE INTERACTIVE COMPUTER SYSTEM

When we think of computers, we often visualize a single piece of physical equipment (hardware); however, in reality, a computer is a system of interconnected components that interact with each other (Lockard et al. 1990, Long 1988, Bitter 1984, Simkin 1990). The primary components of any computer system are the central processing unit, memory, input devices, output devices, and external storage (see Figure 1).

Central processing unit The main piece of hardware for a microcomputer system is the central processing unit (CPU). It is sometimes called the "brain" of the system because it is where most of the data processing tasks are performed. The CPU is made of two parts, the control unit and the arithmetic/logic unit.

The *control unit* acts as a monitor for the computer itself in that it makes sure that all the components work together. Many computer experts liken the control unit to a police officer because it directs the data flow from one part of the computer to another. In addition, it regulates and synchronizes the operations of all parts of the system so that these components work together as an integrated unit. The *arithmetic/logic unit* (ALU) performs all the arithmetic and logical functions. The ALU receives all data and instructions from the control unit and performs the necessary mathematical calculations and logical operations. These decision-making capabilities of the computer are quite simple in nature. Only basic arithmetic operations (adding, subtracting, multiplying, and dividing) and the logic operations (equal, greater than, and less than comparisons) are performed on all data, numerical or otherwise.

The larger computer systems, such as mainframes, have special-function processors to help improve efficiency of the entire system; these include a host processor, a front-end processor, and perhaps a back-end processor (Long 1988).

Memory Memory is an internal component of the system in which information can be

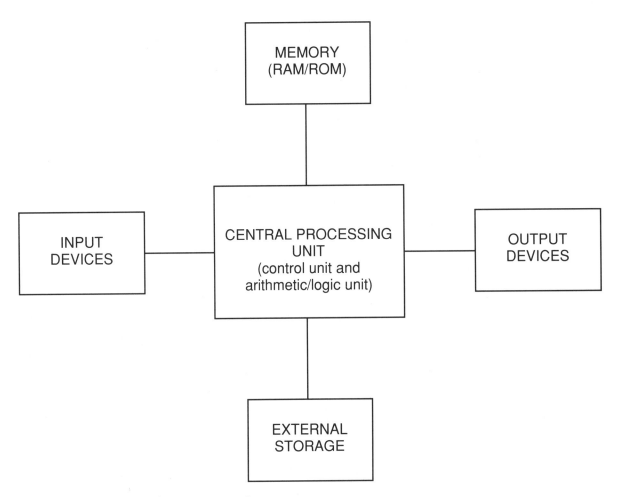

FIGURE 1. Components of a computer system.

stored, accessed, and routed through the system. The two types of memory within a microcomputer are random-access memory and read-only memory. *Random–access memory* (RAM) is a series of chips that can store, change, and retrieve information provided by the user. Information in RAM can be erased by the user when it is no longer needed. This type of memory is temporary, or volatile, in that any data in RAM will be lost when the computer system is turned off. An analogy often associated with RAM is post office boxes into which one can place items for storage until retrieval. The capacity (memory space) of RAM determines the amount of data it can accept and retain. *Read–only memory* (ROM) is the second type of internal memory in a microcomputer. This type contains information necessary for the system to run properly; this information is programmed by the computer manufacturer at the time the computer is built. Read-only memory is permanent and cannot be erased or lost when the computer is off.

Differences in memory among the types of computer have to do with capacity. Microcomputers have the smallest amount available typically measured in thousands of bytes, whereas mainframes measure memory capacity in terms of billions of units.

Besides the information held in internal memory, computers can use information that has been stored by means of external storage devices. Diskettes and disk drives are in this category. *Diskettes*, or floppy disks, generally come in two formats: a 5¼-inch flexible disk and a 3½-inch diskette in a hard plastic case. Both are used to store information such as programs and data for later use. Diskettes can also be erased and reused. *Disk drives*, in combination with the diskette, allow for data to be read and written at very high speeds, which allows for fast access to large amounts of information. Most microcomputer systems require floppy disk drives. A second type of drive is the hard disk drive, which is permanently mounted in the computer and can store a large quantity of data that can be accessed at very high speeds.

Magnetic drives serve as external storage components for the larger systems. Minicomputers, as well as mainframes, typically have more than one magnetic disk drive and/or magnetic tape drive to store vast quantities of data.

Input devices For the CPU to perform a variety of functions and tasks, information needs to be provided. The user may enter information or data into the system through a variety of input devices. All systems include one primary input device, a keyboard. The *keyboard* resembles a typewriter, and sometimes has an additional set of calculatorlike numeric keys or a set of special-purpose keys (function keys). It is the most common method for entering data into a computer system; however, other secondary input devices, such as light pen, mouse, and touch screen (to be discussed later), are also available for most systems.

Output devices Once the computer performs the task, the results need to be displayed back to the user. Information from the CPU is converted back into an understandable form through the output devices. The primary output devices for most computers are the video monitors and printers. The *monitor*, a high-quality television set that displays data on a screen, is the most common way of receiving information from a computer system. It is often referred to as a screen, CRT (cathode-ray tube), or tube. Monitors vary in terms of resolution (clarity of the text or graphics), color (monochromatic or color), and size (5- to 25-inch screens). The materials displayed on the screen of the monitor are sometimes referred to as a soft copy. *Printers* provide a hard copy (or paper copy) of the data and are also typically added as a peripheral (add-on device) to a computer system. Printers differ greatly in terms of speed, print quality, and method of printing (dot matrix or letter quality).

INTERACTIVE PERIPHERALS

In addition to the most common types of input and output devices, modern computers have other peripherals that allow the user to interact with the computer in a variety of ways. These peripherals may be used to enter data as well as to display results of the computer operations.

Currently on the market are such peripherals as the light pen, the touch screen, and the mouse, which allow for the input of data in a unique manner (Lockard et al. 1990, Long 1988, Bitter 1984, Simkin 1990). A *light pen* looks something like a ballpoint pen attached to the computer by a cable, or cord. With a light pen, the user is able to select from choices displayed on the screen simply by touching the item. A *touch screen* is much like the light pen, only easier to use. A touch screen allows the user simply to touch the monitor screen with a finger to select from choices displayed on the screen. A *mouse* is a hand-sized device that the user moves across a flat surface to indicate certain meaningful sections of the monitor screen. The mouse allows the user to input data and make selections from screen menus simply by pointing and clicking the mouse on the specified item on the screen. *Optical scanners* provide a way to write certain data into the computer. Scanner technology uses a light beam that is bounced off an image; then the reflected light is measured to determine the value of the image. Scanners can recognize printed characters, graphics, and various types of codes. *Voice recognition*, or voice data entry, can be used to enter limited kinds and quantities of data at present. In the future, more applications of voice data entry will be available as this technology evolves.

In addition to monitors and printers, such output devices as plotters, voice synthesizers, and voice recognition units can be used to obtain information or data from the computer (Lockard et al. 1990, Long 1988, Bitter 1984, Simkin 1990). A *plotter* is a device that converts computer-generated graphs, charts, and line drawings to high-precision hard-copy format. *Voice synthesizers*, or speech synthesizers, convert raw data to produce speech electronically. At present, only limited vocal inflections and phrasing are used. Yet in spite of this limitation, the number of uses is growing from words in a child's word recognition lesson to the "simple" installations in automobiles that warn "a door is ajar." *Voice response units* use recordings of the human voice and other sounds that are then changed into output. Telephone companies are big users of this technology in their recorded messages to customers; however, such recordings are also used in educational applications and in helping the visually impaired.

HISTORY OF INTERACTION AND COMPUTER SYSTEMS

Although we think of today's computers systems in terms of being interactive and powerful, these capabilities did not always exist. In the early days, the capacity of the computer was quite limited as was the capability of the machine to interact directly with the user. The following historical review outlines the increased capabilities of the computer as it evolved and the progression toward direct user interaction.

TABLE 1. Computer Generations

	Characteristics	Examples
First generation (1940s–1950s)	Vacuum tubes were introduced. Computers were large, slow, and expensive, and required computer operators to process data. Use of binary systems began and information was stored on magnetic tape. Computers were to operate.	Mark I Colossus Mark II ENIAC EDVAC EDSAC UNIVAC
Second generation (1959–1964)	Transistors were introduced. Computers became much smaller, required less power, and were more reliable. Speed was limited. Programming languages such as assembly languages and FORTRAN increased the number of computer users.	IBM 1401 (business) IBM 1620 (science)
Third generation (1964–1971)	Integrated circuits were introduced. Computers became faster, data storage and reliability increased, and cost was reduced. Use of peripherals greatly increased. Compatibility problems were almost eliminated. The developed programming languages were widely used. Worldwide use of computers occurred. Multiple users were able to access the same computer at the same time.	IBM 360
Fourth generation (mid-1970s to present)	The microprocessor is the processing component of the small, inexpensive, but powerful microcomputer. The terminal allows the user to work directly with the computer system in real time. The interactive computer system eliminates the need for keypunch machines and punched cards. Minicomputers and mainframes were built in the early 1980s for large database systems.	Apple (education) IBM 3081 IBM XT IBM AT Cray-1 CYBER 205
Fifth generation (present to future)	Memory chips that can store millions of characters of data and parallel data processing characterize this generation. The capability of processing millions of instructions simultaneously will allow many microproccessors to work together in a coordinated manner. Other technologies will tend to merge with the interactive computer systems.	Expert system Neural network

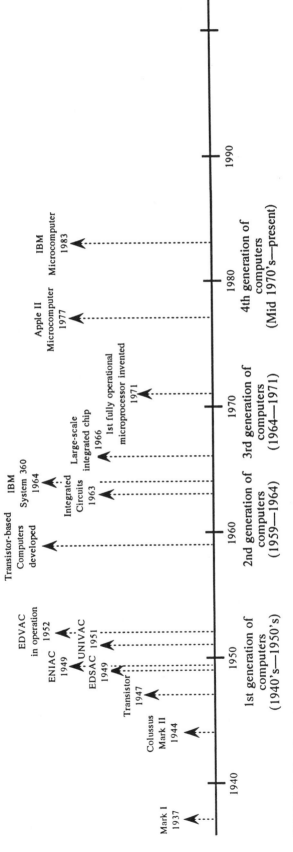

FIGURE 2. Timeline of computer generations.

The Early Electronic Computer Age

The first generation of computers was born with the use of vacuum tubes. Vacuum tubes allowed electrical current to flow through an empty space (a vacuum) in a glass tube. Vacuum tubes controlled the electrical current that indicated numerical values in the computer's memory. All of the computers during this era of vacuum tubes required manipulations by a computer operator with very little interaction between the machine and the end user of the information (those people who requested the data be analyzed).

Howard Aiken began developing the Mark I, an automated calculating machine in 1937. The Mark I stood 8 ft tall and 51 ft long and was made up of 500 miles of electric wire. Actually it was a combination of mechanical and electronic circuits. A computer professional operated the computer by turning 3,000 switches on and off. The Mark I also used paper tape with coded instructions (Bitter 1984). Because of the mechanical linkages, the Mark I was slow. To improve the speed of processing, developers had to discover a way to replace mechanical parts with electrical ones.

The Colossus Mark II was completed around 1944. Colossus Mark II had 2,500 vacuum tubes, but contained electrical parts rather than mechanical linkages. It was used to decipher supposedly secure German codes during World War II; however, not much more is known about the Colossus because it remains protected by British government secrecy regulations (Alessi and Trollip 1985). According to Lovington (as cited in Hofmeister 1984), it supposedly had all of the components of a modern computer except for internal program storage capability. These computers were designed to solve linear equations. Punched cards were the means by which data were input by a computer professional.

Following the Mark I, the first actual computer with no moving parts was an American computer, ENIAC (Electronic Numerical Integrator and Computer), developed by John MAUCHLY and J. Presper ECKERT based on the ideas of John Atanasoff. ENIAC was developed for calculating firing tables for new weapons for the military; however, it

was not used for its original purpose because it was completed after World War II (Alessi and Trollip 1985). ENIAC was programmed by means of electrical switches and connections. The system consumed large amounts of electricity through its 20,000 vacuum tubes and, thus, generated a lot of heat. It performed up to 5,000 additions in 1 second, which was 1,000 times faster than the Mark I (Bitter 1984). A computer professional was required to manage the flow of data through the system. ENIAC was difficult to program because it required the operator to physically rewire parts of the computer to change a program or sequence of tasks (Hofmeister 1984). In spite of its limitations, ENIAC was used at the Aberdeen Proving Grounds for many years.

John VON NEUMANN served as a consultant on the ENIAC and EDVAC (Electronic Discrete Variable Automatic Computer) projects. According to his theory, a computer should have three parts: (1) an arithmetic part for calculations, (2) a control part for regulating the machine functions, and (3) a memory for storing information for later use. Operationalized in 1952, EDVAC was such a computer—capable of storing instructions, eliminating the need for human intervention and reducing operation time (Bitter 1984).

EDSAC (Electronic Delayed Storage Automatic Computer) was the first stored-program computer built in England. It was built in 1949 about the same time that EDVAC was being built by Mauchly and Eckert. Stored-program computers contained sets of instructions in their memories (Alessi and Trollip 1985). Von Neumann's major contribution to these machines was that of converting all decimal numbers into the binary number system of ones and zeros, each representing ons and offs. Binary systems reduced all computations to simple on–off switches within the programs. These stored programs were used to direct the step-by-step operations of the computer on command from an operator. The use of binary numbers improved the reliability of transferring information, and internal storage was much faster than paper-tape storage. EDSAC also used plug-in boards, which made changing programs more practical; the cost to the end user was reduced because of efficient program handling (Bitter 1984, Hofmeister 1984, Long 1988).

In 1951, UNIVAC I, developed by Eckert and Mauchly, became the first commercially available stored-program computer to be produced in quantity for business uses. Prior to that time, most computers were used by governments. Although programs were generally stored on punched paper cards, UNIVAC computers began storing information on magnetic tape in 1957. UNIVAC was capable of performing 1,000 instructions per second and had a memory capacity of about 16,000 characters of data (approximately four typed pages) (Alessi and Trollip 1985, Bitter 1984, Long 1988).

In the 1940s and early 1950s, the work of such people as Mauchly, Eckert, and von Neumann, among others, resulted in the first true computer systems. Data could now be processed faster by machine than by hand.

During this early period, each new advancement in technology made computers easier to operate, faster at data processing, and smaller in size; however, they remained temperamental and expensive to maintain and still required computer operators rather than the end users to process the data (Bitter 1984, Hofmeister 1984).

Second Generation of Computers

Second-generation computers evolved between 1959 and 1964, when the transistor replaced the vacuum tube. The transistor, developed in 1947 by John Bardeen and others at Bell Laboratories, is a semiconductor that regulates the flow of electricity like the vacuum tube. Electricity flowed in less space (200 transistors could fit into the space occupied by one vacuum tube) (Bitter 1984) and with less energy demands. Even though computers required less power and size was reduced, they remained expensive to develop. Each transistor had to be individually inserted into the holes in a plastic board and wires had to be fastened with solder. The speed of internal operations was limited by the physical distance between transistors.

During this era, IBM dominated the computer market, producing the IBM 1401, which was a business-oriented computer, and the IBM 1620, which was a science-oriented computer.

The second generation also saw advances in the development of new programming languages. Programming languages, such as assembly languages and FORTRAN, made communication and interaction between the computer professional and the system easier than before. These languages were closer to English. For first-generation computers, all programs had been written in machine language, which comprised the binary system of ones and zeros. Although the computer could understand the machine, it was not easily understood by humans. The new, high-level programming languages also allowed more people to become programmers and increased the numbers of people using computers (Alessi and Trollip 1985, Bitter 1984).

The batch system, in which the program and data are submitted to the computer and the results are then inserted as required by the program, was still being used, however. This mode of processing, one in which a program runs without interaction between user and computer, would exist until the invention of the microcomputer (Bitter 1984).

Because of transistors, computers became physically smaller, power requirements were reduced, and science- and business-oriented computers were more reliable. Punched cards were read at a reasonably fast pace, which allowed quality reports to be produced; however, computers were to take another evolutionary step with the development of integrated circuits.

Third Generation of Computers

The third generation of computers (from 1964 to 1971) was born with the development of integrated circuits in 1963. Long (1988) considers April 7, 1964, one of the single most important days in the history of computers. On that date, IBM announced their System 360 line of computers with integrated circuits. The integrated circuits allowed computer systems to operate more rapidly and to process and store more data than second-generation computers. The use of peripherals, such as magnetic tape and disk drives, grew markedly (Bitter 1984, Alessi and Trollip 1985). The third-generation computers of IBM, Honeywell, Control Data Corporation, Burroughs, General Electric, and others made the previous generation of computers obsolete.

The compatibility problems of second-generation computer systems were almost eliminated with these new machines. One major factor was the upward compatibility. For instance, a company that purchased a small computer (minicomputer) would be able to upgrade to more powerful machines without having to redesign the existing information systems. Digital Equipment Corporation and Data General Corporation became sales leaders in the minicomputer industry because the demand for small computers in business and science was so great (Long 1988). The programming language developed in the second generation continued to be widely used.

Because of their reliability and reduced cost, computers were beginning to be used worldwide for data processing. Computers were no longer single-purpose systems; they could be used for both science and business purposes (Bitter 1984, Alessi and Trollip 1985). Multiprogramming, in which more than one program is run concurrently in the computer, was now a possibility because of the speed of these machines (Long 1988, Simkin 1990).

The speed of the systems also enabled multiple users to access the same computer at approximately the same time. Time sharing made the computer available to users one at a time; but because the elapsed time between contacts is so minute, each person entering data was unaware of the gap.

Fourth Generation of Computers

The fourth generation evolved with large-scale integration during the mid-1970s. A large-scale integrated (LSI) chip is a microelectronic "system" that can perform a complete job, as opposed to an integrated circuit chip, which can perform only one function.

Several early LSIs to reach the marketplace during this time were the pocket calculator, the digital watch, and the video game. Each employed an LSI chip that contained several thousand transistors on a single chip. With these LSIs, use of computer systems became more commonplace. Not far behind was the microprocessor.

The microprocessor, sometimes called a "computer on a chip," contains nearly all of the subsystems of a computer in one-twentieth of a square inch. More than 15,000 transistors were combined to form a device that could store, process, and retrieve data at the same capacity of computers of the previous decade. The first fully operational microprocessor was invented in 1971 (Long 1988, Bitter 1984).

The microprocessor is the processing component of the small, inexpensive but powerful microcomputer, also called personal or desktop computer. Besides microprocessors, these microcomputers incorporated terminals. The terminal comprised a cathode-ray tube (CRT) and a keyboard that allowed the user to work directly with the computer system in real time. A user could enter data (numerals, letters, and symbols) into the computer and see them instantly on the screen. The interactive computer system eliminated the need for keypunch machines and punched cards as the input data devices. Thus, the first truly interactive computer system had evolved.

New companies such as Radio Shack and Apple Computer Corporation came into existence. These manufacturers, among others, made it possible for small businesses and individuals to own computers. For instance, in 1977, Apple Computer Corporation came out with the microcomputer with the education sector of society in mind. By 1980, IBM had created the Model 3081, which was twice as powerful as previous computer systems. Developed with the very large-scale integrated (VLSI) circuits, this IBM system completed more work in less time (Bitters 1984, Long 1988, Alessi and Trollip 1985, Hofmeister 1984).

FIGURE 3. The logic board, or motherboard, of the Macintosh IIFX microcomputer. Attached to the logic board is the microprocessor, a device based on large-scale integration technology that makes interactive personal computing possible. *Photo by Will Mosgrove, courtesy Apple Computer.*

In 1983, IBM announced the IBM XT microcomputer, one of the first devices to integrate the hard disk as a standard feature and, shortly thereafter, the IBM AT with improved keyboard and more megabytes of primary memory (Simkin 1990).

The overall effect of the microcomputer era was that computers became more affordable to a large base of industries and individuals. In addition, other electronic devices became less expensive, clones appeared, punched cards disappeared, and computers performed many tasks once performed by office personnel.

Minicomputers and mainframes were not, however, eliminated with the advent of microcomputers. The supercomputers, such as the Cray-1 by Cray Research and the CYBER 205 by Control Data Corporation, were built in the early 1980s. Both of these systems were typically for multiusers who had need for large database systems. These huge systems cost between $10 and $15 million and maintained incredible processing speeds because several hundred thousand transistors were placed on a single chip (Bitter 1984, Simkin 1990).

The Future of Computers

Even though progress races on, predicting the future of microcomputer technology is a difficult task. Long (1988) suggests that because the advances in technology are being made so rapidly, we are already in the era of generationless computers; however, according to Simkin (1990) both Japanese and American companies continue to work on a fifth generation of computers. Fifth-generation computers are expected to use memory chips that can each store millions of characters of data, with the memory capacities nearing that of the human mind. Although today's computers process instructions sequentially, fifth-generation computers are predicted to use parallel data processing. The capability of processing millions of instructions simultaneously would allow many microprocessors to work together in a coordinated manner.

In addition, fifth-generation computers are expected to possess artificial intelligence. These computers would exhibit deductive logic that has been programmed by a software engineer. An example from today's systems is expert systems, which are computer programs that attempt to capture the thought processes of experts into prescribed rules of thumb. These systems are then able to evaluate evidence, request additional information, and recommend courses of action based on their findings; they are currently used in medical professions. Another example, neural networks, attempt to mimic human learning processing. Simkin (1990) suggests that such programs hold great promise if they can help computers to function more like the human mind.

Finally other technologies will tend to merge with the interactive computer systems, as has already occurred with interactive videodisc and compact-disk read-only memory interfacing with computer systems. The ability to capture realistic pictures and sound enables the user to interact more effectively with information.

SUMMARY

The primary components of the computer system are input, processing, output, and storage/memory. These components are typically associated with any type of computer system whether it be a microcomputer (the smallest system), a minicomputer, or a mainframe (the largest system). Based on the size of the computer system, these primary components tend to differ in processing speed and power. For instance, the input/output components of the microcomputer are slower than those of larger systems. In addition, microcomputers have a small storage component compared with the larger systems. The trend, with the exception of the supercomputer, is toward smaller, more powerful, and less expensive computers.

Computers have evolved over the last 50 years. We can distinguish four distinct generations, and perhaps a fifth on the horizon. During the 1940s and 1950s, the first generation of computers was characterized by the vacuum tube, with little interaction between the end user and the computer. A computer professional was needed to process data into information with delayed time. From the mid-1950s to the mid-1960s, second-generation computers were characterized by their transistors and solid-state circuitry as well as by advanced programming languages. Third-generation computers revolutionized the market with integrated circuits on wafer chips. The continued development of programming languages enabled widespread use of computers in business and science; however, a computer professional was still necessary as an intermediate between the end user and the computer system.

It was not until the 1970s, during the fourth generation, that computer systems became truly interactive. Users were now able to communicate directly with the computer system. Fourth-generation computers with real-time data processing capabilities have made lengthy delays between data submission and dissemination of results a thing of the past. With the advent of new peripherals, today's computers allow the user to interact easily, in a variety of ways, with the computer.

Key advances in technology such as artificial intelligence, parallel data processing, megachip memories, and integration of other technologies, are the central features of a potential fifth generation of computer systems; however, because the advances in technology are so numerous and occurring so rapidly, some experts suggest that we may have reached a generationless age of computers. It can be assured that as computer technology advances the interactions of users with computer systems will become effortless.

References

Alessi, S. M., and S. R. Trollip. 1985. *Computer-based instruction: Methods and develop-*

ment. Englewood Cliffs, N.J.: Prentice-Hall.

Bitter, G. G. 1984. *Computers in today's world.* New York: Wiley.

Hofmeister, A. 1984. *Microcomputer applications in the classroom.* New York: Holt, Rinehart & Winston.

Lockard, J., P. D. Abrams, and W. A. Many. 1990. *Microcomputers for educators.* Glen-

view, Ill.: Scott, Foresman.

Long, L. 1988. *Introduction to computers & information processing.* Englewood Cliffs, N.J.: Prentice-Hall.

Simkin, M. G. 1990. *Discovering computers.* Dubuque, Iowa: Wm. C. Brown

Gayle V. Davidson

J

JACQUARD, JOSEPH-MARIE

Joseph-Marie Jacquard was born on July 7, 1752, in the village of Couzon, about 3 miles from Lyons in central France. Lyons, the second largest industrial city in France, hummed with the noise of silk looms. Both of Jacquard's parents worked in the weaving trade. His father, a weaver of gold- and silver-embroidered silks, and his mother, a pattern maker, were a modest, practical couple who believed in the virtues of thrift, loyalty, and hard work.

At the age of 10, Jacquard went to work as a "drawboy" in the weaving trade. Patterns were created in silk material by drawboys who lifted and returned the weighted vertical warp threads by hand. In later life, Jacquard became obsessed with eliminating the tedious function of the drawboy in silk manufacturing.

Jacquard invented the loom that made automatic weaving practical for the first time. Named the Jacquard loom after its inventor, it was the most important stage in the evolution of textile weaving by mass production methods. The Jacquard loom started a technological revolution in the textile industry and is the basis of the modern automatic loom. He first formed the idea for his loom in 1790, but his work was disrupted by the French Revolution, in which Jacquard fought on the Republican side. Jacquard returned to his loom design as soon as he was free to do so. At the Paris Exhibition of 1801, he demonstrated a new improved type of silk drawloom, and in 1805 he produced the Jacquard loom in its final form. It linked a system of punched cards with sprung needles that lifted only those threads corresponding to the punched pattern on the card. In this way it was possible to weave patterns of remarkable complexity in silk materials for table cloths, wall hangings, and bedspreads. In 1806 the loom was declared public property, and Jacquard was rewarded with a pension and a royalty on each machine.

The Jacquard loom aroused bitter hostility among the silk weavers, who feared that its introduction would deprive them of jobs. The weavers of Lyons not only burned machines that were put into production but attacked Jacquard as well. Eventually, the advantages of the loom brought about its general acceptance, and by 1812 there were 11,000 in use in France. In 1819, Jacquard was awarded a gold medal and the Cross of the Legion of Honour. His loom spread to England in the 1820s and from there achieved virtually worldwide use. By 1833, about 10,000 looms were in operation in England. In 1834 there were 30,000 looms in use in Lyons alone.

Charles BABBAGE admired a portrait of Jacquard. About 30 inches square, as precise as a line engraving, but made in beautiful colors, it had been woven in silk thread on a Jacquard loom, using some 24,000 cards. It inspired Babbage with the idea of "programming" his analytical engine by means of punched cards. Punched cards were also used by Herman HOLLERITH to feed data to his census machine.

Jacquard died on August 7, 1834, in Oullins, France, at the age of 82 with his mission completed. The drawboy had been replaced by an automated loom.

For Further Reading
Giarratano, J. C. 1982. *Foundations of computer technology*, p. 21. Indianapolis, Ind.: Howard W. Sams & Co.

Donald D. Spencer

JOBS, STEVEN PAUL

Steven Paul Jobs was born on February 24, 1955, orphaned, and raised by adoptive parents, Paul and Clara Jobs. Steve's adopted father was a machinist at Spectra-Physics. When Steve was 5, he moved with his parents to Palo Alto, California, because his father had been transferred. It was from his father that Steve acquired his first interest in mechanical things and electronics.

Steve was 12 when he saw his first computer at Hewlett-Packard. The company had invited a group of schoolchildren to the plant for lectures and some hands-on practice. The experience left Jobs in awe of the device and he wanted one of his own. Several months later, Steve phoned directly to William Hewlett, co-founder of Hewlett-Packard, to ask for some help in building a frequency counter, a device used to measure the speed of electronic impulses, for a school project. Hewlett provided Steve with some parts. He also offered him a job for the summer after his high school freshman year, putting screws in frequency counters at Hewlett–Packard.

Steve Jobs was 16 when he met his eventual business partner, Stephen WOZNIAK, then 21. Both had a gift for putting technology to lighthearted uses. One idea they marketed was a "blue box" that permitted its users to make long-distance telephone calls free. They sold about 200 boxes and then stopped producing them, as it bordered on the illegal. Jobs further developed his business skills in high school, fixing stereos and selling them to classmates.

In 1972, Jobs graduated from Homestead High School in Cupertino, California. That fall he went to Reed College in Portland, Oregon, but dropped out during the second semester. He stayed around campus for another year, attending classes occasionally and reading a good deal about Eastern religions. He left Reed College for good in early 1974. He then returned home and got a job as a video game designer for Atari. Jobs worked at night, and Wozniak often came by to play with the company's video games.

The introduction of the Altair micro-computer had led to the formation of computer clubs all over the country. The turning point in Jobs's life came when he began dropping by the Homebrew Computer Club, an organization of computer enthusiasts in Silicon Valley. Wozniak, a founding member of Homebrew, had been designing calculators at Hewlett-Packard during this time.

In 1975, Wozniak and Jobs started building their own microprocessor-based computer. They used an 8-bit 6502 microprocessor designed by MOS Technology. The computer consisted of only a printed circuit board without a keyboard, case, memory, or power supply. It could, however, be used for developing programs, playing games, and running BASIC language programs. The computer was called the Apple I. Jobs and Wozniak set up a partnership, Apple Computer, Inc., to market the product. All told, they sold about 175 Apple I computers for $500 each, netting about half that sum in profit. (The retail price of the Apple I was $666.66.)

In 1977, Jobs and Wozniak went on to develop a more sophisticated computer, the elegant-looking Apple II. This computer had a sleek, lightweight, beige plastic case; the keyboard and computer merged in a modular design. The $1,350 Apple II weighed 12 pounds and was easy to use. It became known as the Volkswagen of computers. Two milestones in Apple history are especially noteworthy. One was the announcement in the summer of 1978 of the availability of a disk drive, which provided faster, more efficient access to the computer's memory. The second milestone was the arrival of the spreadsheet program called VisiCalc. It was at first available exclusively on Apple II computers, beginning in October 1979, and sold for only $100. By September 1980, more than 130,000 Apple II computers had been sold. By the end of 1983, 6 years after its incorporation, Apple Computer had almost 4,700 employees and $983 million in sales.

In January 1984, Apple Computer announced the Macintosh computer. This was Steve Job's electronic baby. He shaped it, nourished it, and pampered it into life. Working on the Macintosh project was the most exciting and absorbing thing Jobs had ever done. The Macintosh became one of the most exciting and easy-to-use computers of all time.

In September 1985, after a management disagreement with Apple president John Sculley, Jobs resigned as chairman of Apple Computer. He established a new firm, called NeXT, Inc. His plan was to market a sophisticated "scholar's workstation" for under $10,000 to universities and colleges.

In 1988, after 3 years of secretive designing and building, Jobs unveiled the NeXT computer system. The machine, which sold for $6,500, was so sophisticated it could animate almost lifelike three-dimensional images. It was as easy to use as a personal computer, but as powerful as workstations used by scientists and engineers that cost twice as much.

For Further Reading

Slater, R. 1989. *Portraits in silicon*, pp. 309–21. Cambridge, Mass.: MIT Press.

Donald D. Spencer

JOURNALISM, COMPUTERS IN

From the front page to the classifieds, from the news services that send articles nationwide to the food writer who indexes columns on a home computer, there is almost no part of the news business that does not use computers.

Computers revolutionized print newsrooms and the areas that support them; reporters and printers who retired in the late 1960s probably would not recognize the 1990s newspaper plant. By 1990, most daily newspapers had desktop computers or smart terminals hooked up to at least a minicomputer, though some smaller newspapers and many weeklies managed with desktop computers, either alone or in networks. The largest newspapers had mainframes, as did television networks and large TV stations.

PRINT JOURNALISM

Typesetting

Typesetting was the news business's first use for computers. Until this century, printing presses were still basically the same machine Gutenberg invented in the 1450s. They were larger, faster, and fancier, but frames still filled by dropping in a letter at a time. The teletypesetter, a 1930s machine that used perforated paper tape to feed in copy, was limited by the speed at which its operators could hyphenate words that ran past the ends of lines and justify lines so that the right and left margins were even. Turning justification and hyphenation over to computers in the 1960s nearly tripled the speed at which type could be set, to 14 lines a minute. But "cold type," a photographic process being developed over the same period, brought that speed up to 150 to 175 lines a minute.

Lasers now etch printing plates for computer-driven presses at large newspapers, whereas the smallest newspapers can use desktop publishing programs and laser printers to prepare layouts for phototypesetters. But even the 1960s cold-type machines set type far faster than news staffs had stories ready. The next use for computers was to prepare copy faster and to make editing easier. When they first received their cathode-ray tubes (CRTs), many editors grumbled that the machinery slowed them down, but the next generation of writers and editors found typewriters impossibly slow and tedious.

Editing

In the 1960s and early 1970s, newspaper articles were generally typed, triple-spaced, on "books" of carbons with two or three flimsy copies. After an editor went through the copy, it was retyped into a typesetting machine. Edited wire service stories were "punched" onto a teletype that chunked out 66 words a minute; newspapers also could get the stories on paper tape.

Those books of carbons and reels of punched paper tape are gone. Reporters now work at personal computers or smart terminals hooked up to one or more minicomputers or mainframes. Most papers also have laptop computers for use on assignments outside the newsroom, allowing reporters to send copy into the computer rather than dictate it over the phone. Some newspapers also put laptops rather than desktops in regional bureaus.

Freelance writers also write and edit on computers. Some magazines now require regular freelance "stringers" to send in copy over the phone, modem-to-modem; other publications ask for a disk in addition to or instead of paper copies of an article.

Research and Analysis

Reporters use computers both to gather and to analyze information.

Computer terminals are handy note pads during telephone interviews, especially for those reporters whose handwriting tends toward the illegible. And computers themselves revolutionized newspaper libraries, just as they had the newsroom. Instead of rows on rows of file drawers filled with envelopes stuffed with clippings, newspapers could create cross-indexed electronic databases from articles already in memory.

But that change took time, not to mention an additional minicomputer. By July 1990, about 165 U.S. and Canadian dailies had electronic libraries; there were about 1,600 daily newspapers in the United States alone (Rykken 1990). Many computer morgues were part of commercial on-line databases such as DataTimes and VU/Text. Many also could be reached through more general networks such as CompuServe, Prodigy, and GEnie, which also offered quick access to experts who exchanged messages with other members of special interest groups.

On-line databases can be used in several ways for one story. For instance, a science reporter bones up on what's new in orthopedic medicine before a surgeon's news conference, also preparing a list of people who might provide insightful comment. Afterward, a more specific check may reveal whether the announcement was as new as its author said or a refinement of work done in previous years.

Reporters log into on-line databases themselves or work with news librarians who track down articles for them. Many reporters do not want to know any more about computers than the commands needed to edit and store notes and articles. Some also learn how to use databases. Only a few use analytical tools such as spreadsheets and statistical programs. These tools are useful for such diverse questions as what differences among schools appear to have the most effect on students' performance and which candidate is most likely to win the race for governor.

The change from clipping morgue to database prompted thoughts of another change in newspaper libraries. Most newspapers with circulation over 50,000 closed their libraries to the public in the mid-1970s and 1980s because they no longer had the staff both to serve their reporters and to answer questions from the outside (McBride 1990); however, at least one newspaper with an electronic library was selling information to telephone callers, and others were thinking of doing so.

Page Layout and Pagination

What happens after editing depends on the newspaper or magazine. Some send it directly to a teletypesetter, which prints it out in columns, to be cut and pasted onto a page; the layout is then photographed for cold type. Others have dropped scissors, X-acto knives, and rubber cement in favor of keyboard and mouse. Programs help them decide where to put advertisements; how much news will be needed to fill the remaining "news hole"; where to position each story, photograph, or drawing on a page; what size and style type to use for the headline; and how much of a story will fit on a section's front page before it has to "jump" inside.

News Services

In a wire service newsroom, copy written and edited on a CRT is sent from minicomputers and mainframes directly into the computers of subscribing newspapers and radio and television stations. Some news services receive stories by modem from member newspapers; groups of newspapers also exchange stories by modem.

As technology improved, transmissions zipped from 66 words a minute to 300 and then 1,200 baud, or about 1,000 words a minute. In the 1990s, some transmissions moved up to 9,600 baud, about 8,000 words a minute. Faster transmissions let news services send more and longer stories than they did in the 1960s. Instead of ripping up and paging through reams of printout, subscribers use their own computers to sort by topic and pull out the latest version of the stories they want, or to page through the day's report and see what looks interesting.

Codes in the "headers" that open each computer file route stories to different terminals in a subscriber's newsroom—sports to the sports department, stock tables and financial stories to the business section, and other articles to the editors most likely to want them. They also sort the wire into queues so that urgent, "breaking" stories get in line ahead of other general news of the day, and "advances"—usually features—move a week or two ahead of their release dates whenever nothing else is in line.

Graphics

Nor are words all that go through computers. Graphics computers, often Macintoshes, became almost universal in the 1980s. Artists incorporate computer-generated graphs into pictures designed to attract readers' attention. They use drawings and a few words to show readers the mechanics of catching a satellite in space or the steps of a popular football player's victory dance. They turn stored maps into "here's where it happened" charts, with inset drawings and text to explain just what happened.

Graphics, which once moved on the same wire service transmitters as photographs, by the late 1980s moved Mac-to-Mac; brief descriptions were sent on news wires to let editors know what was available.

Photography

Meanwhile, photographers moved into electronic darkrooms. By and large, they still developed film in a chemical bath in 1990,

though a few digital cameras were in use. But those with electronic darkrooms no longer had to expose, "soup," and dry a series of prints, using filters and papers with varying sensitivity to light to change contrast, and lightening or darkening smaller areas by blocking the enlarger's light in some areas while letting it shine longer on others. Instead, they manipulated a digitized image scanned from a negative or a print sent in from outside to get the best contrast and range of color or blacks and grays.

The first electronic news darkrooms were installed in 1978 at Associated Press (AP) headquarters; by 1990, at least a half-dozen other companies provided them. Both AP and United Press International announced in 1990 that they were moving from wirephoto receivers requiring special chemically treated paper to digital transmissions over telephone lines. Each paper transmission took about 8 minutes; a computer transmission at 9,600 baud took about one-eighth that time. Instead of flipping through a 4-inch stack of prints, subscribers could check out electronic "contact sheets" with a dozen small pictures on a screen and decide which merited a closer look. And photographs, like news stories, can be routed to specific departments.

Outside the Newsroom

Computers also classify and alphabetize the classified ads, and keep track of subscribers, payroll, and billing. By and large, spreadsheets were more likely to be found in a newspaper's data processing department than in its newsroom in 1990.

BROADCAST JOURNALISM

Broadcast journalism, a medium of spoken words and moving pictures, was slower than print journalism to move to computers. But the move was well underway by 1990.

Cable News Network, the first network to automate its news operation, did so in 1978. ABC, CBS, and NBC followed later. By May 1990, 80 percent of all stations in the top twenty markets had automated newsrooms (McBride 1990); however, only 35 percent of network affiliates in the top seventy-five markets had any newsroom computers at all and most of those were used only to write and edit scripts. Like newspapers, radio and TV stations also use computers to sort and edit wire service copy and network "feeds" and to call up material used in the past for background or reuse. But many uses are unique to broadcast, and in 1990 at least twenty-four companies were selling programs to fill those needs.

Editing and Production

For radio and television, editing means deciding not only which words best explain a story but which "actuality"—snippets of tape from a disaster site, war zone, interview, or other event—best illustrates it. Then comes production: the job of making sure that all of the bits and pieces that make up a television newscast are on screen when needed.

Computers can automate much of this. For instance, a reporter's script can include commands to bring in specific bits of sound or video stored on a tape cartridge. The television producer can add commands for captions and "stillstorers," machines that hold those portraits and graphics usually shown in the upper right-hand corner of the screen, over an anchor's shoulder. Commands also could be included for cameras mounted on robotic pedestals to change position or zoom in or out.

If the order or time allotted to one item is changed, the commands set up for all of the other stories are automatically reshuffled or modified to fit.

Text

On television, printed text is used to cut the number of spoken words and to convey spoken words to viewers who cannot hear them. While a chubby man in a suit talks about timber, a caption superimposed on the bottom of the screen identifies him as Sen. Stumpy Tree, D-Ore. Later, a view of muddy floodwaters swirling around rooftops is identified as Baton Rouge, Louisiana. Computers

make it easy to add those captions. And, for the hearing-impaired, the close coordination of script and picture easily allows closed-captioned service.

Graphics

Newspaper graphics move only when a page is turned. But television requires far more. The final frame of one report turns like a page in a book to open the next, related story. The title of a special report turns, twists, and is transformed into a drawing of the subject. A description of how the Space Shuttle will capture a satellite is accompanied by an animated graphic, shaded to appear three-dimensional.

Animation, whether done by hand or computer, is a drawn-out process. A second's action may need several drawings for a smooth movement from one position to the next. But many of the programs and computers sold for television stations include effects such as wipes, rolls, folds, and turns. They draw in shadows and imitate the effects of camera movement.

And with time to plan ahead, a desktop computer with a graphics program can spend an untended night or weekend drawing up the intermediate steps needed to get an animated figure from point A to point Z.

References

McBride, J. 1990. Newsroom computers. *Television Engineering* 26(5):27–31.

Rykken, R. 1990. Newspaper libraries: Opening their doors to revenue. *presstime* 12(7):12–14.

For Further Reading

Anderson, D. A., and B. D. Itule. 1984. *Contemporary news reporting*, chap. 13, pp. 233–52. New York: Random House.

ANPA/TEC Report. *presstime* 12(7):20–29. A group of articles including "Joint Ventures Highlight Show" and "Electronic Darkroom Technology Sparks Debate."

Chapman, J. (76100,261). 1990. KYW TV upgrades BASYS newsroom computer system. News release about production control software, uploaded April 20, 1990, to the Journalism Forum of CompuServe Information Service.

Hynds, E. C. 1975. *American newspapers in the 1970s*, chap. 7, pp. 234–55. New York: Hastings House.

Newspapers in the year 2000 envisioned. 1990. *Editor & Publisher* 123(5):28.

Overturf, D. (75360,560). 1990. An overview of Comprompter's ENR software package. News release uploaded April 4, 1990, to the Journalism Forum on CompuServe Information Service. 15,955 bytes.

Perrien, T., Editor for Technology, *The (New Orleans) Times–Picayune*. Interview, August 1990.

Rosenberg, J., M. Fitzgerald, and G. Garneau. 1990. Integrating standard platforms: Variety proliferates in editorial and advertising front-end systems, ad makeup terminals and electronic darkrooms. *Editor & Publisher* 123(5):13–15, 50–51, 55–57.

Special Report/NAB 90: Focus on technology. 1990. *Broadcasting* 118(17):52–56.

Janet McConnaughey

JOYSTICKS

Users communicate with computers through input and output devices. Input, or data entry, devices are the tools we use to put information into our computer systems. Many users are familiar with the keyboard, with which they communicate with their computers. In recent years, however, many devices have appeared that make entering information into computers easier and more efficient. Such devices increase the power of the computer user. There is yet another class of data entry tools that do not involve a user. Such tools include instruments connected to the computer that directly collect data from the environment and input these data into the computer for processing. This article does not focus on these "automatic" data entry devices, nor on communications devices, such as modems, or on storage devices,

such as disk drives. Instead this article describes one type of user-interactive input device, the joystick.

CHARACTERISTICS

Joysticks are cursor positioning devices that give the user far more control of the cursor than the simple up, down, left, and right arrow keys on a keyboard. Joysticks let users move the cursor in lines across the screen display, or in curves, quickly. Although there are a variety of joysticks, they all have some type of handle that the user grasps and moves to control cursor movement. They also usually have one or a few selection buttons located on their housing, on the top of the handle, or nearby, if they are keyboard mounted.

Joysticks are used to tell the computer where to position the cursor, but some joysticks also tell the computer how fast to move the cursor across the screen.

Joysticks are typically used in computer systems as input devices with games, such as "Flight Simulator," driving games, and other types of applications in which the computer allows the user to simulate operating equipment; however, joysticks are also useful for pointing and selecting items from the screen display and for relatively simple graphics applications. Berliss and Borden (1989), in fact, describe joysticks as mouse emulators. They describe joysticks with programmable selection buttons that allow the joysticks to perform many functions normally performed by a mouse. They also describe a joystick designed for people who cannot use their hands. It can be mounted on a gooseneck stand or held in the person's mouth. The selection button can be operated with the tongue.

The design of the joystick varies depending on the tasks it will perform; the application software with which it will be used; and "ergonomic factors," that is, factors related to human use, such as avoiding fatigue, ease of use, and the "feel" of the joystick. Usually small handles, operated by the user's fingertips, are used in joysticks for graphics applications; larger handles are often used in simulators, equipment operation, and games.

Many joysticks are mounted in a housing that rests on a surface. This arrangement is designed for user comfort and ease. For example, the housing often has a place to rest the hand. The housing may also include the selection buttons. The entire unit is connected to the computer by various means, most commonly through the RS-232 port. Alternatively, some joysticks and their corresponding sensors and software are built directly into a computer.

TYPES OF JOYSTICKS

There are several basic types of joystick. Doran (1988) classifies them as either displacement joysticks, force-operated joysticks, or a combination of these. Arnaut and Greenstein (1988) create a separate category out of the switch-type displacement joystick commonly used in games. Schumann (1988), in his article about joysticks used to operate industrial equipment, also describes joysticks that use inductively coupled movement. This article uses Doran's classification.

Displacement joysticks are often used in simulators and games. Usually, the user moves these joysticks physically back and forth or sideways in a horizontal plane along x and y axes. They may have very small handles, which are operated with just two or three fingers, or they may have full-size hand grips. The handle, when not being moved, usually rests in a center position through springs or friction. Displacement joysticks are connected mechanically to a rotary shaft. The mechanical motion of the stick is converted into an electrical signal that tells the computer where to move the cursor. Displacement joysticks might use potentiometers, switches, optical encoders, or fiberoptics to convert the mechanical motion into an electrical signal. Switches are often used in joysticks for games. For example, four switches allow a handle to indicate one of eight positions for the cursor. The signal is not proportional to the movement of the handle in a switch-type joystick. Switches are not usually used for graphics joysticks because they do not allow for the refined movements that graphics require, but are very suitable for joysticks used in games. Potentiometers are often used because they are reliable and readily available, and thus they keep the cost of displacement joysticks relatively low. The other types of converters are used in more specialized applications, such as where long equipment life is needed or, in the case of fiberoptics, in critical and environmentally rugged environments, such as in industry or the military.

Joysticks used for graphics control need at least one selection button, which can be used to execute commands and make menu selections. Another axis can be added to displacement joysticks to allow screen cursor positioning in three dimensions, by allowing the handle to rotate and thus interact with another signal converter. Some joysticks such as grip controls for aircraft have a fourth axis accessed by moving the joystick up and down. These types of grip handles might also have as many as four or five selection buttons to control the computer.

Force-operated joysticks do not move in the same way as do displacement joysticks. The user's fingers exert pressure on the handle, which moves only slightly to give the user the feeling of movement; however, the force joystick responds to the pressure and generates electrical signals. As with displacement joysticks, force joysticks are available with many different types of handles; usually the smaller handles are most common in graphics applications. Force joysticks with a third control axis are also available. This may be accomplished by allowing the user to twist the handle clockwise or to turn a lever on a control on the base of the joystick.

The force joystick works by converting the pressure exerted on the handle into an electrical signal. Usually this is accomplished through sensors bonded to the rod, forming a network across which a voltage source is applied. The sensors measure the force applied.

An additional type of joystick used in operating heavy equipment is the inductively coupled joystick, described by Schumann (1988). These joysticks are rugged and mechanically simple, yet they allow for movement along more than two axes.

ADVANTAGES AND DISADVANTAGES

One advantage of joysticks is that they do not usually require much computer experience to operate. Operating joysticks is easy and almost intuitive; that is why joysticks are so often incorporated into games and public information systems.

Several additional advantages of joysticks have been described by Arnaut and Greenstein (1988) in their review of human factors considerations in input devices. For example, joysticks require very little desk space, and can also be incorporated directly into the keyboard. Numerous models are available, and many of these, particularly the switch-operated types, are low in cost. Most joysticks can be used for long periods without tiring the user, and they allow the user to adjust the feel (e.g., the tension) of the handle.

Another advantage of joysticks is that they can automatically return to a center position, usually through spring loading or friction. Some joysticks allow the user to set whether or not the joystick returns to center. The centering advantage, however, is not viewed as very important for business applications (Howard 1987), so joysticks are not often seen on business computer systems. Joysticks, particularly the force type, are often, however, components of graphics systems, because joysticks allow users to move a cursor easily on a screen.

The primary disadvantage of joysticks is that they are not well suited for some types of graphics applications, because they are usually low in accuracy and resolution, cannot be used to trace or digitize drawings in graphics applications, and cannot be used to input hand-drawn images or single characters (Arnaut and Greenstein 1988).

CHOOSING A JOYSTICK

It is important when choosing a joystick to ensure that it will operate with the particular computer system at hand and will do the desired work. Fischer (1987) also reminds users to take care that the joystick is designed to operate with the application software the user has chosen.

Joysticks are periodically reviewed by authors in popular computer journals. For example, Jones (1987) reviewed four joysticks particularly suitable for game applications. The four joysticks ranged in price from about \$35 to about \$55. They each had one button on top of the handle and two on the housing. They each also had a switch to allow the user to decide whether or not the handle should automatically return to center. Each handle could be adjusted or "trimmed" by the user. The reviewer evaluated the joysticks on several characteristics, including size, "feel," amount of unwanted drift, comfort such as lack of cramping, optional adjustment for handle tension, button placement, and ease of controlling the cursor. Berliss and Borden (1989) reviewed three joysticks ranging in price from about \$55 for a relatively simple joystick to about \$350 for a joystick designed for individuals without the use of their hands.

CONCLUSION

Joysticks are only one type of input device. In examining the entire range of input devices, it is clear that there is no one right tool for any particular job. Rather, when the user considers the work to be performed, the computer system at hand, and the selected application software, several input device choices will become clear. The user can then select the most economical, comfortable, and flexible tool for the job.

In general, keyboards are the input tool of choice for entering text and are still the standard data entry device. Pointing or selection devices, such as mice and trackballs (a version of mice, or vice versa, in which the ball remains stationary), are becoming another common standard as computer systems become more object-oriented and graphical interfaces become more common. When users are not very familiar with computers and will perform limited or infrequent computer tasks, screen input devices, such as light pens and touch screens, are often selected, because users simply touch their choices on the screen in relatively natural motions like pointing. When extensive drawing is to be done, particularly when the artist would want to easily select multiple commands as well, graphics tablets, which can be used with ink or pressure styluses, or by touch, are the most useful input devices. When the user wants to enter data from images that are already printed in visual, text, or coded form, machine "readers," such as scanners, digitizers, optical character readers, bar code readers, and wands, are used. When the data to be entered are in video or audio form, video and audio digitizers are available.

Advanced input technologies are rapidly being developed. These include human voice recognition devices that allow users to enter commands and input data by talking to the computer. "Notepad" software allows users to input data in their own handwriting. Input technologies that allow users to communicate more naturally with computers now include controller gloves, eye tracking devices, and even human gesture readers (Foley 1987).

The simple joystick is the input tool of choice when the user needs a quick and easy way to position the cursor on a screen or move the cursor across the screen in two or even three dimensions. The joystick is particularly well-suited to use in simulations and games and as a selection and drawing device in simple graphics applications. The joystick is also moving into more advanced input applications. It has been incorporated into a T-shaped force-feedback device called a joystring, which the user grasps and moves to control servomotors that control other equipment (Foley 1987). It appears the serviceable joystick will be a part of computer systems for many years to come.

References

Arnaut, L. Y., and J. S. Greenstein. 1988. Human factors considerations in the design and selection of computer input devices. In S. Sherr, ed. *Input devices*, pp. 71–121. New York: Academic Press.

Berliss, J., and P. Borden. 1989. Building a better mouse. *MACUSER*, October, pp. 124–37.

Doran, D. 1988. Trackballs and joysticks. In S. Sherr, ed. *Input devices*, pp. 251–70. New York: Academic Press.

Fischer, S. 1987. Keep application, ease of use in mind when choosing alternative input device. *PC Week*, September 29, p. 127.

Foley, J. D. 1987. Interfaces for advanced computing. *Scientific American* 257:127–35.

Howard, B. 1987. Point-and-shoot devices. *PC Magazine*, August, pp. 95–96. This issue of *PC Magazine* was devoted to input devices, and also includes good articles on voice recognition, touch screens, light pens, graphics tablets, and mice.

Jones, M. 1987. Top guns: 4 joysticks on the job. *PC Magazine*, September, p. 478.

Schumann, D. D. 1988. What's behind that joystick. *Hydraulics and Pneumatics*, June, pp. 55–58.

For Further Reading

Brawer, J. 1988. A+ teachers' toolbox. *A+ Magazine*, February, pp. 106–11.

Bulkeley, D. 1987. Choice of entry. *Design News*, May 4, pp. 79–82.

Heppenheimer, T. A. Machines that read. *Popular Science* 330:82–84, 107–9.

Jenner, D. 1988. Points of order. *Audio-Visual Communications*, February, pp. 26–27, 46–47.

Ostroff, D., and B. Shneiderman. 1988. Selection devices for user of an electronic encyclopedia: An empirical comparison of four possibilities. *Information Processing and Management* 24(6):665–80.

Pepper, J. 1989. Handwriting recognition makes its mark. *PC Week*, May 1.

Phillip, G., and E. S. Young. 1987. Man–machine interaction by voice: Developments in speech technology. Part 1: The state of the art. *Journal of Information Science* 13:3–14.

———. 1987. Man–machine interaction by voice: Developments in speech technology. Part II: General applications, and potential applications in libraries and information services. *Journal of Information Science* 13:15–23.

Poor, A. 1987a. Keyboards beyond the ordinary. *PC Magazine*, August, pp. 99–102.

———. 1987b. Trackballs: Stationary mice. *PC Magazine,* August, pp. 199–202.

Rosch, W. L. 1989. Digitizing tablets, pointing the way to easier input. *PC Magazine,* November 28, pp. 227–81.

Trackballs: A worthy mouse alternative. 1990. *PC Week/Reviews* 7(5):79–88.

Wilton, J. A., and R. S. McLean. 1984. Evaluation of a mouse as an education pointing device. *Computing Education* 8(4):455–60.

Wilhelmina C. Savenye

K

KEMENY, JOHN G.

John G. Kemeny, co-designer of the BASIC programming language, was born in Budapest, Hungary, on May 31, 1926. Kemeny's father believed that Hitler's march into Vienna in early 1938 augured worse things, so he left on his own for the United States. A year and a half later, in early 1940, he sent for his wife, daughter, and teen-aged son John. The family sailed to America without incident. Kemeny attended school in New York City. In 1943, he entered Princeton University, where he studied mathematics.

In 1945, during his junior year at Princeton, he was drafted and sent to Los Alamos, New Mexico, where organizers of the Manhattan Project had undertaken a crash program to accelerate development of the atom bomb. Here he worked in the project's computing center (using IBM bookkeeping calculators) solving mathematical problems.

After the war he returned to Princeton, where he received a doctoral degree in mathematics. While completing his dissertation, he served as Albert Einstein's research assistant at the Institute for Advanced Study. Einstein always had a mathematician as a research assistant. Kemeny worked 3 or 4 days a week with Einstein, who at the time was completing his work on unified field theory. Kemeny spent a considerable amount of time checking Einstein's calculations.

Kemeny taught mathematics for 2 years and philosophy for another 2 years at Princeton. In 1953, he started teaching mathematics and philosophy at Dartmouth College. He served as chairman of the mathematics department from 1956 to 1968 and as president of the college from 1970 to 1981.

At 4:00 A.M. on May 1, 1964, the first BASIC program ran on a General Electric Company time-sharing system. Kemeny, along with Thomas KURTZ, was responsible for this major event in computing history. The time-sharing concept, pioneered by Fernando Corbato and John McCarthy at MIT, would enable a new breed of users to have better access to, and quicker turnaround time on, the computers of the day. The Dartmouth Time-Sharing System was very popular with students who became computer literate almost overnight. What those novice users needed next was a user-friendly language to make real use of that newfound literacy. The Beginner's All-Purpose Symbolic Instruction Code (BASIC), developed by Kemeny and Kurtz, was the solution to this problem. BASIC, which eased the process of developing and debugging programs, soon became the most popular programming language for beginners.

In 1985, Kemeny and Kurtz developed True BASIC, a more powerful version of their legendary language.

Kemeny has published several books on computers and the BASIC programming language.

For Further Reading

Slater, R. 1989. *Portraits in silicon*, pp. 241–49. Cambridge, Mass.: MIT Press.

Donald D. Spencer

KEYBOARDS

The most common way users communicate with computers is through input from keyboards. Virtually all personal computers include a keyboard as standard equipment. Computer keyboards are probably the components most influenced by historical precedents. While technological advances can be seen in the hardware, the key layout and operating principles are remarkably similar to those of a century ago. Although computer keyboards can trace their roots to the development of the typewriter, they have many additional special-purpose keys beyond those found on a typewriter and they interact with the computing system in a much different way.

TYPES OF KEYS

The keys on computer keyboards can be classified into groups by location and purpose. The most recognizable group is the set of alphanumeric keys, the four rows of keys in a typewriterlike layout for the numbers and letters of the alphabet. Most computer keyboards include special keys that can be used in combinations to achieve different results.

One group is the mode change keys, such as the Shift key, which is used to change from uppercase to lowercase, and the Caps Lock key, which is used to type all capital letters without constantly pressing the Shift key. Another group, the editing keys, contains the keys for inserting or deleting characters or altering text. The function keys are a group of programmable keys often placed together at one side. Cursor movement keys are normally labeled with arrows indicating the direction or movement of the cursor, which highlights the current location where characters will be entered on the screen. In an auxiliary numeric keypad, a set of numeric keys are conveniently grouped together for easy entry of numeric data.

KEYBOARDING VERSUS TYPING

Although computer users strike the keys much as typists do, the effective use of computer keyboards requires skills beyond those of typing. The common term *keyboarding* describes the use of the computer to input information. Skilled keyboarders use the other special keys as well as the keys involved in typing.

When a key or combination of keys is pressed on a computer's keyboard, the object is not to produce an image on paper, but to convey information to the computer. Most computer keyboards feature a Return or Enter key that must be pressed to register information in memory.

When a particular key such as the *P* key is pressed, the result may be the appearance of the character *P* on the screen. It could just as well result in the printing of a particular file by a printer with no changes to the screen. The action that occurs when a character or combination of characters is input depends on the program that is running at the time of the input.

The information that is received by the computer is a numeric code rather than an image of a letter. Most computers recognize some standard code, in which each character is converted to a series of bits or binary digits, with each character or character sequence having a different code value. The number of bits in the code determines the maximum number of different possible characters. This allows the system to differentiate an *A* from an *a* as well as determine that the space bar was pressed to enter a blank space or that the sequence Ctrl-D was entered.

QWERTY KEYBOARD LAYOUT

Perhaps the element of computing systems most influenced by historical precedents is the layout of the numeric and alphabetic keys on computer keyboards. The current standard for alphanumeric machines, approved by the American National Standards Institute in 1982, is the QWERTY layout. The QWERTY layout, featuring the numeric keys across the top row of the keyboard, and the letters of the alphabet in the next three rows, is named for the alignment of the first six characters on the top alphabetic row.

The QWERTY layout was developed by the inventor C. L. Sholes, who did pioneer work in the 1860s that led to the introduction of commercial typewriters. Sholes's Type-Writer, which featured the QWERTY arrangement, was marketed by the Remington Company in 1874. The original Type-Writer used only capital letters. The Shift key feature to achieve uppercase and lowercase characters was added later.

Some critics have complained that the QWERTY arrangement is inefficient and confusing, the result of a deliberate attempt by Sholes to slow down fast typers. Most sources attribute the unusual arrangement to the crude technology available at the time. Sholes's motivation seems to have been to place keys such as T and H, which often appear in combination in English words, on opposite sides of the keyboard to keep the mechanical type bars from jamming.

ALTERNATIVE LAYOUTS OF THE PAST

After the introduction of the Type-Writer, other inventors searched for more effective layouts. Most new designs concentrated on the shape of the keyboard, the arrangement of the keys, or the number of keys on the keyboard. Some of the more popular keyboard arrangements at the turn of the century were the double keyboards with separate keys for each uppercase and lowercase character. The chief advantage for typists at that time, who used mostly the one-handed "hunt-and-peck" system, was that only one keystroke was needed for any character.

Other popular designs were the 1884 Hammond Typewriter, in which the keys were arranged in two semicircular rows, and the 1893 Blickensderfer, which used a type wheel to print. Blickensderfer studied the frequency of letters in English text and placed the ten most frequently appearing letters on the bottom row to increase typing efficiency. Once two-handed touch typing became standard in the 1900s, most companies abandoned the alternative layouts and adopted the QWERTY layout.

DVORAK LAYOUT

The major recent rival to the QWERTY has been the Dvorak layout, developed by August Dvorak in 1932. Dvorak's keyboard was also based on frequency counts. It features a *home row* (the middle row of letters) of AO-EUIDHTNS, with the five vowels on one side and the consonants on the other for efficient alternating hand typing.

Dvorak produced studies that showed that approximately 70 percent of the work of the typist could be done on the home row using the Dvorak layout, compared with 32 percent on QWERTY. Further studies have shown that novice typists may be able to be more productive on a Dvorak keyboard. Retraining experienced QWERTY typists on Dvorak keyboards has not produced significant results.

At the time that computers and computer keyboards were being developed, QWERTY was firmly in place as the standard and was easily adapted for computer keyboards. The Dvorak keyboard, now an official alternative standard layout, is meeting with some success, particularly on computing systems where the keyboard may be reconfigured to match the typist.

DESIGN AND LAYOUT OF OTHER KEYS

Keyboard designers must make decisions about how many special-purpose keys to include on keyboards and how to position them so that they can be used efficiently without interfering with other functions. The IBM Corporation has led the way in modern keyboard design. The 84-, 102-, and 122-key keyboard layouts on IBM personal computers have become a sort of industry standard in the United States, along with a 102-key international version.

Layout conventions for numeric keypads involve arrangements of ten keys, one for each numeric digit. The keys are usually placed in a 3×3 matrix or grid, with the zero key centered below the grid. The most common layouts are the calculator layout, starting with the 1-2-3 on the bottom row and moving up in value, and the telephone layout, normally used on touch telephones, with the 1-2-3 at the top.

Cursor movement key layouts normally include four keys for moving the cursor left, right, up, and down. Keys that perform the cursor movement functions are frequently labeled with arrows to indicate the direction of movement. In one common layout, four single-function keys are positioned in a crosslike combination. Another option is to build cursor movement functions into the numeric keypad keys, by having the user invoke the cursor movement function by hitting the Shift key and a numeric key.

Special-function keys are usually arranged according to importance and frequency of use. Typical layouts include those in which the function keys are grouped on the side of the keyboard or in a line at the top of the keyboard. Function keys are used to enter commands such as invoking user help screens or moving the cursor to the beginning or end of a line. They are often labeled generically as function keys with the letter *F* and a key number, for example, F4. In some applications, the function keys have preassigned meanings, and users receive a template or overlay to put on the keyboard to mark what each key does. In other applications, they can be programmed by the user to match the application. Some standards, such as the use of F1 as the user help function key, are evolving. Even though the specific functions and keys still vary widely from application to application, the use of function keys and their role in effective keyboard use are major issues in future keyboard design.

LOOK AND FEEL OF THE KEYS

Many of the design issues involving keyboards are human factors or ergonomic considerations (see ERGONOMICS). The keyboard must not only look right but also feel right to the user.

Most users prefer the keys to look and feel like typewriter keys. The keys are normally plastic-capped boxes that are rectangular or square in shape and slightly concave to fit the fingers. The standards are for keys 0.5 inch in diameter, with a uniform spacing of 0.75 inch from the center of one key to the next. Other factors in user satisfaction include the degree of resistance offered by the keys, and the length of time a key may be held down before the computer responds by repeating the character indefinitely (many systems let the user control this variable).

Alternative designs have met with little success. One alternative is membrane key-

boards, where pictures of key tops were drawn on flat plastic membranes and the user pressed on the membrane to register the keystroke. Another is the "Chiclet" design, where keys were bubble-shaped. The advent of portable and laptop computers brought new keyboards, including compact keyboards, which combined more functions on fewer keys, used smaller keys, and placed the keys closer together.

SENSING THE KEYSTROKE

Keyboards embody a variety of techniques for sensing and registering the keystroke. Some keyboards must be "industrial strength" and perform consistently over years of constant use in harsh environments. Designers must consider cost, reliability, and durability when choosing a sensing mechanism.

Two current electronic switching techniques, membrane and conductive-elastomer keyswitches, are the most common switching technologies. These methods are cost efficient and reliable because of the small number of moving parts but have a life span of approximately 30 million keystrokes. Other technologies, including mechanical contacts, Hall effect, reeds, and capacitance, which have life spans as high as 100 million keystrokes, have been used effectively.

ALTERNATIVE KEYBOARDS

One-handed keyboards, which allow the user to manipulate some other device with the free hand, are advantageous in some settings. A primary category of one-handed keyboards is sequential keyboards, on which each key is limited to one function and operation proceeds one key at a time. These keyboards are typically much larger than the multifunction two-handed models, because there are no Shift or other mode-change keys to use in combination to create patterns. If space is not a factor, these keyboards can result in high performance because of increased speed from the single-key entry mode.

Another class of one-handed keyboards is chord keyboards, which require users to press two or more keys simultaneously to generate most of their characters. Typical chord keyboards have only a few keys, often arranged in a semicircle to operate with a single hand. Chord keyboards with keys for each hand, usually one per finger and one or more for each thumb, can generate over 1,000 combinations, thus matching the capabilities of much larger keyboards in a smaller space.

Chord keyboards were originally developed for specific applications, such as postal letter sorting. In the 1970s, researchers began to apply the technology to computer keyboards, expanding designs to rectangular patterns. The main advantages of chord keyboards are the rapid data entry possibilities and the flexibility gained through the compact size. Chord keyboards have not yet found widespread use for general applications. There are no standards and training users is a key issue. For certain applications, involving standard, repetitive data entry or requiring use of only one hand, chord keyboards are good alternatives.

One approach to simplifying the keyboard for "hunt and peck" users is to arrange the keys alphabetically, an order familiar to most people. Alphabetic keyboards were designed to aid occasional typers in searching for keys in a less hostile environment. Although studies have shown that the typing performance of experienced alphabetic keyboard typists is not significantly better than that of QWERTY typists, alphabetic keyboards offer a good alternative in such cases as working with young children or handicapped individuals, where the reinforcement of the traditional alphabetical ordering is an asset.

THE HUMAN ELEMENT

The main function of computer keyboards is to provide a mechanism for interaction between humans and computing systems. Many of the factors involved in keyboard design are human factors, those that make a device more pleasing, comfortable, useful, or safe for the human user. Some aspects of keyboards, such as minimum height and slope of the keyboard, are already mandated by occupational health and safety standards.

Typical human considerations involving the appearance of the keyboard include the layout, number of keys, size and shape of the keys and keycaps, labeling of the keys, keycap spacing, reflectance of the keycaps, and keyboard background. Tactile feedback, or feel of the keyboard, as well as audible feedback, the presence of an audible click when keys are pressed, are major concerns for users.

The IBM Personal Computer keyboard, a versatile and aesthetically pleasing and practical keyboard, revolutionized the standards for keyboards. IBM introduced such features as detachable keyboards, optional flat or tilted keyboards, and extensive programmable function keys to the personal computer market. The keyboard contained its own keyboard buffer, a small amount of memory that stored characters as users typed ahead while the computer was still busy processing prior input. The keyboard had its own microcomputer that controlled the encoding of keystrokes. This allowed users to reconfigure the keyboard, as all keys were equal in the eyes of the keyboard. The keyboard was easily converted to include special symbols for other languages or mathematical symbols. By simply typing Ctrl-Enter, the keyboard was changed to the Dvorak layout. This keyboard contained a number of features that have been copied and enhanced and are now considered standard for most personal computer keyboards.

THE FUTURE

Ergonomics and technology will continue to drive developments in keyboards. Most keyboards now have their own memory and processors, allowing users to customize or reconfigure them in some way. Few manufacturers produce "dumb" keyboards. The major differences lie in how intelligent the various keyboards are. New standards are evolving for human comfort and safety. Keyboards of the future will themselves be computers that help users interact more efficiently with other computers.

For Further Reading

American National Standards Institute. 1982. *American National Standard for Office Machines and Supplies—Alphanumeric Machines—Keyboard Arrangement,* ANSI X4.23-1982.

———. 1983. *American National Standard for Office Machines and Supplies—Alphanumeric Machines—Alternative Keyboard Arrangement,* ANSI X4.22-1983.

Berardinis, L. A. 1989. Keyboards that handle tough jobs. *Machine Design* 61(4):76–84.

Booth, T. L. 1984. *Introduction to computer engineering hardware and software design,* pp. 377–78. New York: Wiley.

Glasco, D. B., and M. Sargent. 1983. Using IBM's marvelous keyboard. *Byte* 8(5):402–414.

Greenstein, J. S., and L. Y. Arnaut. 1987. Human factors aspects of manual computer input devices. In G. Salvendy, ed. *Handbook of human factors,* pp. 1450–89. New York: Wiley.

Greenstein, J. S., and W. H. Muto. 1988. Keyboards. In S. Sherr, ed. *Input devices,* pp. 123–78. Orlando, Fla. Academic Press.

Gunn, L. 1988. The evolving keyboard. *Electronic Design* 30(24):151–56.

Monty, R. W., H. L. Snyder, and G. G. Birdwell. 1983. Keyboard design: An investigation of user preference and performance. *Proceedings of the Human Factors Society, 27th Annual Meeting, Norfolk, Va., October 1983,* pp. 201–205.

Noyes, J. 1983. Chord keyboards. *Applied Ergonomics* 14(1):55–59.

Rehr, D. C. 1990. QWERTY-DVORAK: The keyboard wars. *The Office* 12(4):19.

Sullivan, D. R., T. G. Lewis, and C. R. Cook. 1988. *Computing today—Microcomputer concepts and applications,* 2nd ed., pp. 53–56. Boston: Houghton-Mifflin.

Harriet Taylor

KNOWLEDGE BASES AND EXPERT SYSTEMS

Beginning in the mid-1950s, Allen Newell, Cliff Shaw, and Herbert Simon inspired research directions in ARTIFICIAL INTELLIGENCE (AI) by investigating chess-playing programs, the Logic Theory Machine (LTM), and the General Problem-Solver (GPS). These early projects, as well as the relations between the Rand Corporation and the Carnegie Institute of Technology, resulted in exciting new directions for AI research that eventually resulted in the expert systems of the 1970s. Early expert systems included DENDRAL, a system used to determine the molecular structure of an unknown organic compound; MYCIN, a system to assist a physician in the treatment of blood infection; and many more. Since then, applications of expert systems in fields such as science, engineering, medicine, social science, law, and many more have been developed. In catalogs of expert systems one may find exciting applications in management, physics, chemistry, electronics, geology, manufacturing, military science, space technology, process control, and agriculture, to name just a few.

What are these systems? How are they designed?

Expert systems are knowledge-intensive systems designed for the solution of problems that require a high level of human expertise. These systems use digital computers in ways that differ from conventional data processing applications. Experts have a body of knowledge that is unfamiliar to the layman. Usually an expert will be versatile and able to make a sensible judgment about the type of answer or detail required. In a practical context, two important features of an expert system are the capabilities to infer reasoning in order to perform tasks that a lay expert could do, and to explain the conclusions and reasoning. This last capability—that in the same way in which human experts should be able to explain their conclusions and reasoning, an expert system should be capable of concise or detailed explanations—is an essential part of the system.

Two of the main questions regarding expert systems involve what makes the expert system expert and how expert systems differ from conventional software. The answers to both questions have to do with the structure of expert systems. Expert systems must have knowledge, together with some means of handling that knowledge, and they must be able to communicate with users.

An acceptable model of the components of an expert system includes:

1. *The knowledge base,* comprised of domain knowledge: facts or rules of thumb to add upon experience.
2. *The inference engine,* a program that allows the hypotheses to be generated from the information in the knowledge base and is the means by which the knowledge is handled.
3. *The input/output interface,* which serves as the language interface, enables the user to supply data and facts to the system, and enables the system to ask questions or supply advice and explanations to the user.

Some people prefer the term "knowledge-based systems" to "expert systems." A model of the basic elements of such a system is shown in Figure 1.

In contrast to human experts, however, expert systems do not resort to reasoning from first principles, drawing analogies, or relying on commonsense knowledge. In essence one can think of an expert system as a consulting system designed to support experts' reasoning on complex problems arising in a narrow domain of knowledge. They evolved from several important concepts in AI. The first is that AI programs, to succeed, must be given large and sufficient amounts of knowledge regarding the problem itself. The second is that the specific description of this knowledge must be completely independent of the control procedures necessary to manipulate that knowledge. This has become the major feature of knowledge systems, namely, the separation of knowledge from the reasoning mechanism of that knowledge.

The knowledge base part of the expert system is analogous to the long-term memory of facts, structures, and rules that represent experts' knowledge regarding the domain of expertise. The inference engine carries out the reasoning tasks and is analogous to the method of reasoning of a human expert in solving problems.

In addition to the knowledge base and the inference engine, the expert system environment contains several tools for constructing or using the expert system. These include building tools for acquiring knowledge, compiling, debugging, and validation. Once the system has been designed, users usually employ a variety of additional tools to interact with the expert system. These tools include graphical environments, interfaces to real-time systems, interfaces to external databases, etc. Four knowledge representation schemes that have dominated knowledge system development tools are:

1. formulas in first-order predicate calculus
2. rule-based systems
3. frame-based systems
4. semantic networks

Predicate calculus, a system of formal logic based on determining whether a proposition is true or false, allows relationships between these propositions to be specified and generalizations to be made.

The second way of representing knowledge in a knowledge base is via production rules. These take the form of IF (antecedent or condition)-THEN (consequence or conclusion), or SITUATION-ACTION.

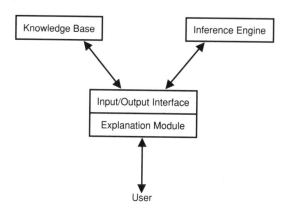

FIGURE 1. Basic elements of an expert system.

The rules in rule-based systems are, in most instances, very similar to the IF-THEN structure of rules appearing as conditional statements in procedural programming languages. Each rule is a modular element of knowledge. The process of transforming basic knowledge into the proper rule syntax of a particular knowledge-based development tool is a major part of "knowledge engineering." Rule-based knowledge systems are generally categorized as exhibiting "forward" or "backward" chaining in the manner in which they process knowledge bases.

When the intelligent system sequences forward from facts to a final conclusion, the process is called "forward chaining." When the system sequences backward from the final conclusion to facts, the process is called "backward chaining." Another form of reasoning is inductive reasoning, which is the process of generalizing from examples. Systems that do inductive reasoning accept a group of examples and form generalized rules covering them.

Another method of knowledge representation and inference are found in the frame-based and object-oriented technologies. Frames are data structures based on Marvin Minsky's theory about how humans think (Minsky 1975) and are used for the representation of stereotyped situations. To each frame one attaches several kinds of information, including relations and procedures.

Frames are used for declarative knowledge, which is more descriptive than procedural. Semantic networks (or associative networks) represent in essence semantic knowledge by showing relationships among various entities. Semantic networks can be used to describe systems, ideas, and relations to be manipulated by the system. A major advantage of frames over semantic networks is that frames may be used for storing procedures and for partitioning complex domains in addition to representation of descriptive knowledge.

Generally speaking, frame-based and object-oriented programming evolved from attempts to implement the "semantic network" class of models for human memory that emerged from cognitive psychology. *Object-oriented programming* emphasizes the underlying concepts (objects) in an application area and the possible linkages between or among them. In such a system the designer begins by specifying the attributes attached to the object. These systems allow the knowledge engineer to specify the hierarchical relationships among objects. It should be noted that one may also associate rules or procedures with objects and attributes. These rules or procedures are used by the system to find values of specific attributes and are specified in the objects' frame structure.

The view that much of the structure of any problem-solving system exists because of the system's need to maintain, structure, and provide information for decision making has given rise to the concept of *knowledge engineering* and to *knowledge management.* The first includes issues that arise in the development of expert systems (e.g., knowledge acquisition, the design of the inference engine, etc.). The second set of issues are those that concern themselves with relationships between expert systems and other computer-based decision aids available to managers.

Automated reasoning strategies such as metaknowledge issues are very important in the design of knowledge-based systems. Various automated-reasoning systems such as PROLOG and OPS5 incorporate built-in control mechanisms. Some of these systems enable us to represent statements similar to those given by predicate calculus. Generally speaking, they employ some kind of a procedure, usually resolution, to prove the consistency of these statements.

Logic programming refers to the use of logic as a programming language. There is a similarity between logic programming and automatic theorem-proving, since both involve the mechanization of inference. The difference is, however, that automatic theorem-proving refers to the generation of proofs, whereas logic programming deals with the use of logic as a computer programming language. One major problem in applying logic to the task of problem solving is that logic does not prescribe which inferences one should draw at any given point in the search for a solution; it only describes which inferences one is entitled to draw according to the rules, frames, or semantic nets.

Logic programming languages appear to be suitable implementation vehicles for many expert system applications. Two important AI languages for this purpose are LISP and PROLOG. In the beginning there was LISP, a programming language based on a mathematical system known as the lambda calculus. A LISP program is basically a set of functions defined in terms of each other, or recursively in terms of themselves. The basic data structure is the list, and LISP programs themselves are basically lists.

Structured programming techniques and abstract data types helped in creating a variety of dialects of LISP. In some cases the hardware and software have been merged in the form of complete development systems known as LISP machines.

On the other hand, in PROLOG a fact is a statement that some entity has a particular property or that some relationship holds between or among two or more entities. Facts are expressed by applying a predicate to a list of arguments. The language has procedural and nonprocedural aspects. Rather than describe a procedure with an explicit sequence of steps, a PROLOG program is basically a declarative set of rules and facts that state relationships. The PROLOG rules are executed by an underlying inference engine, which does impose an order of execution. It is exactly this implicit order that gives PROLOG rules a procedural interpretation.

With all of these languages, the efficiency of execution is measured by logical inferences per second (LIPS).

Expert systems are used in a variety of knowledge-based manufacturing applications, such as planning, scheduling, monitoring, project management, distribution, and diagnosis. Application examples in knowledge-based business systems come from fields such as portfolio analysis, financial statement analysis, assets and liabilities, data processing, and office automation. A variety of applications exist in scientific research, mechanical engineering, seismic analysis, oil-well logging analysis, medical applications, the design of very-large-scale-integrated circuits, circuit-board troubleshooting, pattern recognition, computer vision, and many more.

In recent years substantial efforts have been expended in dealing with the management of uncertainty in expert systems as well as in the design of cooperating expert systems. Managing the imprecision and uncertainty in knowledge-based systems together with the principle of division of labor and specialization of expert systems create a cooperative environment that provides the possibility of functioning in parallel and thus increases the speed of execution.

New techniques also provide a *hybrid intelligent environment* wherein expert systems and neural networks cooperate in the successful execution of tasks. The growth of interest in such hybrid systems has been nothing short of phenomenal. By their very nature, hybrid systems provide not only a reasoning-oriented environment but also a learning environment. When these and similar research efforts will produce better results, intelligent systems will be much stronger and in some ways more humanlike. At this point, however, euphoria should be balanced by healthy skepticism. Machine learning in an uncertain or unknown environment is of vital interest to those working with intelligent systems. Such techniques provide the ability to garner new information, process it, and increase performance of autonomous systems. The field of AI provides two major approaches to the problem of knowledge engineering: expert systems and neural networks. Harnessing the power of these two techniques in a hybrid, cooperating system holds great promise.

Knowledge representation in expert systems is most often in the form of rules garnered through consultation with human experts. Coupling the method of approximate reasoning with knowledge-based techniques yields systems that model human decision making. It is clear that expert systems provide a ready mechanism for explaining why certain decisions are made, even when the human expert is unavailable to articulate the chain of reasoning leading to a decision. This trace of the reasoning process is often crucial to those maintaining the system.

A major disadvantage of knowledge-based systems is their reliance on consultation with human experts for new information. Furthermore, *autonomous* learning in an expert system does not usually include the capability to synthesize new knowledge but is limited to dependence on structures the designer builds in to assess the similarity between situations or to generalize on sets of similar rules.

Neural networks are data-driven systems based on an architecture of many simple, interconnected processing units. The knowledge of a neural net resides in the connections. Neural networks are especially applicable to problems that involve large numbers of weak constraints. They have been successfully applied to perceptual tasks such as pattern recognition, vision processing, and speech synthesis.

The ability to handle minor inconsistencies or conflicts in the data gracefully is an advantage that neural network systems hold over most expert systems. A robust intelligent system must be able to handle conflicting information from different experts, or some degree of contamination in incoming data, without too much degradation in performance.

There are many scenarios in which both types of reasoning—knowledge based and data driven—are appropriate. Harnessing the power of both expert systems and neural networks in a system that allows for imprecise information and/or uncertain environments would yield a system more powerful than either system standing alone.

Learning is an essential component for any intelligent system. One focus of this proposal is on learning in a hybrid system, especially learning in an autonomous or unsupervised mode. The system should be able to learn in an unsupervised situation by experimentation, classification, recognition or similarity, generalizing and applying appropriate previous solutions, or hypothesizing new solutions to situations never before encountered by the system.

Learning in a neural network without the benefit of an initial base of knowledge can be very slow to converge. Therefore the premise in this proposal is that learning can be implemented more efficiently in the neural network when the expert system supplies the metaknowledge to begin the learning process as well as accumulated knowledge in the system.

There is considerable interest in the integration of rule-based expert systems and neural networks. The two methods of knowledge representation represent, respectively, knowledge-driven and data-driven means of knowledge acquisition. There is a growing body of literature that explores the similarity of the underlying structures of these two methods of knowledge representation (expert systems and connections in neural networks).

The certainty factors, which indicate the strength of belief in hypotheses as well as rules from the expert system, are identified with weights in the neural network. Antecedents and consequents from the expert system are identified with units in the neural network. The structural similarity suggests a possible functional similarity between the two types of systems. If both systems are functionally identical, then the fluid transfer of data between the expert system and neural network becomes an important issue.

The proposed model suggests that the expert system, neural network, and learning algorithm be implemented as separate functional units. The only means of communication between the units is the relevant data structure. As shown in Figure 2, the data structure common to the expert system and neural network is the rule base, whereas the data structure common to the neural network and the learning unit is the collection of state arrays.

Each functional unit can be implemented using a different language and/or architecture best suited to the task at hand. For example, the expert system can be implemented using LISP on a minicomputer, whereas the neural network can be implemented using special network hardware. The central processing unit (CPU)-intensive learning algorithm can be executed remotely on a supercomputer or a connection machine.

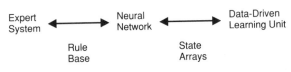

FIGURE 2. A model for integrating expert systems and neural networks.

The transfer of knowledge between system components is bidirectional, and it is precisely the learning capabilities of neural networks that enable the intelligent system to infer new rules or modify existing rules based on neural network performance. This division of labor, by providing the system with whatever knowledge is available a priori through the expert system and the knowledge base, and by developing optional learning strategies for the neural network, is precisely the technology that will provide us with fast, autonomous, effective learning on top of previously acquired knowledge.

It is the *cooperation* of an expert system with a given knowledge base and a neural network with learning capabilities that enables the proposed technology to execute tasks in an autonomous, imprecise, and somewhat unpredictable environment. From a practical point of view, we use neural networks to acquire new knowledge from the environment and replace a computationally intensive form of processing with a more efficient one. On the other hand, the expert system uses knowledge it had acquired from experts and thus relieves the neural network from learning things it already knows, and by that makes the entire system more effective and efficient.

Reference

Minsky, M. 1975. A framework for representing knowledge. In P. H. Whinston, ed. *Psychology of computer vision*, pp. 221–77. New York: McGraw-Hill.

For Further Reading

Buchanan, B., and E. Shortliffe. 1984. *Rule-based expert systems: The MYCIN experiments*. Reading, Mass.: Addison-Wesley.

Gupta, M. M., A. Kandel, W. Bandler, and J. B. Kiszka, eds. 1985. *Approximate reasoning in expert systems*. Amsterdam: North-Holland.

Hall, L. O., and A. Kandel. 1986. *Designing fuzzy expert systems*. Cologne: Verlag TÜV Rheinland.

Harmon, P., and D. King. 1985. *Expert systems*. New York: Wiley.

Hayes-Roth, F., D. Waterman, and D. Lenat.
1983. *Building expert systems*. Reading, Mass.: Addison-Wesley.

Kandel, A. 1986. *Fuzzy mathematical techniques with applications*. Reading, Mass.: Addison-Wesley.

Michalski, R. S., J. G. Carbonell, and T. M. Mitchell, eds. 1986. *Machine learning*, vols. I and II. Palto Alto, Calif.: Tioga.

Pearl, J. 1988. *Reasoning for intelligent systems*. Los Altos, Calif.: Morgan Kaufmann.

Schneider, M., and A. Kandel. 1988. *Cooperative fuzzy expert systems—Their design and applications in intelligent recognition*. Cologne: Verlag TÜV Rheinland.

———. 1989. Fuzzy sets and their applications to artificial intelligence. In M. C. Yoritz, ed. *Advances in computers*, vol. 28, pp. 69–105. New York: Academic Press.

Tamir, D. E., and A. Kandel. 1990. *A schema for knowledge representation and its implementation in a computer-aided design and manufacturing system*. Cologne: Verlag TÜV Rheinland.

Waterman, D. A. 1986. *A guide to expert systems*. Reading, Mass.: Addison-Wesley.

Weiss, S. M., and C. A. Kulikowski. 1983. *A practical guide to designing expert systems*. London: Chapman and Hall.

Zadeh, L. A. 1975. Fuzzy logic and approximate reasoning. *Synthese* 30:407–28.

Zemankova, M., and A. Kandel. 1984. *Fuzzy relational database—A key to expert systems*. Cologne: Verlag TÜV Rheinland.

Abraham Kandel

KNOWLEDGE REPRESENTATION

See Artificial Intelligence

KURTZ, THOMAS E.

Thomas E. Kurtz, co-designer of the BASIC programming language, was born on February 22, 1928, in Oak Park, Illinois. In 1950 he graduated from Knox College in Galesburg, Illinois, with a degree in mathematics. Kurtz received a doctoral degree in mathematics from Princeton University in 1956. His thesis was on a problem of multiple comparisons in mathematical statistics.

Kurtz joined the Dartmouth College faculty in 1956 and began teaching mathematics. Almost immediately he became involved with computers. In his first year, he traveled to General Electric Company in Lynn, Massachusetts, to use their computers. For the following 2 years, he used an IBM 704 computer at MIT.

In the early 1960s Kurtz and John KEMENY designed the BASIC programming language. Their goal was to develop a simple and powerful programming language that students of all disciplines could learn easily. The result was Beginner's All-Purpose Symbolic Instruction Code (BASIC). BASIC is the most common programming language used on computers today. Kurtz and Kemeny tried to impress on members of the college and university community the philosophy that an understanding of computers is as necessary to life as being able to read and write, and that computers should be as accessible as a library. At Dartmouth College, all students can use the library computers at little or no cost. This philosophy is now being implemented in other colleges and universities throughout America.

Kurtz is the co-author (with Kemeny) of one of the original BASIC books (*BASIC Programming*, Dartmouth College, Dartmouth, N.H., 1969). Kurtz has been a member of the President's Science Advisory Commission (1965–1966) and Director of Dartmouth's Kiewit Computation Center and Director of the Office of Academic Computing at Dartmouth.

In the summer of 1983, Kurtz and Kemeny started work on an improved version of the BASIC programming language. Their new language, called True BASIC, was introduced on March 5, 1985. A more powerful language than BASIC, it incorporates interactive graphics, a window manager, formatting tools, and a high-level debugger. It has an interface and command structure that are identical regardless of what computer is being used; this was meant to overcome problems that arose with the original BASIC, requiring different versions for different computers.

For Further Reading
Slater, R. 1989. *Portraits in silicon*, pp. 241–49. Cambridge, Mass.: MIT Press.

Donald D. Spencer

L

LABORATORY INFORMATION MANAGEMENT SYSTEMS

The data generated in chemical laboratories are extremely valuable. These data are used to make decisions affecting the food we eat, the drugs we use to fight disease, the water we drink, the air we breathe, the level of illegal drugs in a person's body, the level of compounds like cholesterol in our blood, and the purity of raw materials and final products. The resources in a modern laboratory are also very valuable. Common laboratory instruments cost about $50,000 and some specialized instruments can cost from $500,000 to over $1 million. The technical staff of a modern laboratory is also valuable, as many years of training are required to operate the instruments and analyze the data properly. The valuable resources in a laboratory, the data generated, the instruments, and the people are the focus of a laboratory information management system, commonly referred to by its acronym, LIMS.

Many regulatory agencies such as the Environmental Protection Agency (EPA) and the Food and Drug Administration (FDA) require specific documentation to show that analysis of samples has been performed properly. All of the supporting data to generate these documents should be a basic part of a LIMS. Many LIMSs have been specifically developed to store and report the data required to produce the documentation required by EPA or FDA.

FUNCTIONS

There is no single definition covering all the functions encompassed by a LIMS. Each LIMS is developed to meet the informational needs of its users. Here are some common functions usually found in a LIMS.

Sample Tracking

When a sample is submitted to the laboratory for analysis, the LIMS tracks the sample and is always aware of the sample's location, the tests that have been performed on the sample, and the tests that need to be performed. The LIMS can generate a chain of custody showing all personnel in the laboratory who had possession of the sample.

Sample tracking is started by a process called sample log-in. In this process the sample is given an identification code used by the system and the tests needed to be run on the sample are identified. Usually at this time, sample labels showing the identification code are printed and an inventory list of samples accepted from a particular customer is generated. Many LIMSs use bar code labels so samples can be easily identified with bar code readers rather than by operators having to input long sample identification codes. The labeled samples are then routed into the laboratory for analysis.

Lists, sometimes called worklists, can be generated showing the samples that must be analyzed by a specific test, instrument, or work location. The samples to be analyzed can be prioritized by the LIMS to ensure that the samples that must be completed most rapidly are analyzed first.

Some LIMSs include with sample tracking the ability to set a price for each test. With this information, an invoice for the testing service can be generated along with the inventory of samples accepted for analysis.

As tests are performed, the test results are entered into the LIMS along with a date and time of completion and the identification of the instrument operator. When all of the tests for a sample have been performed, the LIMS can generate a report showing the results of the tests. The analysis of the sample is then complete and the date and time of the completed analysis are entered into the system.

With this information alone, a wide variety of sample tracking management reports can be generated. Some common management reports generated by a LIMS using these data cover the following areas:

- Volume of samples analyzed in the laboratory over selected periods
- Volume of tests performed in the laboratory over selected periods
- Samples that are currently in the laboratory ready to be analyzed
- Tests to be performed on a specific sample or set of samples
- Amount of time a sample was in the laboratory for analysis
- Number of tests performed by a particular instrument operator in the laboratory

All of this information is extremely valuable for proper management of laboratory resources.

Test Results

Entering test results into the LIMS is done basically using two different methods, which depend on the type of analysis and the capabilities of the analytical instruments. The simplest method is to enter the results manually. In this method, the operator enters the test results, the instrument operator, and the date and time of completion into the system through a series of prompts on the computer screen. A good LIMS will check to ensure that the range of test results entered is plausible. This ensures that values well out of range are not accidentally entered because of operator error.

If an instrument generates a large volume of data for each sample tested or a large number of tests are performed, then manual entry is not very efficient. In this case, if the instrument can be interfaced to the computer system, the results can be transmitted electronically from the instrument to the LIMS. The operator in this method needs to check the results, but does not have to enter each piece of data manually. As many laboratory instruments include computerized data systems (see CHEMICAL INDUSTRY, USE OF COMPUTERS IN THE), electronic transmission of instrument data is now very common.

Usually the data from an instrument contain many more pieces of information than are needed in the database. As part of the instrument-interfacing process, programs are written to filter and parse the data sent from the instrument. The data of interest, obtained after the original instrument data are filtered and parsed, can then be loaded into the LIMS.

Calibration and Check Standard Results

The generation of valid test results requires the analysis of both calibration standards and check standards. Calibration standards are used to generate the calibration curves or lines used to compute the actual amount or concentration of a particular analyte in the sample. Check standards are analyzed to show that the complete analysis system is in statistical control. The calibration and check standard results are usually entered into a LIMS.

Using the calibration standard data, the LIMS can generate the calibration curves or lines for each analyte tested. Using the check standard data, the LIMS can generate control charts showing whether the analysis system is in statistical control.

Stored along with the calibration and check standard data are maintenance or instrument component changes performed on the instrument. These changes can dramatically affect the calibration, check standards, and sample results. With the change recorded in the LIMS, when data are reviewed in the future any dramatic changes in values can be easily explained. Some LIMSs include modules that alert operators when routine maintenance is required on an instrument.

Making Data Widely Available

The valuable data generated in a laboratory should be widely available within a particular organization. This is one of the functions of a LIMS. This usually means the data must be available to a wide variety of computers and computer systems via networks or electronic mail or interactively through resources like bulletin boards.

IMPLEMENTATION

Implementation of a LIMS, like most computer system solutions, requires three major components. First you need computer hardware: the actual computers, instrument interfaces, and printers. Then you need software. The central software component of a LIMS is usually a database management system. A database management system can perform the bulk of the data handling functions required for a LIMS. Finally, you need brainware: people with the knowledge to use the LIMS, and procedures that the LIMS operators can follow to ensure that data are properly entered so they can be easily retrieved from the system.

BRAINWARE

The importance of brainware in implementing a LIMS is usually underestimated. Brainware is needed most when planning the LIMS. Even before any computer hardware or software has been purchased, the entire LIMS should be planned in as much detail as possible. What functions will the LIMS perform? What data will be captured, where and how? What will the reports look like? Are the informational needs of the LIMS users being met? Every possible detail should be planned so that when the actual components of the system are purchased, all of the functions planned for the LIMS can be included.

After the LIMS has been developed or installed, brainware is needed to train the operators and the LIMS users. Operators must learn which procedures should be used for the system, which data should be entered and when, which results should be entered by hand, and how data will be captured electronically from instruments. LIMS report users must learn how to generate and read the reports.

The success or failure of a LIMS is dependent on brainware. A well-planned LIMS with knowledgeable operators and users will meet the informational needs of the users. A poorly planned and implemented LIMS simply will not be used, as the information it contains will not be of value to potential users. A poorly planned and implemented LIMS robs the users twice. First the resources used to develop the LIMS are lost, and second, the valuable data and resources of the laboratory itself are not available as needed.

COMPUTER HARDWARE

The earliest LIMSs were developed on the only computer hardware available at the time, mainframes and minicomputers. Today, computer hardware used to implement a LIMS covers a wide range of computers from personal computers all the way to mainframes.

The rapid development of personal computer–based and workstation-based local area networks (LANs) has provided a good match for the hardware needs of a LIMS. These systems can use the same computer hardware used by most modern laboratory instrument data systems. Through insertion of a LAN card and use of LAN software, the data communication needs between computers interfaced to instruments and the computers of LIMS users are met. Data generated by an instrument in the LAN can be easily entered in the LIMS.

LANs can also be used by minicomputer- and mainframe-based LIMSs to gather data from personal computers and workstations. These data can then be transmitted to the mainframe or minicomputer and loaded into the LIMS.

COMPUTER SOFTWARE

A DATABASE MANAGEMENT program plays the central role in most LIMSs. In early LIMS development, the vendor or user had to develop a system of programs that could perform most of the functions you now find in "off-the-shelf" database management systems. This was a monumental task. Today, most LIMSs use an "off-the-shelf" database management system that provides all the major functions needed. These functions include the ability to

- Create a database
- Enter data into the database
- Easily create data entry forms or screens
- Check data entered to ensure they are valid
- Edit data already entered
- Sort the data using multiple fields
- Query the data to obtain data that meet a specific criterion
- Report the data
- Easily create various report formats
- Print reports and graphs using a number of different printers, plotters, and laser printers

To program these features and functions into a system of programs from scratch is far from a trivial task. Luckily, database management programs provide most of these features so that the LIMS developer is actually creating an application of a database management system (DBMS) rather than creating both the DBMS and the application.

Powerful "off-the-shelf" DBMS software is available on virtually all of the hardware platforms one would consider for a LIMS. Multiuser DBMS software written to run on networked computers is available and it has been used to create many user-developed LIMSs.

The other software that must be developed is usually viewed as part of an instrument interface. This software must have the ability to communicate with an instrument to capture the needed data. Then the data needed for the LIMS must be filtered and parsed from the captured data and loaded into the database. Usually these programs are written in a high-level language like C, Pascal, or BASIC.

The data captured from instruments are usually streams of text in the American Standard Code for Information Interchange (ASCII) format. This ASCII text can then be parsed and filtered to create an output file of comma-delimited ASCII text. In this common data format, each numerical value is separated from others with commas and pieces of data that are delimited with quota-

tion marks. This is the most common format used to transport data between various programs and computer systems because nearly all computer systems can handle ASCII data and most application programs can both read and write in this type of file format. Note this example of two lines of comma-delimited ASCII text:

123.45, 345.6,"benzene",45689,
"GIO","09/23/90"
234.43, 903.4, "ethanol",90234,
"GIO","09/23/90"

Most database management programs can read a file with this format. Each piece of data delimited with a comma will be placed in a separate field in the database, and each line of data will be an individual record in the database. To load ASCII data, the order of the data separated by commas in the ASCII file must be the same as the order of the fields in the table where the data are to be loaded.

VENDOR PURCHASED OR USER DEVELOPED?

If you need the features of a LIMS, you have two major sources. You can purchase a LIMS from a vendor or you can develop the LIMS yourself. As you can already see, the LIMS is not a product category in which a single product can fit the needs of many potential users. In essence, a good LIMS is customized for a particular laboratory, operators, and users.

A LIMS vendor will normally have a core product that uses a specific DBMS running on a specific set of computer hardware. This system can then be customized to meet your particular needs. Normally, the more customization needed, the more the system will cost. Each instrument interfaced to the system will probably require some custom programming. Often overlooked are the brainware costs. Do I have a plan showing I will meet all my laboratory informational needs? Who will train the LIMS operators and users? Who will set up the data handling procedures? Usually these tasks are left to the user unless the vendor specifically contracts to make these plans.

If you choose to create your own LIMS, you must first invest in brainware to plan the LIMS. Then you can select the DBMS and hardware platform. You must develop the LIMS application using the DBMS and other programs where needed. Finally, you must train the LIMS operators and users. The steps you must follow are not that different whether you purchase a LIMS from a vendor or develop your own.

VALUABLE LABORATORY DATA

As laboratory data are so valuable, the management of the data and the resources that produce the data is a critical part of any laboratory's well-being. With the cost of computer hardware and database management software decreasing rapidly, the overall costs of implementing a LIMS have dropped substantially. The costs are in a range now where a laboratory of nearly any size can afford to invest in a LIMS. Because laboratory data are so valuable, all laboratories will soon have some form of LIMS.

For Further Reading

Laboratory PC User, 16 pages per issue. Published since June 1986, 12 times a year. Monthly newsletter of the Laboratory PC Users Group, 5989 Vista Loop, San Jose, CA 95124. Telephone: (408) 723-0947. This newsletter provides valuable tips and applications on using personal computers in scientific laboratories, with special emphasis on laboratory data management and instrument interfacing.

Mezei, L. 1989. *Laboratory Lotus: A complete guide to instrument interfacing.* Englewood Cliffs, N.J.: Prentice-Hall. A guide for using Lotus Symphony or 1-2-3 for instrument interfacing.

———. 1990. *Spreadsheet statistics & curve fitting for scientists and engineers.* Englewood Cliffs, N.J.: Prentice-Hall. A guide for using spreadsheet programs for performing scientific statistical and curve fitting applications.

Moore, J. H., C. C. Davis, and M. A. Coplan. 1983. *Building scientific apparatus: A practical guide to design and construction.* Reading, Mass.: Addison-Wesley. This hands-on book describes techniques for building scientific apparatus for experimentation. More than 140 pages are dedicated to electronics and electronic components.

Ouchi, G. I. 1987. *Personal computers for scientists: A byte at a time.* Washington, D.C.: American Chemical Society Press. Introduction to scientific personal computer applications using off-the-shelf software programs.

———. 1988. *Lotus in the lab: Spreadsheet applications for scientists and engineers.* Reading, Mass.: Addison-Wesley. Book showing applications of Lotus 1-2-3 solving scientific problems.

PC Magazine, Ziff-Davis. Published 22 times a year. This is the best source for personal computer information including product reviews, hands-on applications, and computing trends.

Personal Computing Tools Catalog. Published quarterly. Contact Personal Computing Tools, 17419 Farley Road, Los Gatos, CA 95030. Telephone: (408) 395-6600. Valuable catalog of products for scientific computing.

Ratzlaff, K. L. 1987. *Introduction to computer-assisted experimentation.* New York: Wiley. Good book on basic electronics and computerized data acquisition and control.

Seyer, S. 1984. *RS–232 made easy.* Englewood Cliffs, N.J.: Prentice-Hall. Good book on RS-232 interfacing.

Glenn I. Ouchi

LANGUAGES, COMPUTER

[There are various means of transmitting instructions and data to computers; all such means are called computer languages, *but such languages vary extensively in form, complexity, and ease of use.*

The most primitive of computer languages is machine language, in which instructions are given to a computer as binary information, the equivalent of the on/off signals that computers use to carry out operations. A slightly more advanced language is assembly language (also referred to as assembler language), which renders instructions as simple combinations of alphabet letters, for the convenience of human users.

Neither machine nor assembly languages are intuitively easy to use, though, and so there has been rapid development of increasingly sophisticated languages, the goal of which is ease of use by human operators in various fields. Some specific fields have developed computer languages that accommodate their demands, as FORTRAN does for science, APL for engineering, and COBOL for business. ADA was developed specifically by the U.S. government. Other languages, such as BASIC, PASCAL, and C, were developed for general-purpose programming.

In addition to these high-level languages, various software manufacturers have developed special languages, called very-high-level languages, that operate as part of database management or other software (see LANGUAGES, VERY-HIGH-LEVEL). Regardless of the form, syntax, or usage, though, all computer languages have the same basic function: the transfer of instructions to a computer.

For information on still other computer languages, see ALGOL 60 AND ALGOL 68, FORTH, LISP AND PROLOG, LOGO, MODULA-2, PL-I, RPG, and SMALLTALK.]

A computer language is an interface between man and machine. Computers understand only one language: the binary language of zeros and ones. While it is possible for a human to communicate with a computer on the computer's terms, it is far more efficient to communicate in a language that is more easily understood by humans. Scientists communicated with the earliest computers in the computer's native language; those early computers had toggle switches on the control panel that the operators used to toggle in instructions bit by bit, byte by byte. It wasn't long, however, before they started looking for a better way than this first generation of computer languages.

The better way was assembly language. Assembly language, and its immediate predecessor, machine language, are organized so there is a one-to-one relationship between the language statement and the instruction issued to the computer. The difference between assembly language and direct entry of the machine language is that assembly language is written using mnemonics, or shorthand that is more meaningful to the human than the binary language of the machine. Assembly language is commonly referred to as the second generation of computer languages.

The third generation arrived when scientists developed the compiler. The first compilers were only slightly more efficient than assembly language, but they provided a more human-comprehensible description of the program's algorithms than did assembly language.

A program that will be compiled or interpreted by a computer language is written using a text editor to create a file containing human-comprehensible language statements. This file, containing the source code, is either interpreted or compiled to produce machine code, the language understood by the computer.

Languages can be either interpreted or compiled. An interpreted language is one in which each source code statement is parsed before execution. Whether a given language is interpreted or compiled is determined by the language vendor. Interpreters offer the advantage of immediate feedback—make a change to a source code statement and immediately see the result of the change. However, interpreted languages are less efficient than compiled languages because interpreters typically do not provide optimization facilities. In a compiled language, by contrast, the compiler examines the generated code and, depending upon how sophisticated it is, performs several kinds of optimization. At the simplest level, in a loop construct, a compiler will move repeated instructions to the outside of the loop. By doing this, the compiler speeds up the execution of the code because the expression is evaluated once, instead of each time through the loop.

Compiler writers have many tricks available to optimize the generated source code. Languages can be block-structured or unstructured. Block-structured languages are an outgrowth of the research that led to the discipline of structured programming. Probably the most influential person in structured programming is Larry Constantine, whose book *Structured Design,* coauthored with

Edward Yourdon (Yourdon and Constantine 1979), introduced the computing world to the advantages of structured programming.

Constantine's work built on an earlier demonstration that any computer program could be reduced to three constructs (or blocks): sequential, selection, and iteration. In a sequential block, program control consists of each statement being executed one after the other. In a selection block, choices are made typically with an IF . . . THEN . . . ELSE structure or an ON CASE structure. The third—and final—block structure is iteration, also known as the loop structure. Loop structures typically have controls that specify how many times a loop will be executed. Typically, a loop structure will specify the beginning value, how much the counter is to be incremented at each iteration, and the termination value for the loop counter.

Once computer scientists realized the value that accompanied breaking a program into these three components, they began designing languages that encouraged and facilitated use of block structures. Languages such as Pascal, Algol, and Modula-2 were designed to provide the modularity that block structuring offered. These competed with nonblock-structured languages such as BASIC, FORTRAN, and LISP.

A block-structured language is identifiable by its reliance on modular construction. Each module in a block-structured language typically begins with a "BEGIN" statement and ends with an "END" statement. A higher (calling) module need not know what happens inside such a block; it views the block as a "black box" into which it feeds data and reads it transformed in some way upon exit.

Most modern languages are block-structured. Even languages that began life as unstructured languages have evolved to provide more structures. BASIC and FORTRAN are examples of such languages. COBOL is an interesting exception because it is semiblock-structured. Early versions of COBOL provided only limited modularity. The paragraph in COBOL appears to define a block structure, but the blocks do not have absolute endings. While it is possible to write COBOL code in a block-structured manner,

it is up to the programmer to make sure it is done so.

Computer languages can also be categorized on the basis of whether they are line oriented or not. Both COBOL and FORTRAN are veterans of the earliest days of computing, when programs were punched into a Hollerith card. Because these languages began life with card orientation, it was natural for the designers to assign a meaning to certain card columns. When you have only eighty columns available for a statement, it makes the compiler writer's job easier if he or she knows that the "nine" number for a statement is found in columns one through six, the level declaration of a COBOL data division statement is found in columns eight and nine, and so on.

Languages developed since the advent of interactive terminals tend not to be line oriented. Whereas in FORTRAN each statement is separated by an EOL (end-of-line) token (typically a CR/LF, or carriage return/line feed pair), in a language such as Pascal the "white space" conveys no information content to the compiler. The program

```
program Hello;

begin
  writeln("Hello, World");
end.
```

is exactly the same to the compiler as

```
program Hello; begin writeln("Hello, World");
end.
```

The first thing any compiler does is to parse the program—it identifies each of the relevant tokens. (In the above example program, the lexical analyzer, which does the parsing, will strip out all tabs, spaces, EOLs, etc., and will replace each occurrence with one space. The second program above demonstrates how the source code will look to the compiler after the lexical analyzer has removed all the white space.)

Although a program such as the second example could be written, doing so would obviate one of the most important reasons for having a high-level language: It enhances human understanding of the program logic. When we see "program Hello;" on a line by itself we automatically recognize it as the statement that begins a program. If each such statement is buried in a continuous stream of undifferentiated words, understanding suffers.

Many people make the mistake of assuming two languages with the same syntax will produce functionally identical code. That's not necessarily true, because although the syntax may be the same, the semantics of that syntax may not be. For example, the Pascal statement

$a = b$

is used to inquire whether variable a is equal to variable b; however, the same statement in the C programming language is an assignment statement—that is, the value contained in the variable b is placed in the variable a.

Thus, to program effectively using computer languages, the programmer should have a working knowledge of how each source code statement in his or her source code file will be rendered into machine language by the compiler to be used. Compiler vendors have different goals in mind when they develop compilers. One vendor may be most interested in a product that will compile the source code as fast as possible (to give the programmer the quickest possible feedback) but in doing so is willing to sacrifice generated code size or execution speed. Another vendor may be targeting programmers for whom execution speed is paramount; the compiler may take longer to compile the same source code but result in an executable that is smaller and/or faster than the executable produced by the competition's compiler. Therefore, the dedicated programmer will examine the generated machine code and learn how his tool performs when processing different types of source code instructions.

What does the future hold for computer languages? An important trend that will continue to accelerate is the use of computer-aided software engineering (CASE) tools to generate language source code. Programmers will spend less time writing individual language source instructions and more time analyzing the job the program is to perform. These requirements will be expressed in graphical terms—that is, the programmer will use a graphical environment to create an abstract picture of the overall job to be performed by the system he or she is creating. Using the CASE tool, the programmer takes the graphical description of the problem domain and creates a functional description of how the program will be organized. Another way of describing the two phases of development is to consider the first phase as one in which the programmer explores *what* the program or system is to accomplish; this phase is called analysis. In the second phase, the developer translates the *what* derived in the preceding phase into an abstract description of *how* the system will perform the task defined in the analysis phase; this phase is known as *design*.

Because CASE tool vendors in general are moving toward tools that offer an integrated, seamless path from analysis to code generation, the languages the programmer uses will become increasingly abstract. This is a continuation of the trend begun with the migration from first- to second- to third-generation languages. However, as always, the effective programmer needs to understand what his or her tools are doing for him or her.

Reference

Yourdon, E., and L. L. Constantine. 1979. *Structured design: Fundamentals of a discipline of computer program and system design.* 2nd ed. Englewood Cliffs, N.J.: Prentice-Hall.

Warren Keuffel

LANGUAGES, VERY-HIGH-LEVEL

Since the beginning of the electronic digital computer, a tremendous amount of work has been dedicated to the task of making computer programming easier. Originally, computers were programmed directly in their own language, which consists entirely of ones and zeros; over time, the computer languages have become more and more like human, or "higher-level," languages.

In addition to becoming more human, computer languages have become more abstract, more capable of dealing with rules and concepts; still, computer languages, even at the highest levels, are much more symbolic, and have a much smaller vocabulary, than human languages.

Very-high-level languages attempt to make available to more people the data stored in computers by making the necessary programming as much like human speech and thought processes as possible. Of course, since the computer still only understands ones and zeros, the human-readable program, or source code, must be translated into computer-readable, or object-code, form by a compiler or interpreter.

Instructions in the computer's own binary code, or machine language, was the first programming method, and it is considered to be the lowest-level computer language. Machine language is also the most difficult to translate into another language so that the program can be used on another computer.

At a somewhat higher level is assembler language; it is human-readable and can be translated, with some difficulty, so programs can be used on different types of computers. Assembler language programming is quite time-consuming and requires a very high level of programmer training and skill, since it still requires knowledge of the architecture of the central processing unit (CPU) as well as the operating system under which the program will run. Assembler language is also considered a low-level language, but it is the second generation of computer languages.

Most computer programming is still done in third-generation languages such as COBOL (from "COmmon Business-Oriented Language"), FORTRAN ("FORmula TRANslator"), Algol ("Algorithmic language"), LISP ("LISt Processor"), BASIC ("Beginner's All-purpose Symbolic Instruction Code"), or Pascal (named for Blaise Pascal, the seventeenth-century mathematician who built the first mechanical calculating machine). Programs written in these high-level languages can generally be moved from one type of computer to another fairly easily; they are said to be "portable."

Because high-level languages are designed for human rather than computer convenience, they must be compiled or interpreted in order to run on the computer. The compiler or interpreter, itself a computer program that converts the human-readable computer language into the ones and zeros the computer understands, takes care of a great number of machine- and operating system-dependent details, freeing the programmer to concentrate on the solution as a whole.

There is a price for this convenience, however; programs written in high-level languages usually require more memory and run more slowly than those written in low-level languages. Computers, particularly personal computers, have been getting faster during the same period that languages have become less efficient; the net effect is that programs written in high-level languages run as fast on modern computers as those written in low-level languages did on older computers.

C (so called because its predecessor was called "B") has the characteristics of both second- and third-generation languages; some programmers call it a "high-level assembler language." A C program requires more statements than a COBOL program but is as portable; it requires fewer statements than an assembler language program but will run almost as fast. As a result, C is a very popular language among skilled programmers and software developers.

Very-high-level languages, also called fourth-generation languages, typically consist of English-like words and phrases; when implemented on microcomputers, some include graphic devices such as icons and on-screen "push-buttons" both in the programming task and in the resulting application.

Many fourth-generation languages use Structured Query Language (SQL) as a basis for operations; there is an ANSI standard for SQL.

Oracle, from Oracle Corporation of Redwood Shores, California, was the first very-high-level language to be made commercially available; it was released in 1979. In the years since then, this SQL-based relational database management system has been implemented on many types of mainframes, minicomputers, and microcomputers, including IBM's VM/CMS and MS/SP, DEC's VAX/VMS, and DG's AOS/VS.

Because SQL is standardized, it is possible to develop an Oracle application on a microcomputer, then move it to a mainframe that runs Oracle or IBM's DB2.

Oracle Card, a recent development, includes both microcomputer and mainframe components, and combines the ease of use of the microcomputer with the massive data storage of the typical mainframe. It runs on an Apple Macintosh or an IBM PC (using Microsoft Windows) and allows a user to build a microcomputer application with a graphical user interface that resembles the interface to Apple's HyperCard but that has access to an Oracle mainframe database. The application could have multiple windows into the host database for data entry, browsing, or extracting information, and data in the database may be viewed and edited one row at a time, or several rows can be displayed at once.

The direction that language development will take is difficult to predict, but with languages such as PROLOG (an artificial intelligence [AI] language that applies rules to data to arrive at solutions), Occam (a parallel-processing language), and PARLOG (another parallel-processing language) gaining ground, it is very possible that the programming languages of the future will include SQL and other elements from very-high-level languages, combined with "rule-based" parallel processing, to achieve unparalleled power and ease of use.

For Further Reading

Bodner, M. S. 1990. *Micro to mainframe data interchange.* 2nd ed. Blue Ridge Summit, Pa.: TAB Books.

Hancock, L., and M. Kreiger. 1982. *The C primer.* New York: McGraw-Hill.

Keenan, V. 1991. Oracle Card eases client development. *MacWEEK* 5(15):12.

Walter, R. 1991. *The secret guide to computers.* 14th ed. Somerville, Mass.: Russ Walter Publications.

Sheldon T. Hall

LAW ENFORCEMENT, COMPUTERS IN

Like any business that deals with massive amounts of information on a daily basis, the typical law enforcement agency has become dependent on computers for management and record keeping. The usefulness of these tools to law enforcement personnel has been demonstrated over the past decade: computers save time in keeping accurate records and in obtaining summaries of required information. Just as businesses have become more dependent on computers to make their activities more efficient, local, state, and federal law enforcement agencies would find it difficult to function without access to law enforcement information systems, and many agencies depend just as heavily on computers to facilitate clerical and office tasks.

Law enforcement agencies have become dependent on the utilization of computers for operations and administration, including communications, manpower design, and management; and for training, including the use of teaching computers and advanced individualized instructional techniques to enhance learning and retention (Swanson et al. 1988). Each of these categories is briefly discussed here.

For current information on other software applications, refer to information systems and applications in the law enforcement literature and the reader services of magazines in the law enforcement field, for example, *Police Chief* (International Association of Chiefs of Police, 1110 North Glebe Road, Suite 200, Arlington, Virginia 22201) and *Law and Order* (1000 Skokie Boulevard, Wilmette, Illinois 60091). The Annual Conference of the International Association of Chiefs of Police features the world's largest collection of police products and services.

The availability of manufacturers' representatives for product explanations and demonstrations gives attendees a unique opportunity to comparison shop for nearly every law enforcement–related product and service on the market.

LAW ENFORCEMENT OPERATIONS AND ADMINISTRATION

Law enforcement agencies record information about persons, places, and things. The information may be as routine as a person's traffic arrest record or as complex as an analysis of crime trends in an area. Traditionally, noncomputerized systems involved the tasks of preparation, filing, and retrieval of original police reports by hand. The time used for such labor-intensive activities and the growing volume of police reports to be analyzed provide the impetus for computerized records systems. Thus, many law enforcement agencies are making use of computer software tools for search, retrieval, and records processing in addition to other applications for operations and administration (Hernandez 1987). Some police departments are even providing field personnel with portable laptop computers and software for writing reports. Handheld computers are being used by the Long Beach and San Diego Police Departments in California to issue citations for parking and moving traffic violations.

Computerized Records Systems
A computerized records system provides police agencies with opportunities to maintain large databases with an immediate search and retrieval capability. Cooperating police agencies have almost instantaneous access to information about persons (outstanding warrants, arrest records, and missing persons), places (incident locations), and things (stolen property). Some selected examples follow:

National Crime Information Center. The National Crime Information Center (NCIC) is a nationwide on-line computer/telecommunications system containing millions of stolen property, wanted person, missing person, and unidentified person records that are instantaneously available to local, state, and federal criminal justice agencies across the United States (Federal Bureau of Investigation 1987).

Violent Criminal Apprehension Program. The Violent Criminal Apprehension Program (VICAP) is a national data center designed to collect, collate, and analyze information regarding homicides, missing persons, and unidentified dead bodies. The VICAP staff determines whether similarities exist among the individual cases reported and cases in the VICAP database. Once a multiagency case is established, on-site major case analysis, multiagency cooperation, forensic science laboratory coordination, and other case consultations are available (Brooks et al. 1987).

Automated Fingerprint Identification System. All police departments have files of fingerprints, some containing thousands or millions of records; however, effective use of these files presents a problem because comparing fingerprints manually is extremely time consuming. Now, with the Automated Fingerprint Identification System (AFIS), participating police departments can run searches on a subject's inked fingerprint card, or on identifiable latent fingerprints found at crime scenes, and make rapid suspect identifications. The AFIS system represents a milestone in fingerprint identification techniques. Elzerman (1990) observes that

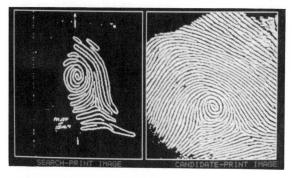

FIGURE 1. The Automated Fingerprint Identification System generates a list of possible candidates to match a latent print (*left*) found at a crime scene. *Courtesy Illinois State Police.*

the AFIS system does not identify individuals; it searches a database consisting of minutiae data and provides a list of possible candidates whose images are then examined by a fingerprint technician to determine if an identification can be made. Elzerman states that "AFIS systems are probably the most important thing that has happened in the law enforcement field since the two-way radio." By networking the central AFIS processing system with remote input stations and booking and verification terminals, one can perform on-line searches from offices located almost anywhere. When several law enforcement agencies install AFIS systems and use a combined database, fingerprint matching becomes possible over a wider area. Such a system does exist in the northwestern part of the United States.

Automated Facial Composite Systems. Compusketch and comPHOTOfit are two computer programs being used by police departments to assemble composite pictures of criminal suspects for subsequent identification by victims and witnesses. Axiom Research Corporation's (1990) comPHOTOfit is a computerized facial composite system capable of creating a photographic likeness of a suspect. It gives law enforcement agencies the ability to convert eyewitness recall of a suspect's likeness from a hazy recollection to a computer-enhanced graphic. The database is an immense library of facial features that permits interchange of the eyes, nose, mouth, forehead, and chin with supplemental selection of mustache, beards, eyeglasses, and head wear, and is capable of producing numerous facial combinations.

Crime Statistics

Analysis of data on crimes known to the police into manageable summaries provides law enforcement with important information with which to combat crime. The purpose of crime analysis is to forecast specific future trends from the use of databases and automated records systems. Auten (1987), investigating a means of improving substantially both effectiveness and efficiency in a medium-sized police department, reports

FIGURE 2. Laser-printed sketch of a suspect, generated by the ComPhotofit facial identification system. *Courtesy Sirchie Finger Print Laboratories.*

the use of an off-the-shelf database management program for crime analysis as an example of selecting compatible hardware and software to meet locally assessed needs. Nationwide, for more than 60 years, the U.S. Department of Justice's Uniform Crime Report (UCR) Program has operated successfully and has benefited not only law enforcement but federal, state, and local governments as well. The data have been utilized by those in the academic field to measure the effects of crime on the populace and to identify areas for social reform. As the official recipient of the data for the U.S. Department of Justice, the Federal Bureau of Investigation (FBI) has benefited greatly from the close harmony and comradeship with local law enforcement that has grown through managing the program. The willingness of more than 16,000 law enforcement jurisdictions, which represent 96 percent of the population of the United States, to participate in the UCR Program attests to its importance and stature. The yearly UCR report *Crime in the United States* and preliminary reports are used not only by law enforcement agencies but also by news media, tourism agencies, and others with an interest in crime in the United States (Federal Bureau of Investigation 1990).

Management and Administration

Computers have become commonplace as tools to assist in management activities of law enforcement. Colton (1979) reports on studies and surveys designed to determine the impact of computers on law enforcement. Among the applications reported are police patrol inquiry and information retrieval, traffic information processing, administrative data processing, crime statistics information services, resource allocation, criminal investigation applications, and command and control. Hernandez (1987), in a review, reports that the emergence of the microcomputer has brought on a new era in police administration. Decision support systems (DSSs) and expert systems (ESs) are among numerous applications of the microcomputer discussed. Hernandez observes the use of DSSs for serving the needs of managers and administrators by taking the modeling power of spreadsheets, as an example, to manipulate data and provide precise information regarding personnel resources and capability. He also observes the emergence of numerous applications in administration, due to advances in expert systems to clone expertise and scan massive amounts of data. Hernandez concludes that managers must be prepared to exploit the technology because the microcomputer can be used to increase the productivity of personnel and improve both operations and decision making. Examples of ESs include the FBI's VICAP (Brooks et al. 1987) and VP-Expert: Rapist Profiling (Burian 1991). These are ES knowledge-based systems that use the reasoning patterns of experts to create computer programs that emulate those experts.

LAW ENFORCEMENT TRAINING

Numerous computer applications in training of law enforcement personnel have been reported in the literature. These include (1) simulations of practical situations, (2) review of law enforcement procedures, (3) record keeping and report preparation, (4) testing and evaluation, and (5) computer literacy for criminal justice personnel.

Only the first two activities are discussed here because they involve delivery of actual instruction to trainees. The next two, record keeping/report writing ("Southeast Florida Institute . . ." 1985) and testing/evaluation (Olsen 1977; Dennis et al. 1979; Walker and Flammang 1980, 1981), use technology in training in other ways. All, however, are reported to make important contributions to the quality of training in law enforcement and thus are included in this list.

Before the full potential of computers can be realized, personnel who use them must be adequately trained. Computers are unique management tools that have both on-the-job roles and potential for supporting the training of personnel for their respective roles. The utilization of computers is described here from an occupational training perspective since computers both act as the subject of instruction and provide the means to deliver it. For other information about how computers are being used in law enforcement training in the United States, refer to information systems and applications in the literature (Roblyer 1989).

Simulations of Practical Situations

Computer simulations are programs that allow trainees to interact with realistic presentations of situations they might encounter. The usefulness and cost effectiveness of these resources are well documented in the literature on law enforcement training. Law enforcement personnel encounter many hazardous situations for which prior training is essential, but which are impossible to provide on a trial basis without computer simulation. Simulations have been reported to assist examples of various training functions.

Firearms Training. By far the most commonly reported training simulation is one designed to prepare police personnel for situations in which they must use weapons to defend themselves or others. O'Connell (1989) reports one such system, the Firearms Training System (FATS). It is described as a system consisting of "a large screen video projector, a laser disc player, a scoring computer, and two S&W [Smith and Wesson] .357 magnum 4-inch revolvers that are modified with special equipment for this simulator." The FATS disc has about 40 scenarios in which a person draws a weapon on the trainee. Each time the trainee responds by firing the specially modified weapon, simulated "bullet holes" are projected on the screen. The screen also indicates whether trainees hit the target, how fast they reacted to the situation, and whether or not they were "killed" in the process. As Nowell and Stinchomb (1988) observe, FATS training not only helps law enforcement officers learn essential skills they will need on the job, it has also been used successfully in court to convince juries that officers received adequate firearms training.

Johnston (1983) created another firearms training system called Computer Assisted Target Analysis (CATA). Available on the PLATO computer system, CATA is not a computer simulation like FATS, but it does assist in simulated firearms training by providing information to help trainees analyze and improve their performance in target practice situations. Trainees record their "hits" during target practice in the field on a score pad, then enter the data into the PLATO terminal. The resulting performance record, together with the instructional lessons, provides a support system for improving trainees' skill in this area.

Basic Training. The California Commission on Peace Officer Standards and Training (POST) (1989) has developed a large-scale interactive video project for the training of police recruits. Working with designers and developers, the Commission has transferred course material that represents 56 hours of traditional classroom training to videodiscs. The course covers a wide range of subject matter vital to new recruits, including an introduction to the criminal justice system; professionalism and ethics; an introduction to law, including search and seizure, use of force, and evidence collection; firearms training, including weapon cleaning and firing range procedures; report writing; transportation of prisoners; arrest procedures; and investigation techniques. Study guides for each subject content area are provided.

Crisis Training. Moore (1988) recommends the use of computers and interactive videodiscs with communications systems (telephone/radio) to simulate crisis situations during training of police officers. He points out that a program called the Casualty Reporting, Information Sorting, and Identification System (CRISIS), produced in England for use in helping to identify victims of major disasters, can also be a powerful training tool for those who must deal with such situations in real life. Another program in crisis training, described by Clede (1986), is the Interactive Crisis Simulator (ICS) developed by September and Associates East, Inc. This simulation shows trainees various situations, reacts to cardiovascular monitors attached to the trainees, and branches the scenarios according to the stress levels detected. As an officer's heartbeat increases, the severity of the situation increases, thus encouraging trainees to master their emotions. "The longer the trainee can remain calm, the more likely the scenario will be resolved quickly and without undue use of force. . . . Instructors can compare profiles of trainee performance and rate them on 28 crisis management and problem solving skills" (p. 64).

Accident Reconstruction. Badger (1989) reports several simulations that are currently being used to assist police officers as they investigate accidents. Officers enter information on the characteristics of the accident and the software gives various kinds of information on what probably took place. These packages can also be used to train officers in accident investigation techniques.

Child Abuse Training. Flammang and Walker (1990) report an investigative case strategy lesson on sexual abuse of children. This lesson was manually tested with both police and social work practitioners before it was first made a part of PLATO courseware in 1980, and then converted to microcomputer in 1990. This simulated case study causes the student to encounter a dynamic field situation. Flammang and Walker (1981) report that the simulation permits achievements not otherwise available. First, each student is able to take the officer role individually, not relying on other students in a group to assist or to take over. Second, a wide variety of situations can be offered. These range from routine to somewhat complex situations that would take the new officer several years of field experience to encounter. Before leaving the training setting, it is possible for police students to have dealt with a vast array of decisions, all in a no-risk setting. Such opportunities have proved to be beneficial in decision-making aspects of medical training. Kemmis (1977) presented results showing that students who experienced patient simulations performed, on evaluations of their behavior, more like conventional graduates with 1 to 2 years of actual experience. The surrogate experiences derived from simulation produced the learning normally derived from actual professional practice. Thus, Dennis et al. (1979) observe, as in the medical field, that a police trainee can acquire such learning with much less expense and risk by using a responsive computer simulation of the phenomenon.

Review of Law Enforcement Procedures

A variety of resources are available to help police officers learn correct operational procedures. The University of Illinois Police Training Institute (PTI) is by far the most active in developing and using computer-based training (CBT), with some 46 titles currently available on the PLATO system (Roblyer 1989) and on IBM-compatible microcomputers (Van Meter 1986; Walker 1991) using the TenCORE Language Authoring System (1990). Walker (1991), utilizing instructional techniques found effective in training more than 18,000 sworn police officers in PTI during the 1980s, reports that the objectives of his IBM-compatible microcomputer lessons address major operational law enforcement problems in crime scene search-

ing and processing, vehicle theft, stabilization of the traffic accident scene, human behavior, conflict management, stress behavior, interviewing, interrogation, child abuse/neglect allegations, child sex exploitation, police community relations, and so on. Walker and Flammang (1980, 1981) describe several benefits of providing training in this way by computer, noting that "police training can benefit from . . . individualizing instruction because of . . . disparities between student background knowledge and learning rates" (p. 224). LeDoux and Stanley (1985), in a study of CBT usage of FBI trainees, found that CBT-only and combination groups scored significantly higher than the lecture-only groups, and that attitudes toward instruction were significantly better in the groups that used CBT. Wilkinson and Chattin-McNichols (1985) found similar results in their study of police personnel in the Port of Seattle Police Department. These findings parallel those of many reviews of experimental studies in other areas (Roblyer 1989) that indicate that technology-based methods are usually at least as effective as non–technology-based methods and, depending on the types of skills and learning needs, are sometimes significantly more effective. When technology is found to be more effective, the reasons are usually that technology-based methods make learning much more interactive than the more typical lecture-based methods in which trainees are more passive participants in training. As Flammang and Walker (1982) observe, police trainers and law enforcement administrators are becoming aware that training must be more practical and performance oriented than it has been in the past if it is to give trainees the on-the-job skills they will need. It is also becoming apparent, however, that providing this interactive training through traditional methods is practically impossible.

CONCLUSIONS

In conclusion, a few statements can summarize the findings of this review and the information given in the literature by computer users in law enforcement:

- Computer-based methods can be potentially powerful in law enforcement. They have been demonstrated to be effective in many important areas of operations, communications and manpower design, management and administration, and training.

- Trainers should be prepared to exploit the technology, as the introduction of CBT begins a new era in law enforcement training.

It seems apparent from this review that the leadership of law enforcement organizations who keep these recommendations in mind can have a resource at their disposal that can greatly enhance their capability to provide effective operations, communications and manpower design, management and administration, and training. The microcomputer can help them revolutionize the police department in the same way that it has changed the face of business and industry in our country. The questions that remain revolve around when, where, and how to use technology to take maximum advantage of what it has to offer.

References

Auten, J. 1987. Using R:Base 5000 in a police department. *Law and Order,* January, pp. 250–56.

Axiom Research Corporation. 1990. comPHOTOfit. (Available from Sirchie Finger Print Laboratories, Raleigh, N.C.)

Badger, J. E. 1989. Crash course in accident investigation. *Law Enforcement Technology,* January, pp. 30–33.

Brooks, P. R., M. J. Devine, T. J. Green, B. L. Hart, and M. D. Moore. 1987. *Police Chief,* June, pp. 37, 41, 42, 44, 45.

Burian, J. J. 1991. *VP-Expert: Rapist profiling* [computer-based training program]. (Available from J. J. Burian, Moraine Valley Community College, 10900 South 88th Ave., Palos Hills, Ill. 60465.)

Clede, B., ed. 1986. Computers in technical operations. *Law and Order,* October, pp. s58–65.

Colton, K. W. 1979. The impact and use of computer technology by the police. *Communications of the ACM* 22(1).

Dennis, J. R., C. Flammang, and R. O. Walker. 1979. Instructional use of computers in police training. *Police Chief,* October, pp. 82–84.

Elzerman, T. R. 1990. Personal communication with author, Aug. 8, 1990. (Theodore R. Elzerman is Assistant Bureau Chief, Bureau of Identification, Illinois State Police, 260 N. Chicago St., Joliet, Ill. 60431-0260.)

Federal Bureau of Investigation. 1987. *National Crime Information Center: Off-line search.* Washington, D.C.: U.S. Govt. Printing Office.

Federal Bureau of Investigation. 1990. *Uniform crime reports 1989: Crime in the United States.* Washington, D.C.: U.S. Govt. Printing Office.

Flammang, C. J., and R. O. Walker. 1981. *Training: The search for alternatives.* In V. Webb (Chair), *Education and training. Symposium conducted at the Meeting of the Academy of Criminal Justice Sciences, Philadelphia, Pa.* (Available from R. O. Walker, Associate Professor, University of Illinois, Police Training Institute, 1004 South Fourth St., Champaign, Ill. 61820.)

Flammang, C. J., and R. O. Walker. 1982. Training—a rationale supporting computer-based instruction. *Police Chief,* August, pp. 60–64.

Flammang, C. J., and R. O. Walker. 1990. Investigative case strategy [computer-based training program]. Champaign: Board of Trustees, University of Illinois. (Available from the Police Training Institute, University of Illinois, 1004 S. Fourth St., Champaign, Ill. 61820.)

Hernandez, A. P. 1987. *Police Chief,* June, pp. 46–50.

Johnston, A. J. 1983. *Computer assisted target analysis.* Unpublished paper for Computer Science 317, University of Illinois, Urbana, Ill. 61801.

Kemmis, S. 1977. *How CAL simulations work.* Monograph on Student Learning in CAL. Glasgow, Scotland.

LeDoux, J. C., and C. J. Stanley. 1985. A comparative study of computer-based instruction vs. lecture. *Proceedings of the ADCIS,* pp. 10–14.

Moore, T. 1988. Police training for crisis: The

use of simulation. *Police Journal* 61(2):119–36.

Nowell, C., and J. B. Stinchomb. 1988. Firearms training: Targeting effective programs. *Corrections Today*, July, pp. 160–61.

O'Connell, R. 1989. FATS-II combines tactics, lethal weapons, low-cost in training today's officers. *Training Aids Digest*, January, pp. 1–2.

Olsen, B. T. 1977. Using the computer in a regional criminal justice training center. *Police Chief*, October, pp. 37–38.

POST: Peace Officer Standards and Training. 1989. *Introduction to law enforcement* [interactive videodisc computer package]. Atlanta, Ga.: COMSELL (500 Tech Parkway, Atlanta, Ga. 30313).

Roblyer, M. D. 1989. *Technology in criminal justice training: A review of literature.* (The Florida A&M University, College of Education Contract No. 00363.) Tallahassee: Florida Department of Law Enforcement, Division of Criminal Justice Standards and Training, Bureau of Training.

Southeast Florida Institute offers microcomputer training for police, corrections officers. 1985. *Crime Control Digest*, August, pp. 2–3.

Swanson, C. R., L. Territo, and R. W. Taylor. 1988. *Police administration: Structures, processes and behavior*, 2nd ed., pp. 365–97. New York: Macmillan.

TenCORE Language Authoring System, Edition 4.2 [computer software]. 1990. (Available from Computer Teaching Corp., 1713 S. State St., Champaign, Ill. 61820.)

Van Meter, C. W. 1986. PTI briefs: 1975–1985 the transition years. *IPA Official Journal*, pp. 23–25.

Walker, R. O., ed. 1991. *On-scene police response courses: Investigation procedures; crisis intervention, stress and variant behavior; interviewing and interrogation; child abuse/neglect investigation;* and *correspondence courses.* (Available from the author, 2316 Winchester Dr., Champaign, Ill. 61821.)

Walker, R. O., and C. J. Flammang. 1980. Law enforcement training: Entering the 1980s. *Police Chief*, November, pp. 60–64.

Walker, R. O., and C. J. Flammang. 1981. Instructional application of computer-based education in police training. *Journal of Police Science and Administration* 9(2): 224–30.

Wilkinson, T., and J. Chattin-McNichols. 1985. Effectiveness of computer-assisted instruction for police officers. *Journal of Police Science and Administration* 13(3):230–35.

Roy O. Walker

LEARNING

See Education, Computers in; Machine Learning

LEGAL APPLICATIONS OF COMPUTERS

The legal profession has for many years been at the forefront of the computer revolution in office automation. Its specialized needs to perform legal research, manage evidentiary information, and generate standardized legal documents have driven the state of the art in full-text information retrieval, word processing, automated document drafting, and even in some branches of artificial intelligence (AI). Computers are now in widespread use in law offices of all sizes.

AUTOMATED TIME ACCOUNTING AND BILLING SYSTEMS

The computerization of the legal profession began in the late 1960s, when systems were introduced into the largest law firms to accept hourly time charges and cash disbursement records and to sort them into draft client bills. The firms that did this soon learned that the systems could generate a variety of useful reports—for example, reports for each attorney of missing time charges and reports for each attorney and each department of monthly and annual charges billed and recovered from clients.

While implemented simply to reduce manual labor, it was quickly discovered that these systems increased the net income of many law firms by 20 percent or more, revealing gross inefficiencies in the ways that attorneys managed their businesses.

Today, systems of this type are available for firms of all sizes and are widely used. The trend is toward networked systems that permit each attorney to enter time charges on his or her own personal computer's screen and to have the information automatically routed over the network to a centralized computer.

Reports generated by these systems have had a profound sociological impact on the practice of law. Previously, a young associate working for four or five attorneys focused on learning the law and serving the client's needs without much concern about gross billings and without much direct supervision by any one individual. Now the office manager can determine from the computer just how many hours each associate (and each partner) is billing, what type of work each associate (and each partner) is doing, and what percentage of time billed is actually recovered from paying clients. Many firms now set "billable hour quotas" for associates, demanding that they bill eighteen hundred to two thousand hours or more each year and forcing them to work long evenings and weekends to achieve these goals. Firms that previously focused on professionalism and service thus find themselves focusing more and more on maximizing their income, sometimes even giving up practice areas where the return is not deemed adequate.

Institutional law practices such as poverty law offices, prosecutorial offices, and legal defender offices also use time management systems to some extent; but since they do not have clients to bill, the reports generated in these practices tend to focus on how many cases of a given type are processed to completion each month and each year by each attorney, rather than on hours worked. These reports can be generated from docketing systems of the type described below, so time accounting systems may not be needed in such practices.

DOCKET MANAGEMENT SYSTEMS

All law firms, all prosecutorial and legal defender offices, and all courts and agencies need to manage and control their dockets. At the very minimum, precautions must be taken to see that cases are filed prior to the expiration of statute of limitations dates, beyond which a case cannot be filed. Also, court dates, brief due dates, and other critical deadlines must be carefully scheduled, recorded, and reported.

Manual card file systems are still used for docketing in many law firms, but the trend is toward computerized database systems that can generate lists of the docketing deadlines sorted in various useful ways. For example, each attorney is provided with a list, in date order, of his or her own deadlines, with every case reported to at least two attorneys (supervising attorney and responsible attorney). Separate lists of deadlines are also provided for each department and for the firm as a whole. In this manner, responsibility for meeting all deadlines is shared by at least four individuals within the firm.

Numerous useful reports can be pulled from the docketing system, which normally keeps track of what attorneys are assigned to which case and of each case's current status. These reports reveal how evenly work is distributed throughout the firm and can be useful in making hiring, promotional, and reorganization decisions.

Corporate counsel use specialized systems to manage the activities of their outside counsel, keeping track of total costs as well as docketing activity. These systems can generate warnings when the costs of a given matter or of a given outside law firm are out of line with preestablished norms.

Courts and agencies also maintain elaborate docketing systems that can assist a judge in scheduling a hearing so it does not conflict with other hearings and with the lawyers' other court appearances. Generally, judges prefer to keep pressure on the attorneys to move each case along toward trial or settlement (preferably the latter, since trial time is limited in all court systems). These systems can inform the judge of which cases are progressing more slowly toward disposition and can inform the supervisory judge of which judges are developing excessive backlogs of pending cases.

Some court systems permit attorneys to view both their own and the court's docketing records to ensure that they agree. Court dockets previously published in newspapers are now available on-line. A few courts even permit lawyers to enter motions onto the court's calendar from their office by dialing into the court's computer.

CRIMINAL HISTORY RECORD INFORMATION (CHRI)

Similar to docketing information, criminal records of formal events such as arrest, filing of charges, conviction, and dismissal are maintained on police, prosecutorial, and court computers. These records are used by the police in investigations, by the courts in setting bond and in sentencing, and to some extent by the public. The FBI gathers much of this information from the states into its centralized computer system. While this information is public, the U.S. Supreme Court has ruled that centralized collections of CHRI are protected by the Federal Right to Privacy Act and are not available to the public. Public access to state CHRI varies from state to state.

In many states, this CHRI information is entered manually into several different computers, and it is difficult to match up the records obtained from the different computers to form a complete criminal history. Arrest information not augmented by disposition information (such as "acquitted" or "convicted") is incomplete, and the dissemination of this incomplete information raises significant privacy concerns.

The police normally maintain separate investigatory files, which are sometimes computerized but which are not generally available to the public.

COMPUTER-ASSISTED LEGAL RESEARCH

Attorneys pioneered the use of large mainframe computers for searching through the cases and statutes, looking for precedents.

After an initial demonstration of full-text word searching at the 1960 American Bar Association meeting, the Air Force established their LITE (later FLITE—Federal Legal Information Through Electronics) computer system and loaded it with cases relating to military justice. That system was later updated to contain all of the U.S. federal cases.

The earliest successful commercial venture was LEXIS, initially established by OBAR (Ohio Bar Automated Research), a not-for-profit entity of Ohio attorneys. LEXIS is now run by MDC (Mead Data Central, Inc.), a subsidiary of Mead Paper Company. A not-for-profit corporation of attorneys called NCAIR (National Center for Automated Information Retrieval) assisted MDC in establishing a full-text database containing federal and state judicial decisions, statutes, administrative regulations, and law review articles. MDC also maintains NEXIS, a database of magazine and newspaper articles.

West Publishing Company uses large computers to organize materials into a variety of helpful publications for attorneys. West publishes all of the state and federal cases—in books, and in their own full-text retrieval system, WESTLAW, which is comparable to LEXIS. In addition, West writes one or more issue summaries called headnotes for each case it publishes and indexes these headnotes within a master outline/index of the law, the Key Number System. Each headnote also contains the citation of any relevant statutory section. These headnotes are included within the WESTLAW database and enable attorneys to narrow their searches for words and phrases to selected cases indexed in a particular way.

Using either LEXIS or WESTLAW, one wishing to find all the court opinions relating to a particular topic types into the computer a "search request"—a formal statement of what words and phrases each opinion found by the computer and displayed to the attorney is to contain. For example, to find all the judicial decisions that discuss recovering (under the Illinois Dram Shop Act) from an owner of a tavern for a gunshot injury committed by an intoxicated patron, one might formulate the following search request:

"dram shop" and "gun" or "rifle"

On both LEXIS and WESTLAW, this search retrieves and displays all the judicial decisions that contain the phrase "dram shop" and also one of the two words "gun" and "rifle." In this search request, the quote marks identify the phrase, the "or" conjoins synonyms, and the "and" conjoins groups of synonyms.

West also uses a mainframe computer to sort the case headnotes into a variety of useful hardbound indices. For example, West publishes a federal digest that contains the headnotes taken from all federal cases sorted into order by legal topic and subtopic. West publishes similarly organized state law digests and also a national law digest. Using the statutory section references as a sorting guide, West sorts these same headnotes into statute section order, merges in the statutory language, and then publishes annotated statutes (state or federal) in which each statutory section is followed by the relevant case headnotes for all cases that have construed the meaning of the statutory language.

Shepard's, a subsidiary of McGraw-Hill, has for many years published in bound form a reverse citation index that tells which more recent cases have cited any given earlier case. Every citation to court authority in every brief must be "Shepardized" by a law clerk to see if the court's decision has been reversed or overruled. West integrated this Shepard's database into WESTLAW so that when viewing an earlier case, one may jump directly to later cases that may have cited and reversed or overruled the earlier case. Later, MDC added this feature to LEXIS.

Lawyers' Cooperative Publishing Company developed an in-house computer system to assist editors in checking out citations to cases. When one typed a citation (volume, report name, and page) into this AUTOCITE service, one received back the proper full name of the case, the proper citation for the decision, the proper parallel citations to other services, and the relevant subsequent history of the case—whether it was affirmed on appeal, whether it has been overruled, etc. This information is also useful to attorneys preparing briefs, where correct case names and parallel citations are essential. The

AUTOCITE service is now integrated into LEXIS. More recently, West has introduced a comparable service as part of WESTLAW.

In conjunction with JURISOFT (now owned by MDC), LEXIS has introduced a service that searches a brief for citations, checks them for proper style and form, and prepares a report concerning the appropriate form and subsequent history of each citation.

The trend in full-text retrieval systems is toward more utilization of optical disk databases, incorporation of hypertext citation and word definition linkages into databases, and much better retention and management of retrieved information in the attorney's workstation. The CCH (Commerce Clearing House) ACCESS system, for example, provides pop-down menus for selection of index categories and documents to be searched and retains all the information retrieved from a central computer in a specialized database on the attorney's workstation. The attorney can go back and browse through the retrieved material repeatedly without having to download the same material repeatedly.

THE ATTORNEY'S WORKSTATION

A recent survey by Professor Ronald Staudt at the Illinois Institute of Technology's Chicago Kent College of Law reveals that in large law firms half of all attorneys have a personal computer on their desk—typically an IBM PC or compatible Intel 286 or 386 model equipped with WordPerfect (first choice) or Microsoft Word (second choice) for word processing.

Word processing is the primary use attorneys make of computers. Personal computers are now employed in preference to terminals for computer-assisted legal research (WESTLAW, LEXIS, ACCESS, etc.). Many lawyers use spreadsheets for trust accounting, for computation of the present value of future earnings in personal injury litigation, and for recomputing real-estate closing payments (particularly tax prorations) when the closing date changes. Some attorneys use computers for electronic mail and conferencing, but standalone fax machines now predominate in law. Error-free document transfer is frequently used between branch offices and between attorneys and regular out-of-town clients.

Most young attorneys insist on being provided their own computers nowadays. Many young lawyers do all their legal drafting on these machines, but dictation is still popular and highly cost-effective. Fewer secretaries are needed today than previously, and it is now commonplace for two or three attorneys to share a secretary.

EXPERT SYSTEMS IN LAW

Expert systems of the conventional variety relating to law have been created, but generally they are used only as teaching vehicles. A few experimental systems employ artificial intelligence techniques to represent legal knowledge. But the current trend in practical systems is toward specialized hypertext databases on optical disks that relate explanatory materials to the underlying statutes, regulations, and cases. These are just now emerging from publishers such as West, MDC, and others.

Specialized document assembly systems (CAPSOFT, SCRIVENER, XPERTEXT, WORKFORM, and FLEXPRACTICE) that can conduct a client interview, assemble legal boilerplate into a form legal document, and save the client data in a client data file for use in other documents at a later time have recently emerged. These systems complement the features of word processors and enable attorneys to design and share automated law practice systems. Most are compatible with WordPerfect. Not many fully implemented and supported law practice systems are available—there is a shortage of attorney-authors with the necessary computer skills to design and maintain these systems.

LITIGATION SUPPORT

A specialized application of computers is management of evidence in major litigation. These systems vary from full-text retrieval systems (similar to LEXIS or WESTLAW) to simpler conventional database systems that store abstracts of documents along with such information as the name of the sender, the name of the recipient, the date, and manually applied index terms. Control Data Corporation pioneered this use of computers in its antitrust suit against IBM in the early 1970s, and IBM later developed a similar system for use in its defense of the government's antitrust suit against IBM. Many public accounting firms provide litigation support system design services for attorneys.

These systems are particularly useful in any litigation where there are thousands of documents, where multiple attorneys and paraprofessionals screen the documents, and where multiple parties may share the discovered documents. Either the full text (as by scanning) or an abstract of each document is prepared and entered into the computer for later access. InMagic is a popular program for management of abstract databases on personal computers, and ZYIndex is popular for full-text searching, because of its search language resembling that of LEXIS and WESTLAW.

BRINGING IT ALL TOGETHER

With the launch of multiwindowed operating systems and multitasking environments, and with the introduction in the near future of computers that will not need to be shut down but that will simply suspend and then relaunch all the multiple applications that may be running (using the Intel 386 SL microprocessor), the attorney's workstation of the near future will have multiple tasks running at all times: the multiwindowed outliner and word processor where the briefs are written; the client interviewing and document assembly engine; the client data file management system; the time accounting and billing charge entry system; the windows granting access to the local optical disk and remote legal databases (LEXIS, WESTLAW, ACCESS); and the personal database containing all the attorney's personal notes.

For Further Information:

The American Bar Association offers two sources of information on legal applications of computers: the Law Practice Management Section, 750 North Lake Shore

Drive, Chicago, Ill. 60611 (312-988-5619) (publishes books, pamphlets, and newsletters on law office automation and supports user groups); and the Legal Technology Resource Center, 750 North Lake Shore Drive, Chicago, Ill. 60611 (312-988-5465) (a vendor-supported exhibit of legal software and hardware; accepts telephone queries concerning law office automation).

The National Center for State Courts, 300 Newport Avenue, Williamsburg, Va. 23187 (804-253-2000, ext. 343) is a clearinghouse for information concerning court automation. They have a court technology laboratory.

For Further Reading

Ayres, J. J. 1990. *Law office software: Attorney's guide to selection.* New York: Wiley.

Braeman, K., and F. Shellenberger. 1991. *From yellow pads to computers: Transforming your law office with a computer.* 2nd ed. Chicago: American Bar Association. For beginners.

deBessonet, C. G. 1991. *A many-valued approach to deduction and reasoning for artificial intelligence.* Norwell, Mass.: Kluwer. Highly technical; describes an experimental AI system developed by an attorney to represent the knowledge content of the Napoleonic Code.

Gardner, A. 1988. *An artificial intelligence approach to legal reasoning.* Cambridge, Mass.: MIT Press.

Harrington, W. 1987. *Lawyer's guide to online data bases.* Homewood, Ill.: Dow Jones-Irwin.

Johnson, D., and P. Mode, eds. 1985. *Improving law firm productivity by encouraging lawyers' use of personal computers.* San Diego, Calif.: Harcourt Brace Jovanovich.

Kely, T. F. 1987, 1990. *Using litigation data bases.* New York: Wiley.

Kinney, E. H., and R. W. Staudt. 1985, 1990. *Litigation support systems: An attorney's guide.* Deerfield, Ill.: Callaghan & Co.

Lauristan, M., ed. 1988. *Technological evolution of the legal profession: Computers as your expert partner.* Chicago: American Bar Association.

Maggs, P. B., and J. A. Sprowl. 1987. *Computer applications in the law.* St. Paul, Minn.: West.

Martino, A., and N. Fiorenze, eds. 1986. *Automated analysis of legal texts: Logic, informatics, law.* Amsterdam: North-Holland.

Mason, M. A. 1988. *Using computers in the law: An introduction and practical guide.* St. Paul, Minn.: West.

Nagel, S. S. 1990. A reference guide on computers and legal decision making. *Jurimetrics Journal of Law, Science, and Technology* 30(2):235. A bibliography in this article lists sixty-four books relating to computers and law practice.

Robbins, R. L. 1990. *The automated law firm: A guide to systems and software.* 2nd ed. Englewood Cliffs, N.J.: Prentice-Hall.

James A. Sprowl

LEIBNIZ, GOTTFRIED WILHELM VON

Gottfried Wilhelm von Leibniz was born on July 1, 1646, in Leipzig, Germany, the son of a professor of moral philosophy at the University of Leipzig. Because the Leibniz family lived in a university community and were part of the academic circle, Gottfried was exposed to a scholarly environment early in life. His father's library was available to him, and before the age of 10, he had consumed books on the Romans, Plato, and the Greeks. He taught himself Latin, was soon reading Greek, and at age 14, was immersed in Aristotle. Years later, he was to admit that the ancient writers had a great effect on his understanding of the world's knowledge. He had learned to use words to attain clarity and to use them properly. There was no school in his day in which a boy of his genius could be educated; he was therefore left to the guidance of his own interests and he became self-taught.

At age 15, he entered the University of Leipzig as a law student; there he came in contact with the thought of men who had revolutionized science and philosophy, men such as Galileo, Francis Bacon, and René Descartes. He received a bachelor's degree at 17. At 20, he received a doctorate in jurisprudence from Altdorf, and for 6 years thereafter pursued a career of law and diplomacy, attempting to stop Louis XIV's march on Holland. Although Leibniz never did get through to the king, he found it easy to gain favor with such figures as Christian Huygens, a leading physicist and mathematician. Huygens presented him with a copy of his mathematical essay on the pendulum. Gottfried quickly became impressed with the power of the mathematical approach, and Huygens became his mentor.

It was during this period that Leibniz became fascinated with mechanical contrivances. He was extremely impressed by the idea of a calculating machine and set out to study in detail the works of Blaise PASCAL and Samuel Morland, and to construct a more perfect and efficient machine.

In 1671, he invented a calculating machine that could not only add and subtract, but could also laboriously multiply and divide. In 1694, he exhibited a working model of his calculator in London, and was made a member of the Royal Society, largely on the strength of his new invention. His calculator consisted of a series of stepped cylinders, each with nine teeth of different lengths. Smaller gears, each representing a digit of the multiplicand, were set above them and placed so each could be engaged by that number of the cylindrical gears' teeth. A complete turn of the set of long gears, therefore, registered the multiplicand once; the multiplier was expressed by the number of times the long gears were turned. Although the machine established many important principles to be used three centuries later in mechanical calculators, it was mechanically unreliable, like Pascal's machine, and unmarketable.

Late in 1675, Leibniz laid the foundations of both integral and differential calculus. For the process of integration, he proposed the familiar symbol $\int$, an elongated "s" signifying "summation." Leibniz also introduced the symbol ∂ (for differentiation). Sir Isaac Newton had laid claim to inventing calculus in the 1660s, but Leibniz was apparently unaware of it.

In 1676, Leibniz left Paris for Hannover, where for the next 40 years he devoted his time to serving the Duke of Brunswick as historian, librarian, and chief advisor, and intermittently working on his calculating machines. Leibniz's later years were divorced from mathematical and scientific pursuits as he turned to philosophy. He developed the ingenious theory of monads—minute copies of the universe out of which everything in the universe is composed, as a sort of one-in-all, all-in-one. His last important contribution came in 1700 in Berlin, where Leibniz organized the Berlin Academy of Sciences and became its first president.

He died in Hannover on November 14, 1716, at the age of 70 during an attack of gout. His death aroused no interest in London or Berlin, and the only person present at his burial was his secretary.

For Further Reading

Evans, C. 1981. *The making of a micro.* London: Harrow House.

Donald D. Spencer

LIMS

See Laboratory Information Management Systems

LISP AND PROLOG

Most of the existing programming languages can be categorized into two broad groups: procedural and nonprocedural (or declarative). In procedural programming languages, the programmer lists the steps that must be taken by the computer to obtain a result. In a declarative programming language, the programmer is expected to specify the problem only and not the details of computational steps. There are several types of nonprocedural languages, among which functional languages and relational (or logical) languages are the best-known.

Using a functional language, the programmer defines a number of functions that form a program. The programmer can then ask a question of the form: "What is the value of a certain expression?" Thus, essentially, users of functional languages define some functions and then specify a desired result by applying these functions to each other and to data objects. The most well-known and widely used functional language is LISP.

The primary task of a programmer using a logic programming language is to define relationships between objects and values. Having a collection of relationships (stated in expressions called Horn clauses), the programmer can ask whether certain relationships exist between some objects of interest or not. Currently, PROLOG is the most popular logic programming language.

Both LISP and PROLOG are general-purpose programming languages in the sense that they can be used for writing programs in almost any domain; however, the artificial intelligence community has been the primary user of these two languages. Both LISP and PROLOG are conversational languages in that the programmer interacts with the system during the course of programming.

LISP

LISP (an acronym for *LISt* Processing) has its roots in a model of computation called lambda calculus, which was developed in the early 1930s by Alonzo Church. Further development of the lambda calculus model by a number of other logicians led a well-respected computer scientist named John McCarty to develop the language LISP in the late 1950s. Since its initial design and implementation, LISP has undergone numerous changes, improvements, and extensions. Complete programming environments have been developed around the language, and specialized hardware for high-speed LISP machines has improved the efficiency of LISP environments considerably.

The existence of several dialects makes it difficult to define what the exact notation of the language is. These dialects share the same foundation but differ significantly in notation. In particular, as each one is tied to a specific hardware and implementation,

none of the dialects are portable, and therefore a program written in one dialect may not be easily transportable into another system. Among the more popular versions are Common LISP, Franz LISP, MacLISP, and INTERLISP. A new dialect, called Scheme, not only extends the set of traditional operators of the language but modifies the interpretations of some of the operators.

The basic data structure of LISP is a list. In fact, a program written in LISP is also a list. Simply put, a list is a sequence of atoms (symbols) or other lists. Here is an example of a list:

```
(+ 5 9)
```

The preceding list happens to be an expression that may be evaluated by LISP. Such expressions are called symbolic expressions, or s-expressions for short. In the preceding example, LISP assumes that + is an operator that must be applied to the operands 5 and 9. This notation is known as prefix (or Polish) notation. Obviously, evaluation of the above s-expression will yield the value 14. Let us look at a more complex s-expression:

```
(*(+ 5 9) (+ 8 (− 5 2))).
```

In the process of evaluation, LISP will compute the expression $((5 + 9)*(8 + (5 − 2)))$.

Defining new functions in LISP is very easy. For example, a function that computes the square of a number can be defined as

```
(defun square (i) (* i i))
```

where *defun* identifies the expression as one that defines a function, *square* is the name of the function, *i* is a variable, and (* *i i*) is an s-expression representing the body of the function. We can now evaluate the function by giving it an argument. By typing

```
(square 5)
```

we get the result 25.

Functions may be used in the definition of other functions. Here is the definition of the function *sum-square* in which the function *square* has been used.

(defun sum-square $(i j)$ $(+$(square $i)$ (square $j)))$)

Now, we can evaluate this function with arguments 3 and 5 by typing

(sum-square 3 5)

This computation yields the value 34.

PROLOG

PROLOG, which stands for *PRO*gramming in *LOG*ic, was the result of many years of research on symbolic logic. After the formalization of predicate calculus around the turn of the century, a group of logicians focused their attention on a more specific form that is now known as the Horn clause (or definite clause). The invention of the unification algorithm in the mid-1960s by J. A. Robinson and its subsequent computational refinements led to the design of PROLOG.

Unlike procedural programming languages, such as FORTRAN and Pascal, in PROLOG the programmer merely specifies some relationships between objects and then presents the system with questions. On the basis of the existing properties and relationships, a PROLOG interpreter decides whether the relationships in question hold or not. A PROLOG program consists of a sequence of *facts* and *rules*. Facts represent the basic assertions and the unconditional relationships between data. Rules, however, are defined by means of conditions that, when met, will imply that a certain relationship must hold. Rules in PROLOG are written in the form

A :- $B1$ and $B2$ and . . . Bn

where A, $B1$, $B2$, . . . , and Bn are predicates (or relationships) and :- represents the implication sign (i.e., "if"). From a computational point of view, the above rule says: "In order to show that A holds, show that $B1$, $B2$, . . . , and Bn hold."

Whenever the conditional part (i.e., the right side of :-) of a rule is empty, then the rule degenerates to a single predicate. This is called a fact in PROLOG.

As an example, let us look at a program for computing factorials:

factorial(1,0)
factorial(X,Y) :- factorial($Z,Y-1$) and $Z = X^*Y$

The first line is a fact that asserts "factorial of 0 is 1." The second line states what conditions must hold between two values X and Y for X to be the factorial of Y. The program makes use of the predicate *factorial*, which stands for "X is the factorial of Y." We can now ask for the factorial of any number, say 6, by typing

factorial(A,6)?

The result $A=120$ will be displayed because the interpreter can show that factorial(120,6) holds.

Lists in PROLOG appear in square brackets, []. So, [sam, joe, mary] is a valid list. The symbol | distinguishes the head of a list from the rest. Thus [A | B] is a list whose head is A and the remainder (called "tail") is B. Below is a program that determines membership in lists:

belongs-to(X, [X | _])
belongs-to(X, [_ | A]) :- belongs-to (X,A)

The first line says "an object X belongs to any list whose first element is X." As the tail of the list is of no interest, in PROLOG we can use the nameless variable "_" in its place. The second line states that "if X is not the head of the list, then X belongs to that list if X belongs to its tail." We can now test membership in lists. By typing

belongs-to(joe,[sam, joe, mary])?

we can test whether joe is a member of the given list. Or we can ask "What belongs to the list [sam, joe, mary]?" in the following way:

belongs-to(X,[sam, joe, mary])?

The answer will be the elements of the given list.

SAMPLE PROGRAMS

Following is a program written in LISP (called SUM) for summation of the elements of a list. The following LISP commands are used:

- cond (selects and executes those statements whose conditions are true)
- equal (tests for equality of two terms)
- car (returns the first element of a list)
- cdr (returns the list without its first element)
- princ (prints a string that is placed within quotes)
- print (prints the value of a given symbol)
- setq (assigns values to variables)

```
(defun sum (1)
    (cond
        ((equal (car 1) nil)
            (princ "The sum of the
            numbers is")
            (print y))
        (t (setq y (+ y (car 1)))
        (sum (cdr 1)))))
```

The program may be executed as follows:

```
(sum ' (1 2 3 4 5 6 7 8 9))
The sum of the numbers is
45
```

The above program may be written in PROLOG by using predicates in the following manner:

```
sum_list :- write ('Enter list of numbers you
            wish to sum'),nl,read(Y),
            sum(Z,Y), write('The sum of the
            numbers is'), write(Z).

sum(Z,Y) :- sum1 (Z,0,Y).
sum1 (X,X,[]).
sum1 (Z,X,[Y1|Y]) :- Z1 is X+Y1, sum1
            (Z,Z1,Y).
```

The execution of this program will yield:

```
| ?-
sum_list.
Enter list of numbers you wish to sum

|:
[1,2,3,4,5,6,7,8,9].

The sum of the numbers is 45
```

For Further Reading

Sterling, L., and E. Shapiro. 1986. *The art of PROLOG.* Cambridge, Mass.: MIT Press.
Winston, P. H., and B. K. P. Horn. 1987. *LISP.* 3rd ed. Reading, Mass.: Addison-Wesley.

Forouzan Golshani

LISTS

Most computers today are used for the management of information. This may be as simple as managing the checks and balances of a bank account, or as complex as retrieving large amounts of archival research information in searches that could otherwise not be done because of the researcher's limited time and resources. To accomplish both these functions, computers use list and file management software.

A list file is any type of data file that holds resource information in sequence for later retrieval. *Database* is another term for this type of file. The machine in the post office that produces a zip code to match an address typed in is an example of a list manager. In this case, the zip code file is a long series of data "cells," each one holding a specific code. These zip code cells are then referenced to corresponding cells holding the information on which zip code matches which address. When the researcher types in an address, the software searches for that address in the file and its corresponding zip code cell, thus producing the match. This type of list file is known as a *flat file*. It is called flat because the searches and matches are made across one dimension throughout the file.

Database and file management software first became commercially available for microcomputers in 1978 with the introduction of VisiCalc by Robert Frankston and Dan Bricklin in Cambridge, Massachusetts. The product was made commercially available the next year for the Apple I computer. The combination of VisiCalc and Apple computers remained strong until the introduction of 1-2-3 by Lotus Development in 1983.

By the early 1980s, the IBM personal computer had become the hardware standard for business applications, in part because of its faster processing speeds. As an important feature of a file processing software package is its ability to process numbers and sort lists of data, speed became an important selling factor in the hardware that drove the software.

Lotus Development's 1-2-3 brought to the IBM hardware base an integrated approach to file management. It was possible to "link" a data cell in one 1-2-3 spreadsheet with a cell in another 1-2-3 spreadsheet. The software allowed for an automatic update across the links so that a change made to a range of cells in one spreadsheet would affect the data in the linked file. This technology was the predecessor of the relational database file. Soon, it would be possible to construct a file in which all data fields were linked together, rather than one particular cell in one file to one cell in another.

The flat filer software package most generally resembles its manual equivalent, accounting ledger paper. Such programs, called SPREADSHEETS (after their paper equivalent), are "pages" of columns and rows; each intersection of a column and a row is called a cell. The user constructs the database by entering numbers or text into the *cells* of the electronic spreadsheet. In most instances, the size of the file increases as cells are filled with data. That is, an empty spreadsheet file will be smaller than a similar file made up of numerous columns and rows.

The flexibility of the flat file results from its ability to be sorted by a number of criteria. The more complex the software, the more sorting fields the researcher has. A field is a particular column or row axis that can be sorted either numerically or alphabetically.

It is possible to sort across selected cells within a field rather than sort the entire file. This selection of cells is a data range. In large files, it is usually more convenient to sort a selected range of cells rather than to sort the entire file.

A common use for a data sort is reconstruction of a list of data into a usable sequence. For example, the researcher may wish to see all data in a range sorted in numerical order. Or, if the sortable range is a date, the user may sort the file to appear in chronological order.

One of the major commercial uses of flat files today is in mailing list management. Most mail order companies have extensive lists of customers to whom they have sold merchandise in the past. These lists of names are then sorted by certain criteria for mailing new offers. The list management industry, which started as an adjunct to mail order sales, has now become an enterprise all its own. Most catalog mailers rent their names to other mailers for more than one dollar per name. With such a large investment in rented names, accurate list management is essential to the mailer.

It is not economically feasible to mail an offer to every name on a mailing list if a majority of those names are not good potential customers. Most often, these names are sorted on a criterion known as RFM, which stands for recency, frequency, and money. The higher classifications (and thus the greatest potential for selling merchandise) are given to the names on a list who have bought most frequently, who buy more than once from the same company, and who spend the most money. As these names age, the less frequent buyers will move to the lower classifications on the list. When a mailing list is sorted in this way, it is possible for the catalog mailer to save mailing costs by sending catalogs only to those customers who are most likely to respond to the offer.

Another factor in mailing list management is the elimination of duplicate names and addresses and the elimination of names registered with the U.S. Postal Service as not wanting to receive mail order offers. In the first instance, the file is run against itself to eliminate any duplications, as there is no reason to send more than one offer to the same address. In the second, the main mailing list is compared with the Postal Service list. When a "hit"—a name that appears on both lists—is found the name is dropped from the mailing list and that person will not receive an offer. By running both of these eliminations, the mailer is saving production and postage costs, thus making the overall mailing more profitable.

After a mailing list has been pared down by removing duplicates and do-not-mail requests, the file is sorted according to the criteria sought by the mailer. When the RFM selection has been made on the list, it is sorted by zip code for address label printing. This sort is necessary as the mailing pieces must be sorted by zip code to keep postage costs as low as possible. All of these operations, from RFM selections to zip code presorts, are done by the mailing list manager.

A second type of file often used is a relational database. Relational files are indexed in such a way that each piece of information in the database is connected to every other piece. Therefore, a search or sort becomes three-dimensional across the entire file. An example of this would be to place a text file into a database in which every word was indexed. In this instance, the researcher asks the file for every instance of a particular bit of information. The software then searches the index and brings forward every "hit" within the file.

In devising searches for a relational indexed file, the more generalized the search criteria, the more "hits" the software will find. For example, searching a text file for the word *atrophy* will produce fewer hits than would searching for the first letter of the word, "a." In the case of searching a flat file, the results of a search are always win/lose. The flat filer will look to a particular cell for the requested information. If the search succeeds, there is one answer. If the search fails, the software will show no matches. In the case of searching a relational database, the end results are limited by the discrimination of the search criteria.

The relational database is most useful in researching large text files. A number of attorneys are now using relational databases on portable computers in the courtroom. It is much simpler to look up a piece of evidence in a data file on a computer than it is to shuffle quickly through large amounts of paper. This practice will become more commonplace as more and more pieces of information are brought into evidence in court cases.

Another example of the relational file is a computerized encyclopedia. By entering search criteria, the researcher can find all instances of a desired term or entry much faster than by manually searching through a printed index.

For Further Reading

Bodian, N. G. 1986. *Encyclopedia of mailing list terminology and techniques.* Winchester, Mass.: Bret Scot Press.

Crown, P. 1973. *What you should know about building your own mailing list.* Dobbs Ferry, N.Y.: Oceana.

Dinerstein, N. T. 1985. *Database and file management systems for the microcomputer.* Glenview, Ill.: Scott Foresman.

Fidel, R. 1987. *Database design for information retrieval.* New York: Wiley.

Hanson, O. 1982. *Design of computer data files.* Rockville, Md.: Computer Science Press.

Kim, K. 1988. *A study of the interactions between operating systems memory management and database buffer management strategies.* Urbana: Department of Computer Science, University of Illinois.

Mayre, A. J. 1983. *Introducing relational database.* Manchester: NCC Publishers.

John L. Myers

LITERARY ANALYSIS, COMPUTERS IN

Literary scholars were, with very few exceptions, relative latecomers to academic computing. This was due partly to the belief that literature cannot be easily quantified, and therefore, there is little place for computing in most literary work; partly to the perceived division between science and the humanities; and partly to a lack of funding for literary computer studies. Other, more sensible reasons for the delayed entry include the difficulty of locating computer-ready texts in conjunction with the struggles of the literary scholars themselves to define what is an acceptable text: Can the mere words on a screen replicate a text in its entirety?

Prior to the development of accurate optical character readers (OCRs), all the texts a researcher might want to use had to be typed in by hand. In the early uses of computers for literary analysis, the researcher had to devise a code for each word that indicated its place in the original text, its function in the sentence, and any other attribute of the word or text in which the scholar might be interested. Then this code, however complicated, had to be transferred to keypunch cards, one word per card. The awkwardness of this process, and the rather advanced knowledge of programming required, deterred many scholars from further investigating the possible uses of computers.

CONCORDANCES

One of the early literary uses for computers was the computer-generated concordance, a list of all the words in a work or works, together with an illustrative quotation. The Reverend John W. Ellison's 1957 concordance of the Revised Standard Version of the Bible was a milestone achievement, having taken "only" 400 hours for processing, a very significant savings over hand-generated concordances. Of course, the 400 hours does not include the time needed to develop a useful code, nor the time needed to enter and proofread all the text. Despite the length of time needed to prepare Ellison's concordance, the significance of his achievement cannot be overstated; the February 18, 1957 issue of *Life* magazine even devoted a full page to the publication of the concordance. The production of concordances continued to dominate literary computing for many years, with several beneficial side effects. First and foremost, each concordance generated also produced a computer-readable text, which allowed literary scholars to develop new ways to use a computer in analyzing a text, although because of changing storage technology, many early computer-readable

texts have been lost. One of the most widely accepted early concordance programs was COCOA, written in FORTRAN, which made the program machine independent. COCOA's direct descendant, the Oxford Concordance Program (OCP), is still very popular, and is now available for use on personal computers. The concordances thus generated, and variations of the concordances, have also been useful. Advanced concordance programs are able to generate rhyme lists, frequency counts, and reverse indices. A reverse index is an index of words in which the words are alphabetized from right to left, as opposed to English's standard left to right. In this manner all the words with the same suffix are grouped together, as are related words, for example, absent/present, malediction/benediction, fortune/misfortune. This type of listing can also facilitate the exploration of elements of pronunciation, such as the common characteristics of all words ending in -ate or -ite.

Another common early use of computers was the comparison of variant texts. Prior to the introduction of computers, multiple editions and texts had to be collated by hand. With the invention of accurate OCRs, able to read and compare variant typefaces, much of the drudgery of collating differences between texts has been removed, and the editor is responsible only for choosing the texts compared, and deciding which of the variant readings is to be the editorial choice. Analyses run on various computer texts can also be helpful in defining the component parts of an author's style: Does the author begin a large percentage of sentences with subordinate clauses? Does the author use an unusually large percentage of gerunds? Do the stylistics of document A, by an unknown author, duplicate the stylistics of document B, and is it possible that documents A and B were written by the same person? The wider availability of computer-readable texts, combined with concordance programs—such as WordCruncher and Micro-OCP—able to run on a personal computer, will no doubt open uses for concordances never thought of before. There are text retrieval programs such as Personal Librarian, which not only searches for keywords, but searches for two or more keywords used in significant co-occurrence, for example, all uses of the word *light* that occur within fifteen words of the word *fire* in Milton's *Paradise Lost.*

Although this sort of analysis was always possible, computers have removed much of the tedious compilation of statistics. The problems remaining are of a less mechanistic and more scholarly nature. The best computer concordance program in the world is useless without a well-defined search, and learning to define significant keywords, and the ability to develop a working inference from the statistics gathered this way, is, and is likely to remain, the province of a skilled and patient researcher.

Concordances have also been of great use in the field of historical linguistics. With enough texts, the researcher is able to determine early uses of a word, and to trace its changes of meaning over time by examining the contexts provided by the concordance program. This ability has already revolutionized the production of historical dictionaries such as the *Oxford English Dictionary.*

STYLE AND GRAMMAR CHECKERS

An increasingly common popular outgrowth of literary computing has been grammar checkers. The first truly useful program to attempt this function was AT&T's Writer's Workbench, developed in the 1970s to help engineers with their writing. Running under UNIX, Writer's Workbench checks for, among other things, frequency of passive verbs, consistency of capitalization, and sexist language. Writer's Workbench is capable of printing a style analysis and comparing the style of the material with a previously chosen criterion such as *The New York Times* or a children's book. The simplest and earliest of grammar checkers indicated possible areas of problems, based on a list of common errors. Style analysis programs attempt to go beyond simple grammatical errors, and enter into the work's readability. The early style analysis programs for microcomputers focused on readability indices, which compute the relative percentages of short and long sentences and words, and frequently give an approximate grade level for the work based on these calculations. Other grammar and

style analysis programs look for passive verbs, number of prepositions, lack of agreement between subject and verb, and other mechanical errors.

The major flaw in all grammar and style checkers created so far is their tendency to enforce agreement with the authorities accepted by the programmer. The creation of a more useful grammar and style analysis program must await the development of a full natural-language parser. A natural-language parser is a computational device that would, ideally, be able to read a natural sentence, such as this, without being misled by the innate ambiguities of language. A parser can also be an algorithm for arriving at the objects in a grammar, or a set of well-formed structured objects. The difficulty of creating a program that would be able to read and interpret language can be seen from this example: "Flying planes made her duck." Any native speaker of English understands immediately what is meant by this sentence, but there are several other ways to interpret it: "When she flew planes, she ducked"; "Her duck was created by flying planes." The computer has little or no way to assign probabilities to the various readings, and a duck born of a 747 is as likely as a woman reacting to a low-flying plane. At this stage of their development, grammar and style checkers are an aid, not a replacement, to editing and revision. Without the creation of a fully functional natural-language processor, it is likely such checkers will never be more than simplistic aids. (See also NATURAL-LANGUAGE PROCESSING.)

TEXT RETRIEVAL

The most useful aspect of computers in academic work has not been limited to the literary field. Annual compilations of bibliographies in a field, for example, the *MLA Bibliography* or the more general *Reader's Guide,* are rapidly becoming available in electronic form, both as on-line searchable databases and as compact-disk read-only memory disks. As with the concordances, however, availability is not a substitute for thinking; a search must be predefined to be of any use. For example, someone wanting to write a paper on John Donne's wife would be ill-advised to run a search with the keywords *Donne, women,* and *love.* With practice in choosing keywords and narrowing searches, a literary scholar's research time can be cut drastically, with possibly more comprehensive results. The availability of abstracts and on-line thesauri for alternative search terms has been shown to be of great utility in the development of accurate and complete searches.

The major problem of databases such as these is their coverage. The *MLA Bibliography* is available in an electronic form from 1963 forward, the *German National Bibliography* from 1986 forward, and the *French National Bibliography* from 1975 forward. Other bibliographic databases have similar, frequently greater, chronological limitations. Another current limitation to the usefulness of on-line databases is the cost of these services. On-line services such as DIALOG and BRS, which have such databases available, charge by the time used and sometimes by the number of matches, or "hits," for the defined search. The only other current technology able to handle informational databases as massive as these is compact-disk read-only memory. Such drives and disks are still very expensive, and the disk must be updated on a regular basis; however, the falling costs of both the hardware and the software may mean that one day scholars will be able to run a complete search for all academic papers on, for example, "Computers in Literary Analysis" on their home computer, without incurring the costs of an on-line search.

FUTURE

The decreasing cost and increasing speed and storage capabilities of computers will make ever more sophisticated text searches and comparisons possible. If a fully functional natural language parser is developed, then sophisticated literary analyses will be able to be performed by computers, with fewer misreadings of ambiguous words and referents and greater flexibility of term definitions. Educational uses for computers continue to grow: Litterms, a software package, teaches the basics of literary analysis (terms such as

simile, metaphor, verse forms) using a preestablished text. With the development of a natural language parser, a program could be designed to analyze any text, although the sophistication and usefulness of the analyses would still be dependent on the sophistication of the scholar instructing the program.

For Further Reading

Burrows, J. F. 1987. *Computation into criticism: A study of Jane Austen's novels and an experiment in method.* Oxford: Oxford Univ. Press. A literary analysis based on computer work.

Computers and the humanities. Paradigm Press/Kluwer Academic Publishers. The best scholarly journal on the use of computers in the humanities.

Gazdar, G. and C. Mellish. 1989. *Natural language processing in PROLOG.* Wokingham: Addison-Wesley. Textbook introduction to computational linguistics and programming.

Howard-Hill, T. H. 1979. *Literary concordances: A complete handbook for the preparation of manual and computer concordances.* Oxford: Pergamon Press. A good overview of the problems involved in creating any concordance.

The humanities computing yearbook. Various editors. Oxford: Clarendon Press. Annual compilation of important work in humanities computing.

Miall, D. S., ed. 1990. *Humanities and the computer: New directions.* Oxford: Clarendon Press. Excellent overview of the current state of computer use in both research and teaching of the humanities.

Oakman, R. L. 1980. *Computer methods for literary research.* Columbia, S.C.: Univ. of South Carolina Press. Complete and accessible, if dated, view of the development of literary computing.

Williams, F., et al. 1989. *Computer-assisted writing instruction in journalism and professional education.* New York: Praeger. Excellent overview of word processors and general analysis programs, albeit focused on instruction.

Wisbey, R. A., ed. 1971. *The computer in literary and linguistic research.* New York: Cambridge Univ. Press. Technical aspects are dated, but a good overview of the various functions of computers in literary and linguistic programs.

Margaret J. Campbell

LOCAL AREA NETWORKS

A computer network is a set of computers and computer-related devices (called stations) connected to each other by communication links. There are several kinds of computer networks. In this article we focus on local area networks. A local area network (LAN) is a relatively smaller network with a maximum span of 10 kilometers (6.2 miles). In contrast to LANs, we have citywide networks called metropolitan area networks (MANs) as well as networks called wide area networks (WANs) covering an entire country or continent. Besides geographic range, local area networks differ from MANs and WANs in several other respects. A local area network provides high-speed transmission and exhibits a much lower error rate than a WAN. A LAN is installed for private use and owned by a single organization.

Local area networks are in widespread use today. They are popular for several reasons. The communication of information is a vital part of modern life. A LAN, like a telephone, connects the people in an organization by allowing them to exchange electronic information freely and efficiently. A LAN facilitates sharing of computing resources to everyone connected to the LAN. Not only does one save money by sharing expensive resources such as laser printers, plotters, hard disks, write-once read-many (WORM) drives, and CPUs (central processing units), but also easy access to information enhances productivity.

The most prevalent types of networks are in-house terminal networks, which are the precursors of LANs. A terminal network consists of a number of terminals that communicate with a central computing facility. In terminal networks, because of limited computing power of terminals, communication protocols are simpler than in LANs.

Research literature devoted specifically to LANs began to appear in the early 1970s, and commercial LAN products were announced in the late 1970s.

CHARACTERISTICS OF A LAN

A local area network is built from various hardware and software components. Major hardware components are network interface cards (circuit boards) that fit inside the stations, cables to provide communication links, taps to hook onto the cable, and repeaters/amplifiers to regenerate/amplify signal for propagation across cable segments. At the lowest level of software we need communication protocol software to move data from computer to computer. At higher levels we require user interface software or an application programming interface (API) that allows users to access communication services from their programs. Further, frequently used application software is made available as part of a LAN installation. Examples of such services are file servers, printer servers, and electronic mail software.

Topologies

Several classifications of LANs are possible based on topology, transmission medium, and medium access method. A topology defines the logical configuration in which stations are interconnected. There are three basic topologies used in LANs: star, bus/ tree, and ring.

Star topology. In star topology there is a central node, called a star coupler, to which each station is connected by two point-to-point links, one for transmission in each direction. When it receives a message on one of its incoming links, the star coupler forwards it on all its outgoing links. Thus, although the individual links are point-to-point, each message transmitted is effectively broadcasted, and only one station at a time may successfully transmit. There are two kinds of star couplers: passive and active. In a passive coupler, the input signal is physically directed to all outgoing links, the actual mechanism of which depends on the transmission medium. Both coaxial cable and optical fiber have been used in a passive coupler-based LAN. An active star coupler acts as a repeater, which regenerates each bit received and retransmits it on all outgoing links. In addition to coaxial cable and optical fiber, unshielded twisted pairs are also used with active star couplers.

Star topology is considered the least attractive because of several disadvantages, the biggest of which is that failure of the star coupler brings down the entire network.

Bus/tree topology. In bus topology all stations are attached to a single link or cable, referred as a bus. Each station on the network has a unique address. When a message is transmitted on the bus, it reaches everywhere; however, it is logically accepted only by the stations whose address matches the one contained in the message. Because of technical limitations and layout constraints, only a small number of attachments can be made to a single piece of cable. To overcome these limitations, several cable segments are usually connected to form a treelike configuration. However, the bus topology is retained at the logical level. In other words, like a single cable segment, only one station can transmit at a time, and each transmission must reach everywhere on all segments.

The choices for transmission media for bus LANs are twisted pair for low speed, and baseband or broadband coaxial cable for higher speeds.

Ring topology. An alternative to the bus/tree topology LAN is the ring. A ring LAN consists of a number of repeaters. Each station hooks to a distinct repeater. Each repeater is connected to two adjacent repeaters by point-to-point links, to form a single loop configuration. Data propagate sequentially in one direction from one repeater to the next around the ring. Each repeater regenerates and retransmits each bit received.

The repeater-to-repeater links can be formed by twisted pair cable, baseband coaxial cable, or fiber-optic cables. A potential problem with ring topology is that a break in any link or the failure of a repeater brings down the entire network. This problem, however, can be dealt with by a refinement of the layout of cables. Because of point-to-point links, a ring can easily use fiber-optic links, which provide very high data rates. This is a distinct advantage of ring over bus topology.

Medium Access Control

All LAN types discussed above have one thing in common: the broadcast nature of communication. Having to broadcast each message farther implies that only one station can successfully transmit at a time. This necessitates use of an arbitration protocol that determines which station gets to transmit next. Medium access control (MAC) protocols are used for this purpose. A *collision* occurs when two or more than two stations transmit simultaneously. Broadly, there are two kinds of MAC protocols: those that allow collisions to occur, and those that prevent collisions. The commonly used protocols in each category are briefly described next.

CSMA/CD. This media access protocol is used for bus/tree topology and has resulted from work on the Ethernet local network. Ethernet was developed by Xerox Corporation in the mid-1970s and is supported by Xerox, Digital Equipment Corporation, Intel, and many other network vendors. The CSMA/CD (carrier sense multiple access with collision detection) protocol requires special hardware to listen to the medium (carrier sense hardware) to determine when the medium is idle and, while transmitting, to notice when a collision occurs (collision detection hardware).

CSMA/CD works as follows. A computer sends a message when it finds the medium idle. During transmission, if collision occurs, each of the colliding stations backs off for a random amount of time, then tries again. This process is repeated until there is a successful transmission. It would seem that CSMA/CD is an inefficient protocol because of time wasted due to collisions and retries. However, the whole process is so fast that the delay due to collision handling is noticeable only under heavy traffic conditions.

Control token. Unlike CSMA/CD, in a token-based MAC protocol, collisions are prevented. A control (permission) token is used for regulating access to the medium. A station can transmit only when it possesses the token. To guarantee fairness to all stations, a station is allowed to hold the token for a limited amount of time. A token-based media-access protocol consists of rules for the circulation of the token and for dealing with several failure conditions, such as loss of token or duplicate token. These protocols differ depending on the topology of the network. The token is simply a series of data bits created by one of the computers on the network. The token moves around the network in a logical ring pattern. In a ring LAN, the logical ring is the same as the physical ring. In star or bus LANs, the MAC protocol has the additional responsibility of building and managing a logical ring.

A commercial star topology network that uses a token-based MAC is Arcnet, developed by Datapoint Corporation in the early 1970s. After Ethernet, Arcnet is the most installed network. In Arcnet, all stations on the network have an address, from 0 to 255. The token circulates in the numerical order of station addresses. When the token reaches the highest addressed station on the network it moves to the lowest addressed station, thereby creating a logical ring. Once a computer has the token, it can send only one packet of data. The station receiving the message then issues the token to the next station in order.

In a bus LAN, the logical ring is maintained by requiring for each station two addresses—one each for its predecessor and successor in the logical ring. A station always receives the token from its predecessor. When a station receives the token and has nothing to transmit, it immediately forwards the token to its successor. If the station has something to transmit, it can do so by holding the token, but only for a predetermined finite amount of time.

In both bus and star LANs, the token is circulated by forwarding it from one station to the next, irrespective of whether a station wishes to transmit or not. In a token-based ring LAN, however, the token circulates freely around the ring without any involvement of stations. A station wishing to transmit must seize the token to get its turn. If a station has higher-priority messages to transmit, it can also reserve the token for the next turn.

The advantage of token-passing over CSMA/CD is the former's predictability. Because of the upper limit on how long a station can hold the token, it is possible to calculate at most how long a station will have to wait before it get its turn. This in turn allows one to put an upper bound on the transmission time of a message. This characteristic of token bus LANs makes them very attractive for use in real-time traffic. The disadvantage of the token-passing access protocol is its complexity, since the protocol must deal with all kinds of malfunctions for the token-based access method to work properly.

LOCAL AREA NETWORK STANDARDS

The standardization of local area networks is important because it permits a smooth integration of use of existing diverse systems and facilitates addition of new systems. A number of organizations contribute to the process of standardization, principally ISO (International Standards Organization), CCITT (International Telegraph and Telephone Consultative Committee), and IEEE (Institute of Electrical and Electronics Engineers). In the context of LANs, IEEE Project 802 has had the most impact. Because of conflicting requirements and to reach a compromise among differing views of involved parties, the IEEE 802 committee came up with four standards supporting four different technologies. These standards are: 802.3 (CSMA/CD Standard), influenced by the success of Ethernet; 802.4 (Token Bus Standard); 802.5 (Token Ring Standard), influenced by the pioneering work by IBM in token ring LANs; and 802.6 (the standard for MANs). The other pertinent standards from the IEEE 802 committee are the internetworking standard (802.1) and the logical link control standard (802.2).

An aspect of LANs that is of considerable importance but has received relatively less attention so far is network management. The IEEE term for LAN management is "systems management." The objective of

LAN management is to allow continuous and efficient operation of the network. Management of a LAN may be subdivided into five subtasks: configuration management, fault management, performance management, access control management, and accounting management.

For Further Reading

Bertsekas, D., and R. Gallager. 1987. *Data networks*. Englewood Cliffs, N.J.: Prentice-Hall.

Doll, D. R. 1980. *Data communications: Facilities, networks, and system design*. New York: Wiley.

Halsall, F. 1988. *Data communications, computer networks and OSI*. 2nd ed. Reading, Mass.: Addison-Wesley.

Hutchison, D. 1988. *Local area network architectures*. Reading, Mass.: Addison-Wesley.

Stallings, W. 1990. *Handbook of computer-communications standards*. Vol. 2: *Local area network standards*. 2nd ed. Carmel, Ind.: Howard W. Sams.

Tanenbaum, A. 1988. *Computer networks*. 2nd ed. Englewood Cliffs, N.J.: Prentice-Hall.

S. P. Rana

LOGIC PROGRAMMING

See Knowledge Bases and Expert Systems

LOGO

Logo is the name of an expanding family of computer languages and applications designed for educational use. It is widely used throughout the world as an introductory programming language and mathematical learning environment for students in elementary and secondary schools. Versions of Logo are available for most popular microcomputers and for most of the world's widely spoken languages as well. During the early 1980s Logo was extremely popular in schools throughout the United States as an introductory computer programming language in elementary schools. Although Logo's popularity has waned somewhat in recent years, its use has become more sophisticated and it is used for a greater variety of applications, and with students of a greater range of ages. Thus it appears to have become an established part of the educational computing scene.

Logo was first conceived during the late 1960s by a research team at Bolt, Beranek and Newman, Inc., a Cambridge, Massachusetts, consulting firm (Feurzeig et al. 1969). With support, first from the Office of Naval Research and later from the National Science Foundation, early Logo researchers set out to make an environment that would allow elementary and junior high school students to learn mathematics and computer programming through nonnumerical applications. Logo's developers based their language on LISP, a language used extensively in artificial intelligence (AI) applications (see LISP AND PROLOG), because it allowed students to manipulate lists of language information as well as mathematical formulas. Logo, like LISP, allowed programmers to solve complex problems in small pieces, by defining and naming small procedures that could be combined to create more complex programs (Feurzeig et al. 1969).

In the early 1970s, the MIT Logo Group, under the leadership of Professor Seymour Papert (Papert 1971), was established at the Massachusetts Institute of Technology. Papert, who has remained Logo's best-known proponent, described Logo as a "mathland . . . [in which] . . . children learn mathematics as a living language" (Papert 1980). He compared the learning of mathematics to the learning of natural language, observing that although all children learn to be fluent in their native languages, relatively few children become fluent in mathematics. Papert sought to correct this by using Logo. He set out to create a computer-based learning environment in which children could learn mathematics by communicating with a computer using an English-like mathematical programming language. Logo was designed to be "a context which is to learning mathematics, what living in France is to learning French'' (Papert 1980).

Papert's approach to learning grows out of the *constructivist* school of learning theory. Constructivists, following the work of the Swiss psychologist Jean Piaget (with whom Papert worked for about 5 years), believe that learners construct their own knowledge about the world, test their ideas by trying them out, and modify them when they no longer work. Papert himself coined the term *constructionist* to define his philosophy of education. He believes that children construct knowledge most effectively while constructing *something* meaningful to themselves. The object or design they are constructing gives them a concrete framework for inventing and trying out their ideas. Logo and all its associated applications are designed to support this approach to learning (Papert 1990).

THE LOGO TURTLE

The key element, symbol, and construction tool of Papert's mathland is the *Logo turtle,* which is used to draw geometric figures on a computer screen. Computer-controlled ''robot turtles'' are also available. Turtle commands such as ''forward,'' ''back,'' ''right,'' ''left,'' ''penup,'' and ''pendown'' are built in to Logo as primitive commands. Logo learners typically begin by defining simple procedures to draw mathematical shapes

such as squares and triangles. Once defined, Logo procedures can be used as building blocks for more complex geometric designs or cartoonlike drawings (Watt 1983; Watt and Watt 1986). For example, the following Logo procedures make the pictures shown in Figure 1:

```
to square
    repeat 4[forward 50 right 90]
end

to triangle
    repeat 3[forward 50 right 120]
end

to house
    square
    forward 50 right 30
    triangle
    left 30 back 50
end

to flower
    repeat 12[triangle right 30]
end
```

In a typical Logo classroom, students are not *directly* taught how to write procedures such as these. Instead, they are supported to discover their own procedures and to invent their own mathematical descriptions in the process. Once students have learned to write simple Logo procedures, it is relatively straightforward to add variables, conditional commands, and simple *recursive* procedure

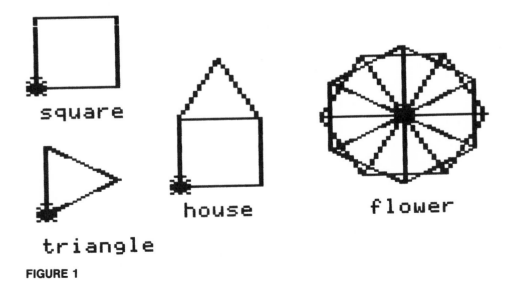

square

triangle

house

flower

FIGURE 1

calls (in which a Logo procedure calls a copy of itself as a subprocedure). For example, the Logo procedure poly requires two variable inputs to specify size and angle and calls a copy of itself to create a variety of regular geometric shapes, including polygons and stars (Watt 1983; Abelson and diSessa 1981). The following Logo procedure makes the pictures shown in Figure 2:

```
to poly :size :angle
  if heading = 0 [stop]
  forward :size right :angle
  poly :size :angle
end
```

Elaborate variations of this are possible by using a third variable to increment the size or angle and by letting the computer run indefinitely until a design begins to repeat itself or fills the screen (Watt 1983; Abelson and diSessa 1981). The following Logo procedures make the pictures shown in Figures 3 and 4:

```
to polyspi :size :angle :increment
  forward :size right :angle
  polyspi (:size + :increment) :angle :increment
end
```

```
to inspi :size :angle :increment
  forward :size right :angle
  inspi :size (:angle + :increment) :increment
end
```

Logo users can learn mathematics by exploring the behaviors of procedures such as these. As they make predictions about what they think will happen when they use different inputs and as they observe patterns among the designs that result, students approach mathematics as a lively experimental science rather than as a series of axioms and proofs to be memorized. A large variety of exploratory math activities such as these have been developed by Logo students and teachers over the years, bringing Papert's vision of mathland at least part of the way to reality.

BEYOND THE TURTLE

The Logo turtle, turtle drawing procedures, and the associated mathematical and problem-solving knowledge involved in using the turtle constitute the most common introduction to Logo. However, as Logo learners gain experience, they are able to understand some of the language's more sophisticated features, such as list processing (which involves manipulating lists of data that may include words, numbers, and other lists) and embedded recursion (more complex recursive programs in which the recursive call is not the last line in the program). And as new versions of Logo are developed, Logo can be used to construct interesting programs in a variety of intellectual and artistic domains.

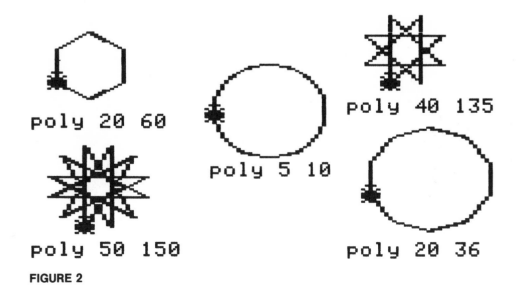

poly 20 60

poly 5 10

poly 40 135

poly 50 150

poly 20 36

FIGURE 2

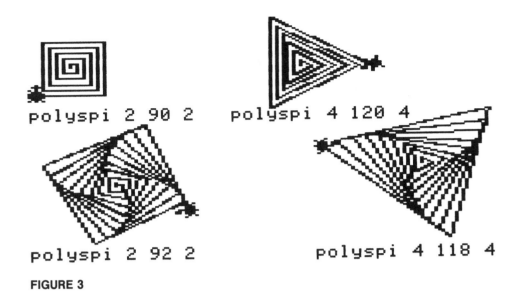

polyspi 2 90 2

polyspi 4 120 4

polyspi 2 92 2

polyspi 4 118 4

FIGURE 3

In addition, Logo can serve as an excellent language for teaching formal and informal computer science (Harvey 1985, 1986, 1987). Understanding Logo can lead naturally to understanding LISP, the AI language from which it was originally derived, and Logo itself can be used for AI projects on computers with enough speed and memory (Friendly 1988).

Versions of Logo are available for most of the world's widely spoken languages. These versions of Logo allow students and teachers to write programs covering a broad range of educational domains, including turtle geometry, many other aspects of mathe-

matics, music, word processing, computer animation, the grammatical structures and syntax of natural languages, general symbol manipulation, simple robotics, object-oriented programming, and AI. Some of the most common educational uses of Logo include:

• Creating computer animations and interactive games. The newest versions of Logo (especially LogoWriter and Logo for MSX computers) allow for multiple turtles and the creation of turtle shapes, which can be changed under program control. Changing the turtles' shapes allows for simple ani-

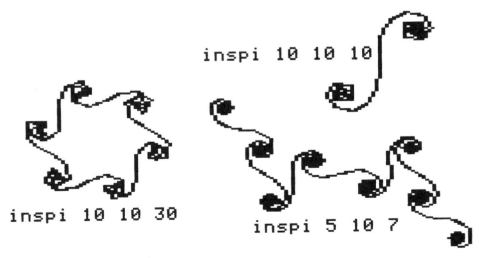

inspi 10 10 10

inspi 10 10 30

inspi 5 10 7

FIGURE 4

mation. Interaction among different-shaped turtles allows Logo programmers to construct their own computer games.

- Combining Logo with word processing. LogoWriter includes programmable word processing capabilities. This expands the usefulness of Logo as an expressive tool, fostering the notion of a "dynamic book" in which text, graphics, and animation are combined. This can be used for creative writing, for reporting on research, and even for designing educational software (Harel 1990).

- LEGO TC Logo. This system provides links between a Logo-speaking computer and the popular LEGO construction system. LEGO TC Logo includes the familiar LEGO bricks, gears, pulleys, and motors as well as touch and light sensors that can send information to the computer. This allows creation of a great variety of computer-controlled models, including robots that incorporate cybernetic feedback. LEGO TC Logo is used as a computerized construction environment for young children and for the study of mechanics and robotics by older students (Harel 1990).

- Logo music. Rudimentary music capabilities in various personal computers allow for a procedural approach to music. Musical composition can be explored as a process of putting musical blocks (procedures) together, carrying out mathematical operations on the notes in those blocks, and recombining them (Bamberger 1979, Harel 1990).

- Logo and language. Logo's list processing capabilities allow for construction of grammatical structures. Students can explore the underlying structures of language by building various structures and comparing them to more naturalistic forms of expression (Friendly 1988; Goldenberg and Feurzeig 1987; Sharples 1985; Watt 1983, 1984, 1985a, 1985b).

- Logo and AI. Logo's list processing, derived from its ancestral language, LISP, provides opportunities for learning about AI by constructing Logo programs (Allen et al. 1984; Friendly 1988; Harvey 1986, 1987).

- Logo microworlds. A microworld is a small, self-contained, exploratory learning environment. The Logo turtle, with its associated commands and programming language, is an example of a microworld. Since its inception, Logo teachers have used Logo as a programming environment to build microworlds to help students explore specific domains such as language, music, physics, and feedback systems (Friendly 1988; Hurley 1985; Lawlor 1982, 1985; Papert 1980; Watt 1985c).

LOGO IN THE SCHOOLS: VISION AND REALITY

Several factors made Logo one of the most popular computer applications in elementary schools in the early 1980s: Seymour Papert's 1980 book *Mindstorms* offered a forceful vision of how computers might transform educational practices rather than merely support existing ways of teaching and learning. Papert's book was interpreted as saying that children who used Logo could easily gain significant understanding of mathematics, problem solving, and computer science without a great deal of direct instruction from a teacher. Logo software had early support from leading computer manufacturers—Apple, IBM, Atari, Texas Instruments, and Commodore all had their own official versions—and the commercial success of Logo made it profitable to develop versions of the language for newer microcomputers as well. Drawing on a decade of federally funded research and development at MIT, Logo was available well before other high-quality software reached the educational market. And Papert's philosophy of student-centered learning fit the then-prevalent desire to teach computer literacy by allowing students to control computers by programming them.

By the late 1980s, Logo's popularity had faded somewhat. Other student-centered tool programs such as word processors and databases had become part of the educational scene. By the late 1980s, many computer literacy programs focused on the use of productivity software such as word processors, databases, and spreadsheets, which were seen as having more immediate applicability to the world outside of school. Furthermore, educational research focusing on the educational benefits for Logo-using students in ordinary classrooms produced mixed results (Clements 1985). Most of all, experience with Logo in schools showed that learning environments were not magically transformed just by the presence of a Logo-speaking computer or two. Also, students who become proficient in turtle geometry do not necessarily improve their abilities in arithmetic, word problems, or algebra. Therefore, taking advantage of the mathematical aspects of Logo turned out to require a more radical revision of the mathematics curriculum than many educators were ready to adopt.

Finally, it became apparent that effective Logo learning requires knowledgeable Logo teachers. Preparing such teachers takes more than the 1 or 2 days of training workshops school districts usually provide for introducing new programs (Watt and Watt 1986). Because different students learn Logo in different ways, at different rates, and apply it to different types of projects, Logo instruction requires a more flexible teaching approach than that used by many classroom teachers—a good Logo teacher works in ways that are more like the practices of a good creative writing teacher or art teacher than those of a conventional math teacher (Watt and Watt 1989).

Considerations such as these led many school districts that embraced Logo enthusiastically in the early 1980s to reconsider its use 5 or 6 years later. Nevertheless, Logo continues to have a place in many school programs. Starting in elementary schools, Logo courses are now taught in many middle and secondary schools as Logo's more advanced applications have become more widely known. Settings for Logo instruction vary. In some schools Logo is taught as part of computer literacy and computer science. In others, Logo is integrated into the mathematics curriculum at different levels. Some schools use LogoWriter to support language arts and creative arts programs, while others use LEGO TC Logo in science, industrial technology, and robotics classes. Non-English-language versions of Logo are used in some foreign-language courses.

As we approach the twenty-first century, a number of developments will influence the future of Logo as an educational tool:

- Educators are expanding their knowledge of Logo, using it as a flexible tool with a range of uses, rather than as a quick fix for computer illiteracy or low scores on math tests.
- Logo researchers and software developers continue to make more powerful versions of the language, connected to more learning domains.
- Mathematics and science curricula are transformed to meet the educational needs of the twenty-first century.

If these trends continue, Logo will continue to have an important place in educational settings throughout the world.

References

Abelson, H., and A. diSessa. 1981. *Turtle geometry.* Cambridge, Mass.: MIT Press.

Allen, J., R. Davis, and J. Johnson. 1984. *Thinking about [TLC] Logo: A graphic look at computing with ideas.* New York: Holt, Rinehart, and Winston.

Bamberger, J. 1979. Logo music projects: Experiments in musical perception and Design, *MIT Logo Memo No. 52.* Cambridge, Mass.: Epistemology and Learning Group, The Media Lab, Massachusetts Institute of Technology.

Clements, D. 1985. Research on Logo in education: Is the turtle slow but steady, or not even in the race? *Computers in the Schools* 2 (2–3).

Feurzeig, W., S. Papert, M. Bloom, R. Grant, and C. Solomon. 1969. *Programming languages as a conceptual framework for teaching mathematics,* Report No. 1889. Cambridge, Mass.: Bolt, Beranek and Newman.

Friendly, M. 1988. *Advanced Logo: A language for learning.* Hillsdale, N.J.: Lawrence Erlbaum Associates.

Goldenberg, E. P., and W. Feurzeig. 1987. *Exploring language with Logo.* Cambridge, Mass.: MIT Press.

Harel, I., ed. 1990. *Constructionist learning.* Cambridge, Mass.: Epistemology and Learning Group, The Media Lab, Massachusetts Institute of Technology.

Harvey, B. 1985. *Computer science Logo style: Intermediate programming.* Cambridge, Mass.: MIT Press.

——. 1986. *Computer science Logo style, Vol. 2: Projects, styles and techniques.* Cambridge, Mass.: MIT Press.

——. 1987. *Computer science Logo style, Vol. 3: Advanced topics.* Cambridge, Mass.: MIT Press.

Hurley, J. 1985. *Logo physics.* New York: Holt, Rinehart, and Winston.

Lawlor, R. 1982. Designing computer-based microworlds. *Byte* 7(8):138–60.

——. 1985. *Computer experience and cognitive development: A child's learning in a computer culture.* New York: Wiley.

Papert, S. 1971. Teaching children to be mathematicians, versus teaching about mathematics. *MIT Logo Memo No. 4.* Cambridge, Mass.: Epistemology and Learning Group, The Media Lab, Massachusetts Institute of Technology.

——. 1980. *Mindstorms: Children, computers and powerful ideas.* New York: Basic Books.

——. 1990. Introduction. In I. Harel, ed. *Constructionist learning.* Cambridge, Mass.: Epistemology and Learning Group, The Media Lab, Massachusetts Institute of Technology.

Sharples, M. 1985. *Cognition, computers and creative writing.* Chicester, West Sussex, Eng.: Ellis Horwood.

Watt, D. 1983. *Learning with Logo.* New York: Byte Books/McGraw-Hill.

——. 1984. *Learning with Apple Logo.* New York: Byte Books/McGraw-Hill.

——. 1985a. *Learning with Commodore Logo.* New York: Byte Books/McGraw-Hill.

——. 1985b. *Learning with IBM Logo.* New York: Byte Books/McGraw-Hill.

——. 1985c. Teacher-made microworlds. In J. Wilton, ed. *Proceedings of Joint Conference of the Educational Computing Organization of Ontario and the Association for Educational Data Systems,* pp. 143–46. Washington, D.C.: Association for Educational Data Systems.

Watt, D., and M. Watt. 1989. Rethinking Logo pedagogy using a process approach. Paper presented at the National Educational Computing Conference, Boston.

Watt, M., and D. Watt. 1986. *Teaching with Logo: Building blocks for learning.* Palo Alto, Calif.: Addison-Wesley.

For Further Reading

Turkle, S. 1984. *The second self: Computers and the human spirit.* New York: Simon and Schuster.

Developers and Vendors of Logo Software

LEGO Dacta, 555 Taylor Road, Enfield, Conn. 06082.

Logo Computer Systems, Inc. (LCSI), 3300 Cote Vertu, Suite 201, Montreal, Que. H4R 2B7, Canada.

Paradigm Software, Inc., PO Box 2995, Cambridge, Mass. 02238.

Terrapin Software, Inc., 400 Riverside Street, Portland, Me. 04103.

Daniel Lynn Watt

MACHINE LEARNING

Machine learning is the research area concerned with building machines (or equivalently, writing computer programs) that improve their performance through experience. Machine learning is a subfield of artificial intelligence (AI); many researchers consider it an essential subfield, claiming that a machine that does not benefit from its experience cannot be considered intelligent. Its history generally parallels that of AI; it has employed the devices used for mechanized reasoning as they appeared. Although results of such efforts have been published since the 1950s, machine learning is still considered a new field and there are still disputes among scholars about what is and is not machine learning and how it should be investigated. The First Machine Learning Workshop took place in the summer of 1980 at Carnegie-Mellon University and the first journal devoted exclusively to machine learning appeared in 1986.

Human learning takes many forms, including skill refinement, learning by being taught, learning by analogy, learning from examples, and learning by exploration or experimentation. All these types of learning have been exhibited by machines, but a comprehensive theory or a single programming paradigm that encompasses them all has yet to emerge.

In general, learning machines have had the following components: a store of knowledge, a performance component that applies its knowledge, and a learning component that modifies its knowledge. In addition, there is a learning protocol that specifies the type of task the system can learn and the type of feedback on its performance the system requires in order to learn.

To provide some sense of this dynamic research field, several historically important systems are described in the following section. The important topic of learnability theory is introduced and finally some aspects used to compare and contrast these systems are mentioned. Related topics not discussed include neural networks or connectionist learning, the field of PATTERN RECOGNITION and the engineering discipline of adaptive control.

SOME IMPORTANT LEARNING SYSTEMS

The field of building learning machines might be said to have begun with the checkers playing programs of Arthur Samuel in the 1950s (Samuel 1959). The approaches he adopted contained many elements still found in learning systems today. Samuel did not propose to build a general learning machine, but one for a specific task: checkers. This task is a relatively simple one with clearly defined actions. The possible states of the world the machine must face are limited to the configurations of the board, which allows one to safely assume the machine has complete knowledge of all important information needed to act wisely. Nevertheless, there was no known algorithm for making flawless decisions. Samuel's program planned its moves by first generating possible moves, looking ahead several moves from each, and computing a value for each resulting situation. This value was a weighted sum (i.e., a polynomial) of features (such as the piece advantage and the number of exposed pieces). The learning task was to find what features and what weights produced the best checkers playing by most accurately predicting the "desirability" of future board situations. This set of features and numbers constituted the system's knowledge. The machine could learn by playing against humans, standard book moves, or itself. To adjust its polynomial, the value computed for each board position encountered in play was compared with the value computed by looking ahead. Those weights that correlated positively or negatively with the difference were adjusted slightly in the direction of the correlation. After many such adjustments, if a feature's weight was too low (indicating that it contributed little to the evaluation), it was dropped from the polynomial and a new term was added (from a predefined set). An evaluation polynomial would look like:

position value = + 0.45 (mobility and
                  control of the center)
              − 0.40 (king center
                  control)
                    . . .
              + 0.13 (threat moves).

After learning, the program was able to beat not only its author but prominent checkers players as well.

With the growth in the 1970s of rule-based approaches to machine reasoning, systems were developed that were able to learn their own rules. Among the first was Waterman's Poker Player, which played against another program (a teacher) assumed to have perfect knowledge in the form of an algorithm. If the learner made an incorrect play, it was instructed by the teacher what play was correct and what game features were relevant (error-driven learning). By this interaction, the learner was able to acquire rules that allowed it to approach the teacher's level of proficiency. A few years later, an article described another program, Meta-Dendral, which used a rule-based knowledge representation and learned to classify unknown substances from their mass spectrographs. Some researchers consider this article to be the first research paper coauthored by a machine.

In the mid-1970s, learning machines were developed that used Boolean expressions, rather than sets of feature-weights or rules, as their representation of knowledge.

The learning protocol often used was called "learning from examples" and has important ties to pattern recognition and to the psychological study of concept acquisition. In this protocol, a machine is shown a number of training instances, each described by a list of features and correctly classified. The machine must find a Boolean expression that allows it to classify correctly instances that it has not previously seen. An example was Michalski's AQ11 system, which learned to diagnose soybean diseases (among other things). Each instance was a known case of soybean disease characterized by features such as the month the disease appeared, the amount of precipitation, the temperature, the type of spots on the leaves, etc. AQ11 was able to learn to classify soybean diseases more accurately than an expert system built with knowledge from human experts. The resulting Boolean expressions were of the form:

IF [precipitation > normal] and [temperature
    < normal] and . . .
      or
[month_of_appearance = April to August]
and . . .
THEN diagnosis = *Phytophthora* root rot.

AQ11 works by selecting a small set of the instances and forming an initial "hypothesis" (a Boolean expression called a cover) that discriminates one class of instances (called a concept) from the rest. It then incrementally improves its hypothesis by examining the other instances for classification errors of two types: concept instances not covered by the hypothesis and nonconcept instances covered by the hypothesis. AQ11 made almost exclusive use of a general cover algorithm, but other systems of this type had special operators for generalization (relaxing the Boolean terms to cover previously excluded concept instances) and for specialization (restricting the Boolean terms to exclude previously covered nonconcept instances). Decision trees, a related knowledge representation, have also been successfully used to learn classification tasks. ID3 and its derivatives (Quinlan 1986) are among the best known systems using decision trees.

Another approach, the genetic algorithm (GA), also emerged in the 1970s. Conceived as an extremely general approach to adaptation, it is based on the idea of Darwinian evolution. Unlike other algorithms that try to make incremental improvements in a single hypothesis, the GA maintains a set of hypotheses called a population. Each hypothesis is represented as a string (a chromosome) of symbols, most often bits. The control cycle of the GA is called a generation and involves a survival-of-the-fittest step in which the better-than-average chromosomes reproduce in proportion to their fitness. Then new hypotheses (offspring) are formed by recombining the parent chromosomes using a cut-and-splice operation called crossover (Figure 1). A mutation operator that will, with low probability, randomly alter some of the bits in some of the offspring and an inversion operator that will cause a reordering of the bits are also used. These operators differ significantly from the operators (like generalization and specialization) of the previous systems in that they manipulate strings without trying to achieve a specific improvement. Effective search results from the interplay between selection and recombination yielding a phenomenon called *implicit parallelism*, in which many coadapted sets of symbols (*schemata*) simultaneously proliferate in proportion to their observed fitnesses. This gives the G.A. its generality; it is not restricted to any particular problem domain or knowledge representation. Holland and Reitman (1978) designed a coding scheme for production rules that allowed the evolution of knowledge by trial and error. The first such system, CS-1, was able to learn a simple maze running task. Later, Smith (1983) demonstrated that a similar system was able to beat Waterman's teacher program at poker. Because its learning protocol was simple trial

and error learning, it was not limited to acquiring the teacher's knowledge. Recently, some researchers have begun evolving neural networks using GAs. Because of their reliance on very low level knowledge representation, GAs (and some neural networks) are sometimes called *subsymbolic* learning systems (Goldberg 1989; Carbonell 1990).

Learning general concepts from sets of examples is often called similarity-based learning (SBL) because the program works by discovering common features of the examples that are classified together. To discover these regularities without any prior knowledge, SBL systems require many training instances to learn reliably. Another form of learning, capable of generalizing from a single instance, emerged in the early 1980s. Called explanation-based learning (EBL) (Ellman 1989), it requires a considerable store of prior knowledge, usually represented as rules. When given a new instance of a known concept, an EBL system uses its knowledge to verify the truth of the instance, by constructing a reasoning chain from the instance features to the concept (conclusion). This logical chain is called an explanation. The EBL system then examines this explanation and determines the sufficient conditions on the instance features that allow the explanation to be valid. It then formulates a new rule that allows the conclusion to be drawn immediately (in one step) not only for the given instance, but also for any other instances that satisfy these conditions. From one perspective, one might say that an EBL system does not learn anything it did not already know, but it does reformulate its knowledge allowing it to quickly reach conclusions after learning that would have required extensive searching before learning.

A learning protocol requiring a minimum of input from a teacher (including none at all) is that of learning by "discovery." An influential discovery system, called Automated Mathematician (AM), was developed by Lenat (1982). The AM was initialized with a small set of concepts from the field of mathematics, such as "set" and "equality," represented as *frames* (sets of attributes with their values). It also had some operators that allowed it to create new concepts (e.g., by generalizing, specializing, or combining old-

FIGURE 1. The action of the crossover recombination operator.

er concepts), generate some examples of concepts, and form conjectures by looking for regularities among these examples. Its operation is analogous to a theorem prover that begins with a set of axioms and rules of inference and proceeds to derive theorems. Similarly, its behavior would be combinatorially explosive; therefore Lenat provided a set of heuristic rules to control its actions. The AM maintained an agenda of tasks it might perform, and each was rated for "interestingness." AM's only mission in life was to spend its time on interesting knowledge derivation. In the process, AM discovered such concepts as prime number, de Morgan's Law, and the Prime Unique Factorization Theorem.

LEARNABILITY THEORY

Attempts to formulate formal theories of inductive inference made relatively little impact on machine learning until Valiant (Valiant 1984) formulated the notion of learning in the "probably approximately correct" sense (PAC learning). In PAC learning, two probability thresholds are specified, p_1 and p_2. A learned concept is said to be correct (approximately) if its probability of misclassifying unseen instances is less than p_2. The probability that a correct concept will be learned is p_1. The protocols involve learning from examples where the examples are randomly drawn from some unknown probability distribution. These protocols require only access to a supply (possibly very large) of examples of the concept and a teacher capable of telling the algorithm whether examples it poses are or are not instances of the concept. A concept is a Boolean expression that divides the universe of possible examples into two sets, those that are examples of the concept and those that are not. Using this notion, Valiant and others have begun to prove theorems showing that machines can learn whole classes of nontrivial concepts and do so in feasible (i.e., polynomial) numbers of steps. Such theorems can also be used to set bounds on the number of training examples needed to reach specified error tolerances (p_2) for these classes of concepts.

ASPECTS OF LEARNING SYSTEMS

Learning systems have been compared and contrasted using several criteria, among them the learning protocol, the knowledge representation, and the research orientation. Perhaps the simplest protocol is rote learning, in which the machine remembers every event from its experience, and the right action for it. Another protocol is learning by being told, which spans a spectrum from explicit programming (the teacher plants knowledge directly into the machine) to various forms of advice taking. A protocol involving less teacher effort is learning from examples, in which the system begins as a tabula rasa and learns from positive (or positive and negative) examples that have been infallibly classified. Variations include features that may be missing or erroneous, erroneous classifications, prior knowledge (e.g., EBL), and different sources of examples (e.g., there may be a fixed set, they may be generated by a teacher, they may be randomly generated, the system may generate its own for the teacher to classify). Learning by analogy involves finding a mapping between internal representations of similar objects. Systems using the learning-by-exploring (or discovering) protocol require no teacher; they simply interact with a problem environment and adapt.

Knowledge representations used in machine learning research have included numeric parameters, decision trees, formal grammars, production rules, logic-based expressions, graphs/networks, frames/schemas, and computer code. Because learning performance is so influenced by the representation, research has begun to explore self-modification of knowledge representation.

Research orientations of three types have been identified. Researchers may be trying to build a system to perform a specified task (engineering orientation), to gain theoretical insight (theoretical orientation), or to model some aspect of human learning (cognitive modeling). To explore further, the reader is directed to four recent books on the subject (Cohen and Feigenbaum 1982; Michalski et al. 1983, 1986; Carbonell 1990) and to the journal *Machine Learning* (Kluwer Academic Publishers).

References

Carbonell, J. G., ed. 1990. *Machine learning paradigms and methods.* Cambridge, Mass.: MIT Press.

Cohen, P. R., and E. A. Feigenbaum, eds. 1982. *The handbook of artificial intelligence.* Vol. 3. San Mateo, Calif.: Morgan Kaufmann.

Ellman, T. 1989. Explanation-based learning: A survey of programs and perspectives. *ACM Computing Surveys* 21(2):164–221.

Goldberg, D. E. 1989. *Genetic algorithms in search, optimization, and machine learning.* Reading, Mass.: Addison-Wesley.

Holland, J. H., and H. S. Reitman. 1978. Cognitive systems based on adaptive algorithms. In D. A. Waterman and F. Hayes-Roth, eds., *Pattern-directed inference systems.* New York: Academic.

Lenat, D. B. 1982. AM: An artificial intelligence approach to discovery in mathematics as heuristic search. In R. Davis and D. Lenat, eds., *Knowledge-based systems in artificial intelligence.* New York: McGraw-Hill.

Michalski, R. S., J. G. Carbonell, and T. M. Mitchell, eds. 1983–1986. *Machine learning: An artificial intelligence approach.* 2 vols. San Mateo, Calif.: Morgan Kaufmann.

Quinlan, J. R. 1986. Induction of decision trees. *Machine Learning* 1(1):81–106.

Samuel, A. L. 1959. Some studies in machine learning using the game of checkers. *IBM Journal of Research and Development* 3(3):210–29. Reprinted 1963 in Feigenbaum and Feldman, eds., *Computers and thought,* pp. 71–105. New York: McGraw-Hill.

Smith, S. F. 1983. Flexible learning of problem solving heuristics through adaptive search. In *8th International Joint Conference on Artificial Intelligence, Karlsruhe, Germany, August 1983.*

Valiant, L. G. 1984. A theory of the learnable. *Communications of the ACM* 27(2):1134–42.

For Further Reading

Carbonell, J., and P. Langley. 1987. Learning, machine. In S.C. Shapiro, ed. *Encyclopedia of artificial intelligence.* New York: Wiley.

J. David Schaffer

MANAGEMENT INFORMATION SYSTEMS

Management information system (MIS) is the most common name applied to the technology-based information system supporting organizational operations and management. Within an organization, the term is also applied to the organizational function providing and managing the technology and services. It is used for the academic field that studies the information management function and information systems. Management information system is not the only term that is used to refer to the system, the function, and the academic field. Other common terms that are reasonably similar in meaning are information management (IM), information resources management (IRM), information systems (IS), and information technology management (ITM).

The historical evolution of information systems in support of organizational operations and management began with the introduction in 1954 of computers for business data processing. The use of the computers was usually termed *data processing* or *electronic data processing* (EDP). The scope of use tended to be limited to simple transaction systems (processing invoices, payroll, inventory, etc.) and simple reports; however, many leading practitioners and academics began in the late 1950s and early 1960s to design computer-based systems that were more comprehensive and provided a wide range of support to organizations.

The term *management information system* was applied in the mid-1960s. In 1968, the Society for Management Information Systems (SMIS) was formed (later renamed the Society for Information Management). The first academic research center specifically designed for MIS was also founded in that year (The Management Information Systems Research Center at the University of Minnesota). The academic study of MIS is distinguished from computer science by its emphasis on the application of information technology to organizational needs. The academic relationship of MIS to organizational and management studies has resulted in most MIS academic research and degree programs being part of schools of management.

DEFINITION

A well-known definition in 1974 (with minor updating in 1985) summarizes the concept:

> an integrated, user-machine system for providing information to support operations, management, analysis, and decision-making functions in an organization. The system utilizes computer hardware and software; manual procedures; models for analysis, planning, control and decision making; and a data base. (Davis 1974, p. 5, Davis and Olson 1985, p. 6)

Some important elements of the definition follow.

Computer-based. One can conceptualize a management information system without information technology, but it cannot be implemented fully as a manual system. Information technologies including electronic communications are therefore an essential part of a management information system.

User–machine. The MIS concept recognizes the fact that the most effective system is designed to use the capabilities of both humans and computers. The division of labor uses computers and other information technology to enhance and expand the capabilities of human operators and users of the system. This aspect is often referred to as man–machine or human–machine systems.

Integrated system. Organizations share information internally and externally. Information captured or developed in one part of

the organization is needed by other parts of the same organization. A well-designed MIS recognizes the information interrelationships and designs systems to support sharing and joint use. The individual systems that compose the MIS are designed to operate as component systems of an overall system.

Database. The concept of databases follows from the concept of sharing and integration. The implementation of databases (instead of separate files belonging to applications) supports the shared use of data. It fits with the concept of data as an organizational resource to be managed like other organizational resources. An organization will generally employ several databases that fit together in an overall data architecture.

To support . . . functions in an organization. The objective of an MIS is to support an organization. The functions being supported include operations, management, analysis, and decision making. The support may be structured in the form of models that support specific methods or approaches to these functions. It may also be unstructured and provide support through access to data and software capabilities. Users develop their own models and analyses. The personnel being supported range from clerical personnel performing basic transactions to high-level executives performing strategic planning. The information system support can include systems for routine data processing and reporting, systems for automation of operations, and systems to achieve competitive advantage and support organizational strategy.

MANAGEMENT INFORMATION SYSTEMS IN SUPPORT OF DIFFERENT LEVELS OF MANAGEMENT ACTIVITY

The MIS concept is comprehensive and envisions support to all levels of operations and management in an organization. As illustrated in Figure 1, the information system is congruent with the concept of a pyramid of organizational information activity.

At the bottom are routine transaction

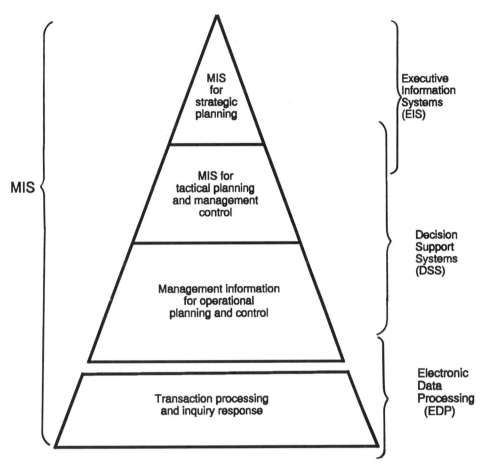

FIGURE 1. Management information systems in support of organizational operations and management.

processing and processing of inquiries seeking data from the databases. In terms of volume of activity, transaction processing and inquiries take up much of the information processing system time and capacity.

The next level of activity consists of applications in support of operational planning, control, and decision making. Typical activities are scheduling production and controlling purchases.

The management information at the next level is focused on management control through tactical planning and decision making. Budgets, management reports, and variance analyses are typical at this level.

The highest level in the management information support pyramid is strategic planning and related policy planning and decision making.

DECISION SUPPORT SYSTEMS AND EXECUTIVE INFORMATION SYSTEMS

The management information pyramid is useful in understanding the relationship to MIS of systems labeled decision support systems and executive information systems. In the early 1970s, some academics and researchers identified an important component of the MIS as being computer software and applications that support decision makers in their decision processes, especially unstructured decision making (Gorry and Scott Morton 1971). These support systems were labeled decision support systems or DSS (see article on DECISION SUPPORT SYSTEMS). The design and implementation of DSS form a subfield within MIS and an area of both practitioner and academic research and development. Early DSS development focused on individual decision makers; subsequent development in the 1980s included support for group decision support systems (GDSS) or computer-supported cooperative work (see article on COOPERATIVE WORK SYSTEMS).

A similar interest in a component of the MIS has resulted in a support system labeled executive information system (EIS) or perhaps executive support system. The needs of high-level executives differ from those of personnel charged with management control and operational control. The executives performing strategic planning must deal with much more external information and data not normally available in the organization's information processing systems. Therefore, support for strategic planning and high-level executive decision making requires additional data and sets of analytical routines that are more or less unique to this level of management. An executive information system provides this support (see article on EXECUTIVE INFORMATION SYSTEMS).

The relationship of the MIS concept to the concepts of DSS, GDSS, and EIS are illustrated in Figure 1. In this figure, MIS is the comprehensive concept and DSS and EIS are component systems. This view is most consistent with the development of the MIS concept; however, an alternative view is that MIS was an early, report-oriented concept and DSS and EIS are higher-level concepts. Those who support the latter view note that there was little industry adoption of the DSS and EIS components until these were identified with different labels.

STRATEGIC APPLICATIONS OF INFORMATION TECHNOLOGY

The basic competitive strategies of an organization are either to be a low-cost producer or to offer differentiated products or services that will command a premium price. Early use of computers in organizations tended to be oriented to cost reduction. This was followed by systems that changed the operations of organizations. On-line reservations systems and automated teller machines are examples. These systems represented new ways of performing fundamental services. Both cost reductions and new ways of performing services can be strategic or nonstrategic to an organization. The applications are strategic if they change the nature of competition or support the firm's competitive strategy. This identification and development of strategic systems have become an important activity of strategic planning by management (in conjunction with MIS management). The concept of an MIS therefore includes strategic applications of information technology. (see STRATEGIC USES OF INFORMATION SYSTEMS).

SUPPORT FOR ORGANIZATIONAL FUNCTIONS

Although it is conceptually simple to think of the MIS as being one large encompassing system, such a massive system would be cumbersome and difficult to build and maintain. Instead, there are natural groupings or subdivisions around which subsystems of the MIS are built. The different business functions such as marketing, production, logistics, human resources, finance, and accounting have unique needs requiring information processing applications designed specifically for the functions and databases used primarily for them. The concept of applications that support transactions, operations, control, and strategy is applicable for each function. Therefore, an MIS for the marketing function will have applications for marketing transactions, marketing operations, marketing management control, and strategic marketing planning. The MIS for each function is, however, not completely isolated. These system are designed to transfer data, share data, and operate as part of the larger MIS system within an enterprise information architecture.

EVOLUTION OF THE MANAGEMENT INFORMATION SYSTEM CONCEPT AND NAMES APPLIED TO IT

The MIS concept has been expanded since its original formulation; the basic concept still applies. This expansion and sharpening of the concept have been evolutionary over a

25-year period. The first major sharpening of the concept involved significant focus on systems for support of decision making (both individual and group). This was followed later by systems for executive information use. The MIS concept as originally described tended to concentrate on the information system as support for information processing needs of an organization. By the early 1970s the scope was expanded to include systems incorporating information technology that changed the way organizations functioned. A later development in the early 1980s placed attention on information systems applications as an important component of competitive strategy.

What to call the system and the organizational function responsible for it is still in evolution. Although MIS is the dominant name for the comprehensive concept of a system based on information technology to support organizational information needs, there is a trend to identify the function that provides the services by the term *information management* and the systems by the simple term *information systems*. The range of names related to MIS are illustrated by the names of two professional organizations: the Society for Information Management (SIM) composed of information management executives and the Data Processing Management Association (DPMA) with a broad range of information processing personnel as members. Two journals devoted to the field also illustrate the variety of names. The *MIS Quarterly* is a leading journal with articles for both scholarly business readers and academics. A leading academic research journal is called *Information Systems Research.*

SUMMARY

Although other terms may be used, the term *management information system* is the one most commonly applied to the organizational technology-based information system, to the information management function, and to the academic field of study. The MIS concept began as a comprehensive view of computer-based information systems as support for organizational operations, management, analysis, and decision making. The concept

has been sharpened and expanded by a focus on component systems for individual and group decision support and executive information systems. The scope of the MIS has been expanded to include not only information processing as organizational support but also information technology as an essential component of new operations and services and information technology applications as an essential part of an organization's competitive strategy.

[*See also:* Database Design, Automated.]

References
Davis, G. B. 1974. *Management information systems: Conceptual foundations, structure, and development.* New York: McGraw-Hill. Ranked as a classic in the field.

Davis, G. B., and M. H. Olson. 1985. *Management information systems: Conceptual foundations, structure, and development.* 2nd ed. New York: McGraw-Hill.

Gorry, G. A., and M. S. Scott Morton. 1971. A framework for management information systems. *Sloan Management Review* 13(1):55–70. A classic framework article.

For Further Reading
Aaron, J. D. 1969. Information systems in perspective. *Computing Surveys,* December, pp. 216–36. Very early survey.

Davis, G. B. 1987. Information systems as an academic discipline. In H. K. Achleitner, ed. *Part III: Concepts of information, intellectual foundations for information professionals,* pp. 115–41. Boulder, Colo.: Social Science Monographs.

Dickson, G. W. 1981. Management information systems: Evolution and status. In M. Yeats, ed. *Advances in computers.* New York: Academic Press. A historical review.

Ives, B., J. S. Hamilton, and G. Davis. 1980. A framework for research in computer based management information systems. *Management Science* 19(6):910–34. Defines MIS as a field of research.

McFarlan, F. W., and J. L. McKenney. A series of three articles in the *Harvard Business Review:* The information archipelago —Maps and bridges. September–October 1982. The information archipelago—Plotting a course. January–February 1983 (with P. Pyburn). The information archipelago—Governing the new world. July–August 1983.

Gordon B. Davis

MANUFACTURING ENGINEERING, COMPUTERS IN

Manufacturing engineering is the discipline, within engineering, that specifies the systems and processes to be used for transforming raw materials into usable goods. Manufacturing engineers start with the design specification of products and determine the best way in which such products can be made to meet (or exceed) specifications. A central tenet, applied across the board, is that the process of manufacturing must be as efficient as possible. In any manufacturing system, several types of inputs are typically applied, in an incremental way, toward the transformation of raw materials into final products. These inputs, in addition to the raw materials themselves, include human labor, capital equipment, energy, tools, and specific types of data. This branch of engineering focuses on determining the precise inputs required, as well as generating plans for combining all inputs in the most effective way so that the resulting product meets all customer expectations.

In preparation for a career in manufacturing engineering, interested individuals must undertake the basic engineering training and then proceed to specialize in the study of various methods for transforming certain raw materials into final products. Manufacturing engineering practice includes the use of a variety of analysis methods to determine the best way in which inputs should be applied during the process of manufacturing. Because of the extreme variety of product types that exist, manufacturing engineers typically posses expertise in the manufacturing design of only a small set of product types. As an example, the process of manufacturing electronic goods is quite different from that of producing automobiles.

Nonetheless, a common thread exists for all types of manufacturing, that is, the requirement to be efficient and, at the same time, produce high-quality goods.

ROLE OF COMPUTERS

There are two main areas in which computers currently play a prominent role in manufacturing. First, as manufacturing systems and processes have become more and more complex, computers now serve as the primary tool to assist manufacturing engineers in performing much of the analysis they need to carry out. This then facilitates better manufacturing decision making in the face of increasing complexity and marketplace uncertainty. Second, computers are often used to control and manage manufacturing systems and processes. This often contributes dramatically to the quality and efficiency with which manufacturing operations can be performed.

The task of product design usually precedes that of manufacturing engineering, yet they are both highly dependent on each other. Decisions made during product design could severely limit the feasible set of alternatives available during manufacturing design. Historically both of these functions have been isolated from each other, but current trends suggest that better integration of design and manufacturing engineering can yield major improvements in terms of reduced cost, improved quality, and reduced product development lead times. We will see in a subsequent section how computers assist in this respect.

In the 1990s, the competitive challenges that face most manufacturing firms include a need to reduce cost, enhance product quality, achieve rapid product realization, and make their products, processes, and facilities more flexible. Each of the four challenges listed presents unique and unprecedented opportunities for the use of computers to achieve a competitive edge. As an illustrative case, we can see that the most important determinant of cost competitiveness is the efficiency with which manufacturing inputs are used. Manufacturing efficiency is determined by processing efficiency, resource efficiency, and facility efficiency. In general, if everything else remains equal, the fewer input resources that go into manufacturing a product, the lower its final cost will be.

SOME APPLICATIONS OF COMPUTERS

This section describes some applications of computers in manufacturing engineering and points the way in which each helps to improve productivity directly or indirectly by assisting in the complex analysis tasks that have to be performed. Computer applications in manufacturing can be characterized, for convenience, into four areas:

1. Product processing
2. Handling of materials
3. Planning and design tasks
4. Management of manufacturing systems

At least one example is presented of each of the first three categories. A common attribute, held in common by each of these applications, is that they are tasks that humans perform quite poorly or that humans generally find unattractive. Despite advances in artificial intelligence, tasks that require any degree of creativity continue to be reserved almost exclusively for humans. Most successful applications represent a complementary combination of human and computer capabilities.

Robotics

Robots are applied in two main areas of manufacturing. The first is in processing, assembling components, for example, and the second is in material handling. From a physical point of view, robots are typically made up of two or more jointed linkages. To operate as required, every robot has at least one computer that controls the coordinated motions of its linkages. The computer control is also responsible for monitoring for unsafe conditions and making the robot operate in response to external inputs or according to a user's program. The programming of robots is usually accomplished by a combination of off-line programming, in one of the several robot programming languages, and programming-by-teaching, in which the robot is led through a sequence of motions that it can then repeat as desired. Most tasks for which robots are suited either are repetitive in nature, require great amounts of consistency, operate in hazardous environments, or are otherwise unattractive to human operators. Recent advances in robotics include the design of robots that operate at faster speeds, are easier to program and operate, and have computer controls that operate on more sophisticated algorithms. Vision systems are also being used in conjunction with robots. Typically, the vision system is used to identify one part from among several within its view, and then different algorithms are used to determine the particular action the robot must take. Using robots to automate the process of manufacturing, where appropriate, shows considerable potential for manufacturing cost reduction as well as for improvements in quality and consistency.

Machine Tools

Machine tools for manufacturing come in a wide variety of types, each type corresponding to a different type of manufacturing process. The processes, and hence machine tool types, range from those for machining metallic parts to those for producing plastic components. By using computers to control machine tools, many manufacturing processes can be automated and be programmable at the same time. This provides some flexibility as well as improved levels of efficiency over manual machine tools. As with robots, machine tool programming can be performed off-line by using one of the many available languages. To automate the programming tasks, some computer software now exists to produce part programs directly from a part's design information, which exists in computer format. Many computer-controlled machine tools now go even one step further to provide automatic part loading and unloading as well as automatic changing of tools. Recent advances in this area include adaptive computer controls, which make the machines not only easier to program, but also more robust in the face of unusual processing conditions. They also help the machines operate more consistently and efficiently.

Material Handling Systems

The ability to move parts through a factory as rapidly and cost effectively as possible is an important aspect of efficiently operated manufacturing systems. An added requirement often encountered is for manufacturers to provide material handling flexibility, to allow rapid responses to unexpected occurrences, at a low total cost. Traditional methods of material handling, which are essentially manual, often do not meet this need. Automated material handling, without any programmability, also falls short in terms of flexibility. The introduction of automated and programmable material handling devices has been a major improvement over traditional methods. In all cases, these devices have computer controls. This provides considerable flexibility as a number of different algorithms can be provided to help the material handling system to adapt to changes in the operating environment. The most popular type of programmable and computer-controlled material handling vehicle is known as the automated guided vehicle (AGV). These vehicles often have the ability to load and unload parts without manual intervention. They are also able to navigate independently across a factory floor. Typically they navigate by following a path defined by thin wires embedded beneath the factory floor. A new class of more flexible vehicles, known as autonomous vehicles, can navigate from one place in the factory to another without the use of guidewires. These vehicles use combinations of dead-reckoning, triangulation, and code detection technologies to accomplish this task.

Manufacturing Simulation

Computer simulation has developed into an important tool for a variety of manufacturing planning tasks, primarily as a result of the increasing complexity of most manufacturing operations. Traditional analysis tools have often been shown to be unable to handle a lot of the complexity that exists in real manufacturing systems. Some manufacturing engineering analysis tasks that are routinely performed using computer simulation include manufacturing system design, plant scheduling, product cost analysis, and process optimization. A variety of computer simulation languages currently exist to model different components of manufacturing systems, such as material handling, plant control, processing, equipment reliability, and process scrap rates. Typically, the analyst uses one of the available simulation languages to develop a model of the system. The simulation model can then be run under a number of hypothesized operating conditions to predict what the performance of the system will be like. In this way several options can be investigated with the aim of arriving at the best system design or to find optimal operating conditions. Using simulation permits manufacturing engineers to explore a wider range of alternatives more rapidly. The ultimate result of using simulation, if applied appropriately, is that better manufacturing decisions can be made and manufacturing systems can be designed and operated much more cost effectively. Future trends in manufacturing system simulation include increasingly sophisticated computer simulation languages that permit models to be developed much more intuitively. Object-oriented simulation is also an important advance that allows the user to model manufacturing system objects directly as simulation objects on the computer.

COMPUTERS AND INFORMATION

Traditional manufacturing systems, with few or no computers, have relied on paper documents and word-of-mouth communication to keep records, transmit instructions, and move data from one area to another. There are several obvious problems with these methods. First, the methods are highly unreliable and the information is often subject to loss and damage. Second, they often cause miscommunication and must, in many cases, be transcribed from one form to another to be useful. The existence of computers in various manufacturing areas, as described earlier, provides a good opportunity to avoid these problems. When computers are networked together, manufacturing data can be transferred electronically from one process to another. Two main types of manufacturing data require transmittal. Planning data such as product designs and production plans must be transmitted from the planners to the plant where the actual work takes place. Also, operational data, which includes information for managing and controlling plants, are often transmitted within manufacturing systems. In both cases, electronic transmission permits all manufacturing tasks to be much better integrated. This yields several benefits, including better management and control of all manufacturing processes, thus reducing cost and increasing manufacturing efficiency.

HUMAN ISSUES

Any discussion of the role of computers in manufacturing engineering must, by necessity, also touch on the human aspects of introducing these new technologies. There is a common misconception that computer technologies, when applied on a large scale in manufacturing, will ultimately result in widespread unemployment. In general, this is not so. Certainly, computer controls permit many hazardous, boring, and complex jobs to be eliminated; however, these are jobs that are hardly ever attractive to human workers, so this can actually be seen as a positive development. Nevertheless, the opportunity that is presented by the introduction of computers into manufacturing is that many jobs can now be upgraded. Instead of asking people to perform undesirable jobs, such as spray-painting cars and trucks, they can now face the more attractive prospect of programming the computers and robots and designing the complex manufacturing systems to make this all happen. This introduces a new challenge to society, however. To handle these higher-level jobs, workers must have much higher levels of training and be better skilled. As long as workers are willing to upgrade their skills, the future looks bright. On the other hand, if education and training are not given a high priority, then the doomsday scenario of widespread unemployment could unfortunately come to pass.

FUTURE

As far as we can tell, the current trend of increasing computer applications in manufacturing planning, analysis, and operations can be expected to continue. There is certainly no letup in the competitive pressures that brought about these developments. Furthermore, we expect that there will be increased levels of integration among the various manufacturing tasks. This will lead to greater cost efficiency as well as opportunities to manage the system as a whole rather than as isolated areas. The end result will be lower-cost products, improved manufacturing decision making, and, above all, more rapid and robust responses to changes in the marketplace. This is the ultimate goal of computer-integrated manufacturing.

For Further Reading

Allegri, T. H., Sr. 1984. *Materials handling: Principles and practice.* New York: Van Nostrand Reinhold.

Baudin, M. 1990. *Manufacturing systems analysis with application to production scheduling.* Englewood Cliffs, N.J.: Yourdon Press.

Groover, M. P. 1987. *Automation, production systems, and computer-integrated manufacturing.* Englewood Cliffs, N.J.: Prentice-Hall.

Groover, M. P., and E. W. Zimmers, Jr. 1984. *CAD/CAM: Computer-aided design and manufacturing.* Englewood Cliffs, N.J.: Prentice-Hall.

Kulwiec, R. A., ed. 1985. *Material handling handbook.* New York: Wiley.

Law, A. M., and Kelton, W. D. 1991. *Simulation modeling and analysis.* New York: McGraw-Hill.

Luggen, W. W. 1991. *Flexible manufacturing cells and systems.* Englewood Cliffs, N.J.: Prentice-Hall.

Maleki, R. A. 1991. *Flexible manufacturing systems: The technology and management.* Englewood Cliffs, N.J.: Prentice-Hall.

Pegden, C. D., R. E. Shannon, and R. P. Sadowski. 1990. *Introduction to simulation using SIMAN.* New York: McGraw-Hill.

Stark, J., ed. *Handbook of manufacturing automation and integration.* Boston: Auerbach.

O. O. Mejabi

MANUFACTURING RESOURCE PLANNING

Information systems for planning and control in manufacturing management, or manufacturing resource planning (MRP II) systems, directly address such problems as the need to reduce costs, improve quality and customer service, cut inventory investment, increase responsiveness to change, and increase management control. This paper describes the basic set of MRP II tools for planning and controlling a manufacturer's resources, not only material but also labor, equipment, and capital.

MRP II concepts have evolved into a professional body of knowledge about management of manufacturing. The original concepts were defined in the 1950s. Packaged software solutions were developed in the 1970s. Continuous extensions since that time have made MRP II a companywide manufacturing planning system (not just a production and inventory control system). It is applicable to the entire spectrum of manufacturing environments, from project/job shop to repetitive/process operations.

An explanation of MRP II starts with the basic manufacturing equation: define what you plan to make (the master schedule), what resources you need (the bill of material/resources), what resources you have (inventory and capacity), and then determine what you need to get (purchasing and production). In defining what you plan to make, the master schedule must account for higher-level aggregate plans, typically determined through business planning, sales/marketing planning, production planning, and rough-cut capacity planning.

MRP II consists of the concepts, procedures, and software to perform the activities for manufacturing planning and to update all related computer files. In an organization, it is necessary to coordinate the activities of different functions. Coordination requires timely and accurate transfer of information. This article explains the use of MRP II to manage information and coordinate various manufacturing-related functions.

The basic master files and major information flows required to support manufacturing decisions, shown in Figure 1, provide the organizing focus for further explanation.

BASIC MASTER FILES

Several master files form the basic building blocks for an MRP II system. These include information about the general ledger chart of accounts, product/process definition, locations/lots for inventory, customers, and vendors.

General ledger chart of accounts. The general ledger chart of accounts identifies the financial activities that will be budgeted and tracked, where the account number format also identifies the organizational structure. When normal transaction processing (such as a receipt or shipment) affects the general ledger, the equivalent financial transaction uses predefined interface accounts (such as inventory or cost of goods sold) to update the general ledger.

Product/process definition. Product design is defined in the item master and bills of material, which reflect relationships between salable end items, raw materials, and any intermediates. The bills or product specifications can express a dynamic product design by defining engineering changes with effectivity dates or revision level control. For custom product environments, a unique bill is defined for each sales order, although standard options and features may have predefined bill structures. In addition to the engineering function, the bills serve the purposes of cost accounting (for calculating product costs), material planning (with lead times and lot sizing logic), and sales order processing (with pricing schemes).

Process design is defined in the work center master and routing (or bill of resources). The routings express the various activities that consume resources (such as equipment and labor) and provide the basis for activity-based cost accounting, capacity planning, and control/tracking of production activity.

Locations/lots for inventory. The location master identifies the physical locations that

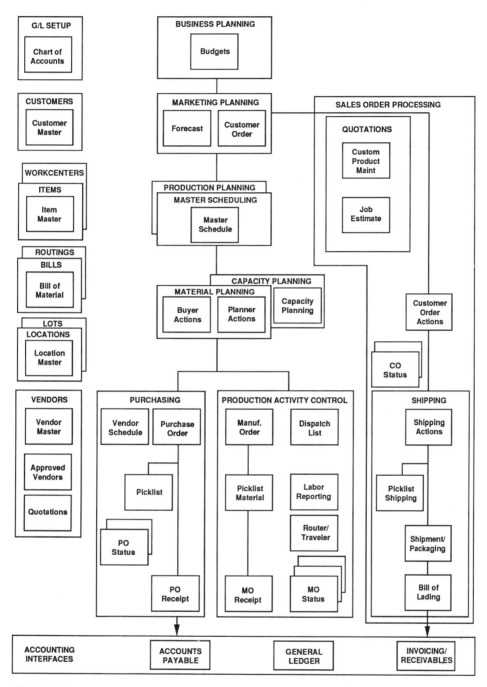

FIGURE 1. Major information flows.

contain inventoried items, which can be uniquely differentiated by lot number. Material planning must account for inventory status (such as on-hand, in-inspection, or on-hold), and lot traceability must track material from raw material receipt through intermediate levels to customer shipment.

Customers. The customer master identifies the firms that purchase products/services, and includes multiple ship-to and bill-to locations, credit limits and terms, general ledger and accounts receivable policies, and text information for each customer. Other setup information related to customers includes tax code, commission code, and price book (e.g., for contracts) information.

Vendors. The vendor master identifies the firms who supply goods/services. Vendors may be approved by the purchasing/quality functions for supplying certain items, and quotations may be established to define agreed-upon prices and contract terms.

BUSINESS PLANNING

Business planning defines the business mission of the company and its markets, profit objectives and resources. Business planning ultimately results in an annual budget that establishes the baseline for financial planning and measurement purposes, as well as for communicating with the financial community. Additional sets of budget numbers may need to be developed to reflect contingency planning or anticipated changes (e.g., by reviewing/updating them on a monthly or quarterly basis based on new information).

SALES/MARKETING PLANNING

Sales/marketing planning focuses on defining all demands being placed on the factory, both the actual customer orders and the estimated/forecasted demands. A sales forecasting system can be used to project estimated demand based on sales history. Forecasts by product families can be used for aggregate planning. Planning bills are used to disaggregate the forecast into salable end items on the basis of product mix percentages. In custom product environments, the planning bill reflects the product mix and typical configuration quantities of options, features, and key resources.

SALES ORDER PROCESSING

Sales order processing starts with entry of the customer order, where availability should be checked for each item. Given available finished goods inventory in a standard products environment, the item may be shipped immediately; however, the item may not be available until a future date (based on production schedules and other customer commitments), so that recommended actions about forward orders must be summarized for customer service representatives in terms of exception conditions (such as release for shipment, shipment past due, or credit limit exceeded). Customer inquiries about customer order status must also be supported.

In a custom product or job shop environment, the customer order defines what should be built and a quotation (the first step in the order processing cycle) may need to be developed. Several approaches can be used to define the custom product, such as copying a previous order and modifying it, selecting options from a predefined list, or defining a new, original bill and routing. The configuration forms the basis for a job cost estimate, and ongoing changes to the custom product configuration result in a revised estimate.

Required shipment activity can be summarized in terms of recommended actions, such as printing consolidated picklists (for assembling the order) and packing lists. Material may be moved (picked) to a staging location, and then packaged and shipped with corresponding box labels and a bill of lading. Shipment transactions update the inventory and costs of goods sold general ledger accounts, and also pass information to invoicing about the sales, freight, tax, and commission charges.

PRODUCTION PLANNING AND MASTER SCHEDULING

Production planning is performed first at the aggregate level. The plan is typically expressed in terms of planned rates of output by product family (to satisfy the rate of demand). The master schedule is the specific statement of production for end items in a standard products environment, or for predefined intermediates in a custom products environment. For custom products, a final assembly schedule is used in conjunction with the master schedule. The master schedule (and final assembly schedule for custom products) drives the operations of the entire organization; materials management schedules purchase/production deliveries, production management adjusts capacity and priorities to make it happen, sales makes customer commitments based on it, and accounting performs financial planning.

CAPACITY PLANNING

Capacity planning takes the schedules defined by the production plan/master schedule, extends them by the routing for each item, and calculates the load on each resource. By comparing load against capacity for bottleneck resources and highlighting overloaded periods, capacity planning can be used to determine the degree to which the master schedule is realistic. In overloaded periods, the load can be reduced (by rescheduling production) or the capacity increased (by overtime, additional equipment/personnel, and so forth).

MATERIAL PLANNING

Material planning takes the schedules defined by the production plan/master schedule and explodes them into material requirements based on the bills of material and lead times. The system should provide recommended actions to planners (responsible for scheduling each area of production) and buyers (responsible for obtaining raw material) to meet the master schedule. In an exception-oriented approach, the recommended actions would identify when orders should be released to production (and when availability of all components should be checked prior to starting production); when orders need expediting or follow-up or are past due; when customer order commitments have overconsumed the planned factory capacity; and when paperwork (production instructions) should be printed or reprinted (e.g., because of changes in the report specifications).

PURCHASING

Purchasing involves periodic review of approved vendors and quotations and daily coordination of vendor deliveries through a vendor schedule. In this case, the purchase order simply confirms the agreed-on date and quantity for delivering items. For subcontracted items, the components may need to be picked and sent to the vendor. Receipts are matched against the original purchase order and may be placed in receiving inspection areas for disposition by quality control.

Purchase orders are also required for one-time items and operations specially purchased for a custom product, for outside operations on a manufacturing order, and for expense and capital equipment items. Inquiries about purchase order status must also be supported.

When receipts are recorded, information is passed to accounts payable for the purpose of matching receipts to invoices, and to the general ledger for the purpose of updating inventory, unvouchered payables, and purchase price variances.

PRODUCTION ACTIVITY CONTROL

A manufacturing order defines the quantity and start/complete dates for producing a given item. On a given order, the standard bill and routing may be modified to become an "order-dependent bill" that reflects material substitutions and/or alternate operations. Material usage and labor/resource expenditures are reported against this order-dependent bill. As an alternative to picking material components prior to starting production, the components may be "backflushed" or postdeducted after completion of an operation or receipt of the parent (e.g., in chemical production).

Coordination of various areas of production activity (or work centers) is critical to meeting the master schedule, and dispatch lists provide a key coordination tool. The dispatch list identifies, in due date priority order, manufacturing orders that must be completed in a given work center (on the basis of the routing), and is constantly updated to communicate changing priorities immediately. In custom product environments, the router/traveler also acts as a coordination tool, because it provides detailed instructions (defined in the routing) for producing an item. In repetitive environments with standard routings, visible scheduling systems (such as the use of KANBAN tokens) can be used as the coordination tool.

By reporting actual material and resource consumption, one can compare actual costs with standard/estimated costs and calculate variances. Manufacturing transactions (such as the consumption of material and resources, and manufacturing order receipts) automatically generate the financial transactions for updating the general ledger.

INTERFACES TO ACCOUNTING

The primary interfaces to accounting involve invoicing/receiving, accounts payable, and the general ledger. Normal transaction processing automatically generates the information that needs to be passed to the accounting applications. Shipment information is passed to invoicing for the purposes of generating accurate invoices and subsequently generating customer statements and tracking receivables.

Purchase receipt information is passed to accounts payable for the purposes of matching receipts to invoices (if applicable) and authorizing payments to suppliers.

Costed manufacturing transactions (such as shipments, receipts, resource expenditures, and material consumption) are passed to general ledger to track inventory, manufacturing expenses, and actual-against-budgeted costs.

HOW MRP II RELATES TO OTHER MANUFACTURING SYSTEMS

MRP II forms the heart of the planning and control system for manufacturing. In the case of computer-integrated manufacturing (CIM), connectivity between MRP II and the various CIM components is achieved by data import and export. Computer-aided design applications use/update information about items and bills in the MRP II system. Decision support system applications require ad hoc access to the MRP II database. In the case of the just-in-time (JIT) manufacturing approach, the planning and control system provided by MRP II supports the simplification and continuous improvement efforts of

JIT (e.g., to reduce lead times, lot sizes, safety stock, and inventory).

For Further Reading

Hamilton, S. 1991. *Information systems for manufacturing management.* Minneapolis, Minn.: Microtechnology Sources Ltd.

Ling, R., and W. Goddard. 1983. *Orchestrating success: Improve control of the business with sales and operations planning.* Essex Junction, Vt.: Oliver Wight Ltd.

Wight, O. 1984. *Manufacturing resource planning: Unlocking America's productivity potential.* Essex Junction, Vt.: Oliver Wight Ltd.

Scott Hamilton

MARKETING AND MARKETING RESEARCH, COMPUTER USE IN

Computers have changed the way marketers analyze potential markets, develop new products and services, and promote these products and services to consumers. For example, a product manager can use a demographic database to identify rapidly growing metropolitan areas, another database to profile the consumption habits of those living in an identified area, and a statistical analysis package to compare these habits with those of the company's current customers to determine whether the proposed market has adequate potential. The manager can choose other software to determine potential retail locations within the city based on specific demographic patterns within the city, to choose appropriate radio, television, and newspaper coverage, and to select street addresses for a direct-mail campaign. Another package can dial the phone numbers of everyone living in the city and connect the phone call to an operator only when a live voice answers. The telemarketer can then use a script shown on a television monitor in front of them to deliver a sales pitch tailored to the individual's responses. Desktop technology continues to improve; Kirchner and Thomas (1989) report that by 1995 it is expected that new video technology and satellite mapping will allow managers to "see" buildings, street corners, and other geographic features as they make their plans.

Marketing encompasses a wide variety of activities, as detailed in the definition of marketing adopted by the American Marketing Association in 1985: "Marketing is the process of planning and executing the conception, pricing, promotion, and distribution of ideas, goods, and services to create exchanges that satisfy individual and organizational objectives." This article presents an overview of the major areas of marketing that now make use of computers.

MARKETING RESEARCH

Four areas in marketing research where computers have had a dramatic impact are sampling, data acquisition, data analysis, and simulation.

Sampling. Sampling as we know it today would not be feasible without information systems that have the capability of storing large amounts of information and sorting through this information at great speeds. Mailing list companies are often used to provide random samples of certain populations. These samples can be defined very broadly, for example, heads of households, or very specifically, for example, physicians of a certain specialty (see Kaehler 1988).

Data acquisition. The process of acquiring information from consumers has improved through the use of certain information technologies. For example, audience tracking, a process by which researchers determine which television programs people are watching, has recently become totally automated (*Marketing News* 1987, Schlossberg 1990). As soon as the television is turned on, selected consumers "log in." A computerized device then monitors which programs are being watched. Subsequently, the data are uploaded, giving networks and advertisers immediate feedback about who has been watching their programs.

With bar codes on more than 90 percent of the products we purchase (see BAR CODE SYSTEMS), researchers are able to get a much better picture of what consumers are buying. Many point-of-sale systems are set up to track spending patterns of consumers (Stanat 1989). In addition, these bar codes can be used by members of consumer panels to record their purchases. For a long time consumer panelists were forced to manually log each of their purchases; however, now some companies provide these consumers with optical scanning devices, which are used to record each purchase in a relatively easy manner (Prete 1991). This makes it easier for the consumer to participate, decreases the errors in recording purchases, and results in faster availability of panel data.

Certain data acquisition/analysis techniques are also now being done by computers. For example, perceptual mapping (in which consumers' perceptions of several products are graphically portrayed on a single "map") was once done by manually sorting cards; however, the software is now available to carry out much more sophisticated perceptual mapping techniques on personal computers (Minno 1990).

Data analysis. Data analysis is a central part of most marketing research applications. Whether the researcher is compiling simple cross-tabulations or completing very sophisticated multivariate analyses, computerized statistical software packages are available for completing the task. A decade ago, these packages were available only on large mainframe computers; however, today, most popular packages are now available on microcomputers.

Simulation. For some types of marketing research, it is prohibitively difficult or expensive to actually survey consumers, so researchers turn to simulation software. The effects of changes in price, promotional expenditures, inventory level adjustments and routing, or business locations can all be simulated with available software (*Marketing News* 1991a, 1991b; Zufreyden 1989).

DIRECT MARKETING AND TELEMARKETING

Direct marketing is the process of selling directly to consumers (bypassing intermediaries). This process is heavily reliant on computer databases for developing customer lists (Holtz 1985), refining customer lists (Schley 1990), and tracking customer purchases (Miller 1989).

Telemarketing broadly refers to the use of telephones in the marketing of products. Inbound telemarketing occurs when potential customers are provided with a telephone number (usually toll-free) that can be called to place an order, obtain product information, and so forth. In outbound telemarketing, the marketer calls the consumer to promote a product or service. Whether inbound or outbound, the telemarketer is usually assisted by a computer. Inbound telemarketers usually sit in front of a computer that allows them to place an order, check on what products are in stock, make purchase adjustments, and so on. Outbound telemarketers often use technologies such as computer-assisted dialing (Schley 1990) in which a computer dials the telephone. If a person answers the telephone, the call is then immediately routed to a telemarketer; in this way the telemarketers do not spend their time on busy signals or calls where the phone is not answered. One firm was able to almost double the productivity of its telemarketers by using this technology (Schley 1990).

MARKETING COMMUNICATION

Desktop publishing and desktop presentations have revolutionized the way marketers and salespeople develop proposals (Holtz 1985), brochures (Holtz 1985), reports (Holtz 1985), presentations (Taylor 1990a), and newsletters (Holtz 1985). Computers have decreased the cost of developing such communications and have decreased the time required to do so. They have also allowed marketers to customize such communications toward individual customers or subsets of the market.

RETAILING AND THE POINT OF SALE

The place where the market transaction takes place, the point of sale (POS), has been dramatically affected by advances in information technology. Point-of-sale systems, including scanners and credit card verification systems, have greatly increased the efficiency and effectiveness of the sales transaction. One researcher estimated that, when humans manually enter transaction information, one mistake is made for every 300 keys entered. In contrast, scanners make a mistake once in every 200,000 to 300,000 tries. In addition to providing more efficient means of completing the transaction, POS systems also provide information that can help companies track their inventory, identify what products are selling and what products are not, and make quick price changes for products that are not selling. Computers are also now being used to dispense coupons at the supermarket checkout stand (Berger 1988).

Computer graphic techniques are now being used to help retailers plan shelf placement of products (Steinhagen 1990). This can result in more efficient use of shelf space and store layouts that increase sales of higher margin items.

The computer is now being used, though on a limited basis, for actual shopping. As more consumers have access to microcomputers, modems, and on-line services, more firms are considering this as a way to expedite the sales transaction (Strauss 1983).

Computerized point-of-purchase displays are being used to provide consumers with individualized product information. Consumers can enter relevant information into the computer that can provide the consumer with the information needed to make a decision. One firm, using 21,000 such units, achieved a sales increase of 200 to 300 percent (Miller 1987).

Computers are being used to provide demonstrations at customers' homes and offices (Schell 1990). One computer manufacturer uses such a program to provide a general product description, a generic cost comparison, an on-line tutorial demonstrating the product's use, and an "interview" of the prospective purchaser that prepares their sales representative for a follow-up sales call. The single diskette can be passed around to all of those involved in the decision process, providing each with an individual opportunity to become acquainted with the product.

The same program can also be used by the company's salespeople as refresher training for a product line that they seldom sell.

MARKET ANALYSIS/STRATEGY DEVELOPMENT

Market analysis and strategy development constitute the process by which upper management sets the strategic direction of the firm and then analyzes potential markets to achieve the organization's objectives. Mass amounts of data are often needed to properly conduct such analysis/development. Computer systems have been developed to specifically support such decision making (Stanat 1989, Hawk 1990).

Kirchner and Thomas (1989) described a computer application called "desktop demographics." With this technique marketers can plan their targeting strategy by integrating information from several different databases. Customers can be described and differentiated relatively easily by the marketing decision maker.

Geographic factors are often a crucial part of a marketing strategy. Geographic information systems (GIS) software (Taylor 1990b) combines maps of geographic areas with information about those areas. This can help in understanding market potential, working with "planned roll-out strategies" (strategies where a product is introduced sequentially to different geographic regions), developing retail sites, developing market coverage strategies, and locating distribution centers. Marketers today are also going beyond the geographical boundaries of the United States, and looking for international marketing opportunities. McClenahan (1990) describes software that helps firms decide whether they should consider exporting their products.

Marketers also try to determine what group of current or potential consumers may be most likely to purchase their product. This process of market segmentation is now available to more marketers. For example, Seldon (1990) describes software that allows hotel managers to track the number of registrations, charges per stay, geographic sources of business, advance registration patterns, daily arrival and departure patterns, and other information of different classes of hotel visitors.

SALES MANAGEMENT/PERSONAL SELLING

The geographic software just mentioned can also be used by sales managers. It is currently being used to assist in the geographic placement of sales people (Taylor 1990b) and in deciding on a location for a sales meeting (Wiesendanger 1990).

As so many tasks are associated with managing a sales force or making a sales call, several software packages have been developed to assist the sales manager or salesperson (see Goldenberg 1990, Licciardi 1990, *Sales & Marketing Management* 1990). These packages help carry out such tasks as lead tracking, territory management, sales forecasting, database management, and contact management. Special software packages for electronic mail have been developed to help salespeople and their managers communicate field information and share information about customers (Taylor 1990c).

References

Berger, W. 1988. Electronic coupons—And push-button recipes. *The New York Times* 138 (November 27):F11.

Goldenberg, B. 1990. How to pick the best from the rest. *Sales and Marketing Management* 142(15):58.

Hawk, K. 1990. More marketers are going online for decision support. *Marketing News* 24(23):14.

Holtz, H. 1985. *The consultant's edge: Using the computer as a marketing tool.* New York: Wiley.

Kaehler, K. 1988. Medical supply firm enhances targeting with the aid of computerized data base. *Marketing News* 22(23):12.

Kirchner, R. J., and R. K. Thomas. 1989. Desktop decisions. *American Demographics* 11(8):34–37.

Licciardi, S. 1990. Paper-pushing sales reps are less productive. *Marketing News* 24(23):15.

Marketing News. 1987. People meter to be

sole tool for '87 Nielsen TV ratings. *Marketing News* 21:1.

———. 1991a. 1991 *Marketing News* directory of software for marketing. *Marketing News* 25(9):24–31. Contains descriptions of more than 100 software products useful for marketing managers.

———. 1991b. 1991 *Marketing News* directory of software for marketing research. *Marketing News* 25(9):15–22. Contains descriptions of more than 100 software products useful for marketing researchers.

McClenahan, J. S. 1990. Ready to export? "Expert" software promises an answer. *Industry Week* 239(18):60.

Miller, C. 1987. Trend in fashion retailing is to make a "video statement." *Marketing News* 21(25):1.

Miller, S. 1989. Mine the direct marketing riches in your database. *Journal of Business Strategy* 10(6):33–36.

Minno, J. 1990. Microcomputer tools assist with perceptual mapping. *Marketing News* 24(23):28.

Prete, D. D. 1991. Advances in scanner research yield better data quicker. *Marketing News* 25(1):54.

Sales & Marketing Management. 1990. Directory of PC-based sales and marketing applications software. *Sales & Marketing Management* 142(15):69ff. This directory should be especially helpful to sales managers.

Schell, E. H. 1990. On the cutting edge of sales technology. *Sales and Marketing Management* 142(9):86.

Schley, S. 1990. Keeping that personal touch in telephone sales. *Sales & Marketing Management* 142(12):102.

Schlossberg, H. 1990. Case of the missing TV viewers: Everyone knows they're gone, but no one knows why. *Marketing News* 24(19):1.

Seldon, W. L., Jr. 1990. Computers used to fill rooms, and they still do. *Marketing News* 24(1):51, 57.

Stanat, R. 1989. *The intelligent corporation: Creating a shared network for information and profit.* New York: AMACON.

Steinhagen, T. 1990. Space management shapes up with planograms. *Marketing News* 24(23):7.

Strauss, L. 1983. *Electronic marketing: Emerging TV and computer channels for interactive home shopping.* White Plains, N.Y.: Knowledge Industry Publications.

Taylor, T. C. 1990a. Making the best of the "generation gap." *Sales & Marketing Management* 142(11):158.

———. 1990b. Bytes replace pins for better strategic mapping. *Sales & Marketing Management* 142(11):158.

———. 1990c. When a car phone isn't good enough. *Sales and Marketing Management* 142(7):150.

Wiesendanger, B. 1990. Need help choosing a facility for your next sales meeting. *Sales and Marketing Management* 142(8):93.

Zufreyden, F. S. 1989. How much should be spent for advertising a brand? *Journal of Advertising Research* 29(2):24–34.

James A. Muncy
Donald A. McBane

MATHEMATICAL USE OF COMPUTERS

The computer has revolutionized the way mathematics is done and the way it is taught. It serves both to perform complex calculations and to develop mathematical intuition. Paradoxically, it both enhances and diminishes the status of the professional mathematician, for the access it provides to powerful mathematical techniques is available to everyone, even to those with little or no background in mathematics.

NEW MATHEMATICS

The ability to rapidly resolve and display complex functions has literally changed the way in which mathematicians, both pure and applied, think about their subject. For the applied mathematician, statistician, physicist, and engineer, the desktop computer has replaced both pencil and paper. Both amateurs and professionals now use the computer to solve large systems of simultaneous linear equations through matrix, linear program, and regression techniques. Attacks on problems that lack explicit solutions are made through special-purpose software capable of implementing finite-difference methods, Monte Carlo simulation, and iterative nonlinear fits. And symbolic equations and logical relations are resolved as readily as numeric.

The ready availability of powerful mathematical software has shifted the emphasis in applied mathematics from computation to problem formulation and model verification. New branches of applied mathematics have arisen within the field of computer science devoted to the development of rapid algorithms for mathematical computations (called variously algorithms, numerical analysis, statistical computing, and systems and simulations) and of calculation-intensive computer architectures (Stone 1987). The computer has created new mathematical disciplines that deal with problems of computability (Garey and Johnson 1979) and numerical analysis.

Even the pure mathematician has been affected. Recent advances in at least four branches of pure mathematics—number theory (Riesel 1985), graph theory, combinatorial optimization (O'Heigeartaigh 1985), and nonlinear oscillations, also known as nonlinear dynamics (Peitgen and Saupe 1988)—seem always to have been made with a computer at hand. The classic four-color problem, for example, was resolved by showing that a certain computer program converged, rather than by providing an explicit solution (Appel and Haken 1976).

These developments in pure mathematics have fostered revolutions in the applied sciences: biology (May 1976), mathematical physics (Yuan and Feng 1988), and statistics (Noreen 1989). Today, operations research (network routing, scheduling, and resource allocation) relies almost entirely on the computer for solutions.

EARLY SOFTWARE

The first computer software developed specifically to aid with mathematical and engineering problems were general-purpose languages: FORTRAN, a formula translator; Algol, for the development and execution of algorithms; SIMula, MuSIMP, MacSyma,

and Reduce, for the evaluation of symbolic expressions; APL, for array and vector processing; and (in the 1970s) PROLOG, for the verification of proofs and programs. These formula-oriented languages are still in use today; in fact, FORTRAN remains the primary language for the analysis of large-scale systems on supercomputers.

Subroutine libraries constituted the next generation of mathematical software. On the one hand, there are broad-spectrum libraries like the IMSL Math/Library for mainframe computers, UNIX workstations, and MS-DOS desktops, which contain nearly 500 subprograms for basic matrix and vector operations, evaluation of linear systems, integration and differentiation, generation of sets of orthogonal functions, and nonlinear optimization. On the other hand, there are special-purpose languages like CELSIM, GASP, GLIM, GPSS, SAS, and SLAM II for use in modeling and simulation.

Although languages and subroutine libraries remain the primary software tools on supercomputers and mainframes, their complexity and steep learning curve limit their use to individuals with a strong background in computer programming and a willingness to persevere through endless documentation. Fortunately, the advent of the microcomputer was accompanied by the introduction of menu-driven mathematical software that is no more difficult to use than a spreadsheet or a word processor.

The simple, intuitive spreadsheet approach can be used to balance a checkbook (Lotus 1-2-3), solve a linear program (What's-Best), and explore the effects of random variation on a set of outcomes (@Risk). And although a spreadsheet will perform the arithmetic for anyone who can set up the calculations, new symbolic manipulators such as TKSolver and Mathematica will do the algebra, convert the units, and find the general solution to an integral or differential equation.

The newest mathematical software makes use of icons and ideographs. With the LabView environment on the Macintosh, the bench scientist with little or no mathematical background can manipulate icons of knobs, dials, meters, and fast Fourier transforms to program data acquisition and signal processing. With GPSS-PC and SlamView under Windows on the IBM-PC, the executive can use icons to build simulations of a factory floor or a grocery store checkout line (Pritsker 1974).

CATEGORIES

Categories of mathematical software include (1) calculators, which can range in complexity from a few arithmetic functions to several hundred complex mathematical expressions; (2) equation solvers for underdetermined (linear program), determined (matrix), and overdetermined (regression) systems; (3) graphics programs for displaying results and developing intuition; (4) math editors for editing and displaying symbols and formula as well as text; (5) symbol manipulators for resolving algebraic, finite and infinite sum, integral, and differential equations; (6) signal processors and filter simulators; and (7) simulators (discrete and continuous, analog and digital, deterministic and Monte Carlo). Although these categories are convenient for describing program function, in practice, few programs fit neatly into any single category.

Calculators

Almost every computer system incorporates some sort of pop-up calculator, complete with a point-to-and-click keyboard identical to a handheld calculator. On a Xerox GlobalView desktop, the various calculator keys are labeled $+$, $-$, $/$, $*$, and $=$, as well as sin, cos, and tan. A press of the $=$ key displays the result of a calculation that then can be pasted into other GlobalView documents.

The Scientific Wheel provides similar capabilities for any MS-DOS-based computer and pops up to display a multifunction calculator that provides for units conversion, numerical integration, differentiation, and graphics.

Equation Solvers

Today, even a salesperson with only marginal knowledge of linear programming techniques can use a spreadsheet and What'sBest

to resolve underdetermined systems with up to 4,000 variables and 1,500 constraints. These limits apply only to the named software and an IBM-AT. With other software and a computer processor that supports virtual memory, the number of equations that can be resolved is limited only by the processor's address space (up to 2^{128} entries on the largest of supercomputers) and not by the memory available. Calculations can be made 100–200 times faster with a math coprocessor (i.e., a microprocessor support chip that performs mathematical computations using binary-coded decimal notation and floating-point calculation).

Graphics Programs

Graphics programs can clip and transfer data from a spreadsheet, accounting, or other computer program to create instant multicolor x–y, log–log, R-theta, and scatter plots, two- and three-dimensional bar charts, and pie charts; enhance them with figures and drawings; resize, rescale, and rotate images; add text and arrows; and then paste them back into the text of a report. New developments in computer graphics have resulted in the ability to display three-dimensional surfaces in perspective with hidden-line removal, creating renewed interest in digital reconstructions among clinicians, biologists, and bioengineers.

Math Editors

This set of mathematical software tools arose not for the purpose of solving equations but for documenting and reporting results. The mathematician now has a choice of several dozen text editors that can display mathematical equations—Greek as well as Latin letters—and organize and display formulas and symbols with subscripts and superscripts.

Exact, for example, can be used with any MS-DOS word processor and lets the user incorporate equations into text, with Greek symbols, integral and summation signs, radicals, fractions, superscripts, and subscripts. All symbols are aligned automatically; thus, the bar separating the numerator and denominator of a fraction appears on the line with the equals sign.

MathCad, for the Macintosh and MS-DOS-based systems, combines a math editor with a text editor, a calculator, graphics, and array manipulation. It is the ideal engineer's scratchpad, making it easy to produce reports that include formulas, symbols, and graphs.

Symbolic Processors

What was once an exercise in computer science, the development of translators that could process symbols, may liberate all of us eventually from fear of algebra the way calculators freed us from fear of arithmetic. Derive, for example, lets desktop users solve symbolic equations (algebraic or trigonometric) and obtain series in closed form along with limits, derivatives, Taylor approximations, and integrals. TKSolver provides personal computer users with automatic units conversion and does table lookup while solving explicit or implicit sets of simultaneous equations (Konopasek and Jayaraman 1984).

Signal Processors

Signal processing programs provide for analysis and pattern classification via digital filtering, auto/cross spectral density, and transfer function/impulse response. New computer chips, specifically designed for digital signal processing, support the execution of a 256-band fast Fourier transform in a single pass (Cochran et al. 1967).

Today's signal processing software is characterized by remarkable ease of use, and thus may be used by an engineer who is not familiar with programming. DADisp, an MS-DOS-based program with 150 built-in data manipulation and signal processing functions, treats digital waveforms as individual entries in a spreadsheet, and can display up to 64 waveforms simultaneously. LabView for the Macintosh lets even naive users program data acquisition and signal analysis using icons that represent the various signal processing functions. Other signal processing software provides for the design and

execution of IIR, FIR, and Kalman filters. Signal processing chip-sets speed up calculations by a factor of 100 to 1000.

Simulators

Simulation software can be used by planners in four ways (Pritsker 1984): (1) as explanatory devices to define a system or problem, (2) as analysis vehicles to determine critical components and issues, (3) as design assessors to synthesize and evaluate proposed solutions, and (4) as predictors to forecast and aid in planning future developments.

Simulation software ranges from function generators like @Risk that add random variables to spreadsheets, to comprehensive languages like CELSIM (for modeling interacting populations of animal and plant cells) and the icon-based SlamView. Tutsim for the Apple II and the IBM-PC converts a digital computer into an analog computer for use in servo-control design.

MULTIFUNCTION MATHEMATICA

One program, Mathematica, which runs on the Macintosh and MS-DOS- and UNIX-based computers, fits into almost all of the preceding categories. Mathematica is the ultimate scientific calculator with more than 400 built-in mathematical functions—sines and cosines; power series; Bessel functions; Chebyshef, Legendre, Gegenbauer, and Jacobi polynomials; spherical functions; and matrix operators. It can solve algebraic equations, differential equations, integrals, and integrodifferential equations, and provides both numeric and symbolic solutions. An exact solution is provided if one is available and a numeric solution if one is not. Numeric results may be obtained to any degree of precision.

With the appropriate hardware, Mathematica is capable of displaying shaded three-dimensional graphs in color to aid in developing intuition into complex mathematical relationships. On the Macintosh, pull-down hypertext notebooks permit the user to read about and then display specific functions.

Mathematica offers wide latitude in *how*

instructions are entered. The user can create procedures with branches and loops as in FORTRAN, use recursive functions as in C, nest functions as in LISP, create objects as in SmallTalk, and set out rules and constraints as in PROLOG.

On the down side, Mathematica gains its flexibility through the use of an extraordinarily complex command language, putting it beyond the reach of the casual user.

References

Appel, K., and W. Haken. 1976. The existence of unavoidable sets of geographically good configurations. *Illinois Journal of Mathematics* 20:218–97.

Cochran, W. T., et al. 1967. What is the fast Fourier transform? *Proceedings IEEE* 55:1664–77.

Garey, M. R., and D. S. Johnson. 1979. *Computers and intractability.* San Francisco: Freeman.

Good, P., ed. 1990. *Annual report on statistical and mathematical software.* 6th ed. Huntington Beach, Calif.: Information Research.

Konopasek, M., and S. Jayaraman. 1984. *The TKSolver book.* Berkeley, Calif.: Osborne/McGraw-Hill.

May, R. M. 1976. Simple mathematical models with very complicated dynamics. *Nature* 261:459–67.

Noreen, E. W. 1989 *Computer-intensive methods for testing hypotheses.* New York: Wiley.

O'Heigeartaigh, M., et al., eds. 1985. *Combinatorial optimization: Annotated bibliographies.* New York: Wiley.

Peitgen, H.-O., and D. Saupe, eds. 1988. *The science of fractal images.* New York: Springer-Verlag.

Pritsker, A. A. B. 1984. *Introduction to simulation and Slam II.* West Lafayette, Ind.: Systems Publishing Corp.

Riesel, H. 1985. *Prime numbers and computer methods of factorization.* Boston: Birkhauser.

Stone, H. S. 1987. *High-performance computer architecture.* New York: Addison-Wesley.

Yuan, L. D., and D. H. Feng, eds. 1988. *Proceedings, International Conference on Computational Physics.* Singapore: World Scientific.

Wolfram, S. 1988. *Mathematica.* Redwood City, Calif.: Addison-Wesley.

Phillip I. Good

MAUCHLY, JOHN WILLIAM

John Mauchly was born in Cincinnati, Ohio, on August 30, 1907. His father was a physicist at the Department of Terrestrial Magnetism of the Carnegie Institution in Washington, D.C. Mauchly grew up in Chevy Chase, Maryland. He attended John Hopkins University on a scholarship, receiving a doctoral degree in physics in 1932 at the age of 24.

The following year he became a professor of physics at Ursinus College in Collegeville, Pennsylvania, near Philadelphia. During his 8 years at Ursinus, he began a project on weather analysis that led him to the conviction that a high-speed computer was necessary. Realizing that the speed problem could be solved by electronics, he began experimenting with equipment he purchased himself.

In 1941, Mauchly left Ursinus College to join the staff of the Moore School of Electrical Engineering at the University of Pennsylvania, in Philadelphia. It was there that he met J. Presper ECKERT.

The following year, Mauchly and Eckert submitted a proposal to the U.S. Army describing an electronic computer, which resulted in a contract from the Army's Ordnance Department to build the machine.

Basically conceived to help develop new weapons during World War II, the Electronics Numerical Integrator and Computer (ENIAC) was completed in 1946. It was this nation's first large-scale electronic digital computer and it was certainly a landmark leading to the development of many future computer designs.

Mauchly was an idea man of tremendously good instincts. He was a conceptualizer, a catalyst, and a pioneer who championed ideas before their time. He was certainly the prime mover in securing the contract for the first large-scale electronic digital computer. He was one of the founders and an early president of the Association for Computing Machinery (ACM) and the Society for Industrial and Applied Mathematics (SIAM).

Both Mauchly and Eckert had become employees of the Remington Rand Corporation, which later became Sperry Rand Corporation and then Unisys Corporation.

In 1959, Mauchly left Sperry Rand and his partner of 18 years to form Mauchly Associates. While working in his own company, Mauchly developed the critical path method (CPM) for job and resource scheduling. In 1968, Mauchly formed Dynatrend, a systems consulting company that specialized in forecasting weather and stock market trends.

Mauchly died January 8, 1980, while undergoing heart surgery in Ambler, Pennsylvania. He was 72 years old.

For Further Reading

Wulforst, H. 1982. *Breakthrough to the computer age.* New York: Charles Scribner's Sons.

Donald D. Spencer

MEDICAL IMAGING, COMPUTER-ASSISTED

Until the discovery of x-rays less than a century ago, medical treatment was hampered by the inability of doctors to view internal organs. The first x-ray pictures, more properly termed *radiographs*, made it possible to see dense structures such as bones and widened the vision of physicians dramatically. But radiographic imaging has always had drawbacks. First, imaging with x-rays depends on differences in density of body tissues and their ability to absorb, or attenuate, x-rays. Subtle differences in tissue density have always been difficult to capture on film, so that x-ray differentiation of one organ from another has often been trou-

blesome. Second, radiographs are two-dimensional pictures of three-dimensional structures, which makes internal spatial relationships difficult to evaluate. Over the years, several strategies were invented to attempt to resolve the problems encountered with plain radiographs. One such method is known as tomography. Tomography employs synchronous rotation of an x-ray source and a receptor around a stationary object. Traditional tomography was devised to sharpen the focus on a structure within the body and to differentiate it from overlying and underlying tissues. Unfortunately, plain tomography results in blurring of the film because of the contribution of surrounding tissues to the image.

The quest for sharper radiographic images led to the development of computed tomography (CT). In the early 1970s, Godfrey Hounsfield employed a mainframe computer to reconstruct a tomographic image of brain tissue using measurements of attenuation of the radiation. Rather than making a tomographic picture directly on x-ray film, Hounsfield made a computer-generated picture that was based on measurements of attenuation of a beam of radiation passing through a slice of preserved tissue. Because dense tissues attenuate radiation more than soft tissues, it is possible to calculate tissue density by knowing how much the x-rays employed are attenuated as they pass through the body from different angles. Hounsfield's work, which later earned him a share of the Nobel Prize, led directly to the first CT scanner, placed in operation in 1972. Computed tomography, sometimes called computed axial tomography or "CAT scanning," employs an x-ray source that rotates around a stationary subject, passing a divergent beam of x-rays through the subject and onto an array of several hundred stationary detectors. The detectors, in turn, report the strength of radiation each receives to a microcomputer that serves as the main computer for the entire system. The main computer then passes the data to another computer known as a parallel processor. The parallel processor is actually multiple computers linked in parallel, which allows for much faster calculation of tissue densities. The parallel processor calculates the density of small units of tissue, assigning each pixel (picture element) of the resulting image a numerical value, which is in turn translated into a shade of gray and placed in proper position in the generated image. The first data acquisition and imaging done by Hounsfield required several hours, but today's CT scanners, because of vastly expanded computing power and better mathematical image construction techniques, can acquire data and form an image of a discrete portion of the living body in less than 4 seconds. Computed tomographic images today are incredibly sharp and they reveal subtle structures of living tissue in detail (Figure 1).

In the past few years another type of computerized imaging has also become important in medicine though it employs magnetism instead of x-rays. Nuclear magnetic resonance (NMR) imaging or magnetic resonance imaging (MRI) is based on the magnetic properties of atoms in the body, especially hydrogen atoms, which are most abundant. When an atom is exposed to a magnetic field its spin axis will align more or less along the field's lines of force. If trans-

verse magnetization is then produced by applying radio-frequency (RF) pulsations at a 90° angle, the spinning atoms will tend to tilt, and when the RF pulses are removed, the atoms will return to their initial orientation, though there is a delay in their realignment, known as relaxation time. Differences in relaxation time of atoms of various elements in the body is the reason magnetic resonance imaging is possible.

In practice, an MRI scanner uses a strong magnetic field to align atoms of the body; then an RF generator is employed to impart a tilt to them. The tilt gradually resolves as the atoms undergo relaxation, and because the spinning atoms are magnetic, their changing orientation results in emission of RF signals. Because tissues of the body have different densities and compositions, there are significant variations in their atoms' relaxation times, and hence variations in the frequency of the RF signals emitted. These signals are detected by a receiver coil and, in turn, induce varying voltages in the coil that are proportional to variations in atomic spin axis. These voltages are employed by the MRI computer to generate an image of whichever portion of the body is

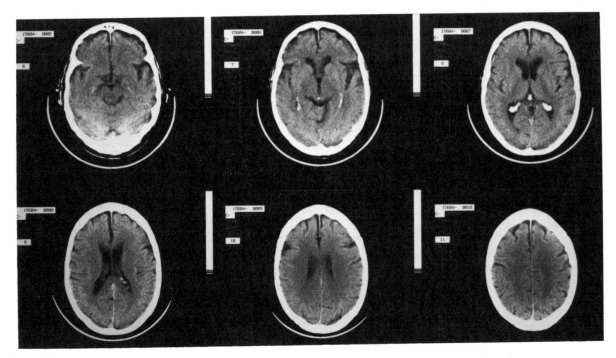

FIGURE 1. Computed tomographic brain scan. Note detail of brain surface and internal cavities.

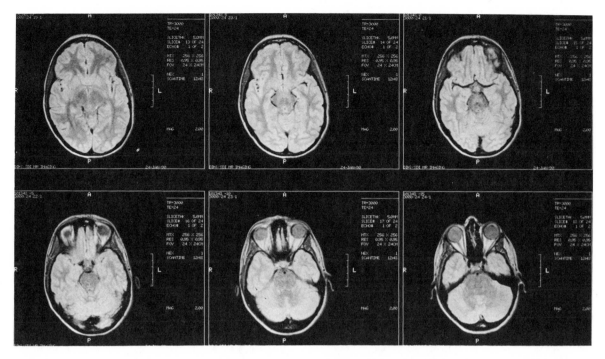

FIGURE 2. Magnetic resonance image of the brain showing differentiation of gray matter and white matter.

exposed. The computer uses a mathematical method known as a two-dimensional Fourier transform to construct a two-dimensional image. Magnetic resonance images have even more detail than CT images and they can be constructed in several planes instead of being limited to transverse sections as are most CT images. Magnetic resonance imaging is currently most used in imaging soft structures of the body such as brain and neural tissue and in imaging various joints of the body (Figures 2 and 3), though imaging of other structures will doubtless be important in the future.

Besides their use in radiographic imaging, computers are being applied throughout modern medicine to enhance human vision. Currently, computers are employed in the specialties of cardiology, neurology, otolaryngology, pathology, and surgery, to name only a few. In cardiology, for example, computer-generated images of blood flow patterns through the heart assist in the diagnosis of diseased heart valves. In plastic surgery, computerized images of a patient's face can be changed in such a way that a possible postoperative result may be shown to a patient or used in teaching resident physicians.

Pathologists use computer-generated, digitized imaging of tissue and organ specimens to enhance their ability to make sophisticated diagnoses. Surgeons use computers to construct and manipulate three-dimensional images of portions of the body to allow them to plan complex surgical procedures.

Computers, mostly minicomputers or microcomputers, will likely be employed

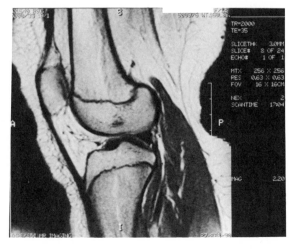

FIGURE 3. Magnetic resonance image of the knee joint. Note the sharp detail.

even more widely in the future for sophisticated imaging, especially as more computing power is packed into smaller units. The ability to archive images will be especially important as medical informatics continues to advance toward an entirely paperless medical record.

For Further Reading

Barnes, G. T. 1989. Computed tomography: Physical principles and image quality consideration. In J. K. T. Lee, S. S. Sagel, and R. J. Stanley, eds. *Computed body tomography with MRI correlation*, pp. 1–21. New York: Raven Press.

Evens, R. G. 1989. The history, economics and politics of CT and MRI. In J. K. T. Lee, S. S. Sagel, and R. J. Stanley, eds. *Computed body tomography with MRI correlation*, pp. 1113–23. New York: Raven Press.

Maisey, M. N. 1989. The quest for an image of man. *Lancet* 2(8678–8679):1493–1500.

Gary L. Hoff

MEDICAL INFORMATICS

Medical computer applications have increased exponentially since the beginning of electronic computing. The suggestion that electronic digital computers might have utility in medicine was made as early as the 1950s, but it was not until 20 or more years after the initial papers published on the subject that computers began to emerge from the hospital business office. Before 1970, the uses of computers in medicine were limited; generally computers were mainframe units dedicated to one or two applications such as collation and reporting of data in the medical laboratory or billing for hospital services, but little progress was made in the management of other kinds of medical information. Interest in applying computers to the particular needs of medicine was high during the 1960s (the American Medical Association sponsored a conference early in the decade dealing with the computer and its use in keeping medical records), but available hardware was cumbersome and software limited. With the emergence of smaller personal computers in the 1970s, however, and with the evolution of more easily understood software, it became feasible to explore ways not only to collect, compare, and record discrete pieces of data such as individual laboratory values but also to systematize larger bodies of medical information. The evolution of computer programs has proceeded so far since then that the knowledge of expert physicians is now being used in conjunction with systems of artificial intelligence to design sophisticated programs that can assist the medical practitioner in clinical decision making, though these programs have yet to achieve the diagnostic accuracy of a trained medical subspecialist.

While computers and software have advanced spectacularly over the past several decades, the body of medical knowledge has continued to expand, making management of information in medicine one of the most staggering intellectual tasks of the practicing physician. As a result of the avalanche of medical information and the need for a way to systematize it an entirely new discipline, known as medical informatics, has developed over the past 20 years. Medical informatics has been defined as the basic science of computers in medicine, dealing with the exchange of information through computer-based systems.

Although methods of management of medical information have their roots in the latter years of the nineteenth century, the term *medical informatics* seems to have gained acceptance as a result of its use by the International Federation for Information Processing (IFIP) at its first triennial World Conference on Medical Informatics in 1974. Since then, there have been other such international conferences sponsored by IFIP and societies devoted to medical information systems, including the Society for Advanced Medical Systems (SAMS) and the Society for Computer Medicine (SCM). The American Association for Medical Systems and Informatics was formed by the merger of SAMS and SCM in the early 1980s. In the following years the American College for Medical Informatics (ACMI) was established to recognize experts in the field, and by 1989 approximately 100 fellows of the college had been recognized. The Symposium on Computer Applications in Medical Care (SCAMC) was established in 1977 and has been held annually thereafter. In 1988 AAMSI, SCAMC, and ACMI merged to form the American Medical Informatics Association (AMIA).

Medical informatics includes such diverse applications as gathering, maintenance, and review of individual patient records; monitoring of patients in special or intensive care units, including recording and correlation of the information obtained; retrieval of bibliographic materials; dissemination of medical news; interactive medical education; and assistance to the physician in clinical decision making.

This article discusses the use of computers in medical information processing. (For another way in which computers are used in modern medical practice, see MEDICAL IMAGING, COMPUTER USE IN.)

APPLICATIONS

Medical Records

Medical records have traditionally been kept as hard copy in the form of handwritten and typewritten notes and reports generated by doctors, nurses, and other health workers, accompanied by printed reports from departments such as the laboratory and radiology and other paper-based items such as electrocardiograms and specialized tests in graphic or text form. The chief limitation of the current, traditional system of medical recordkeeping has been the lack of ready availability of the patient record, coupled with the difficulty of searching it for specific data. Although efforts have been made to systematize the individual patient record in its current form, such efforts have been hampered by the sheer size of some records, which can be hundreds of pages in length. Besides the obvious difficulty in finding specific information in a large, hard-copy record, the potential to overlook important information is also high. Even when a record is readily available and well organized, poor handwriting or poor reproduction of printed material may make information retrieval difficult, if not impossible. Additionally, when patient information is not readily available, critical mistakes in medical care can easily occur.

A number of centers in the United States have explored the uses of personal computers to initiate, update, and maintain individual health records. Unfortunately, no comprehensive, uniform, or generally acceptable system of computer-based medical record keeping has yet been developed. The difficulty arises partly from the need to establish first an agreed-on and precise medical vocabulary for data entry; partly because capture of data to computers has most often been as discrete, numerical data rather than as text; and partly because of the time needed for physicians to learn to use microcomputers and the various programs currently being tested.

These problems aside, a computer-based medical record has significant advantages over a paper record. Access to the record is greatly enhanced, especially when multitasking computers are employed, allowing for easy review of pertinent information. The use of terminals or networks can make it possible to store a record electronically in one location and access it in any location in a system. In contrast to paper records, once data on a patient are stored in a computer, they may easily be displayed in any number of combinations. Summaries and reports of a person's past illnesses, current and past laboratory values, and medications and modifications of treatment can be easily generated and compared with current problems and treatment, giving the clinician a much clearer view of the individual patient.

Besides its role as a passive information receptacle, a computer might be employed to assist in automatically reviewing and correlating the information entered into the medical record, reviewing the record for problems that may be overlooked such as rare diagnoses and drug interactions. In this way, the computerized record may assist the otherwise overextended physician by flagging abnormal findings and generating reminders suggesting therapeutic strategies. Several medical records systems now available for computers have the capability to review and flag patient charts. One study, using a medical record system known as COSTAR to draw attention to abnormal results, showed a reduction in the percentage of overlooked positive streptococcal throat cultures to nearly zero. Clearly, such reminder systems will have an increasingly important role in the practice of medicine in the coming decades.

Computerized medical records will provide another benefit to medical practitioners in the future that is difficult to obtain from current hard-copy systems. Using computerized records, it is possible to review the clinical experience of a hospital or clinic with regard to specific illnesses and therapies and form opinions regarding efficacy and efficiency of previous medical strategies. Computers may be used to research the record and estimate future risks for patients with certain serious illnesses such as heart attacks, for example, and through such estimates allow for modifications of treatment that can reduce mortality in higher-risk patients and allow for earlier release of those at lower risk. Lower-risk patients would therefore be subjected to less testing in such a system, lowering the cost of hospital care.

Presently, totally computerized medical records do not exist, for several reasons. Generally, physicians prefer to keep records as text rather than enter information in the kind of multiple-choice format used in many computer programs for data entry (new methods integrating text with more structured information may resolve this difficulty). Also, changing an entire medical record to an electronic format means that graphic materials such as electrocardiograms must also be converted or the record will necessarily be split into electronic copy and hard copy. Although compact disk technology will likely allow for such conversion in the future, it is not widely available at present. Finally, the cost of computerizing the records of an entire clinic or hospital is likely to be very high, further slowing conversion. Despite these roadblocks, it is likely that computerized medical records will eventually replace paper records.

Decision Assistance

Because computers can allow rapid searches of bibliographies, databases, and patient re-cords, there has been increasing interest in the use of microcomputers to aid physicians in making clinical decisions. As mentioned earlier, programs that provide signals of abnormal findings have been available for many years. Most laboratories in large hospitals now use programs that draw attention to a significant deviation from the expected normal range, for example. These programs provide the simplest kind of assistance in clinical decisions by calling attention to important information on which to base clinical decisions, but they give no guidance to the decision itself.

Besides entry of patient information into a database or personal record, information management also includes retrieval of pertinent medical articles and papers that may assist in patient management. Until less than a decade ago, the clinician searching the medical literature was forced to spend hours personally reviewing bibliographic sources such as *Index Medicus*. But with the advent of telecomputing and the establishment of medical bibliographic services such as MEDLINE, it is now possible to search the entire international body of published medical papers in a short time by connecting with such services, using either a personal computer or a terminal and a modem. There have been reports in medical journals that rapid availability of bibliographic services via modem has made it possible to immediately alter the management of patients during surgery or in an emergency department. Although bibliographic services also provide information necessary to manage difficult or baffling clinical problems, they do not help the clinician make use of that information, nor can these programs suggest diagnoses.

Programs that do make diagnoses have been studied in several university medical centers around the United States. Initial attempts at such clinical decision systems were based on simple algorithmic logic, and the limitations of numerical statistical methods became clear in early research. Algorithms and simple statistical methods were found to be too simplistic to emulate the complicated thought processes by which a trained clinician arrives at a medical diagnosis, and diagnoses made by such systems were often wildly inaccurate. To emulate human problem-solving methods, researchers have instead turned to the field of ARTIFICIAL INTELLIGENCE. Artificial intelligence substitutes conceptual analysis for numerical analysis and, by using a given set of rules for making choices, simulates the way human experts in any field make sophisticated, reasoned decisions.

Early reported work on artificial intelligence in medicine actually involved only a few experimental systems, all of which were designed and run on mainframe computers. One system, INTERNIST-1, was directed at complex problems in internal medicine; another, the Present Illness Program (PIP), was intended to provide hypotheses about disease processes in patients with kidney disease. These two systems involved the entry of large volumes of medical information obtained from experts and from the medical literature and employed problem-solving methods based on human reasoning processes. These kinds of artificial intelligence systems are also known as *expert systems* because of their debt to the knowledge and decision-making prowess of experts in a particular field of endeavor. Expert systems show great promise, but have yet to consistently reach human standards of accuracy in medical diagnosis. For example, a group of cases were reviewed and diagnosed by INTERNIST-1, and the diagnoses were compared with those made by a number of human medical experts. INTERNIST-1 made twenty-five accurate diagnoses out of a possible forty-three, while the human physicians made thirty-five accurate diagnoses. Much work clearly remains before expert systems can be relied on for more than diagnostic assistance, and whether such systems can ever reliably replace complex human reasoning seems doubtful at present.

To date, use of artificial intelligence programs in medical diagnosis continues to be limited mostly to research. Commercial artificial intelligence programs with medical applications are starting to become available, however. In addition, at least one diagnostic support program that is an expert system, DXplain, has already been widely available to physicians with telecomputing capability. This program was accessible by use of the American Medical Association's nationwide telecomputational network, AMA/NET. It reviewed clinical manifestations supplied by the user to generate a list of possible diagnoses. This remarkably easy-to-use program required little computer experience or training. The physician entered clinical findings in the form of common, recognizable terms and was given a plausible and complete list of differential diagnoses, ranked in the order of probability supported by the information entered, rather than one most likely correct diagnosis. Because of its wide availability, ease of use, planned updating, and relatively simple format, DXplain was the first widely useful expert system in medical diagnosis, though AMA/NET ceased operating in late 1990.

Medical Education

Computers were initially thought to be useful in education as teaching machines—that is, machines that could automatically present information to students, but in traditional ways. Very early in the development of computerized education programs, however, experts in medical education saw that computers could provide more than facts. Medical educators argued that computers might teach clinical skills by providing realistic simulations of actual patient encounters, complete with opportunities for simulated clinical decisions. Clinical simulations can also provide students with experience in diseases that might otherwise not be encountered. Potentially dangerous procedures can also be taught in simulation without danger to actual patients. Furthermore, computer-based learning programs can be used without regard to the kind of regular scheduling that traditional methods require, giving students more flexibility and allowing for self-pacing.

Early work in computer-assisted learning was confined to tutorials and drills, so-called programmed learning, though some early mainframe systems did concentrate on clinical simulations. In the 1970s, through the National Library of Medicine, computer-based tutorials and patient simulations were shared by more than 150 institutions. But further progress was slow, for a number of reasons. First, hardware and software were often incompatible at different institutions. If one center wished to use the system of another, it often could not do so without considerable financial outlay. Upkeep of mainframe systems and telephone access was also quite expensive. Additionally, development of computer-assisted learning systems required the efforts of a number of people, including clinicians, programmers, and professional educators, not all of whom were available at any given center. Until personal computers became more widespread in the 1980s, computer-based education stagnated.

Although early programs used traditional methods such as tutorials and drills as well as clinical simulations, programs today are mostly simulations of patient encounters. And whereas early programs were confined to the use of text only, the powerful graphics capability of current microcomputers coupled with new videodisc technology has made simulations very realistic. Several programs now in use allow the student to make free-text inquiries in the same manner as a doctor does when taking a patient's history; in addition, the student may review other pertinent materials, such as electrocardiograms and radiographic images stored on videodisc, and make decisions regarding further testing and management of the "patient." Compared with the compatibility problems of the earlier systems, current systems are more standardized as most will run on MS-DOS systems, and hence they are more likely to achieve wide use. A great deal of educational software became commercially available during the 1980s. For example, *Scientific American* has published simulations for personal computers on floppy disk called Discotest, and simulations originated by the Massachusetts General Hospital, previously available via AMA/NET, have been offered for sale for personal computers as *RxDx* from Williams and Wilkins. Other commercial products are also available.

Simulations of clinical situations have gone even farther. A system integrating a personal computer and patient simulation program with a manikin representing a human torso has been developed to train health professionals in critical care. This system employs software that runs on a Macintosh computer to generate real-time displays of electrocardiograms and blood pressure tracings that change in response to interventions made by the trainee. Recognition and treatment of abnormal cardiac rhythms and pressures can thus be taught to medical students and other health professionals without endangering critically ill patients. In addition, a library of cases may be built by use of the software, allowing for incorporation of new medical information and tailoring of the system to specific groups of trainees.

Today, virtually all medical schools in the United States employ computer-assisted learning in some form, and the personal computer has become the standard device employed. At some schools of medicine, curriculum reform is an ongoing process that involves heavy use of both mainframe computers and microcomputers as an essential ingredient in undergraduate medical education, supplementing more traditional classroom methods. In the future, with decreased cost allowing for increased availability of personal computers for students, the traditional medical curriculum will no doubt be supplanted by newer and potentially more effective methods to impart the vast knowledge required to practice medicine.

THE FUTURE

Although a handheld diagnostic computer is not likely to become feasible in the near future, a number of fascinating possibilities exist for the use of portable computers in medicine. Small, portable units are already being routinely employed by many practitioners to record pertinent patient data for later download into office or clinic computers, to calculate drug dosages, to correlate clinical information obtained in intensive care units, and to serve as memo machines. It is likely that as more memory is built into these small, handy computers they will become portable workstations for physicians, incorporating the ability to download, store, and correlate data obtained from computers in such locations as intensive care units and medical laboratories. Such small, compact, yet powerful computers may one day incorporate artificial intelligence systems to allow for decision assistance. Word processing software will allow the physician to write progress notes that could then be directly loaded into the central, computerized patient record. Data input will likely be by voice rather than by keyboard, though optical scanning equipment will make it possible to enter printed material if necessary. Compact disks will likely be employed to store pictures, x-rays, and graphic materials such as electroencephalograms for ready review. Indeed, an entire hospital might be interconnected by linking personal workstations of physicians, nurses, and ancillary personnel with central mainframe computers, which would not only store patient records but also assist in records research and in comparison of critical information. No matter what form computers take in the future, they have already changed the practice of medicine irrevocably.

For Further Reading

Barnett, G. O. 1984. The application of computer-based medical-record systems in ambulatory practice. *New England Journal of Medicine* 310(25):1643–50.

Barnett, G. O., J. J. Cimino, J. A. Hupp, and E. P. Hoffer. 1987. DXplain: An evolving diagnostic decision-support system. *Journal of the American Medical Association* 258(1):67–74.

Collen, M. F. 1986. Origins of medical informatics. *Western Journal of Medicine* 145(6):778–85.

Collen, M. F. 1989. Evolution of medical informatics societies in the United States. *M. D. Computing* 6(1):192–98.

DeTore, A. W. 1988. Medical informatics: An introduction to computer technology in medicine. *American Journal of Medicine* 85(3):399–403.

Haynes, R. B., K. A. McKibbon, C. J. Walker, N. Ryan, D. Fitzgerald, and M. F. Ramsden. 1990. Online access to MEDLINE in clinical settings: A study of use and usefulness. *Annals of Internal Medicine* 112(1):78–84.

Greenes, R. A., and E. H. Shortliffe. 1990. Medical informatics. An emerging academic discipline and institutional priority. *Journal of the American Medical Association* 263(8):1114–20.

McDonald, D. J., and W. M. Tierney. 1988. Computer-stored medical records: Their future role in medical practice. *Journal of the American Medical Association* 259(23): 3433–40.

Manning, P. R. 1986. The computer and the future of continuing medical education. *Western Journal of Medicine* 145(6):872–73.

Miller, R. A., H. E. Pople, and J. D. Myers. 1982. INTERNIST-1, an experimental computer-based diagnostic consultant for general internal medicine. *New England Journal of Medicine* 307(8):468–76.

O'Desky, R. I., M. J. Ball, and E. E. Ball. 1990. Computers in health care for the 21st century. *Methods in Informational Medicine* 29(2):158–61.

Pickell, G. C., D. Medall, W. S. Mann, and R. J. Staebler. 1986. Computerizing clinical patient problems: An evolving tool for medical education. *Medical Education* 20(3):201–3.

Piemme, T. E. 1986. Computer-assisted learning and evaluation in medicine. *Journal of the American Medical Association* 260(3):367–72.

Saliterman, S. S. 1990. A computerized simulator for critical-care training: New technology for medical education. *Mayo Clinic Proceedings* 65(7):968–78.

Shortliffe, E. H. 1986. Medical expert systems—knowledge tools for physicians. *Western Journal of Medicine* 145(6):830–39.

Shortliffe, E. H. 1987. Computer programs to support clinical decision making. *Journal of the American Medical Association* 258(1):61–66.

Starkweather, J. A. 1986. The computer as a tool for learning. *Western Journal of Medicine* 145(6):864–68.

G. L. Hoff

MENUS

Since the late 1970s, the menu has become an increasingly popular human–computer interface. Today's user of a computer-controlled device, a microcomputer system, a workstation, or a computer terminal, most often taps into the rich resources of the computer's power through an interactive human–computer interface and has a real-time "conversation" with the computer. In a typical computer session the user issues an instruction or command, waits for the response, and then issues another instruction. However, a user new to a system or software application usually does not know what all the possible instructions are. Even someone who has used the system in the past may have forgotten some of the correct commands. A menu alleviates these problems by displaying a list of currently viable instructions. The user need only understand or recognize the various choices and select the appropriate one. Errors are reduced, since incorrect or inappropriate choices do not appear on the menu.

Menus are used in a wide variety of applications and occur in many forms. In the most common form, menus appear as a list of possible options on a video display terminal or screen. Menus are used in automatic teller machines, video arcade games, some museum and hotel automated information retrieval systems, and telephone answering services (an example of an auditory menu) as well as in many software products, such as in word processors, spreadsheets, and programming language systems. Almost everyone has had an opportunity to select an instruction for a computer software product or a computer-controlled device from a menu.

ITEM REPRESENTATION AND SELECTION

A menu presents a set of possible instructions or commands. Often instructions for selecting one of the instructions appear as well. Menu items are typically words or short phrases descriptive of the instruction or activity represented. Two example menus are shown in Figure 1. In one simple format (see Figure 1a), menu items are displayed in a numbered list. A user makes a choice by typing the number of the desired instruction and pressing the Enter key. Single mnemonic alphabetic characters (see Figure 1b), function keys, or specially labeled keys may represent the choices so a user can indicate a selection with a single keypress.

In some menus, one of the choices appears in a highlighted form. For example, it may be brighter than the other items, appear in a different color, or be surrounded by a different background color. A user issues an instruction by highlighting the desired menu item and then pressing the Enter key. The Tab key or arrow keys are often used to move the highlighted area through the various menu items. Sometimes a command may be highlighted by typing its number or letter. A mouse, trackball, or joystick may be used to highlight the appropriate menu item. It is possible for several different methods of highlighting to be available in a single menu.

Other possibilities for selecting a menu item include pointing to it with a light pen or, on a special touch-sensitive screen,

```
┌─────────────────────────────┐
│        MAIN MENU            │
│                             │
│ What would you like to do?  │
│                             │
│ 1 - Database Processing     │
│                             │
│ 2 - Games                   │
│                             │
│ 3 - Programming             │
│                             │
│ 4 - Word Processing         │
│                             │
│ Type a number and press     │
│ the return key. _           │
└─────────────────────────────┘
```

```
┌─────────────────────────────┐
│        MAIN MENU            │
│                             │
│ What would you like to do?  │
│                             │
│ D - Database Processing     │
│                             │
│ G - Games                   │
│                             │
│ P - Programming             │
│                             │
│ W - Word Processing         │
│                             │
│ Type a letter representing  │
│ your choice. _              │
└─────────────────────────────┘
```

    (a)   Numeric Selection   (b)   Alphabetic Selection

FIGURE 1. Example menus.

touching the screen itself. Menu items do not always appear as words or phrases; they may be pictures (called icons). For example, a picture of a trash can might represent a remove or delete instruction. With icons, it is often possible for a new user to infer actions without specific instructions.

MENU ORGANIZATION AND STRUCTURE

Menu items are organized and structured to minimize the amount of time a user needs to make a selection. No single method works best in every situation. Some items have a natural order, as in the days of the week or the months of the year. If a natural sequence exists, it is typically used to order the items on the screen. If items are designated by mnemonic characters, the choices may be ordered alphabetically. Groups of related items may be presented together. The most often used or the most important instructions may be listed first, followed by the less often used or less important ones.

If there are too many items to be listed on a single screen, the menu must be divided into two or more screens, which are logically connected to each other in some way. One simple structure is a linear sequence—a first screen followed by a second screen, etc. The user scrolls forward and backward through the menu screens to find the one with the appropriate item. The most common nonlinear structure for a multiscreen menu is a tree. Each choice on the main screen represents a different second-level screen with additional choices. Figure 2 shows level-two menus for

the Games and Programming choices from the menu in Figure 1. Research suggests limiting a tree-structured menu to four levels, with four to eight items per screen. These limits are not overly restrictive, since a menu structure conforming to these guidelines can still offer a selection from 4,096 items. More complex menu structures may be built, but they present navigational problems for beginners. Even with a tree-structured menu, it is possible for a user to become "lost" in the system by making a selection that turns out to be incorrect and having insufficient knowledge to return to the previous menu screen or the starting point. Researchers offer several suggestions to help users move around in a menu structure. The top-level menu screen should always be clearly labeled as the main menu. From each menu screen (except the first) the user should be able to return to the previous screen. In some applications, the screen at each successive level partially overlays the previous screens, leaving a visible trail of menu traversal. Figure 3 illustrates three levels of a tree-structured menu in overlay form. Printed menu maps can help the user form a mental model of the menu structure.

MENU DISPLAY

Menus require screen space for their display. A menu may be displayed initially over the entire screen and disappear once an item is selected. In some applications—for example, certain word processors and spreadsheets—a menu remains visible at all times.

```
 ┌─────────────────────────────┐
 │   GAMES MENU                │
 │                             │
 │ Which game would you like   │
 │ to play?                    │
 │                             │
 │   A - Asteroids             │
 │                             │
 │   H - Hunt the Wumpus       │
 │                             │
 │   S - Snake                 │
 │                             │
 │ Type the letter of your     │
 │ choice. _                   │
 └─────────────────────────────┘
```

```
 ┌─────────────────────────────┐
 │   LANGUAGE MENU             │
 │                             │
 │ Which language would you    │
 │ like to program in?         │
 │                             │
 │   B - BASIC                 │
 │                             │
 │   L - Logo                  │
 │                             │
 │   P - Pascal                │
 │                             │
 │ Type the letter of your     │
 │ choice. _                   │
 └─────────────────────────────┘
```

FIGURE 2. Level-two menus.

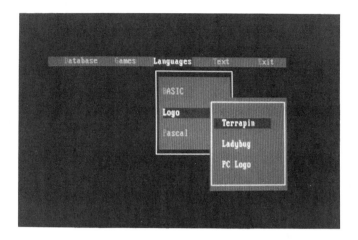

FIGURE 3. An overlay menu. *Photo courtesy Susan R. Wallace.*

Permanent menus must require minimal screen space. They typically occupy one or two lines at the top or bottom of the screen. To conserve space, instructions listed in a permanent menu are often represented by a single letter. Such menus are not as self-explanatory as full-screen menus with less cryptic items. Pull-down and pop-up menus appear on the screen when requested by a user and temporarily overlay part of the screen. Pull-down menus typically represent lower levels in a tree-structured menu with a permanent main menu screen. Pop-up menus appear when the user presses a special key, called a "hot key," associated with that menu.

ADVANTAGES AND DISADVANTAGES

Empirical evidence suggests that menus offer many advantages to the new, inexperienced, or intermittent user. They guide users through the range of possible choices, hide incorrect or inappropriate options, reduce typing errors by requiring a minimum number of keystrokes, and eliminate the need for extensive training and memorization. Even beginners will become frustrated with a menu system, however, if it takes too long for the desired instruction to appear. The two system parameters that affect how quickly a user can move through a menu structure are the system response time and the display rate. The system response time is the amount of time it takes for the system to start responding after an instruction is given by the user. The display rate is the time needed for the screen to change from one configuration to another. The frustrating effects of a slow display rate may be partially offset if the user can enter a choice before the entire menu is displayed. Menus that require fewer screens by listing more choices per screen help offset the negative effects of a slow system response time.

An extensive menu structure can slow down an experienced user by requiring him or her to navigate through the early screens of a long serial menu or the upper levels of a tree-structured menu. However, shortcuts can be provided to speed up the instruction selection process for these users. One possible shortcut is a type-ahead buffer, which allows a user to enter all the necessary keystrokes to traverse a menu structure without waiting for each menu to be displayed. Another shortcut requires naming each menu screen. A knowledgeable user can go directly to the appropriate menu, accessing it by its name. A macro definition facility provides a third possible shortcut. A long sequence of keystrokes used to traverse a menu can be defined as a macro and assigned a name. When the user types the name of the macro, the keystroke sequence is executed automatically.

RESEARCH RESULTS

Menus have become the standard human–computer interface for applications accessed by noncomputer specialists. However, research studies have not conclusively demonstrated their superiority over command language or natural language interfaces. Paap and Roske-Hofstrand (Helander 1988) discuss some of the attempts to compare menu and commands as well as the difficulties inherent in such attempts. In none of the cases they cite did users at any experience level perform significantly better with a menu-driven system than with a command language.

Many commercial products are available

that allow even inexperienced computer users to design menu-driven interfaces for their own computer systems. Once a decision has been made to utilize a menu system, research results can provide some guidance in choosing the best structures and screen layouts. Both Baecker and Buxton (1987) and Shneiderman (1980, 1987) summarize a number of menu studies. Research findings include the following: Users do not employ optimal search strategies when using menus, so alphabetizing a list is less helpful than organizing the items by category. If a letter is used to designate a menu item, the letter chosen should have some relationship to the item. Shorter lists are easier to search than longer ones. However, the fewer levels in a tree structure, the better. The amount of space required for a menu should be kept to a minimum. Menus should be displayed to novice users only or on request. The user should be able to toggle between automatic and nonautomatic menu displays. Although many design questions have been answered, additional work is needed to find the optimal method of human–computer communication.

References

Baecker, R., and W. Buxton. 1987. *Human-computer interaction: A multidisciplinary approach.* San Mateo, Calif.: Morgan Kaufmann.

Helander, M., ed. 1988. *Handbook of human-computer interaction.* New York: Elsevier Science.

Shneiderman, B. 1980. *Software psychology: Human factors in computer and information systems.* Cambridge, Mass.: Winthrop.

———. 1987. *Designing the user interface: Strategies for effective human–computer interaction.* Reading: Mass.: Addison-Wesley.

For Further Reading

Laurel, B., ed. 1990. *The art of human-computer interface design.* Reading, Mass.: Addison-Wesley.

Martin, J. 1973. *Design of man-computer dialogues.* Englewood Cliffs, N.J.: Prentice-Hall.

Vassiliou, Y., ed. 1984. *Human factors and interactive computer systems.* Norwood, N.J.: Ablex.

Susan R. Wallace

METEOROLOGICAL USE OF COMPUTERS

In the atmospheric sciences, two general subdisciplines use computers—the fields of meteorology and climatology. The former focuses on analysis of observations of the present state of the weather, numerical representations of atmospheric characteristics over short intervals of time, and development of numerical weather-forecast technology. The need for quick and accurate representation and prediction of atmospheric conditions is crucial, for example, to the aviation industry, to the issuing of warnings for severe storms and their effects, and in general to the everyday welfare of the nation. Climatology emphasizes a systems view of how the atmosphere behaves on average, and the importance of the geographic variation of earth surface conditions in terms of the evolution of the climate system. Knowledge in this area is critical for strategic planning purposes and evaluation of past events (e.g., why did droughts occur over several years?) and long-term future prospects (e.g., are we going into a global warming period?).

Without the advent of computers in the first place and the continual advance of computer technology, research and operations in these two fields would long ago have come to a standstill. In fact, historical advances in meteorology and climatology have often been coincident with advancements in computer technology (see, e.g., Burks et al. 1946; Goldstine 1972; Thompson 1983; Tribbia and Anthes 1987; Rollwagen 1989; Shuman 1982, 1989).

Covered below are selected topics that illustrate the role of computers in these two fields: computer use in operational forecasting; computer use in broadcast meteorology; new technologies in meteorology and related computer needs; and research on the climate system with supercomputers. These are examples of important areas in which computers have been used successfully to accomplish basic and applied research objectives in the fields of meteorology and climatology.

METEOROLOGY

Operational Forecasting

The theoretical foundations of meteorology and climatology were largely in place in the early decades of the twentieth century, but significant improvement in specifying accurate atmospheric behavior and in developing numerical weather prediction (NWP) was not possible given the computation capabilities then available. The idea of NWP is attributed to V. Bjerknes (1904), who applied physical principles to problems of atmospheric processes. Some 18 years later, L. F. Richardson (1922) essentially created the modern-day approach to producing a numerical weather forecast. His problem, however, was inadequacy of computational facilities. He used a 10-inch slide rule and a table of logarithms. At this rate, he calculated that 64,000 human computers would be required to keep up with the numerical calculations necessary to produce a daily forecast in time to have meaning to the public.

Electric computers were invented in the mid-1940s, and John von Neumann organized the Electronic Computer Project at the Institute for Advanced Study (IAS) in Princeton, New Jersey. One of the major uses of computers at this institute was numerical weather prediction. Charney et al. (1950) ran a successful NWP forecast on the ENIAC (Electronic Numerical Integrator and Computer); however, it still took 24 hours to make a 24-hour forecast. On the IAS computer, it took 5 minutes to develop the forecast.

In 1954, the U.S. Joint Numerical Weather Prediction Unit (JNWPU) was organized, consisting of the U.S. Weather Bureau, the Air Weather Service, and the Naval Weather Service. An IBM 701 was installed in 1955 and numerical weather forecasts were made twice daily. In 1960, the National Meteorological Center (NMC) was organized; it still exists and is now located in Suitland, Maryland. Automated weather prediction products started to replace manual methods around 1960. Today, 95 percent of the NMC's products are computerized. Table 1 presents a brief summary of computer technology changes at NMC, a measure of skill of forecasts, and numerical models used from 1955 to the present. Numerical weather predictions began with the electronic computer and improvements in NWP have been driven primarily by advances in computer technology (Shuman 1982, 1989). Today, increases in supercomputer power have allowed for better NWP procedures and theory construction in addition to better field observation technology and communication capability. There is still a need for regional refinement of weather predictions and enhancements of the man–machine mix that provides for better local forecasts. In the age of satellite technology, various satellites are heavily used in meteorology and climatology, and computers are also at the core of these systems.

Broadcast Meteorology

The use of large mainframe computers for generating accurate weather forecasts is vastly important to the operations of the national weather services. Most Americans, however, do not obtain weather information directly from the U.S. National Weather Service (NWS); instead they rely almost exclusively on the broadcast media. More specifically, television weather forecasts have assumed the dominant role in providing the public with up-to-date weather forecasts and warnings.

The visual nature of television has led to the development of specific computer technologies designed to summarize large amounts of meteorological data in an eye-pleasing, uncomplicated fashion. Since many television weather people are not trained meteorologists, the bulk of computer technology in broadcast meteorology has focused on preparing graphical images rather than providing the computational power necessary for numerical weather forecasts. The specific hardware and software used

TABLE 1. Historical Development of Numerical Weather Prediction and Computers[1]

Year	Percent Skill[2]	Computer	Model[3]
1955–58	40	IBM 701/704	Subjective
1958–62	50	IBM 7090	Barotropic (one level)
1962–66	55	IBM 7094	Three-layer (primitive equation)
1966–71	60	CDC 6600	Six-layer (primitive equation)
1971–77	70	IBM 360/195	Winds input (limited fine mesh)
1977–80	77	IBM 360/195	Increased resolution (limited fine mesh)
1980–85	82	IBM 360/195	Twelve-layer spectral (nested grid model)
1985–present	85–90	Cyber 205	Better physics and resolution (nested grid model)

[1]Source of information: Shuman 1989.

[2]Annual average skill in predicting the 500-millibar geopotential height over North America 36 hours in advance. Forecast made at the National Meteorological Center. Skill of 100 percent is defined as a perfect forecast; zero percent is average success. Skill percentages extracted from Tribbia and Anthes 1987.

[3]Numerical weather prediction model used. See Shuman (1989) for details on models.

vary by station and by the size of television market.

Most stations receive their meteorological data through a subscription with a private company. These companies make available the latest nationwide observations along with NMC forecasts, weather maps, and satellite images. The data are usually obtained in real time, either by satellite link or via dial-in telephone lines. A dedicated personal computer collects data from the subscription service 24 hours per day, and stores the information on hard disk. Custom software packages allow the weathercaster to convert these data into draft-quality graphical images. Many of these packages provide the means to animate the still-motion satellite images to produce "movies" depicting cloud movement through time.

Once the draft images have been produced, they are often fed into specialized graphical workstations for enhancement. The images can be overlaid on user-created basemaps showing political boundaries and/or physical features. Using a digitizing tablet, the television weather person can add any additional graphical features, such as cold and warm fronts, or the location of high and low pressure cells. Once completed, the

images are placed in a sequence for display during the broadcast.

New Technologies

As the 1990s began, the meteorological services in the United States were on the verge of introducing a variety of new technologies designed to increase the skill level in generating forecasts and to increase the warning time during severe weather events. All of these technological advances will rely heavily on the ability of computers to process large volumes of data rapidly on a real-time basis.

ASOS. Currently, most weather observations by the NWS are taken by human observers. These meteorologists typically take a variety of weather measurements once per hour (more frequently during storm events) and type these observations into a computer. The observations are then transmitted through a high-speed communications network to all other offices of the NWS, to the NMC, and to a variety of other users. This system has remained largely unchanged since the late 1950s.

In an effort to reduce costs and to take advantage of the technological advances of the past three decades, the NWS has initiated a program to replace the human weather observers with automated instrumentation. This program, called the Automated Surface Observation System (ASOS), was scheduled for installation beginning in 1992. Each observing site was to be equipped with an extensive array of weather observing instruments. On-site computers would pre-process the sensor data and apply necessary calibration/correction factors. These computers would then transmit the information over the standard high-speed data network, and over local communication networks to end users.

Nexrad. A new weather radar system called NEXRAD, for "next-generation radar," was under development in the early 1990s as a network of over 100 Doppler radar units, capable of detecting not just the location of precipitation but also its velocity and direction of motion. These new radars were expected to allow significant improvements in detecting the precursors of violent storm activity (such as tornados). Because of the complexity of the NEXRAD radars, and the enormous amounts of data generated by them, an entire new line of computer hardware and software was also required.

The NEXRAD system consists of three major components: the Radar Data Acquisition Subsystem (RDA), the Radar Products Generation Subsystem (RPG), and the Principal User Processor Subsystem (PUP) (Milner 1986). The RDA is unmanned and comprises the radar unit and pre-processors. The pre-processors acquire the data and transmit it to the RPG.

The RPG forms the heart of the data processing system; it is composed of several computers with a variety of tasks. The Doppler radars are capable of providing large amounts of data in a short period of time. They can search over 25 million cubic kilometers of atmosphere every 5 minutes, and generate a variety of base data including reflectivity, radial velocity, and spectral width. In order for forecasters to make use of NEXRAD, it would be necessary for the system to sift through a myriad of data streams and provide relevant output products. To accomplish this, complex numerical algorithms were developed that could analyze the data and identify weather features such as tornadic activity, intense rainfall, and high winds. The RPG generates tabular and graphical products in real time and transmits them to the PUP subsystem.

The PUP subsystem is the user interface to the NEXRAD system, linked to the RPG through 9,600-bit-per-second telephone lines. Users would poll the RPG for desired products, which would then be displayed on specially designed graphical workstations.

Graphical presentation of data. Until recently, meteorologists have been forced to use two-dimensional media to display atmospheric data that are three-dimensional. This has typically been accomplished by plotting weather data on maps and using isolines to depict the inherent spatial patterns (an isoline is a line connecting locations where a particular value of a quantity is recorded). Several like maps are produced for different layers in the atmosphere. This technique does not make it easy to visualize the three-dimensional nature of the atmosphere. In addition, it is important for meteorologists to visualize changes in the atmosphere with time. This further complicates attempts to use two-dimensional graphics techniques.

With the advent of supercomputers, researchers have begun to develop techniques for the visual display of three-dimensional images through time (Grotjahn and Chervin 1984; Schiavone and Papathomas 1990). Early products have been quite remarkable, such as full-color animated movies of the development of a hurricane. These visualization techniques have combined the skills of mathematicians, computer scientists, psychologists, and meteorologists in an attempt to develop graphical products that convey the maximum amount of information to the user. They allow meteorologists to assimilate information quickly that might typically take hundreds of two-dimensional graphics to display. These new visualization techniques are becoming available in widespread use as computers employing the necessary computational power to generate such images become cheaper and more available.

CLIMATOLOGY

At the Federal Level
In the United States, computers are used in support of climatological research sponsored both by the federal government and by state and regional agencies. At the federal level, two fundamental activities dominate computer usage: basic research on the global climate system; and archiving, management, and dissemination of quality-controlled climate information for operational and strategic planning purposes. The former is typified by the activities of the National Center for Atmospheric Research (NCAR) in Boulder, Colorado (Hess 1985). Founded in 1959, NCAR has as its mandate to conduct basic research and to complement the work of universities in an alliance between teaching and research, and is endowed with large research facilities, including an enormous amount of computing power. A Community Climate Model was constructed to assist in providing an understanding of physical and dynamical processes that govern the behavior of the global atmosphere on time scales ranging from a few days to millions of years. Large, complicated numerical models have been developed, are well documented, and have become "user friendly" to the many scientists tackling atmospheric modeling problems at both regional and global scales. In May 1976 NCAR purchased the first Cray computer at a cost of approximately $4 million. Since then, supercomputing power has meant quantum jumps in handling general circulation models that are used to project changes in climate. For example, one of the most important computer modeling areas is projection of greenhouse warming due to current and anticipated increases in carbon dioxide emissions. These projections are virtually impossible without the aid of supercomputer technology. As of 1985, NCAR was the only major research center in the country that provided CRAY-class computers for research in the atmospheric sciences (Hess 1985).

Also at the federal level are many agencies that make use of weather and climate information in decision-making frameworks. The major agency that archives and dissemi-nates climate information is the National Climatic Data Center (NCDC) in Asheville, North Carolina (Crowe et al. 1988). This agency is part of the National Oceanic and Atmospheric Administration (NOAA) and the U.S. Department of Commerce. Another important information center is the Climate Analysis Center, a subdivision of the NMC (Finger et al. 1985). Both of these centers house computerized weather and climate data on magnetic tapes, compact disks, and personal computer–compatible diskettes. For example, at NCDC, original weather data from the field are archived on microfilm and microfiche. The data are also digitized and quality-controlled with a series of computer programs to minimize data errors (Heim 1988). The quality-controlled data are then added to magnetic tape archives. Climate data users can then request data in taped or diskette form. For the latter, data are loaded from tapes to a UNISYS 2200 mainframe and downloaded to diskettes via a personal computer. In addition, NCDC has developed a software system called CLICOM, which is a menu-driven climatological-data management and analysis system for use on low-cost personal computer systems. This system provides for data entry, quality control, inventory, and storage of meteorological observations. The system has a meteorological-station history, data-dictionary subsystem, and can generate several statistical and graphical summary products (Heim 1988). Many systems of this kind, compatible with personal computers, are now available for the meteorological and climatological researcher. Similar systems are available at the Climatic Analysis Center (CAC). A data user may obtain near–real time weather and climate information via the CAC Computer Communication System in order to develop assessments of agricultural crop status, water resource management, irrigation requirements, forest fire potentials, health risks, drought probabilities, insect infestations, and stock market risks, among other important considerations.

Regional and Local Levels
Weather and climate information transmitted from weather stations to the national centers

is also communicated by computer networking to regional and local levels. Regional Climate Centers have been instituted in the United States and equipped with computer systems interconnecting with those at the state and federal levels (Changnon et al. 1990). The major purpose of the centers is to provide a better-integrated assessment, through computer technology, of regional peculiarities and anomalies of weather and climate impacts on society; and to ensure accessibility to data users, preferably by inexpensive personal computer systems, of critical weather and climate conditions that affect regional activities. State climate offices interact by computer communication with these regional centers. An excellent example of computer linkages at a state level between those who collect data and those who need to use data is the Illinois system (Changnon et al. 1984). At the Illinois State Water Survey a computer system and network was established to assimilate state weather records, put them in a useful form for water specialists and agriculturalists, and enable the user with an inexpensive personal computer to obtain data each day via telephone.

References

Bjerknes, V. 1904. Das Problem der Wettervorhersage, betrachtet vom Standpunkte der Mechanik und der Physik. *Meteorologische Zeitschrift* 21:107.

Burks, A. W., H. H. Goldstine, and J. von Neumann. 1946. Preliminary discussion of the logical design of an electronic computing instrument. Report to Ordinance Department, U.S. Army (Electronic Computer Project, Institute for Advanced Study, Princeton, N.J.).

Charney, J. G., R. Fjortoft, and J. von Neumann. 1950. Numerical integration of the barotropic vorticity equation. *Tellus* 6:309–318.

Changnon, S. A., P. J. Lamb, and K. G. Hubbard. 1990. Regional climate centers: New institutions for climate services and climate-impact research. *Bulletin of the American Meteorological Society* 71(4): 527–37.

Changnon, S. A., J. L. Vogel, and W. M.

Wendland. 1984. New climate delivery system developed in Illinois. *Bulletin of the American Meteorological Society* 65(7):704–705.

Crowe, M., T. Reek, and R. Mattingly. 1988. Operational automated graphics at the National Climatic Data Center. *Bulletin of the American Meteorological Society* 69(1): 28–38.

Finger, G. G., J. D. Laver, K. H. Bergman, and V. L. Patterson. 1985. The Climate Analysis Center's User Information Service. *Bulletin of the American Meteorological Society* 66(4):413–20.

Goldstine, H. H. 1972. *The computer from Pascal to von Neumann.* Princeton: Princeton University Press.

Grotjahn, R., and R. M. Chervin. 1984. Animated graphics in meteorological research and presentations. *Bulletin of the American Meteorological Society* 65(11):1201–1208.

Heim, R., Jr. 1988. Personal computers, weather observations, and the National Climatic Data Center. *Bulletin of the American Meteorological Society* 69(5):490–95.

Hess, W. N. 1985. NCAR and the universities. *Bulletin of the American Meteorological Society* 66(5):515–29.

Milner, S. NEXRAD—the coming revolution in radar storm detection. *Weatherwise* 39(2):72–85.

Richardson, L. F. 1922. *Weather prediction by numerical process.* Cambridge: Cambridge University Press.

Rollwagen, J. 1989. The integral role of supercomputers for the advancement of environmental prediction. *Bulletin of the American Meteorological Society* 70(10): 1279–84.

Schiavone, J. A., and T. V. Papathomas. 1990. Visualizing meteorological data. *Bulletin of the American Meteorological Society* 71(7):1012–1020.

Shuman, F. G. 1982. Numerical weather prediction. In *The federal plan for meteorological services and supporting research for fiscal year 1983*, pp. 1–13. Washington, D.C.: NOAA, U.S. Department of Commerce.

———. 1989. History of numerical weather prediction at the National Meteorological Center. *Weather and Forecasting* 4:286–96.

Thompson, P. D. 1983. A history of numerical weather prediction in the United States. *Bulletin of the American Meteorological Society* 64(7):755–69.

Tribbia, J. J., and R. A. Anthes. 1987. Scientific basis of modern weather prediction. *Science* 237:493–99.

Anthony J. Brazel
Tomas J. Miller

MICROCOMPUTERS (PERSONAL COMPUTERS)

Few technological developments in recent history have spawned the interest of the general public as have microcomputers. In 10 short years, microcomputers have become as commonplace in the American home as stereo systems or microwave ovens. Although electronic computers have a comparatively long history, dating to the 1930s, microcomputers became commercially available only in the mid-1970s. Often, microcomputers are simply described as "the smallest computers" and their physical size is offered as the distinguishing feature when contrasted with minicomputers or mainframe systems. This distinction is correct, but there are other aspects to be considered such as cost, computational power and speed, and applications. As microcomputer technology advances, however, it becomes increasingly difficult to define classifications of computers.

Early first-generation computers were all "mainframe" computers. They evolved from the first digital computers such as ENIAC, the ABC, and UNIVAC I, and derived this name because they were built around racks or a metal frame chassis into which electronic components were placed. Computers were necessarily large because the technology of the period relied on vacuum tubes, switches, and relays. In addition to their large physical size (some mainframes would require as much space as an average family dwelling), early computers consumed large amounts of electrical power and generated considerable heat because of the many vacuum tubes. Even though present-day mainframe computers use state-of-the-art technology, they are still large computers with many powerful peripheral devices (e.g., input, output, and storage), and serve many users at the same time.

As semiconductor technology became prevalent in the second generation of computers, components could reside on a single circuit board rather than multiple racks. These smaller systems became known as "minicomputers." Currently, minicomputers are in the midrange of data processing systems, between mainframes and microcomputers.

Large-scale integration (LSI) permitted miniaturization of electronic components to a scale that enabled an entire computer to reside on a silicon chip. This microelectronics technology led to the term *microcomputer*. One of the main distinguishing characteristics of a microcomputer is that it generally serves one user at a time, hence the term *personal computer*, which is practically interchangeable with *microcomputer*.

Today we often speak of microcomputers in terms of cost, ranging from $1,000 to $10,000. The two principal manufacturers are IBM and Apple, though many other companies offer similar microcomputers, components, and peripheral hardware. Minicomputers are popular in smaller organizations and generally range in cost from $10,000 to $100,000. They may serve multiple users via remote terminals. Wang and Digital Equipment Corporation (DEC) are two major vendors of minicomputers. Mainframe computers may cost several hundred thousand dollars to several million dollars depending on the type of system. They are often found in large organizations such as financial institutions, universities, industry, and government, and may serve many users or groups. A fourth category of computers may also be considered—"supercomputers." Supercomputers are large systems used for unique and specialized uses that only they may handle (such as scientific applications, meteorology, and complex calculations). Major manufacturers of mainframes and supercomputers are IBM, Control Data Corporation, and Cray.

A BRIEF HISTORY OF MICROCOMPUTERS

Development of microcomputers began in 1971 with the 4-bit programmable Intel Corporation 4004 microprocessor for a Japanese calculator. The microprocessor, or the central processing unit (CPU), is the center or "brains" of the microcomputer. Interest in this technology led to introduction of the more powerful Intel 8080 microprocessor, or chip, in 1974. This event was significant, as it heralded the real beginning of the microcomputer industry. The 8080 chip contained the equivalent of 4,500 transistors and could address 64K of random-access memory (RAM). This evolution of microprocessors continues to the present. Microcomputer clock speeds, a measure of the rate at which electrical signals move through the CPU, have increased almost tenfold in 10 years.

A milestone in computer technology occurred in 1975. In that year Micro Instrumentation and Telemetry Systems Inc., a small business in New Mexico, marketed a computer kit, the Altair 8800, for about $400. Based on the Intel 8080 chip, the Altair was a desktop computer that could support the BASIC programming language and sufficient memory for important applications. The commercial response to the Altair, after it appeared on the cover of the January 1975 issue of *Popular Electronics,* was overwhelming. In a sense, a new market for small, affordable microcomputers was born.

The Altair and the growing public interest in microcomputers resulted in a need for software development for these new systems. As there was no existing microcomputer software industry, little was available. This need led to the development of the Microsoft Corporation, the first major computer software company. Microsoft would prove to be a potent force in the microcomputer industry's evolution and, as will be seen later, was the supplier of the operating systems for the IBM microcomputer in addition to many popular software packages.

Many other computer companies appeared and rapidly disappeared because of a lack of commercial success during the mid-1970s. One of the most important success stories, however, began in 1977 with the appearance of the Apple II, a marvelous system developed by Stephen WOZNIAK and Steve JOBS. The Apple II series of computers, which included the Apple II Plus, IIe, IIc, and IIGS, employed the 6502 microprocessor, an 8-bit CPU, which meant it operated on instructions and data 8 bits at a time. By 1978, the Apple II was enjoying considerable commercial success, even though by present microcomputer standards it was not inexpensive. For example, in the late 1970s, an Apple II Plus with 48K of RAM, one 5.25-inch floppy disk drive, BASIC resident in read-only memory (ROM), a powerful operating system, and a monochrome monitor would cost about $2,400. A dot matrix printer and interface card would add an additional $800 to $1,000 to the total cost of an Apple II Plus system.

Also introduced in 1977 were the Commodore PET (which later evolved into the more powerful VIC-20 and Commodore 64) and the TRS-80 Model I from Tandy Corporation. Both of these microcomputers would continue to be popular commercial systems.

A number of factors shaped the amazing success of the Apple II series of microcomputers. Perhaps most important, it was sold preassembled rather than as a kit. Another extremely important factor was the early offering of the Disk II floppy disk drive in mid-1978. Also, its operating system, color, sound, high-resolution graphics capabilities, and expansion possibilities made the Apple II a popular choice among hobbyists, educators, enthusiasts, and businesses. Applications in schools and colleges were also special contributors to the Apple success story, as the system was quickly embraced by educators. The selection of Apple microcomputers by the Minnesota Educational Computer Consortium (MECC) further accelerated the acceptance of Apple by educators throughout the nation. The MECC had held a large catalog of software for educational applications. These were converted from various sources for use on the Apple II, giving Apple a major advantage over its competitors.

Electronic spreadsheets are often credited with establishing the success of the microcomputer industry. The first spreadsheet for a microcomputer, VisiCalc, appeared in 1979 for the Apple II. Originally marketed for about $200, VisiCalc was an immediate success and sold over 100,000 copies the first year—an impressive sales figure given the infancy of the microcomputer industry.

Other computer companies entered the marketplace during the late 1970s and early 1980s but were largely unsuccessful. Even Apple was not immune to failure. In 1980, the Apple III was released but was such a dismal failure that its production was halted almost immediately.

A preview of modern portable computers was given by the Osborne I microcomputer in 1981. This small, suitcase-sized system included 64K of memory, a monochrome monitor, a keyboard, and a disk drive, all self-contained. It was marketed complete with WordStar word processing software, SuperCalc spreadsheet, BASIC, and the CP/M operating system and utilities. By late 1983 the company entered bankruptcy in spite of considerable growth and acceptance. This was not an uncommon phenomenon in the microcomputer industry, and, as the microcomputer industry entered the 1980s, no undisputed winner had emerged. The leaders were Apple, Tandy, and Commodore along with Osborne, Northstar, Exidy, Hewlett-Packard, Texas Instruments, and others.

This situation rapidly changed in August 1981 with the announcement of IBM's entry, the IBM Personal Computer or IBM PC. The IBM PC was an instant success, with orders far exceeding corporate expectations.

Unlike most other personal computer makers, IBM was a large, established company. It was also the country's leading supplier of business equipment. Its first personal computer, known simply as the IBM Personal Computer, or PC, had one disk drive and 16K of RAM. As with the Apple II, its "open" design meant that the machine's specifications were readily available to any hardware or software developer who was interested in designing products to work with it.

The PC's great advantage was that it carried the IBM name. IBM had an extensive, enviable sales network among businesses, and the company's solid reputation led companies to take a serious look at personal computers for the first time. The continued popularity of VisiCalc in an IBM version further helped establish the PC as a standard piece of office equipment.

Many design features of the IBM PC also contributed to its immediate acceptance. One unique and significant feature was the use of the Intel 8088 microprocessor, a 16-bit CPU, at a time when other microcomputers were 8-bit systems. It was a faster microcomputer, performing about a quarter of a million instructions per second at a clock speed of 4.77 MHz (megahertz). Disk storage was an improvement over existing systems, allowing about 360,000 characters or bytes of storage on a double-sided floppy disk. Random-access memory could easily be expanded to 640K.

In 1983, IBM added its first member to the PC family, the IBM XT, which included hard (fixed) disk storage in addition to the floppy disk. Then in late 1983 came IBM's first microcomputer disappointment, the IBM PCjr, also known as "the Peanut." Although everyone expected the PCjr to enjoy the same popular acceptance as the PC, its production was terminated in 1985. Criticisms of the PCjr included a difficult-to-use keyboard, expansion problems, lack of full compatibility with the PC, and other technical problems. Just as the PCjr was fading from the computer scene, an important new IBM entry arrived, the IBM AT model, with much greater computing speed and power.

The mid-1980s witnessed the appearance of numerous IBM PC-compatible microcomputers or "clones." These machines used the MS-DOS operating system (or a minor variation) and were capable of running all or almost all of the software supported by the IBM PC. Popular clones were the Tandy 1000 and 1200, Leading Edge, and Compaq. Generally, these machines were less expensive than the PC and could be an excellent alternative.

Computing speed and power increased even more with introduction of the Intel 80286 CPU, which debuted in 1982. In addition to faster processing speeds, the Intel 80286 could address 16 MB (millions of bytes) of RAM and supported multitasking (execution of more than one program at a time). Such microcomputers far exceeded the capabilities of predecessors, allowing numerous new tasks to be performed that were previously the province of minicomputers and mainframes. This computing power increased even more with the advent of the 32-bit, 16-MHz Intel 80386 chip in 1985 and the 33-MHz 80486 chip in 1990.

In 1984 Apple introduced the Macintosh, a small, lightweight, 32-bit computer that represented a radical departure from the popular Apple II series. The Macintosh's black and white, 9-inch monitor generated an incredibly crisp display and also came with a detached keyboard and mouse. Software resembled that designed for an earlier unsuccessful Apple computer, the Lisa, in that many software operations could be executed by moving the mouse, pointing at various symbols on the screen, and clicking the mouse's button. The Macintosh, and later versions, the Macintosh SE and Macintosh II and IIx, were well-received by the public because of their user friendliness. They continue to be popular microcomputers, especially for desktop publishing and graphics applications.

MICROCOMPUTER SYSTEMS AND COMPONENTS

In principle, microcomputer systems and components do not significantly differ from minicomputers or mainframe computers in purpose or main components. The purpose of a computer is to process data, a formal representation of facts, ideas, or instructions. This is the case regardless of the size, power, speed, or cost of the computer. Data processing systems have four necessary, fundamental functions: input, storage, processing, and output. The components of a computer that accomplish these functions are generally classified into two categories: hardware and software. Hardware refers to the physical equipment and mechanical/electronic devices (e.g., input and output devices, processing devices, and storage devices). Software typically refers to computer programs, instructions and documentation, and systems procedures. These two categories, hardware and software, are discussed in the following paragraphs.

The most immediately recognized microcomputer hardware components are in-

FIGURE 1. The Macintosh Classic personal computer. *Courtesy Apple Computer, Inc.*

put and output devices. Input devices provide a means of communication of data between the user and the microcomputer. The most common input device is the keyboard. The keyboard resembles an ordinary typewriter keyboard with a few additional keys (such as Enter, Escape, Control, and Break) and the necessary circuitry to connect it to the computer. Other types of data input hardware are page scanners, optical character readers, the hand-held mouse, graphics pads, bar code readers, joy sticks, and numerous sensor-type input devices for scientific or computer control systems.

Output devices communicate to the user the processed data in a form that can be understood by the person using the microcomputer. The two most common output devices are the monitor (also called a video display or cathode-ray tube) and printer. There are many varieties of monitors and printers; usually they differ in their ability to produce high-quality symbols and graphics. For example, monitors may be monochrome or color and may produce various image qualities depending on the resolution (number of dots per unit area that produce the image). Printers are generally of the dot matrix, laser, ink-jet, or impact type.

As mentioned earlier, the "brains" of the microcomputer is the central processing unit, microprocessor, or chip. The CPU stores and processes data, interprets instructions, manipulates data, and sends data to other places in the system. The CPU resides on the microcomputer motherboard, a printed circuit board that connects all the microcomputer hardware. This motherboard also includes receptacles and slots for other important components such as random-access memory and read-only memory chips, the power supply, buses (wires that transfer information from one place to another), and expansion cards (which permit additional devices such as a modem, extra memory, terminal emulation, and video output).

External data storage (sometimes referred to as secondary or mass storage) is usually handled by magnetic disk systems. Magnetic disks are of two types: removable and fixed. Removable disks were the first systems available for microcomputers. Today the two most common types are the older 5.25-inch floppy disk and the 3.5-inch disk.

FIGURE 2. The motherboard of the Macintosh IIci personal computer. *Courtesy Apple Computer, Inc.*

Fixed or hard disks are permanently mounted in a drive unit. They have a larger storage capacity than the removable disks, and operate considerably faster. In fact, 40- and 80-megabyte drives are common in microcomputer systems. Other types of external storage technologies for microcomputers are compact-disk read-only memory (CD-ROM) and magnetic tape. Magnetic tape systems operate, in principle, like audiotape or videotape recorders. They are frequently used with microcomputers for archival or disk backup/data protection. The CD-ROM devices use laser optical technology much like digital audio compact discs. They provide enormous potential for data storage, permitting storage of an entire encyclopedia or large database, for example, on a single disk.

Even the most advanced technology in microcomputer hardware is of little use without software. The software that is closest and most essential is the operating system. The operating system is a set of instructions that start up ("boot") the computer and manage the interactions of all the various components. In a sense, it is a supervisor or manager as well as a resource. A microcomputer without an operating system is analogous to an automobile engine without gasoline. Generally speaking, the operating system is not applications software (e.g., word processors, spreadsheets, filing systems), but it does provide the means for using such software.

The selection of an operating system for a microcomputer is typically defined by the hardware. The IBM PC and compatible microcomputers use the MS-DOS operating system (or some variation of MS-DOS) from the Microsoft Corporation. The newer IBM PS/2 family of microcomputers uses the OS/2 operating system, which provides a "windows environment." Apple II microcomputers use ProDOS or the older Apple DOS 3.3 operating systems. Macintosh computers use the Macintosh System, with user interface utilities called Finder and Multi-Finder. Additionally, many other microcomputer operating systems are available, notably UNIX by AT&T Bell Labs and CP/M, an early microcomputer operating system by Microsoft.

APPLICATION SOFTWARE

Commericial software to run on microcomputers falls into six major categories: word processing, desktop publishing, spreadsheets, databases, graphics, and communications.

Word processing is the most popular application and has all but eliminated the typewriter. Word processing software lets users easily compose documents that range from simple letters to complicated, lengthy publications. Word processing packages routinely automate a document's pagination, footnotes, and index. Many come with an on-line thesaurus and are programmed to check the accuracy of a document's grammar and spelling.

An increasingly popular use of microcomputers is in the area of desktop publishing, an application that offers much more sophisticated text-handling capabilities than does word processing software. With desktop publishing programs, users can ready pages for publication in magazines, newsletters, catalogs, and other documents that previously required professional typesetting services. The programs permit users to set text into columns and lay out pages, and also to add graphics, drawings, and photographs to the pages they compose. The graphics-based Apple Macintosh computer handles images and graphics more deftly than the IBM PC and compatibles, and it is considered the superior system for desktop publishing activities.

The ability to mix numbers, text, and graphics is an important part of the newest generation of spreadsheets, which have become increasingly fast and sophisticated since VisiCalc's 1979 debut. In 1984, a spreadsheet called Lotus 1-2-3 appeared and overtook VisiCalc's lead. In addition to its computing wizardry, Lotus 1-2-3 had database and graphics capabilities. Millions of copies of Lotus 1-2-3 were sold. There are dozens of spreadsheets on the market, and most come with a variety of functions that let users "spiff up" the visually dull rows of numbers. With a few keystrokes, users can display numbers as charts or graphs and add shading or color and text.

Electronic databases, like electronic spreadsheets, have revolutionized work for those who use them. A database is a collection or list of information on a particular subject. Once users enter information into a computerized database, the computer takes only seconds to sort it into dozens of categories. For example, a list of customers can be broken down by product, geographic area, purchase date, and amount of expenditure. Computerized sorting quickly generates information that otherwise may remain buried amid the data.

Graphics software performs a variety of commercial art tasks, including design, layout, illustration, and photographic touchups. In addition, artists are working in the electronic medium, using "paint" software, for example.

Regardless of the application, computer users often need to transmit their documents, spreadsheets, and graphic designs electronically to others. Attaching a modem and a telephone line to a microcomputer turns the computer into a tool for communications.

Today, communications is gaining momentum as a critical part of microcomputing. Many businesses run internal networks that distribute memos and financial reports and allow employees to communicate with each other. They also hook up to external electronic mail services, which allow users to send data over phone lines to another mailbox. In addition, computers can be outfitted with facsimile boards that allow documents to be routed to a facsimile machine.

MICROCOMPUTER FUTURE

A forecast of the future of microcomputers is difficult, if not impossible, and filled with many uncertainties. It is almost certain, however, that microcomputers will continue to become smaller, more powerful, less expensive, easier to use, and increasingly user friendly. Advanced technologies promise almost unlimited data storage and processing speeds not unlike those of supercomputers. A wider variety of software will emerge for new and different applications. Voice recog-

nition/communication and the understanding of natural languages will almost certainly be a practical reality in the near future. Already many advancements have been made in this area. Pattern recognition systems, artificial intelligence, expert systems, and even game playing software will expand microcomputer usage to previously unconsidered areas. Portable laptop computers will undoubtedly continue to grow in popularity, especially as display and battery systems are improved. Word processing, spreadsheets, database management systems, and graphics applications, along with desktop publishing, electronic mail/communications, and software development, will continue to account for much of the microcomputer applications activity. But as to what precisely lies ahead, no one really knows. One can be certain, however, that technological advancements will drastically alter the methods our schools use to deliver instruction, the way our offices and industries are run, the delivery of health care, and almost every other facet of our society.

For Further Reading

Alexander, R. C., and D. K. Smith. 1988. *Fumbling the future: How Xerox invented, then ignored, the first personal computer.* New York: William Morrow.

Bitter, G. G. 1984. *Computers in today's world.* New York: Wiley.

Butcher, L. 1988. *Accidental millionaire: The rise and fall of Steve Jobs at Apple Computer.* New York: Paragon House.

Ingalsbe, L. 1989. *Using computers and applications software.* Columbus, Ohio: Merrill.

Levy, S. 1984. *Hackers.* New York: Doubleday.

Malone, M. S. 1985. *The big score: The billion dollar story of Silicon Valley.* Garden City, N.Y.: Doubleday.

Navell, S. B. 1989. *Introduction to microcomputing.* New York: Wiley.

Norton, P. 1986. *Inside the IBM PC.* New York: Prentice-Hall.

Pylyshyn, Z. W., and L. J. Bannon. 1989. *Perspectives on the computer revolution.* Norwood, N.J.: Ablex.

Ritchie, D. 1986. *The computer pioneers: The*

making of the modern computer. New York: Simon and Schuster.

Rose, F. 1989. *West of Eden: The loss of innocence at Apple Computer.* New York: Viking.

Stine, G. H. 1985. *The untold story of the computer revolution: Bits, bytes, bauds, and brains.* New York: Arbor House.

Sumner, M. 1988. *Computers: Concepts and uses.* Englewood Cliffs, N.J.: Prentice-Hall.

Tomczyk, M. 1984. *The home computer wars: An insider's account of Commodore and Jack Tramiel.* Greensboro, N.C.: Compute! Publications Inc.

Vinsonhaler, J. F., C. C. Wagner, and C. G. Gentry. 1989. *People and computers: Partners in problem solving.* St. Paul, Minn.: West.

Deborah Asbrand
William C. Bozeman

MILITARY USE OF COMPUTERS

The use of computers in the military has both been parallel to and provided impetus for their development and use in the private sector, starting with the British use of primitive computers to assist in cryptanalysis during World War II. For example, ENIAC, the first general-purpose electronic digital computer, was originally developed during World War II to calculate data for ballistic trajectories. WHIRLWIND, the first digital computer built for real-time applications, was originally conceived shortly after the war with the idea of providing a simulator for flight training, and was later used during the early 1950s to assist in the management of radar tracking data for air defense systems. Military applications have also stimulated the development of programming languages. For example, COBOL, a business language still widely used today, was developed under the sponsorship of the U.S. Department of Defense. JOVIAL, one of the first high-level programming languages, was developed for use in U.S. Air Force command, control, and communication systems. It is not widely used today outside of the Air Force, but many of the concepts that were developed in the design of JOVIAL have been used in other languages, such as PL/I.

Development of systems for military applications has also provided techniques and impetus for development in more specialized areas of computing. Research in developing automated mobile systems for use in combat has led to robotics technology that can be used in the private sector for automated production in factories. The early work done in the development of automated command, control, and communication systems such as SAGE (see below) has been applied in the development of automated air traffic control systems.

However, although many of the computer systems used by the military have their counterparts in systems used by businesses and individuals, the military requirements differ in that the losses in case of failure, whether as a result of no response, untimely response, or an inappropriate response (such as the release of classified data to an unauthorized user), can be much greater. Not only money and time—as would be the case in most commercial applications—but also thousands of lives may be lost in case of failure, and the national security could be endangered. These concerns are the reasons behind much of the military interest in use of computers to begin with, but use of computer technology, while it may solve such problems in one area, will create new problems in others. Moreover, the conditions under which military systems must operate may be much more strenuous, so the difficulty of attaining these properties will be much greater. Finally, the benefits of even a slight advantage in these areas may be greater than in the private sector; for example, a slight advantage in response time may make the difference between winning and losing a battle.

There are two main areas in which the military has requirements that go beyond the usual needs of information processing. The first is the use of embedded computer systems in weapons systems, airplanes, etc., to provide information to a human operator, operate the system automatically, or do both. One such example is in the guidance system in the Tomahawk cruise missile, which relies in part on a computerized system that compares a stored map generated from satellite photographs with the terrain actually covered to help the missile locate itself. This information is used not only to supplement information gained via more conventional techniques, but also can be employed to program alternative courses and random-path "zigzag" flights. A similar system is utilized when the missile approaches its target.

The second area is in automated command, control, communication, and intelligence (C^3I) systems. An automated C^3I system is a specialized one that assists in the planning and direction of battles and other military activities in a number of ways. It generally includes several databases to manage different kinds of data, a set of communication functions so that data can be shared with other systems and other components of the same system, a set of data collectors, and possibly some simulation tools that can be used to simulate the outcome of various decisions. Since the system is relied on to coordinate data from various different sources, it should also include analytical tools to process different and sometimes contradictory data—for example, tracker correlation tools to reconcile tracking data. The exact form such a system takes will depend on its application. A strategic C^3I system will be used to protect a country from attack and usually will comprise a number of large, fixed installations. A tactical system, intended for use during combat, would be more mobile and would have to be able to operate under more adverse conditions.

The earliest example of an automated C^3I system was the Semiautomatic Ground Environment (SAGE) Air Defense System, which was implemented in the mid- to late 1950s. This system gathered and analyzed information collected by radar to provide early warning of air attack on North America. A current example of a strategic system is the Worldwide Military Command and Control System (WWMCCS) and the WWMCCS Intercomputer Network (WIN). WWMCCS was established in 1962 and consists of personnel, communications equipment, facilities, and procedures used to plan and direct operational activities of U.S. military forces. The C^3I information and support are accom-

plished on processors interconnected with WIN, which became fully operational in the early 1980s. WIN provides the resources of a computer network, such as teleconferencing and electronic mail, and retrieval of files from remote hosts. It also provides security and control measures to prevent loss of information in transit. It is used by the U.S. military to share information needed for its operation; for example, the Navy Command and Control System employs WIN to distribute processing of position and status information on Navy units among the fleet commanders in chief.

The U.S. Naval Tactical Data System (NTDS) is an example of a tactical command, control, and communication system. It is the oldest such system currently in operation; it was first installed on Navy ships in the late 1950s and has been continually updated since then. A ship's NTDS system gathers data from sensors, aircraft, and other NTDS-equipped ships. These data are sent to a number of computers installed on the ship that process the data and reconcile them so an accurate picture can be given of all contacts, whether surface, subsurface, or air. This information is displayed to the operations officer in the ship's combat information center and also is used to set the vector coordinates of the ship's missile armaments and aircraft and to manage the airspace for aircraft carriers. The NTDS system can interface with other, similar systems such as the Airborne Tactical Data System and the Marine Tactical Data System.

The usefulness of computers in the military was well illustrated in the Persian Gulf War of 1991, in which systems employed ranged from the twenty-year-old Patriot missiles, which were among the first to use software-based controls, to the developmental U.S. Air Force/Grumman joint surveillance target attack radar system (Joint-STARS), which located Iraqi ground and moving targets, including mobile Scud missile launchers. Other systems employed include the Pioneer and Pointer unmanned aerial vehicles, tiny unmanned aircraft (the Pointer is about the size of a model airplane) provided with sophisticated navigational systems that were used for target observation and damage assessment, and electronic warfare equipment on manned aircraft that allowed them to detect and fire missiles to destroy air defense sites. Command and control systems were also tested to the hilt; throughput for the worldwide command and control system was tripled during Desert Storm. The Gulf War also pointed out some areas in which improvement was necessary: Problems with friendly fire casualties have resulted in increased concern about developing ground-based Identification Friend or Foe systems. Computer technology also was of vital importance to the other side; the main goal of the air war was to destroy the Iraqi command and control system.

The necessity of ensuring that military systems are safe and reliable is well acknowledged, and various steps to guarantee that such systems are indeed safe and reliable are being taken. One area in which the military's concern has been particularly visible is in development of computer languages that will support sound software engineering. The Ada language, the U.S. Department of Defense standard language for embedded computer applications, is intended to be such a language. It originated as a result of a higher-order language working group started by the U.S. Department of Defense in cooperation with the defense departments of several West European countries in the mid-1970s to define requirements. Ada is highly modularized, which makes it easy to reuse pieces of code; it is strongly typed, which reduces the chance of errors; and Ada compilers must go through a rigorous validation procedure, which ensures that the language is highly standardized. Ada has been both praised and criticized by the software engineering community. It has been praised because of the support it provides for sound software engineering practices. It has been criticized for the large number of instructions, which many fear could make it behave unpredictably, and for the slow progress in building Ada compilers. Ada compilers have been slow to arrive; they are not generally very fast; and, ironically, most currently available compilers do not support some useful features for embedded systems provided for in the specification of the Ada language, such as interrupt handlers and physical address storage. The slowness of

progress in the development of compilers has been blamed, in part, on the rigor of the standards. However, the situation has been improving; second-generation Ada compilers are in general twice as fast as first-generation ones, and considerable progress has been made in developing support tools for Ada, including specification languages such as Task Sequencing Language (TSL) and Annotated Ada (Anna). (See also ADA.)

Another area of computer reliability that the military is particularly concerned with is security. With the advent of viruses, computer security has interested the general community recently, but the possibility of unauthorized release of sensitive military data due to violation of a computer system's security mechanisms has been a concern of the U.S. military since the mid-1960s. The U.S. military's security standards for operating systems in which sensitive data are stored are provided in the Department of Defense's Trusted Computer System Evaluation Criteria (TCSEC), first published in 1983 and revised in 1985. The TCSEC gives several different sets of criteria that must be met by operating systems that store classified information, depending on the level of assurance required. An interpretation of the TCSEC requirements for networks has been published, and an interpretation for database management systems is in preparation. As in the case of Ada, the TCSEC requirements have been criticized for their extreme rigor, particularly for the length of the evaluation process at the higher assurance levels. However, in recent years systems that are intended to be evaluated at the higher assurance levels have slowly begun to appear and receive ratings.

For Further Reading

Andriole, S. J. 1986. *High-technology issues in C³I*. Washington, D.C.: AFCEA Press.

Beckett, B. 1983. *Weapons of tomorrow*. New York: Plenum Press.

Ganapathi, M. and G. O. Mendal. 1989. Issues in Ada compiler technology. *IEEE Computer* 22(2):52–60.

Gasser, M. 1988. *Building a secure computing system*. New York: Van Nostrand Reinhold.

Metropolis, N., J. Howlett, and G. C. Rota.

1980. *A history of computing in the twentieth century*. New York: Academic Press.

Schleher, D. C. 1986. *Electronic warfare*. Dedham, Mass.: Artech House.

U.S. Department of Defense. 1983. *Reference manual for the Ada programming language*. Washington, D.C.: U.S. Government Printing Office.

U.S. Department of Defense. 1985. *DoD trusted computer system evaluation criteria*. Washington, D.C.: U.S. Government Printing Office.

Wexelblatt, R. L. 1981. *History of programming languages*. New York: Academic Press.

Catherine Meadows

MINORITIES

See Equity Issues and Computers

MODULA-2

Modula-2 is a computer programming language designed in 1978 by Niklaus WIRTH. On its publication in 1980 it gained immediate and widespread attention. It was intended to be a systems programming language for the Lilith computer system, but has been accepted as a general-purpose programming language and is now taught as the first language in many universities. It is an improvement in many ways over Wirth's widely used language, Pascal. The structure of the language encourages modular programming and other programming practices recommended by software engineers, while allowing machine-level access by means of low-level types and functions. Compilers for Modula-2 are available on the VAX system (VMS and UNIX), IBM mainframes and personal computers, and Apple's MacIntosh computers.

Modula-2 supports functional and data abstractions, thus providing improved reliability and savings in software maintenance and upgrade costs. Modula-2 extends Pascal both upward (with data abstraction) and downward (with facilities for access to low-level features of the machine). Modula-2 encourages the design and construction of reliable, robust, and maintainable programs.

HISTORICAL DEVELOPMENT

The computer programming languages of the 1950s were designed for efficiency of object code and compatibility with existing hardware systems. In the 1960s the importance of the language as a system component was recognized, and hardware designers began to take into consideration the languages' characteristics while they designed the computer hardware. During the 1970s the "software crisis" developed. Software costs (design, writing, debugging, and maintenance) were rising steadily while hardware costs continued to decrease. The discipline of software engineering was born in response to this problem, and language designers began to incorporate into their languages features that would encourage programmers to design readable, correct, reliable, and robust programs.

The first problem-oriented language that was defined in a precise and formal way was Algol-60, designed by an international (IFIPS) committee. The design effort continued beyond the publication of the Algol-60 specifications, and during the early 1960s the committee considered ways to improve Algol. The designers split into two camps concerning the best approach. One group argued for increased formalism, and the other, of which Niklaus Wirth was a member, argued that programming languages should be simple and manageable. Algol-68 was the product of the Formalism Group, and Algol-W (the W is for Wirth) was designed by the Simplifiers.

Pascal was the next language designed by Wirth, in 1968, and it soon became the most popular programming language with educators, because its structure taught good programming habits to its users. The available control structures in Pascal made the feared "GOTO" (Dijkstra 1968) unnecessary. Even a novice programmer no longer was tempted to write programs containing "spaghetti."

In 1977, Wirth was the leader of a project called Lilith, which included the concurrent development of a hardware system and a base language that could be used for the development of all the software for that machine. Modula-2 was that language, and its design allowed the writing of systems programs without any lapses into assembly or machine language. Lilith was expected to serve one user and its architecture included only one processor, simplifying the job of the operating system, but the system language still had to include access to machine functions. Modula-2 provided this capability with procedures and data types in its "SYSTEM" module.

LANGUAGE STRUCTURE

Modula-2 was an evolutionary development from Pascal, to which Wirth added several new features: modules, separate compilation, data abstraction, machine-level access, and coroutines. At the same time he took the opportunity to correct some of the minor flaws and inconveniences of Pascal that had been the subject of numerous articles in the literature since 1968 (e.g., Welsh et al. 1977, Johnson and Munro 1984). Because of Modula-2's close relationship with Pascal, the discussion of its structure will include occasional references to Pascal. The language's structure is usually described by means of syntax diagrams, but extended Backus-Naur Form notation can also be used. In the following discussion both are found.

The most important feature of Modula-2, according to its creator (Wirth 1984), is the MODULE. This structure allows the programmer to define a package of constants, data types, variables, data structures, and procedures that can be separately compiled and then linked at run time with user programs ("client" modules). At the top level, any Modula-2 program is made up of a collection of MODULEs, some of which may be found in libraries. Three kinds of MODULEs are available: PROGRAM, DEFINITION, and IMPLEMENTATION. The syntax diagram for each of these structures is shown in Figure 1. The user's program is packaged in a PROGRAM MODULE. Objects such as procedural and data abstractions can be shared between modules. Such an object is packaged in a pair of associated modules consisting of a DEFINITION MODULE and an IMPLEMENTATION MODULE. The

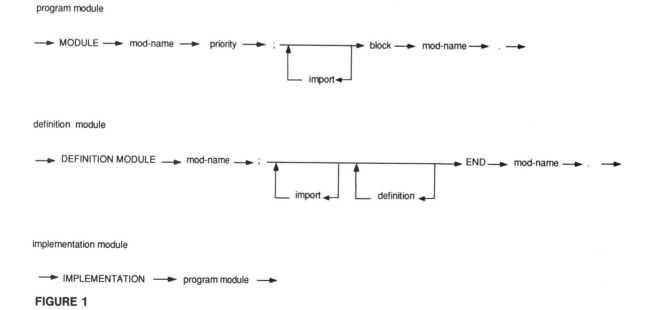

FIGURE 1

DEFINITION MODULE contains declarations of constants, types, variables, and data structures, together with specifications (name, type, and parameter list only) of procedures and functions. The accompanying IMPLEMENTATION MODULE contains the complete declarations of all the procedures specified in the DEFINITION MODULE. Objects defined in these two MODULES are automatically made available for IMPORTing into any other MODULE. To make use of the object the using MODULE simply includes an IMPORT statement.

The general structure of a module comprises a header line that tells the kind of module and its name, IMPORTs if appropriate, declarations, and a body (Figure 1).

The block is made up of a series of declarations followed by a sequence of statements bracketed by a BEGIN–END pair. The declarations include constants, types, variables, procedures, functions, and modules, and can be listed in any order that the programmer thinks appropriate. This flexibility of ordering allows the programmer to group declarations in a way that might make the program more understandable.

Modula-2 includes eleven statement types. The most noticeable difference from Pascal is that the requirement for matching BEGINs and ENDs has in many cases been relaxed. If a compound statement or statement sequence is to be included in an IF, WHILE, FOR, LOOP, or CASE statement, it is easy for the compiler or interpreter to discern the beginning and end of the statement sequence, and so the BEGIN (and sometimes the END) is omitted. This can be seen in the following sample IF statement:

Pascal
```
IF <Boolean exp> THEN
  BEGIN
    stmt-1;
    stmt-2
  END
ELSE
  BEGIN
    stmt-3;
    stmt-4
  END;
```

Modula-2
```
IF <Boolean exp> THEN
  stmt-1;
  stmt-2
ELSE
  stmt-3;
  stmt-4
END;
```

The eleven statement types of Modula-2 are listed here:

1. *Assignment statement:*
   variable name := expression
   The expression on the right is evaluated, and the resulting value is assigned to the variable named on the left.

2. *If statement:*
   IF Boolean expression THEN statement sequence
   { ELSIF Boolean expression THEN statement sequence }
   [ELSE statement sequence]
   The value of each Boolean expression causes control to be transferred to either the statement sequence following THEN or the statement sequence following ELSE.

3. *Case statement:*
   CASE expression OF case { | case }
   [ELSE statement sequence END]
   The value of the expression causes a transfer to the corresponding case label (if it exists). If not, the sequence of statements following ELSE is executed.

4. *WHILE statement:*
   WHILE Boolean expression DO statement sequence END
   For as long as the Boolean expression is found to be true, the statement sequence is repeatedly executed. If the Boolean expression is false the first time it is evaluated, the statement sequence is not executed at all. The syntax is given in Figure 2.

5. *For statement:*
   FOR ident := expression TO expression [BY constant expression] DO statement sequence END
   The DOWNTO alternative of Pascal is not available. The default stepsize is 1,

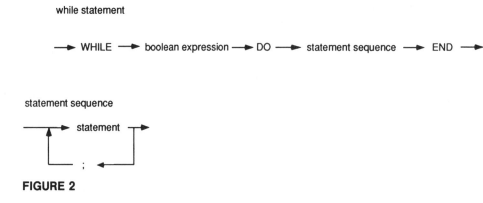

FIGURE 2

but an optional BY part can specify some other stepsize (either positive or negative). The counter variable (ident) can be any ordinal type.

6. *REPEAT statement:*
REPEAT statement sequence UNTIL Boolean expression
The statement sequence will be repeatedly executed as long as the Boolean expression is false. It will be executed the first time regardless of the Boolean expression.

7. *LOOP statement:*
LOOP statement sequence END
This is new in Modula-2. It is an iterative statement in which the terminating condition can (must) be placed within the enclosed statement sequence. At least one EXIT (or RETURN or HALT) statement is included in the statement sequence, controlled by the terminating condition. If such a statement is not included, the LOOP will continue until an error stops it.

8. *WITH statement:*
WITH designator DO statement sequence END
As in Pascal, the designator provides qualifiers that can be prefixed to identifiers in the statement sequence if those identifiers are field names within record definitions (and therefore meaningless without the qualifiers).

9. *PROCEDURE call:*
procedure name [actual parameters]
A PROCEDURE can be declared in two different ways, as a function or as a "proper" procedure. Depending on the declaration, the PROCEDURE call can be used as a component of an expression or as a statement.

10. *EXIT statement:* EXIT
This one-word statement can be used only inside the body of a LOOP statement, and when it is executed, control passes from the inside of the LOOP to the statement following the END of the LOOP.

11. *RETURN statement:* RETURN [expression]
This statement causes termination of a procedure invocation, returning control to the statement following the call of the procedure. If the word RETURN is followed by an expression (optional), a value is returned by the procedure. In this case it acts like a Pascal function.

Modula-2's built-in data types include all those of Pascal, without change, as well as a few new ones:

- INTEGER: A number with no fractional part, for example, 3, −85
- CARDINAL: A nonnegative INTEGER, for example, 0, 234.
- REAL: A larger class of numbers, those with or without a fractional part, for example, 0.01, 14.0, −324.64, 14.3E-2
- CHAR: A single character
- BOOLEAN: A variable, expression, or constant that can have one of only two values, TRUE or FALSE
- Enumerated: A data type defined by the programmer, in which all the possible values of the variable are listed. Thus, the

programmer can define a type called pet, and give it a list of values such as (cat, dog, bat, mongoose, unicorn).

- Subrange: A data type defined by the programmer that consists of a part of one of the types above (except REAL), for example, [100..199], ['A'..'Z'], [−3..3], and [dog..mongoose]
- SET: A data structure that has as its value a group of atomic elements chosen from one of the above types (except REAL), for example, { 1, 3, 6, 10, 15, 21 } or { '?', '.', ',', '!' }.
- ARRAY: An ordered homogeneous list of elements of any type (including ARRAY) that can be accessed by use of a subscript.
- RECORD: A heterogeneous list of elements that can be accessed by means of "field names," for example, information about a student, airline flight, or automobile part.
- String: A string constant is a sequence of characters enclosed in single or double quote marks. A string variable is an ARRAY of CHARs.
- POINTER: An indirect reference to (address of) an anonymous data item. This data type is used by a Modula-2 (or Pascal) programmer to define data structures (e.g., stacks, trees) that are not built into the language.
- BITSET: Permits bit operations on machine words.
- ADDRESS and WORD: System-dependent data types that permit determination of run-time addresses.

MODULA-2 PROBLEM DOMAINS

Scientific. By virtue of its standard library, MathLib0, and its variety of data types (ARRAYs, RECORDs, and REALs), Modula-2 is equipped to solve scientific problems. The most recent version of Modula-2 also includes the LONGINT and LONGREAL data types to give additional precision to scientific calculations.

Business: Modula-2 has a very flexible RECORD data structure, but there are no input, output, or file operations defined as part of Modula-2. All such operations are provided in the standard library modules: FileSystem, InOut, RealInOut, and Terminal. Each input and output procedure from these libraries is capable of reading or printing only one value of a particular type. This makes programs that do a lot of input and/or output operations relatively lengthy. Business problems can be solved in this language, but there are probably better languages for this task.

Systems programming. Since Wirth's purpose in designing Modula-2 was to make a system programming capability available in a high-level language, we might expect this to be a strong point of the language. It has POINTERs for the definition of complex data structures, and includes the data type BITSET, which permits bit operations on machine words. Also included are the dependent data types, ADDRESS and WORD, as well as the ADR procedure, which allows the program to determine the run-time address of a variable.

COMPARISON WITH PASCAL

With Modula-2, Wirth has indeed improved on Pascal. Many of the improvements have already been described. Here is a list of those changes:

- Separate compilation of MODULEs
- Data abstraction facilities (DEFINITION and IMPLEMENTATION MODULEs)
- Coroutines
- Multiple variant fields (permitted anywhere in the RECORD structure)
- Open arrays (When a one-dimensional array is used as a procedure parameter, the upper bound of the array need not be specified.)
- Conditional evaluation of Boolean expressions
- Optional ELSE clause in CASE statement
- Order of declarations relaxed
- Low-level programming (using BITSET, WORD, ADR, etc.)
- Relaxation of BEGIN..END bracketing
- Optional ELSIF clause in IF statement

- Optional specification of stepsize in FOR statement
- RETURN/EXIT/HALT statements
- New numeric data types (CARDINAL, LONGINT, and LONGREAL)
- Standard procedures INCrement and DECrement
- Identifiers of unrestricted length
- Constant expressions permitted wherever a constant value is allowed.
- Case sensitivity (In Modula-2, an identifier that is declared as Foot cannot later be referred to as FOOT or fOoT. All reserved words and standard identifiers must be written in full caps.)
- All Input, Output, and File operations in libraries
- Standard libraries (FileSystem, InOut, RealInOut, Terminal, MathLib0, and Storage)

SAMPLE PROCEDURE: INTEGER POWER

An example program that makes genuine use of Modula-2's strongest abilities (the MODULE, low-level programming, concurrency, and data abstraction) would be too long for this article. See any Modula-2 text (especially King 1988) for more extensive examples. The procedure to raise a REAL or INTEGER number to an Integer power follows:

Modula-2

```
PROCEDURE IntPower (Num : REAL;
Exponent : INTEGER) : REAL;
(* returns the value of Num raised to the
Exponent power *)
VAR   Neg : BOOLEAN;
      Ans : REAL;
      Pow : INTEGER;

BEGIN     (* IntPower *)

  Neg := FALSE;

  IF Exponent < 0 THEN
     Neg := TRUE;
     Exponent := − Exponent
  END; (* IF *)
```

```
  Ans := 1.0;

  FOR Pow := 1 TO Exponent DO
     Ans := Ans * Num
  END; (* FOR *)

  IF Neg THEN
     RETURN 1.0 / Ans;
  ELSE
     RETURN ANS
  END (* IF *)

END; (* IntPower *)
```

Pascal

```
Function IntPower (Num : Real; Exponent :
Integer) : Real;

  { returns the value of Num raised to the
  Exponent power }

Var   Neg : Boolean;
      Ans : Real;
      Pow : Integer;

Begin     { IntPower }

  Neg := False;

  If Exponent < 0 Then
     Begin
        Neg := True;
        Exponent := − Exponent
     End; { If }

  Ans := 1.0;

  For Pow := 1 to Exponent Do
     Ans := Ans * Num;

  If Neg Then
     Ans := 1.0 / Ans;

  IntPower := Ans

End;     { IntPower }
```

References

Dijkstra, E. 1968. GOTO statement considered harmful. *Communications of the ACM* 11(3):147−48.

Johnson, M., and A. Munro. 1984. Pascal's design flaws—Modula-2 solutions and Pascal patches. *Byte*, March, pp. 371−88.

King, K. 1988. *Modula-2. A complete guide.* Boston: D. C. Heath. Contains an extensive bibliography and a thorough description of the language.

Welsh, J., W. J. Sneeringer, and C. A. R. Hoare. 1977. Ambiguities and insecurities in Pascal. *Software—Practice and Experience* 7(6):685–96.

Wirth, N. 1984. History and goals of Modula-2. *Byte,* August, pp. 145–52.

For Further Reading

Bohm, C., and G. Jacopini. 1966. Flow diagrams, Turing machines, and languages with only two formation rules. *Communications of the ACM* 9(5):366–71.

Jensen, K., and N. Wirth. 1974. *Pascal user manual and report.* Heidelberg: Springer-Verlag.

Wirth, N. 1982. *Programming in Modula-2.* Heidelberg: Springer-Verlag.

———. 1985. From programming language design to computer construction. *Communications of the ACM* 28(2):159–64.

———. 1987. *Algorithms + data structures = programs.* Englewood Cliffs, N.J.: Prentice-Hall.

Denis Conrady

MULTIMEDIA

Multimedia is a technology platform that allows the user to combine text, graphics, animation, voice, music, and full-motion video in computer-controlled applications. The evolution of the technological capabilities of computers, television sets, and audio systems has encouraged such diverse industries as publishing, telecommunications, computers, and others to invest considerable time and money in research and development activities tied to multimedia concepts. The term *multimedia* applies to a very broad range of systems composed of varied combinations of sound, visuals, and text. Standards have not yet been established by the industry or international standards bodies and will take several years to evolve.

What distinguishes current multimedia from past manifestations created on film and videotape is the inclusion of the interactivity provided by the computer. Multimedia modules that are computer based provide the user with control of the direction and pace of the learning environment. The potential for information delivered by these platforms is extensive and exciting. Research has long shown that multisensory learning can be very effective and efficient. Similarly, learner-paced materials are superior to fixed-paced materials in most situations. These facts combined with the learner control of branching provide a sound basis for the utilization of multimedia systems. There are several areas in which this technology proves to be successful. The first is in overall learning situations in both education and training. Learning at home, school, and work benefits from the development of integrated hardware and user-friendly multimedia software. The human–machine potential is considerable. A second area of promise is in the formulation of business presentations and workshops. The diversity of multimedia will allow the creation of attention-getting and motivating units with plenty of "show." Third, desktop video is quickly evolving its own multimedia configuration. Local video production may see the same revolution that the printing industry saw with desktop publishing. The fourth area is in the development of new delivery styles and methods that will benefit from the prototyping abilities of the multimedia format.

There are many stimulating possibilities for this technology. Both education and training seek applications that take advantage of the ability to combine sound, graphics, and text in interactive modes that address more than one learning style. The ability to synthetically reproduce key learning environments by employing capabilities such as split screen for side-by-side comparisons, text-over-graphics screens for emphasis and review, and interactivity to allow individual control of branching leads to intriguing possibilities. ABC News Interactive released *The '88 Vote: Campaign for the White House* in a multimedia format. This videodisc provides political speeches and announcements, along with biographical information and electoral information, for all thirteen presidential candidates on side 1. Side 2 offers speeches, statements, and commercials by Bush and Dukakis including complete Election Day coverage with final results. This information can be used as an interactive module by the instructor. By adding a software program, users can create their own documentary on the spot.

From a design and development perspective, digital technology adds a dimension to the computer-aided design (CAD) business. Simulations are more three-dimensional in appearance and can allow an architect to display a realistic representation of a building without having to build a model. Interactivity and overlay capabilities then allow evaluation of alternative designs and specifications with relative ease. Sales and promotion productions can also take advantage of animated graphics and video simulations. A landscaper could create a point-of-sale environment in which trees were added, flowers changed, and sidewalks relocated, all at the push of a button. Synchronized audio could be provided to create an automatic promotion without the expense of an attendant for use in malls and other public places.

The capability is there, but at present multimedia consists mostly of promise. It will take several years of development before computer stores stock user-friendly multimedia applications that run flawlessly on a compact, affordable system with standard interfaces and interchangeable hardware components. The present state of the technology is a ruleless system in which hardware and software elements are combined depending on the particular sources the developer wishes to incorporate into that presentation.

TYPICAL HARDWARE

Multimedia can be created and presented on several levels of sophistication. In general, more sophisticated programs encumber the user with problems of incompatibility and/or significant cost increases. Entry-level multimedia can be very effective. Students can produce video book reports on a system consisting of a computer, a video cassette recorder (VCR), a paint program, and a cas-

sette tape recorder. As this system is upgraded by addition of a video camera for input and speakers for higher-quality audio playback, the system begins to shift to an intermediate platform.

Color video cameras, digitizers, improved graphics, and inexpensive hand scanners add impact and polish to this level of utilization. Users can produce a video program with overlays, original graphics, and images captured via the camera.

Advanced interactivity and motion video are the key ingredients to advanced multimedia platforms. Larger and faster storage devices, music interfaces such as Musical Instrument Digital Interface (MIDI) keyboards, laser printers, audio and video capture boards, and full-motion video packages provide extraordinary opportunities for multimedia development.

Platforms for application development and advanced playback situations require rather costly and extensive systems. Certain basic components will be found in most multimedia development systems. A typical system would include the following items:

- Computer (IBM 386/486-based/Mac II/ Amiga 3000)
    VGA level graphics
    Color monitor and video card (high resolution/multisynch)
    Audio capture board
    Video capture board
    Authoring software
    Large hard disk (100–300 megabytes)
    3½-inch drive
    Printer
- Digitizers
    Color scanner
    Frame grabber
    Audio sampler/digitizer
- Video
    Camcorder
    VCR with small monitor
    Video projector for presentations
- Audio
    Speakers (self-powered)
    MIDI keyboard

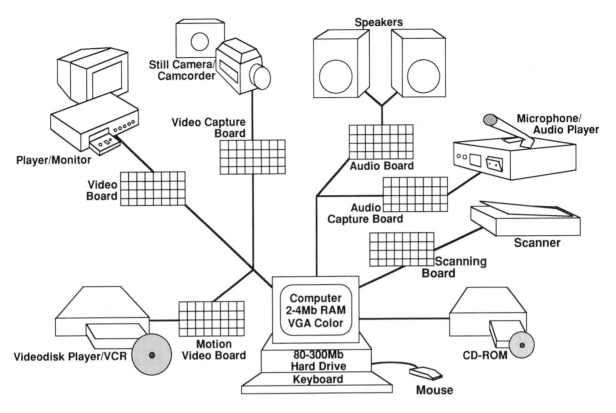

FIGURE 1. Multimedia production system.

• Other optical equipment
  Compact-disk read-only memory (CD-ROM)/Digital Video Interactive drive
  Laser disk
  Overhead projector

Indiana University and IBM have cooperated in developing a prototype of a movable multimedia playback system for an instructional environment. It consists of a personal computer with an overhead projection camera system, a 35-inch television, an audio cassette player, a video cassette player, a laser disk, powered speakers, and a remote control "black box" with fiber-optic links to their remote control mechanisms. All hardware is contained in an entertainment center on wheels. The unit is made to be hooked into a cable TV system to add standard news broadcasts and other programming.

The hand-held, infrared, remote unit activates programs in the black box that then send signals via the fiber optics to set up and begin playback of programs. For example, a single input on the remote unit will initiate a program in the control unit that will turn the TV on, change it to channel 3, and then start the videodisc. Although in early development, this system provides a peek into the future of multimedia education. Software is being developed to provide an interactive audience response system to the platform. This software will record responses and provide statistical displays of the data for the instructor and/or the learner.

MULTIMEDIA SOFTWARE

The many disparate elements of multimedia software create many difficulties for authoring software vendors. Several features must be included within the programs to ensure seamless presentations. Tools that are commonly included are an outliner, a relational database, editing utilities, a synchronizing tool, previewing/evaluating capabilities, and possibly a custom programming module.

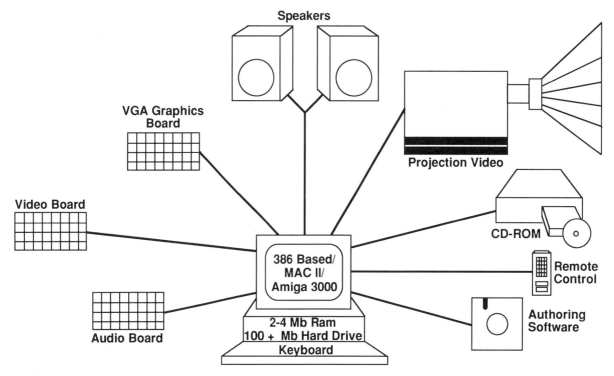

FIGURE 2. Multimedia playback system.

The outlining function may be referred to as storyboarding or flowcharting in some programs. This important tool allows the user to organize his or her thoughts and to ensure proper sequencing. Authors commonly use writing design tools to outline the presentation before gathering data, creating graphics, or preparing animation.

Keeping track of text, still visuals, video, and audio can be very difficult without a data management tool. Indexing of items in order to locate file names, graphics files, file lengths, and similar elements is vital to multimedia programming.

Sound and visual materials are often acquired from preexisting materials such as clip art files and recorded tapes. Commonly, these items must be edited for inclusion into the multimedia program. Audio and video editing utilities need to be added to the standard drawing utility for any authoring package.

Whether icon based like MacroMind's Director or card file based like Hypercard, a synchronization tool permits you to choose the sequence that will be followed for display of the various elements. This tool can be very complex and needs to be as user friendly as possible.

A critical but often overlooked authoring utility is a full-screen preview function that allows the user to evaluate a program to ensure that it works properly before duplicating and using it. Incomplete or reduced-size representations allow problems to slip into the final presentations.

Owl International has released Guide multimedia development software with most of the tools mentioned above. Graphics features similar to Microsoft "Windows" are used by Guide to supply hypertext functions that permit the mix of multimedia information in logical, organized modules. Guide could be used to design technical manuals or to develop problem-solving units to aid training and support functions.

Most corporate and educational multimedia producers prefer to work with more basic and user-friendly authoring packages often referred to as multimedia presentation programs. Hypercard systems have been used for early development on the Apple Macintosh. MacroMind's Director software is also a rich multimedia authoring tool for this environment. This software is constructed in two modules: Overview and Studio. The first module is used for simple animations via preset templates. The Studio module is also used for animations but can also be used to paint pictures, move objects, add sounds, and script overall animations. One drawback to most multimedia packages, including Director, is that they require fairly large storage space. A CD-ROM drive, a cartridge drive, or a large hard disk is recommended.

Commodore Amiga platforms have presentation software such as The Director and Commodore Authoring Software, now known as AmigaVision. AmigaVision is supplied with all 2000 and 3000 computers. This icon-based authoring and presentation program manipulates icons to create sequenced presentations. For multimedia authoring, Commodore users have CanDo from INOVAtronics. CanDo utilizes "cards" and "decks" to create a variety of educational and training applications.

Turnkey multimedia from IBM can be delivered via The Audio Visual Connection (AVC). AVC is a combination of hardware and software that permits digitizing, storage, and manipulation of images, sound, and text for complete multimedia presentations. The package consists of the authoring software, the AVC language, and two optional boards: the Video Capture Adapter and the Audio Capture and Playback board. Two important distinctions between AVC-type software and basic linear screen shows exist. In addition to the linear presentation, AVC can interact with the user and use these data to branch to different levels as needed. Second, AVC allows the user to integrate all of the multimedia elements into a coordinated unit.

This powerful program can provide valuable application tools, but, as with other such multimedia packages, it demands a large volume of disk space. This huge appetite for storage space highlights the current main drawback to multimedia development —standardization.

NEED FOR STANDARDS

In the future, the different approaches to multimedia may converge. But, at present, a user must be willing to learn four different strategies, each based on a corporate plan for multimedia. Presently Commodore, Apple, IBM/Intel, and Sony/Phillips are each creating their own paths. Each tried to mold multimedia into existing systems and then searched for its own best strategy for mass storage needs. This approach has led to four somewhat different tactics.

Commodore led the crowd with the introduction of the Amiga in 1985. Early Amigas were touted as desktop video systems and they easily synchronized standard video signals. The recent Amiga 2500 and 3000 machines have been pitched as multimedia platforms. They offer multitasking, color graphics, and speech synthesis as well as basic audio capabilities. With the addition of a *genlock*, these machines can be synchronized with just about any video from 8-millimeter to NTSC RS-170A. Genlock is a hardware device that allows a video system to match its timing or synchronization to the timing of the incoming signal.

Apple calls multimedia "desktop media." It has added high-quality sound, live-action video, and animation to the solid base offered by the Apple Macintosh platform. The binder for the Apple Macintosh multimedia system is Hypercard and authoring packages such as MacroMind's Director. Apple has developed a set of protocols to control the information path between Hypercard and Macintosh multimedia peripherals. Apple is developing "symmetrical video compression" to help solve the massive storage problems of multimedia. Symmetrical systems provide for both storage and playback of compressed data. Apple stresses the need for users to be able to create and edit their own productions, in contrast to the IBM/Intel game plan, which is pursuing canned presentations created and compressed by a larger computer system.

IBM has joined with Intel to attempt to move the PS/2 microcomputers into the multimedia marketplace. The IBM strategy has been built around the fact that the PS/2 microcomputers do not have multimedia-quality built-in hardware. Add-on peripherals from both IBM and outside vendors allow the creation of an IBM multimedia workstation. Present IBM promotions offer laser disk and CD-ROM-based multimedia; however, it is very clear that Intel's Digital Video Interactive (DVI) system is an integral part of IBM's future multimedia plans.

Sony and Phillips are working with all three of the major companies vying for multimedia sales. They are developing optical storage devices to deal with the large storage problems facing all vendors. They are also developing compact-disk interactive (CD-I) technology that provides the capacity for standalone, embedded-computer multimedia presentation systems. Sony and Phillips are also looking at transitions between multimedia and consumer electronics that might lead to new markets and products.

The result is that we have diverging rather than converging technologies. Commodore moves forward with its powerful graphics and video compatibility with user-friendly authoring systems. Apple shifts from desktop publishing to Hypercard desktop presentations via interlocked, interactive peripherals. With limited antecedents, IBM aligns with Intel to look at futuristic systems with full-motion video via DVI technology. Concurrently, Sony and Phillips pursue current optical solutions while researching CD-I as a future device for not only the computer multimedia market, but also new developments in consumer electronics.

FURTHER DEVELOPMENTS

Computers use digital audio or video information that requires considerably more storage space than analog information such as music stored on an LP record. Video requires even more than audio. High-quality multimedia systems demand full-motion video and CD-quality audio processed as digital information. In general, microcomputers do not have the power and storage necessary for this to happen. To find a solution to this dilemma, vendors have been spending research and development dollars to focus on new systems. One pair of solutions is to speed up the computers and to increase their storage capacity. Central processing unit (CPU) clock speeds of 33 MHz are now common and hard drives with 300 mega-

bytes of storage are available for most platforms. The "faster and larger" trend is evident in new planned releases, but more help is needed. Work to improve the data transfer rate between the CPU and the disk will help, but new technologies must be developed. Video images and audio files must be reduced and the costs must be contained to make development and presentation cost effective.

Elimination of unneeded or repetitive information can be realized by compressing and decompressing video and audio digital data. Compression systems will allow these data to fit onto a reasonably sized unit like a 5-inch compact disc. One such compression technology is DVI, being developed by Intel and IBM.

Digital Video Interactive Technology

Digital Video Interactive technology can access motion and still images, audio, graphics, computer data, and text (see Table 1). These inputs are digitized and compressed and stored on a random-access device such as a CD-ROM or a hard disk. Real-motion video can then be presented in full-screen and full-color programs with synchronized sound, all done by the computer.

To understand the significance of DVI technology it is helpful to review the developments that led to this advance. Laser videodiscs were first introduced in the 1970s. They could deliver 54,000 analog video frames per side or 30 minutes of video. But videodiscs are bulky read-only devices. They are also limited by the cost of producing the raw video and program data and pressing the master disc. Inputting video from analog videodiscs remains a viable procedure, but interactive, edited full-motion video demands better technology. Capture cards such as TrueVision's Targa board can be used to create a weak replication of motion video by capturing a series of successive video frames and replaying them at ten to fifteen frames per second. This technique provides a method for small jobs but demands extremely large memory capabilities and therefore does not lend itself to larger projects. The motion sequences are also perceived as soft

TABLE 1. Highlights of Digital Video and Compact-Disk Interactive Sytems

Compact-Disk Interactive (CD-I)
Audio characteristics
    Excellent for music and multilingual uses
    Over 19 hours of audio available
    Provides 16 parallel channels
Video characteristics
    Capable of partial-screen, full-motion video
    16 million color combinations, with over 32,000
        for user graphics
    Up to 7,000 photo-quality pictures can be used
Text/data
    Provides programming equivalent to over
        1,800 floppy disks
    Capable of 300,000 typed pages[a]

Digital Video Interactive (DVI)
Audio characteristics
    Up to 40 hours of AM-quality monaural
        (or 5 hours FM stereo)
Video characteristics
    Over 1 hour of full-screen, full-motion video
        (2 hours of half-screen, full-motion video)
    5,000 very high resolution still images
        (10,000 high-resolution still images)
    Can be edited if stored on magnetic media
Text/data characteristics
    Up to 650,000 pages[a]

[a]DVI "pages" are smaller than CD-I pages. The amount of actual text is similar. Both provide enough space for over 100,000 printed pages.

Sources: Intel and American Interactive Media.

focused and pulsating. Basic math pinpoints the storage problems. The standard rate for video broadcasting in the United States is thirty frames per second. One minute of full-motion video consumes roughly 2 gigabytes of storage. In 1982, the first CD-ROM prototype was unveiled. A personal computer could now access over 600 megabytes of prerecorded digital information from one source. But even with these improvements motion video development continued to search for more powerful solutions. Some form of compression technology had to be applied to these massive data files. Digital Video Interactive technology grew from the limitations of these earlier formats. In 1987 a demonstration exhibited a DVI prototype that could deliver 72 minutes of highly compressed, full-motion video and FM quality audio.

Digital Video Interactive technology solved the storage problem with a compression scheme that can crush video files to almost 1 percent of their original size, allowing over 1 hour of playback on a standard CD-ROM. Audio signals also take advantage of this significant compression. The result is a motion video sequence with CD-quality audio merged with text and graphics that demands much less storage than most other technologies. Although the video produced is somewhat smudged, the process is distinctly ahead of any competitors for full-screen, full-motion, color video.

Implementation of DVI is through a set of add-on boards: a video board containing random-access memory (RAM) and pixel/output display processors, and an audio board with a digital processor plus utility functions such as additional memory, CD-ROM interface, and joystick capabilities.

Digital Video Interactive applications are being developed for the Intel Pro Application Development System. Authoring tools, resource databases, and corporate applications are being released, but the degraded video quality and the high cost of early systems will limit growth until improvements and volume production are realized.

Compact Disk Development

Compact-disk interactive technology is another compact disk–supported technology developed by Phillips that provides CD-quality audio, color graphics, animation, and text (see Table 1). The CD-I machine is based on the 68000 processor (Macintosh, Amiga, Atari) and gives the user the ability to interact with the finished video. It does not offer motion-video editing. This standalone device connects to existing television or audio equipment rather than to specialized computer equipment to provide multimedia functions.

Phillips, Sony, and Microsoft are developing a format now called *CD-ROM-XA* (XA = extended architecture). This system uses digital signal processing that allows interleaving of full-range audio with text and image data. Although sharing many similarities with CD-I, the CD-ROM-XA is being marketed strictly as a computer peripheral rather than as a standalone product. One of the first applications of CD-ROM-XA was a presentation jointly produced by the University of Houston and Compaq Computer Corporation to encourage President George Bush to support construction of a presidential library in Houston.

Other Developments

Digital Video Interactive and compact-disk interactive technologies also face competition from a new class of compression chips, based on the work of the Joint Photographic Experts Group (JPEG), that support high-quality video applications such as random-accessed editing. Digital electronic cameras, improved color image storage, and networking to include color printers and scanners are incorporated into these new international standards. Limitations, including some video standards and motion video storage, have spawned a parallel research program entitled Motion Pictures Experts Group (MPEG), which is striving for a completely standardized, symmetrical system. The strength of the two programs is that they are developing international standards.

The latest innovations in motion video research are plug-in video and audio boards for microcomputers. Several companies (including Video Logic, New Media Graphics, and IBM) have developed circuit boards that not only allow translation of video data from analog to digital and back, but additionally provide extensive editing capabilities. Special-effects editing features include inversion, copying, placing into "windows," and size alteration. Sound effects can be imported from music libraries, captured by the audio boards, and edited for user-designed productions.

IBM has released the M-Motion Video Adapter/A aimed at their PS/2 line of microcomputers. The video adapter was developed along with a software tool kit to provide multimedia authoring with full-motion color video and high-quality audio. Video images can be imported via videodiscs, cameras, VCRs, and closed-circuit television. Users can digitize and store music, voice, or other sound input from two standard stereo sources and listen to the audio through headphones, powered speakers, or amplified systems. Although the board and tool kit originally released constituted more of a standalone product, later releases support the AVC software program (discussed previously).

One additional development has been the release of LD-ROM by Pioneer. This additional specification to their 12-inch laser disk systems provides the user with the ability to add computer digital instructions on the same disk as the video and audio tracks.

LIMITATIONS, CAPABILITIES, DIRECTIONS

Multimedia presentations cannot be used passively. Built-in interactivity forces participation with the development and direction of the programming. Instructional materials can also take advantage of the ability to align pacing more closely with the proficiency of the learner. But if multimedia is going to persist and help guide us to new plateaus of information transfer, several potential roadblocks must be avoided. Initially, the applications must be functional. They must be perceived as part of the process of the user's work environment and not seen as an "add-on" versus embedded applications. Hardware and software developments must be readily available and reasonably priced. Simultaneously, multimedia training must address evaluation procedures to ensure that applications are appropriate for the medium and the message. Technology is not a substitute for substance.

The potential of multimedia is vast. A system that allows instructors to become facilitators of learning rather than bestowers of information is painfully needed in this time of information explosion in every area of daily life. Multimedia is the future of computers in education and training. The present limitations of speed, storage, and price will soon disappear. The motivation is there and education, business, and the military will invest significant energy in the development of multimedia modules that will facilitate efficient and effective communications with target audiences.

[*See also:* Presentation Graphics.]

For Further Reading

Ambron, S., and K. Hooper. 1990. *Learning with interactive multimedia.* Redmond, Wash., Apple Computer, Inc.

Arnett, N. 1989. Multimedia. *Infoworld,* January, pp. 35–40.

Barker, J. 1989. Behind the hype: Multimedia is a buzz word but what is it? *Times Educational Supplement,* November, p. 54.

Birkmaier, C. 1990. Opening the door to multimedia computing. *Videography* 15(7):90–93.

Butler, C. 1990. Understanding multimedia. *Audio Visual Communications,* April, pp. 34–37.

Desktop editing: The wave of the future is now. 1990. *Audio Visual Communications,* February, pp. 37–49.

D'Ignazio, F. 1990. Multimedia sandbox: An inquiry-centered classroom of the future. *The Computing Teacher,* March, pp. 16–19.

Frenkel, K. 1989. The next generation of interactive technologies. *Communications of the ACM,* July, pp. 872–80.

Holland, C., and J. St. Lawrence. 1989. *Amiga in desktop video.* Westchester, Pa.: Commodore-Amiga, Inc.

Lippincott, R. 1990. Beyond hype. *Byte,* February, pp. 215–18.

Lockwood, R. 1990. Multimedia in business: The new presentations. *Personal Computing,* June, pp. 116–26.

Long, K. Y. 1990. Multimedia: Coming thing or passing fad? *CBT Directions,* May, pp. 32–33.

Multimedia: An educator's guide. 1990. *Electronic Learning,* Special Supplement, January.

Raskin, R. 1990. Multimedia: The next frontier for business? *PC Magazine,* July, pp. 151–92.

Ripley, G. D. 1989. DVI—A digital multimedia technology. *Communications of the ACM,* July, pp. 811–22.

Robinson, P. 1990. In depth: The four multimedia gospels. *Byte,* February, pp. 204–12.

Rosenthal, S. 1990. A multimedia glossary. *PC Magazine* 19(13):158–59.

Sands, O., III, and L. R. Wallace. 1990. Multimedia is the message. *Amiga World,* February, pp. 23–24.

Stefanac, S., and L. Weiman. 1990. Multimedia: Is it real? *Macworld,* April, pp. 116–23.

Worthington, P. 1990. Market potential for multimedia is strong. *Infoworld* 12(5):43.

Terry L. Holcomb

MUSIC, COMPUTER APPLICATIONS IN

Computer music in general can be divided into two primary categories: sound production methods (e.g., commercial sound synthesizers) and music composition methods. When computer music began during the mid-1950s both the sound production and compositional processes were carried out in a single environment—the mainframe computer. Here, the composer used tedious programming methods to specify digitally the character of each individual sound component (instrument) of the musical texture, then meticulously notated the composition in computer music format as a stream of numbers standing for various features of the musical texture: pitch, rhythm, dynamics, tone color, and so forth. Additionally, the composer could ask the computer to aid in the composition of the music score on some level. For example, the computer might have been programmed to generate some random numbers, test them for suitability against a stored rule base, and assign them to one or more of the common musical elements. All the notes of a composition were entered on punch cards before the complete deck was submitted to the computer for batch processing. Then, the deck (music score) was compiled and converted to audio signals via a digital-to-analog converter, a process that often required a long delay between the act of composition and the first hearing of the result.

Although this method, called direct synthesis, is still in use today, its tediousness, the impossibility of real-time performance of the music score, and the inaccessibility of mainframe computers to musicians unaffiliated with universities and research institutions led to a separation of functions. Over several decades the areas of sound production and score composition became distinct through the advent of viable real-time, microprocessor-based music performance devices. The most notable catalyst to musical productivity was developed during the 1970s by a Stanford University computer music researcher, Dr. John Chowning. His theoretical work in the area of frequency modulation (FM) sound synthesis techniques gave rise to a generation of powerful digital tone generators that gradually replaced the analog sound synthesizers in use at numerous electronic music studios around the world.

As digital synthesizers evolved from their analog counterparts, manufacturers such as the Yamaha, Korg, Casio, New England Digital, Kurzweil, and Roland companies began (1982) to equip their instruments with MIDI (Musical Instrument Digital Interface). MIDI was originally intended to provide means for communication between synthesizers, but its environment rapidly grew to include the personal computer as composer's assistant, conductor, performer, and music publisher. During the late 1980s, MIDI and the development of polyphonic, multitimbral, digital synthesizers (which could convincingly emulate the sound qualities of traditional acoustic instruments such as the violin, clarinet, and trumpet) revolutionized every dimension of commercial music production.

It is likely that, as technology advances, these separate functions will be reunified within a single piece of hardware. In fact, the Motorola 56001 Digital Signal Processor, a powerful sound-generating device, is already being included as a standard component in at least one professional computer (the NeXTcube). This machine is capable of sampling, digitizing, storing, and reconverting external analog sound signals as well as providing means for composers to generate directly any definable sound event sequence (music score).

MUSIC INTELLIGENCE

How can the computer (rigid and mechanistic) be brought to bear on the musical arts (organic and intuitive)? Is it really possible to treat music as something that can be quantified, tested, and systematically codified in the same way that one would develop and study a computer-simulated model of a new spacecraft?

Although it may be argued that the act of creating a spiritually moving piece of music remains a mystery (aesthetics, the philosophy of artistic value systems, is still unable to adequately explain how and why an art object comes to be considered beautiful), care must be taken not to transpose this view to other, more accessible dimensions of musical structure. Leaving aside the act of creation, almost every domain of the musical event is susceptible to computational methods.

Investigators in a variety of musical disciplines are devising ways to enlist the computer's help in solving problems. A few of the major research areas are music theory, computer-aided instruction, and algorithmic composition.

Computer-Aided Instruction

Since 1975, interest in computer-aided instruction has grown rapidly. Although the most intense efforts to prepare effective computerized educational materials have been in the area of music theory, researchers in all musical disciplines are discovering ways to enlist the computer as teacher's aid. Instructional systems will continue to develop, thereby freeing the classroom teacher to deal with problems other than routine testing and drill exercises.

Algorithmic Composition

Music composition can be defined as the process of selecting from a finite set of elements (pitches, rhythms, tone colors, etc.) certain possibilities over others for presentation as a work of art. Beginning in the 1950s, musicians began to bring the computer into their employ as a tireless assistant in the composition of musical structures. Of these, two composer/experimenters, Lejaren A. Hiller in the United States and Iannis Xenakis in France, independently contributed many important techniques to automated music composition. Figure 1 is a block diagram of the structure of an interactive computer program to compose a music score, and Figure 2 illustrates the complete process of using compositional algorithms to generate a music score for performance by a digital synthesizer.

DIGITAL SOUND SYNTHESIS: HOW A COMPUTER PRODUCES SOUND

Traditional musical instruments function by setting in motion a vibrating mechanical body, which in turn produces excitations of the air waves, which, when received by a human being, are perceived as sound. We can say this takes place entirely in analog form, because the resultant sound waves are of a continuous nature and the nerve impuls-

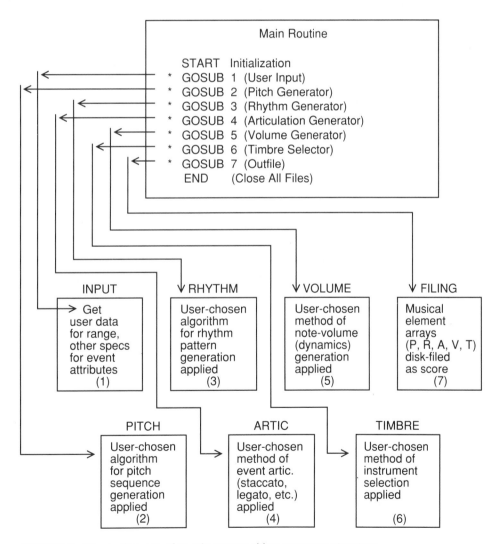

FIGURE 1. Block diagram of music composition program structure.

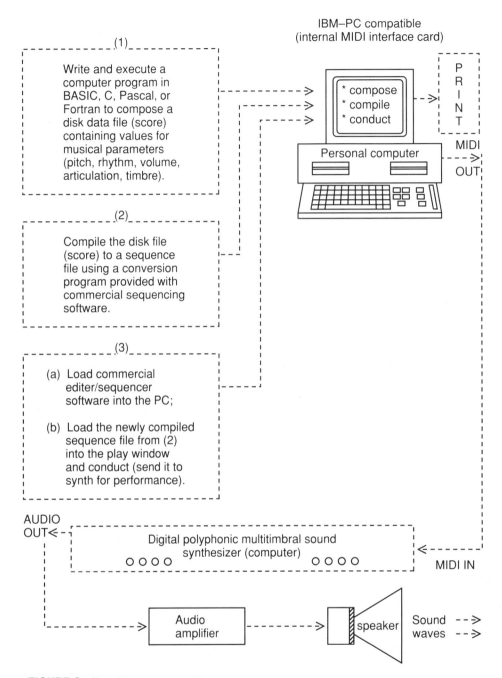

FIGURE 2. Algorithmic composition process.

es (electrical) transmitted from the human ear to the brain vary in direct proportion to the intensity of the air wave striking the eardrum. The computer, however, does not deal with continuous electrical voltages. By contrast, it consists entirely of finite-state switches, which can take on one of two possible states, on or off. (In practice, this is accomplished by a voltage that assumes either a low or a high value.) How, then, can a set of switches produce a continuous waveform intended to be perceived as a musical sound?

To create a sound wave, the computer produces a rapid stream of numbers, scaled to represent many vertical slices of an analog sound wave. It digitizes the wave by providing enough samples to allow a digital-to-analog converter to neatly fill in the blanks, or "smooth" the sound wave while converting it to an analogous electrical signal. Figure 3 is an example.

The beauty of this technique is that, because the wave information is stored in computer memory (wave table) prior to conversion, the numbers representing the sound wave can be manipulated and edited in minute detail to transform the shape, intensity, duration, and tone color of the resultant sound.

When computer music began in the 1950s, this was all done with software running on mainframe computers. Pioneer computer music researcher Max V. Mathews is credited with developing (1957) the first usable compilers (programs) for the digital synthesis of sound at the Bell Telephone Laboratories in Murray Hill, New Jersey. Mathews's compilers allowed the composer to ask the computer to produce all the numbers necessary for the description of musical sounds in all their details. To grasp the significance of this approach to sound generation, imagine a traditional musical instrument such as the clarinet that could, from one note of a score to the next, completely change its nature. That is, while playing the first pitch of a composition it might sound like an oboe, on the second pitch a pipe organ, on the third pitch an imaginary musical instrument never heard before.

During the 1960s and 1970s Mathews's compilers were used at a small group of computer music studios located at major universities such as Stanford, Princeton, and the University of Illinois. In the 1970s, research in digital technology led to the development of commercial, digital keyboard synthesizers (such as New England Digital Corporation's Synclavier) that could generate numbers fast enough to allow real-time production of sound. This created a state of affairs in which an external microcomputer was interfaced with the "hardwired" digital sound synthesizer to control macrodimensional aspects of producing the music score. The culmination of this development was in the advent of MIDI protocol, which allowed

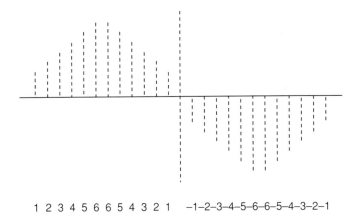

1 2 3 4 5 6 6 5 4 3 2 1   −1−2−3−4−5−6−6−5−4−3−2−1

FIGURE 3. A wave in digital form.

the transfer of control information between digital synthesizers and standard microcomputers such as the Macintosh and IBM-PC.

In a typical MIDI-based system, the microcomputer serves as "brain" to help compose, record, conduct, and print the music, as illustrated in Figure 4.

MUSIC REPRESENTATION AND ENCODING

Contemporary music notation is a synthesis of logical, symbolic, and graphic (also called iconic) elements, a hybrid system that has evolved over hundreds of years and that requires considerable practice to master. Although it allows people to communicate their musical thoughts to one another reasonably well, it is of no use in communicating with computers unless it is converted into machine language.

Because the computer is only a complex network of many on/off switches whose positions are symbolically represented as either low or high (0 or 1), a method must be devised to meaningfully translate musical information into patterns of numbers. For instance, the individual pitches of the piano keyboard can be represented by the integer set 1 to 88.

Musical parameters. Composers use the term *parameter* to refer to any quantifiable dimension of a musical structure that can be isolated and scaled according to a range of discrete numeric values along a finite continuum.

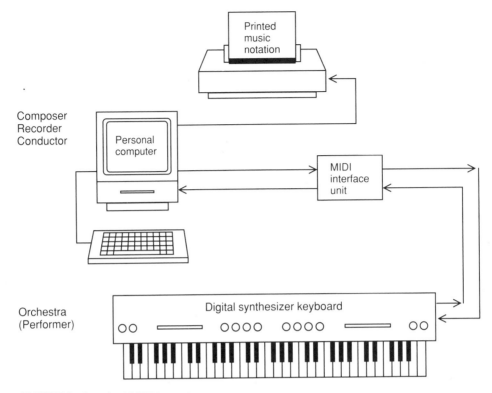

FIGURE 4. A typical MIDI-based system.

The lower-level parameters are similar to what are called the elements of music: pitch, rhythm, articulation, dynamics, and tone color. Often they are stored as a group, called a vector. It is said that a vector contains the key to an aggregate of "attributes/variables" that totally defines the important characteristics of one note event. For example, a hypothetical event vector containing data for five parameters (musical elements) can be visualized as shown in Figure 5.

In computer terms, a vector is a multidimensional array used to store the specific values (states) of every musical variable associated with each note event. The total collection of array addresses along an imaginary line (1 to n) that contain the succession of note events is termed the *notelist*. Figure 6 is a

two-dimensional array that holds values for the pitch and rhythm parameters of a note-list (sequence of pitches) of order (length) ten.

Today, a great deal of microcomputer software is available for MIDI-interfaced synthesizers that allows extensive viewing, editing, and polishing of musical material. The musician can use this software either to enter the notes of the score from a computer or synthesizer keyboard or to compile a score from the output of an interactive algorithmic composition program. Subsequently, the score can be performed by the computer and/or printed in conventional music notation on standard printers.

FUTURE RESEARCH AND DEVELOPMENT

Although it is impossible to foresee with certainty the direction research will take in the coming years, products will undoubtedly be developed in the following areas:

- Music notation optical scanning devices and software to interpret various notation

NOTE–EVENT #1

PITCH	DURATION	VOLUME	ARTICULATION	TIMBRE
C#3	Eighth–Note	fff	Staccato	Clarinet

FIGURE 5. Example of an event vector.

systems and automatically perform music scores on MIDI synthesizers

- Devices and software to sample digitally music improvised by various acoustic instrument ensembles and convert it to music notation
- Complex sound synthesis devices built into personal computers
- Automatic composition software geared to the needs of the entertainment industry (programs that will instantly compose music in a variety of styles)

[*See also:* Arts, Computer in the.]

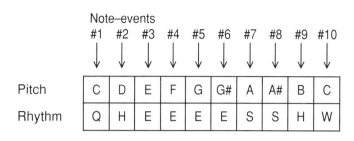

Rhythm Key: W = Whole–note   H = Half–note
Q = Quarter–note   E = Eighth–note
S = Sixteenth–note

FIGURE 6. Example of a notelist.

For Further Reading

Bateman, W. 1980. *Introduction to computer music.* New York: Wiley-Interscience.

Cope, D. 1987. *Experiments in music intelligence.* San Francisco: Computer Music Association.

———. 1987. An expert system for computer-assisted composition. *Computer Music Journal* 11(4):30–46.

Dietrich, F. 1987. The computer: A tool for thought experiments. *Leonardo* 20(4):315–25.

Dodge, C., and T. Jerse. 1985. *Computer music synthesis, composition, and performance.* New York: Schirmer Books.

Evans, B. 1987. *Integration of music and graphics through algorithmic congruence.* Proceedings of the International Computer Music Conference, University of Illinois, Urbana, 1987.

Hiller, L., and L. Isaacson. 1959. *Experimental music.* New York: McGraw-Hill.

Holtzman, S. R. 1981. Using generative grammars for music composition. *Computer Music Journal* 5(1):51–64.

Jones, K. 1985. Compositional applications of stochastic processes. *Computer Music Journal* 5(2):45–56.

Lidov, D., and J. Gabura. 1973. A melody writing algorithm using a formal language model. *Computer Studies in the Humanities* 4(3/4):138–48.

Roads, C. 1979. Grammars as representations for music. *Computer Music Journal* 3(1):48–55.

———, ed. 1985. *Composers and the computer.* Cambridge, Mass.: MIT Press.

———. 1985. Research in music and artificial intelligence. *ACM Computing Surveys* 17(2):163–90.

Roads, C., and J. Strawn, eds. 1985. *The foundations of computer music.* Cambridge, Mass.: MIT Press.

Scarborough, D. L., B. O. Miller, and J. A. Jones. 1989. Connectionist models for tonal analysis. *Computer Music Journal* 13(3):48–61.

Tipei, S. 1988. MAIDEN VOYAGES—A score produced with MP1. *Computer Music Journal* 11(2):49–58.

———. 1990. The computer: A composer's collaborator. *Leonardo* 22(2):189–95.

Todd, P. 1989. A connectionist approach to algorithmic composition. *Computer Music Journal* 13(4).

Whitney, J. 1980. *Digital harmony: On the complementarity of music and visual art.* New York: McGraw-Hill.

Winograd, T. 1968. Linguistics and the computer analysis of tonal harmony. *Journal of Music Theory* 12:2–49.

Winsor, P. 1987. *Computer-assisted music composition.* Princeton, N.J.: Petrocelli Books.

———. 1989. *The computer composer's toolbox.* Blue Ridge Summit, Pa.: Windcrest Books.

———., and G. Delisa. 1990. *Computer music in C.* New York: McGraw-Hill.

Xenakis, I. 1971. Free stochastic music from the computer. In J. Reichardt, ed. *Cybernetics, art and ideas.* Greenwich, Conn.: New York Graphic Society.

———. 1971. *Formalized music.* Bloomington: Indiana University Press.

Phil Winsor

N

NATURAL COMPUTING

See Cybernetics and Natural Computing

NATURAL-LANGUAGE PROCESSING

Computers can process text with ease, but computer *understanding* of text is still more dream than reality. It's one thing to search for a word in a database; it's quite another to determine the meaning that the writer intended in a sentence. But there are now programs that can be said to understand natural-language texts—that is, texts written in human languages such as English and Japanese (see also SPEECH TO PRINT).

Language itself is extremely complex. People comprehend language with such ease that it's often hard to see where the problems are until one starts programming. Modern theoretical linguistics dates only from the 1950s—a science no older than computing itself. It's easy to forgive the pioneers of computational linguistics for thinking that fully automatic machine translation would require little more than a bilingual dictionary and some rules of inflection.

The enormous advantages to be gained from computer understanding of natural languages have spurred the field on despite the failures due to its initial naïveté. If the computer can communicate in the user's language, database interfaces and computer-aided instruction can be made easier and more effective. The comprehension of full written texts is the basis for applications such as machine translation and the automatic creation of KNOWLEDGE BASES AND EXPERT SYSTEMS.

"Understanding" is a nebulous concept. What would it mean for a computer to understand something? In a paper published in 1950, not long before his death, computing pioneer Alan TURING suggested that behavior was what counted. If a computer responds to some linguistic input the way a human would in the same situation, then it has understood it. Although no one would suggest that today's natural-language understanding programs are as good as humans—certainly, the programs lack the breadth and flexibility of human understanding—they nevertheless can perform their tasks well, though limited to narrow domains.

This article deals only with computer processing of written language. For the special problems of speech input and output, see SPEECH TO PRINT and SPEECH RECOGNITION AND SYNTHESIS.

WHAT'S INVOLVED IN UNDERSTANDING

A basic natural-language understanding system (see Figure 1) typically contains a *parser* and *grammar*, a *semantic interpreter*, and an *application module*. In addition, it needs a *lexicon* or *dictionary*, and possibly a *knowledge base*.

The job of the parser is to analyze the input for its syntax, creating a tree structure that shows, for each word in the sentence, what its part of speech is and how it fits into the larger structure of the sentence, much as is often taught in high-school language classes. For example, Figure 2 shows the result of parsing the sentence "Peter Piper picked a peck of pickled peppers."

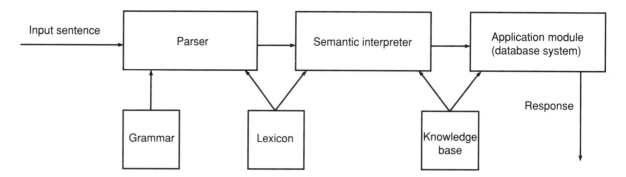

FIGURE 1. The organization of a typical natural-language interface to a database system.

In theory, at least, the parser is independent of any particular language. It is given a grammar and a lexicon (a list of words) for the language that it is to operate upon. For example, a very simple grammar might say that in English a sentence (S) is made up of a noun phrase (NP) followed by a verb phrase (VP), and a verb phrase is a verb (V) followed by a noun phrase. This might be written like this:

$$S \rightarrow NP\ VP$$

$$VP \rightarrow V\ NP$$

Given, in turn, rules for what constitutes a noun phrase and a lexicon that says, for example, that *pick* is a verb, a parser could use these rules to analyze the sentence in Figure 2. Parsing has received considerable attention, for there are now grammars of considerable sophistication for English and other major languages.

The stage after parsing is semantic interpretation—taking the parse tree and figuring out what the sentence actually means. This includes deciding which sense the speaker or writer intends if a word or phrase is ambiguous, deciding what the pronouns stand for, and so on. Generally this stage involves translating the sentence into some kind of representation of its meaning. This representation could be a logic of some kind—possibly one of the many formalisms for knowledge representation developed in ARTI-

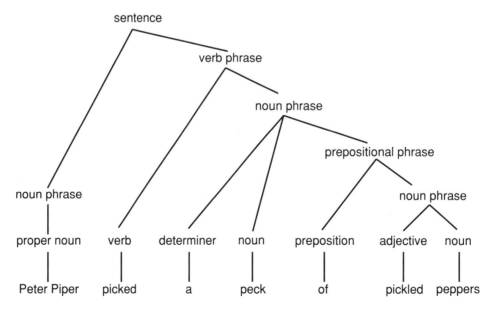

FIGURE 2. Tree structure created by a parser for the sentence "Peter Piper picked a peck of pickled peppers."

FICIAL INTELLIGENCE (AI)—or a statement in the input format for some other program.

In practice, parsing and semantic interpretation are frequently run together in parallel. That's because often the meaning of the earlier parts of a sentence will influence how the later parts are to be parsed. For example, consider these sentences:

> The tourists told the guide that they couldn't understand.

> The tourists complained about the guide that they couldn't understand.

In the first sentence the clause "that they couldn't understand" describes what the tourists said; in the second, it describes the guide. To decide how the words should be parsed in each case requires knowing what the earlier part of the sentence means.

The final stage of understanding is for the system to act upon what the sentence is saying. If it is a question, that would probably mean answering it; if it is an assertion of fact, it would probably mean storing it. Often this final stage is a separate, preexisting program to which the natural-language program is acting as an interface.

DATABASE INTERFACES

Perhaps the simplest application of natural-language understanding is in interactive interfaces to DATABASES and the like. The most basic interface need understand only a single sentence at a time, and if an input should defeat it, it can ask the user to clarify or to choose from one of several interpretations. Typically such interfaces parse the input, translate it into a database query language, and send it off to the database, whose response is then presented to the user. The kinds of questions that could be asked might be "What companies reported a loss last year?" or "Where is Boise?"

Of course, if the system is to be more of a help than a hindrance, it will usually require additional features. A sentence should be interpreted in context, with pronoun references to previous input or output being resolved. The system should not have to ask for clarification too often, and certainly not have to ask again if a subsequent sentence contains the same difficulty. In addition, it must be able to cope with badly spelled, ungrammatical, and *elliptical* input, just as any human could. An elliptical utterance is one in which words that are obvious are left out; this is especially common in follow-up queries. For example, a user who asks, "What companies reported a loss last year?" should be able to follow up with "In 1984?" or "A profit?" and have the system infer how that fits into the context.

Nor should a system be too literal. A user who says "I need the phone numbers of all the New Mexico sales staff" expects some names to appear next to the list of phone numbers. A user who asks for "the sales staff making more than $40,000 and less than $80,000" should get a list of people whose salary meets both conditions simultaneously; but one who asks for "the sales staff based in New York and Montreal" should get staff in either city and not be told there aren't any (because some are in New York and some in Montreal, but none are in both places at once).

The first commercially available piece of natural-language software was a database interface. The Intellect system, released in 1981 by the Artificial Intelligence Corporation of Waltham, Massachusetts, was for many years alone on the market. Intellect runs under the major IBM mainframe operating systems and can interface with a variety of database systems. But natural-language systems are also available for personal computers. The first such system, and probably the best-known, is Q&A, by Symantec Corporation of Cupertino, California. Q&A includes a full database system and a natural-language interface that the user can customize to his or her own database by supplying an appropriate lexicon.

TEXT UNDERSTANDING AND KNOWLEDGE REPRESENTATION

The problems of understanding a single sentence are complex enough. Machine comprehension of an extended coherent text is an order of magnitude more difficult again. That's because it requires understanding not only each individual sentence but also the implicit relationships among them that form the larger picture being built up.

Consider this text of just two sentences:

> The governor is sure to be defeated. The new tax system is very unpopular.

A full understanding of this text includes realizing that the first sentence is a conclusion that has been drawn, and the second sentence is some evidence that the speaker or writer is presenting in its support. But it's not the order of the sentences that matters, for they might just as easily have been reversed:

> The new tax system is very unpopular. The governor is sure to be defeated.

Rather, what's needed is not just knowledge about the structure of arguments, but also knowledge about politics and elections—and about how other people might reason, whether one happens to agree with their conclusions or not.

In other words, for a computer (or a human) to understand a text requires extensive knowledge of the *domain of discourse*—of the topic that's being talked about. Research in text and discourse understanding, therefore, has focused both on the nature and structure of discourse itself and also on the more general problem, from AI, of how knowledge about the world can be represented in a computer and deployed as necessary. Quite a number of knowledge representation formalisms have been developed, though none yet has anything close to the expressive power required—the ability to express not only anything that can be said in natural language but also all the knowledge that we carry in our heads that defies linguistic expression.

OTHER APPLICATIONS

There are many conceivable applications for intelligent text understanding systems. For example, an expert system for advising physicians could keep its knowledge up to date by reading the new medical literature each week. And systems with extensive encyclopedic knowledge bases could answer questions for people by actually understanding and digesting the text at their disposal.

Such systems are still far off. But an application that is much closer to hand is *machine translation.* That's because in machine translation, systems can be built to operate with human assistance to get them over the parts that are still too difficult for any computer program. For example, Siemens's METAL system (described by Slocum) for German-to-English translation relies on a well-maintained terminology bank and simple semantic features. But METAL's translations must be "postedited" by professional translators to correct errors and make the output more readable. Current research in machine translation emphasizes methods of giving the system greater ability to recognize the meaning of the text and thus minimize the amount of human help needed.

NATURAL-LANGUAGE GENERATION

Understanding language is only half of how humans use language. The other half, of course, is producing it in the first place. Natural-language generation—computer creation of natural-language text—is rapidly becoming an important subfield. Synthesizing text has always been required in machine translation systems, where understanding the input is just the first half of the problem; a translation has to be produced. But there is now a greater emphasis on systems that can take a representation of what is to be said and turn it into a coherent, well-expressed paragraph. Like any writer, the system has to decide what order to say things in, how the ideas are to be incorporated into sentences, what is to be emphasized and how, and perhaps even what is to remain unsaid. For example, the Pauline system of the Information Sciences Institute of Los Angeles (described by Hovy) can describe the same situation from many different perspectives and can also vary its style in response to the "situation" in which it is "speaking." It can be formal or informal, respectful or disrespectful.

But many problems stem from an inability, so far, of systems to deal with the more subtle aspects of language. For example, a machine translation system should be able to preserve in its translation all the stylistic nuances of the original—its degree of formality, dynamism, simplicity, or even deliberate obscurity. Achieving the same stylistic effect in different languages may require quite different words and structures in each. The Stylistique system, developed at the Universities of Toronto and Waterloo by DiMarco and Hirst, is "goal-directed"—that is, it tries to determine exactly what effect the original writer intended, and then do what's necessary to carry that effect over into the translation.

THE FUTURE

As natural-language understanding techniques continue to develop, software of increasing sophistication will enter the market. Ovum Ltd., a London-based market consultancy, has predicted that natural-language systems will be a $2 billion industry before the end of the century.

For Further Reading

Allen, J. 1987. *Natural language understanding.* Menlo Park, Calif.: Benjamin/Cummings. A university-level introduction to the field.

Cohen, R. 1987. Analyzing the structure of argumentative discourse. *Computational Linguistics* 13(1):11–24.

DiMarco, C., and G. Hirst. 1990. Accounting for style in machine translation. Paper presented at 3rd International Conference on Theoretical Issues in Machine Translation, Austin, June 1990.

Gazdar, G., and C. Mellish. 1989. *Natural language processing in LISP; Natural language processing in POP-11;* and *Natural language processing in PROLOG.* Wokingham, Eng.: Addison-Wesley. A series of introductory textbooks, each based on a particular programming language.

Grishman, R. 1986. *Computational linguistics.* Cambridge, Eng.: Cambridge University Press. A university-level introduction.

Grosz, B., K. Sparck Jones, and B. Webber. 1986. *Readings in natural language processing.* San Mateo, Calif.: Morgan Kaufmann. A collection of important research papers.

Hovy, E. 1990. Pragmatics and natural language generation. *Artificial Intelligence* 43:153–97.

McTear, M. 1987. *The articulate computer.* Oxford, Eng.: Basil Blackwell. A good, detailed introduction to the field that requires no previous background.

Schank, R., and C. Riesbeck, eds. 1981. *Inside computer understanding.* Hillsdale, N.J.: Lawrence Erlbaum Associates. Examples of some natural-language systems and how they are programmed.

Slocum, J. 1988. *Machine translation systems.* Cambridge, Eng.: Cambridge University Press. Includes a history of machine translation, and descriptions of a number of projects.

Turing, A. M. 1950. Computing machinery and intelligence. *Mind* 59:433–60. Reprinted in E. A. Feigenbaum and J. Feldman, eds. *Computers and thought.* New York: McGraw-Hill, 1963, pp. 11–35, and A. M. Collins and E. E. Smith, eds. *Readings in cognitive science.* San Mateo, Calif.: Morgan Kaufmann, 1989, pp. 6–19.

The following journals specialize in papers on current research in natural-language understanding:

Computational Linguistics. Published by The MIT Press, Cambridge, Mass., for the Association for Computational Linguistics, Morristown, N.J.

Computer Speech and Language Processing. Academic Press, London.

Machine Translation. Kluwer Academic Publishers, Dordrecht, Netherlands.

Graeme Hirst

NAVIGATIONAL USE OF COMPUTERS

The computer has been a key part of navigation from the very beginning. Until recently, though, that computer was the gray one between the ears of the navigator.

The navigator's job is divided into three parts: (1) estimating an initial, working position; (2) checking the working position with a second position called a fix; (3) weighing the relative merits of these two positions (they are usually close, but never agree exactly) and making a judgment of the vessel's most probable position.

As all voyages, flights, and trips begin from a known place at a known time, the position of any floating, flying, or rolling vehicle at any time can always be estimated by looking at the record of the direction steered and the distance run from the point of departure. This is essentially what anyone traveling a highway from one city to another does almost without thinking: keeps mental track of the car's speed and the time on the road. At sea and aloft, a compass course takes the place of the road. The navigator keeps a record of courses and speeds in a notebook called a *log* and, at regular intervals, marks the craft's approximate position on a map or chart.

The position found in this manner is traditionally referred to as the *dead reckoning position* or (*DR*). The phrase is supposed to be a corruption of *deduced reckoning*, but no one really knows the origin.

When land is in sight, a navigator can check this DR by taking compass bearings to find the angles between landmarks and applying plane trigonometry. Centuries ago, this was the only position-confirming technique available to navigators. If there was no land visible, dead reckoning was the sum and total of navigation.

When Christopher Columbus set out across the Atlantic for China in 1492, for example, his ships kept their dead reckoning by turning over a sand glass every half-hour and recording the course steered by inserting a peg into a plank on which compass courses were represented by columns of holes. It was navigation by egg timer and cribbage board.

The ability to check the DR when out of sight of land had to await the development of a clock that could go to sea without going haywire, and that did not happen until 1736.

Once dependable clocks were available, however, timetables of the stars' positions, called *ephemerides* or *almanacs,* could go to sea as the basis for the position-fixing technique of celestial navigation.

The basic theory of celestial navigation has been known since about 200 B.C. and the data needed to make it work—tables of the hourly positions of the sun, moon, stars, and planets—had been piling up in observatories for centuries. But without an accurate

clock, these ephemerides were useless to seafarers.

Given a source of reliable time, a navigator now could look up the locations of two or more stars in an almanac, measure their angles above the horizon with an instrument called a sextant, determine his or her distances from the points on the earth directly underneath those stars by applying spherical trigonometry, and put an "X" on a chart where the distances crossed. Because this position, called a celestial fix, is produced by reference to something other than the shipboard compass and speedometer, it is a means of confirming the DR. Until the advent of radio, celestial fixes were the only means of checking the DR when out of sight of land. Over the next two centuries celestial navigation developed into an extremely useful part of navigation, aloft as well as afloat, and it is still widely used today.

Before the electronic microchip arrived, the computer in navigation was the navigator. The navigator made observations, and solved mathematical equations into which he or she entered data from those observations and almanacs. To solve the equations the navigator usually used tables of logarithms. Putting it into contemporary computer terms, these observations were the input, the almanacs and other tables were the databases, the formulas were the programs, and the navigator was the central processing unit.

This was essentially the situation until the invention of the microchip. Then, of course, the personal calculator and, finally, the microcomputer came along and took over the tasks of storing data and solving equations. To the navigator was left the role of making the observations—collecting the input for the calculator or computer.

The electronic chip made possible an even more momentous change, however: digital instruments, instruments the output of which was in a form a computer could understand. For example, digitizing the compass and speedometer made it possible to hook them to a computer and create an automatic dead reckoning keeper. One such device is the dead reckoning analyzer indicator (DRAI). At the start of a trip the navigator enters the latitude and longitude of the departure point; from then on, the DRAI keeps track of courses and speeds and continuously displays the resulting latitudes and longitudes.

The navigator can check the DRAI positions by celestial fixes or can make use of fixes produced by one or more of the other new devices made possible by the marriage of radio receiver and microchip. Colloquially known as "black boxes," the ones most widely used these days are Omega and Loran. Like celestial navigation, Omega and Loran produce fixes by reference to things external to the vessel or aircraft, not stars in this case, but radio waves transmitted by towers strategically placed around the globe.

The ultimate dead reckoning machine is the inertial navigator. Inside this device three gyroscopes hold a reference plane perfectly level and sensors called *accelerometers* detect the slightest movements of the plane up, down, or sideways. A computer keeps track of all these little movements and resolves them into a DR that shows not only latitude and longitude, but also altitude above or depth below the starting point. Inertial navigation systems, as these are called, are widely used in submarines, long-range aircraft, and the space shuttle.

Any DR, even one produced by a state-of-the-art inertial navigator, needs to be checked, of course. Checking and cross-checking are the most important jobs of the traditional, human navigator: to periodically get a fix from the stars, Loran, Omega, radar or optical bearings; to compare the fix with the DR; and to arrive at a judgment of the vessel's most likely location. As a rule, if a navigator judges the DR and fix to be in tolerable agreement, the fix is taken as correct and a new DR track is begun from it. If a navigator does not think the DR and fix agree closely enough, the DR is continued until another fix can be had.

Although judgment cannot come from a computer, a very close approximation of it can be achieved by statistical programs that weigh the relative accuracies of a fix or fixes compared with the DR and arrive at a most probable position. It is then up to the human who rides herd on the machine to decide if its decision makes sense or not. (An example of a computer that stopped making sense is HAL, costar of the movie *2001*.)

Just as computers have made it possible to automate the dead reckoning side of navigation, they have also been used to automate the position-fixing side. One system, for example, is a computer containing a highly accurate internal clock and almanacs of all the celestial bodies. To it is hooked a digital sextant on which the navigator pushes a button when he or she has the stars in its sights. The computer reads the angles, notes the times, looks up the data in the almanac, computes the fix, and displays it.

The next step in automating celestial navigation was elimination of the human being and the sextant. The replacement for this venerable instrument (through the ages, the virtual symbol of navigation) is the automatic star tracker, a computer-guided photo-electric telescope that constantly tracks three or more stars and can be set to produce either a continuous string of fixes or fixes on demand. In continuous mode they are used in long-range fighter–bombers. In demand mode they are used through the periscopes of submarines as one source of checking or updating the positions given by the inertial system.

The ultimate position-fixing devices made possible by the computer are satellites, manmade electronic stars in orbits high above the earth. They do not twinkle; they talk—send coded radio messages to yet another kind of black box that translates these signals into latitudes and longitudes. Currently the United States has six of these satellites in operation in the so-called NAV-SAT program. These navigational satellites went into service for the U.S. Navy in 1964 and became available for civil use in 1967.

As of 1990 an even more sophisticated satellite program is underway. It is called the Global Positioning System and is referred to as GPS or NAVSTAR. Compared with NAV-SAT, GPS uses many more satellites (18 with 3 spares) in higher orbits (11,000 miles versus 700 miles). More satellites means no gaps in the coverage, better internal cross-checking to detect faulty satellites or transmissions, and the ability to give the altitude as

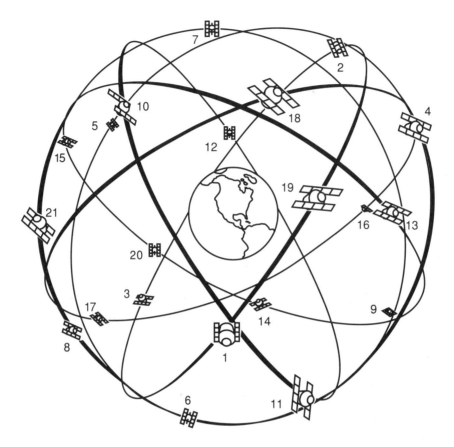

FIGURE 1. The NAVSTAR operational constellation: eighteen satellites plus three active spares.

well as the latitude and longitude of a fix. When fully operational it will replace NAV-SAT.

Inertial navigators can also be updated by other position-fixing devices or techniques, that is, by radar or optical ranges and bearings when in sight of land, and by Omega and Loran when along shore or at sea. In a fully automated inertial navigation system, all fix-generating devices are linked directly to a main computer that continuously monitors and evaluates the incoming data, compares and cross-checks fixes and DRs, and displays the most probable position from moment to moment.

At present such complete systems are used only on missile-carrying submarines and capital ships such as aircraft carriers and cruisers. A total Ships Inertial Navigation System, as it is called, is large, heavy, and very expensive. Commercial ships and yachts usually rely on Loran, Omega, or NAVSAT. Long-range commercial aircraft normally have more than one inertial navigator on board. Updated by Omega, Loran, or NAVSAT, they also can cross-check each other.

When all is said and done, navigation is the art and science of checking one thing against another. If the vessel is slow or the available methods of cross-checking few, a human can do it. But when the craft is speedy or a lot of information is coming in from a swarm of electronic devices, only a computer can keep up.

For Further Reading

American practical navigator, 2 vols.: NVPUB-9V1 (1984) and NVPUB9V2 (1981). Washington, D.C.: Defense Mapping Agency Hydrographic/Topographic Center. Called "The Tome" or "Bowditch" after its originator, Salem shipmaster Nathaniel Bowditch. Exhaustive: 2,000 pages of the lore, science, and art of navigation.

Dutton's navigation & piloting, 14th ed. 1985. Annapolis, Md.: Naval Institute Press. Textbook of the U.S. Naval Academy. Descriptive and practical. Great deal less math and theory than Bowditch, especially on inertial, radio, and satellite navigation systems.

Navigation. Journal of the Institute of Navigation, Washington, D.C. Professional journal. Highly technical.

Ocean Navigator, Portland, Maine. General boating magazine with emphasis on navigating and voyaging in small craft (roughly, 30- to 65-footers).

Hewitt Schlereth

NETWORK DATABASES

See Database Management

NETWORKS, COMPUTER

With widespread automation, more and more information is being captured in electronic form and processed by computers as data. When information required in an application originates from several sources located at different sites, computers at these sites must communicate to exchange data. We encode data as electronic or optical signals for propagation over a transmission medium that provides the communication link between the communicating sites. A computer network is a set of computers and computer-related devices connected to each other by communication links. In a computer network, communication links may be constituted of a variety of media, ranging from copper wire to air.

A direct link by way of a transmission medium between two computers is called a point-to-point link. When communicating units are far apart, it is often impractical to provide a point-to-point link between them. In such situations, the computers are attached to a communications network, a collection of interconnected functional units that provide a data communications service among computers attached to the network. In most communication sessions there is one transmitter or source of data and a corresponding receiver or destination. The transmitter and the receiver must follow a complex set of rules and conventions called *protocols* for proper communication. Two communicating partners can exchange messages only if they follow the same protocol. To facilitate the development of networks and networking applications that can run on diverse platforms, international standards for communication protocols are developed.

This article is an introduction to various aspects of computer networking. The following topics are included: data communication concepts, communication media for networking, characterization of computer networks, and communication protocol standards.

DATA COMMUNICATION BASICS

From the transmission standpoint, there are two kinds of data: *analog* and *digital.* Voice and video are examples of analog data. Text and integers are examples of digital data. Digital data assume values from a discrete set, whereas analog data take values from a continuously varying set of values. It is the signals that transmit data along a suitable medium. Like data, signals may be analog or digital. An analog signal is a continuously varying electromagnetic wave. A digital signal is just a sequence of pulses. A signal has three characteristics: amplitude, frequency, and phase. These characteristics are varied to represent data. Data encoding is the process of transforming input data or signals into signals that can be transmitted. The *amplitude* indicates the voltage level of the signal. The *frequency* of a signal is described in units of hertz (Hz). One hertz means one oscillation per second. Both analog and digital data can be propagated by either analog or digital signals. The term *signaling* refers to the propagation of signals along a transmission medium.

For the communication system, digital data are nothing but a sequence of 0s and

1s. Digital data, like text, which is a sequence of characters, are converted to binary data by using a code such as ASCII (American Standard Code for Information Interchange) or EBCDIC (Extended Binary Coded Decimal Interchange Code). In EBCDIC, a character is represented by a unique 8-bit pattern. In ASCII, 7-bit patterns are used for the same purpose. However, characters are usually transmitted in units of 8 bits called *octets* or *bytes.* In ASCII, the eighth bit can be used for parity.

By using different voltage levels for binary digits 1 and 0, digital data can be easily represented by digital signals. One may also use analog signals to represent digital data. The device used for this purpose is called a *modem* (modulator/demodulator). A modem accepts digital bits and changes them into an analog signal. This transformation process is known as *modulation.* At the receiving end, the modem receives the analog signal and converts it back to its original digital representation. This reverse transformation is *demodulation.*

To represent analog data by an analog signal is simple. An analog signal of the same frequency as the given analog data will directly encode it. It is also possible to represent analog data by digital signals. The device used for this purpose is analogous to a modem. For voice data, the above device is a *codec* (coder/decoder). The codec takes an analog signal representing voice data and approximates that signal by a stream of 0s and 1s. At the receiving end, the sequence of binary digits is used to regenerate the original analog data.

Both analog and digital signals may be transmitted on appropriate transmission media. A transmission system may treat the signals differently during propagation. As with data and signals, there are two ways of transmission: analog and digital. In *analog transmission,* the transmission system propagates analog signals (representing analog or digital data) as such without any interpretation. All signals become weaker (attenuate) after a certain distance. Therefore, after appropriate distances, amplifiers are used to strengthen the signal during propagation. Unfortunately, the amplifiers enhance not only the signal but also the noise in the

signal. This distortion in the signal is not always tolerable. However, in the case of analog data such as voice, a distorted signal may still be intelligible. In *digital transmission,* the transmission system employs repeaters before the signal distorts. A repeater, upon receiving the digital signal, extracts the pattern of 1s and 0s from it and regenerates the signal. The regenerated signal has no noise in it and is as good as the original signal. The current trend is to move toward digital transmission.

TRANSMISSION MEDIA

Many characteristics of a computer network —its speed, cost, and physical range—depend largely on the medium it uses to transmit messages. Most common types of transmission media use a physical cable to carry the transmitted information. However, one can also transmit data without a cable by using electromagnetic waves through free space. Some common types of transmission media are discussed next.

Twisted Pair Cable

A twisted pair cable is made with a pair of copper wires twisted together. The twisted pairs are usually bundled together and enclosed in a single cable. With some twisted pair cables, an additional insulating material is wrapped around the two twisted wires. The resulting cable is called a shielded twisted pair. A shielded twisted pair is more immune to interference than an unshielded twisted pair.

Twisted pair cable is used extensively in the telephone system to carry voice. It is inexpensive and easy to install. A major disadvantage of twisted pair cable is its relatively low bandwidth—that is, its low capacity for carrying information. Therefore, twisted pair cable is used only in low-speed networks (transmission speed of 1 megabit per second or less).

Coaxial Cable

Coaxial cable has four parts. The first is the inner conductor, a solid metal wire. It is surrounded by the second part, insulation.

The third part, a thin, tubular piece of metal screen, surrounds the insulation. Its axis of curvature coincides with that of the inner conductor (therefore the term *coaxial*). The fourth part is an outer plastic cover that surrounds the rest. Coaxial cable offers much greater speed than twisted pair cable (up to 100 megabits per second) and is impervious to external electrical signals.

Fiber-optic Cable

A fiber-optic cable is a bundle of strands of glass or plastic. It differs from metal cables in that it carries the transmitted data in the form of a fluctuating beam of light rather than an electrical signal. Because of the use of a light beam, fiber-optic cable is immune to electromagnetic interference. Fiber-optic cables are rapidly replacing metal cables, because the former are lighter, cheaper, and capable of extremely high transmission speeds. A standard coaxial cable can transmit 5,000 voice conversations at once, whereas a fiber-optic cable can transmit ten times as many.

Microwaves

Wires and cables are suitable for connecting computers and devices in the same room or building. With computers located far apart, it is very costly, and even impossible in some cases, to lay down and maintain cable connections. Since the telephone networks were already in place before the arrival of computer networks, it is possible to employ the communication services of telephone networks for interconnecting computers. Telephones and modems provide a low-speed method of connecting remote computers. For a higher transmission speed, it is possible to lease a special dedicated telephone line to connect a pair of computers. A dedicated point-to-point line is useful when there is a need to transmit large amounts of information continually.

An alternative to cables is the microwave. Microwaves are extremely short radio waves that have a high bandwidth. Microwave relay stations transmit data and voice signals between distant locations. Microwaves are commonly used for transmitting voice and video images. Microwave trans-

mission is quite focused, and microwaves cannot bend around the earth's curvature. This puts an upper limit on the length of a point-to-point microwave link. This limitation is overcome using communication satellites for microwave transmission. A communication satellite provides an indirect link between two or more microwave transmitter/receivers known as ground stations. The communication satellite receives transmissions on one frequency from the sending station but transmits on a different frequency for the receiving station. Furthermore, a satellite repeats or amplifies the signal before retransmission. An important difference between a direct microwave link and indirect link by satellite is that transmission in the former case stations is quite focused, but not so in the latter case. The satellite microwave transmission is broadcast transmission. In other words, a transmission from a satellite can be received by many ground stations, and many stations can directly transmit to the same satellite. In addition to microwaves, radio waves of other frequencies may also be used for communication between computers.

COMPUTER NETWORKING

A computer network involves many components, such as terminals and computers, spread over large distances. It is obvious that a direct point-to-point link between all pairs of communicating partners is impossible to provide. In the absence of a point-to-point connection between two computers, messages exchanged by them must pass through several intermediate processors. The role played by the intermediate processors in assisting message propagation is referred to as *switching*. One way to characterize a computer network is by the switching technique it employs.

There are two major switching techniques: *circuit switching* and *packet switching*. In circuit switching, a direct communication path is first established through the communication network between the transmitter and the receiver. This path is then exclusively used throughout the communication session. A circuit-switched data network (CSDN) employs circuit switching in its operation. Public telephone networks are prime examples of CSDNs.

Packet switching is an alternative to circuit switching and is designed specifically for communication of data. In contrast to circuit switching, no communication path is established in advance between the transmitter and the receiver. Each message to be transmitted is first divided into smaller chunks, called packets. Each packet is then forwarded one hop at a time. When an intermediate processor receives a packet, it stores the packet and inspects it. If that processor is not the final intended receiver of the packet, it is forwarded to an adjacent (directly connected) processor. Eventually, after several hops the packet reaches the destined receiver. A data network employing packet switching in its operation is referred to as a packet-switched data network (PSDN). The prime examples of PSDN are ARPANET, BITNET, and TYMNET. ARPANET is the network created by the Defense Advanced Research Projects Agency of the U.S. Department of Defense and interconnects computer science departments of a large number of universities. ARPANET became operational in 1969. The network TYMNET is contemporary to ARPANET but was set up for accessing time-sharing mainframe computers by remote terminals rather than for computer-to-computer communication. The network BITNET, started in 1981, is a worldwide university network and unlike ARPANET is not confined to just computer science departments.

The networks described above are all made up of point-to-point links between intermediate processors called switches or IMPs (intermediate message processors). These networks span very large distances and therefore are also referred to as long-haul networks or WIDE AREA NETWORKS (WANs). In contrast to a WAN, a LOCAL AREA NETWORK (LAN) is a smaller network, covering at most 10 kilometers (6.2 miles). A LAN interconnects computers and devices owned by a single organizational unit. Furthermore, a LAN employs a broadcast medium that is either a common bus or a ring. Ethernet, pioneered by Xerox Corporation, is a popular bus-based LAN technology. In the ring arena, the IBM token ring is the standard. A LAN is a broadcast network. The message transmitted on the media physically reaches every connected device but is accepted only by the unit to which it has been addressed. A message can be addressed to more than one or to all recipients. Such a style of communication is referred to as multicasting or broadcasting. Many local area networks are set up to allow many microcomputers to share an expensive resource, such as a large hard disk or a laser printer. Other networks are established to share global information conveniently.

There are other broadcast networks besides LANs. A *packet radio network* is a broadcast network that uses radio waves for transmission. Ground-based antennas provide broadcast links among multiple locations. The first packet radio network was developed by the University of Hawaii. Called ALOHANET, the network became operational in 1970.

COMMUNICATION PROTOCOLS AND STANDARDS

A communication protocol is a set of rules that must be followed by communicating partners for proper communication. A message sent by a transmitter can be received correctly by a receiver only if the receiver follows the same protocol as the transmitter. Computer networking has evolved rapidly and over several different platforms. As such there are many dissimilar approaches for designing communication hardware and software. To deal with this confusion, the International Standards Organization (ISO) has proposed the ISO/OSI Reference Model for Open Systems Interconnection as a standard for describing and categorizing network components. The reference model consists of seven layers: physical, data link, network, transport, session, presentation, and applications. A brief description of the purpose of each layer is given next.

The *physical layer* is the lowermost layer. It defines the electrical characteristics of signals passed between the computer and communications devices, such as a modem or other network interface hardware. The voltage levels and other transmission characteristics are determined at this level.

The *data–link layer* controls the transmission of a message along a single point-to-point link. The main purpose of this layer is to make the link appear totally reliable to the network layer. It does so by detecting and correcting any errors caused during physical transmission.

The *network layer* provides a transparent data transfer service to the higher layers. By transparent we mean that the higher layers using data transfer service need not know anything about the underlying network configuration or technology. A major function performed in the network layer is routing of messages through the network.

The *transport layer* is in one way similar to the data-link layer because the purpose of the transport layer is also to ensure that data are delivered error-free and in correct sequence. The data-link layer concerns itself with transmission over a single link, whereas the transport layer must ensure error-free transmission between the source and the end receiver.

The *session layer* establishes, maintains, and terminates a logical connection, called a session, for data transfer. A session temporarily links two devices in the network in a manner analogous to the way a telephone call links two telephones. The session layer also provides a means for controlling the dialogue in a session.

The *presentation layer* defines control codes, how data should be formatted, and other attributes of the message being transmitted. The purpose of the presentation layer is to hide the differences in data representation among heterogeneous computers and applications.

The *applications layer* provides the user interface to a range of networkwide services to support distributed applications. The services include file transfer access and management (FTAM) and general document and message interchange services, such as electronic mail.

The ISO/OSI standard includes service definitions and protocols for the seven layers described above. Other major institutions involved in the standardization efforts are IEEE (Institute of Electrical and Electronics Engineers) and CCITT (Comité Consultatif International de Télégraphique et Téléphonique), a committee of ITU (International Telecommunication Union). Several ISO standards are adopted from IEEE and CCITT standards. X.25 is a popular CCITT protocol for the third layer of the ISO model. A collection of protocol standards for all layers in a network model is often called a protocol *suite*. Besides the OSI protocol suite, another widely popular set of protocols is the Internet protocol suite, which has evolved in the ARPANET project. The Internet protocol suite is referred to as the TCP/IP protocol suite; TCP (transmission control protocol) and IP (Internet protocol) are two protocols at the transport and network layers, respectively. There are many proprietary protocol suites that have evolved over private vendors' networks. Notable among these is the SNA (systems network architecture) protocol suite of IBM.

INTEGRATED SERVICES DIGITAL NETWORKS

The most significant trend in telephone systems is certainly the gradual change from analog transmission to entirely digital transmission. Telephone networks with digital transmission can transfer any type of digital traffic, such as voice, data, alarms, and video. The Integrated Services Digital Network (ISDN) concept has evolved to explore this potential. Since 1980, CCITT has been working on ISDN-related definitions and standards.

In ISDN, an abstract digital pipe provides subscribers with access to communications facilities through a standard network interface. The main thrust of the ISDN concept is to support a wide range of voice and nonvoice applications in the same network. Examples of important categories of new services that could be provided through ISDN are facsimile, teletex, and videotex. The facsimile (also called fax) services relate to the transmission of graphics as well as handwritten and printed material. The teletex service is an enhanced electronic mail service and is likely to become quite popular. The videotex service allows a person sitting at a terminal to interact with a remote database. Once the videotex system is in place, it would be possible to perform many common transactions, such as banking and reservations, from a remote terminal.

For Further Reading

Bertsekas, D., and R. Gallager. 1987. *Data networks.* Englewood Cliffs, N.J.: Prentice-Hall.

Comer, D. 1988. *Internetworking with TCP/IP: Principles, protocols, and architecture.* Englewood Cliffs, N.J.: Prentice-Hall.

Davidson, J. 1988. *An introduction to TCP/IP.* New York: Springer-Verlag.

Doll, D. R. 1980. *Data communications: Facilities, networks, and system design.* New York: Wiley.

Guruge, A. 1987. *SNA: Theory and practice.* Elmsford, N.Y.: Pergamon Press.

Halsall, F. 1988. *Data communications, computer networks and* OSI, 2nd ed. Reading, Mass.: Addison-Wesley.

Henshall, J., and S. Shaw. 1988. *OSI explained: End-to-end computer communication standards.* New York: Wiley.

Land, J. 1987. *The integrated services digital network (ISDN).* Manchester, Eng.: The National Computing Centre.

Martin, J., and K. Chapman. 1987. *SNA: IBM's networking solution.* Englewood Cliffs, N.J.: Prentice-Hall.

Scientific American, Sept. 1991 (special issue: Communications, Computers and Networks).

Stallings, W. 1990a. *Handbook of computer-communications standards,* Vol. 1: *The open systems interconnection (OSI) model and OSI-related standards,* 2nd ed. Carmel, Ind.: Howard W. Sams.

———. 1990b. *Handbook of computer-communications standards,* Vol. 2: *Local area network standards,* 2nd ed. Carmel, Ind.: Howard W. Sams.

———. 1990c. *Handbook of computer-communications standards.* Vol. 3: *The TCP/IP protocol suite,* 2nd ed. Carmel, Ind.: Howard W. Sams.

Tanenbaum, A. 1988. *Computer networks,* 2nd ed. Englewood Cliffs, N.J.: Prentice-Hall.

S. P. Rana

NETWORKS, LOCAL AREA

See Local Area Networks; Networks, Computer

NETWORKS, WIDE AREA

See Networks, Computer; Wide Area Networks

NONSTANDARD DATABASE SYSTEMS

Database technology and the three common data models (i.e., hierarchical, network, and relational) were developed in response to the requirements of commercial data processing, which may be characterized by large volumes of homogeneous, record-oriented data. These models, however, are less effective when data objects vary in size and do not conform to any rigid structure. In addition, database languages based on these models have a limited expressive power and, in general, are not responsive to the complex requirements of sophisticated users. Recently, a number of systems that extend the capabilities of ordinary databases have been developed. These systems can be identified as expert databases, temporal databases, spatial databases, deductive databases, object-oriented databases, and office information systems (OISs). A short description of each system follows.

EXPERT DATABASE SYSTEMS

Conventional database systems are mainly concerned with efficient storage and retrieval of data. Generally, all data must be explicitly stored, and there is no mechanism for deriving new facts from the existing information. In expert systems, which are often idealized as systems that can imitate the expertise of a human being, the emphasis is largely on deduction of new facts, and they are not confined to the stored data. Expert database systems attempt to integrate the capabilities of expert systems and database systems into one coherent system. These systems provide, on the one hand, constructs for the representation of knowledge in the form of rules or frames along with capabilities for search and inferencing, and on the other hand, the ability to efficiently and reliably store, retrieve, and update large volumes of data.

The integration of databases and expert systems may be achieved in several ways.

- A database system may be enhanced to include rules and inferencing power. This technique is suitable for a large database that has been in operation for a long time. The knowledge base and the accompanying inference engine are similar to other application programs that receive data from the database. In certain types of expert databases, called *active* databases, the system has triggers (or rules that when executed invoke a transition) and transition constraints. Some rules are tied to constraints; and once a constraint is violated, a rule or a collection of rules is executed. Some of these rules may be used for user notification, in which case they are called *alerters*.

- Alternatively, an expert system may be extended with database capabilities and transparent access to data. In contrast to the previous method, the underlying database system in this method has no autonomy because it is generally used in conjunction with the expert system.

- A third method requires interface of an expert system and a database system. In this cooperative mode, the expert system, which knows the structure and the schema of the database, formulates its queries according to the modus operandi of the database. In return, the database system presents its answers in a format readily usable by the expert system. This scheme is advantageous because the two systems exist and operate independently of each other.

- A fourth method requires development of expert database systems in an integrated framework that allows both database capabilities and inferencing power. In this approach, one unified system executes both functions. (See the section on deductive databases below.)

IBM's STARBURST project extends Structured Query Language (SQL) and aims to support the increasing demands of a variety of applications including expert systems (Haas et al. 1988). KEEConnection, on the other hand, is an example of efforts to extend expert systems with database capabilities. It enhances the expert system KEE with database functions (KEE 1988).

TEMPORAL DATABASE MANAGEMENT SYSTEMS

Current database systems do not maintain a history of attribute values. In effect, each update destroys the old fact. In certain applications, keeping track of all previous information is important (e.g., maintaining histories of previous illnesses and medications in a hospital's patient database). To meet this need, temporal databases were designed with the aims of incorporating time in database systems and allowing multiple versions of data items to be stored in and retrieved from the database. Generally, temporal databases separate time-dependent data from time-independent data and provide some sort of time-keeping scheme for their management. *Attribute time stamping* is a simple method for managing temporal data. Each new attribute value is augmented with a timestamp that records the time of the update and thus distinguishes the current value of an attribute from its previous versions. By assigning a timestamp to each value, the database system can process queries that involve temporal relationships, such as "before," "after," and "during" (see Clifford and Tansel 1985 for more details).

SPATIAL DATABASES

As temporal databases incorporate time into the system, spatial databases extend the ordinary database systems by modeling the space dimension. The word *space* is used loosely to capture such entities as lines, drawings, and graphs and such spatial relationships as proximity and boundary. There are many applications for spatial databases, including computer-aided design and manufacturing, geographic information systems, and geometric modeling and design.

Spatial databases must store both spatial and nonspatial information. The former is the representation of drawings, regions, and lines, whereas the latter consists of alphanumeric values as in conventional systems. Specific operations in a spatial database depend on the type of information it contains. For example, in a geographic database system in which maps consisting of several regions are stored, the following operations (among many others) are essential: union, projection, fusion, selection, and superposition. Figures 1 through 5 illustrate these operations.

For further reading, see Buchmann et al. (1989) and Kasturi et al. (1989).

DEDUCTIVE DATABASES

The emergence of PROLOG in the mid-1970s generated interest in investigating a more active role for logic in the design of database query languages and database processing. Deductive databases are the confluence of ideas from logic programming and relational databases. Thus, as in PROLOG, data and knowledge are represented as Horn clauses (or rules) of the form

$$A :- B1 \ \& \ B2 \ \& \ \ldots \ \& \ Bn,$$

where A, B1, B2, . . . and Bn are predicates. A is called the head of the clause, and B1 & B2 & . . . & Bn is called the body or the condition of the clause. The condition part of a clause may be empty, in which case we call it a *fact*. A database is essentially a collection of Horn clauses of the above form. In deductive databases, however, most of the Horn clauses have no conditions (i.e., they contain mainly facts.) Queries to the database are formulated as they are in PROLOG.

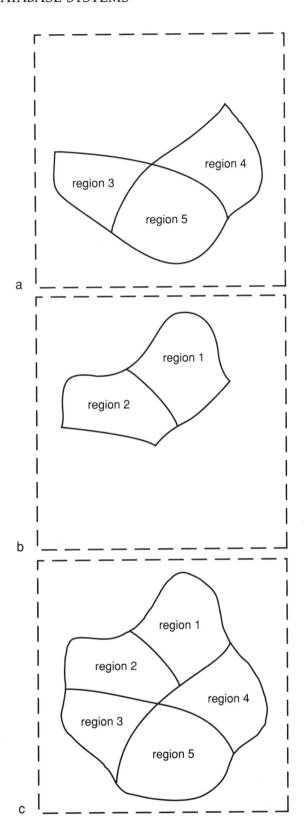

FIGURE 1. Union of two maps: (a) map m1, (b) map m2, (c) the union of m1 and m2.

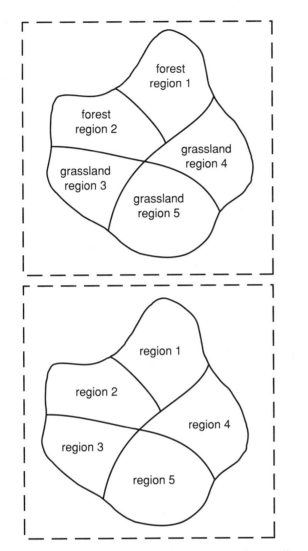

FIGURE 2. Projection on the attribute "landscape."

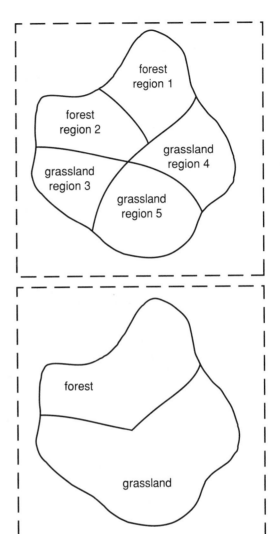

FIGURE 3. Projection on the attribute "region" and fusion on attribute "landscape."

Deductive databases are more powerful than ordinary databases because they allow storage of rules in addition to facts. In addition, certain tasks such as computation of transitive closure are naturally provided in deductive databases. Ordinary relations are given by listing the instances of the predicate that represents that relation. Deductive databases allow virtual relations (or views), which may be specified by rules. Other positive aspects of deductive databases include a well-defined semantics based on first-order logic, a simple notation, and representational uniformity for both knowledge and data. This topic is discussed further by Lloyd and Topper (1985).

OBJECT-ORIENTED DATABASES

Although there is no consensus as to what the term *object-oriented* means or what it implies, there are a few main ideas that are generally agreed upon. The following features are commonly expected from object-oriented database systems:

The Power of Abstraction

Objects are described by their properties and behavior, independent of their internal representation and independent of any method of implementation. An object's definition consists of a name, a set of proper values,

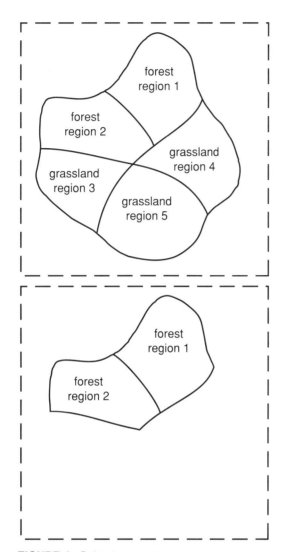

FIGURE 4. Selection on "landscape = forest."

and a set of appropriate operations (or methods) applicable to that object.

Object Identity

The object identity property requires each object to have a unique identity that distinguishes it from other objects, particularly from objects of the same type that have the same values for most or all of the attributes.

Provisions for Hierarchical Classes (or Types)

Two types of hierarchical structures should be permitted.

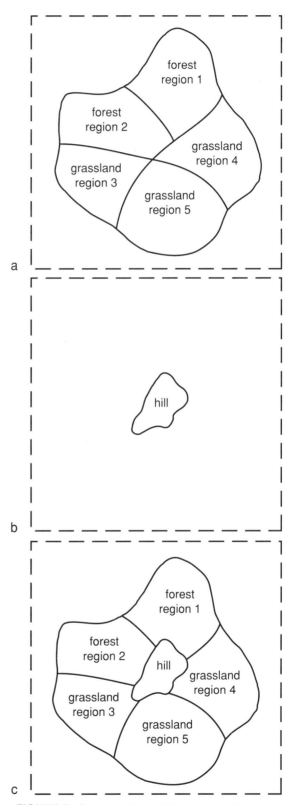

FIGURE 5. Superposition of two maps: (a) map m1, (b) map m2, (c) superposition of m2 onto m1.

- General classes may be refined by providing subordinate classes. Each subordinate class inherits the properties of the more general class. A simple example is the class "persons," which may be characterized as having three subclasses: women, men, and children. The class "men" may be further refined to have its own subclasses, say, "married-men" and "single-men." The subclass "single-men" inherits all the properties of its superclasses, namely, "men" and "persons."
- Complex objects should be subdivided into simpler components. For example, the complex object "car" may be subdivided into several components such as "body," "engine," and "wheels," and each of these components may be further subdivided into other components.

Persistence

Although persistence is a common feature of all database systems, from a programming point of view it is considered a novelty. Persistence enables a system to preserve the results of one program, after the completion of its execution, for later reuse.

Extensibility

In conventional databases, the schema of a database is fixed at the time the database is created. Generally, no changes are possible without substantial redesign and programming. In an extensible object-oriented system, the user may introduce new classes of objects and use them just as predefined types are used.

In the object-oriented model, objects are grouped into classes. A collection of attributes associated with a class represents the properties of the objects belonging to that class. The relationship "instance-of" identifies the objects that belong to each class. In Figure 6, this relation is used to specify that Apollo IX is an instance of the class of spacecraft. Classes may form a class hierarchy in which each subclass is a specialization of its superior classes. By using the relation "is-a," the relationship between subclasses and superclasses can be represented. For example, the class "spacecraft" is a subclass of the class "carriers." Therefore, the relation "is-a" is used to connect the classes "spacecraft" and "carriers."

Several prototype object-oriented database systems have been developed by both the computer industry and academic re-

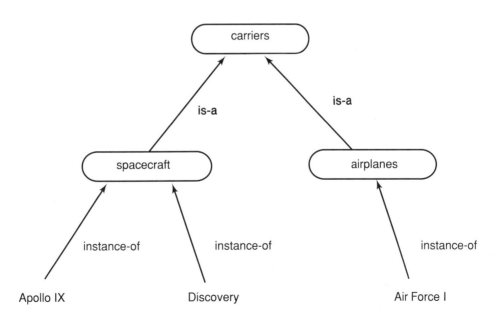

FIGURE 6. Relationships "is-a" and "instance-of" in object-oriented systems.

search centers. The ORION system developed at the Microelectronics and Computer Corporation (MCC) is an object-oriented system that emphasizes persistence and sharability of objects (Banerjee et al. 1987). One of the notable features of ORION is its ability to deal with schema evolution and changes to class definitions and object structures. The system provides support for composite objects and allows a hierarchical collection of component objects to be considered as a logical entity.

Iris was developed at Hewlett-Packard Laboratories (Fishman et al. 1987). Iris supports a number of novel and extensible data types such as graphic images, text, and vectors. Iris is expected to be the underlying database system for integrated systems such as office information and engineering testing, measurements, and design.

At Xerox, the PROBE system and its data model PDM provide a simple framework for the design of database systems. PDM is an extension of the data model DAPLEX and attempts to integrate ideas from the relational, functional, and object-oriented approaches (Dayal et al. 1988).

Another system, Gemstone, was developed with the view that object-oriented languages, specifically SmallTalk-80, may be combined with traditional storage management mechanisms to ease the modeling process and reduce the efforts needed for application development (Maier and Stein 1987).

OFFICE INFORMATION SYSTEMS

One of the fastest-growing applications of database systems is automated office information systems. These systems store and process a variety of objects such as texts, reports, messages and other types of communications, letters and their subsequent annotations, forms, and addresses. Office information systems (OISs) typically involve totally unstructured objects and operations. Time plays a prominent role in OISs, since the system must deal with a variety of time constraints and time-critical events. In addition to keeping calendars and schedules, the system should capture and monitor duration of activities, response time to messages and letters, circulation time of a document within the office, and appropriate deadlines for generating reminders. One important requirement of these systems is to provide adequate browsing and navigation interfaces by which a complex group of users, each performing a variety of tasks, may access and view documents. Ideally, the user should be able to browse through various forms of information, zoom in as necessary, and augment information on the points of interest.

Typically, an OIS demands a high degree of interconnectivity among office workstations. Reliable communication may be achieved through electronic mail, facsimile transmissions, and audio and video digitizers/interfaces. In most offices, information must be summarized or reformatted before being passed on to a higher level. OISs cater to this need by filtering unnecessary information at each level, thereby ensuring that information is presented in the proper degree of detail.

Not all of the above features are present in existing OISs. Office-By-Example (OBE) is a system under development at IBM (Whang et al. 1987). It supports many activities, such as electronic mail, word processing, and handling of images and database tables. The OBE is an extension of the database query language Query-By-Example (QBE). The Office Task Manager (OTM) is an object-oriented office system that can collect and store documents, act on these documents as needed, delete documents when appropriate, set deadlines, and manage time schedules (Lochovsky et al. 1988).

References

Banerjee, J., H.-T. Chou, J. F. Garza, W. Kim, D. Woelk, N. Ballou, and H.-J. Kim. 1987. Data model issues for object oriented applications. *ACM Transactions on Office Information Systems* 5(1):3–26.

Buchmann, A., O. Guntner, T. R. Smith, and Y. F. Wang, eds. 1989. *Design and implementation of large spatial databases*. Lecture Notes in Computer Science 409. New York: Springer Verlag.

Clifford, J., and A. Tansel. 1985. On an algebra for historical relational databases:

Two views. In *Proceedings of ACM SIGMOD Conference on Management of Data, Austin, Texas, May 1985*. New York: ACM Press.

Dayal, U., A. Buchmann, U. Chakravarthy, M. DeWitt, D. Goldhirsch, S. Heiler, F. Manola, J. Orenstein, R. Rosenberg, and A. Rosenthal. 1988. *Overview of PROBE: An object-oriented, extensible database system*. Xerox Advanced Information Technology Reference 171. Cambridge, Mass.: Xerox Corp.

Fishman, D. H., D. Beech, H. P. Cate, E. C. Chow, T. Conners, J. W. Davis, N. Derret, C. G. Hoch, W. Kent, P. Lyngbaek, B. Mahbod, M. A. Neimat, T. A. Ryan, and M. C. Shan. 1987. Iris: An object-oriented database management system. *ACM Transactions on Office Information Systems* 5(1): 48–69.

Haas, L. M., W. F. Cody, J. C. Freytag, B. G. Lindsey, G. M. Lohman, K. Ono, and H. Pirahesh. 1988. An extensible processor for an extended relational query language. IBM Research Report RJ-6182 (60892), IBM Almaden Research Center, San Jose, California.

Kasturi, R., R. Fernandez, M. L. Amlani, and W. C. Feng. 1989. Map data processing in geographic information system. *Communications of ACM* 20(12):10–21. (This special issue of CACM, edited by Grosky and Mehrotra, is dedicated to image database management.)

KEE Software development user's manual, version 3.0. 1988. Mountain View, Calif.: IntelliCorp.

Lloyd, J. W., and R. W. Topper. 1985. A basis for deductive database systems. *Journal of Logic Programming* 2(2):93–109.

Lochovsky, F. H., J. S. Hogg, S. P. Wieser, A. O. Mendelzon, and U. Toronto. 1988. OTM: Specifying office tasks. *Proceedings of Conference on Office Automation Systems, Palo Alto, California, March 23–25, 1988*, pp. 46–54. New York: ACM Press.

Maier, D., and J. Stein. 1987. Development and implementation of an object-oriented DBMS. In B. Shriver and P. Wegner, eds. *Research directions in object oriented programming*. Cambridge, Mass.: MIT Press.

Whang, K.-Y., A. Ammann, A. Bolmarcich, M. Hanrahan, G. Hochgesang, K.-T. Huang, A. Khorasani, R. Krishnamurthy, G. Sockut, P. Sweeny, V. Waddle, and M. Zloof. 1987. Office-By-Example: An integrated office system and database manager. *ACM Transactions on Office Information Systems* 5(4):393–427.

Forouzan Golshani

NORRIS, WILLIAM C.

William Norris was born on July 14, 1911, on a farm in Red Cloud, Nebraska. Obtaining an education was not simple for Norris. He had to walk or ride a pony, no matter what the weather, to a one-room schoolhouse a mile from home. While in high school, Norris developed a strong interest in physics. In 1932 he received a bachelor's degree in electrical engineering at the University of Nebraska. With few jobs available, Norris ran the family farm for the next 2 years. He later took a civil engineering job that involved laying out terraces and dams.

In 1934, he joined the Westinghouse Company and sold x-ray machines and other equipment. In 1941, he took a job as an electrical engineer for the U.S. Navy in Washington, D.C. After Pearl Harbor, Norris was commissioned in the Naval Reserve, where he worked with mathematicians and engineers from corporations and universities in top-secret cryptography work, trying to break German and Japanese codes.

After the war (1946), at the government's suggestion, Norris and other technical specialists found private financing and formed Engineering Research Associates (ERA), which specialized in producing customized data processing equipment for the navy. By 1952, ERA had built over 80 percent of all American-built electronic computers.

Engineering Research Associates was purchased by Remington Rand in 1952. After Remington Rand and Sperry Corporation merged in 1955 (becoming Sperry Rand), Norris became vice-president and general manager of the new St. Paul, Minnesota-based electronic computer division called Univac. Frustrated because Univac was not able to keep up with IBM in building and marketing new computers, Norris decided to venture out on his own. In 1957, Norris along with Seymour CRAY and seven others left Sperry Rand Corporation to found Control Data Corporation (CDC). Cray was given a free rein by Norris to develop a supercomputer line. The first computer produced by CDC was the CDC 1604. When it reached the market in 1958, it was one of the first fully transistorized computers and the largest scientific computer at the time. The CDC 1604's early success was phenomenal. Control Data could not make them fast enough to keep up with the demand.

In 1959 CDC released the Model 160 desk-sized computer. A year later, Cray began working on the CDC 6600. When the CDC 6600 appeared in 1963, it was twenty times faster than any other computer. It could execute an average of over 3 million instructions per second.

Control Data Corporation continued building fast scientific computers; the next step was the CDC 7600, followed by the Star 100 in 1974. Then came the CYBER 205, one of the first supercomputers to introduce vector processing, in which the computer works on many different parts of the problem at once. The CYBER 205 is capable of up to 800 million operations a second.

By the mid-1960s, Norris had become convinced that total dependence on mainframe computers was unwise. He looked for other businesses. Norris took the company into the peripheral products business. It proved to be a wise decision. Between 1969 and 1971, when the large computer market suffered a setback, CDC was able to fall back on the peripherals business.

Norris continued to build his empire by developing a strong line of peripherals, two service bureaus, and a technology information service. The company also made substantial investments in the development of the PLATO system—computer-aided educational hardware and software.

In 1986, Norris, at age 76, retired from the company he founded 29 years earlier. During his more than 40 years in the computer business, he took on many very big and controversial projects.

For Further Reading

Reflections. 1988. Manhasset, N.Y.: CMP Publications.
Slater, R. 1989. *Portraits in silicon*, pp. 113–25. Cambridge, Mass.: MIT Press.

Donald D. Spencer

O

OBJECT-ORIENTED PROGRAMMING

One of the most exciting developments in computer languages in recent times is the increasing popularity of a family of languages called *object-oriented programming languages*. The goal of a good computer language is to make it as easy as possible for a programmer to translate ideas about how the computer should behave into a precise set of instructions, a program, that tells the computer what to do at each moment. The idea of an "object," whether it is a concrete object such as a rock or a tree or an abstract object such as the United States, is central to human thinking. Object-oriented programming is a style of programming in which a programmer describes the objects that make up a program, and says what information each object must contain and what actions the object can perform.

In the early days, computers were thought of primarily as manipulators of numbers. Early high-level programming languages, such as FORTRAN, were oriented primarily toward working with numbers and had operations to add, subtract, multiply, store, and retrieve numbers. A few other kinds of data, such as *arrays,* which organize collections of numbers, and *strings,* which represent ordered sequences of letters, were added to high-level programming languages, but the data types present in conventional languages always lagged behind the needs of applications. A number-oriented language is fine for a program whose job it is to operate directly on numbers, such as a program that adds up all the numbers representing the salaries of workers in a particular business; however, as the number of computer applications increased, computers did not work exclusively with numbers anymore.

The computer could store a database of employees, and it could be asked to retrieve a list of only those employees whose names begin with M. To design a new office building, a computer could display a picture of a floor plan, with the office of each employee labeled with the employee's name. How could a program that needed to represent information about people, or pictures of a building where they worked, be written in a language that did not have people or pictures as primitive concepts, but only numbers and a few ways to organize them?

The good news is that, surprisingly, a language that works with numbers is sufficient, in a theoretical sense, to write any program imaginable. The bad news is that doing so is often difficult in practice. The trick to dealing with a mismatch between the vocabulary of the application and the vocabulary of the programming language is to establish a *representation*. A representation is a kind of code that establishes a correspondence between the objects that you need to model in the program and a set of numbers.

For example, a set of "employee numbers," 1 for Jane, 2 for Fred, 3 for Bob, and so on, can be used to represent the employees. Other examples of such representations in everyday life are social security numbers, bank account numbers, and airline flight numbers. The problem with using numbers as representations in programming, like the use of identification numbers in everyday life, is that it is often difficult to remember what the numbers mean, it is easy to make a mistake about a number, and there is no obvious relation between the number and what it represents. In an object-oriented programming language, there is no need for the programmer to make numerical codings for the concepts that make up a program. Such codings are done automatically by the program that implements the programming language. Instead, the language provides means for directly describing the characteristics of an object.

In an object-oriented programming language, we could create an object named "Jane," which represented some particular employee of a company. Objects are characterized by their knowledge, that is, what information they have, and their behavior, that is, how they act when they communicate with other objects. You can think of each object in an object-oriented programming language as being an imaginary person. You can ask questions of that person, and the person can either respond directly or, in turn, ask questions of other objects. The information stored in the object for Jane might consist of her name, social security number, age, and other information particular to her. She might respond to questions asking for this information or requests to get a particular job done.

Even inanimate objects in the real world can be represented by objects in an object-oriented language. An object representing Jane's office might answer the question "Whose office are you?" You could ask the office object to draw itself on a graphics screen if it were part of an architectural floor plan. It would know such information as its color and position on the screen.

Now for some terminology: The questions and requests that an object responds to are called *messages* in an object-oriented language. The object usually stores the program that controls its behavior as a set of procedures that are specific to each kind of message it may receive. Each procedure that responds to a specific kind of message is called a *method*.

Many objects tend to be similar to other objects in certain ways, and most object-oriented languages have some way of capturing those similarities so that a programmer does not have to repeat descriptions of objects that are similar to those that already exist. One way of doing this is to have objects

called *classes* represent behavior common to a set of objects, and *instances* represent the knowledge and behavior of individual objects. In the previous examples, "Employee" might be the name of a class that represents the behavior that all employees share in common, and Jane is an instance of the class Employee. All employees might have the same behavior when responding to a message like "start lunch break," but individual employees would differ on other items, such as a social security number.

Furthermore, in addition to the similarity between a class and its instances, classes can have similarity to each other. Some classes can be further subdivided into smaller classes that contain more specific information. The class *Employee* can be broken down into specific kinds of employees, for example, Manager, Secretary, and Salesperson. Each of these specialties may have knowledge and behavior that is shared between all others of that specialty but not by others outside it. Subdivisions of a class are referred to as *subclasses*. The sharing of behavior between a class and its subclasses is referred to as *inheritance*.

Organizing a program as a collection of objects that act in response to messages is the central idea of object-oriented programming. It is important to remember that object-oriented programming is really a philosophy, or style of programming, not a specific programming language. It is possible to do object-oriented programming in a program written in practically any language, as long as the organization of the program conceptually corresponds to the ideas of objects and messages; however, it is easier to do object-oriented programming in some languages than in others. Object-oriented programming languages are those programming languages that have been specifically designed with the object-oriented programming model in mind. The built-in operations of the language directly support programming in an object-oriented style. A typical object-oriented programming language will have constructs for defining a new object, defining behavior for an object, and sending messages.

One of the earliest and still most popular object-oriented programming languages is

SmallTalk. SmallTalk was invented in the early 1970s by Alan Kay at the Xerox Research Center in Palo Alto, California, inspired by an earlier language named Simula. SmallTalk was originally designed for use by nonexpert computer users such as children, and has now grown into a large and elaborate system that can be used for substantial programming projects. It has a graphically oriented user interface based on windows and menus. This interface, from the ParcPlace implementation of SmallTalk-80, is illustrated in Figure 1.

The SmallTalk interface is centered around a *browser* window. The purpose of a browser window is to let the user find information about existing classes and methods and define new ones. The browser window is divided up into smaller windows, or *panes*, which contain lists from which the user can select. Classes and methods are organized into *categories*. The four small panes at the top of the browser window are, respectively, lists of class categories, specific classes, method categories, and specific methods. By selecting from these windows, the user can browse through a system of objects the way one would browse through a library by searching the card catalog and book stacks organized by subject matter.

The larger pane in the bottom portion of the browser window shows the text of a selected method, or of a class definition. There is a word processor in this window, so that the user may modify the definition of an existing class or method if he or she wishes. A new class of method can also be added by editing the text of this window. Pop-up menus offer operations such as executing an expression and finalizing an editing change. The screen may contain multiple browser windows or windows with other specialized interfaces.

The syntax of the SmallTalk language for writing methods is as follows. Each expression consists of the name of the recipient followed by the message and a period. For the simplest messages, those that need not contain other objects in the message, the message is simply represented by a word, as in

Jane printSocialSecurityNumber

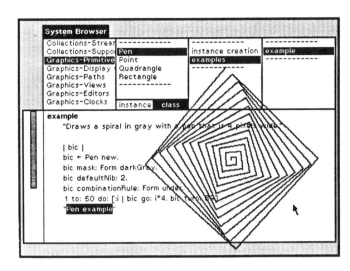

FIGURE 1. Interface from the ParcPlace implementation of SmallTalk-80. *Reproduced with permission from Goldberg 1984.*

A more complex message may have more than one part, and is composed of several keywords, each a word followed by a colon, then an object that forms that part of the message.

JanesOffice displayOnScreen: myScreen
inColor: officeColor.

In the preceding example, **JanesOffice** is the recipient, and the message consists of two parts, one part named **displayOnScreen,** with a variable that names a screen, another **inColor,** with a variable for the color. Like other programming languages, SmallTalk has variables, assignment statements, and arithmetic expressions and conditionals. Although the syntax of these constructs resembles that of other programming languages, all aspects of SmallTalk are implemented using the object and message metaphor.

SmallTalk is not the only object-oriented programming language. Another early language was Actors, developed by Carl Hewitt and his colleagues at MIT for artificial intelligence applications and to help understand the theoretical nature of computation. Many other languages have been designed since that time. Currently, an area of great activity is the design of object-oriented extensions for previously existing procedural languages. This permits people who have experience with existing programs in other languages to enjoy some of the benefits of object-oriented programming. This works more or less well, depending on how closely the style of the existing language fits the philosophy of object-oriented programming.

The Common LISP Object System, CLOS, is an extension to the LISP programming language, which provides most of the same ideas as SmallTalk, but also includes the novel idea of being able to tailor behavior that depends on several different kinds of objects at once, rather than just a single object. C++ is an object-oriented extension to the lower-level programming language C. C++ is less similar to SmallTalk and to the spirit of object-oriented programming, but has achieved wide popularity because of its speed and because the C language is widespread. Conventional procedural languages like C and Pascal lack the crucial facility of *dynamic memory management* necessary to achieve full object orientation in the sense of SmallTalk or LISP-based languages, but nevertheless can implement some form of object and message passing.

There are many application areas for which object-oriented programming affords a decisive advantage. SmallTalk was originally designed for educational applications, because explaining programming in terms of objects and messages was considered more intuitive for beginners than the conventional explanations of programming in terms of hardware registers and processors. Dynamic simulations were another area of early application, because object-oriented programming allowed a clear mapping of objects being simulated to objects that made up the program. Actors was designed for artificial intelligence applications, because the "anthropomorphic" metaphor of objects as active agents that can communicate among themselves encouraged the building of intelligent problem-solving capabilities into any component of a program.

Object-oriented databases, which provide objects whose storage resides permanently on a disk rather than temporarily in the memory of the machine, are beginning to become a viable and more flexible alternative to conventional file systems. Many systems for graphics and graphical user interfaces use

object-oriented programming, because visual objects are naturally represented. In the next few years, parallel machines will become more common, and object-oriented languages provide a good base for exploiting parallelism. The natural parallelism of objects acting in the real world is well modeled by parallelism between objects in an object-oriented language. As the benefits of object-oriented programming become more widely recognized, this style of programming will find an ever-widening range of applications.

For Further Reading

Cox, B. 1986. *Object-oriented programming, an evolutionary approach.* Reading, Mass: Addison-Wesley.

Goldberg, A. 1984. *SmallTalk-80: The interactive programming environment.* Reading, Mass.: Addison-Wesley.

Goldberg, A., and D. Robson. 1983. *SmallTalk-80: The language and its implementation.* Reading, Mass.: Addison-Wesley.

Keene, S. 1988. *Object-oriented programming in common LISP.* Reading, Mass.: Addison-Wesley.

Kim, W., and Lochovsky, F. 1989. *Object-oriented concepts, applications and databases.* New York: ACM Press.

Yonezawa, A., and M. Tokoro. 1987. *Object-oriented concurrent programming.* MIT Cambridge, Mass.: MIT Press.

Henry Lieberman

OFFICE AUTOMATION

Some of the most visible applications of computer technology are now found in offices. Professionals, managers, and clerical workers use them. Computers are found in offices of organizations that are very small as well as very large, manufacturing as well as service-oriented, and in the public as well as private sector.

Automating the office has provided many advantages in terms of the quality and flexibility of the finished products. An early goal of office automation was to enable the "paperless office," but paper consumption increased dramatically as a result of the technology. It is now apparent that realistic goals are needed for appropriate application of office technology.

GOALS AND FUNCTIONS

According to Gremillion and Pyburn (1988), an office performs cognitive, social, procedural, and physical activities. Cognitive activities include tasks that support decision making and planning. Social activities involve many forms of communication. Procedural activities often focus on completing forms and checking documents. Physical activities are those that are visible, including writing, typing, and delivery. These physical activities support the other three activities and involve interaction with computer equipment.

A surprisingly wide variety of equipment is used to automate the office. Some examples are typewriters, copiers, fax (facsimile) machines, computers, and dictating machines. Office technology has evolved considerably over the years, and should continue to progress in the future. But the targets of this technology will probably always be data, text, images, and voice. In an office, these resources are manipulated, communicated, stored, and retrieved.

One goal of office automation is to enable these resources to be integrated rather than independent. For example, a team that is working on a large project might prepare a final report. This report could involve cost figures (data), arguments for action (text), and pictures (images). Members of the project often communicate their comments to each other (voice) as the work progresses. In the office of yesterday, the data were found only on the firm's accounting system, the text on sheets of paper, the images on photographs or drawings, and the voice on tape. In the office of the future, all of these items might be found at a workstation, organized and contained in computer files. As computer storage becomes even more affordable and developers discover better ways to make these items easy to access, an office worker might be able to "point" in some way to the project report, and retrieve the report. Symbols on the report shown on-screen could indicate voice messages that apply in certain sections; pointing to each symbol might make the system "play" the associated message. Graphics and pictures could be stored as high-resolution color images. Data on which the report is based might be included for easy review or manipulation. Gates (1990) describes how such a system might be used.

Figure 1 illustrates how today's data, text, images, and voice resources and technology fit together (Hirschheim 1985, p. 6). This figure is an excellent view of just what is office automation. In addition, a good verbal definition is offered by Pick (1986): "Office automation is the use of computer and telecommunications technologies to simplify and support routine office functions, improve communications, increase office productivity, and generally enhance the quality of clerical output" (p. 398).

Figure 2 provides a highly graphic view of an automated office (Pick, p. 399). Dictation or printed facsimile documents are entered on word processors or standard typewriters, or read by optical readers. These computer-readable documents are then stored or sent to other offices via data communication lines. Further modifications might be made to these documents and stored, transmitted, printed, or reduced to microfilm size. These and other actions are enabled by several tools, described in the next section.

TECHNOLOGY SYSTEMS IN THE AUTOMATED OFFICE

Automated office tools include office publishing systems, electronic communications systems, electronic meeting systems, image processing systems, and office support systems (O'Brien 1990).

Office Publishing

Office publishing systems include word processing and desktop publishing. Word processing is one of the most visible and widespread office technologies, and involves

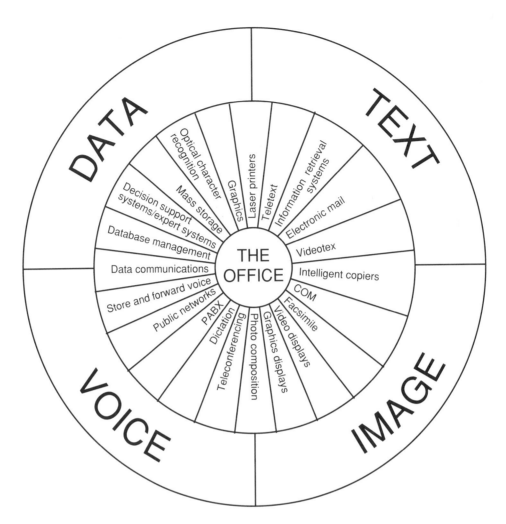

FIGURE 1. Integrated view of office technology. *Adapted from Hirschheim 1985, p. 6.*

a great range of hardware and software, from inexpensive memory typewriters to terminals attached to mainframe computers. Desktop publishing is a growing application of office technology, and focuses on production of high-quality printed materials.

Word processing systems allow entry, editing, storage, retrieval, and printing of text. A typical word processing system allows words and sentences to be typed and viewed on a display screen. Changes can be made by moving a *cursor,* or arrow pointer, to the appropriate screen location, eliminating unwanted characters, and inserting new text. If words, sentences, or paragraphs must be copied or moved to new locations, it is easy to mark the section and initiate the copy or move function. For example, in a typical graphical interface system, a user can use a

"mouse" device to move the arrow on the screen. Dragging, or moving the mouse, causes the arrow to move on the screen in a corresponding direction. For instance, dragging the mouse to the right causes the arrow on the screen to move to the right. Dragging the mouse toward the back of the desk causes the arrow to move up the screen.

If a user wishes to move a sentence, he or she can move the arrow to the beginning of the sentence, then press and hold a button on the mouse and drag it to the end of that sentence. As soon as the entire selection is displayed in reverse video (white letters on a black background), the user can then let go of the button. By pressing one or two keystrokes or pointing to words at the top of the screen that become "pull-down" menus, the word processing program can move the se-

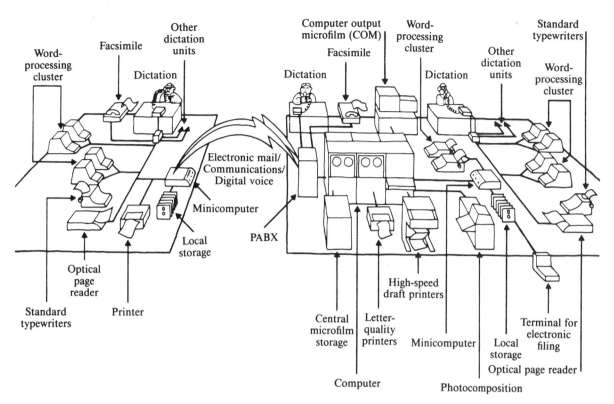

FIGURE 2. Schematic drawing of an automated office. *Reproduced with permission from Pick 1986, p. 399.*

lection elsewhere. Copying is done in a similar manner, and can greatly accelerate entry of repeating words or symbols. Systems that do not make use of a mouse allow cursor movement to be performed via arrow keys, and usually require special combinations of keystrokes for other functions.

Many other kinds of commands are available to word processing systems. For example, the user can search for certain letters or phrases, replace every instance of one set of letters for another set of letters, save the current document on disk, request a list of synonyms for a certain word, activate a spell checker, change the size or style of what will be printed, and so on. There are perhaps hundreds of commands that can be included in a word processing program; some very elaborate systems will perform desktop publishing functions.

Desktop publishing is a natural extension to word processing, and allows users to produce professional-looking documents. Many users routinely produce newsletters, proposals, presentations, and reports. Often

users who are quite knowledgeable about word processing as well as their own areas of specialty (e.g., law, product design) must undergo some training in printers' terms and practices, page layout, and graphic design.

Desktop publishing software is most often found on IBM PC-compatible computers as well as computers by Apple and NeXT. Laser printers are most commonly used so that the print quality is as high as possible. For documents that are highly important, users often take their diskettes to a printing shop, because specialized printing equipment provides much crisper printing. Rather than the 300 dots per inch (90,000 dots per square inch) of a common laser printer, professional-looking results often require the use of printers that achieve 1,200 dots per inch (1,440,000 dots per square inch).

Electronic Communications Systems

Included in electronic communications systems are voice mail, electronic mail, and facsimile (fax) technology. These systems are used to a great extent today, and each provides unique advantages.

Voice mail systems operate much like personal telephone answering machines. Most often, the voices are digitized rather than stored on tape, and there are advanced capabilities of sending messages as well as receiving them. Messages can also be sent to multiple recipients in many systems.

Electronic mail provides the ability to send and receive typewritten messages or computer-readable files. Most systems allow users to "check their mail" as they do at their postal mailbox, and indicate how many messages are waiting to be read. As a message appears on the screen, the user can save (or discard) it, print it, reply to the sender, or forward the message to another recipient.

Fax machines became widespread in the 1980s. A fax machine, like voice mail, allows the user to avoid typing altogether, and is essentially a long-distance copy machine. The document is fed, page by page, into a feeder on the sending fax machine. Each page is pulled past a scanning device that converts the image into audible codes. These codes are sent over an ordinary phone line to the receiving fax machine, which converts the codes into a printed copy of the original. Any image, including text and graphic images, can be sent. Unfortunately, the quality of the image suffers a little, and small images might be unreadable. It is common to see fax machines employed to send quick drawings or sketches, detailed plans, signed contracts, and orders.

Electronic Meeting Systems

Electronic meeting systems include group decision support systems, teleconferencing, and telecommuting. These systems allow information to flow quickly between computers, and permit collaboration in new ways.

Group decision support systems very often enable meeting participants to combine ideas in solving a particular problem. Most often, participants gather in a specially designed room, and a projection screen of some kind is used to display the current status of the meeting. For example, ideas can be listed, spreadsheet models can be built,

drawings can be modified, votes can be tallied, or documents can be created.

Teleconferencing is a remote form of group decision support. Participants in remote locations are linked by computer, video, and/or voice, and can send information to and receive information from each other as they try to make their decisions. The video option is quite costly and is therefore used less than the other options.

Telecommuting is seen by many people as a solution to the ongoing energy crisis. Many jobs do not require physical presence at a central work site. In many cases, workers can write documents or perform clerical functions at their homes just as effectively as they can at their offices. Difficulties are the level of trust in the workers that must be held, the lack of satisfaction that comes from social interaction, and the potential for household interruptions.

Image Processing Systems

Image processing systems provide one of the first opportunities to move closer to the paperless office promised many years ago. Such systems include optical scanning, storage, and filing, as well as interactive video.

Images of any kind can be captured and saved for future retrieval in image processing systems. Important documents such as orders, forms, signed contracts, drawings, and even income tax returns have been managed on such systems. A scanner converts the image to digital form, which is saved on high-volume storage devices like optical disks.

Interactive video systems often include full-motion video clips as well as stationary images, and portions are displayed when deemed appropriate by the programs that control access to them. Such systems are particularly appropriate for educational purposes, when students need to see how something works rather than simply be told facts.

Office Support Systems

This final category of office automation includes electronic calendaring and project management. Both functions involve management of time, but at different levels of specificity.

Electronic calendaring allows users to determine the need for a meeting and select members that should be involved. The software can scan the calendars of the others and select a date where all are free. When the date is found, the calendars of all members are updated to reflect this meeting. Naturally, the others must check their systems so that they are aware of this meeting.

Project management scheduling systems allow users to determine which organizational members need to perform specified functions on projects and when these functions need to be completed. These systems do not specify exact dates and times as do calendaring systems, but address tasks in general so that groups of people can be managed.

CONCLUSIONS

Office automation has been designed to reduce paperwork, increase productivity, and increase the quality of what is produced. Although it appears that paperwork has not been reduced, productivity and quality are believed to have improved as a result of office technology. Increased integration of technologies used in the office should result in further improvements.

References

Gates, W. 1990. *Information at your fingertips.* Keynote address at COMDEX, Las Vegas, Nev., Nov. 12, 1990. Available on videotape from Microsoft, Inc., Redmond, Wash.

Gremillion, L., and P. Pyburn. 1988. *Computers and information systems in business: An introduction.* New York: McGraw-Hill.

Hirschheim, R. A. 1985. *Office automation: Concepts, technologies and issues.* Wokingham, England: Addison-Wesley.

O'Brien, J. A. 1990. *Management information systems: A managerial end-user perspective.* Homewood, Ill.: Irwin.

Pick, J. B. 1986. *Computer systems in business: An introduction.* Boston: PWS Computer Science.

Dennis F. Galletta

OPERATING SYSTEMS

The basic and historical function of operating systems is to instill order in the request, use, and release of resources in a computer system. The operating system manages the available resources needed by different users. In the 1950s, a user reserved the whole computer system for the duration of the user's program: There was virtually no operating system. Later, batch processing emerged, and operating systems began managing the input/output devices. Batch processing consists of three phases. In the first phase, jobs are read by a card reader onto a magnetic tape. In the second phase, an operator brings the tape to the machine room where the computer executes the programs on the tape. Any output is written onto another tape. In the last phase, the operator loads the tape to print the output stored in it. Examples are the FORTRAN Monitor System and the IBSYS (IBM's operating system for the 7094). In the 1960s, operating systems offered not only batch processing but also time-sharing and real-time processing (Rosen 1969; Weizer 1981). Such systems constituted a trend toward a general-purpose operating system offering several services to a user. Time sharing is a technique that allows multiple users to be served simultaneously by a single computer. Examples of these systems are the Digital Equipment VMS, AT&T Unix, and IBM VM.

Recent developments in computer systems have included the function of providing users with a virtual machine for writing application programs. Modern systems consist of raster displays, laser printers, large physical and virtual memories, large disks, and multiprocessors either centralized or distributed using local area networks or gateways. Users of a modern computer system are faced with a multitude of available resources, and the operating system must hide the complexities of the computer system from the user, thereby presenting the complex computer system to the user as a virtual machine ready to provide service in a variety of applications. Examples of these systems are the Cedar File System (Gifford et al. 1988), the V Distributed System (Cheriton

1988), the Andrew System (Satyanarayanan 1990), the Mach Operating System (Black 1990), and the Amoeba System (Mullender et al. 1990).

Our discussion of operating systems would not be complete without mention of personal computer operating systems. The most popular, Microsoft's MS-DOS, supports program loading and local disk drive. This is a single-user environment and therefore does not need many of the features discussed above. Recently, however, the Unix operating system has been integrated with the personal computing environment. This brought the capabilities of mainframe computers to personal computers. Thus, the cycle experienced by the development of operating systems for mainframes was extended to personal computer operating systems.

STRUCTURE OF OPERATING SYSTEMS

The structure of operating systems is usually a layered structure. The highest layer consists of an interface with the user, presenting an environment for writing application programs easily and conveniently. The lowest layer deals with the basic machine—registers, memory addresses, and other hardware features. The intermediate layers consist of specific function(s) and hide the detail of the lower layers.

A typical layer structure of an operating system is shown in Figure 1.

The most common user interface is a command language. An interpreter executes the wish of the user through the command language. A typical set of commands includes starting and terminating a session, executing programs, obtaining information about the system, and managing files. The command interpreter is resident in memory and executes any command entered into the computer through the keyboard. MS-DOS command language consists of a set of textual commands that are typed on the keyboard. Other systems such as the Macintosh have a more convenient way of inputting commands through a combination of windows, menus, and mouse pointing devices.

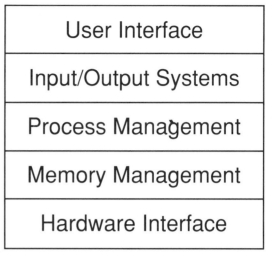

FIGURE 1. Layered structure.

The following sections describe how each of the intermediate layers makes the basic machine more conveniently accessible to a user.

INPUT/OUTPUT SYSTEMS

It is one of the main functions of an operating system to provide control over the use of input/output (I/O) devices: how to issue commands to devices, how to interrupt devices, and how to present a uniform set of I/O services independent of the type of devices. The most common I/O devices are random-access memory (RAM), disks, printers, tapes, pointing devices, and terminals.

Device drivers are programs that actually perform the reading and writing operations on an I/O device. These programs are concerned with the low-level hardware feature of the device, such as addresses of the blocks making up the file, position of the read/write arm, and size of the memory buffer in which data read from the device are to be stored. These programs are executed in the device controller. Through the device drivers, data can be transferred between memory and the I/O device.

Interrupt handlers are a set of programs that a central processing unit (CPU) executes when a particular event occurs. The most common type of operating system is interrupt-driven. The operating system is forever waiting in a loop for an interrupt. When an interrupt occurs, the CPU checks the type of event that has occurred and what to do to service the interrupt, finding it in a table called the interrupt vector, which is resident in memory and contains the type of event and the beginning address in memory of the program to be executed.

For I/O systems, the interrupt handler is a very important mechanism. When a *process* (defined below under "Process Management") requests an I/O operation, it interrupts the CPU. The CPU recognizes this interrupt and puts the process in blocked state. The CPU then starts the I/O process for the user process that requests I/O and then picks up another ready process for execution. When the I/O process finishes executing the I/O request, it interrupts the CPU to inform it that the I/O operation has been completed.

File systems provide the user with external storage of programs, data, object modules, and library functions. The operating system is responsible for providing the user with a convenient way of storing, retrieving, and maintaining files. Access to files must be device independent; that is, the same set of primitive commands can be used in accessing the files no matter what type of device the files are stored in. Several file structures are now used. They may be as simple as a sequence of bytes or a sequence of records, or they may have a complex structure such as linked-list or tree structures.

PROCESS MANAGEMENT

A *process* is the execution of a program by the CPU given a set of inputs and producing a set of outputs. A process has three states: running, blocked, and ready. A process is *running* when it is being served by the CPU. The process is *blocked* when it is waiting for some event (e.g., waiting for I/O or allocation of memory). A process is *ready* when it is waiting for its turn to be served by the CPU. A process can be classified as either a user process or a system process. A user process is generated by the user's program, and a sys-

tem process is generated by the operating system to perform tasks used only by the operating system (e.g., the memory management process, the file management process, and the I/O device process).

Each process gets its chance to be executed by the CPU. The technique of determining which process will be served by the CPU is called process scheduling; the program that performs this task is called the scheduler. Some process-scheduling techniques are first-come-first-serve, round-robin, and priority scheduling.

First-come-first-serve is the simplest process-scheduling technique. A ready process is served according to its time of arrival at the CPU. Thus, the oldest process is always executed first and the newest process is served last.

Round-robin gives each ready process a slice of time to be served by the CPU. A process not completed within this time slice waits again for its turn. Thus, it is fair in distributing service to all the ready processes waiting for the CPU, and several programs are active at any particular instant. This is known as multiprogramming. For interactive systems, each terminal user is given a time slice for his or her request to be served. Because the CPU serves so quickly, terminal users believe that the CPU is always ready to serve their requests. Furthermore, several tasks can be in different stages of execution simultaneously (e.g., in a windows operating system, each window currently being used represents a task, but only one window or task is active at a particular time).

Priority scheduling serves its ready processes according to the urgency of the need to be served by the CPU. It is possible to implement a scheduling process in which system processes receive higher priority than user processes.

Processes communicate with one another in the system. When two or more processes share a resource, their access to the shared resource must be synchronized in order not to interfere with their operations on the shared resource. A common situation in operating systems is the producer/consumer condition, in which one process (the producer) is producing items and putting them in a shared buffer and another process (the consumer) is removing items from the same buffer. We do not want the producer to attempt to put an item in a full buffer or the consumer to attempt to remove an item from an empty buffer. Examples of shared resources in the operating systems are the shared buffer for the read/write operation by the disk controller, the shared queue of processes waiting to be executed by the CPU, and the shared screen of the monitor when multiple processes are displaying data on it.

MEMORY MANAGEMENT

Memory is one of the limiting resources of a computer system. The source program is translated by the compiler into a machine-specific low-level language. This translated program contains all symbolic instructions, operands, and addresses. They are in the language understandable only to the CPU executing the instructions. The translated program is called the object module or an executable module. Next, the different object modules needed in executing the program are linked and loaded in memory for execution. The operating system is responsible for managing allocation of memory to the object modules. Several techniques are used in memory management: fixed partitions, variable partitions with compaction, overlays, and virtual memory.

A simple memory management technique is fixed partitions. Memory is divided into fixed partitions; each partition may have different sizes to accommodate different memory requirements of programs. This technique is simple but has its drawback. The size is fixed, and the memory needed by a program may be less than or equal to the fixed size. This results in fragments—pieces of memory not used by the program.

To remedy this drawback, memory is allocated in variable partitions, that is, according to the size the program requires. In time, however, fragments develop because programs are terminating and new ones are admitted into the system. Periodically, the operating system recovers these fragments by relocating the allocated partitions to make one contiguous partition of all the fragments. This is called compaction.

Overlaying is a technique that swaps between memory and secondary storage sections of the program being executed, when there is not enough memory to allocate all memory requirements of a program. The operating system allocates memory on a demand basis; that is, when the section of the program is not yet to be executed, it is not loaded into memory. Thus memory is initially loaded with the minimum set of sections of a program to start it. Later, when a section is needed, a section already in memory is selected to be swapped to secondary storage, and the needed section overlays the vacated partition.

The last memory management technique is virtual memory, in which memory is partitioned into fixed sizes called *pages* (about 2K–4K). A program is allocated several pages at a time. On a demand basis, when the program needs a section of the program that has not yet been loaded in memory, a certain number of pages are replaced by the needed section and the previous contents of these pages are placed in secondary storage.

RECENT DEVELOPMENTS

The availability of multiprocessors has led to the operating system meeting new requirements. Multiprocessors consist of several CPUs that cooperate in the execution of a computational task(s). Memory can either be shared by the CPUs or be distributed among them. The former is called a tightly coupled system, and the latter is called a loosely coupled system. Thus, the design of the operating system for multiprocessors takes into account the following aspects: CPU load balancing, locking algorithms for shared resources, and intercommunication among CPUs. These are aspects not considered in centralized operating systems. Some examples of multiprocessor systems are Cray X-MP, IBM 3081 and 3084, and Cyber 170.

In the past 10 years, networking has made interconnection of computers very easy and efficient. Ethernet, a popular local area network, combined with single-user workstations has ushered in the era of distributed computing systems. These systems share resources and are very robust because they provide redundant files and servers. If one file or server goes down, a backup copy takes over. This may result in performance degradation, but the whole system will not go down. The operating system controlling the distributed environment is called the distributed operating system. Some of its requirements are load balancing, file and resource assignment and locking, transparency, resilience, and security.

For further reading on operating systems, refer to Deitel (1983), Peterson and Silberschatz (1985), and Tanenbaum (1987).

References

Black, D. L. 1990. Scheduling support for concurrency and parallelism in the Mach operating system. *IEEE Computer* 23(5):35–43.

Cheriton, D. R. 1988. The V distributed system. *Communications of the ACM* 31(3):314–33.

Deitel, H. M. 1983. *An introduction to operating systems.* Reading, Mass.: Addison-Wesley.

Gifford, D. K., et al. 1988. The Cedar file system. *Communications of the ACM* 31(3):288–98.

Mullender, S. J., et al. 1990. Amoeba: A distributed operating system for the 1990s. *IEEE Computer* 23(5):44–53.

Peterson, J. L., and A. Silberschatz. 1985. *Operating system concepts.* 2nd ed. Reading, Mass.: Addison-Wesley.

Rosen, S. 1969. Electronic computers: A historical survey. *Computing Surveys* 1(1):7–36.

Satyanarayanan, M. 1990. Scalable, secure, and highly available distributed file system. *IEEE Computer* 23(5):9–21.

Tanenbaum, A. S. 1987. *Operating systems: Design and implementation.* Englewood Cliffs, N.J.: Prentice-Hall.

Weizer, N. 1981. A history of operating systems. *Datamation* 27(1):119–26.

Arturo I. Concepcion

OPERATIONS MANAGEMENT

Operations management deals with managing the design and operation of a process (factory, restaurant, airport, hospital, etc.) that converts inputs (materials, labor, etc.) into outputs (finished products, food, healthy patients, etc.). For example, the operations management decisions in a hospital involve facility expansion, bed capacity, operating room capacity, doctor and nurse staffing levels, doctor and nurse scheduling, inventory control, and quality control. Similarly, operations management decisions in an automobile factory affect capacity, staffing, scheduling, inventory, and quality control. This article describes how computer systems assist managers in making operations management decisions.

PROCESS DESIGN

Operations management involves many process design decisions including where to locate and how to lay out the facility. Computer-based DECISION SUPPORT SYSTEMS (DSSs) are often used to assist managers in making these process design decisions. The DSSs apply operations research models to help managers find a near-optimal location, lay out a factory, and so forth. For example, analysts for a large retail chain applied a mathematical model to locate 200 new stores in the United States. The model considered income, population, home values, and the location and sizes of competing stores. The model was embedded in a DSS that allowed analysts to access databases containing demographic information (e.g., average income) organized by geographic areas comparable to zip codes. The DSS allowed the analysts to try different locations and to find suitable alternatives to propose to management. Demographic databases, geographic databases, and graphic mapping software made this DSS very useful.

The DSSs for facility layout are similar to those for facility location, except that the goal is often to minimize the total materials handling cost given the expected number of times that batches of materials must move between machines. Computer-aided design (CAD) systems are very useful for facility design.

Computer-based DSSs have been developed for a number of other process design decisions including those involving technology (equipment) selection, capacity expansion, and worker task assignment (line balancing). Computer simulation, queuing theory, and linear programming models are valuable tools for studying many of these problems.

FORECASTING

A good forecast of demand for goods or services provides very important information for planning capacity and inventory requirements. Forecasting seasonal demand is especially important for distributors and manufacturers that need to stock inventories in anticipation of peak seasonal demand. Forecasting is also important for service companies such as airlines that need to adjust their capacity as demand changes by time of day, day of the week, and week of the year.

Computer-based DSSs can assist management in making longer-term forecasts such as annual sales forecasts. These systems are based on econometric (regression) models that use historical relationships between many variables to make forecasts. Several databases with time-series data are available from both government and industry sources.

Many operations management problems require routine daily or weekly forecasts to support short-term decisions. These forecasting models are often embedded in the applications software. For example, most inventory control software will forecast weekly sales for all inventoried items with a technique called exponential smoothing. Management uses this system to determine which items should be reordered, how much should be reordered, and which items deserve special attention from management.

Short-range forecasts can also serve as a check on new input data to make sure the values are reasonable. An exception message can warn the user that the input data may be wrong. Management is also given exception messages whenever the demand for an item changes radically. This calls management's attention to this item so that future problems (e.g., stock running out) can be avoided and so that management can learn from exceptional trends.

SCHEDULING

Many operations management decisions involve scheduling and sequencing issues. Typical scheduling problems include aircraft scheduling, nurse scheduling, vehicle scheduling, and robot scheduling. These scheduling problems are often very difficult to solve. For example, it is possible to schedule a trip to 10 cities in 3,628,800 different ways. High-speed computers are well suited for these combinatorial problems.

Computer-based approaches for scheduling are either *exact* or *heuristic*. Exact procedures are guaranteed to find the mathematically optimal (best) solution. Heuristic procedures attempt to find the optimal solution, but do not guarantee optimality. Even with extremely fast computers, many scheduling problems require too much computer time to solve with exact algorithms. As a result, most scheduling programs use heuristics that generally find satisfactory but not necessarily optimal schedules.

LOGISTICS AND INVENTORY MANAGEMENT

The logistics and inventory aspects of operations management concern the storage and transportation of inventories from the manufacturer to the market. Inventories represent a very significant asset in many organizations.

Computer technology has had a major impact on both logistics and inventory management. A typical manufacturing or distribution company has 40,000 items and 30,000 transactions per week. It is simply too difficult for paper-based systems to keep up with so many items and transactions. Computer-based inventory management systems have three basic types of transactions: (1) receipts, (2) issues, and (3) corrections. A receipt increases the on-hand inventory with the arrival of a purchase or shop order. An issue decreases on-hand inventory when items are removed.

The inventory policy dictates when a purchase order is released (sent) to a supplier or to the in-company manufacturing facility to request replenishment inventory. The *reorder point policy* is a common policy that requires that a purchase order be released whenever the on-hand plus on-order quantity falls below R units. The best value of the reorder point R for each item can be calculated based on a statistical analysis of historical data stored in the computer. The quantity ordered is determined to balance the cost of placing an order (the order cost) and the cost of carrying inventory (the carrying cost).

PRODUCTION PLANNING AND CONTROL

Production planning and control systems deal with inventory management and production scheduling problems from purchasing all of the way through to the *end item* sold to the customer. In addition to managing inventories, production managers must also manage machines, tools, workers, and suppliers so that the entire organization works together to meet the customer's requirements with respect to timeliness, quality, and cost.

The most popular computer-based approach for managing batch manufacturing is called MANUFACTURING RESOURCE PLANNING or material requirements planning (MRP). Manufacturing resource planning systems provide a comprehensive framework for managing large complex manufacturing organizations. These systems are used by engineers, inventory managers, purchasing managers, production planners, production managers, and accountants.

The top three boxes in Figure 1 deal with the strategic planning and the annual budgeting process. The result of this planning process is a consistent set of business, marketing, and production plans that specify how many units of each product family should be built in each time period (usually months or quarters).

If the necessary resources are available, the production plan is broken into the master production schedule, which is a set of schedules for each end item in the product family. The item master database describes each item (item number, description, unit of measure, etc.). The master production schedule is then "exploded" by the MRP module into material plans for each item needed to build the end items. (Note that the MRP module performs the planning function within the MRP system.) The "explosion" process is based on the bill-of-material database, which contains the list of the "child" items required for each "parent" item.

After the material plans are complete for all items, the capacity requirements planning (CRP) module translates all open and planned shop orders into the number of hours of work required at each work center during each time period. This process requires the routing database, which specifies how many hours of work are required at each work center to build each item. Capacity requirements planning *load reports* provide a graphic summary of the hours of capacity required at each work center in each time period. If load reports predict that the work load will exceed capacity, management may schedule overtime or adjust the material plans.

Shop floor management responds to the material plans by canceling, releasing (starting), or rescheduling shop orders. Similarly, purchasing management may cancel, release, or reschedule purchase orders. The system also provides dispatch lists to work center supervisors so they can start shop orders in the right sequence.

Process manufacturing companies deal with oil refining, chemicals, food processing, and so on. Many of these companies have adapted MRP systems for their purposes; others have developed special-purpose scheduling systems that fit the particular product and process technology. Linear programming computer software packages are particularly useful for developing plans for oil refining and feed formulation systems where it is important to find frequently the optimal mix of end products or raw material inputs.

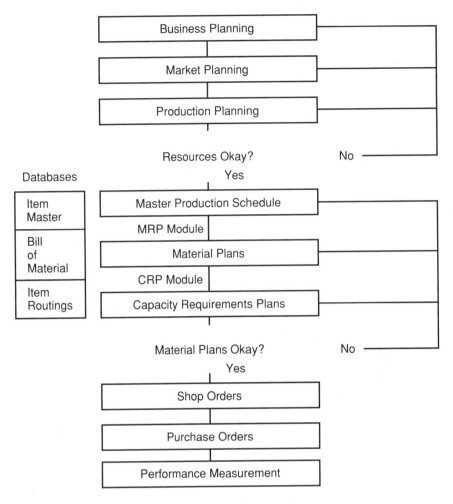

FIGURE 1. Material requirements planning framework.

QUALITY CONTROL

From an operations management perspective, quality is best defined as "conformance to standards." Although quality cannot be "inspected into the product," inspection does play an important part in quality control. Computer technology can support both the acceptance sampling and the process control types of inspection. Acceptance sampling checks a few parts from a batch to decide if the batch is acceptable. Process control collects data as the process is operating to make sure that the process is not going out of control. Computers are useful for storing and displaying both types of inspection information. Many companies also have extensive supplier monitoring software systems that evaluate suppliers on quality, timeliness, cost, and other performance measures.

PROJECT MANAGEMENT AND SCHEDULING

Project management and scheduling software can help manage large projects such as constructing a skyscraper, launching a spacecraft, or managing a software development project. Project management software requires that the user define all of the tasks (activities) needed to complete the project. For each task the user must define the task time, resources, costs, and precedence tasks. Project management software helps plan and control the project in terms of start dates, due dates, resource requirements, costs, and budgets.

DATA COLLECTION SYSTEMS

Computer-based data collection systems are used for operations in many organizations. Bar-coding, optical character recognition (OCR), optimal mark recognition (OMR), and other optical scanning devices allow for transaction data to be collected at low cost so that the current status of the system can be known at all times. These technologies are particularly useful for high-transaction-volume inventory systems in warehouses and retail outlets.

DATA COMMUNICATIONS

Computer-based data communications systems can enhance productivity in data-intensive operations management environments. For example, express mail services use handheld data entry devices that can communicate a "batch" of data periodically to a main computer so that management can help keep track of the location of all packages. Many field service engineers for computer companies now communicate with their dispatchers via handheld brick-sized microcomputers that support data communications over phone lines or radio channels. Waller (1990) notes that electronic data interchange is playing an increasingly important role in the communication of purchase orders to suppliers. Facsimile (fax) transmissions are also becoming very popular. Electronic data interchange is also being used to send material plans to suppliers for purchased parts far in advance of actual purchase orders. Some banks send digitized images of checks so that no paper needs to be moved.

CONCLUSIONS

Computer technology plays an important role in several operations management environments. For the high-level decisions, such as facility location, computer-based decision support systems provide useful information summary and analysis. For more routine decisions, such as inventory control and quality control, computers can handle the clerical work and provide insightful excep-

tion reports. In today's "data-rich" world, the application of computers to operations management has greatly enhanced the productivity of many manufacturing and service operations.

Reference

Waller, D. G. 1990. The evolution of EDI partnerships. *Production and Inventory Management Review*, Nov.:30–31.

For Further Reading

Ballou, R. H. 1973. *Business logistics management.* Englewood Cliffs, N.J.: Prentice-Hall.

Murdick, R. G., B. Render, and R. S. Russell. 1990. *Service operations management.* Boston: Allyn and Bacon.

Orlicky, J. 1974. *Material requirements planning.* New York: McGraw-Hill.

Plossl, G. W. 1985. *Production and inventory control—Principles and techniques.* 2nd ed. Englewood Cliffs, N.J.: Prentice-Hall.

Schroeder, R. G. 1989. *Operations management.* 3rd ed. New York: McGraw-Hill.

Vollmann, T. E., W. L. Berry, and D. C. Whybark. 1988. *Manufacturing/planning and control systems.* 2nd ed. Homewood, Ill.: Irwin.

Arthur V. Hill

OPERATIONS RESEARCH

See Queueing Theory

ORGANIZATION OF THE INFORMATION SYSTEMS FUNCTION

The idea that there should be something called the information systems (IS) function is a recent development in organizational life. Prior to the spread of modern digital computers into organizations in the late

1950s and early 1960s, the vast majority of information processing work done in organizations was carried out by the functional units where information originated and was needed. Even organizations with intensive and sophisticated information handling activities tended to treat information processing as a specialized and relatively low-level function, usually carried out by data processing clerks using mechanical tabulation equipment. In most cases, this equipment was distributed throughout the organization as needed, and not consolidated into a central processing unit.

Throughout the 1960s general-purpose digital computers became more powerful, and were applied to an increasing number of tasks in the organization. The complexity of handling information to be processed with the new technology increased steadily. In a short time the practices for managing the low-level tasks of data processing on tabulation equipment were inadequate for coping with the complicated environment created by use of expensive, general-purpose digital computers. Of particular concern to organizational leaders was the high purchase cost of these computers, often the largest capital investments organizations made outside of buildings. Making full and efficient use of the expensive computing resource was high on the priority list of senior managers. The fact that the processing power of a computer rose at a rate equal to the square of the cost of the processor made it practical to bring all processing jobs to a central location for maximum efficiency. This was the main impetus for consolidating information processing activity in organizations.

Initially, the computer was placed under the control of the functional department that used it the most. This was often the organization's accounting or finance department. Other departments needing to use the computer brought their work to this department for processing. As demands for computer processing grew, the responsibilities and authorities of those performing the processing function grew. In time, this function took on a life of its own in the organization, and identifiable data processing departments were established. These departments embodied those tasks that grew into what we

now call the IS function. It is important to note that the IS function as we think of it today is shaped more by this history than by functional activities unique to the processing of information.

BASIC ISSUES IN ORGANIZING THE INFORMATION SYSTEMS FUNCTION

There are three basic issues to consider in organizing the IS function. The first is what the function is to contain or involve. The second is the governance structure and mechanisms for the function. The third is the means for allocating and controlling resources dedicated to the function.

Components of the IS Function

The exact configuration of responsibilities and tasks contained in the IS function will depend to some extent on the governance structure and mechanisms adopted. Thus, these two issues must be seen as tightly coupled. The key in determining what to include in the IS function is the nature and role of information processing in the work of the organization. In organizations where information collection, handling, and storage are disaggregated and linked only to specific functional tasks, the IS function can be narrowly defined. It might, for example, include nothing more than provision of computer processing and storage services. On the other hand, where the work of the organization is dependent on highly integrated flows of information in various forms, both within and outside the organization, a much more comprehensive scope might be warranted.

In the early days of the IS function, the primary components were provision of computer processing, computer operations, tape and disk storage, printing, programming of applications, and data entry. All of these might still be appropriately included in the package, but over the years conditions have changed such that some are no longer necessarily part of the IS function per se. For example, the emergence of efficient data communications technology made it possible to place data entry terminals in the user departments, where data originate, and move the entire data entry function to the users. Similarly, it is possible to give responsibility for the programming of applications to users or to purchase applications software from outside vendors. Over the past decade, all forms of electronic communication have become more tightly coupled to computing activities, and many organizations have added voice communications to the IS function, meaning the IS function includes the telephone system. Some organizations take an even broader view, gathering together all "information" activities such as copying, reprographics, public information, telephone communications, radio communications, and so on, along with the traditional IS functions.

The choice of which activities to include in a definition of the IS function will depend on the history of the organization, the existing deployment of authorities and responsibilities, the capabilities of the existing work force, and the objectives of senior managers. There is no ideal set of activities to be included. Nevertheless, the choices of what is included are important, for they will determine the kind of IS function the organization builds.

Governance Structure and Mechanisms

Selecting the appropriate governance structure and mechanisms for the IS function is crucial. The fundamental question of who will direct the function determines the kind of function the organization will have. The brief history above shows that the governance of the IS function in most organizations was historical accident, due to the economies of scale offered by centralizing information processing in one computer system, and the assignment of responsibility for the computer system to the department making the most use of the system. The questions whether to centralize or decentralize computing and where to locate control over computing resources have been hotly contested for many years. Improvements in technology have brought highly distributable computing capability in the form of minicomputers and microcomputers, and the costs of computing processor power have dropped dramatically. There is no essential economic reason to centralize processing.

Improvements in applications also have extended the utility of computing to many functional units, so the rationale for maintaining control over computing resources in a particular functional unit has been called into question.

There is no simple answer to the question whether to centralize or decentralize the IS function. For one thing, there are different aspects of the function that might be centralized or decentralized. Three are obvious: (1) control over the resources and policies related to information processing, (2) control over the physical technology, and (3) control over the functional expertise in applying the technology. Centralization of control basically means that one person or a small group of people decide how the IS function is to be set up and managed. Decentralization of control means that decisions regarding the IS function will be made by many individuals and groups, with no expectation of cooperation among them. By centralizing control, it is possible to create and maintain centralized physical technology and centralized functional expertise if desired. Yet, centralized control can also permit decentralized deployment of technology and decentralized functional expertise. Centralized control usually has the full weight of the organization's decision authority structure behind it, so the policies of those in control can be enforced even if they are difficult to carry out.

Decentralization of control clearly makes possible the decentralization of technology and expertise. But it is usually very difficult under conditions of decentralized control to maintain centralized technology and centralized expertise. This is because real control comes through the means to enforce policy. No decentralized decision maker can bring the full weight of the organization's decision authority structure to bear, so the only sources of genuine local control are to obtain possession of both the technology and the expertise necessary to meet local needs. Thus, a decision to decentralize control of the IS function is very difficult to reverse as time goes on.

The most common arguments for and against centralization of the IS function are most easily understood in terms of a tradeoff between efficiency and effectiveness. As a general rule, it is more efficient to centralize expensive resources because they can be more readily used by all who need them, and idle time is reduced. The economies of scale in early mainframes made this particularly important. On the other hand, decentralization usually permits more effective use of the resource because those actually doing the work that requires the resource can get access to and apply the resource more readily. The changing capabilities and economics of computing technology have made it impossible to settle this trade-off in any conclusive manner.

The more important issue in the centralization decision concerns organizational philosophy. It is usually best to organize the IS function in a manner that corresponds to and complements the larger organizational structure. If the organization operates as a highly centralized entity, a centralized IS function is probably best. Conversely, a highly decentralized organization is unlikely to work comfortably with a centralized IS function. There are exceptions to this rule of thumb, but they are not common. They arise most often when the specific information processing needs of parts of the organization require organization of the IS function in a manner different from the larger organization's structure.

The advent of minicomputers and microcomputers prompted many observers to predict that the IS function would inevitably become decentralized. This is an ungrounded proposition. There are important reasons why an organization might want to maintain highly centralized control over IS policy, IS technology, and IS expertise. The fact that the economics of computing favored centralization of the IS function in the early days was not proof that the function *should* be centralized. In the same way, the fact that IS activities can now be economically decentralized is not proof that the IS function should be decentralized. Rather, organizations now have real options with respect to centralization and decentralization, and the question of what an organization should do depends on the character of information processing in the business of the organization and the organizational philosophy of

the organization's leadership. There are pros and cons with either direction.

If an organization pursues a strategy of centralized control of the IS function, the question of where to locate that control in the organizational hierarchy becomes critical. There are basically two options. One is to locate control within the authority of an existing division or department, such as the finance department or an administrative services department. The other is to make the IS function an independent department reporting directly to a high-level organizational executive. Most management experts recommend the latter to increase the likelihood that the needs of the whole organization will be served well. Placing the IS function under the control of one functional group makes it too easy for the needs of that particular group to be favored over others' needs. In spite of this advice, a large number of organizations have stayed with the traditionally common arrangement of locating the IS function in the organization's accounting or finance department. There is little empirical evidence to show which arrangement is preferable. The decision where the IS function shall be located will turn mainly on the beliefs and biases of senior organizational leaders.

Decentralized IS functions usually work well to serve the local needs of specific user groups, but they sometimes do not work well in serving the organizationwide IS needs. Conversely, centralized IS functions can serve organizationwide needs well while neglecting the needs of local groups. In either case, a useful strategy for avoiding unmet needs is to form a representative committee to discuss shortcomings in existing operations. The idea of the "steering committee" arose in the days of the centralized IS function to hear and accommodate the needs and concerns of the local IS user communities. A typical complaint was that the centralized IS group served only the needs of the department it reported to (usually accounting or finance) and perhaps top management. The steering committee was intended to put IS service under the scrutiny of an authoritative body of representatives from other functional areas needing IS attention.

The steering committee concept has had

a mixed history. It worked well in those cases where the top management of the organization truly empowered the steering committee to set IS policy, and where the IS managers were willing and able to respond to the needs articulated by the steering committee; however, in cases where the committee was merely a sounding board with no real authority, meetings of the committee usually degenerated into meaningless exercises as the high-level members of the committee sent subordinates with less influence to take their places. Similarly, in cases where the IS managers were determined to restrict service to only those departments with the greatest resources and political power, the purposes of the steering committee were easily subverted. The key to making a steering committee work as planned is to match the real charter of the committee with the requisite authority to do the job, and to make sure the IS managers understand that their performance will be evaluated in significant measure by the steering committee. In the most extreme cases, the resources of the IS function are controlled by the steering committee.

In organizations that have adopted highly decentralized structure for the IS function, steering committees serve a different purpose. The representatives are brought together to find ways to cooperate and compromise in the interests of objectives that span across departments. Good examples of such coordination objectives include data communications networking, establishment and maintenance of shared databases, consolidated purchasing and training, and setting of standards for equipment, data, and operations. These kinds of committees almost always are the result of action by high-level, central executives who feel that organizationwide concerns are not being met by the decentralized structure. The key to success of these committees is a strong presence of a powerful central authority with good negotiating skills who has the power to require the decentralized IS groups to come together and reach compromises. The most direct source of power is control over resources for the IS groups.

The final issue in governance structure and mechanisms for the IS function is the internal organization of the IS unit. A common approach is to organize around discrete functional specialties, such as computer operations, data communications, systems development, and data entry. This arrangement has advantages because the work is divided according to the kinds of tasks being done, and there is relatively little overlap between the tasks. The most serious question in internal organization has to do with the work structure in the systems development area. Most IS units do four kinds of software-related systems work: systems programming, systems analysis, applications programming, and applications maintenance. Systems programming generally has to do with creation and maintenance of basic system utilities and the operating system itself. It also usually involves installation of applications that require system-level modifications. Systems analysis is the task by which requirements for new systems are ascertained and the systems themselves are designed. Applications programming usually involves only the programming and testing of new systems, or major enhancement features of existing systems. Applications maintenance refers to fixing of problems in existing systems and making modifications and enhancements to existing systems.

The key issue to address in work arrangements among systems development personnel is whether to split the systems analysis, applications programming, and applications maintenance functions. On one hand, these functions require somewhat different skills and work habits, so they can be easily divided. On the other hand, the typical life cycle of systems is messy rather than neat, and problems that show up in maintenance are often traced back to systems analysis and programming. Thus, these activities are all part of the same package when it comes to utility of the application to the users. A significant problem that arises when the activities are split is failure to take ownership and responsibility of important tasks and products. The analyst or programmer might give insufficient attention to the maintainability of the system because he or she will never have to maintain it. The systems maintenance person might defer fixing a problem or making a modification on the grounds that the original analysis or programming will not permit such changes. The main problem in such cases is misplaced authority and responsibility, and no one is really accountable for the long-term welfare of the system's users.

When organizing the IS function internally, it is very important to pay close attention to the motivations and reward systems for various functional groups. To the extent possible, specialties that must work together harmoniously to achieve effective service should be under the same supervisory structure.

Allocating and Controlling Resources

The IS function is expensive, and it is becoming increasingly so. The rapidly declining price and growing capabilities of computing technology have stimulated the application of the technology to such a great extent that the overall costs of the IS function now constitute a significant part of many organizations' budgets. Moreover, the conventional understanding of what constitutes an IS "resource" has shifted over the years to include the very information being processed. It is important to keep separated the issues of resources for dealing with information and the resources of information. The organizational responses for managing the two can be quite different. The resources for dealing with information can be measured by counting all direct and indirect costs related to collecting, storing, processing, and making use of information. The commonly accepted cost components include the following: First are the labor costs for all those whose primary jobs consist of collecting and entering information into storage or processing systems, those who create the hardware and software systems inside the organization used for processing information, and those who install, operate, and maintain the information processing technologies used in the organization. Second are the purchase and contract costs for the equipment and software required for information entry, processing, storing, printing, displaying, and so on. Third are the costs of supplies and services (including training) consumed in dealing

with information. Finally, there are the costs of managing and directing the people involved in these activities. Together, these costs form the basis of the IS function's budget.

If the IS function is centralized, there will be a single budget. If it is decentralized, there might be many budgets, or the costs of the IS functions will simply be bundled into the overhead costs of the functional units in which the functions are located. It does not really matter how costs are accounted for and how budgeting is done unless there is a desire to control allocation and consumption of resources involved in the IS function. This is usually the case, given the high profile of IS costs in today's organizations. The question, then, is how to allocate and control the resources of the IS function.

There are two general strategies for resource allocation and control. The first is to treat the IS function as an overhead item, a kind of public good available to the organizational units that use IS services. The main mechanisms of allocation and control are to set a specific limit on the resources available for the IS function, usually via a budget allocation, and to establish policies for deciding what those resources shall be spent on. This usually means setting priorities for new system development or rewriting of old systems and placing limits on use of particular resources (e.g., disk storage or processor time) by different user groups. This strategy can work very well, but has two potential drawbacks. One is that the policies might be set in arbitrary or unfair ways, so some user groups are disadvantaged. The other is that there is an incentive for user groups to make constant demands for resources as they are not directly paying for what they receive.

The second strategy is to create a kind of internal market for IS services through use of a pricing or chargeback system. The common way of constructing a chargeback system is to assess the costs of providing each chargeable aspect of IS service, develop cost-based prices for these, establish some kind of monitoring or metering to measure use, and then charge users for the amount they use. Naturally, the resources to buy these services must be made available to the user groups.

The theoretical advantages of pricing are significant. With an appropriately constructed and applied pricing system one can simultaneously establish efficient allocation (because users buy only what they need), recover costs (because the users pay for what they use), and gain important information for capacity planning. Differential pricing (e.g., higher charges in peak load periods) also permits load leveling.

In practice, chargeback schemes often run into trouble. One problem is that the costs of administering a chargeback system can be substantial. The main difficulty, however, is the fact that there is no real market in which the logic of pricing can obtain. Most organizations do not permit their departments to "go outside" for IS services, so the internal IS function can behave as a monopoly. The typical monopoly seeks to restrict supply and raise prices, not the best strategy for the welfare of the organization or the IS users. On the other hand, the lack of a real market places the IS function itself in an inefficient position because it cannot easily sell surplus capacity on the outside market and thereby recover costs for carrying that capacity. In such cases, the IS function has only three choices: restrict capacity to reduce excess supply, charge the users for the entire supply even though they do not use it, or run a deficit. Restricting supply below reasonable levels can be very damaging to the organization's welfare, and charging users for unused capacity destroys the whole incentive to be economical. The only sensible way to deal with this problem is for the IS function to run a deficit on a regular basis. But this usually does not reflect well on the IS managers unless the senior management of the organization are particularly enlightened about the complexities of chargeback schemes for IS functions.

The choice between providing IS services as a public good and using chargeback is not easy. Both approaches have drawbacks. Generally, the simplest solution is to provide services as a public good, and use policies to restrict runaway costs; however, an effectively designed and implemented chargeback system can be of real use in an organization where the IS function has many different user groups, placing high demand on the IS resource base. It is also possible to mix the strategies, using policies to allocate some resources (e.g., programmer and analyst time) and chargeback to allocate other resources (e.g., computer processor time and disk storage).

The treatment of information as a resource is quite a different issue from controlling the resources of the IS function. The idea that information is an organizational resource came into vogue in the early 1980s, first through the recognition of the data administration function and later in the concept of information resource management. The data administration notion was built around the practical observation that certain kinds of data require special attention and handling. For example, databases essential to the work of the organization often must be built to allow multiple uses of data elements, thereby increasing the importance of maintaining data accuracy and integrity. Some kinds of data, such as names, identifiers, and so on, serve multiple purposes and must be treated as special. The first concern of data administration was the data, not the processing of the data. This was an important shift in philosophy in the management of the IS function.

The information resources management (IRM) concept stems from somewhat different principles than the data administration concept. The basic view of IRM is that information is an essential resource for organizations, in the same vein as land, labor, and capital. Information must therefore be treated in the context of resource economics and managed by specialists equivalent to those who manage other organizational resources. The idea is attractive in principle, but it has serious shortcomings. To begin, information is not a resource in the sense of resource economics. Resources in the economic sense are defined by their scarcity. Information does require an investment initially, when it is created, discovered, or otherwise obtained. But unlike resources in the economic definition, information can be used over and over again at almost no cost without losing its inherent value. Once it is available, it is no longer scarce. This makes many features of resource economics inapplicable to information and deprives the IRM concept of its most significant technical base.

The most significant development in the IRM scene occurred in the early 1980s when the federal government of the United States adopted the IRM concept as the organizing philosophy for all executive-branch IS activities. Information resources management officers were created in all executive departments, and IRM plans were required for all IS activities. In the years since IRM was adopted, the changes in federal IS activities have been minimal. Most of the IRM managers are merely the IS managers renamed.

On the other hand, the IRM concept in practice serves a somewhat different purpose than the resource economics perspective suggests. It is mainly a means of mobilizing organizational attention around the fact that information is important, that it is expensive to manage well, and that greater care in managing information can have real payoffs.

For Further Reading

King, J. L. 1982. Organizational cost considerations in computing decentralization. In R. Goldberg and H. Lorin, eds. *The economics of information processing*, vol. 2, pp. 68–81. New York: Wiley.

———. 1983. Centralized vs. decentralized computing: Organizational considerations and management options. *ACM Computing Surveys* 15(4):319–45.

———. 1988. The changing political economy of chargeout systems. *Information Systems Management*, Spring, pp. 65–67.

King, J. L., and K. L. Kraemer. 1988. Information resource management: Is it sensible and will it work? *Information and Management* 15:7–14.

King, J. L., and E. Schrems. 1978. Cost-benefit analysis in information systems development and operation. *ACM Computing Surveys*, March, pp. 19–34.

Kraemer, K. L., J. L. King, D. Dunkle, and J. P. Lane. 1989. *Managing information systems: Change and control in organizational computing*. San Francisco: Jossey-Bass.

John Leslie King

ORGANIZATIONS

See Appendix: Computing Assocations

ORGANIZING INSTITUTIONAL INFORMATION SYSTEMS INFRASTRUCTURE

Information used in an organization can be classified into two general types: Type I information, used for overall operation and management of the organization, such as accounting, purchasing, and personnel; and Type II information, used to support the work of the specialized needs of professionals in the organization, such as scientists, engineers, and economists. Type I information is common to all large organizations, while Type II varies, based on the type, nature, and objectives of an organization. Before the advent of digital computers, highly labor-intensive but well-organized systems were created to store, manipulate, and distribute Type I information. Because of difficulty in handling this information, the uses were very limited. Type II information was handled in an ad hoc manner by each professional group interested in it. As early as 1952, large enterprises recognized the advantages of digital computers and began applying them to Type I information. A new class of professionals evolved whose job was to understand the enterprises' information needs and the information systems required for handling them. These early systems mimicked the manual processes they replaced. In the 1960s the use of computers expanded to Type II information. In this case, however, the computer professionals provided the computational means and left the information handling to the specialist in each field. The 1970s saw an expansion of functionality beyond what was conceived with manual systems. In particular, distribution of information throughout the organization improved as on-line systems became available. A dramatic change came in the 1980s as graphics presentation, user-friendly interfaces, capable data networks, massive memories capable of storage, and presentation of nontextual material expanded the use of Type I information and created totally new ways of using Type I and Type II information. There is a general attempt to collect information at the point of origin and enhance and deliver it to point of use without any human handling. There is also an understanding that information systems should be used to add value to the transactions necessary in running large organizations. Nevertheless, at this writing the use of information systems in the United States is nonuniform, with many instances of inadequate or even undesirable application of information systems. A majority of large organizations have frozen their usage in the 1960s style, although state-of-the-art equipment and systems are used. Part of the reason is that the organizations, which were created in the 1960s to bring about change and modernize their information systems, have become powerful obstacles to change. This is particularly the case in public and governmental organizations.

USE OF INFORMATION IN LARGE ORGANIZATIONS

Type II information and its processing are normally controlled and managed by professionals in various fields of endeavor. The research staff of an organization shapes the nature of information systems used for research. The engineering staff deals with systems in engineering. The organizationwide issue is the creation and operation of a data network. The networking is required to allow sharing of expensive equipment and systems across an organization and to help the transfer of data to and from various operations. For example, engineering data are shared with manufacturing, or quality assurance data are shared with engineering. Data networks are also used to allow the entire organization to get access to external information resources essential to the organization's various endeavors. Bank databases used for economic forecasting, access to supercomputers for engineering modeling, transfer of documents to and from colleagues

and customers, and sharing of high-speed printers are but a few examples of the need to create and operate a data network.

Type I information is used in all aspects of the day-to-day operation of an organization. To support the overall operation of an organization, information systems are developed to support such functions as purchasing, inventory, and accounting. These transaction systems, initially developed in the 1960s, were originally run in batch modes— usually overnight. The new trend is to fully interactive systems that can provide instant feedback, resulting in more responsive operations.

The data collected and generated by these transaction systems are also used in tactical decision making to change and improve operations. Data generated by an inventory system are used to control inventory size better or to reduce waste; financial data could suggest new patterns of investment; student enrollment data could suggest changes in class schedules. A new important trend is the development of expert systems in support of transaction systems. These expert systems will directly analyze data generated by the transaction systems of an organization and suggest improvement in operations.

Finally, all data generated and collected within the organization, and acquired from outside, are used in the development of short-term and strategic plans. Simulation and modeling techniques, graphics representation, simultaneous sessions with several information services, and the means to integrate information from many sources are important tools for all planning activities of an organization. These systems reduce planning time, provide means for monitoring the implementation of plans, and allow the timely modification of plans as circumstances dictate.

STRATEGIES FOR INFORMATION MANAGEMENT

Information management strategies in large organizations, unlike most other management strategies, are not mature and vary greatly from organization to organization.

Several trends, however, are noteworthy. It is recognized that a high-level position in a large organization should be established to set policies and standards and to coordinate the information system activities of various parts of the organization. The holder of this position, referred to as chief information officer (CIO) in many organizations, usually reports to the chief executive or chief operating officer and is responsible for overall planning of information systems. In organizations that are centrally controlled, the various information system operations report to the CIO.

Many organizations recognize that knowledge of information systems throughout the organization is required for their proper use and integration into the work of the organization. The internal training program of these organizations reflect this recognition.

It is recognized that organizationwide standards for hardware, software, and networking could reduce overall costs, including training costs. Also, it is recognized that limiting the number of vendors that provide equipment, software, and services simplifies the management of information systems and results in efficiencies.

A number of organizations consider information systems strategic tools for creating market niches by personalizing or specializing products and services. It is also recognized that information systems could shorten the reaction time of an organization to changing markets and circumstances beyond its control.

The board of directors, auditors, and others concerned with the well-being of an organization recognize the devastating impact that information systems failure could have on the organization. For that reason, a substantial amount of efforts and funds are expended to set up safeguards, such as disaster plans and security policies, to protect the operation and integrity of these systems. The distribution of computing systems throughout the organization, while creating many new opportunities for automation and improvement in the effectiveness and efficiency of the organization, has created new security and information integrity issues that are not adequately managed at this writing.

IMPACT

Three major trends dictate attention to careful management of information systems in a large organization. First, there is an increase in the number of knowledge workers in large organizations, in response to the move from a materials to an information-based world economy. The effectiveness of these workers is partially determined by the capability and quality of the information systems available. Second, the rate of change in factors affecting large organizations continues to accelerate, thereby requiring a much quicker response time by the organization to these events. Third, the increase in capability and reduction in cost of information systems have resulted in the proliferation of these systems throughout large organizations.

As we approach the end of this century, the management of information systems is becoming the most vital issue for many large organizations.

For Further Reading

Bullinger, H. J., E. N. Protonotarios, D. Bouwhuis, and F. Reim, eds. 1988. *Information technology for organizational systems.* New York: North-Holland.

Feigenbaum, E., P. McCorduck, and H. P. Nii. 1988. *The rise of the expert company.* New York: Times Books.

Holsapple, C. W., and A. B. Whinston. 1988. *The information jungle.* Homewood, Ill.: Dow Jones-Irwin.

Martin, J. 1989. *Strategic information planning methodologies.* New York: Prentice Hall.

Masuch, M., ed. 1990. *Organization, management, and expert systems.* Berlin and New York: Walter de Gruyter.

Stinchcombe, A. L. 1990. *Information and organizations.* Berkeley: University of California Press.

Morteza A. Rahimi

OUTER SPACE

See Aerospace, Computer Applications in; Astronomy, Computers in

P

PARALLEL COMPUTING

The ever-growing demand for faster computation is approaching the limits for a single processor, which is the speed of light (3×10^8 meters per second). A number of approaches to speed up computation time on a computer exist, and parallel processing is one of them. In the 1940s, John von Neumann devised the first digital computer, which performed instructions sequentially, or one after the other. For example, an instruction would be fetched from memory, decoded, and executed, in that order. Parallel processing, on the other hand, consists of a number of methodologies that increase computation speed by performing selected computations or instructions concurrently, or at the same time. A parallel processor or parallel computer implements any parallel processing technique. In other words, parallel processing performs several things simultaneously.

A problem may have areas of computation that are "parallelizable" (that can be processed independently yielding the same final result). Many typical problems have computation areas that can be parallelized. For example, problems that are expressed in vectors or matrices have sections of computation that are well suited to parallel processing: these problems have blocks that can be done simultaneously, because each individual result will not affect the other results; therefore, the final result will be correct. Some physical problems that can take advantage of parallel processing are fluid flow calculations, simulations of complex systems, intelligent robots, weather prediction, economic forecasting, artificial intelligence, image processing, nuclear reactor modeling, seismic geophysical exploration, and special medical diagnosis. Each of these applications is characterized by a large amount of data that can be analyzed much faster when parallelized. For example, simulation of the heat flow on a two-dimensional metal plate can be represented on a parallel computer with 1,024 processors by dividing the plate into a grid of 32×32 segments. Each segment contains the temperature distribution of the portion of the metal plate that is assigned to one processor.

A number of additional implementation questions must be addressed in parallelizing a problem: Is the memory associated with each processor global, local, or a combination of the two? Local is convenient but liable to produce incorrect results (the local will not have the latest result); global is more accurate but contention problems may arise when two processors need the same data. What will the overall connection scheme be (more connections are handy but harder to keep track of)? How much can we spend for the parallelization? What languages can be implemented? How many processors are needed? How extensible or flexible is the parallel solution (general solutions are nice but more difficult to produce because of the complexity involved)? Not only must these questions be posed, but there are trade-offs between the factors. Figure 1, for example, shows the trade-offs between two of these factors, time and number of processors. In other words, overhead increases with more processors, computation time increases with fewer processors, and execution time is minimum where computation time intersects with overhead.

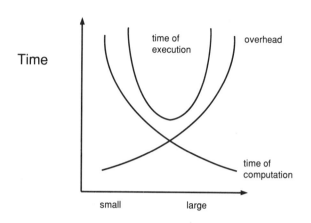

Time

FIGURE 1. Number of processors versus time.

TYPES OF PARALLEL PROCESSING

Parallel computing can be implemented with hardware, software, or a combination of the two. Several techniques exist to implement parallel computing, including pipeline computers, multiprocessor systems, and neurocomputers. Once a parallel computation has been identified, either the parallelizable segments must be divided among the processors, or the parallelization must be specified automatically. Some overhead for this parallelization exists, and affects the degree of parallelization (in other words, some tasks will be done faster sequentially than in a parallel system). Very large system integration (VLSI) hardware is often mentioned in

conjunction with parallel processing, because VLSI technology allows the processors and memories to be located on the same small chip. The software and coordination for these many processors can become quite complex and challenging, however.

Several methods of classifying parallel computation schemes exist. Flynn's classification scheme consists of four categories based on a multiplicity of instructions and data. The categories are single instruction, single data (SISD); single instruction, multiple data (SIMD); multiple instruction, single data (MISD); and multiple instruction, multiple data (MIMD). The last three categories (SIMD, MISD, and MIMD) relate to different types of parallel systems. This classification scheme depends on the computer's behavior, not on granularity (which is a measure of how fine the parallel partitioning is) or synchronization method. Figure 2 shows the relationship among these parallel types of classifications and some commercial examples of parallel computers.

There exist other classification schemes that depend on factors other than the multiplicity of data and instructions. For example, Skillicorn gives a classification scheme that mentions the degree of parallelism (or the number of processors in parallel) and their structure. Other factors that could distinguish parallel computing systems are communication characteristics, data distribution characteristics, and mathematical techniques. Once a parallelizable section is identified and described, a number of approaches

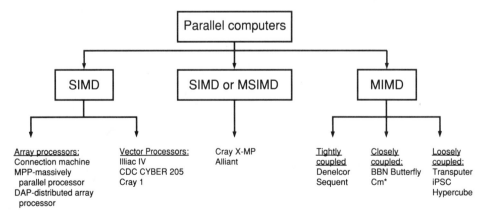

FIGURE 2. Parallel computer classification.

exist to implement this parallelism. The following sections describe parallel computing systems.

Pipeline Processors

The idea of pipelining requires overlapping instructions, as with assembly lines in a manufacturing plant. The input processes are subdivided into subprocesses, each of which is executed at the same time as other subprocesses from other tasks in the pipeline. The idea of pipelining improves the overall speed of a computer system just as the assembly line improved the overall speed of the automobile plant. The parallelism is introduced when a number of these dividable sequential tasks are performed simultaneously. Figure 3 demonstrates the idea of pipelining. When instruction 3 is fetched, instruction 2 is decoded, and instruction 1 is executed, during the same time interval $t2$. This explains the speedup. The type of problems performed on the pipeline processor have to be able to be divided up into overlapping tasks.

Connection Machine

The Connection Machine, developed by Hillis in an award-winning thesis in 1985, consists of a large number of small processors that are capable of performing parallelizable computations very quickly. Thinking Machines Corporation has developed an operational 64K processor machine, with 1,000 MIPS (millions of instructions per second). Each processor is extremely simple, with only 4K of memory, and 8 bits of internal state flags. The Connection Machine inte-

grates hardware and software for use on very large amounts of data. Each processing element is assigned one element for processing and the entire operation is performed in parallel. The massive number of processors requires both a master computer and a microcontroller, as shown in Figure 4. The master computer controls the communication between the processors, and the microcontroller transfers data through a high-bandwidth input/output channel. The large number of processors (each with its own memory of 4,096 bits) allows a fine granularity in calculations.

Hypercube

The hypercube is a type of parallel computer in which 2^n loosely coupled processors form a "cube" of 2^n vertices (or corners) of an n-dimensional cube. Parallelism arises in the hypercube when the different elements in the cube perform parallel program segments concurrently. For example, a three-dimensional hypercube contains eight processors (which could each calculate one-eighth of a parallelizable algorithm). A seven-dimensional hypercube has 128 nodes and 896 communication channels. Each processor has direct communication with n other neighbor processors through the directly connecting edges, and may have a shared connection to a host or master computer (for program coordination). If the dimension is higher, the communication capacity is higher in relation to computational capacity. A six-dimensional hypercube will require at most six hops from one node to another. There are

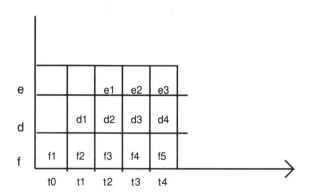

FIGURE 3. Pipelining of instruction sequencing.

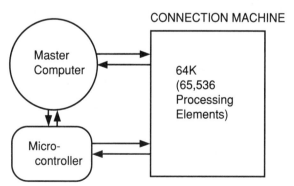

FIGURE 4. Block diagram of the Connection Machine.

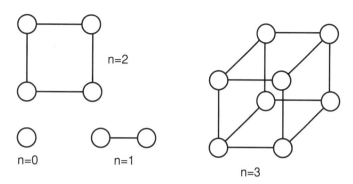

FIGURE 5. Hypercubes of dimensions 0, 1, 2, and 3.

other advantages to the hypercube: there are no special case edges (as in systolic arrays); there is a good balance between number of links and cost; two nodes are at most n links away from each other; and many arbitrary algorithms can be embedded in the hypercube architecture. For example, meshes of all dimensions, as well as a variety of parallelizable algorithms (fast Fourier transformations are one example), can be embedded in a hypercube. Figure 5 shows hypercubes of dimensions 0, 1, 2, and 3 and their connections.

Data Flow Machines

Data flow machine structure consists of machine instructions linked by the data dependencies between them. Data flow computers can be easily represented by the data flow graph, which is a bipartite graph having two nodes, called *actors* (circles) and *links.* Links denote the communication; the actors represent the operation to be performed. The links

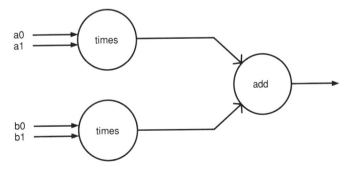

FIGURE 6. Data flow diagram.

receive tokens from one actor and send them to another actor. The actors correspond to places and the links correspond to transitions in the Petri net (see next section). The data flow machine exhibits parallelism because chunks of data can be transferred, in the form of vectors or arrays. A typical instruction can be executed when all the data that it depends on are available, and this information is given by those data dependency links. For example, Figure 6 shows a data flow graph for computing the dot product of two two-element vectors.

Only when the data are represented as a number of discrete data entries (as in a vector or array) will a data flow machine operate as a parallel processor. A big advantage to the data flow computer is the simplicity of the parallelism (the chunks of data are just sent and calculated), and some models (see discussion of Petri nets below) can easily reflect this parallelism. A disadvantage to the data flow approach is that the system will wait until all data specified are available (whether necessary for the calculation or not). A dynamic and more precise definition can alleviate this problem. Many of the same problems that face other parallel processing systems are present in data flow systems, for example, error detection, deadlock avoidance, program flexibility (this computer may not be suitable for some types of problems), and increased programming complexity.

Neurocomputers

Neurocomputers are modeled on biological neural systems, which are naturally very parallel. A worm's brain is estimated to have 1,000 neurons (nerve cells), and a human's brain, about 100 billion neurons. In the context of computers, neurons, or neural elements, are defined as units that operate when a specific threshold value (which is based on input values) is reached. The inputs to the neuron are summed (or weighted and then summed), and the output is based on the calculation for the threshold value (typically a transfer function). Several layers of neurons (each successive layer supplies input to the next) constitute the neurocomputer. Neural networks algorithms are promising for solving conventional problems in a parallel processing manner. They are being applied in a variety of software algorithms such as those for artificial intelligence, system identification, error detection and communication, and a host of other problems for which the conventional procedures have been highly involved. Figure 7 shows a single typical neuron representation, which is the unit of the neurocomputer. Let $x1$, $x2, \ldots, xn$ be the inputs to the neuron, and $w1, w2, \ldots, wn$ be the weights. The inputs and the weights correspond to stimulation levels and biological neuron synaptic strengths. The neuron output is given by

$$Z = x1 * w1 + x2 * w2 + \ldots + xn * wn$$

or

$$Z = \sum_i x_i * w_i$$

or

$$\mathbf{Z} = \mathbf{X} \cdot \mathbf{W}.$$

Systolic Arrays

Systolic arrays, proposed by Kung, consist of interconnected general processing elements in a highly regular format. Parallelism is introduced in the systolic array when the different elements in the array perform segments of a parallelized algorithm. The communication to the outside world is tightly controlled, because only boundary elements are involved. The exact interconnection pattern is flexible, so that the designer can exactly specify the connections. *Systolic* refers to the regularity of heartbeats (systole is

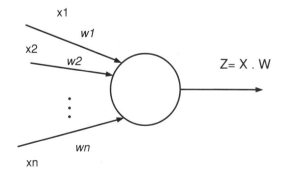

FIGURE 7. Neuron representation.

literally the contraction of the heart): the function of the systolic array is highly regular.

SOFTWARE FOR PARALLEL PROCESSING

When an algorithm is parallelized, either the software, the hardware, or both must be changed from the sequential implementation. Often the hardware is given, and so software implementation is the key to parallel processing. Software issues include language, compiler, and operating system; these are very critical in the parallel programming environment.

The sequential implementation language must be modified to reflect the parallel implementation. For example, C++ has a special feature called PARMACS, which is a set of macros that implement shared memory constructs for the programmer. Often, the parallel processing software addresses one of the parallel processing issues (in the preceding example, shared versus local memory), but this can make the language more complex and in some cases less flexible (again, the preceding example makes local memory less attractive). According to several authors, the future of programming, and parallel programming in particular, includes software engineering workstations, expert systems, automated techniques, graphical user interfaces, portability across architectures, interoperability (off-the-shelf LEGO approach), more complex embedded applications, security and privacy, and object-oriented programming.

Some parallel languages (languages with some facility for parallel processing) are OCCAM, ADA, extended Fortran 77, C++, and concurrent Pascal. Several models for representation of parallel software exist, including Markov chains, queueing models, and the traditional models (data flow diagrams, Pert charts, HIPO charts, Warnier diagrams, Jackson methodology diagrams, etc.). The next section discusses the Petri net, a representative model useful for parallel computing systems.

Petri nets constitute a modeling technique particularly well suited for representation of parallel processing, because the Petri net can represent both hardware and software aspects simultaneously—the hierarchical system layers, the control factors, and the conflict/parallelism inherent in the system. Typically, parallel programs are described somewhat informally. When the program is being debugged, the programmer may have difficulty discovering whether the error is in description or implementation. The parallel program, therefore, may require a more rigorous description method than the sequential program (this may be due to the sheer complexity).

Petri nets are a modeling tool adequate for parallel program description. Petri nets are bipartite graphs and have two types of nodes: places (circles) and transitions (bars on directed arcs). This model can show control aspects, the hierarchization of the problem, concurrency (temporal or otherwise), and conflict (an important issue in parallel computing systems). The dynamic control aspects of the graph are represented by a graph primitive, called a token (shown as a dot on a place). The tokens move through the net whenever a transition "fires." A transition is enabled to fire when each input place contains at least one token, and after the transition fires, each output place gains one token (and each input place has one token reduced). Tokens are not conserved (more tokens may be added than subtracted when a transition fires). Also, the choice as to when or if a transition may fire once enabled is not strictly given in the traditional Petri net. A specialized type of Petri net, called a probabilistic Petri net, can specify the probability of firing for each transition.

Figure 8 shows a Petri net that contains both conflict and concurrency, which are essential components of a parallel computing system. If both places $p1$ and $p2$ contain a token, both transitions $t1$ and $t2$ are enabled to fire; however, they both cannot fire simultaneously, because the enabling token at $p2$ can serve only for one transition to fire. In other words, if $t1$ fires, it will disable $t2$ (because the token in $p2$ will be removed). This concept is known as "conflict." Concurrency, on the other hand, can also be seen in

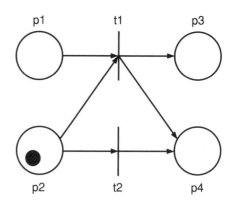

FIGURE 8. Petri net with conflict and concurrency.

this diagram. If $p1$ and $p2$ contain one token each, $t1$ will be enabled. If $t1$ fires, both $p3$ and $p4$ will receive a token simultaneously.

An example for parallel processing could be the summation of numbers. The first $1/n$ numbers could be summed on one processor, the second $1/n$ summed on another processor, and so on to the nth $1/n$ numbers summed on the nth processor. The following Extended Fortran do-loop shows 100 numbers to be summed, which are parallelized among four processors:

```
SUM.TOTAL = 0
DO 5 I = 1,100, 4
5 SUM.TOTAL = SUMTOTAL + SEGMENT(I)
END.
```

Here, "4" indicates the number of processors that the algorithm will be divided among and SEGMENT(I) indicates the segment of the array of 100 numbers that has been divided among the four processors. This minor extension to the operating system can reflect the potential parallelization.

Other structures for parallelization of software are cobegin/coend and fork/join, which are actually delimiters for the area of the algorithm that is to be parallelized and are inherent with the specific parallel language chosen. For example, the preceding example (which consists of summing the numbers from 1 to 100) can be stated with cobegin/coend statements that frame the parallelized algorithm segments:

```
BEGIN
  So;
  SUM.TOTAL = 0; let n = 1 for processor 1,
  26 for processor 2, 51 for processor 3, 76
  for processor 4 and m = 25 for processor 1,
  50 for processor 2, 75 for processor 3, and
  100 for processor 4;
  COBEGIN
    FOR I = n to m do
    SUM.TOTAL = SUM.TOTAL + I;
  COEND;
  Si;
END.
```

In this program, the parallelized segments are set off, or delimited, with the cobegin/coend statements. The parallelized algorithm can be divided up statically (specified exactly as it is here) or dynamically (changing with every execution).

SELECTED COMMERCIAL PARALLEL PROCESSING EXAMPLES

Some successful commercial parallel processing computers are the BBN Butterfly, which has 32 processors, a Butterfly switching system, and a UNIX-like operating system supporting C language; the Alliant FX/8, which has eight computational elements, six interactive processors, a common memory bus, and Fortran 77 with array extensions; the Intel iPSC, which has thirty-two processors with 0.5 MB each and a XENIX operating system with Fortran 286 language; the CRAY X-MP, which has two central processing units with 2M 64-bit words, supporting Extended Fortran 77 language; the IBM 3090, which has two processors with one vector unit each and Fortran 77 language; the FPS T, which has sixteen processors with a Transputer operating system and OCCAM language; and the Sequent Balance 21000, which has thirty processors and a DYNIX operating system with Fortran 77 with extensions. The main issues in the various commercial parallel processors are the difficulty of programming, the flexibility of architecture (does the architecture suit the particular problem, or was it configured with another problem in mind), the cost, the num-ber of processors, the interconnection system, the choice of operating system, and deadlock and race. Deadlock is indefinite waiting on shared information; races occur when the final state is indeterminate or alternates between two continuously changing values.

PERFORMANCE MEASURES

Several different factors affect the decision to parallelize a system and to what degree the system will be parallelized. Some overhead is associated with the parallelization, and some small tasks will be more efficiently done on a sequential machine. Minimum processing time is a general reason to use a parallel processor. Two other reasons for parallelization are flexibility (the parallel processor can handle many types of computations efficiently) and reliability (the processor interconnections can be reconfigured to avoid a faulty processor) or "fault tolerance" (the system can operate adequately even when some processors fail). The processing time is typically given as MIPS, millions of instructions processed per second, or MFLOPS, millions of floating point operations per second.

Three rules of thumb may offer some help in the decision to parallelize:

1. *Amdahl's law:* Speedup $= n/(1+(n-1)f)$, where n = number of processors and f = fraction of nonparallelizable operations (so if 5% of an algorithm is unparallelizable, the maximum speedup is 20, no matter how many processors are there).

2. *Grosch's law:* The computing power of a processor increases in proportion to the cost (the cost will be a limiting factor at some point).

3. *Minsky's conjecture:* Because of communication overhead between n processors, the actual performance of the parallel computer is approximately proportional to $\log_2 n$ instead of n, limiting the actual parallelization that can be achieved.

Two performance measures for parallel processing commonly used are:

1. Speedup = time for sequential calculation/time for parallelized calculation.

2. Efficiency = speedup/degree of parallelism or number of processors.

One major problem in the implementation of parallel processing systems (outside of the earlier discussion of the measurement of such systems) is the synchronization in the system. In other words, the degree of connectivity between processors and the degree of independence of the processors are in conflict. The memories (global and/or local), the algorithms, the communication, the data, and the results all must be properly synchronized to avoid deadlocks (when the system is waiting for results from two processors, each of which is waiting on the same data, causing the system to deadlock, or wait indefinitely, because of poor synchronization).

For Further Reading

Babb, R., ed. 1988. *Programming parallel processors.* Reading, Mass.: Addison-Wesley.

Chandy, K., and J. Misra. 1988. *Parallel program design: A foundation.* Reading, Mass.: Addison-Wesley.

DeCegama, A. 1989. *Parallel processing architectures and VLSI hardware.* New York: McGraw-Hill.

Flynn, M. 1966. Very high speed computing systems. *Proceedings of the IEEE,* December 1966, pp. 1901–9.

Hayes, J. 1988. *Computer architecture and organization.* New York: McGraw-Hill.

Hecht-Nielson, R. 1988. Neurocomputing. *IEEE Spectrum,* March 1988.

Hillis, W. 1988. *The Connection Machine.* Cambridge, Mass.: MIT Press.

Hwang, K., and F. Briggs. 1987. *Computer architecture and parallel processing.* New York: McGraw-Hill.

Kogge, P. 1981. *The architecture of pipelined computers.* New York: McGraw-Hill.

Kung, H. 1982. Why systolic architectures? *IEEE Computer,* January 1982, pp. 37–46.

Marsan, M., G. Balbo, and G. Conte. 1987.

Performance models of multiprocessor systems. Cambridge, Mass.: MIT Press.

Peterson, J. 1981. *Petri net theory and modeling of systems.* Englewood Cliffs, N.J.: Prentice-Hall.

Skillicorn, D. 1988. A taxonomy for computer architectures. *IEEE Computer,* November 1988, pp. 46–57.

Special Issue on Supercomputer Technology. *Proceedings of the IEEE,* December 1989, pp. 1793–1999.

Harpreet Singh
Lisa Anneberg
Devinder Kaur
Ece Yaprak

PARALLELISM

See Distributed Computing; Hardware: Computer Architecture; Parallel Computing

PASCAL, BLAISE

Blaise Pascal was born on June 19, 1623, at Clermont-Ferrand, France. His mother died when he was 3. He had two sisters, Gilberte, 3 years older, and Jacqueline, the baby. His father, Etienne, was a lawyer and mathematician. Etienne abandoned his career to raise Blaise and his equally talented sisters. The Pascal children's education took place informally, with Etienne introducing such topics as ancient languages but withholding subjects he felt were above the boy's head. He denied him, therefore, any books on mathematics. He even warned his friends never to mention mathematics in front of his son.

In the end, Blaise managed to beg from his father the most elementary definition of geometry, whereupon he taught himself its basic axioms, and succeeded, with no guidance whatever, in discovering for himself the first twenty-three propositions of Euclid in the correct order. This was enough to convince his father, who set about teaching him everything he knew about geometry.

When he was only 16, Pascal published a book on the geometry of the conic sections that for the first time carried the subject well beyond the point at which Apollonius had left it nearly nineteen centuries before. Descartes refused to believe that a 16-year-old could have written it.

Soon his father moved to Rouen, where he had been appointed tax commissioner. This job called for monumental calculations in figuring tax assessments. The man who had tried to hold back his son now turned to him for help in the thankless labor of hand-totaling endless columns of numbers. In 1642, when he was only 19, young Pascal had invented a calculating machine (called *la Pascaline*) that, by means of cogged wheels, could add and subtract. The calculator could add a column of eight figures. He patented it and had hoped to profit from it, but did not. It was too expensive to build to be completely practical. Nevertheless, it was the first mechanical digital calculator able to do addition and subtraction. For many years Pascal kept improving his calculator, and made more than fifty models, trying to make his calculator handle fractions and square roots. His calculators were admired by the scientific community and made him famous in his time.

Pascal's calculator was a simple device about the size of a shoe box; however, it pointed out three principles that were used in later calculators: (1) that a "carry" could be accomplished automatically, (2) that subtraction could be accomplished by reversing the turning of the dials, and (3) that multiplication could be performed by repeated addition.

In 1646, Pascal's interest moved toward physics. He demonstrated with the help of his brother-in-law that air pressure decreased with altitude as Torricelli had predicted, by taking a mercury barometer to the summit of Puy de Dome (a height of 1,200 m, near Clermont-Ferrand). His interest in hydrostatics also led him to demonstrate that pressure exerted on a confined fluid is constant in all directions. This is called Pascal's principle and it is the basis of the hydraulic press, which Pascal described in theory.

In 1653, a friend, Chevalier de Mere, asked Pascal to solve some problems about dice. Pascal in turn wrote and began active correspondence with Pierre de Fermat. Together, Pascal and Fermat developed the first theory of probability. A year later he refined his generalized theory of numbers. He devised his arithmetic triangle from which Sir Isaac Newton deduced the binomial theorem and Gottfried LEIBNIZ, the integral calculus.

In 1654, he had a narrow escape from death when the horses of his carriage ran away. He interpreted this as evidence of divine displeasure, and his conversion became sufficiently intense to cause him to devote the remainder of his short life to prayer and religious writings. He had given up science, mathematics, and technology, except for some work on the solution of the cycloid (undertaken to distract his mind from a toothache) and the promotion of a scheme for a public transportation system in Paris.

The last years of his life were dominated by illness and pain. He died at 39 on August 17, 1662. He was one of France's greatest mathematicians and philosophers.

For Further Reading

Harmon, M. 1975. *Stretching man's mind: A history of data processing*. New York: Mason/Charter.

Donald D. Spencer

PASCAL

Pascal is a high-level, general-purpose programming language. The language was originally designed for teaching programming theory, but is widely used in developing computer programs for business, science, and education.

HISTORY

Pascal is named after the French mathematician Blaise PASCAL (1623–1662). The language was developed in 1968 by Professor

Niklaus Wirth, at the Eidgenossische Technische Hochschule in Zurich, Switzerland. Wirth designed the language as a tool for teaching structured programming concepts.

The first Pascal compiler was developed in 1970, and by the late 1970s the language was used extensively in introductory computer science classes on both mainframes and microcomputers. Pascal is one of the most widely taught first programming languages at the university and college level.

Outside the classroom, Pascal has always been a favorite language of personal computer users. UCSD Pascal was developed at the University of California at San Diego in the 1970s as a portable development environment and became a popular alternative to BASIC on early microcomputers. Borland International's 1983 introduction of Turbo Pascal, a low-cost compiler and development system, prompted many people to begin programming the recently introduced IBM-PC. The language continues to be popular, with Pascal compilers available for most computers.

In the interest of standardizing the many implementations of Pascal that were appearing, *The Pascal User Manual and Report* was released in 1978. Several years later, in 1983, the International Standards Organization (ISO) established a Pascal standard published in *ISO 7185.* This standard is the basis for both the British and American (ANSI–IEEE) Pascal standards.

Pascal is still evolving as a language. Even though standards exist, most software manufacturers add their own extensions and libraries to the language. For example, data types such as *LongInt* and *String* and string handling routines such as *Concat, Copy, Delete,* and *Insert* have proved popular enough to be included with most Pascal implementations even though they are not defined in the standard.

The most recent language enhancements are object-oriented extensions. Object-oriented languages combine data and procedures into single structures. Many people feel it is easier to learn and more flexible to program with an object-oriented language than to use a procedural language such as Pascal or C. With extended versions of Pascal, such as Apple Computer's Object Pascal,

one can write procedural programs, object-oriented programs, or programs that mix the two styles together. The interest in object-oriented programming has generated proposals to add object-oriented features to existing Pascal standards.

LANGUAGE OVERVIEW

As Pascal was designed as a teaching language, there are relatively few concepts to learn. The language is highly structured and encourages good programming practices. Because of these two factors, Pascal programs tend to be easy to read and understand.

A Pascal program is composed of statements. A statement is an instruction carried out by the computer. In Pascal, statements are separated by semicolons. Sets of related statements that follow each other are called blocks. Blocks are enclosed with the *begin* and *end* keywords. The main block, which occurs at the end of the program, always ends with a period. A sample Pascal program is shown in Figure 1.

Pascal contains predefined and user-defined data types, keywords, and operators for constructing statements and blocks, and standard routines for mathematical, memory, and input/output operations.

DATA TYPES

Pascal has five basic data types:

Boolean	A set of truth values, true and false
Char	A set of alphanumeric characters
Integer	A set of positive or negative whole numbers
Real	A set of positive or negative decimal numbers
Text	A file of characters

The range of *Integer* and *Real* numbers varies depending on the type of computer. Pascal has a predefined constant, *MaxInt,* that is equal to the largest *Integer* for the specific implementation.

In addition to the standard data types, you can create your own types with the *array, file, record,* and *set* keywords.

```
program Sample;
(label
        any program labels would appear
        here)
const
        SampleString = 'A sample string';
(type
        any user defined data types appear
        here)
var
        SampleNumber : Integer;
procedure SampleProcedure;
begin
        Writeln(SampleString);
end;
function AddOne(number; Integer) : Integer;
begin
        AddOne := number + 1;
end;
begin
        SampleProcedure;
        SampleNumber := AddOne(6);
        Writeln('The number is: ',
            SampleNumber);
end.
```

Figure 1. A simple Pascal application demonstrating functions, procedures, and program structure. Comments are enclosed in braces.

Keywords

Pascal is a fairly terse language and contains only a few reserved keywords. These keywords are used to create new data types, control program flow, define blocks, and assign identifiers. Standard Pascal keywords are shown in Table 1. Pascal is not a case-sensitive language. Capitalization does not affect keywords or identifiers (such as variables). For example, the variables *Rate, RATE,* and *rate* are all considered the same.

TABLE 1. Standard Pascal Keywords

and	end	nil	set
array	file	not	then
begin	for	of	to
case	function	or	type
const	goto	packed	until
div	if	procedure	var
do	in	program	while
downto	label	record	with
else	mod	repeat	

Operators

Operators are symbols that instruct Pascal to perform an operation. Operators are used to construct statements, to assign, access, and test data values, and to perform mathematical operations. Pascal operators are listed in Table 2. Operators are always evaluated in a certain order, such as everyday arithmetic precedence; however, you can use parentheses to specify the order of operations in a statement, for example, $(X + Y)*Z$.

Procedures and Functions

Pascal programs are frequently divided into procedures and functions. These are subprogram statements that execute blocks associated with them. When a procedure is called, the statements within the procedure block are executed. A function works the same way, but returns a value when the last statement in the block is executed. Both types of statement can optionally be passed arguments (values provided to the function or

TABLE 2. Standard Pascal Operators

Operator	Description
+	Addition, set union, unary plus
−	Subtraction, set difference, unary minus
*	Multiplication, set intersection
/	Division (Real type), set difference
:=	Assignment
=	Equivalence
<>	Not equal
>	Greater than
<	Less than
>=	Greater than or equal, set inclusion
<=	Less than or equal, subset
∧	Pointer dereference
()	Parentheses
[]	Array index, set literals
(* *)	Comment delimiters
..	Subrange delimiter
.	Record field designator
,	Array and set element separator
;	Statement separator
and	Logical conjunction
div	Integer division
in	Set membership test
mod	Modulus
not	Logical negation
or	Logical disjunction

TABLE 3. Standard Pascal Functions

Function	Argument Type	Returns
Abs	Integer or Real	Absolute value
Arctan	Integer or Real	Inverse tangent
Chr	Integer	Argument converted to Chr
Cos	Integer or Real	Cosine
Eof	File	End of file
Eoln	File	End of line
Exp	Integer or Real	Exponentiation
Ln	Integer or Real	Natural logarithm
Odd	Integer	Whether the argument is odd
Ord	Char, Boolean, or User defined	Ordinal number of the argument
Pred	Scalar (except Real)	Predecessor of the argument
Round	Real	Rounded Integer
Sin	Integer or Real	Sine
Sqr	Integer or Real	Square
Sqrt	Integer or Real	Square root
Succ	Scalar (except Real)	Successor of the argument
Trunc	Real	Truncated argument

TABLE 4. Standard Pascal Procedures

Procedure	Description
Dispose	Deallocates a pointer to memory
Get	Advances to the next component in a file
New	Allocates a pointer to memory
Pack	Packs an array
Page	Inserts a form feed in a file
Read	Reads information from the input device
Readln	Reads a line of information from the input device
Reset	Resets a file to its beginning for reading
Rewrite	Resets a file to its beginning for writing
Unpack	Unpacks a packed array
Write	Writes information to the output device
Writeln	Writes a line of information to the output device

procedure, on which to operate). In addition to defining your own procedures and functions, Pascal has many built-in routines for performing mathematical, memory, and input/output operations. Standard functions and procedures are shown in Tables 3 and 4.

For Further Reading

Cooper, D., and M. Clancy. 1985. *Oh! Pascal!* 2nd ed. New York: W. W. Norton.

Kernighan, B. W., and P. J. Plauger. 1981. *Software tools in Pascal*. Menlo Park, Calif.: Addison-Wesley.

Savitch, W. J. 1987. *Pascal, an introduction to the art and science of programming*. 2nd ed. Menlo Park, Calif.: Benjamin/Cummings.

Wirth, N., and K. Jensen. 1985. *Pascal user manual and report*. 3rd ed. New York: Springer-Verlag.

Joel McNamara

PATTERN RECOGNITION

Pattern recognition theory and practice is concerned with the design, analysis, and development of methods for the classification or description of patterns—objects, signals, and processes. The classification is done using such physical properties of the patterns as the height, width, thickness, and color. These properties are called *features* or *attributes* and the process of obtaining the feature measurements for any given pattern is called *feature extraction.*

Pattern recognition is an important area of multidisciplinary study because of its wide range of applications and the fact that performing pattern recognition occupies a large part of our daily activity. We effortlessly recognize our friends from a distance or their voice over the telephone, identify familiar objects of our everyday use, and note trends in a set of data. The early work in pattern recognition was motivated by the desire to impart humanlike recognition capabilities to computers so that we could communicate with these machines through written and spoken words. As a result, most of the early efforts in pattern recognition were directed toward building character recognition and speech recognition systems. At the same time, many studies were undertaken to develop and understand models of the human perceptual process with the aim of using such models to build pattern recognition systems. One of the best known examples of such an early work is the *perceptron* model of Rosenblatt, which was developed as a model for a biological neuron, an individual nerve cell in the brain. Although the perceptron model exhibited the capability to learn to make distinctions between two classes of patterns, it had some serious limitations in terms of the nature of pattern classes it could deal with. The present-day activity in the area of *artificial neural networks* is an outgrowth of early pattern recognition work in which the limitations of the early perceptron-type neuron models are overcome.

Pattern recognition systems have two major kinds of applications. In the first kind of applications, the pattern recognition systems are employed with the aim of reducing labor to gain cost and speed advantage.

Some examples of this kind of application are found in (1) the industrial environment, where pattern recognition techniques are used for sensing the location and identity of the parts for quality control and automated assembly; (2) the office environment, where different types of optical character recognition (OCR) systems are used to input text to a computer for word processing or desktop printing; and (3) banks, to read checks at high speed. The second kind of pattern recognition system applications are made in those instances where the patterns are complex and difficult for untrained personnel to recognize. Examples of this kind of application include fingerprint identification, flaw and crack detection in tubes and vessels using ultrasonic waves, blood cell classification, and aircraft identification. The list of applications mentioned here is by no means an exhaustive list and the reader should refer to the books and articles listed at the end of this article to find out more about pattern recognition applications.

A SIMPLE PATTERN RECOGNITION EXAMPLE

Let us consider a simple example of agricultural produce grading to understand the different aspects of a pattern recognition system. Let us say that we wish to set up an automatic produce grading system for an apple crop. The crop is to be graded in four categories: (1) AAA for large and shiny apples, (2) AA for shiny but small apples, (3) A for large but less shiny apples, and (4) reject for any apple that does not fit into one of the above grades. Although a human inspector can do the crop grading, speed and fatigue are at least two reasons that favor an automatic system. The various stages of a possible pattern recognition system for produce grading are shown in the block diagram of Figure 1, which is typical of many pattern recognition systems.

The first stage of the produce grading system is the *pattern acquisition stage,* where through a suitable choice of a sensor the pattern to be classified is converted into a representation that is suitable for computer manipulation. In the present example, this

FIGURE 1. Block diagram of a pattern recognition system showing its various stages.

can be done by a video camera imaging the apples as they come along on a conveyor belt. The pattern acquisition stage is followed by a *preprocessing stage* that in this particular case involves the task of locating the pattern (apple) in the video image. The exact choice of preprocessing operations is a function of the nature of patterns, choice of sensors, and operating environment. Once the pattern is isolated by the preprocessing stage, certain predetermined properties of the pattern are measured. This function is performed by the feature extraction stage of a pattern recognition system. In the present case, these properties are size and shininess of apples, measured from their isolated images. In most of the practical pattern recognition systems, the number of properties or features used is many times more than the present example. The output of the feature extraction stage is next passed on to a decision-making stage where a determination of the pattern type is made. This stage is generally called the *classifier stage*. The output of the classifier stage is called the *classification label* and represents the decision made by the classifier on the sensed pattern. In the context of the present example, there are four possible labels for the classifier stage to choose from. These are the three produce grades and the reject option. The classifier selects any of these four labels for a given apple, following the grading rules stated earlier.

A graphical representation of the grading rules is shown in Figure 2 where the horizontal and the vertical axes represent the size and the shininess feature values of an apple, respectively. The outer box of Figure 2 represents the feature or the *pattern space*, the space of all possible apple size and shininess values. The inner rectangular boxes denote possible combinations of size and shininess values for each grade of apple. The process of classification using the graphical representation in Figure 2 can be understood in the following way. Pick an apple and measure its

size and shininess. Plot a point in the feature space of Figure 2 corresponding to the measured size and shininess values. Determine the inner box where the plotted point falls. The grade attached to the inner box is then the grade of the apple picked. Thus, one way of looking at the classification rule is that it divides the entire feature space into many *regions* and each region represents a particular classification label. The process of classification is then nothing but finding the region to which the sensed pattern belongs. It must be mentioned here that the regions in the feature space are not always necessarily rectangular; they can have any arbitrary shape.

In the above example, the classification rule was assumed to be known; that is, the size, shape, and position of the inner boxes of Figure 2 were assumed to be given. However, it is generally not so. In the majority of pattern recognition applications, the classification rule is inferred from a large collection of patterns of known identity. In the context of the above example, this would be done by providing the pattern recognition system designer with apples of all grades. The patterns of known identity used by the designer are called *training* or *labeled patterns*. Once the system designer fixes the type of classifica-

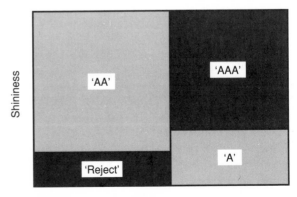

FIGURE 2. Graphical representation of the apple grading rules.

tion rule, the training patterns are used to adjust the parameters of the classification rule. This process is often termed the *training process* for the pattern recognition system.

PATTERN RECOGNITION METHODOLOGIES

The current pattern recognition methodologies can be grouped into three three distinct approaches: *statistical, structural,* and *neural.* The reader should consult the textbooks listed at the end of the article for the details on these methodologies. Here, we shall briefly explain the different methodologies in a conceptual fashion.

Statistical Approach

The statistical approach treats each pattern as a point in the appropriate feature space. Similar patterns tend to lie close to each other, whereas dissimilar patterns, those from different classes, lie far apart in the feature space. This implies that patterns from different classes form different groups of points or *clusters* in the feature space. The tightness of each cluster depends on the variations present in the patterns of the corresponding class. The distance between any pair of clusters depends on the similarity between the corresponding pattern classes. The statistical approach makes use of classification rules that take into account the closeness of a given pattern from different clusters by suitably defining a measure of closeness that incorporates the tightness of different clusters and any a priori information about any particular type of pattern being more likely. Ordinarily, these classification rules are inferred from a collection of patterns of known classification labels; however, there are many instances when such a collection of patterns is not available. An example of such a situation is the classification of remotely sensed data of an inhospitable terrain gathered through airborne or spaceborne platforms. In these situations, part of the collected data is first processed through *clustering techniques*, which make use of similarity between the patterns to put them into different groups. Properties of these groups are then used to derive classification rules for the rest

of the data. Often, the clustering techniques are applied in an interactive environment to get a *feel* for the data. Consequently, the clustering methods are also called *exploratory data analysis* techniques.

Structural Approach

The structural pattern recognition approach takes an entirely different viewpoint. The basic philosophy of the structural approach is to consider a complex pattern as a structure made from simpler patterns. These simpler patterns are called *primitives* and they function as basic building elements. The presence and the arrangement of these primitives define different pattern types. The recognition of an unknown pattern is carried out by finding the primitives and their arrangement. In many instances, the arrangement of primitives to generate complex patterns is described in a formal fashion using a set of *production rules* along the lines of grammatical description of sentences. Consequently, the structural approach is also known as the *syntactic approach* and the process of recognition is often called *parsing.* Although the formal structural approach has had only a limited success, an informal approach using *decision trees* to detect the presence and the arrangement of the various primitive types in a complex pattern has been a popular way of implementing the structural pattern recognition approach.

A decision tree represents a step-by-step decision-making process where a simple test is made at each step of the process. The outcome of the test determines the next action. The tests are planned in such a way that the execution of each test reduces uncertainty about the pattern being examined. As an example of the decision tree–based structural recognition approach, let us consider the problem of stylized hand-printed digit classification. To keep the decision tree small, we will determine only whether the digit under consideration is an odd digit or an even digit; no actual identification of the digit will be done. Each digit to be classified is assumed to have been hand-printed using strokes lying within the unshaded area of a rectangular box as shown in the examples in Figure 3.

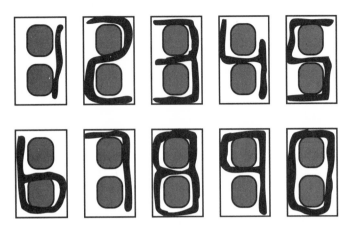

FIGURE 3. Examples of stylized hand-printed digits.

The stylized hand-printing of characters using guiding lines or boxes is popular in those OCR applications where the data are to be read from business forms filled out at various locations. By enforcing a uniform style and constraining the writing area, the task of character recognition is simplified. For example in the present case, each stylized digit can be considered as made up of two primitive strokes: a horizontal stroke (H) and a vertical stroke (V). By division of the stroke area in the guiding rectangular box into seven distinct parts as shown in Figure 4, each stylized digit can be described in terms of the presence/absence of the two stroke types in each divided part of the stroke area. Such a description is given in Table 1 where the letters A to G denote different parts of the guiding rectangle and

TABLE 1

Digit	Box Position						
	A	B	C	D	E	F	G
0	H	V	V	—	V	V	H
1	—	—	V	—	—	V	—
2	H	—	V	H	V	—	H
3	H	—	V	H	—	V	H
4	—	V	V	H	—	V	—
5	H	V	—	H	—	V	H
6	—	V	—	H	V	V	H
7	H	—	V	—	—	V	—
8	H	V	V	H	V	V	H
9	H	V	V	H	—	V	H

the letters H and V stand for the two stroke types. A dash indicates the absence of any type of stroke. A table like Table 1 that provides the complete description for decision making is often called a *decision table*. In many instances, a decision table carries much more information, including the cost of detecting different primitives and their chances of being present in different pattern classes.

The decision tree to determine the odd–even nature of an input digit is shown in Figure 5. The circles in the decision tree stand for tests. The entry within each circle indicates the corresponding test. For example, the entry in the topmost circle in the tree shows *V:E*. This is interpreted as whether a vertical stroke is present in the stroke area E

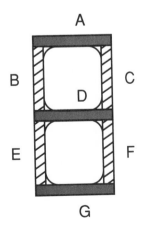

FIGURE 4. Seven stroke regions used to describe stylized hand-printed digits.

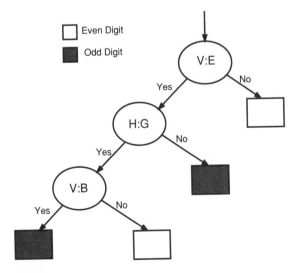

FIGURE 5. Decision tree for odd–even digit identification.

or not. The square boxes in the decision tree stand for the final outcome or the decision. The boxes representing the decision that the digit under consideration is an odd digit are shown shaded. The blank boxes stand for the decision that the digit is an even digit. In the decision tree terminology, the square boxes are called *terminals* or *terminal nodes* and the circular boxes are called *internal nodes* or *test nodes.* The topmost internal node is called the *root node.* Although it is possible to design a good decision tree manually by inspecting the decision table when it is small, a systematic design procedure is needed for problems of large size.

Neural Approach

The neural pattern recognition approach is currently the most popular. In this approach an interconnected network of simple processing elements, called *artificial neurons,* arranged in several layers is used as a basis for pattern recognition following the analogy of the human brain, which is known to have about one hundred billion (10^{11}) neurons, with each neuron having 1,000 to 10,000 interconnections. Figure 6 shows the working of a typical artificial neuron. It has a number of input lines/links that receive information from other neurons. The information coming on each of the input lines is suitably weighted and combined with the information from other lines. If the sum total of combined information is found to be larger than some preconceived value, the neuron passes on this fact to other neurons by firing or letting its output value go high. Thus, we can view each neuron as an elementary classifier capable of making a simple yes/no type of decision on its own input.

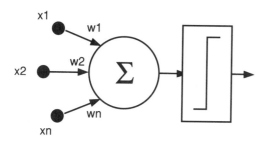

FIGURE 6. Typical artificial neuron model.

Although such an elementary capability is not enough for nontrivial pattern recognition tasks, the combined decision-making power of even a small artificial neural network of a few hundred neurons in two or three layers can be enormous.

The main reason for the current popularity of the artificial neural networks is perhaps their *learning capability.* Each neuron in the network can be made to learn to weigh its incoming information following one of several learning procedures if it is shown a number of patterns of known identity—training examples. In the same way children are taught number and letter shapes by repeatedly exposing them to those shapes, a neural network can be made to adjust the weights of different interconnection links to produce desired classification behavior. The most widely used neural network training procedure is the *backpropagation procedure,* which derives its name from the way the error in the network response is used to adjust the weights. One of the successful applications of the backpropagation training procedure is the handwritten digit recognizer developed to read zip code on mail pieces to speed up mail sorting. Unlike the statistical or the structural approach, the neural recognition approach can develop its own feature extraction stage also. This in essence means that even a nonspecialist can possibly develop and design a pattern recognition system following the neural approach as long as he or she has access to a collection of training examples.

SUMMARY

Pattern recognition has evolved as a mature interdisciplinary area of study over the past 40 years. With rapid advances in computer technology and falling hardware prices, more and more pattern recognition applications are opening up. For example, automatic data/text entry from formatted or unformatted documents using pattern recognition techniques, which until a few years ago was restricted to specialized applications like check reading, is becoming more and more commonplace with the availability of affordable desktop document scanners and personal computer–based recognition software. We can expect to see a proliferation of pattern recognition applications in all facets of our endeavors with further improvements in computer technology and pattern recognition advances.

For Further Reading

Beale, R., and T. Jackson. 1990. *Neural computing: An introduction.* Bristol: Adam Hilger.

Dattatreya, G. R., and L. N. Kanal. 1985. Decision trees in pattern recognition. In L. N. Kanal and A. Rosenfeld, eds. *Progress in pattern recognition 2.* Amsterdam: North-Holland.

Dayhoff, J. E. 1990. *Neural network architectures.* New York: Van Nostrand Reinhold.

Denker, J. S., et al. 1989. Neural network recognizer for hand-written zip code digits. In D. Touretzky, ed. *Neural information processing systems 1.* San Mateo, Calif.: Morgan Kaufmann.

Duda, R. O., and P. E. Hart. 1973. *Pattern classification and scene analysis.* New York: Wiley.

Fukunaga, K. 1990. *Introduction to statistical pattern recognition.* 2nd ed. New York: Academic Press.

Gonzalez, R. C., and M. G. Thomason. 1978. *Syntactic methods in pattern recognition.* Reading, Mass.: Addison-Wesley.

Jain, A. K. 1987. Advances in statistical pattern recognition. In P. A. Devijver and J. Kittler, eds. *Pattern recognition theory and practice.* Berlin: Springer-Verlag.

Jain, A. K., and R. C. Dubes. 1988. *Algorithms for clustering data.* Englewood Cliffs, N.J.: Prentice-Hall.

James, M. 1987. *Pattern recognition.* Oxford: BSP Professional Books.

Miclet, L. 1986. *Structural methods in pattern recognition.* New York: Springer-Verlag.

Pao, Y.-H. 1989. *Adaptive pattern recognition and neural networks.* Reading, Mass.: Addison-Wesley.

Rosenblatt, F. 1962. *Principles of neurodynamics: Perceptions and the theory of brain mechanisms.* New York: Spartan.

Rumelhart, D. E., G. E. Hinton, and R. J. Williams. 1986. Learning internal representation by error propagation. In D. E. Rumelhart and J. L. McClelland, eds. *Parallel distributed processing: Explorations in the microstructure of cognition.* Cambridge, Mass.: MIT Press.

Sethi, I. K. 1990. Entropy nets: From decision trees to neural nets. *Proceedings IEEE.* 78(10):1605–13.

Young, T. Y., and K. S. Fu. 1985. *Handbook of pattern recognition and image processing.* New York: Academic Press.

Ishwar K. Sethi

PERFORMANCE EVALUATION

Performance evaluation is an area of computer science that seeks to measure, evaluate, and improve the speed with which computer programs solve specific problems. The subject also includes the study of entire computer systems, of the effectiveness with which they utilize the hardware and software facilities, and of their capacity to get the required jobs done.

Why worry about the performance of computer systems when computer hardware steadily becomes faster and more powerful each year? The answer consists of two parts. First, while computers keep getting faster, the problems we need solved become increasingly complex and there are still many problems we cannot solve fast enough to be effective. For example, we can predict tomorrow's weather, but doing so usually takes longer than the time we have before tomorrow. Second, computers are designed in a very general manner with many choices in hardware and software such that the choices can influence the time needed for solution by a factor of 2 to 100 or more. Thus, in some cases, it pays to evaluate and improve the performance of a particular computer application. Should we be interested in computer performance all the time or just sometimes? The answer is that performance can be ignored most of the time, except when programs or applications are critical or when a system cannot solve effectively the problems it must solve.

We usually begin to evaluate performance by choosing performance goals, selecting measurement tools to discover how close we are to reaching the goals we set, measuring the actual performance, analyzing the measured results, and possibly changing some performance parameter before repeating the measurement and evaluation steps.

Performance evaluation can be done on an individual computer program or application to determine its effectiveness, or on an entire computer system to evaluate the capacity of a given hardware/software system to solve a specific set of problems. Many clever individual program performance efforts were made in the early days of computers before the 1960s, when computers and input/output (I/O) devices were very slow, main memories were very small, and users often ran the programs themselves. With the advent of multiprogramming operating systems in the 1960s in which several programs were executed concurrently, and of batch processing in which the actual user was not even present at the computer, the progress of an individual program was often not even readily observable and took a back seat to the performance of the entire computer system. The main concerns at that time were how well the hardware facilities were utilized and how well the scheduler distributed system resources to the individual programs or jobs. Individual program performance again became a focus in the 1970s as many computer installations turned to on-line interactive screens or transactions processed by a computer program while users waited at their terminals. One basic premise of performance evaluation until about 1980 was that a computer is an extremely expensive device that should therefore be used to its maximum capacity; this premise was no longer valid for personal computers (PCs), most of which sat idle more than 90 percent of the time. In addition, most operating systems on PCs were so primitive that they executed only one program at a time, so that individual program performance was identical to the performance of the entire system. As PCs and workstations begin using more sophisticated multiprogramming operating systems in the 1990s, interest in entire system performance will again flourish, and individual

program performance will continue to be of interest.

PERFORMANCE GOALS

Performance is often a neglected area in computer use. Although an automotive engineer would never dream of producing a car without first setting down performance goals and specifications in terms of maximum speed, acceleration, and gasoline mileage, most computer programs are still written with few performance specifications or goals. Furthermore, most programs do not measure and report on their own performance, and simply measuring the performance is usually difficult and time-consuming. Even after programs are in production, small changes to correct errors and other maintenance will often change performance of a program, and users will simply accept the new reduced performance as standard, perhaps after grumbling about it for a few days.

Thus, setting performance goals and specifications should be one of the first steps in designing a program. The goal might be a particular response time for an interactive program, or a number of transactions that can be processed in an hour. For a batch program, one must somehow create a measure of performance that relates the volume of data processed to the time it should take. For example, an invoicing system might set up as a measure of performance the number of order records processed per seconds of central processing unit (CPU) execution time. Thus, a performance goal might be to process more than ten order records per CPU second of execution time.

Performance goals and specifications start to take on real meaning only if there is a simple way to evaluate whether the program is reaching that goal. Hardware and software monitors can be used to measure such performance, or such performance can be calculated from data stored in the system log. However, the measurement or calculation of performance results is unlikely to be done unless it is very simple or is done automatically when the program is run. When performance is likely to be important, programs should report on their own efficiency automatically. Thus a batch program could request from the operating system the execution time from the beginning of a program to the end, and at the end print out the performance measure that relates volume of data processed to the CPU execution time used. Similarly, an interactive transaction processing system could keep track of the response time for each transaction and then print out periodically or on demand the response time distribution for the past hour or the entire day.

If performance is critical for an installation, tests should be run before any program is put in production to demonstrate that not only does the modified program work as desired, but it still meets the performance goals set for the program.

WHAT IS MEASURED?

Most of the time we are interested in how long it takes to solve a certain problem, and we seek to measure the *elapsed time* for execution of a specific program. This can be done reasonably with a stopwatch for programs that take more than a few seconds, but most computers keep track of time, and the starting time is often subtracted from the ending time to calculate the elapsed time of execution. For multiprogramming operating systems that execute more than one program simultaneously, the concept of *CPU execution time* is used and includes only the time that the CPU spends working on a specific program. Thus, a particular program may be in the computer for an elapsed time of 10 minutes, but the CPU execution time may only be 2 minutes; the remaining 8 minutes the CPU either spends on other programs in the computer or merely waits for I/O operations to be completed. On systems without multiprogramming, such as MS-DOS for PCs, the only time available is elapsed time, but for multiprogramming systems the operating system makes both elapsed time and CPU execution time available.

Another item of interest in measuring performance is I/O time (i.e., the time spent transferring data to and from external devices). This information is not readily available

in most operating systems, but can sometimes be deduced from a system log file or a job control listing.

Another measure of performance for interactive programs is *response time,* which can be defined as the elapsed time from the moment the user hits the return or enter key for a specific request to the time the user receives the output from the request and the computer is ready to receive the next request. This is a very important measure of performance since in most cases the user can do little more than wait while the computer processes the request. For example, a possible performance goal for a transaction processing system is a response time of less than 3 seconds for at least 95 percent of all transactions.

SOFTWARE VERSUS HARDWARE MONITORS

Once a performance goal such as the response time described above is formulated, a tool to measure the actual time in a specific computer system under a specific work load is necessary. While it is possible to measure and keep track of the actual response times by using a stopwatch, it is not an accurate technique and requires extraordinary effort by all the users. Another technique is to have the program report on its own performance. There are also generalized tools available for making such measurements. What we need is a monitor to measure and keep track of the response time from each transaction. This can be accomplished with a *hardware monitor,* which is often another computer external to the system being measured, but can be simply a specialized piece of hardware external to the measured system. Alternatively, a *software monitor* can measure the response time and be no more than another program running in the actual computer being measured.

A hardware monitor is often connected to the measured computer system with a multitude of wires that sense what is happening inside the measured system by sampling low-level registers such as the program counter, memory address register, and I/O channel status bits. Usually, hardware monitors are used on more expensive mainframes and minicomputers, where the potential savings in improving performance justify the expense and work required in the measurement itself. Hardware monitors require an intimate knowledge of the inner workings of the hardware and software of the measured system and are therefore usually specific to a hardware system running a specific operating system.

Use of a *software monitor* is usually a cheaper technique and can be accomplished by putting some extra routines into the operating system or simply by having another application program running in the computer that makes the measurements. For the latter method, that program often requires some assistance from the operating system to gain access to the relevant information. Such software monitors may be available from the machine vendor, be acquired from a third party, or be written by users themselves. Writing a software monitor is usually not a simple task and requires a systems programmer who has a fair understanding of the workings of the machine and the operating system. Although hardware monitors hardly ever change the timing of the measured events, software monitors are only programs and have the disadvantage that they take time and may actually change the environment they are attempting to measure.

WHAT CAN MONITORS MEASURE?

Besides measuring a response time for an interactive transaction, a hardware or software monitor might be able to:

1. count the number of times a program is run.
2. deduce the amount of CPU execution time a program takes.
3. deduce the elapsed time for execution of the program.
4. deduce the amount of I/O done to each device.
5. deduce the amount of time a program uses specific I/O devices.
6. count the number of times a certain procedure and/or statement is executed in the program.

7. show the percentage of time the CPU spends in executing specific procedures or statements.
8. show the percentage of the time the CPU is
   a. idle,
   b. busy executing the operating system, or
   c. busy executing a user program.
9. show the utilization of main memory.
10. show the paging rate for a given program or the entire system.
11. measure response time for an on-line transaction or an interactive program.

Each monitor is different and can accomplish a different subset (or superset) of the functions listed above. Some of the functions can be used to evaluate performance of specific individual programs; others are geared to measure the performance and workings of the entire computer system.

CRITICAL PROGRAMS

The performance of most computer programs (90 percent or more) is irrelevant to most users. The only ones of interest are the *critical programs*, which typically constitute less than 10 percent of all programs. A program might be considered critical if:

1. the program is time-critical; that is, the program requires results a very short time after input data is supplied.
2. the program is run frequently and consumes considerable computer resources.
3. the program consumes extremely large amounts of computer resources, even if it is not run frequently.

Most sophisticated operating systems maintain a *system log* file that records many system events. Such a log file may be helpful in identifying the critical programs or applications on a particular computer system. It can also serve as a good source of other performance information about the system.

Thus, performance evaluation of a computer system need not involve looking at a large number of programs, since the performance of the whole system is determined largely by a small percentage of the application programs that are the critical programs. Examples of critical programs include most interactive programs that are run frequently, such as an accounts payable on-line transaction used to enter each day's receipts for at least 4 hours a day, or a batch program to generate invoices that takes 30 minutes to run but is run four times a day.

CRITICAL PARTS OF PROGRAM

The performance of a critical program is determined largely by the execution time of a small number of program statements, usually less than 10 percent of the number of statements in the program. Thus one of the steps in performance evaluation of a critical program is to identify the critical parts of the program. Both hardware and software monitors have features that can help to identify the critical parts. In addition, compilers often have options that insert additional code in a program so that after it is executed it lists the number of times each procedure and/or statement was entered during program execution. One can also scan the program visually looking for inner loops and time-consuming statements, but actual measurement is preferable, as even experienced programmers are often surprised to learn where the critical parts of their programs are located.

While tools that measure the number of times each statement or procedure is executed are easier to obtain, they do not directly indicate where the CPU spends its time during execution because different statements require different amounts of time for execution. The most sophisticated tool is one that actually samples the program counter during program execution. Most ideal is a hardware monitor that does this sampling without slowing program execution. A software monitor is also useful but is less accurate because the sampling program may not be able to sample the program counter as often or as regularly as a hardware monitor.

One final difficulty in finding the critical parts of a program is that these parts may change with different data inputs and it is much too complex and time-consuming to do measurements with all possible input data combinations. This problem is normally confronted only to the extent that one tries to sample the program execution with the most probable input data.

IMPROVING PERFORMANCE OF CRITICAL PARTS OF A PROGRAM

Once the critical parts of a program are identified, their performance can be improved with many techniques well known to computer scientists. These techniques range from removing invariant statements from inner loops to avoiding recalculation of common subexpressions to choosing data types carefully. In addition, many language and compiler-specific performance considerations can be explored by studying the performance characteristics of the compiler to be used. A number of articles listed below discuss such techniques in detail.

For Further Reading

Agajanian, A. H. 1975. A bibliography on system performance evaluation. *IEEE Computer* November:64–74.

Drummond, M. E. 1973. *Evaluation of measurement techniques for digital computer systems.* Englewood Cliffs, N.J.: Prentice-Hall.

Heines, T. S., and P. J. Jalics. 1988. Compiler performance analysis tools. *Software Practice and Experience* 18(9):917–21.

Jalics, P. J. 1977. Improving performance the easy way. *Datamation* April:135–48.

———1987. COBOL on a PC: New perspectives on a language and its performance. *Communications of the ACM* 30(2):142–54.

———1989. Realizing the performance potential of COBOL: Programs. *IEEE Software* September:70–79.

Schaefer, M. 1973. *A mathematical theory of global program optimization.* Englewood Cliffs, N.J.: Prentice-Hall.

Svobodova, L. 1976. *Computer performance measurement and evaluation methods: Analysis and applications.* New York: Elsevier.

Waldbaum, G. 1978. *Tuning computer users' programs.* Technical Report RJ-2409, IBM Research Laboratories, San Jose, Calif., December.

Paul J. Jalics

PERIPHERAL MANUFACTURING COMPANIES

See Appendix

PERSONAL COMPUTERS

See Microcomputers (Personal Computers)

PHARMACY PRACTICE, USE OF COMPUTERS IN

Pharmacy practitioners use computers in drug distribution, clinical, functions, and administrative functions. Drug distribution is the process of delivering drugs to patients. The clinical function is the monitoring of patients for the appropriate response to drug therapy. Administrative applications are those that assist with the management of the institutional pharmacy (hospital or nursing home) or community pharmacy.

TYPES OF COMPUTERS IN PHARMACY SYSTEMS

Computer systems used for pharmacy applications range from mainframes to microcomputers. In hospitals with mainframe computers, usually one mainframe computer is used for all the hospital's computer applications. Some community pharmacies may share a mainframe computer system. Phone or satellite connections link these pharmacies together. In the community setting this occurs most frequently with chain pharmacies that share patient prescription and other information. Some hospital and community pharmacies use either minicomputers or local area networks (LANs). Some small hospital pharmacies or community pharmacies support their entire operation on a single microcomputer. Some of the applications described run independent of the day-to-day operations of the pharmacy. A microcomputer usually runs these applications.

DRUG DISTRIBUTION

Community and Outpatient Clinic Practice
Community pharmacy and outpatient clinic pharmacies in institutional settings use computers in the prescription drug dispensing process. The pharmacy system uses numerous databases in the dispensing process. One database will contain patient names and demographics such as birth date, address, and phone number. Another will contain information on physicians. A drug formulary or medication database contains all the medications available in the pharmacy. This medication database also contains information on medication cost, strength, drug class, and National Drug Code (NDC) number. One database or a couple of the databases linked together contain patient medication profiles. These profiles contain information on the medications a patient is taking, how the medications are to be taken, the number of times prescriptions can be refilled, and patient allergies. This database may contain information on patient diseases and adverse reactions to medications. With the filling of every prescription, the pharmacist reviews the patient profile for such problems as drug interactions.

For each new prescription, information is entered into or updated on the patient, physician, drug formulary, and medication profile databases as needed. During the prescription refill, the information is accessed again. The computer also calculates the cost. A printer attached to the computer system prints the label for each prescription and the patient's receipt.

Institutional Pharmacy Practice

Unit dose. Institutional pharmacies that provide services to hospitalized and nursing home patients usually dispense medications using a unit dose system; that is, each dose of a medication is contained in an individual package. Each drawer of a unit dose cart contains the daily medication doses for a patient. This cart is delivered daily to the nursing unit. The institutional pharmacy uses the patient, physician, drug formulary, and medication profiles, which are similar to the community pharmacy databases. The computer prints out a list of the unit dose packages to be placed in the drawers assigned patients on a unit dose cart. The list is updated daily to account for all changes made to the medication profiles. Such changes include discontinuation of a medication and new medication orders.

A few institutional pharmacies are starting to implement dispensing machines connected to the computer system. Using the computer's medication profile database, the dispensing machine produces strips of medications for the patients. A pharmacy technician then separates the strips into the patient drawers. Without the dispensing machine, the technician must select each drug and then place it in the appropriate drawer of the unit dose cart.

Intravenous drug therapy preparation. In the hospital, the pharmacy computer system prints lists of intravenous products that must be prepared daily. It can aid pharmacy personnel with calculation of the correct dosages. It can also help with calculation of the correct amounts of additives to the various intravenous solutions and flow rates. The system can also check for incompatibilities between additives in the intravenous solution.

Medication administration record/solution administration record. In institutional settings, the computer prints out a medication administration record (MAR) for each patient. The nursing staff use the MARs to chart the administration of oral, topical, and injectable medications. Solution administration records (SARs), which are similar to MARs, are printed for those patients receiving intravenous solutions.

CLINICAL FUNCTIONS

Pharmacokinetics

Pharmacokinetics is the study of drug absorption into the human body, distribution throughout the body, and elimination from the body. Part of pharmacokinetics is prediction using mathematical formulas of how a drug is absorbed, distributed, and eliminated based on certain characteristics of a particular patient. The computer is convenient because it does these calculations very quickly and stores information on previous pharmacokinetic calculations for each patient.

Drug Information

Pharmacists require a large amount of information for each drug, including the pharmacokinetics, indications for use, contraindications for use, adverse effects, correct dose, and treatment of an overdose. Popular reference books and drug information sources are also available on compact-disk read-only memory (CD-ROM) or on-line services. Two examples of CD-ROM references are the ASHP Drug Information Source and DRUGDEX.

Drug Use Review

In institutional settings, the pharmacy databases can be linked with laboratory and diagnostic databases. This linkage allows the hospital to check for appropriate treatment and monitoring of patients receiving medications. A search of the linked databases determines whether a patient has had an appropriate diagnosis requiring treatment with a particular medication. The search can also detect trends, such as misuse by a certain group of physicians or problems with a certain patient population. Also, the drug use review can determine whether the medications are monitored appropriately on the basis of laboratory information. These searches can be expanded to include other types of monitoring as the information written in patient charts is entered into a computerized patient database.

Drug Interaction and Therapeutic Incompatibility

In both institutional and community practice the computer system uses various databases to check for problems with medication use, such as drug interactions. One of these databases comprises drugs that interact, as well as information on the severity of the drug interactions and how often they occur. Another database lists reactions between certain diseases or medical problems and medications. Yet another database lists the classification of a drug, for example, antibiotic. Administration of duplicate medications to the same patient is classified as a therapeutic duplication. The pharmacist can request the computer to check for all the possible drug interactions, drug–disease problems, and therapeutic duplications. Some computer systems check automatically for these items with the filling of every prescription.

Compliance Applications

The pharmacist can check the medication profile database for information on patient compliance, that is, whether the patient follows instructions when taking the medication. The computer can also send patients reminders to pick up refills of medications slightly before they exhaust their current supplies.

Clinical Databases

Pharmacists are being given more responsibility for the monitoring of medication therapy, including monitoring to prove that the medication is treating the disease and not causing adverse effects. Software for this purpose usually runs on a microcomputer. Clinical databases contain information on patient demographics, diseases, treatment, adverse effects, laboratory results, and clinical notes. Databases are updated every time

the pharmacist makes contact with the patient and are viewed to determine the performance of appropriate medication treatment and monitoring for each patient. This information is useful for patient care, drug use review, and research purposes such as investigational new drug research.

Patient Education

The computer system can print additional information on each prescription to remind patients how to take the medication, for example, "take on an empty stomach" and "may cause drowsiness." The system can also print out information sheets of very detailed instructions about the medication. This information would include how to take the medication, adverse effects, indications for the medication, and what to do if a dose of the medication is omitted.

New methods of patient education are being developed. One of the newest is the U.S. Pharmacopeia's "USP DI—Visualized —About Your Diabetes." This application runs on a microcomputer with a touch screen and a videodisc player. It shows video examples of the disease, its treatment, and techniques used to monitor treatment.

Pharmacist Education

Computer applications assist with the education of pharmacists and pharmacy students by simulating practice situations. The simulation allows the pharmacist or student to learn from mistakes and gain new experiences. In a common simulation, the computer acts as a patient and participants interact with the computer as they would with the patient in a real situation. Some recently released simulations use videodiscs to allow for audiovisual enhancement of these computer-generated interactions.

ADMINISTRATIVE FUNCTIONS

Purchasing and Inventory Control

In both community and institutional pharmacy settings, the computer system can keep a perpetual inventory. Each time a new shipment of drugs arrives from a drug company vendor, the computer system enters the inventory into the computer database. The computer automatically adjusts the inventory with the filling of every prescription. These high and low inventory quantities are used as the criteria to decide what items to order and what quantity to order. A high inventory and low inventory for each item are calculated by the computer based on the usage patterns of the medications. The drug orders are printed out and sorted by vendor. This information is saved by the computer and verified when the order arrives at the pharmacy. After verification, the order is added to the inventory.

Formulary Management

This administrative function of the pharmacy system allows the pharmacist to add new drugs, delete drugs no longer used by the pharmacy, or update information on drugs currently on their formulary or drug list in the pharmacy. Information includes name, dose, vendor, inventory, location in the pharmacy, cost, and therapeutic classification. The cost data are the most frequently updated. Some vendors allow communication via modem, tape, or diskette to update cost data on a routine basis.

Insurance and Billing

Some community pharmacies bill electronically for prescriptions covered by insurance. They can bill the insurance company directly using a communication application of the pharmacy computer system and a modem. Some pharmacies use a third-party billing company; the pharmacy simply ships all the insurance claims to one source, which then bills all the different insurance companies. The other option is submitting a disk or tape of the billing information to the insurance company. Other pharmacy computer systems print out a bill for each insurance company.

Some insurance companies use point-of-sale (POS) devices. By use of a credit card issued to the patient requesting the pharma-

ceutical service, the POS device verifies immediately that the patient is eligible for the service and indicates how much of the bill the patient has to pay. The POS device then charges the insurance company for the remainder.

Institutional pharmacies usually do not bill directly. The pharmacy ships billing information via a direct link or a tape to the hospital financial department, which then bills the insurance company or the patient.

FUTURE

Two new areas of development for pharmacy applications are robotics and wireless networks. In both community and institutional practice settings, the robot will interface with the computer system to decrease the amount of manual labor in the dispensing process. In institutional settings, the wireless network will allow portable computers to interact with network servers or minicomputer or mainframe computer databases. The nurse using such a system could chart the medication administration record on-line from a patient's room while administering the medication to the patient. In most hospitals this information is kept only as a written record. The wireless network will allow the pharmacist to access and enter data from any location in the hospital.

For Further Reading

Fassett, W. E., and D. B. Christensen. 1986. *Computer applications in pharmacy.* Philadelphia: Lea & Febiger.

Kolb, K. W. 1989. Computerization as an aid in management of clinical pharmacy services. *Topics in Hospital Pharmacy Management* 8(4):26–35.

Lenhart, J. C. 1989. The use of computer-assisted instruction in a pharmacy department. *Topics in Hospital Pharmacy Management* 8(4):55–61.

Mansur, J. M., and E. G. Nold. 1989. The application of computerized clinical files to hospital pharmacy practice. *Topics in Hospital Pharmacy Management* 9(3):68–76.

Rajia, T. C., N. F. Bierschenk, L. C. Knodel, and V. M. Bowden. 1990. Improving access to computer-based library and drug information services in patient-care areas. *American Journal of Hospital Pharmacy* 47:137–42.

Tamai, I. Y., L. Z. Rubenstein, K. R. Josephson, and J. A. Yamauchi. 1987. Impact of computerized drug profiles and a consulting pharmacist on outpatient prescribing patterns: A clinical trial. *Drug Intelligence and Clinical Pharmacy* 21:890–5.

Wordell, D. C. 1989. Distributed processing for pharmacy and drug information at the Hospital of the University of Pennsylvania. *Topics in Hospital Pharmacy Management* 9(3):17–36.

Michael E. Pitterle

PHYSICAL FITNESS

See Health and Fitness,
Computer Applications in

PL/I

HISTORICAL DEVELOPMENT

PL/I, Programming Language 1, was developed during the middle 1960s in an attempt to bring together features of a number of earlier, application-specific languages providing a single general-purpose language for widespread use. Until this time, FORTRAN, COBOL, LISP, and SNOBOL provided the programmer with language options, but no single language provided the tools necessary to solve a variety of problems. A scientific problem required the use of FORTRAN or Algol; a commercial application was best addressed with COBOL; string manipulation was accomplished with LISP or SNOBOL; systems programming required assembly language.

The rapid proliferation of languages during the 1950s and 1960s resulted in two major concerns. First, a computer installation would have a difficult time supporting and maintaining a large number of languages. Second, increasingly complex programs were beginning to require programming tools that spread across several languages. Motivation to find a single-language solution to everyone's programming needs was apparent.

PL/I was created by a committee organized by the IBM Corporation and was first implemented on the IBM 360 series machines. The design philosophy of creating a single language that would satisfy nearly all users required that features deemed necessary in all of the previous languages be made available to the PL/I user. Examination of the language shows that its design drew heavily on earlier languages. For example, PL/I has formatted input and output similar to FORTRAN, PICTURE-type declarations as does COBOL, and block structure similar to Algol.

Many feel that the issues of execution efficiency versus program flexibility and ease of use for the beginner versus detailed control for experienced programmers conflict with the expectation of providing "something for everyone." The result is a powerful and yet complex language that has never been as widely accepted as its creators had hoped.

PL/M, Programming Language for Microprocessors, is a dialect of PL/I developed by Intel as a high-level language for its microprocessors. PL/M+ is an extended version of PL/M developed by National Semiconductor.

OVERVIEW OF THE LANGUAGE

The basic PL/I instruction or program statement has the form

```
label: statement;
```

Labels are optional, may not start with a number, and are of a maximum length of thirty-one characters. The statement consists of some acceptable combination of instructional code, operators, and operands. All statements must end with a semicolon.

Sequences of PL/I statements are organized into procedures. Each *procedure* must begin with a PROCEDURE statement and conclude with an END statement. A typical PL/I procedure would resemble

```
name: PROCEDURE;
         statement;
         statement;
             .
             .
             .
      END name;
```

A PL/I program is organized in terms of procedures, with the simplest type of program consisting of a single procedure. When a program contains more than one procedure, one of these must be designated as a main procedure as follows:

```
label: PROCEDURE OPTIONS(MAIN);
```

Each procedure contains a set of declarations and a set of executable code. Each declaration has a basic form with default options. Defaults are declarations provided by the compiler when not specified by the programer. A wide variety of elementary data types are available including numeric data, character strings, pointers, and labels. Homogeneous and heterogeneous data structure types are available.

A large spectrum of operations are available. Arithmetic and other numeric operations are fully supported, as are input/output operations. Automatic type conversions between different hardware representations and character string data are also provided.

Program control features are standard, including IF-THEN-ELSE, DO, and WHILE statements. Subprogram facilities are emphasized in PL/I, with sequence control including parallel processing and interrupt handling, as well as ordinary subprogram recursion.

The following example provides a glimpse of the syntax of PL/I. This program uses a subroutine called SUM to add the values of a list of numbers.

```
EXAMPLE: PROCEDURE OPTIONS(MAIN);
  DECLARE L FIXED;
  START: GET LIST (L);
    IF L>0 THEN BEGIN;
      DECLARE V(L) DECIMAL FLOAT;
      GET LIST (V);
      PUT LIST ('INPUT VALUES ARE',V,'SUM
        IS', SUM (V,L));
      GO TO START;
    END;
  SUM:PROCEDURE (X,K);
    DECLARE X (*) DECIMAL FLOAT, K
      FIXED,
      TEMP DECIMAL FLOAT INITIAL (O);
    DO I = 1 TO K;
      TEMP = TEMP + V(I);
    END;
    RETURN(TEMP);
  END SUM;
END EXAMPLE;
```

Two special features of PL/I are also worth noting: interrupt handling and macro definitions. Through interrupt-handling features, PL/I allows the programmer to incorporate special error and data-handling procedures, based on run-time conditions. For example, overflow traps and subscript range control may be accomplished based on interrupts handled by the programmer. Program debugging can also be quickened by determination of when a specific statement is executed.

PL/I has also incorporated a number of features to allow program modification prior to compile time. These features involve specialized code that is expanded at compile time into PL/I code, and so resembles macro-type features available in most assembly languages.

DATA TYPES AND OPERATORS

One of the best ways to obtain rapid insight into the power of a language is to examine the types of data, operators, and structures available to the programmer. The following summary of how PL/I establishes and processes its data shows both the breadth and complexity of the language.

Declaration of data types is provided at compile time, either explicitly by programmer code or by default. The declarations are structured in terms of attributes, with allowable values for the various attributes specified within the declaration. The compiler uses these declarations to assign appropriate internal representation for data items and to specify the manner in which the data items are processed.

Numbers are classified on the basis of four attributes: mode, which may be real or complex; scale, fixed-point or floating-point; base, decimal or binary; and precision, number of digits in the number. For most applications, numbers would be real, floating-point, and decimal, of say ten digits in length. The PL/I declaration for such a numeric variable, named NUM, would be as follows:

DECLARE NUM DECIMAL FLOAT (10);

If a numeric variable whose name begins with the letters A to H or O to Z is not declared, a default of real, floating-point, decimal is assigned, with the precision dictated by the internal word length of the computer system. Variables with names beginning with the letters I to N are real, fixed-point integers.

The PL/I arithmetic operators are standard: + (addition), − (subtraction), * (multiplication), / (division), and ** (exponentiation). Numerous built-in functions are also available, such as absolute value and square root.

When a portion of memory is to be reserved under a specified name to accommodate a string of characters, the declaration would be of the general form

DECLARE name CHARACTER(n);

where "name" refers to the variable name and n is a number specifying the length of the character string to be stored. Thus,

DECLARE BOOK CHARACTER(24);

would reserve enough memory to store 24 characters in the variable named BOOK.

Several operators are available for string manipulation including the concatenation operator ‖. Built-in functions for strings are also available. For example, SUBSTR(BOOK, m, n) returns a string of length n, starting at the mth character of BOOK.

Although character strings are an important component of the data types in PL/I, an additional data category is the bit data string. Bit strings serve both to hold binary information and to hold truth function information. The bit string operators are the three logical connectives: & (and), | (or), and ⌐ (not). Bit string operations are performed bit-by-bit, yielding a result of the same length as the operand.

PICTURE data types in PL/I allow the programmer to specify precisely the format of strings or numbers. When a needed format does not conform to one specifically available, PICTURE allows the programmer to set up his or her own.

A data type particularly helpful in list processing is the pointer. A pointer variable contains an address to a data structure. This pointer typically contains the address of a "base" for addressing the complete data structure. Two pointer functions are provided for list processing: ADDR and NULL. ADDR returns a pointer that identifies its argument; for example, ADDR(LISTNAMES) would return a pointer to the variable LISTNAMES. NULL returns a pointer to an empty location, that is, a location that contains no data.

Arrays are data structures that contain homogeneous data items, that is, only elements of the same type. Arrays are named and declared in the same way as are single-valued variables. The only additional specification that is required is the size of each dimension. The declaration

DECLARE BALANCE(10,4) FIXED(10,2);

would allocate storage under the name BALANCE to accommodate forty fixed-point numbers with ten-digit precision, two to the right of the decimal point. Array elements are referred to by giving numerical locators. For example, BALANCE(2,3) refers to the value stored in row 2, column 3 of BALANCE.

Structures are data structure types that

may contain heterogeneous data (elements of different types). Consider the structure

```
DECLARE 1 STUDENT,
        2 NAME,
             3 FIRST CHARACTER(24),
             3 LAST CHARACTER(24),
        2 ADDRESS,
             3 STREET CHARACTER(20),
             3 CITY CHARACTER(15),
             3 STATE CHARACTER(2),
        2 GRADE FIXED;
```

Here, STUDENT is a structure with three components: NAME, ADDRESS, and GRADE. GRADE is a numeric data element, but NAME and ADDRESS are themselves substructures. The syntax used to access a structure is to write the name of the structure separated by periods. For example, STUDENT.ADDRESS.CITY refers to the element CITY of STUDENT. (If subscripts are used within a structure, the subscripts follow the name and precede the period.)

SUMMARY

The variety of data-type options in PL/I further illustrates the creator's desire to serve the needs previously met by multiple languages. The scientific programmer has the needed numeric tools. LISP and SNOBOL users have string manipulation capabilities, and system programmers may even process bit strings without resorting to assembly language code.

As is apparent from the continued proliferation of languages through the 1970s and 1980s PL/I did not reach its design objective of being a general-purpose language accepted by the majority of application programmers. In fact, in the attempt to satisfy everyone, PL/I resulted in a language that indeed was usable by everyone but was acclaimed by few.

For Further Reading

Elson, M. 1973. *Concepts of programming languages.* Chicago: Science Research Associates.

Higman, B. 1967. *A comparative study of pro-gramming languages.* New York: American Elsevier.

Ledgard, H. F., and M. Marcotty. 1986. *Programming language landscape.* 2nd ed. Chicago: Science Research Associates.

Pollack, S. V., and T. D. Sterling. 1970. *Computing and computer science.* Toronto: Macmillan.

Pratt, T. W. 1975. *Programming languages: Design and implementation.* Englewood Cliffs, N.J.: Prentice-Hall.

James L. Poirot

PL/M

See PL/I.

PLANNING OF INFORMATION SYSTEMS

Every organizational function must be planned for in a way that ensures that the function's goals, strategies, programs, and activities are consistent with the objectives and strategies of the overall organization. This is no less true of the information systems (IS) function than of the marketing, operations, and finance functions.

In the early days of computer systems, the focus of attention was on automating activities, such as invoicing and payroll, that had previously been done manually. In such an environment, IS planning focused primarily on efficiency and budgeting considerations. It was important for the IS function to do those things that substituted computers for people in a fashion that maximized the net avoided cost—the costs associated with the manual procedures and systems that were being replaced (less the cost of the new computer system).

As computers and the IS function now play a wide variety of different roles in organizations, the planning focus and its associated criteria have become much more complex. Computer systems are being employed in a variety of new ways, for example, to aid the enterprise in achieving a competitive advantage and to facilitate reductions in the number of layers of management. Information systems planning must ensure that these roles for information resources are well chosen and effectively executed.

VARIETIES OF INFORMATION SYSTEMS PLANNING

Information systems planning takes place in various forms and at many levels in the organization, ranging from the choice of an organizational role for IS to play to the planning of specific computer programs that are to be developed.

It is useful to think of a number of levels and varieties of IS planning. Even though every organization may not conduct an identifiable process for each phase, every enterprise that employs computers must make the choices that define each of these phases:

• IS mission planning
• Strategic IS planning
• IS technology planning
• IS functional planning
• IS portfolio planning
• IS project planning

These varieties of IS planning are interdependent and iterative in the senses that the results of one phase are used in other phases and that the output of a subsequent phase may be fed back to influence the tentative result of a prior phase.

IS Mission Planning

At the highest organizational level, IS mission planning involves the choice of the role(s) that information resources will play in the organization. The alternatives range from a role in which computer systems are to be employed primarily for operational purposes, such as to perform invoicing and required reporting to outside constituencies, to a strategic role in which the systems are an integral element of the manner in which the enterprise competes in its marketplace(s).

If such a formal specification of a role for

IS is ignored because the choice is ill-structured, the choice of an IS role is being implicitly made. For an enterprise to ignore the possibility of selecting a new role for information resources in a dynamically changing environment is equivalent to it choosing the role that IS is currently playing. That role, which may itself have been only implicitly specified, may be inappropriate for current and future environments.

An IS mission plan that prescribes a clear role for information resources to play in the organization provides guidance for lower-level planning and decision making. The IS mission plan informs those at lower levels which new technologies, systems, or applications are consistent with the role and which are not. They are thereby able to focus their energies and to make decisions that are consistent and that will advance the organization's pursuit of its goals.

Strategic IS Planning

Figure 1 shows strategic IS planning as a two-way process that relates organizational-level attributes and IS-level attributes (King 1978). Once the choice of a strategic role for IS is made, strategic IS planning can be employed to transform the "organizational strategy set"—the organization's objectives, its "business" strategy, the role selected for IS, its non-IS resources, its philosophy and culture—into an "IS strategy set"—the selection of the general frameworks ("architectures") that will be employed to acquire, process, and disseminate information. These architectures specify how various elements of the overall organizational information system relate to each other, for example, how various communications networks operate and interconnect, how data stored in various computer memories relate, how computer applications and technologies relate, and

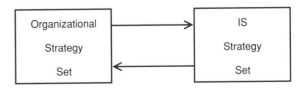

FIGURE 1. Two-way process of IS strategic planning. *Adapted from King 1985.*

how systems development processes conducted at one organizational level relate to those at another level.

A second important dimension of strategic IS planning has to do with the determination of the way in which organizational information resources can be used to influence the organization's strategy (the left-pointing arrow in Figure 1) (King 1985). If, for example, the IS function has a unique strength, the IS strategic planning process must consider how this capability might be used to influence the organization, its strategy, or its business practices. For instance, a proprietary database might be exploited to identify new product or market opportunities, or an efficient processing capability might be offered as a service to other companies to use on a contract basis, thus creating a "new business" for the enterprise.

IS Technology Planning

As IS technology development is so fast-paced and dynamic, the organization must keep abreast of new technologies and of those that are on the horizon. This means that, even though it may not itself be a developer of new IS technology, an enterprise must plan for the way in which it will employ new technologies in the future. Thus, it must monitor and assess newly developed and newly emerging technologies and it must decide on the level of resources it will allocate to each. For instance, many business firms assigned IS resources to developing prototype expert systems and neural network applications when these technologies were in early stages of development, even though they had not decided to employ such systems in significant ways. In these firms, the choice was based primarily on a desire not to be deficient if the significant potential of such technologies were to be realized.

IS Functional Planning

Once the higher-level plans are prepared, the IS function must plan for how it is going to accomplish the goals that have been set. All required IS resources—computers, net-

works, people, methods, and so on—must be identified and a plan must be developed to acquire, develop, and manage them. Thus, IS functional planning is very much like functional planning in other areas of the enterprise. The term *management of information systems* (MoIS) has come into use to describe the many planning, organizing, and control activities that are the essence of managing the IS function (Gray et al. 1989).

IS Portfolio Planning

The typical organization possesses existing information resources and must integrate planned new resources into the existing architectures and applications portfolio. This phase of IS planning determines which changes are made and in what sequence, to ensure that objectives are accomplished and that the overall system that results is fully integrated.

One important aspect of portfolio planning is the prioritization of projects. Typically, every planned change—be it the acquisition of new software, the development of a new application, or the updating of an existing computer program—cannot be performed immediately. A priority and sequence must be developed on the basis of the relative importance of each planned change and the availability of the required scarce resources.

IS Project Planning

The IS development portfolio is made up of individual projects, each with a specific goal. Each of these projects must be planned in terms of the goals and subgoals to be sought, the resources to be employed, the timing of the accomplishment of goals and subgoals, and the methods for performing the various project activities.

INFORMATION SYSTEMS PLANNING METHODS

A variety of methods are available for each of the varieties of IS planning. Greater significance rather than specificity of methods is the criterion that forms the basis for the choices made in each phase of planning.

IS Mission Planning Methods

The primary criterion in IS mission planning is the fulfillment of the organization's basic objectives. Various IS roles will lead to different degrees of attainment of the objectives that drive the organization. Secondarily, the relative "newness" and dynamism of IS suggests that it is prudent to select the IS role in consideration of the new opportunities presented by evolving information technologies.

IS mission planning is the least structured of the phases. These planning choices are generally made on the basis of the judgment of top executives; however, these judgments can be based on frameworks that are useful in focusing executives' attention on critical issues or alternatives.

For instance, the "strategic grid" (McFarlan et al. 1983) depicts four different combinations of the strategic criticality of information resources in current operations and in the future. This grid may be used to focus attention on alternative roles and levels of strategic impact that may be considered in the IS mission planning process.

Strategic IS Planning Methods

Strategic IS planning specifies the organization's information resource architectures in terms of which will best satisfy organizational objectives, satisfy the role selected for IS, and support the implementation of the organization's strategy.

A variety of IS strategic planning processes have been developed. A distinction is sometimes made between "enterprisewide" IS strategic planning approaches and others. This distinction is between the situation in which a specific, comprehensive, and well-developed strategic business plan provides the business strategy inputs to strategic IS planning and all business processes and functions are assessed, and the situation in which there is no formal strategic business plan or a much narrower focus is used. IBM's Business Systems Planning (BSP) (IBM 1981) process is one of the best known step-by-step

enterprisewide procedures for dealing with the various processes that constitute an enterprise. Some strategic planning methods subsume both the IS strategic planning and mission planning phases.

The phase of IS strategic planning that deals with the possible influence of information resources on the organization's strategy and practices is often dealt with by using one or more frameworks that have been developed to guide thinking. For instance, the customer resource life cycle framework (Ives and Learmonth 1984) focuses attention on each stage of the customer's business processes so that opportunities to reach customers through information technology can be identified and explored. Porter's competitive market (Porter 1980) model, which prescribes "five forces" (threat of new entrants, rivalry among competitors, etc.) that exist in any industry, is another widely used framework. Creativity-enhancing methods, which can be implemented either by an individual or by a group, can also be readily used for this purpose. Among the best known of the group methods is the nominal group technique (Van Gundy 1981).

IS Technology Planning Methods

One essential element of IS technology planning is deciding whether to invest in currently available new technology or to defer investment until innovations become available. The classic dilemma of the computer age is the recognition that a technology investment made today will inevitably become obsolete before its potential benefits are fully realized.

Because of the uncertainties in future technological developments, technological forecasting, an element of technology planning, is most often done in generic rather than specific terms. For instance, an enterprise might assess current levels of office productivity and how significantly new IS technology is likely to enable productivity improvements to be made. The enterprise may then plan for such improvements in terms of current versus deferred capital investments, even though it may not be clear precisely which technologies will be used to achieve the planned improvements. Among the methods for forecasting very uncertain technology events and their role in IS plans are morphological analysis and Delphi (Van Gundy 1981).

IS Functional Planning Methods

Often the methods used for planning the IS function are not significantly different from those used to plan for other organizational functions (Gray et al. 1989); however, the criteria employed in planning decisions have become more complex since new roles for information technology have become common.

The primary planning criterion when the IS role is prescribed as purely operational support is efficiency; however, when the IS role comes to involve new elements, such as the development of strategic systems, another criterion—the level of competitive advantage produced by the strategic systems—becomes of concern.

Measures of "user satisfaction" are often employed to assess the impact of the IS function in its organizational support role. New measures of the level of competitive advantage associated with the strategic role for IS are being developed. The absence of an accepted valid metric for assessing the contribution of the IS function in its many possible roles is, however, a significant detriment to the level of specificity and rigor that can be attained in IS functional planning.

IS Portfolio Planning Methods

The critical trade-offs that must be considered in IS portfolio planning are the allocation of resources to maintenance activities versus innovative activities, the "make or buy" decision for any new element that is to be added to existing information resources, and the effective integration of these new elements.

Maintenance activities normally consume a large proportion of IS functional budgets. These activities, although necessary, compete for resources with new applications and new systems. Often, maintenance activities are "defensive" in nature in that they prevent obsolescence in existing systems. Innovations are often "offensive" in nature in that they have the potential to generate new revenues or to support new activities. So, this trade-off is a difficult one.

Once any change in the portfolio is tentatively approved, the organization must determine whether "off-the-shelf" products or services are available from vendors, or whether new development processes should be performed externally or internally. These choices involve obvious economic considerations, but, as well, they often involve less tangible issues of security and competitive advantage. For instance, a firm that believes that a new system can produce sustainable comparative advantage might not wish to involve outsiders in its development, even if the costs of internal development are significantly greater.

The technical and functional integration of new system elements is also of concern in IS portfolio planning. Steps must be taken to ensure that increments are both technically and functionally compatible with existing systems and architectures.

Many organizations use a steering committee composed of representatives of the IS function and user groups to establish priorities for new developments. Often, the "make versus buy" and the technical and functional integration issues are incorporated into the proposal that is made by a "champion," or proponent, of a new system.

IS Project Planning Methods

IS project planning methods are generally similar to those used for any technology-based development project. Project network models and associated techniques such as "critical path analysis" or Program Education and Review Technique (PERT) are fundamental to most of these approaches (Cleland and King 1983). They are the key elements of planning and control techniques that enable the project manager to schedule and coordinate the project activities, to monitor expenditures, and to ensure technical compliance with project specifications.

References

Cleland, D. I., and W. R. King. 1983. *Systems analysis and project management.* 3rd ed. New York: McGraw-Hill.

Gray, P., W. R. King, E. P. McLean, and H. J. Watson. 1989. *Management of information systems.* Chicago: Dryden Press.

IBM. 1981. *Information systems planning guide: Business systems planning,* 3rd ed., GE20-0527. White Plains, N.Y.: IBM.

Ives, B., and G. P. Learmonth. 1984. The information systems as a competitive weapon. *Communications of the ACM* 27(12):1193–201.

King, W. R. 1978. Strategic Planning for MIS. *MIS Quarterly* 2(1):27–37.

King, W. R. 1985. Information technology and corporate growth. *Columbia Journal of World Business,* Summer.

McFarlan, F. W., J. L. McKenney, and P. Pyburn. 1983. The information archipelago—plotting a course. *Harvard Business Review,* Jan.–Feb.

Porter, M. 1980. *Competitive strategy: Techniques for analyzing industries and competitors.* New York: Free Press.

Van Gundy, A. B. 1981. *Techniques of structured problem solving.* New York: Van Nostrand Reinhold.

William R. King

POINT-OF-SALE

See Financial Services, Computer Use in

POLICE

See Law Enforcement, Computers in

POLITICAL USES OF COMPUTERS

Computers are fast gaining a toehold in the legislative and political arenas after years of resistance. Politicians are much like the chief executive officers of major corporations in that their success depends in large measure on their "people skills." Complicated machines such as computers have, therefore, been viewed as alien to the personal contact elected officials know to be the key to their success. It took decades for politicians to understand that the technology involved with the visual medium of television could be used to enhance their contact with people. Today, the use of this technology accounts for a significant portion of the strategy and the cost of political campaigns. As computers are a nonvisual form of technology, their acceptance by politicians has been relatively slow compared with other sectors of society. This tardiness has been compounded by both the rapid advances in computer technology and the complexity of that technology. These factors demand that politicians devote scarce financial resources to hiring experts who understand computers.

TAKING COMPUTERS OUT OF THE POLITICAL CLOSET

Until recent years, computers were relegated by politicians to simple list-keeping duties. Mainframes kept lists of the names and addresses of constituents who wrote elected officials, with the lists being used solely to mail out newsletters and Christmas cards. Political pollsters were among the first to use the number-crunching capability of computers to help them analyze the statistics obtained from public opinion polls. Today, personal computers are commonplace in the offices of elected officials and political campaigns. They have displaced most typewriters for word processing. On a less universal basis, the political world is making use of a wide array of sophisticated computer applications in an effort to increase the effectiveness of both elected officials and candidates for public office.

COMPUTERS IN POLITICAL CAMPAIGNS

Nowhere is this more evident than in political campaigns. Campaigns thrive and succeed on the effective use of information. Knowing every facet of an incumbent's record, a challenger can employ strategies that emphasize the weaknesses of the opponent. Equally important, an incumbent has to make the most of her or his own record of accomplishments as an elected official. There was a time when candidates would give eager campaign workers the task of combing news clippings and sifting the *Congressional Record* to compile these vital data. Today, however, those eager workers can use on-line computer databases to do their job faster and provide more useful information. No longer is it sufficient for campaign managers to have boxes filled with research at their disposal. Information on votes, bills introduced, and attendance records needs to be *analyzed*. How does the candidate's voting record compare with the voting record of the state's most popular member of Congress? How often does the candidate oppose the President? Is the candidate a pawn of special interest groups?

In these days of pragmatic politics, public opinion polls are the nexus of campaign strategies. Politicians have elevated pollsters to the position of pundits. Not only do they determine the mood of the voting public, they often have a major say about what issues a candidate will raise, the position the candidate will take on those issues, and the overall image the candidate will project to the voting public. Computers have come to be used by pollsters not only to analyze public opinion but to differentiate the various segments of the public to which the candidate will appeal. Combining polling data with the type of socioeconomic demographic information used by advertising agencies to market products, pollsters are able to segment the public literally on a block-by-block basis. Mailings and other literature can be targeted to the different audiences identified by this segmentation. Different radio and television advertisements can be prepared to be aired on different stations that appeal to various age, economic, ethnic, or racial groups. None of these sophisticated political campaign techniques would be possible without the use of computers, which distill information from census data, drivers' license files, and other computer-based sources of information.

Campaigns are increasingly using what is known as opposition research to strike the opponent where he or she is most vulnerable. Every incumbent has a record. Incumbents have taken a stand on the issues, often unpopular stands. They also have voted on legislation that often contains unpopular provisions. These votes are all part of the public record. But many incumbents escape attack because their challengers do not have the time or resources to sort through thousands of bills and votes.

The same opposition research techniques that can help launch an attack on the opponent can also help protect the incumbent from attack. Legislative research can find an incumbent's weak spot and help find ways to shield the weak spot, or turn it into a strength.

Both the challenger and the incumbent often find it difficult to turn a voting record to their own advantage. The campaign's staff has to sift through thousands of votes and thousands of bills. And when they have found the key votes and bills, they must decide how to use that information to their greatest advantage. This analytical problem is significant because the legislative process is often obscure. To the unaided eye, things are not always what they seem to be. On occasion, this obfuscation is intentional. For example, key votes often come on a motion to table. A member of Congress may vote to table (or kill) the bill. If this motion fails, the member may then vote for the final bill. The hometown paper may carry the member's vote for the bill and totally miss her or his more important vote to kill the proposal on the tabling motion. Similarly, popular bills that appear to be sure-fire bets for passage can become vehicles for unpopular amendments that may have little or nothing to do with the heart of the legislation. Thus, a vote that appears to be for motherhood can also contain a vote for a less saintly proposal. To make matters even more difficult, important information about a candidate's record can be embedded elsewhere in the *Congressional Record* or in committee reports.

GROWTH OF RELEVANT COMMERCIAL ON-LINE DATABASES

Sifting through reams of paper and library stacks of reports is a daunting research task; however, Congress and most states now maintain computer databases that provide elected officials and the public with information about the content and status of legislation. More significant are the commercial legislative databases that provide even more information than is available to the public on-line. These databases can sort through hundreds of thousands of pages of legislation and seemingly countless votes. Some contain more than a decade's worth of information. Using these databases, campaign operatives can find who voted for what, and who decided not to vote. And with a word- or phrase-based exploration of the text of the *Congressional Record,* the candidate's staff can search for debates and floor statements that can become turning points for the campaign. Equally speedy searches of bills can be performed to obtain their text, their status in the legislative process, who supported them, whether they were mentioned in major publications, and much more. These legislative databases are supplemented by other well-established on-line commercial services that focus on providing easy computer access to newspaper and periodical articles. Other databases can even provide information on the types of businesses in a geographic area and the number of workers they employ. Individuals can now use personal computers to find in minutes information that formerly took days to uncover. In political campaigns, computers not only save time and human resources; they also increase a candidate's ability to acquire and use information vital to the success of the campaign.

Using these databases, a challenger can maintain a dynamic profile of the incumbent. Rather than concentrating on only a handful of high-profile votes, the candidate can search for those votes of interest to a particular constituency. By searching the actual text of bills, a campaign can find politically important provisions embedded in even routine bills. For example, information about funding for abortions in the District of Columbia can be found in appropriations bills. Key labor rights provisions can be found in everything from tax bills to copyright legislation. A search of actual bill text can locate these provisions and help turn obscure legislative detail into a hot campaign issue.

The challenger can also use the on-line database to pick up voting trends or to make unfavorable comparisons to other legislators. Using the system's analytical functions, the campaign can create a report card on issue areas such as trade, civil rights, and defense. Analysis can also compare the incumbent's voting record with that of popular or unpopular colleagues. Is the incumbent another Ted Kennedy? Another Jesse Helms? Is he a knee-jerk supporter of the President even when it comes to voting against an issue that is popular in his home district? Does what the candidate say she did when she visits her district comport with what she actually did when she was in Washington?

As much as this information may seem to be most useful to challengers, on-line computer databases can be of equal help in turning an incumbent's record into an asset. The incumbent's campaign can identify potential weaknesses before they are located by the challenger. This gives the campaign the opportunity to prepare a response or an aggressive promotion of the position.

The incumbent can also use the system to find popular issues on which his or her voting record is excellent. Or the incumbent can identify successful politicians who have a similar voting record. The candidate can then find ways to put these similarities to the greatest advantage.

Money is at the heart of every political campaign, and computers are now vital to soliciting a steady flow of money. Computers are used not only to target direct-mail fundraising appeals, but also to maintain sophisticated lists of contributors. Computer-generated personalized letters spew out thank-you letters and requests for more money. They also are necessary to maintain the political contribution records required by the federal and state governments. Special software packages have been developed to perform these tasks. The Federal Election Commission sponsors an on-line database that provides up-to-date information on political campaign contributions based on the reports all candidates are required to file periodically. This information is used by candidates to determine how much money their opponent has raised and from whom it has been received. By monitoring an opponent's contributions, a candidate knows how much he or she is either ahead or behind in the all-important race for money. Perhaps the most effective use of this service is made by the media who analyze this information in an attempt to determine whether a candidate is receiving large amounts of funding from well-heeled special-interest groups.

Among the tasks to which computers have so far found little use in campaigns is networking, so that candidates of the same party can share information about issues, tactics, and finances. For all Democratic candidates in a state, for example, to make use of at least a computerized electronic bulletin board would stop at least some of the constant reinventing of the wheel that goes on during campaigns. Computer fax boards with broadcast capabilities would enable the quick dissemination of information about late-breaking developments. To the extent that national party organizations can provide on-line issue and public opinion information, they can vastly improve the effectiveness of their candidates' campaigns. The ability of computers to do vote projections and other statistical analyses is used more by academics than by politicians.

COMPUTERS AND THE LEGISLATIVE PROCESS

There are equally as many uses for computers in the legislative, as opposed to the political, process. In the past decade, Congress and most state legislatures have changed dramatically. Legislation has become more complex, party loyalties have diminished, the congressional seniority system is a mere vestige of its halcyon days, and political action committee (PAC) contributions as well as campaign spending have mushroomed. These factors have combined to make legislators ever more sensitive to concerns about the political impact of their votes. As a result, interest groups and professional lobbyists have to work harder to get the votes of elected officials.

The primary use of computers in the legislative arena is to provide quick access to information about either upcoming or historical information about legislative activity such as bills, votes, committee hearings, and

the like. On-line commercial databases enable individuals to search for bills by key words in either their titles or their full text. Similar searches can be done on the federal level for floor votes in the House and Senate as well as committee votes. An individual interested in an obscure subject such as magnetic levitation transportation can use these databases to find every reference to the subject in bills, committee hearings, votes, statements printed in the *Congressional Record*, and even major newspaper articles and network television programs. This type of computer research capability is far more effective and cost-efficient than a roomful of researchers.

Every member of Congress can be profiled by such factors as state, party, district, committee and subcommittee memberships, type of district represented, and victory percentages from past elections. In addition, members' profiles include the bills they have introduced or cosponsored, their votes in committee on the floor, how much PAC money they have received, and the groups that have given them that money.

Although the goal of the paperless office may not be in sight, computers can reduce the amount of paper lobbyists need to handle. For example, almost every day Congress is in session, its committees and subcommittees hold hearings and vote on legislation. In addition, weekly there are dozens of press conferences and television programs that focus on key public policy issues. Devoting human resources to attending these hearings or reading transcripts is far more expensive than scanning them by using an on-line database, especially when the key words and phrases of interest can easily be searched for.

All of this information is of vital interest to the thousands of pressure groups trying to influence elected officials. Slowly but surely, professional lobbyists are beginning to understand that they need a wealth of information about the politicians they are lobbying. Contrary to popular belief, the last two decades have been characterized by a diffusion of political power in this country. Party affiliation has become an unreliable indicator of the positions a legislator is inclined to take. Major interest groups such as business and organized labor have lost power. Such trends make it harder to mount a successful legislative lobbying effort. In an effort to meet this challenge, lobbyists are becoming more sophisticated in their legislative research. They can no longer be satisfied with the knowledge of members of Congress they have gained from years of experience. Now, lobbyists need analysis to tell them which members of Congress are likely to be sure votes, which are the most likely to be persuaded, and which are lost causes.

It is in this analytical targeting of lobbying resources that commercial on-line computer databases are gaining the plaudits of those lobbyists who understand that they cannot possibly know it all. The databases provide more than information about bills and upcoming or past legislative action. They let users perform analysis. Vote information can be analyzed in a variety of ways. You can see how only certain members voted or how all Republicans voted. On a series of votes, you can establish your own vote ratings analysis by ascribing your own "right" and "wrong" positions for each vote. The commercial database will then assign a percentage rating on those votes for a single member or any group of members.

If you want to see how a member voted on trade, you would first search the database for all trade votes. After selecting either all of those votes or only those you wanted, you could establish a trade vote rating for the member (or any group of members). This approach can be used to show that a member is casting votes that either do or do not adequately represent the trade interests of her or his district. The extent of the usefulness of this analytical capability is limited only by the analytical resourcefulness of the user.

There are even more sophisticated forms of vote analysis that have yet to find their way into general usage. Using vote information from an on-line database, for example, it is possible to find which members of Congress are most likely to vote for a proposal to place a tax on imported oil. Database information can also identify informal coalitions of legislators. If Senator Smith is about to offer an amendment to tax oil, an analysis of past votes and other information available from the database can indicate which legisla-

tors have shown a pattern of voting with Senator Smith on similar issues in the past.

Grass roots (or citizen) lobbying has grown in importance at the federal and state levels. To a significant extent, this type of lobbying is orchestrated by various interest groups who understand that elected officials respond best to the people who have the power to vote. Direct mailings produced by computer-driven laser printers are sent out by the thousands to targeted groups of voters who are asked to write, phone, or telegram their elected officials. Some mailed appeals even include what appears to be a letter written on stationery with the constituent's name laser-printed at the top. All the constituent needs to do is sign the letter and mail it in an equally personalized envelope, which is also enclosed. So sophisticated has computer technology become that the direct-mail appeal can include a "handwritten" note from a well-known individual that actually reproduces the individual's handwriting and can vary the text to include a variety of personalized touches.

Only recently have elected officials on the national level begun to use computers effectively for legislative research and constituent service. Gone are the days when mainframes were used for simple list maintenance. Also gone are the ancient machines that once were used to provide "canned" responses to constituent letters. These dinosaurs had forced staff aides to send only the simplest responses to letters that were often complex. Now, elected officials use in-house personal computers or service bureaus to produce more personalized responses that can insert prepared paragraphs that are responsive to constituents who write about different legislative issues in the same letter. Without computers, this type of personalization could be achieved only by devoting scarce staff time to composing letters. Computers are also used to keep track of every constituent contact. Computers not only store the names and addresses of constituents who write letters, but the subject of their letters. That way, letters or newsletters can be targeted to groups of constituents interested in subjects such as the environment, foreign policy, abortion, and other key issues. By using computers to improve constituent communications, politicians are finding that this relatively new technology can help them improve their contact with voters. So much are computers used for such purposes that Congress has been forced to place more stringent financial limits on the prolific mailings of its members.

CONCLUSION

Over the past decade, computers have slowly become an accepted and valuable tool in the legislative and political processes. It has taken that long for them to be accepted as productive tools to be used in acquiring and making more effective use of the vast amount of public policy information available. Over the next few years, the analytical powers of computer software will find greater acceptance as political campaigns, lobbyists, and politicians realize that computer power can be translated into political power.

Howard Marlowe

PRESENTATION GRAPHICS

Computer graphics provide powerful tools for communicating and analyzing data. The computer graphics revolution began in the 1960s and intensified during the 1980s. Inexpensive and easy-to-use graphics software now provides individuals with professional graphic production capabilities at desktop workstations and personal computers. Computer graphics use will accelerate in the 1990s as organizations focus less on gathering data and more on presenting, analyzing, and using data for effective decision making.

Masses of data that currently reside in various public and private databases are often understandable only when presented graphically. Graphic presentations can help identify key variables and trends, while highlighting important relationships among variables. In addition to standalone management graphics packages, advanced graphics capabilities are available with many spreadsheet, database, and statistics software packages running on mainframe, mini- and personal computers. As workstations and personal computers increase in capability, graphics-oriented systems will become even more commonplace.

TYPES OF GRAPHS AVAILABLE

The most commonly used business graphs are line, bar, and pie charts (shown in Figure 1). These types of graphs are readily produced by most graphics software packages. But the computer graphics revolution has created and popularized a number of new graph formats for business applications. These include three-dimensional (3D) graphs, Chernoff faces, star and polar charts, animated graphs, contour plots, and color maps (see Figure 2). Chernoff (1973) developed a graphing technique in which the features of human faces represent varying values for different attributes. For instance, if the two faces in Figure 2 represented the end-of-year performance of two different companies, then the degree of the smile might graphically depict profit margins and the direction of the eyes, the nature of competition. Presumably the company depicted on the right is doing less well and is under attack from new competitive initiatives. Chernoff faces have been recommended for applications such as bankruptcy prediction.

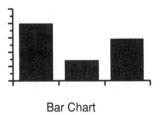
Bar Chart

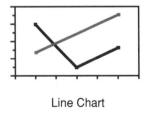
Line Chart

Pie Chart

FIGURE 1. Bar, line, and pie charts.

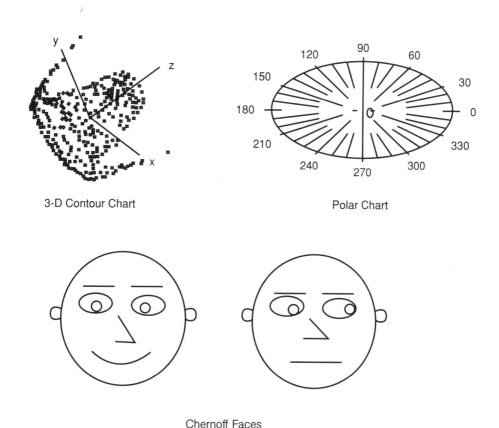

3-D Contour Chart

Polar Chart

Chernoff Faces

FIGURE 2. New graph formats.

Stereoscopic or 3D presentations have also grown in popularity. According to Hopper (1990), stock traders on Wall Street are now using special glasses to study complex data screens. The depth dimension provided by stereoscopic presentations is alleged to permit humans to grasp complex information more quickly. Novel graphs must, however, be used cautiously. A person who is inexperienced with a new format may get little value out of a complex graphic display. No matter how well designed, a 3D contour chart (like that in Figure 2) showing the relationships between trends for a forecasting task is likely to be nothing more than a pretty picture to an untrained eye. Graphic interpretation is a skill that must be learned.

SELECTION OF AN APPROPRIATE PRESENTATION FORMAT

Researchers have found that there is little support for the popular belief that graphics are universally superior to other presentation formats, especially tabular reporting. In some cases, people have been shown to do better using graphics than using tables, but for other tasks tables have been found to be superior to graphics. In many studies research reported no difference between the graphic and tabular information formats.

The effectiveness of graphics appears to be dependent on (1) the purpose or task for which the graphics are to be used and (2) the nature of the graphic format presented. Therefore, different types of information presentation are most appropriate for different types of situations. The two general areas of decision making where graphic presentation have been shown to be superior to the use of tables are in forecasting activities that require trends to be quickly spotted and analyzed and in situations where a vast amount of information is presented and relatively simple conclusions drawn. On the other hand, researchers have been unable to detect systematic differences in performance when graphs are used rather than tables in allowing readers to accurately retrieve information, recall information, or comprehend messages presented in reports.

Designers of graphics and graphic interfaces must not only determine when graphics are appropriate, they must also choose among a large variety of different formats. The specific graphic format that is used impacts what information can be extracted from a data presentation. For example, a 3D bar chart displaying in one picture the sales of different company products over a series of months by market location can be extremely useful in providing a quick understanding of the comparative performance of different sales regions. On the other hand, a pie chart might be more appropriate for a task requiring the relative comparison of the different types of marketing costs in a sales region. Similarly, a 3D contour chart is not likely to provide an accurate reading of a single data point; however, it may be useful in portraying the interactions of time period, geographic area, and product type in a sales analysis. The effectiveness of alternative graphic formats and details depends on the particular situation in which they are used.

A number of reference works provide a wealth of recommendations on the uses of different graphic formats. The work of Tufte (1983) is particularly noteworthy. These recommendations, however, tend to be based on practice and accumulated experience rather than scientific investigation. Figure 3 summarizes the findings accumulated from systematic, controlled research studies that have determined what type of graph is best for what types of tasks.

Bar and line formats appear to be the most appropriate for summarizing data. Although line charts are the most often used format for depicting variables over time, bar charts appear to be equally effective in portraying time series. Placing multiple variables in each graph increases the speed of comprehension as compared with multiple graphs of single variables. Contrary to common usage, grouped bar charts should be used rather than pie or segmented bar charts to present proportions of a whole. Grouped bar charts minimize the perceptual problems associated with pie and segmented bar charts. Perceptual errors in interpreting the graph are also minimized when grouped bar charts are used rather than segmented line or bar charts. Humans can more accurately read graphs that have a fixed common baseline than they can estimate lengths across bar charts or judge areas within pie charts. People also tend to overestimate the length of a vertical bar, thereby suggesting the use of horizontal bars instead of vertical bars in comparing variables or examining the relationships between variables.

Graphics provide no benefits over tables in determining single values from a display or a report. More significantly, graphic charts may even lead to poorer performance. If, however, graphics are used for such a task, the following should be kept in mind: (1) determining points from a line graph is much more difficult than doing so from bars because line graphs do not clearly pinpoint the exact y value for a given x value, (2) readers tend to completely overlook any figures on scales, (3) data values at the end of the bars increase the accuracy of decisions, and (4) placement of values on the bars is more effective than grid lines.

BIAS IN GRAPHIC PRESENTATIONS

Even if the format appears to be correct, the scales, grids, and titles can be manipulated to bias the interpretation of the data. Deceptive graphics, or "lying with statistics," is a serious problem. Over many centuries, graphic artists have evolved generally accepted standards for graphs to reduce misuses and abuses of graphics. Graphics standards are a set of predefined rules that direct the construction of a graph with regard to its components, such as size, color, shading, and scaling. Researchers report a worrisome number of violations. For example, according to Johnson et al. (1980), up to 30 percent of the graphs in corporate annual reports included at least one violation of standards. The most common "error" was the distortion of recent trends. Distortions of trends can occur when the starting baseline of a graph is at a number other than zero or the time frame or scale varies from one graph to another without any notification. Violations of standards are

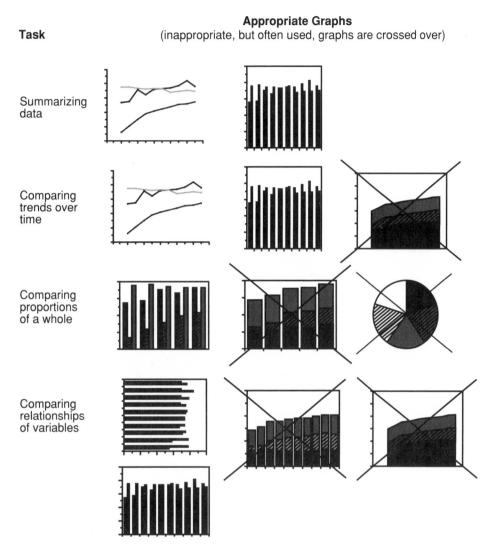

FIGURE 3. Contingency table for graph formats.

likely to escalate as more graphics are generated by personal computer users who have little knowledge of either graphic design or related standards.

Kosslyn (1985) has proposed a computer program that would emulate an expert human graph designer. Whenever a user of graphics software attempts to violate any standards, the expert system would be called to enforce the standards and suggest a corrective action. Although some progress has apparently been made toward developing such a system, today's commercial solutions are far less sophisticated. Some graphics packages are accompanied by chart books that provide predesigned graphic formats. Interactive chartbooks engage the user in a dialogue about the data and the purpose of the chart and then propose acceptable charts. Other packages encourage use of the graphics standards (such as zero origin on y-axis scales) via default options built into the software. Chartbooks and default options are particularly effective for novice users who have not learned to customize their graphs. Training is another way to enforce graphic standards. Both the readers and generators of graphic output should be exposed to materials highlighting the common abuses and misuses of graphics.

FUTURE TRENDS

Increasingly, sophisticated new systems are permitting graphics to be integrated with other modes of presentation. DeSanctis and Jarvenpaa (1989) found that charts that combined numeric and graphic information led to better performance than charts that contained either numeric or graphic information only. Hence, multiple views of data can be much more effective than single views. We must now learn how graphics can be most effectively combined with other modes of presentation.

Graphic presentations are, for instance, the cornerstone of the EXECUTIVE INFORMATION SYSTEMS (EISs) that are becoming more and more common on managers' desks. The power of the EIS graphics software does not, however, result from standalone graphic presentations, but from combination of graphics with other modes of presentation for (1) trend analysis, (2) exception reporting, and (3) "drill-down" analysis. For example, a producer of soft drinks might want to know how its cola products are performing in the U.S. market. Traditionally the firm might have had 50 percent of the market, whereas their major competitor and various regional products shared the remainder of the market. The line chart could quickly highlight the firm's performance relative to their major competitors' over the last year using point-of-sale data obtained from supermarkets. The comparison might reveal that the major competitor has held its market share but the company in third place has increased its share significantly. A drill-down option lets the EIS user recheck the data and calculations used to generate the line chart. Some data points on the line chart might be further exploded to provide regional or store-level data, now perhaps in a table format. Having discovered that the bulk of the increase has come in a particular geographic market segment, the user might ask to see a bar chart, this time comparing prices for the product in various distribution outlets. After making a few confirmatory phone calls, the user might annotate the graph with an explanation and, using electronic mail, forward it to appropriate managers for action.

Advances in multitasking and windowing technology have also increased the use of multimedia interfaces—graphics combined with text, voice, and image presentations. For example, a merchandise buyer for a furniture store might be provided with a sophisticated electronic catalog from a major supplier. One window of the workstation might be open to display a bar chart of last year's sales for a particular line of recliners. In another window, the user might see an image of this year's version of the chair. By manipulating a mouse, the user could turn the chair around to see the back or zoom in to look closely at the fabric of the chair. A palette of colors and prints would permit the buyer to quickly look at other versions. In a third window, the user might see an advertisement for the chair that the supplier intends to run in a popular home furnishings magazine. If requested, an accompanying voice briefly describes the general promotional plans for the piece. A fourth window might provide access to the corporate electronic mail system, permitting the buyer to communicate directly with the supplier's representative. The buyer might later open a fifth window, containing an order form that will be electronically transmitted directly to the supplier.

In conclusion, the 1970s and 1980s were characterized by advances in computer technology helping organizations to gather and store data. The 1990s will be a decade concerned with analyzing, distributing, and using that information to manage the business, but the presentations of these data will not be restricted to one medium. Users will demand multimedia interfaces. The attention of researchers will no longer be on whether graphics are more effective than tables. They will, instead, increasingly focus on how the modes should be best integrated and interwoven to obtain the maximum benefit from gathered data. The increased flexibility in graphics technology will also heighten the concerns about abuses of graphics. Although graphics technology can produce a picture worth a thousand words, it can also lead to misrepresented information in the hands of an unskilled user. Graphics software that contains expertise about graphics standards can help the user make informed decisions.

References

Chernoff, H. 1973. The use of faces to represent points in *k*-dimensional space graphically. *Journal of the American Statistical Association* 68:361–68.

DeSanctis, G., and S. L. Jarvenpaa. 1989. Graphical presentation of accounting data for financial forecasting: An experimental investigation. *Accounting, Organizations, and Society* 14(5/6):509–25.

Hopper, M. D. 1990. Rattling SABRE—New ways to compete on information. *Harvard Business Review*, May–June, pp. 118–25.

Johnson, J. R., R. R. Rice, and R. A. Roemmich. 1980. Pictures that lie: The abuse of graphs in annual reports. *Management Accounting* 62:50–56.

Kosslyn, S. M. 1985. Graphics and human information processing. *Journal of the American Statistical Association* 80(391):499–511.

Tufte, E. R. 1983. *The visual display of quantitative information.* Cheshire, Conn.: Graphics Press.

For Further Reading

Cleveland, W. S., and R. McGill. 1984. Graphical perception: Theory, experimentation, and application to the development of graphical methods. *Journal of the American Statistical Association* 79(387):531–54.

DeSanctis, G. 1984. Computer graphics as decision aids: Direction for research. *Decision Sciences* 15(4):463–87.

Ives, B. 1982. Graphical user interfaces for business information systems. *MIS Quarterly*, Special Issue, pp. 16–47.

Jarvenpaa, S. L., and G. W. Dickson. 1988. Graphics and managerial decision making: Research based guidelines. *Communications of the ACM* 31(6):764–74.

Sirkka Jarvenpaa

PRINTING TECHNOLOGIES

A number of choices are available in printer hardware for today's computer systems. The main criteria now used in selecting a printer are speed of printing, print quality, and price. In all these cases, as the level of technology increases, so does the speed and quality of the printout. Additional features and higher-level technology also increase price.

Three basic types of printer are available, each with different features that are beneficial to different types of users. The three general categories, based on the amount of information that is printed simultaneously, are character printers, line printers, and sheet printers.

CHARACTER PRINTERS

Character printers include any printer that prints a document one character at a time. Two major types of character printers are available: the dot matrix printer and the "daisywheel" printer. Because these two machines print each unique character before moving on to print the next, this class of printers is generally the slowest. Because of the machinery used and the number of repetitive actions, these printers also emit the most noise while printing.

In a dot matrix printer, a moving print head skates along the platen of the printer, imprinting the image of a letter through an inked ribbon. The image of the letter is then transferred to the paper wound around the platen. This printer has only the one moving element, and the letters are formed by a

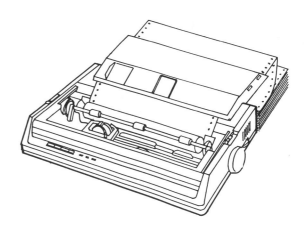

FIGURE 1. A dot matrix printer, the Okidata 320. *Courtesy Okidata.*

number of wires embedded in the print head. As the printer receives the signal from the software to form a particular letter, a certain combination of the wires will extend from the print head to make the impression against the ribbon. Because of this flexibility in character formation, these printers can produce graphic as well as text printouts. The head works in a bidirectional mode: it prints left to right across the page, and then prints the following line right to left on its return trip. This feature saves the time wasted in waiting for a carriage return between each printed line. Dot matrix printers generally print at speeds of 50 characters per second or more. The faster the machine, the higher its cost.

As each letter is made up of a matrix of closely spaced dots (the imprints of the wire ends), the closer the dots are to each other, the sharper is the image of the letter. At the low end of the spectrum are the nine-pin printers using nine wires, at the high end are twenty-four-pin and thirty-six-pin models.

The advantage to using a dot matrix printer is the ability to do "draft quality" printing at low cost. (This is the least expensive printer on the market, and generally uses an inked fabric multiuse ribbon that is inexpensive and easily reinked or replaced.) These machines also use continuous-form printer paper, so that multiple-page printouts can be run unattended; there is no need to insert a blank sheet of paper each time the printer finishes printing a page. This is particularly useful to applications that print out long reports or other documents that do not have to be of "correspondence quality." The print quality of a dot matrix printer is fine for "draft" use; however, most book and magazine editors would not accept a manuscript submitted to them in this low-quality print.

More expensive dot matrix models offer wide-carriage platens for printing on 15-inch-wide accounting paper. Most offer a selection of fonts for changing the appearance of the type on the page. Thus, it is possible to use italics, underlining, and boldface print in a document. The disadvantage to lower-priced dot matrix printers is the lack of "true descenders" in its fonts. A descender is that part of the letter that extends below the line—the bottom half of the lowercase q,

y, p, g, and j. Without the ability to print below the line, lower-priced dot matrix printers pull the letter up above the line, and print the entire letter on or above the line of printing.

The "daisywheel" printer gets its name from the character print wheel used. The wheel is generally a disk-shaped element with each character extending from the apex on a long spoke, resembling the petals of a daisy. This printer uses the same form of "head" element that moves along the length of the platen. The element rotates to the correct character to be printed. Then, a hammer extends from the print head and presses the letter against a ribbon, transferring the image of the character to the paper. Because there is much more physical movement in the skating of the print head followed by rotation of the wheel, this process is much slower than dot matrix printing. Because of the motion of the hammer against the platen, this printer also creates much more noise than would the dot matrix printer.

Most daisywheel printers print bidirectionally, though they work at a much slower pace than would a dot matrix printer. The speed of a daisywheel printer can be as low as 15 to 20 characters per second.

The advantage to using daisywheel over dot matrix is that the printed type is sharper. In fact, it is impossible to differentiate between text printed on a daisywheel printer and that on a typewriter. These machines can also use continuous-feed paper, though most are single-sheet printers, as the type produced is of the "correspondence" quality used for letters and final drafts.

The disadvantages to using a daisywheel printer are the increased price, the overhead expense, and the lack of flexibility in printing. Most daisywheel printers use a carbon-coated plastic ribbon that can be used only once and cannot be reinked. Thus, the ribbons do not last as long as the dot matrix ribbons and cannot be recycled. In addition, as most daisywheel printers use typewriter ribbons, the supplies are initially more expensive than those for dot matrix types.

To change fonts on a daisywheel printer, the user must buy additional type wheels and interchange them, if multiple fonts are used in the same document. Through the use of "overstrike" (the printer types the character, moves the print head slightly beyond the original point, and types the character again) it is possible to create the illusion of boldface print. Underlining is possible, but italics and regular-face type do not appear on the same print wheel.

The major disadvantage to using a daisywheel printer is the lack of flexibility. This printer can produce text file printouts only; because it only has use of the characters on the type wheel, it cannot print graphics beyond what can be produced with typewriter characters.

A new innovation in character printers has been the advent of the ink jet printer. Originally, this machine was created as a means of high-speed printing in industrial applications (such as printing names and addresses on mailing labels). Today, it is quickly replacing both dot matrix and daisywheel printers as an economical, quieter alternative.

The ink jet printer works by shooting a spray of ink through a nozzle in the moving print head directly onto the paper. Because the spray of ink is fine and precise, the shape of the letters is more exact than that produced by the dot matrix, very close to that of the daisywheel. This machine also adds the flexibility of printing in any number of fonts and graphic formats. The cost is low because the machine uses a refillable ink cartridge, much like that of a giant fountain pen. There are few moving parts, and the machine makes virtually no noise.

The disadvantages to using an ink jet printer are the higher cost and the relative impermanence of the ink. Some machines use a water-soluble ink that runs if it gets wet. To have a permanent copy of a printout from such a printer, it is necessary to make a photocopy of the printout. This problem can be remedied by making sure the ink used is not water soluble.

LINE PRINTERS

The line printer is used in industrial applications in which large volumes of print are being produced. It is faster than character printing because these machines print an entire line of print, rather than only one character, in one movement. Most line printers are dot matrix printers. Because of the size, cost, and noise of this type of machinery, line printers have not crossed over to home use.

PAGE PRINTERS

Page printers work by printing an entire page, rather than single characters or lines, in one motion. The technology for this type of machine is known as nonimpact printing (because the print head is not beating against a platen, as is the case with the other types of printers), or as laser printing. The print in this case is transferred electronically to the paper.

The technology of nonimpact printers is very similar to that of modern photocopy machines. The software sends the image of a page to the printer, and this image is transferred to a magnetically charged rotating drum within the printer. Particles of negatively charged toner (a fine dry powder that is used instead of ink) stick to the positively charged magnetic "image" on the drum. The drum rotates as a sheet of paper passes under it, transferring the toner from the drum to the paper. In a final step, the toner is affixed to the paper with heat, thus making a permanent copy. This is done via a small laser beam that heats the toner and "fixes" the printout, giving rise to the name *laser printer*.

The advantages of using a page printer are similar to those of the ink jet printer.

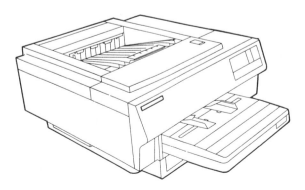

FIGURE 2. A laser printer, the Hewlett-Packard LaserJet series II. *Courtesy Hewlett-Packard.*

With no moving type element, the printer is not limited to one particular print type. It is possible to print both text and graphics on the same page, and to do so in a quality of printing that is "near typeset." The type density of the most commonly used laser printers, although forming characters with a matrix of closely spaced dots on a page, is 300 dots per inch. This density creates a character almost as fine as that produced by the daisywheel. Some more expensive laser printers can produce a type density of up to 1,200 dots per inch. Laser printers are single-sheet feed machines, so they can print only onto single nonbound pages, not on continuous-feed paper. These machines also have bin-style sheet feeders, though; so, once the hoppers are filled with paper, the machine can be left unattended for long print jobs.

Because there are no moving print heads or typing elements, the noise level of the page printer is the lowest of the group. Depending on the capacity of the machine and the number of font changes or graphics in a document, the printing speed for a page printer is between four and eight pages per minute.

The disadvantages are initial up-front cost and the limitations of the types of paper that can be used in these machines. Laser printers are the most expensive printers on the market today. Although they require less maintenance than the other types (a toner cartridge can last as long as 3,000 to 4,000 pages, depending on the type and density of printing done), each toner cartridge costs an average of $100. The per-page cost is lower for the laser printer; however, the initial investment in the printer and supplies is greater than for the other machines.

The page printer is the most sensitive of all these machines as to which types of paper can be used. Most laser printers take paper up to a thickness of 65-pound stock (the thickness of a business card) with no problems. Thicker papers cause the printer to jam, as do papers thinner than 20-pound stock (the weight of regular paper used in photocopiers). Onion skin paper will not run through a page printer if it is of less than 15- to 20-pound weight.

Many people use printers for correspondence printed on preprinted letterheads. This works well with all printers, including laser printers, with some exceptions. Paper that has been engraved, flat printed (like this book), or blind embossed (letters pressed into the paper, giving a raised appearance) works well if it is fed through one sheet at a time. Paper that has been thermographed (a coat of resin is applied over the print to make the letters look "raised") cannot be used. The heat of the laser will melt the resin and cause the plastic to stick to the rotating drum, thus making it impossible to print. Also, self-stick labels cannot be run through a laser printer unless they have been specifically manufactured for laser printers. The heat from the laser causes the labels to work free from their backing and to adhere to the rotating drum, again ruining the printer.

Which one of these printers is the correct choice depends entirely on the end application for which it is needed. Long reports, documentation of software programs, and "daily" work can all be easily done on a dot matrix printer. Large-volume printing, such as weekly reports in an industrial setting, is better done with the line printers. Any work that must be of high print quality, where appearance is paramount, should be printed on the daisywheel, ink jet, or laser printer. If both print quality and speed are important, the laser printer is the best selection.

Dot matrix printers are available for as little as $100 for a 9-pin short (9-inch) carriage printer. The price may go as high as $500 for a wider (15-inch) carriage, 24-pin printer.

Daisywheel printers are slightly more expensive than dot matrix printers, costing from $200 for a short carriage up to $800 for the wide carriage. Some companies offer a hybrid machine that has both dot matrix print for "draft" quality work and daisywheel print for "correspondence" quality. Purchase of such a machine would save the added expense of owning both types of printers.

The ink jet printer starts as low as $200 for a single-character printer, and runs as high as $800 for the same technology in a page printer.

Laser printers generally cost more than $1,000; however, with additional features such as increased memory, large paper bins, and additional font support, the price may go as high as $2,000 for a home-use printer and well over $5,000 for a high-speed multiuser machine.

For Further Reading

The computer and data processing market. 1975. New York: Frost and Sullivan.

Davenport, J. W. 1986. *Graphics for the dot matrix printer.* New York: Computer Books Division, Simon & Schuster.

Ink jet printers—The unfulfilled promise. 1980. San Jose, Calif.: Strategic Business Systems.

Ledin, V. 1984. *How to buy and use a printer.* Sherman Oaks, Calif.: Alfred Publishing Co.

Myers, D. 1989. *The laser printer handbook.* Homewood, Ill.: Dow Jones-Irwin.

O'Reilley, F. J. 1985. *Computer printers: Directions, markets, technologies.* Stamford, Conn.: Business Communications Company.

Output hardcopy devices. 1988. Boston: Academic Press.

Semos, S. M. 1989. *Dot matrix printer reference manual.* 2nd ed. Torrance, Calif.: Epson-America.

Webster, T. 1984. *Terminals and printers buyer's guide.* New York: McGraw-Hill.

John L. Myers

PROCESSING METHODS

One of the most common uses of computers in business is the processing of day-to-day transactions. This could include entering sales receipts into an accounting system or data on hours worked into a payroll system. There are two principal methods (sometimes called modes) that computers use to process transactions: batch and on-line processing. These two methods differ in the way data are prepared and entered into the computer, and in the way the computer updates its records. Below we discuss the two methods and a hybrid approach developed by combining aspects of each method.

BATCH PROCESSING

In the 1960s when many early transaction processing systems were developed, computer hardware was very different than it is today. For example, the primary mode of data storage was magnetic tape and the primary data input device was the punched card reader. Today, data are typically input from the keyboard and stored on disk drives. Both the card reader and magnetic tape are sequential devices. Magnetic tapes are similar to audio cassette tapes: to access a piece of data in the middle of a tape, the computer must read all the preceding data. Disk drives, however, are similar to compact discs or record players: data can be accessed in the middle of a disk directly (without reading all the preceding data). Batch processing was developed to maximize efficiency in the card reader/magnetic tape environment.

Batch processing can be best described using an example. Consider student grades for a large college. The 10,000 student records are stored in a "master file," often on a magnetic tape, sorted by student identification number. One day at the end of the semester several professors have completed their grades. A deck of 200 punched cards is produced containing each student's ID number, course numbers, and new grades. A sort program is then used to produce a transaction file containing these changes sorted by student ID number.

A batch processing procedure is used to produce a new master file containing updated student grades (Figure 1). The first record is read (ID 12345) from the transaction file. The master file is read until ID 12345 is found. For each record up to student 12345, the student's grades are written unchanged onto the new master file. Student 12345's record is then updated with the new grade and written out to the new master file. This process is then repeated for each subsequent record in the transaction file. Any remaining records on the old master file are then written out to the new file. A report is produced that notes the changes made and any errors

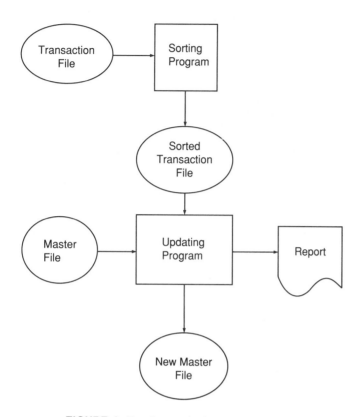

FIGURE 1. Batch processing procedure.

essing is that the master file is almost always out of date. Changes to the master file are not made when they occur. Rather they are accumulated and a batch of changes are all made at once. Batch processing, therefore, would not be appropriate for an airline reservation system, where up-to-the-minute data on the number of available seats are critical.

ON-LINE PROCESSING

Owing to the development of direct-access storage devices such as magnetic disks, the computer gained the ability to efficiently read and write data directly anywhere in a large file. On-line processing (Figure 2) uses this capability, permitting immediate updating of files. We do not have to wait to accumulate a batch of changes before updating the file. In addition, data are processed in the order in which they are received. They need not be sorted before the master file is updated.

The college grading system example can

that occurred in processing. For example, if an invalid ID was found in the transaction file, this would be included in the report.

Because in batch processing data are accumulated for a given period and then processed together, processing occurs periodically. Typically, it would occur at the end of the day or week. Payroll processing and generation of monthly telephone bills are examples of batch processing applications.

One advantage of batch processing is that the master file need be read through from beginning to end only one time. If we were to update each student's grades individually, we would read through the file up to 200 times. Hence, this process is much more efficient when the master file is stored on a sequential device such as a magnetic tape. As sequential devices are typically less costly than direct-access storage devices such as magnetic disks, batch processing is a relatively economical method of transaction processing.

One major disadvantage of batch proc-

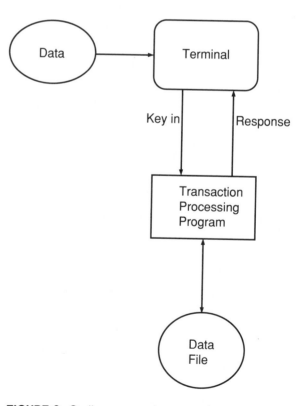

FIGURE 2. On-line processing procedure.

be used to describe on-line processing. When a professor's grade sheet is received, a clerk in the registrar's office enters each grade directly into the student master file. The clerk enters the course number (Accounting 100) and then the ID number and new grade of each student (e.g., ID 12345, A) into the computer terminal. The computer immediately searches the location where student 12345's record is stored, and updates it. The workstations or terminals used by the clerks are directly connected to the computer, permitting immediate update of the master file.

There are several important differences between batch and on-line processing for updating student records. With the on-line method, the clerks need not wait until the end of the day to process a batch of updates. Further, the updates need not be sorted by student ID number. That is, the clerks do not have to worry about whether the order in which the students appeared on the grading sheet is consistent with the order of the contents of the master file. Student 12345's record can be updated before student 12300's record or after student 12350's record, even though the master file is arranged in ascending order of student ID number.

On-line processing is used when quick, real-time responses are crucial. Typical examples of on-line processing include credit card validation, update of patient data at a hospital, airline reservations, and deposits to and withdrawals from a bank account. In some newer examples of on-line processing systems, the clerk's role has been eliminated. For example, when bank deposits and withdrawals are made through automated teller machines, the customer directly enters the transaction data.

One advantage of on-line processing is that the input data can be validated immediately. By echoing the data or presenting error information, the computer can help clerks correct input errors. For example, the computer can flag an invalid student ID number, course number, or course grade. As one of the major sources of computer error is incorrect input data, accuracy can be improved. In a batch environment, errors would be printed to a separate report and corrected in the next batch run.

In an on-line environment, the master file always has more up-to-date information. In our student grade example, clerks or administrators will have a more up-to-date view of each student's records. This is even more critical when financial data, such as bank balances, are involved.

Unlike the situation for batch processing, there is no backup file automatically generated in the on-line environment. Hence, special backup procedures are used. These often involve making a periodic copy of the master file and a separate file containing all changes to the master that were made since the last backup was produced.

HYBRID METHODS

In some circumstances, a combination of batch and on-line processing is used. One common hybrid approach involves on-line data entry and batch master file update (Figure 3). This can be illustrated using the student grade example. As in on-line processing, the student grades are entered by a clerk and verified as they are received in the registrar's office. The master file, however, is *not* immediately updated. With a separate input program, the new grades are checked for valid course and student ID number and for valid grade and then stored in a transaction file. At the end of the day, the transaction file is sorted and the master file is updated. This latter step is similar to batch processing. As on-line data entry allows immediate verification of input data, this hybrid method improves the accuracy of input data, while avoiding the processing effort needed to update the master file frequently.

The hybrid approach is especially beneficial when data entry takes place at many locations. For example, a chain of apparel stores may enter sales transactions in each store at the cash register, when purchases are made. These data would then be stored in a small computer at each store. A master file located at the chain's headquarters and containing sales data for all the stores would be updated nightly. The headquarters computer would call each store's computer to update its master file. This hybrid approach is most

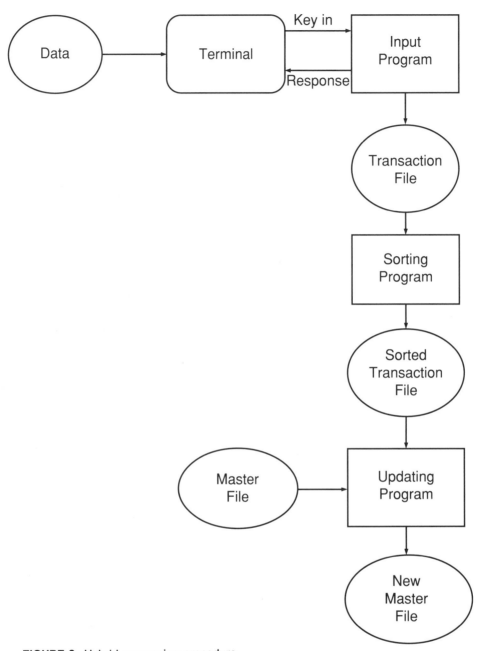

FIGURE 3. Hybrid processing procedure.

useful when immediate input verification is important but current information is not critical to the performance of the business.

For Further Reading
Davis, G. B., and M. H. Olson. 1985. *Management information systems: Conceptual founda-* *tions, structure, and development.* 2nd ed. New York: McGraw-Hill.

Kroenke, D. 1989. *Management information systems.* Santa Cruz, Calif.: Mitchell Publishing.

David K. Goldstein
Namjae Cho

PRODUCTION SYSTEMS

See Artificial Intelligence; Knowledge Bases and Expert Systems

PROGRAMMING LANGUAGE DESIGN

A computer follows a set of instructions that are arranged together by a programmer in the form of an *algorithm*. An algorithm is a precise statement of actions that the computer must execute to solve a given problem; it is a recipe. For example, if we want the computer to find the roots of the equation $3x^2 + 5x = 22$, we could write down a recipe, or an algorithm, for solving equations of the general form $ax^2 + bx = c$. Then, if we submit a particular equation to the computer, it will follow the steps of the algorithm and produce the answers to the problem.

If we were describing an algorithm to another person, we could write it in any number of ways. We could write it in a natural language such as English or French; we could use mathematical notations and terminology; we could use logical formulas. In any case, we use a language to describe an algorithm. A *programming language* is a notation used to describe algorithms for computer execution.

As opposed to natural languages that evolve over time through usage, a programming language is *designed* by people. The designer has the ability to define a language and enforce its rules of usage, which, in general, is not possible with natural languages. This ability also places a responsibility on the designer to create a language that is not only restrictive but also productive, in that its restrictions are intended to help its users write better programs more quickly.

What are the guidelines that a language designer must follow to design a "good" language? What is a "good" language? What kinds of languages are possible? In the early days of computing—the early 1950s—programming languages were very simple, with a binary alphabet consisting of the numbers 0 and 1 only. These languages, called machine languages, were easy for the machine

to interpret but hard for people to use. Since then, there have been many advances in the design of programming languages, both to make languages that are easier for people to use and to make languages that are more appropriate for different application areas such as business data processing and scientific computation. In this article, we look at the evolution of languages since the beginning, look at the different types of languages in existence today, and derive some rules of language design based on these examinations. The field of such a study is called *programming linguistics.*

WHAT MAKES UP A PROGRAMMING LANGUAGE?

There are hundreds of programming languages in existence today. Although they have differences, they also share many common characteristics. In particular, the basic components that make up a programming language are rather constant. We start our study of programming linguistics by examining these basic components.

By considering what a programmer needs to express in writing a program, we can tell what every programming language must contain to allow the programmer to write the needed programs. For example, let us imagine that we want to write a program to *sort* (arrange) a collection of words in alphabetical order. This task might be a part of a larger task of composing a dictionary. The programming language we use must allow us first to read the data, that is, the individual words, from an external medium into the computer. Once the data are input into the computer, they must be represented in the computer in some form of a data structure; then we need to manipulate the data, for example, to count how many words there are and decide whether one word should appear before or after another. Sometimes, we need to select one of several operations to perform. For example, when we compare two words, we might want to perform different operations based on the result of the comparison. Once we are finished sorting the data, we need to produce an output, that is, transfer the data from inside the computer to an external medium such as paper or the computer screen.

Using this simple example, which is fairly representative of the kinds of tasks that a program does, we can divide the components of a programming language according to Table 1. The differences among languages stem from how they treat each of these components and how they combine them. These components are closely interrelated. For example, if the language allows the use of character data, then it must also support appropriate operations for manipulating such data. In the next section, we look at some important existing languages and the different ways in which they treat data, operations, sequencing, and input/output.

SOME EXAMPLE LANGUAGES

FORTRAN

FORTRAN is the first programming language that gained widespread acceptance. Designed during the period 1953–1957 and put in use in 1957, it is still one of the most used programming languages. It is certainly the dominant language for scientific applications. The language has evolved through many revisions from its simple form in 1957 to a much larger and more comprehensive language. The current version is called FORTRAN 77, because it was made official in 1977. Work is proceeding in defining a new version, currently referred to as FORTRAN

TABLE 1. Components of a Programming Language

Component	Purpose
Input/output	Allows the transfer of data into and out of the computer
Data	Allows the representation of the data
Operations or commands	Allows manipulations of the data
Sequence control	Allows the ordering of operations

9X. We examine the components of the original FORTRAN here.

Data. Because FORTRAN was aimed at scientific computation, it supported only two kinds of data: integer (i.e., whole numbers such as -10, 3, 390,939) and floating point (i.e., real numbers such as 3.141592). It has a capability for aggregating data into arrays and matrices. Original FORTRAN, however, reflected the restricted capabilities of the early computers by allowing matrices only up to three dimensions.

Operations. Again, because of the intended application domain for the language, the operations provided are mathematical ones such as arithmetic and trigonometric operations. For example, assuming that the variables A and B represent the lengths of the sides of a right triangle, we can compute the length of the hypotenuse by the following statement:

$$C = SQRT (A**2 + B**2)$$

The operations used in this statement are assignment ($=$), square root (SQRT), exponentiation ($**$), and addition ($+$). We see that the notation adopted by FORTRAN also reflects the scientific notation.

Sequence Control. At the time FORTRAN was designed, the importance of the sequence control mechanisms of a language was not recognized. As a result, FORTRAN's features are quite limited in this area. It supports an IF statement that allows the programmer to test for a condition (e.g., some number being positive) and execute (or not) a given operation based on the result of the test. It also supports a GOTO statement that allows the programmer to transfer control to any other operation in the program. This next operation must be labeled by a number, and the label is used in the GOTO statement to identify the operation to branch to. The combination of the GOTO and IF sequencing operations is quite powerful and allows any form of sequence to be constructed because we can test a condition to decide whether to branch to another operation or simply continue the sequential execution. This powerful (but, as we will see, error-prone) combination of sequence controls is supported by all computers directly. FORTRAN also supports a form of a selection to choose which of two or three operations to execute next.

Another important control structure introduced by FORTRAN is the DO-loop construct, which allows a sequence of other statements to be executed a fixed number of times. This facility is also supported directly by a "decrement and branch" instruction that is available on many computers. This instruction decrements a value (which must be initially set to the number of times we want the loop to execute); if the result is greater than zero, it branches to the beginning of the statement sequence; it exits the loop if the result is zero.

The most useful sequence control mechanism supported by FORTRAN, however, is the SUBROUTINE feature, which allows the programmer to group a sequence of operations together and give them a unique name. This named unit, called a procedure or subroutine, can then be called from different points of the program. A procedure call causes the procedure to execute and, on completion, to return control back to the calling point. This mechanism not only allows the code for the procedure to be written only once, but also, more importantly, allows the programmer to use the power of abstraction. For example, if we write a procedure to sort a set of words, we can use this procedure without thinking about how it does the sort, that is, the internal operations used in the sort procedure. In effect, the procedure mechanism allows us to build new operations that are not provided as basic ones in the language. Proper use of the mechanism helps a programmer design programs that are easier to write, read, and modify (e.g., extend).

Input/Output. FORTRAN supports the transfer of data from and to cards, disks and tapes, paper printers, computer screens, and so forth. It allows the data to be formatted while they are being transferred.

C

As experience with FORTRAN grew, both the validity of its approach (using a human-oriented rather than a machine-oriented notation) and its shortcomings (limited data and control facilities) became apparent. As a result, a succession of languages were designed to continue in the path that FORTRAN had created and to improve on its capabilities. Algol 60, PL/I, Pascal, C, Ada, and many other languages fall into this category. Here we examine the language C to see in what ways it differs from FORTRAN.

Data. The language C was designed to support, in the first place, the writing of so-called systems programs—programs that are used to control various functions of computers to make the computer easier to use—as opposed to applications programs that are used to make the computer support a particular application. For this reason, C supports not only data types based on mathematical number systems, integer and real, but also types based on computer memory organizations. In particular, C supports data of type *char*, which can be used to store character data and corresponds to one byte of memory. A very powerful data type supported by C is called a pointer; it allows one data item to contain the "address" of another data item, that is, to point to another data item. This data type allows the programmer to represent interrelated information, such as a family tree, relatively easily. In general, graphs can be represented this way.

In addition to providing additional primitive data types, C also has a richer set of mechanisms for grouping these data types together. Arrays collect a set of items that are all of the same type; records or structures collect a set of items that are not necessarily of the same type; enumerated types allow a set of values to be treated as a sequence, for example, the collection *weekdays = (Monday, Tuesday, Wednesday, Thursday, Friday)*. In general, the most important ways that programming languages have evolved over the years are in how they view the role of data and how much flexibility they give the programmer in representing the information needed by the program.

Operations. Naturally, for each of the additional primitive types, C also provides operations for manipulating them. For example, for pointers, there is an operation for accessing the data pointed at by the pointer and there are character operations such as for comparison. There are also operations for dealing with aggregate objects. For example, the successor operation returns the next item in an enumerated sequence.

Sequence Control. Many languages that came after FORTRAN provide additional looping constructs to allow a sequence of statements to be executed repeatedly as long as, or until, some condition is satisfied. This means that the number of times that the loop will execute does not have to be known a priori, as in FORTRAN's DO-loop. Many of these languages also generalize the IF selection to a CASE statement, which allows a selection among any number of operations, not just two. C supports both such loop constructs (*repeat* and *while*) and the case construct (called *switch* in C).

Input/Output. C, like several other languages, takes the approach that input/output should not be part of the language because it is too dependent on the computer and the input/output device being used. Therefore, C depends on a set of "libraries" that contain operations the programmer may call from the program to effect input/output. For example, there is a standard library that provides operations for reading and writing characters, integers, and real numbers from the computer keyboard and onto a computer display or from and into a disk file.

LISP

FORTRAN and C fall into the category of languages that we can call imperative languages. These languages grew out of the attempt to make computers easier to program than was possible with machine and assembly languages. These languages are, nevertheless, based on the underlying capabilities and characteristics of the widely available computers, such as the memory organization and sequential execution of instructions. These two characteristics are re-

sponsible, for example, for the prevalence of arrays and loops in imperative programming languages.

Since the early days of programming languages, however, there have been attempts to base the design of languages on criteria other than computer organization. LISP, one such language, has been based on mathematics and functions. (See also LISP AND PROLOG.)

Data. As opposed to FORTRAN and other languages that deal primarily with numeric data, LISP is aimed at "symbolic" data processing, that is, programs that manipulate primarily symbols rather than numbers. Thus, the data manipulated by a LISP program are either an *atom* (a symbol) or a *list* (a list of symbols). A list is built by using parentheses around the elements that form the list. Each symbol (atom) may have a value associated with it.

For example, the atom TOM is a symbol. The list (FATHER TOM JOHN) may represent the fact that the father of TOM is JOHN. And the list ((FATHER TOM JOHN) (FATHER JOHN JOE) (FATHER JIM JOHN) . . .), which contains sublists, may represent the paternal relationships among a group of men. Although LISP also supports numeric data, the emphasis of the language is on symbols.

Operations. The important operations in LISP are for symbol manipulation, such as finding the first element of a list or the tail part of a list, checking whether a data item is an atom or a list or whether it is the empty list, and so on. Even function application is shown in LISP using the list notation. For example, the operation of adding *A* and *B* is shown as (+ *A B*). In general, LISP operations are functions; whenever a list is to be evaluated, the first element of the list is taken as a function to apply to the remaining elements; the result of the application of the function is the value of the list. As in mathematics, lists (i.e., function applications) may be nested arbitrarily.

Sequence Control. The primary mechanism of sequence control in LISP is function application. To apply a function application, first its arguments are evaluated, which may require other function applications, and then the function is applied to the results. A typical LISP program is a single function application (involving other functions internally). The body of a function is defined naturally as a list.

Input/Output. LISP provides mechanisms for reading in and writing out the values associated with symbols used in the program.

SNOBOL4

FORTRAN deals with numeric data and LISP deals with symbolic data in general; in SNOBOL4 on the other hand, the emphasis is on character data. It grew out of the needs for text processing applications such as language analysis and translation.

Data. The interesting aspects of SNOBOL4 are the character data type that it supports and ways of defining patterns of data. For example, we can define a particular pattern to match any sequence of characters that end in the letter A, or any sequence of characters that contains either the letters B and C or the letters Y and J. The pattern definition facilities of SNOBOL4 are quite sophisticated and, in general, allow the programmer to define a kind of language that the program can then use to validate the correctness of character strings such as the input data or contents of a file.

Operations. We have already referred to the important operations of SNOBOL4 in relation to patterns. There are many operations to support such things as character string concatenation, substring, indexing into a character string, or searching for a particular substring. Finally, the operation *match* tries to match a character string against a pattern. For example, if we have defined a pattern PATERNAL-RELATIONSHIP to consist of a parenthesized list of three items, the first of which is the string FATHER, a single match operation can determine whether a given character string is a paternal relationship and, if so, what are the names of the father and the son.

Sequence Control. The sequence control in SNOBOL4 is traditional in that statements are executed sequentially. In addition, however, each statement may fail or succeed—for example, the pattern may or may not be matched—and control can be transferred to another (labeled) statement based on the success or failure of the current statement. Procedures may also be defined and called.

Input/Output. SNOBOL4 provides extensive facilities for reading character data and printing and formatting output data.

APL

The trio of languages LISP, SNOBOL4, and APL were among the early languages that deviated from the conventional approach of basing the language on the capabilities of conventional computers. This is seen primarily in the way these languages view the data. We have seen that FORTRAN supports numbers and arrays, LISP supports symbols and lists, and SNOBOL4 supports characters and patterns. APL, in turn, emphasizes numbers and arrays (called vectors in APL).

Data. APL assumes that data should be maintained in the form of arrays (of any dimension). Elementary data are primarily numeric. Characters are supported but character strings are represented as vectors of characters.

Operations. Many mathematically oriented operations are provided by APL, most of them dealing with arrays. In general, any operation that works for scalar values also distributes over arrays. For example, simple addition or multiplication can be used to do element-by-element addition or multiplication of arrays. In addition, some high-level operators are provided for composing the primitive operations to easily build new ones that are not already in the language, such as matrix multiplication and inner product.

Sequence Control. In APL, statements are executed sequentially. But while in LISP a program may be a single function application, in APL, because of the power of the basic operations, a program may consist of a single expression that evaluates the desired result. Thus, sequence control is not very relevant and APL provides only rudimentary ones, including a jump.

Input/Output. Facilities are provided for transfer of numbers and vectors.

PROGRAMMING LANGUAGE PARADIGMS

Although the basic components are common to all languages, by studying just the six aforementioned programming languages, we can already see that there are also basic differences among languages as well. These differences stem from the way in which they combine the basic components of the language (data, operations, etc.) and the style of programming they promote. We can say that each language follows and promotes a particular paradigm and we can categorize programming languages on the basis of such paradigms. In general, the languages in the same paradigm have more similarities than differences; the differences, however, are sharp among languages in different paradigms.

Imperative Paradigm

Imperative languages cover the traditional programming languages starting from FORTRAN. They are based on the conventional computer architectures, which consist of a processor for executing instructions and a memory for storing data and program instructions. The structure of a program in an imperative programming language is a collection of statements (instructions) that are usually executed in sequence unless directed by such control structures as loops, branches, or procedure calls. This paradigm started with FORTRAN and has evolved over the years. Some of the prominent languages in this class are FORTRAN, Algol 60, BASIC, PL/I, COBOL, Pascal, C, and Ada. In the early 1980s, the U.S. Department of Defense commissioned the design of Ada through a long, painstaking process, to combine the best-known imperative language features into a single language that could replace the different languages in use by the different groups in the Department of Defense and its contractors. The language has gained popularity for general usage.

Functional Paradigm

The functional programming languages are based on mathematical functions and function applications as we have seen in the case of LISP. As opposed to building a program from a sequence of statements, in a functional programming language, the programmer builds a program by defining functions that are themselves built from applications of functions. These languages are characterized, in general, by heavy use of recursion (functions that call themselves) and functions that use as arguments other functions and may return functions as their result. These facilities are necessary for defining powerful functions. LISP was the precursor of these languages. Interest in them grew substantially in the 1980s. Some of the other prominent languages in this class are Scheme, Miranda, and ML.

Logic Paradigm

The logic programming languages are based on mathematical logic. In these languages, a program consists of (1) a set of logical assertions that establish the facts and relationships governing a set of data, and (2) a set of rules that allow new information to be derived from the set of assertions. An input to the program is matched against the assertions and rules to see if its truth or falsehood can be established. For example, in PROLOG, we might write the assertions

```
father(john, tom).
father(john, joe).
father(jim, john).
```

and the rules

```
ancestor (X, Y) :- father(X, Y).
ancestor (X, Y) :- father(X, Z), ancestor(Z, Y).
```

as a program to define how to determine whether one person is an ancestor of another. Then, the following queries to the program are valid (given along with their interpretation):

```
father(john, tom)?
    is john the father of tom?
    answer: yes
father(Q, tom)?
    who is the father of tom?
    answer: john
ancestor(Q, john)?
    who are all the ancestors of john?
    answer: jim
```

Object-Oriented Paradigm

As we have seen, data types play a central role in all languages. In the object-oriented paradigm, the programmer has the ability to define a particular data type and an associated set of operations as an integrated object. In this paradigm, programming an application consists of identifying the set of objects that make up the application and defining those objects. For example, if we are programming a financial application, we might define objects for invoices and payments. SIMULA 67 was the first language in this class. Other languages are SmallTalk, Eiffel, and C++, an attempt to augment C with object-oriented facilities.

Combining Paradigms

Many languages combine aspects of the different paradigms. Indeed, it is unlikely that one paradigm will satisfy the needs of all applications. Therefore, a language intended to be applicable in many applications must combine elements from the different paradigms. For example, the object-oriented paradigm has been introduced into languages of all the other classes to build, for example, object-oriented imperative programming languages or object-oriented logic programming languages.

DESIGN CRITERIA FOR PROGRAMMING LANGUAGES

Given the diversity of languages and computer applications, it is clear that no single language satisfies all requirements and all users. If such an all-purpose language existed, all the other languages would disappear and there would be no need for any new languages. In practice, however, we see that programming languages are constantly evolving as are rules and criteria for designing them. The following are some of the criteria that all languages must satisfy to one degree or another. The emphasis placed on the criteria differs based on the needs of the language and its intended applications.

Expressiveness

A language must allow the programmer to express all programs of interest in a natural way. In practice, all programming languages are universal in the sense that they are theoretically equivalent and an application that can be programmed in one language can be programmed in any other language. The particular combination of concepts used in a language and the paradigm it follows, however, makes it more expressive for one application over another. In general, a language designer can achieve maximum expressiveness by reducing the number of rules and exceptions in the language. The intended application area guides the choice of paradigm to adopt.

Efficiency

The purpose of a programming language is to write programs that can be executed on a computer. Usually, the efficiency of program execution is important because we may have enough resources (i.e., a powerful enough computer) to run a program only if it is efficient enough. The programming language must, therefore, be efficiently implementable on a computer. Although expressiveness is achieved by reducing the number of restrictions in the language, efficiency is often achieved by placing restrictions on the language (e.g., on the length of data that can be represented). The language designer faces constant trade-offs between expressiveness and efficiency.

Reliability

Expressiveness allows a program to be written easily and efficiency allows the program

TABLE 2. Genealogy of Computer Languages

Language	Year Designed or Introduced	Predecessor Language	Intended Purpose
FORTRAN	1954–1957	—	Numeric
COBOL	1959–1960	—	Numeric
APL	1956–1960	—	Array processing
LISP	1956–1962	—	Symbolic
SNOBOL4	1962–1966	—	String processing
BASIC	1964	—	Interactive computing
PL/I	1963–1964	FORTRAN, Algol 60, COBOL	General purpose
SIMULA 67	1967	Algol 60	General purpose
Pascal	1971	Algol 60	General purpose
PROLOG	1972	—	Artificial intelligence
C	1974	Algol 68, BCPL	Systems programming
Modula-2	1977	Pascal	Systems programming
Ada	1979	Pascal, SIMULA 67	General purpose
SmallTalk	1971–1980	SIMULA 67	Personal computing

to run quickly. Once the program completes and produces the answer, how do we know that the result is correct? A language that is reliable helps the programmer write reliable programs, that is, programs on whose results we can rely. Clearly, reliability must be of utmost importance for any language, especially as programs are used in more critical applications such as life support systems. It has been found that people can write more reliable programs if they use higher-level mechanisms that are closer to the application than to the machine. For example, programs that use the jump control structure have been found to be less reliable than those that use loops. Designers of more modern languages have tried to reduce their dependence on such low-level programming constructs.

Table 2 shows a genealogy for some of today's important and popular languages.

For Further Reading

Ghezzi, C., and M. Jazayeri. 1987. *Programming language concepts.* 2nd ed. New York: Wiley. Textbook covering common concepts of programming languages in detail, along with functional and logic paradigms.

Sammet, J. E. 1969. *Programming languages: History and fundamentals.* Englewood Cliffs, N.J.: Prentice-Hall. Classic collection of hundreds of languages.

Special issue on programming language paradigms. 1989. *ACM Computing Surveys* 21(3), Sept. Includes technical, detailed articles on functional languages, logic languages, and parallel and distributed languages used for multiprocessor machines and multicomputers.

Watt, D. A. 1990. *Programming language concepts and paradigms.* London: Prentice-Hall International. Clear exposition of programming language concepts and paradigms.

Wegner, P. 1976. Programming languages—The first 25 years. *IEEE Transactions on Computers C-25* 12:1207–25. Comprehensive and readable survey.

Wexelblat, R. L., ed. 1980. *ACM History of Programming Languages Conference.* New York: Academic Press. Collection of interesting articles about the historical development of individual languages written by the designers of the languages themselves.

Mehdi Jazayeri

PROGRAMMING LANGUAGES

See Languages, Computer; Programming Language Design

PROTOCOLS

See Local Area Networks; Networks, Computer; Wide Area Networks

PROTOTYPING

The word *prototype* literally means "first of the type." The precise meaning of this word, though, depends on the context in which it is used. *Prototype* can reflect any of the following concepts:

- A model on which something is patterned, for example, a wooden prototype of an airplane
- The first full-scale, and (possibly) functional, form of an object, for example, a full-scale working prototype of an airplane
- A new design or a construction of an object, for example, the first space shuttle

A prototype, in information systems development, is a preliminary version of a computer system. The prototype may be a simple sample of an input screen or a mockup of a complex system that includes interactive screens, reports, databases, and operating programs that use sample data. A prototype can also be a working version of the final system.

Prototyping is the process of building a prototype. It is a technique often used to help in settling the final design of the system. In the prototyping of information systems, such terms as *rapid prototyping, adaptive design, incremental design, heuristic development, piloting, throwaway code,* and *iterative design* are also used.

To understand the usefulness of prototyping when developing information systems, consider two ways of trying to understand football—going to the game or looking at a series of still pictures of the game. One method represents learning from the dynamic model; the other, from a static one. Prototyping is like building and using dynamic models. Developers of information systems prototypes capitalize on the fact that most people can easily point to features they do not like, or spot a missing feature, in a dynamic model.

PROTOTYPING IN INFORMATION SYSTEMS DEVELOPMENT

In information systems development, the prototype is used to do one or all of these: to clarify user requirements, to verify the feasibility of the design, to create the final system, and to train users. The users are people outside the formal data processing or information systems areas of an organization who use computers to solve problems or enhance productivity. Information systems prototyping enables the system builders to present a prototype of an application (albeit often very incomplete) to the users for evaluation. The prototype of the system is demonstrated on the computer.

Prototyping of the information system is performed for one of the following reasons:

1. *To explore:* Emphasis is on clarifying the requirements and desirable features of the final system and on exploring possible alternative system solutions.
2. *To experiment:* Emphasis is on determining the adequacy of a proposed solution before investing in a large final system (as in a pilot project for engineered goods).
3. *To evolve:* Emphasis is on gradually adapting the system to changing requirements that cannot be reliably determined in the early phases of system development.

In prototyping, the information systems developer focuses on the prototyping *process* itself. This helps the system builder elicit the design requirements from the intended users of the system. The underlying assumption is that users know better than system builders what the target information system should do. They know better because they are specialists in the functional business area for which a given information system is intended (for example, production planning). There is no built-in expectation of doing things right the first time. The *initial* analysis and design of the system are always incomplete and need to be revised. During the prototyping process of systems development, designers as well as users of the system expect to make mistakes.

interval between iterations. For the prototyping to work, the feedback from the system evaluators (its intended users) must be given relatively quickly.

GENERAL FLOW OF WORK

In general, the prototyping process follows these steps. A prototyped system is built and evaluated. The necessary corrections and enhancements are determined, and then the prototype is evaluated again. There is recycling and looping (also called iteration) to earlier stages of the system development until the users and builders of the system agree that the requirements are specified. In essence, the users' needs are clarified by actively involving them in the process. All steps focus on the construction of a working prototype of the required information system as quickly as possible. The steps of the prototyping cycle are illustrated in Figure 1.

A key aspect of prototyping is the short

TYPES

Two kinds of prototyping are generally practiced: the throwaway and the evolutionary. Both approaches use software tools, called productivity tools, that help to create prototype systems fast. Fourth-generation languages and many of the computer-aided software engineering tools fall into this category.

The *throwaway* concept is based on an initial test idea of engineering. Once the test is done, the prototype is discarded and a preliminary design is made. The test's goal is to achieve a better understanding of the users' requirements and of the system's performance, because, initially, the users may not be able to define their requirements

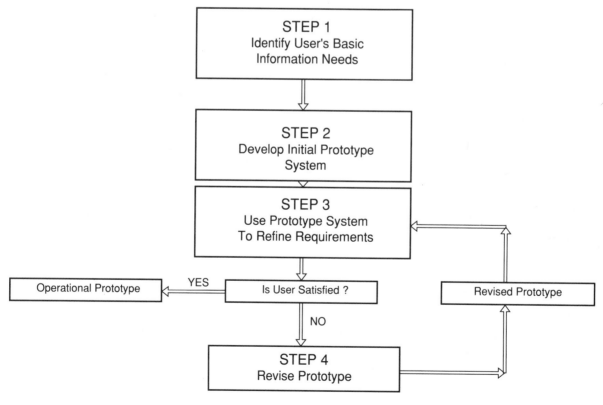

FIGURE 1. Prototyping cycle.

clearly. The prototype is never used as a production system, hence it is a throwaway.

The *evolutionary* approach refines the system under construction, iteratively, over repeated trial periods. It is based on the iterative product development idea of engineering. The system is constructed rapidly, and then it is enhanced and changed as it is *used*. The goal is always to deliver a working model of the system and to try to react to the working model. This interaction is planned, and as subsequent versions of a working system evolve, they come closer to what the user really wants.

ENVIRONMENT

The prototyping environment should have these components:

- Well-managed data resources for easy access to organizational data
- A fourth-generation language or other development tools for the quick creation of prototypes
- Users knowledgeable in their business area, informed about the prototyping process, and willing to use new tools to solve their information systems problems
- A prototype builder or builders—data processing professionals knowledgeable about organizational data resources, prototyping approaches, and tools

In most instances, the prototype is developed with the help of the intended user of the system, who also functions as the application's *designer* (user/designer), working side by side with the systems professional, who functions as the system *builder* (analyst/builder). From the practitioner's point of view, the most productive prototyping arrangement is one in which there is a separate person for each role. That is, the prototype is developed by one builder and one designer. With group decision support system tools constructed for joint application development, efficient prototyping can also be accomplished by a small group of users/designers and analysts/builders.

WHEN IT WORKS

The primary advantage of a prototype is that it gives those who will use the final system an opportunity to see, on the computer, what they will be getting, rather than having to rely on verbal descriptions and multitudes of charts and diagrams prepared by technicians. It is much easier to change a prototype than it is to make changes to a final, fully functional system.

Prototyping, when applied appropriately, offers the following:

- The ability to place a functioning and useful system in the hands of the users quickly when it is clear that the traditional methodology will not get the application system delivered in time
- An effective division of labor between the users and the builders of the system when users are unsure of what is needed, as the information requirements do not have to be complete before one starts to prototype

- The ability to try out ideas without high costs or risks
- An increase in users' interest in and satisfaction with new applications
- The ability to build at low cost systems that are to be used on an irregular or infrequent basis

In general, good applications for prototyping are those that require extensive use of user dialogues. Prototyping is a desirable approach with any medium- to large-scale software development project that demands diversified requirements and expertise. In such cases, use of prototyping draws expertise together. It combines available knowledge into a working model, which can convey the ideas more effectively than volumes of paper specifications and chart presentations.

Prototyping is also a good approach for exploring and evaluating new technologies and tools and determining their applicability and effectiveness before adopting them. New areas of automation present many challenging problems because there are no models to guide software development, no expertise on the applicability of the various tools for the new area, and not even any guarantee that automation can succeed.

Poor applications for prototyping are those that tend to be batch oriented and that involve little or no user interface. Applications that focus heavily on calculation of large quantities of data, such as numerical analysis or statistical algorithms, are not prime candidates for prototyping; however, being a poor candidate for prototyping does not automatically mean that a prototyping approach should not be attempted.

SHORTCOMINGS

There are some disadvantages of prototyping. Prototyping may encourage inadequate problem analysis. As is often pointed out by practitioners, prototyping still requires a disciplined analysis of the problem. As building a model of a system quickly with the help of a fourth-generation language does not guarantee that the model is adequate, the time required to finally fix the problem can exceed the time required to perform a detailed analysis. Prototyping is not a substitute for analysis; it supports analysis.

Users may not adequately understand the prototyping process and may be unwilling to give up the prototype. For example, when users see the prototype running, they may assume that it is ready to be used in a production mode. They may not realize that edit and validation routines have not been included, backup and recovery procedures have not been added, and so on. Users may become impatient waiting for a final version of the system, because the prototype took a short time to construct. Thus, they may resist having anyone work on the production version of the system, erroneously assuming that the prototype is adequate.

The major critique of a prototyping approach is that it draws builders from the work on the ultimate system. The argument concerns building of a working prototype: if one has to build a working prototype, one may as well build a complete system, as the effort required is not a great deal more. How much more, though, depends on the nature of the ultimate system.

HOW PROTOTYPING ACTIVITIES DIFFER FROM THE CLASSICAL SYSTEMS DEVELOPMENT LIFE CYCLE APPROACHES

Systems development is the procedure involved in creation of information systems. In a classical systems development life cycle each developmental step is sharply defined. Steps follow an established order and each produces a clearly defined outcome. For example, the requirements definition stage produces documents that specify what the proposed system is supposed to accomplish and whether or not it is practical to build the system. In systems development life cycles there is no second chance to make things right if mistakes were made in earlier steps.

The prototyping approach is mostly a process of iteration and refinement. Prototyping does not follow sharply defined steps but mixes analysis, design, development, and testing. It gives the prototype users and builders experience with a working version of the intended system early in the systems development cycle. There is a chance to make things right the second and third times around. Experience with a prototype offers an opportunity to adjust requirements and design specifications before spending too much time and money.

Prototyping differs from the classical life cycle methods in that it focuses on the *production* of the system rather than the *sequencing* of work leading to the ultimate system: the system's code. Prototyping can be used to augment, rather than replace, the classical life cycle: both methods are complementary approaches to development. The clearly defined outcomes of the life cycle are retained, but instead of a sequential process based on complete specifications, prototyping, along with fourth-generation languages and other prototyping tools, is used to work from incomplete systems analysis and design specifications to build a working model for experimentation and testing. As discoveries are made from the experiments, information systems specifications and the working model evolve together. In essence, prototyping reduces the risks of producing systems that do not meet user needs.

[*See also:* CASE Tools; Modula-2; Simulation; Systems Development Life Cycle.]

For Further Reading

Boar, B. H. 1985a. Applications prototyping: Trades guesses for experience. *Computerworld* 19(9):45, 56–57.

———. 1985b. Application prototyping: A project management perspective. In *American Management Association handbook.* New York: Wiley. This author gives good reasons for use of prototyping.

Budde, R., K. Kuhlenkamp, L. Mathiassen, and H. Zullighoven, eds. *Approaches to prototyping.* Berlin: Springer-Verlag. Contains a variety of articles on the tactics of prototyping.

Collins, M. 1989. Putting your 4GLs to work. *Computing Canada* 15(4):32–33. Good brief on why fourth-generation languages are suitable prototyping tools.

Connell, J. L., and L. Shafer. 1989. *Structured rapid prototyping: An evolutionary approach to software development.* Englewood Cliffs, N.J.: Prentice-Hall. Describes state-of-the-art disciplined approach to prototyping.

Gane, C. 1989. *Rapid system development.* Englewood Cliffs, N.J.: Prentice-Hall. Presents combination of techniques for rapid production of quality systems. Discusses new tools and their use.

Ivari, J., and M. Karjalainen. 1989. Impact of prototyping on user information satisfaction during the information systems specification phase. *Information and Management* 17(1):31–45. Good reference source for problems with user satisfaction.

Lantz, K. 1986. *The prototyping methodology.* Englewood Cliffs, N.J.: Prentice-Hall. A classic on prototyping methodology.

Mude, T., and G. Willis. 1991. *Rapid prototyping: The management of software risk.* London: Pitman. Explains the use of rapid prototyping within the discipline of software engineering.

Rymer, J. R. 1990. The fine art of not programming. *Personal Computing* 14(3):82–88. Current look at the tools of prototyping.

Vonk, R. 1990. *Prototyping: The effective use of CASE technology.* Hemel Hempstead, U.K.: Prentice-Hall International. Discusses all major aspects of the prototyping approach to requirements definition.

Weber, H. 1989. From CASE to software factories. *Datamation* 35(7):34–36. Good brief on approaches to automation of the software development process.

Willis, T., C. Huston, and E. L. d'Ouville. 1988. Project manager's responsibilities in a prototyping system analysis and design environment. *Project Management Journal* 19(1). A look at prototyping from the project manager's perspective.

Wita Wojtkowski
W. Gregory Wojtkowski

Q

QUERY PROCESSING IN DATABASES

Query processing is a major task of any database system. The major steps in query processing include parsing query statements, performing semantic analysis, applying optimization techniques, retrieving appropriate data from the database, and deriving the desired output. Databases may be structured according to different models, including among others the *relational database* model (Codd 1970; see also DATABASE DESIGN, AUTOMATED; DATABASE MANAGEMENT). Here we present a query processing system for relational databases that describes each of the major steps in query processing. The focus is on developing a relational query processing system that implements the SQL query language (Chamberlin et al. 1976). Some early efforts in designing relational query processing systems include System R (Astrahan et al. 1976), ISBL (Todd 1976), INGRES (Stonebraker et al. 1976), and ORACLE ("ORACLE Introduction" 1980). Query optimization is an important component of a relational query processing system. An early work in this area is that by Wong and Youssefi (1976).

Figure 1 describes a layered software architecture for processing database queries. The query processing system consists of four subsystems: SQL Subsystem (SQLS), Database Object Management Subsystem (DOMS), Storage and Access Subsystem (SAS), and Virtual Memory Subsystem (VMS). Functions of the four subsystems are described in Table 1. Query optimization is distributed among these subsystems.

THE SQL SUBSYSTEM

The SQL subsystem (SQLS) performs syntactic and semantic analysis of the SQL state-

ments. Some of the major components of this subsystem are the SQL parser, the query optimizer, and the task implementer. This subsystem consists of two layers, namely, SQL-PARSER-OPTIMIZER and SQL-IMPLEMENTER (Figure 2). SQL-PARSER-OPTIMIZER gets input tokens from the lexical analyzer, checks the correctness of the syntax, and stores the various SQL command parameters into the appropriate parameter tables. It also creates a parse tree for the query statement. Based on this parse tree, SQL-IMPLEMENTER executes a set of action routines. Action routines execute low-level database operations by calling DOMS. SQL-IMPLEMENTER gets the SQL command parameters from the parameter tables.

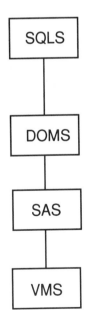

FIGURE 1. Software architecture of the query processing system.

813

TABLE 1. Subsystem Functions

Subsystem	Function
SQLS	Performs syntactic and semantic analysis of SQL statements. Does query optimization. Executes SQL commands.
DOMS	Maintains and manipulates database objects. Transforms "relation" information into "file" information and vice versa.
SAS	Implements and maintains file access structures. Optimizer selects the appropriate access structure.
VMS	Moves pages of the database file from secondary memory to main memory and vice versa. Maintains structures of free and allocated file pages.

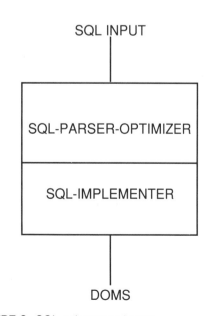

FIGURE 2. SQL subsystem layers.

THE DATABASE OBJECT MANAGEMENT SUBSYSTEM

The purpose of the Database Object Management subsystem (DOMS) is to provide abstract data types for the database information. DOMS defines the database *objects* and the abstract operations performed on these objects. In SQLS, data are accessed through a hierarchy of database objects. This hierarchy of database objects is implemented in DOMS. Three types of database objects are discussed here: the database directory object type (DDOT), the relation directory object type (RDOT), and the relation object type (ROT). The root of the hierarchy of database objects is the database directory object. At the next level of the hierarchy are the relation directory objects. At the bottom of the hierarchy are the relation objects. An object consists of a set of *tuples* (see DATABASE DESIGN, AUTOMATED; DATABASE MANAGEMENT). The database directory object consists of a set of tuples representing relation objects. A tuple in a relation object represents a relation tuple. The SQLS views the database information as a set of hierarchic objects. It does not concern itself with how these objects and their hierarchy are implemented. The SQLS uses the database objects through the operations defined on them.

Before an object can be accessed, it must be opened by creating an object descriptor for the object. The object descriptor maintains run-time information about the object. Multiple objects of type ROT may be opened at any one time; however, only one object of types DDOT and RDOT is opened at any one time. Those are the current database directory and relation directory objects. An object can be opened only when its parent object is opened. Similarly, an object can be closed only when all of its child objects are closed. Each opened object has a currency pointer that is stored in the object descriptor of the object. The currency pointer points to the current tuple of the object. Thus, the currency pointer helps in locating a tuple of the object. An object can be created only in the context of the hierarchy. Thus, to create an object, its parent object must be created first. Similarly, all the child objects must be destroyed before an object can be destroyed.

The association between DDOT and RDOT objects and between RDOT and ROT objects is one to many.

The SQLS initializes and terminates DOMS by the following two commands:

- *Init_DOMS(Status):* It initializes DOMS. Status indicates if the initialization is successful.
- *Term_DOMS(Status):* It terminates DOMS. Status indicates if the termination is successful.

Functional abstractions of the object types are described below:

- *Create_Object(Object_type, Object_name, Object_attributes):* It creates an object of Object_type with the given Object_name and Object_attributes. The new object is the child of the current parent object.
- *Destroy_Object(Object_type):* It destroys the object of Object_type pointed to by the currency pointer of the current parent object. The object should be closed before it can be destroyed.
- *Open_Object(Object_type, Object_descriptor):* It allows for later access of objects. The object of Object_type pointed to by the currency pointer of the current parent is opened. Open_Object sets up the currency pointer in the Object_descriptor of the object.
- *Close_Object(Object_descriptor):* It closes the object corresponding to Object_descriptor. When an object is closed all of its children should be closed.
- *Fetch_Next_Tuple(Object_descriptor,Tuple):* The currency pointer of the object corresponding to Object_descriptor is updated to point to the next tuple of the object. Then, the tuple is returned.
- *Rewind_Object(Object_descriptor):* It rewinds the object corresponding to the Object_descriptor by setting the currency pointer to the first tuple of the object.

The following two operators apply to relation objects:

- *Insert_Tuple(Object_descriptor,Tuple):* The tuple is inserted into the set of tuples of the relation object corresponding to Object_descriptor.

- *Delete_Tuple(Object_descriptor):* The tuple, pointed to by the currency pointer of the object corresponding to Object_descriptor, is deleted.

THE STORAGE AND ACCESS SUBSYSTEM

The primary function of the Storage and Access subsystem (SAS) is to implement file access methods such as pile, B-tree, and hash access methods. The optimizer selects access methods according to case. In this section we describe the pile access method.

A pile consists of a header page followed by data pages. The header page contains information such as the record length and the first page in the pile. The data pages contain the data records and extra information, such as the number of records in the page and the next page in the pile. When a data page overflows, it splits into two. Half of the records of the overflowing page are moved into the new page. The content of underflowing pages is distributed between the neighboring pages.

The pile manipulation routines are:

- *Create_Pile(Record_information,PID):* It creates the header page of the pile and places the Record_information in the header page. It returns the PID number, which is a pile identifier.
- *Open_Pile(PID,Pile_descriptor):* It opens the pile identified by the PID. It creates the Pile_descriptor structure. The pile descriptor structure keeps dynamic information about the pile such as the record currency pointer (RCP) and the record length. The RCP consists of a page number and an offset within the page.
- *Scan_Pile(Pile_descriptor,Record):* It updates the RCP to point to the next record of the pile and returns the current record.
- *Close_Pile(Pile_descriptor):* It deallocates all pile-related information from the Pile_descriptor and closes the pile.
- *Destroy_Pile(PID):* It frees the header and the data pages of the pile identified by the PID.
- *Delete_Record(Pile_descriptor):* It deletes the record pointed to by the RCP and updates the RCP.

- *Insert_Record(Pile_descriptor,Record):* It inserts the Record into the pile corresponding to Pile_descriptor. The record is inserted right after the record pointed to by the RCP. The RCP is updated to point to the inserted record.
- *Rewind_Pile(Pile_descriptor):* It rewinds the pile corresponding to the Pile_descriptor.

THE VIRTUAL MEMORY SUBSYSTEM

All database information is stored in a single file maintained by the Virtual Memory subsystem (VMS). The file is composed of sequential fixed-size pages. The SAS requires the pages to be in main memory. It is the responsibility of the VMS to move information between the main memory and secondary memory and to enforce a page replacement policy. The VMS allocates and frees pages as needed. Maintaining the free and allocated lists of pages requires some link information in each page of the database file. The VMS maintains a data structure that records information about the file pages residing in the main memory.

CONCLUSION

A query processing strategy for a database system has been described. Many of the standard query processing techniques have been exemplified through a software system architecture consisting of four major subsystems. This software architecture provides a basis for partitioning the major query processing responsibilities between various software modules.

References

Astrahan, M. M., et al. 1976. System R: A relational approach to data management. *ACM Transactions on Database Systems* 1(2):97–137.

Chamberlin, D. D., et al. 1976. SEQUEL 2: A unified approach to data definition, manipulation, and control. *IBM Journal of Research & Development* 20(6):560–75.

Codd, E. F. 1970. A relational model for large shared data banks. *Communications of the ACM* 1(3):377–87.

ORACLE introduction. 1980. Menlo Park, Calif.: Relational Software Inc.

Stonebraker, M., E. Wong, P. Kreps, and G. Held. 1976. The design and implementation of INGRES. *ACM Transactions on Database Systems* 1(3):189–222.

Todd, S. J. P. 1976. The Peterlee relational test vehicle—A system overview. *IBM Systems Journal* 15(4):285–308.

Wong, E., and K. Youssefi. 1976. Decomposition—A strategy for query processing. *ACM Transactions on Database Systems* 1(3):223–41.

Sakti Pramanik
Anastasia Analyti

QUEUEING THEORY

A *queue* is a waiting line; *queueing theory* is the mathematical theory of waiting lines. It might seem bizarre at first glance that such a simple concept as a queue would be interesting from a mathematical viewpoint or important from a practical viewpoint, but both are true. Queueing theory is used to model (describe in abstract terms) systems that provide service to "customers" whose arrival times and service requirements are *random* (i.e., unpredictable except in a statistical sense).

Queueing theory is important because many real service-providing systems can be viewed abstractly as queueing systems: customers *arrive* (at random), request a (random) amount of *service time* from a *server*, and if they are *blocked* (i.e., if they find all servers busy) they take some action, such as leaving immediately, or *waiting* (in a *queue*) for a server to become available. Two important examples of such service systems are (1) a telephone system, where a telephone call (customer) requests at a random point in time the use of a trunk (server) for a conversation of random duration; and (2) a computer system where a computer programmer (customer) sitting at a terminal requests at a random point in time access to a central processing unit (server) for the processing of a transaction of random duration. In both cases, the system designer must balance two competing factors: the quality of service provided (as measured by the probability of blocking, or the average delay) and the cost of providing the service (as measured by the cost of each trunk, or the number of terminals that can be supported). Queueing theory permits the designer to quantify this service-cost tradeoff; clearly, it is a useful tool.

Queueing theory is interesting (from a mathematical viewpoint) because the inclusion of randomness in the model, which is necessary for the description of real systems, makes problems very difficult that otherwise would be quite trivial (a phenomenon well known to students of probability theory). These two factors (economic importance, mathematical challenge) have interacted to produce a surprisingly large body of technical literature—literally thousands of papers in engineering and mathematical journals, and many monographs and textbooks.

Historically, queueing theory dates from the early 1900s, when A.K. Erlang of the Copenhagen Telephone Company derived the important formulas for teletraffic engineering that today bear his name. When, following World War II, operations research became a recognized field of study, queueing theory was incorporated as one of its methodologies. The range of applications expanded to include manufacturing, urban planning, air traffic control, and highway design, but the main application remained telephony. With the explosive growth of computer science and engineering, a major new area of application was born in the early 1960s, and new models and theory were developed to meet the needs of this new technology. And with the increasing convergence between telecommunications and computer science beginning in the 1980s, technology again is providing the models and applications for a new era of accelerating growth in queueing theory.

Queueing theory is a subject of some depth and subtlety. This article will discuss some of the most important models and their applications and, in passing, attempt to convey the subtleties that make these models interesting to theoretically oriented computer scientists.

SOME FUNDAMENTAL MODELS

One of the most important models is the *Erlang loss model,* which is widely used in the design and analysis of telephone networks. In this model, calls (customers) arrive at random instants in time to request the use of a trunk (server) for the duration of a conversation (service time). If an arriving call finds all trunks busy (is blocked), the call is *lost;* that is, the call is immediately *cleared* from the system, without waiting and without receiving any service, and we say that "blocked calls are cleared." The fraction of arriving calls that are blocked (the probability of blocking) is predicted by the famous *Erlang loss* (or *Erlang B) formula,* denoted by $B(s,a)$, where s is the number of servers and a is the *offered load,* which is a measure of the amount of traffic:

$$B(s,a) = \frac{\dfrac{a^s}{s!}}{\sum_{k=0}^{s}\dfrac{a^k}{k!}}. \tag{1}$$

This formula is hard to calculate directly from its right-hand side when a and s are large, but is easy to calculate numerically with a computer when the following iterative scheme is used:

$$B(n,a) = \frac{aB(n-1, a)}{n + aB(n-1, a)}$$
$$(n = 1, 2, \ldots; B(0, a) = 1). \tag{2}$$

For example, the following BASIC code, which encodes the iterative algorithm of (2), will quickly and accurately calculate the numerical value of $B(s,a)$ for any given values of s and a.

```
10  INPUT S,A
20  B=1
30  FOR N = 1 TO S
40  B = A*B/(N+A*B)
50  NEXT N
60  PRINT B
```

To illustrate, the above code will produce $B(1,0.8) = 0.4444$, $B(10,8)=0.1217$, $B(100,80) = 0.003992$. The first of these three values is easy to calculate directly from (1), whereas the third is virtually impossible.

To interpret these results, we need to understand the meaning of the quantity a, which was said to measure the amount of traffic generated by the calling population and offered to the trunks. The offered load a equals the product of the call arrival rate and the average call duration; this value, expressed in dimensionless units called *erlangs*, equals the average number of trunks that would be busy simultaneously if there were enough trunks so that no calls would be lost (that is, if there were an infinite number of trunks). Thus, $B(10,8) = 0.1217$ means that if ten trunks are provided to handle the amount of traffic that would produce, on average, eight simultaneous calls if every potential call were to be provided with a trunk, then 12.17 percent of arriving calls would be lost (cleared, not carried) because they would on arrival find all ten trunks busy with other calls. Then the *lost* (or *overflow*) *load* would be $aB(s,a) = 8B(10,8) = 0.9733$ erlangs, and the *carried load* would be $a-aB(s,a) = 7.0267$ erlangs. If we define the *server utilization* ρ to be the carried load per server, then

$$\rho = \frac{a(1 - B(s,a))}{s}, \qquad (3)$$

which, in this case, would be 0.703 erlangs per server (i.e., if the load were evenly distributed over the ten trunks, then each trunk would be busy about 70.3 percent of the time). Application of formulas (2), or (1), and (3) to these three examples of (s,a) pairs illustrates the fact that when a and s grow, but the ratio a/s is held constant, the probability of loss decreases and the server utilization increases; that is, large systems are more efficient than small ones. But this efficiency has its price; if the demand grows larger than the original estimate that the system was designed to accommodate, the more efficient system will experience more degradation of performance than the less efficient (because the less efficient system has more "slack").

It should be apparent that these formulas are invaluable in the design and analysis of telephone networks and other random-demand service systems. Perhaps not so apparent are the subtleties: These formulas presume that the randomness in the call arrival times is of a particular type (namely, a *Poisson process*), and that the system has been in operation under stable statistical conditions for a "sufficiently long" period of time (*statistical equilibrium*); but, incredibly, the results are *insensitive* to the statistical characteristics of the lengths of the calls other than their average. There are many other interesting and important subtleties; the reader is directed to the references cited at the end of this article.

Strictly speaking, the Erlang loss model is not a *queueing* model, because no queueing is allowed to occur; blocked customers are cleared. But the Erlang loss model can be viewed as the extreme case of the model that includes n waiting positions, to accommodate a queue whose maximum length is n. In this context the Erlang loss model is the special case when the queue capacity is $n=0$. At the other end of the spectrum is the case of infinite queue capacity, $n = \infty$; this is the important *Erlang delay model*, in which all blocked customers wait in the queue as long as necessary until service begins. Whereas the Erlang loss model is especially useful in the design and analysis of voice-communications systems, the Erlang delay model finds wide application in the design and analysis of data-communications systems. (Voice messages ordinarily need to be transmitted on demand in real time, whereas data messages can be stored and transmitted later when facilities become available.)

Analogous to the Erlang B (or loss) formula (1) is the *Erlang C* (or *delay*) *formula*

$$C(s,a) = \frac{\dfrac{a^s}{s!(1-a/s)}}{\displaystyle\sum_{k=0}^{s-1}\frac{a^k}{k!} + \frac{a^s}{s!(1 - a/s)}}, \qquad (4)$$

which gives the fraction of arriving customers that will find all s servers busy and therefore be forced to wait in the queue. As with (1), the right-hand side of formula (4) is easy to calculate only when a and s are small; but efficient and accurate calculations can be made by combining the iteration scheme (2) with

$$C(s,a) = \frac{sB(s,a)}{s - a(1 - B(s,a))}, \qquad (5)$$

that is, change the BASIC code following (2) to include

```
55 C=S * B/(S−A*(1−B))
60 PRINT B,C
```

For example, the augmented code will now produce also C(1,0.8)=0.8, C(10,8)= 0.4092, C(100,80)=0.01965. Note that in every case C(s,a)>B(s,a); this can be explained by observing that in the Erlang B model, blocked customers are cleared from the system, while in the corresponding Erlang C model, the blocked customers are retained (in the queue), thereby increasing the probability that future arrivals will find all servers busy. Note also that (4) and (5) are valid only when a<s; when $a \geq s$ the customers are arriving faster than the servers can handle them and the queue length grows without bound. In this case, we define C(s,a)=1. The fact that the Erlang C model is characterized by a "critical" offered load, while the Erlang B model has no such limitation, is one of the major mathematical differences between the two models. Another major difference is that, in contrast with the insensitivity of the Erlang B formula to the statistical properties of the service-time distribution (other than its average value), the Erlang C formula presumes that the service times are *exponentially distributed*. These facts provide further examples of the mathematical subtleties that characterize queueing theory.

Since no customers are turned away in the Erlang C model, the lost load is zero and the carried load equals *min(a,s)*; then the server utilization is

$$\rho = \begin{cases} \dfrac{a}{s} & (a < s) \\[2ex] 1 & (a \geq s). \end{cases} \quad (6)$$

(When $a \geq s$, all the servers will be constantly busy, and each server will carry 1 erlang of traffic.)

If we let w and τ denote the average waiting time and average service time, respectively, then

$$w = \frac{C(s,a)}{(1-\rho)s} \tau \quad (7)$$

when $a<s$, and $w = \infty$ when $a \geq s$. If we assume in addition that the waiting customers are served from the queue first–first out (FIFO), then the probability $P(t)$ that a typical customer will spend at least t waiting in the queue before beginning service is given by the formula

$$P(t) = C(s,a)e^{-(1-\rho)s\frac{t}{\tau}}. \quad (8)$$

For example, suppose that a data-communications system can be represented by an Erlang C model with ten transmission channels, each of which can transmit at the rate of 1,000 bits per second. Suppose furthermore that measurements show that the average message length is 1,500 bits and the channel utilization is 80 percent. Now, since ρ=80 percent and s=10, it follows from (6) that a=8 erlangs; from (4) or (5) the fraction of messages that do not receive immediate service is C(10,8)=0.4092; and from (7), since τ = 1,500/1,000=1.5 seconds, the average time that elapses between the instant a message "arrives" (requests access to an idle channel) and the instant a channel becomes available (and transmission begins) is, from (7), w =0.3 seconds; finally, from (8), if service from the queue is FIFO, then the fraction of messages that wait in the queue more than 1 second is P(1)=5.5 percent.

Clearly, the Erlang C model is as important in data communications as the Erlang B model is in voice communications. But the Erlang C model (unlike Erlang B) presumes that the service times have a particular statistical distribution, namely, the exponential distribution. What happens when the service times cannot be assumed to be exponentially distributed? Unfortunately, the removal of this restriction makes the model very difficult to analyze, except in one very special, but important, case: s=1. The single-server model that corresponds to Erlang C, but without the restriction' to exponentially distributed service times, is well understood and yields some very simple and important formulas. Known in the literature as the *M/G/1 queue*, this model is perhaps the single most important model in queueing theory. It is important not only for direct engineering application, but also as a building block for many more complicated models.

For M/G/1 the fraction of arrivals that

will be blocked (and thus be forced to wait in the queue) is still given by (4) (with $s=1$, $a<1$),

$$C(1,a) = a = \rho; \qquad (9)$$

that is, in M/G/1 the probability of blocking equals the offered load, which also equals the utilization of the server (whether or not the service times are exponentially distributed). The average waiting time w is given by the Pollaczek–Khintchine formula:

$$w = \frac{\rho\tau}{2(1 - \rho)}\left(1 + \frac{\sigma^2}{\tau^2}\right), \qquad (10)$$

where σ^2 is the *variance* of the service-time distribution. (The variance is a measure of the "spread," or variability, of a statistical distribution.) In the particular case of exponential service times, then (it can be shown) $\sigma^2 = \tau^2$, and the right-hand side of (10) agrees with the right-hand side of (7) (with $s=1$), as it must.

It is interesting to compare the behavior of M/G/1 with exponential service times (called M/M/1) with that of M/G/1 with constant service times (called M/D/1). In this comparison, M/M/1 and M/D/1 differ only in their service-time variance; all other parameters, including average service time, are the same. It can be shown that $\sigma^2 = 0$ for M/D/1 (that is, the variability of service times that do not vary is zero). Therefore, the factor $(1 + \sigma^2/\tau^2)$ on the right-hand side of (10) is twice as large when service times are exponentially distributed as when they are constant; and hence the average waiting time in M/M/1 is twice as large as in M/D/1 (all other things being equal). But recall that, according to (9), in both cases the fraction of customers who must wait is the same; thus, the variability of the service times does not affect a customer's chance of being blocked, but does affect his or her waiting time if blocked. This discussion shows how queueing theory provides qualitative as well as numerical information.

In all the models considered above, we assumed that the randomness in the arrival process is of a particular type, namely, a Poisson process; this means that the customer population is so large that the behavior of the population as a whole is not affected by the behavior of its individual members. Sometimes this mathematical idealization is an oversimplification of the real system under study. A typical example is provided by the performance analysis of a time-shared computer system consisting of a single central processing unit (CPU) that serves n terminals, where n is a small value such as 10 or 25, too small to be considered "infinite." In this system, if (a programmer sitting at) a terminal requests the use of the CPU when it is busy, the terminal waits in the queue for the CPU to become available. From the viewpoint of the terminal, an important measure of system performance is the *response time*, defined as the elapsed time from the instant the terminal makes its request for service until the instant the CPU completes the processing of the terminal's transaction (i.e., response time equals waiting time plus service time). From the viewpoint of the system designer or administrator, it is important to know, for example, the relationship between the average response time and the number n of terminals, as a function of the characteristics of the users, such as the *think time* (the average time a terminal "thinks" between receiving a response from the CPU and asking for another response) and the transaction processing time (which depends on the particular type of transaction and the speed of the CPU).

Finite-population models with *quasirandom input,* in which the instantaneous arrival rate depends only on the (finite) number of customers who are eligible to generate a request (i.e., "thinking," not waiting in the queue or being processed by the CPU), are more complicated than their infinite-population (Poisson-input) counterparts. As a consequence, it is easier to calculate their performance characteristics directly from the equations that describe them than from closed-form solutions of these equations.

For example, the following simple-looking (but sophisticated) code embodies a recursive solution of these equations for the quasirandom-input model of a time-shared computer system composed of a single CPU, with exponential service times, serving n terminals. The INPUT values are the number of terminals N (=n), the average think time TH, and the average transaction-processing time T (=τ) of the CPU; the output values are the CPU utilization U (=ρ), the average response time R, and the throughput TP (the average number of transactions processed per second).

```
10  INPUT N,TH,T
20  P = 1
30  AH = T/TH
40  FOR J = 0 to N−1
50  P = (N−J) * AH * P
60  SP = SP + P
70  NEXT J
80  U = SP/(1+SP)
90  TP = U/T
100 R = N/TP−TH
110 PRINT U,R,TP
```

Shown in Figure 1 is a family of graphs, calculated from this code, in which normalized average response time $r = (w + \tau)/\tau$ is plotted against CPU utilization ρ for different values of the number n of terminals. Note the upperbound curve, which corresponds to $n=\infty$; this curve was calculated from the Poisson-input model M/M/1, for which w is given by (7) with $s=1$ (or (10) with $\sigma^2 = \tau^2$) : $r = (w + \tau)/\tau = (1 - \rho)^{-1}$.

For example, consider the following scenario: A single CPU supports thirty terminals, and measurements show that the utilization of the CPU is 80 percent. How would the addition of ten new terminals affect the system's performance? To answer this question, run the program with INPUT values N=30, T=1, and the value of TH that produces U=80 percent (which can be found by

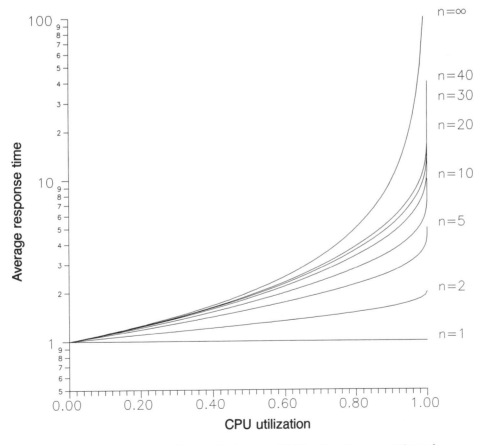

FIGURE 1. Average response time plotted against CPU utilization. *n*, number of terminals.

systematically varying TH, using bisection, for example, until it yields a value for U that is "close enough" to 80 percent). This value of TH, which turns out to be approximately 33.84, is the average think time that characterizes the thirty users in this environment; it yeilds U=0.80 (by construction), R=3.66, and TP=0.80 (TP=U when T=1). Assuming that the same value of TH characterizes the ten additional users, a new run with N=40, T=1, and that characteristic value of TH yields U=TP=0.96 and R=7.94. That is, the addition of ten terminals would increase the CPU utilization from 80% to 96%; the throughput would increase by a factor of 0.96/0.80=1.2; and the average response time would increase by a factor of 7.94/3.66=2.17. Thus, if the actual average transaction processing time were 2 seconds, say, then the addition of ten new terminals would increase the throughput from 0.40 to 0.48 transactions per second (good), while the average response time would increase from 7.32 to 15.88 seconds (bad).

MORE ON QUEUEING THEORY

Queueing theory is both useful and interesting, but also sophisticated and subtle. One should not apply these results without a sufficient understanding of the implications of the technical assumptions, such as Poisson input, quasirandom input, and exponential service times. There are many books that discuss the underlying mathematical theory (probability, stochastic processes) or the more specialized techniques and results that constitute queueing theory.

A good introduction to operations research and stochastic models in general, and queueing theory in particular, is provided by Hillier and Lieberman (1990) in their widely used textbook, written for upper-division undergraduates and master's-level students. A more advanced treatment of stochastic processes that provides a good theoretical background for queueing theory is Heyman and Sobel (1982); another is Wolff (1989).

For the reader who needs more evidence of the utility of queueing theory in computer science and engineering, see, for example, the textbooks by Bertsekas and Gallager (1987), Kleinrock (1976), and Leon-Garcia (1989), and the papers collected by Takagi (1990).

Finally, there are many textbooks and monographs devoted solely to queueing theory. Cooper (1990) is a survey that gives a more detailed and technical overview than the present article, and contains a large and up-to-date set of references, including direct reference or pointers to almost all textbooks on queueing theory; this is a good place to start.

References

Bertsekas, D., and R. Gallager. 1987. *Data networks.* Englewood Cliffs, N.J.: Prentice-Hall.

Cooper, R. B. 1981. *Introduction to queueing theory.* 2nd ed. New York: North-Holland (Elsevier). Reprint 1990. Washington, D.C.: CEEPress, The George Washington University.

Cooper, R. B. 1990. Queueing theory. In D. P. Heyman and M. J. Sobel, eds. *Stochastic models,* chap. 10, pp. 469–518. Amsterdam: North-Holland (Elsevier).

Heyman, D. P., and M. J. Sobel. 1982. *Stochastic models in operations research.* Vol. 1, *Stochastic processes and operating characteristics.* New York: McGraw-Hill.

Hillier, F. S., and G. J. Lieberman. 1990. *Introduction to stochastic models in operations research.* New York: McGraw-Hill.

Kleinrock, L. 1976. *Queueing systems.* Vol. 2, *Computer Applications.* New York: Wiley.

Leon-Garcia, A. 1989. *Probability and random processes for electrical engineering.* Reading, Mass.: Addison-Wesley.

Takagi, H., ed. 1990. *Stochastic analysis of computer and communication systems.* Amsterdam: North-Holland (Elsevier).

Wolff, R. W. 1989. *Stochastic modeling and the theory of queues.* Englewood Cliffs, N.J.: Prentice-Hall.

Robert B. Cooper

R

REAL ESTATE INDUSTRY, USE OF COMPUTERS IN THE

Every parcel of real estate has unique surface, subterranean, and air rights defined by federal, state, and local governments. No two properties are the same. City planners, demographers, politicians, lawyers, mortgage bankers, appraisers, environmentalists, geologists, engineers, architects, investors, developers, property owners, and tenants are a few of the real-estate players who use economic, political, physical, and social information affecting land use, property rights, and market values. The availability and cost of this information is a major impediment to responsible preservation, development, financing, acquisition, and use of land.

There are two major classes of software for use in real-estate analysis and management: financial and geographic. This article will emphasize the use of geographic information systems. Sophisticated and specialized computer software for accounting (cash flow, profit and loss), management (portfolio analysis), tax assessment (regression analysis), design, and risk analysis (Delphi method, probability analysis, exponential smoothing, Box-Jenkins forecasts, etc.) are commonly used financial software in the real-estate industry. The Center for Construction Management Software Evaluation at the University of Colorado at Denver publishes an annual report on real-estate construction software. The Institute of Real Estate Management of the National Association of Realtors maintains an approved list of property management software.

The major impact of computer technology on real estate is in geographic information systems (GIS). Current developments will result in a geographic and demographic database for the entire 3.6 million square miles of the United States. The Topographically Integrated Geographic Encoding and Referencing (TIGER) system will accomplish this by merging the 1990 census data into existing geographic information system (GIS) and compact-disk read-only memory (CD-ROM) technology.

GIS is an organized collection of computer hardware, software, and geographic data, to capture, store, update, manipulate, analyze, and display complex spatially referenced information efficiently. During the 1970s the first commercially available GIS system was developed by the Environmental Systems Research Institute for environmental applications on mainframes. By 1990 this technology had become available for personal computers. Originally the typical use of GIS was in such areas as transportation planning and demographic analysis. With software and databases developed by private industry and government agencies, analysts assign geographic classification codes to addresses, route vehicles, prepare maps, identify markets, estimate property values, delineate high-crime areas, draw political and service area boundaries, and project population growth and housing demands. Local governments use street networks to identify traffic patterns and industrial polluters. Highway departments, civil defense offices, and real-estate firms use these geographic and demographic databases.

Using maps and data together is a powerful analytical tool in real estate, since most of the information dealt with relates to geographical information. Pertinent political (zoning), economic (land values), physical (geographic), and social (demographic) data

823

can be analyzed in visual presentations of a block, neighborhood, census tract, ZIP code, city, area, or region of the country.

OVERVIEW OF DESKTOP MAPPING SYSTEMS

Desktop mapping improves the effectiveness and efficiency of real-estate data processing, since all the information being processed has to do with geographic data. This technology enables one to *graphically* manage, organize, manipulate, analyze, and present data— then view the visual picture of the analysis. One can take available data and place it on a map providing a look at specific data and its relation to geography. An estimated 85 percent of databases contain some sort of geographical information, such as street addresses, cities, states, ZIP codes, and phone numbers with area codes and exchange numbers. Examples of geographic analysis include the geographical distribution of males between ages 30 and 40 with annual incomes between $35,000 and $50,000, the examination of patterns of assessed property values, or the effect of new housing development on traffic flow. A picture shows *where* things are instead of only *what* they are.

GIS packages are used in conjunction with TIGER files, other U.S. Census Bureau data files, and files made available by the private sector such as data files, boundary files, line files, point files, and image files. GIS maps consist of a database and layers that may contain any of four types of graphic objects: line objects, point objects, boundary objects, and image files.

- *Line files* represent line objects, streets, highways, rivers, power lines, railroads, and more. Working with a series of line widths, styles, and colors, maps may be customized to meet individual needs for analysis. For example, major roads may be shown by use of wider lines, minor roads may be shown by a narrow line of a different color, while railroad mainlines may be dark blue and industrial sidings light blue. Power lines and telephone cables may be designated with dotted or dashed lines. However, line object files provide no way to work directly with regions. Regional information is provided through the use of boundary files.

- *Boundary files* are used to represent bounded regions such as countries, states, counties, and census tracts. Each object in a boundary file is one such bounded region. When mappers refer to boundaries, they are referring to a bounded area, not just to the boundary line separating one region from another. These areas can be colored or filled with a hatch pattern (parallel lines, crossed lines, wavy lines, etc.) and used either to differentiate one region from another visually or to encode some type of information about the region (population, seasonal rainfall, per capita income, etc.). Objects (buildings over ten stories, recent sales of more than $100,000, number of banks, etc.) can be counted within bounded regions; however, a more detailed analysis of objects is provided through the use of point files.

- *Point files* represent point objects such as towns and cities, particular street addresses, crime sites, fire hydrants, and pay phones. Each point object is assigned a symbol, which can encode information in three ways: shape, size, and color. Generally, different shapes represent different kinds of objects. Simple geometric figures (circles, squares, or triangles) can be used to represent different objects; or symbols may be more specific, such as the Red Cross to signify a hospital or an airplane for an airport. These symbols are often made different sizes and colors to represent differences between or among objects of the same type. For example, cities and towns may be shown as circles of differing diameters to represent population density or city area. Point files can accommodate more subtlety of detail by having the same object represented in different ways on maps of different scale. On a state map a city may be represented as a point object, while at a different scale the city is shown as a bounded region. More complexity of detail is handled by image files.

- *Image files*, such as labels and legends, are the cosmetics of a map image. These image files have been layered with a boundary or point file. There are two general ways of representing graphic images in a computer: *vector* and *raster*. Vector representation is a computer version of "connect the dots" in which the computer generates images using a few data points and mathematical formulas. In a raster representation, images are stored and displayed as row after row of colored dots, much like an image created with mosaic tiles, or the halftone images in newspaper photographs. Some types of map imagery are generally in raster form: aerial and satellite images and many weather images. These images have a lot of detail, making them look quite realistic. Most maps used by desktop mapping packages are represented as vector images. Vector images can be scaled easily, while raster images cannot. Vector images generally take up less file space than raster images and, in general, can be handled more flexibly. Most of the GIS software packages provide programs to allow for the raster to vector conversion.

Since data are at the heart of desktop mapping, the ability to work with a variety of databases in the mapping package is necessary. GIS packages provide access to existing databases in a variety of popular formats, either directly or through import routines. Because the graphics of the package are linked to database facilities, street, boundary, or point information can be automatically placed on the map, or label points can be positioned by the user. Demographic data contained in databases can be classified into five general categories: (1) population information, (2) household information, (3) household wealth indicators, (4) other wealth indicators, and (5) industry and occupation. This information is combined with location information and linked to a map in a process called *geocoding*. Locational information includes not only street addresses but also street intersections, area codes, ZIP codes, and county, state, and country names. For some purposes it is adequate to geocode to the ZIP code or county level. If general demographic statistics are to be displayed, then exact locational information is probably not necessary. But to set up a database containing specific locational information,

the exact address must be coded. Once the information is geocoded, the data from the database can be used to locate graphic objects on the map. The geocoding software, as well as a variety of existing databases, are available for purchase from GIS software vendors.

For the past several years, the Census Bureau has been building, integrating, updating, and editing the TIGER system and production processes to support the 1990 Census. The TIGER files will provide 100 times more detail than the Dual Independent Map Encoding (DIME) files, which were used for the 1980 Census. The bureau consulted private-sector GIS experts and joined forces with the U.S. Geological Survey (USGS) in 1983 to work toward the common goal of developing a single, integrated geographic database for the entire nation.

TIGER was developed by integrating the updated 1980 DIME files with the Digital Line Graphs (DLGs) from the USGS. The DIME files are street network files of 345 metropolitan statistical areas (MSAs). Each record in the file is related to all other segments in the file because of the census encoding. All street segment record types have address ranges and corresponding census geography codes, such as census tract number and block number. The endpoints or nodes of each segment are expressed in latitude and longitude values. The source materials for the DLGs are 1:24,000 scale maps photographically reduced to a 1:100,000 scale. Each map was then scanned, and hydrography and transportation features were recorded and compiled to include geographic coordinates for streets, roads, railroads, streams, and political jurisdictions. Within metropolitan areas, the files contain address ranges and associated ZIP codes for each side of the street segments. With GIS applications software, these TIGER/Line files can be used as a base layer for vehicle routing, 911 emergency response, redistricting, marketing, thematic mapping, and other applications.

TIGER/Line files contain six record types or files for each county. Record type one contains forty-one items, including feature codes, street names, address ranges, and census codes. Record type two contains shape coordinates. Record type three contains 1980 census codes. Record type four contains alternate names. Record type five is a one-for-one index of all names in the county. Record type six is used for ZIP code and address range exceptions. The Census Bureau plans to release additional versions of the TIGER/Line file to reflect changes from bureau update operations.

APPLICATIONS OF THE GEOGRAPHIC INFORMATION SYSTEM IN REAL ESTATE

GIS is emerging as an important use of information technology for real estate. Some uses are feasible with existing databases; others will become feasible as more geographic databases are made available. Public land records used in the real-estate industry include property cards in the county property assessor's office, transfer records, mortgages, deeds, zoning restrictions, floodplain records, and easements. General land management records are available through the Census Bureau, while specific property records must be gathered individually, or through a private firm. Being able to access all of this information from a personal computer makes most research trips to the courthouse unnecessary. After the initial information is input into the database, file management and update become a routine maintenance activity. Once detailed location-specific databases are developed, one may select a specific property from the map, and GIS will provide all the information pertaining to that parcel, including sales records, property taxes, zoning restrictions, buildings descriptions, square footage, easements, topography, roads, rivers, and floodplains. This procedure can also be performed for a group of properties, with the search procedure restricted to particular fields.

Household data such as income ranges, sex, age, education, zoning, property values, building, and lot size can be overlaid with locations of schools, churches, local shopping centers, transportation systems, and recreational and employment centers. Market analysis and feasibility analysis for a proposed shopping center might include vis-

ual presentation of the primary and secondary market area and competing retail centers. Industrial location analysis requires detailed information on transportation systems, land availability and costs, utilities, labor, climate, costs of living, taxes, housing, education, and recreation. The search procedure of the database can be limited to these and other characteristics and applied to a specific region on the map. GIS processing can layer all of the pertinent geographic and demographic information in a graphic form, allowing examination of viable alternatives.

A real-estate appraisal provides an unbiased estimate of the nature, quality, value, or utility of an interest in a parcel of real estate as of a given date. To do this, an appraiser must research the subject and all factors affecting its value, including recent sales of comparable properties, building and land costs, income data, legal and physical encumbrances, and market demand; then, assemble and process the pertinent data, using appropriate analytical techniques; and finally, use professional judgment to estimate the market value, the highest and best use, and/or the feasibility of development. Using location-specific databases, GIS allows the appraiser to gather much of the necessary data without leaving the office. With digitized processing of satellite images, site inspections can be enhanced. The satellite images provide the same "bird's-eye view" seen with aerial photographs. Satellite images are automatically coded with latitude and longitude references as they are recorded. This means that exact overlays of market information are possible.

Computer software packages (an example package is PRIME-LOCATION) link interactive demographic and geographic databases with satellite imagery. With this software it is possible to integrate property sales data on the system showing every sale of every parcel of real estate in the county. One can see the market as it is analyzed, using up-to-date satellite photos so precise that it is possible to count and display rooftops. A mouse click can pull up exact street addresses and latitude/longitude information. Databases such as Donnelley Marketing Information Services' Market Potential

Report Series can provide detailed current-year breakdowns of consumer spending patterns and can be used in conjunction with other demographic systems in analyzing retail, commercial, and industrial real-estate markets. The layers of information allow the demographic data to be shown thematically as a shaded pattern, with potential sites overlaid as point references on the map. Site locators can immediately see if a site that seems profitable, based on thematic map information, is in an area separated from the target population by poor road access or a river, too close to a competitor or uncomplementary business, or on terrain difficult to develop.

Government uses of GIS that complement the real-estate industry include land use planning, tax assessments, traffic signal work, transportation planning, zoning, sanitation, utility services, emergency response, redistricting, crime analysis, public health, and general resource allocation.

For Further Reading

Benzon, W. 1990. *Desktop mapping the MapInfo way.* New York: MapInfo Press.

Everything becomes clear with PRIME-LOCATION. 1990. *DemoMetrics* 7(2):5.

Langdon, D. R., and J. A. Herbers. 1990. Mapping the future. *Casualty Insurance* 2:13.

MapMaker maps road to health in Tennessee. 1990. *GeoForum* 6(1):5.

PC Week/Reviews. 1990. Desktop mapping enhances planning. *PC Week*, July 2, pp. 81–84.

Rowan, T. 1990. The use of computerized demographic data bases in feasibility studies. *Real Estate Appraiser and Analyst* 54:11–17.

Schroeder, R. 1990. A satellite view for site location. *DemoMetrics* 7(2):1+.

U.S. Department of Commerce, Bureau of the Census. 1989. *TIGER questions and answers.* Washington, D.C.: Bureau of the Census.

———. 1990. *TIGER—the coast-to-coast digital map data base.* Washington, D.C.: Bureau of the Census.

J. B. Pennington

REAL-TIME SYSTEMS

Digital computers are increasingly used for almost all aspects of human life, a large part of which falls into the category of *real-time computing.* Real-time means "sensing the status of a system, processing the sensed data, and effecting the system with the processed results without any delay." Ideally, the definition of real-time requires no delay between sensing and effecting, but, practically, a small delay between these two actions is unavoidable and also acceptable. The magnitude of the delay tolerable depends on the specific system under consideration, for example, a few milliseconds for robot-servo controllers and a few minutes for some industrial control systems. Real-time computing is a discipline concerned with the design, implementation, and analysis of digital computer systems responsible for handling the following three stages in real time: data acquisition from sensors and operators; data processing on, perhaps, multiple processors; and outputting the results to output devices such as display units or actuators (Shin et al. 1985). See Figure 1 for an example of a real-time computing system intended for control applications.

Figure 1 is the block diagram of a typical real-time control system. The inputs to the controller are from sensors that provide data about the controlled process and from the environment. The inputs are typically fed to the controller computer at regular intervals. Data rates are usually low: sensors generally put out fewer than twenty words a second.

Central to the operation of the system is the *trigger generator.* In most systems, this is physically part of the controller itself, but here they are separated for purposes of clarity. It is the function of the trigger generator to initiate execution of a controller job. Triggers can be classed into three categories, as shown in Figure 1.

Although digital computers have long been used for real-time applications, their widespread use began with the development of inexpensive microprocessors in early 1970. Real-time computing systems cover a spectrum from the very simple (e.g., a digital scale) to the very complex (e.g., an automated factory). See Shin (1987) and Krishna and

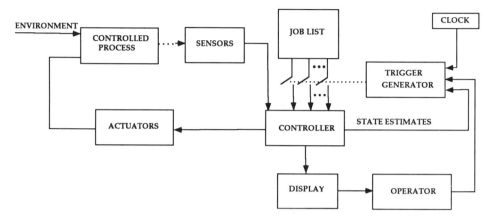

FIGURE 1. Typical real-time control system. *Reproduced with permission from Shin et al. 1985. Copyright 1985 IEEE.*

Lee (1991) for recent research and developments in the area of real-time computing. Examples of current real-time computing systems include control of automobile engines and brakes, industrial robots and numerically controlled machines, flight control and avionics systems of airplanes and spacecraft, nuclear reactor control, electric power generation and distribution, life-support systems, and a great many defense systems.

Three major components and their interplay characterize real-time systems. First, "time" is the most precious resource to manage in real-time systems. Computational tasks must be assigned and scheduled to be completed before their deadlines. Messages are required to be sent and received in a timely manner between the interacting tasks. Second, reliability is crucial, as failure of a real-time system could cause an economic disaster or loss of human lives. Third, the environment in which a computer operates is an active component of any real-time system. For example, for a drive-by-wire system it is meaningless to consider onboard computers alone without the automobile itself.

Every time-critical system must operate within a state-space circumscribed by given constraints. This is the allowed state-space. Leaving this state-space constitutes *dynamic failure.* Dynamic failure is said to occur if the computer used does not respond fast enough to the environment. It expresses the fact that slowness of the computer can be a cause of catastrophic failure. For example, the aircraft

must not touch down with too great a downward velocity or the undercarriage will collapse.

The performance of a real-time system naturally depends on the speed of the digital computer used. If the computer takes longer than a certain duration to compute the output, a dynamic failure or catastrophic failure occurs. This duration is the *hard deadline.* If a system contains one or more tasks with hard deadlines, it is called a *hard real-time system.* Examples of hard real-time systems include digital flight control systems and robot guidance and control systems. On the other hand, even if an automatic bank teller machine does not respond within a specified (by the designer) duration, it will only make the customer discontent. Such a duration is called a *soft deadline,* and a system is called a *soft real-time system* if it contains only those tasks with soft deadlines. Real-time tasks may be periodic or aperiodic. Periodic tasks are triggered at regular intervals, such as once every 100 milliseconds, based on the characteristics of the system, and aperiodic tasks are triggered randomly as such a need arises; for example, the human operator pushes the panic button or an automatic monitor generates a warning task. See Figure 1 for three different ways of triggering real-time tasks.

Although real-time computing requires high speed in executing tasks, it is different from fast computing. The main objective of fast computing is to minimize the average response time of a given set of tasks, whereas real-time computing is intended to meet the individual timing requirement of each task (Stankovic 1988). The most important property of a real-time system should be predictability; that is, its functional and timing behavior should be as deterministic as necessary to meet system specifications. As use of multiple processors is becoming popular to enhance system throughput, it is getting more difficult to achieve predictability by scheduling tasks and intertask communications on the different components within the system. It is therefore essential to tailor the distributed/parallel architecture to meet both the timing and reliability requirements of real-time systems.

Real-time computing adds the additional constraint that not only must the correct input/output data arrive at the correct location, they must also arrive in time. Clearly, a computer can process data no faster than it can acquire the data; this has been the rationale behind the attention paid to memory subsystems and increasing the accessibility and access speed of memories. To meet the need of both performance and reliability, a real-time system usually has provisions for multiple ways of accessing input/output devices in case of component failures in the system (Shin and Dykema 1990).

Future real-time systems are expected to be in a wider spectrum of applications than the current ones, and will be more complex. They will be distributed and capable of making intelligent decisions and adapting themselves to dynamically changing situations.

References

Krishna, C. M., and Y.-H. Lee. 1991. *IEEE Computer on Real–Time Systems*, Special Issue, vol. 24, no. 5, May.

Shin, K. G. 1987. *IEEE Transactions on Computers on Real–Time Systems*, Special Issue, vol. C-36, no. 8, August.

Shin, K. G., and G. L. Dykema. 1990. A distributed I/O architecture for HARTS. *Proceedings, 17th International Symposium on Computer Architecture*, pp. 332–42.

Shin, K. G., C. M. Krishna, and Y.-H. Lee. 1985. A unified method for evaluating real-time computer controllers and its application. *IEEE Transactions on Automatic Control* AC-30(4):357–66.

Stankovic, J. A. 1988. Misconceptions about real-time computing: A serious problem for next-generation systems. *IEEE Computer* 21(10):10–19.

Kang G. Shin

RELATIONAL DATABASES

See Database Management

RELIGION, COMPUTER USES IN

Prior to 1980 computer use in religious organizations was minimal. High costs for purchasing, maintaining, and staffing computer installations kept such technology from all but the largest and most specialized of applications within religious offices. Since that time, with the advent of the personal computer and the reductions in cost associated with it, computer use has grown steadily within these groups. Significant changes in both administration and mission work itself have resulted from the assimilation of computer technology into all levels of these organizations, from the local church, parish, or synagogue to national or world-level judicatory offices.

DEVELOPMENT OF USE

The mainframe computers of the 1970s and early 1980s were unheard of in religious organizations with a few notable exceptions. Those exceptions were national or world religious bodies whose vast financial and administrative systems became too cumbersome to manage by manual methods. Examples of such systems are the administration of pensions and health insurance programs for religious employees. Those agencies invested large sums of money in computers to assist them with their specialized work.

The great majority of judicatory offices

at state and regional levels, such as dioceses, conferences, and synods, did not obtain computer technology until the 1980s. However, during the ensuing decade, computers proliferated in judicatory offices to the point at which virtually no state or district religious office is without a computer today. Three major factors contributed to the increase in the numbers of computer installations in judicatory offices during this time: (1) technology significantly improved, (2) costs greatly decreased to affordable levels for such charitable agencies, and (3) an explosion of information in society required religious offices to find new methods of managing such information for their respective missions.

A small but significant minority of local churches, parishes, and synagogues in various denominations have obtained computers at this time. However, most of these local groups are larger congregations, with over five hundred members. Yet the numbers of local congregations obtaining computers increase every day. Such growth has been encouraged by the availability of official denominational computer software packages.

The majority of local religious bodies, which generally consist of small rural worshiping groups under three hundred members, have not yet obtained computers. It is difficult to discuss computers in such settings when many of these congregations do not have indoor plumbing, or when most are still deciding whether to buy a copying machine to replace their worn-out mimeograph duplicator. Cost is another factor that prohibits many small congregations, especially those under a hundred members, from obtaining computer technology. Cost remains an obstacle in spite of decreasing costs for computers in the general marketplace. The only way many of these small congregations will ever obtain a computer is through a major donation of one or two concerned members.

IMPACT ON RELIGIOUS ORGANIZATIONS

The impact of computers on the life of national and regional religious organizations has required changes in management structures, the ways in which information is perceived, and the methods by which information is maintained and used.

Management Structures

In obtaining computer technology, religious bodies often found themselves lacking the necessary expertise to program, operate, and maintain computer systems. Getting the expertise was an unexpected cost and burden that most religious agencies did not anticipate.

After the expertise was secured, management structures had to be changed to supervise the computer staff. Religious organizations had been accustomed to missionaries, priests, rabbis, and administrative personnel such as bishops and general secretaries operating their organizations. Suddenly, computer staff and executives who sometimes were paid higher salaries than the top executives or bishops had to be included. To complicate matters, some computer staff had difficulty understanding the nature of religious work in a not-for-profit environment, causing further problems. Management structures were redefined to accommodate the new technological "wizards" so the religious mission could continue to be promulgated. In many cases today, computer staffs of national and large state and regional judicatory offices outnumber other departments in size of staff, salaries, and budgets. Many computer executives in religious organizations have migrated to second-level management there and have become part of the power structures that make denominational decisions. In the 1970s and early 1980s, such control by computer personnel was nonexistent. If "information is power" is true, then religious bodies have clearly demonstrated that adage, with computer executives a heartbeat away from top denominational leaders, large computer staffs, and major computer expenditures. The impact on management structures and decision-making authority within religious organizations can arguably be the most significant effect of computer technology on such groups.

Information Perception and Use

Another impact of computers on religious organizations involves the ways in which information is perceived and used. Historically, information in such bodies was considered a liability, except when the information carried the religious message of the group. Beyond the message to be transmitted, information and data needed to make a religious body function were considered important to the function but otherwise superfluous. Computers in the 1980s changed that perception. Almost overnight, information became an asset to these communities. Those who knew how to access it and use it became the power brokers of today's religious denominations. For example, most Christian, specifically Protestant, religious bodies did not care to follow up on members who moved from one city to another. They assumed the moving members would unite with a congregation of same denomination or faith in their new community. However, through computer member tracking, it was discovered that the majority of moving members did not unite with a similar body of the same denomination in their new community. Suddenly, through computer-maintained information, what was a common assumption was exposed as a myth. Then the computers were used to find out why denominational loyalty was disappearing and what moving members were looking for in a church in their new community. Local and judicatory church leaders used that information to further the church's mission and denomination by developing successful membership growth programs. In many instances those persons assumed positions of high leadership. This is not to say that those leaders were wrong or ambitious, but that computers changed the perspective of how information is perceived and used in religious organizations. Numerous other instances of computer-maintained information and its impact on the life of religious groups abound.

Other impacts of computer technology on religious bodies are of lesser importance; nevertheless, they could assume roles of major proportions in the future. Some of these impacts include the following:

Confidentiality of Information

Prior to the advent of computers, confidential information within religious organizations was never an issue. People there trusted one another to maintain confidences. The sacredness of the confessional was assumed by almost everyone and, with a few notable exceptions, such confidentiality was maintained.

With the advent of computers in religious organizations, the confidence of religious constituencies in the judicatory staffs to maintain confidentiality when needed was diminished. This was due in part to the reality that even the most complicated computer security system could be penetrated. However, what most people did not realize is that confidential information in a religious computer is safer than it is on paper in a filing cabinet that could be broken into with a crowbar! Yet, a distrust of the machines was evident, causing an undercurrent that eventually led to many religious bodies creating elaborate computer security systems.

Financial Cost

Most religious executives who decided to obtain computer technology were deluded into believing a popular 1970s and early 1980s myth: Computers save money. In fact, computers cost money, and lots of it. Most religious bodies discovered after the computers were installed and the staffs employed that they were spending more money than in the past. This was disheartening to many, especially to those executives who made great claims of reduced budgets making more money available for mission work, to justify the computer purchase. Since religious groups are often driven by bottom lines, like secular businesses, large computer budgets became an anomaly for a time, causing cutbacks in other areas.

Today, however, computer budgets in religious bodies have ceased to be a major issue, because such groups have learned what computers can do for them when properly applied. They may cost more money, but computers also double and, in some cases, triple productive output. Thus what was a major cost issue for religious organizations became a minor concern due to the massive benefits of managing information more effectively through computers. The cost issue still remains; however, it is seen as a necessary component to the work of religious groups.

Volunteers

One of the significant changes in the life of many religious organizations in the 1980s was the dramatic reduction of volunteers' time at the local church, parish, or synagogue level. Social and economic changes resulting in fewer nonworking adults to serve in what was once a major volunteer work force have significantly reduced the number of volunteers available for religious groups. In smaller local units, the once-strong volunteer work force has become nearly nonexistent. In addition, these same small congregations frequently cannot afford to have even one paid secretarial position.

The development of lower-cost computers and software is helping to fill this gap for secretarial functions. In many cases, word processing has enabled a pastor, rabbi, or priest to continue to produce worship service materials with no secretarial assistance at all. In this sense, computers may have helped to keep alive functions and missions that otherwise would have been lost altogether.

Standardized Data Definitions

Religious organizations at regional and national levels have not realized the full potential of data sharing and transfer because most have not created standardized data definitions. This fact makes transfer of data and data sharing difficult, preventing meaningful data collation and comparison. While business and industry have to a very large extent achieved standardized data definitions, some major religious communities are just beginning to discover the potential benefits of such standardization.

APPLICATIONS IN USE TODAY

Some applications that computers are used for in religious organizations include:

Accounting

The application first used by religious groups through computers was, as in most businesses, accounting. Denominational financial headquarters and pension boards began to employ computerized accounting systems in the 1960s. Fund accounting, unlike profit and loss accounting systems, took several years to develop into equally professional applications, primarily because of lack of funding for administration within religious bodies.

Today, not only do judicatory offices utilize computerized accounting systems, but so, too, do a growing number of local churches and synagogues. While still in its infancy at the local level, growth in religious financial applications is being encouraged by members who have seen the obvious benefits of computers in secular organizations.

Membership Records

Membership records have been computerized to the benefit of many church offices, giving pastors and other church leaders access to information that was previously slow or difficult to obtain. What had been a tedious process of maintaining accurate address lists, especially of members who maintain seasonal residences in two locations, is accomplished easily with computerized membership lists. Obtaining selective lists of members according to residential locations, age, membership category, or any other recorded data has become a simple process.

In some cases, data that were nearly useless prior to the advent of computerized records are being maintained in electronic membership databases. One example is the recording of blood type. There have been a few documented cases in which lives have been saved because a church or synagogue has had on file the blood types of its members, and a blood donor was located quickly in an emergency situation.

At the regional, judicatory, or denominational level such computerized membership record keeping has other benefits. What was previously an impossible task of trying to access membership characteristics for a larger base than the local organization may now be as simple as merging databases into a single database, then using the same software to pull an even more selected group from the larger organization.

Attendance Tracking

By keeping attendance records and using a computer to spot changes in attendance patterns, skilled pastors and congregational leaders have been able to identify persons whose only call for help has been a sudden change, increased or decreased, in attendance patterns at worship services or other functions.

Skills and Interests

Local religious groups have long recorded, either formally or informally, the various skills, abilities, and interests of their members. Then, when a job needs to be done— whether it is finishing off a basement to make additional classrooms, teaching a special study series, or cooking a meal—the leadership has an available talent pool for such services. Maintaining such a pool, however, is difficult when done with an index card type of system, as so many have been.

With a good computer program, membership can be entered into a database and coded with the many different interests and talents that each member has indicated he or she is willing to donate to the community. It is automatically indexed by the computer, may be more easily accessed than a box of index cards, and can be easily kept up to date as members join and leave the organization.

Additionally, using a manual system for this information, with its slower and more tedious access, would frequently result in relying on people's memories. This would further result in some members being overlooked and other members being overworked. Computerized talent pools help the leadership to call on a wider base of the group's members when jobs need to be done. The result is greater participation of all members and frequently organizational growth.

Bible Reference Tools

One of the more creative and useful computer tools for religious use has been the development of several different Bible computer programs. The full text of the Bible is generally stored on-line, and powerful text search features are built into the program. Topical indexes and cross-references are also sometimes added.

The preacher, teacher, or research scholar can then quickly search the Bible for the needed texts by keying in a word, phrase, or topic, and the program will locate all relevant references within a few moments. These portions of the biblical text can then be called up on the screen for reference and possible use in sermons, lesson plans, and other writings. In some more sophisticated programs, two or more versions of the Bible may be displayed on the screen at one time, in columnar fashion. The researcher may then reference the same chapter and verse in different versions, or display two or three different Bible passages about the same topic at one time. The time saved in biblical research is immense. More importantly, these computer programs have been able to enhance writing, preaching, and teaching in churches, synagogues, seminaries, and universities.

Networking

Because most local religious communities belong to a larger, regional body, these parent religious organizations are natural candidates for the development of computer networks. Several networks have been formed to date, primarily within the regional and national structures. These networks have served to link clergy and laity alike through electronic mail, bulletin boards, and in some cases on-line meetings. Members from disparate locations may participate in discussions through computer networks, when they would otherwise be prevented from such participation because of the cost of face-to-face meetings. Additionally, religious news networks have been created similar to secular news networks, so that reporters may transmit their stories immediately into their home office, and news releases may be posted on bulletin boards for downloading by any newspaper or other communications medium.

Desktop Publishing

Religious organizations need to communicate with their memberships on local, regional, and organizationwide bases. Such contacts are frequently maintained through newsletters. Special events that need to be publicized, as well as printed programs for the events themselves, formerly demanded a great deal of time from the largely volunteer base generally available for such work. Further, local religious groups frequently have had less than adequate typewriters, duplicators, and other office equipment available to them.

The advent of desktop publishing has changed many religious organizations, providing them with tools to produce professional-quality newsletters and announcements. Desktop publishing programs coupled with a high-quality printer can reduce the time needed to produce such materials by half or more while vastly improving the quality of the printed material. Volunteer time can then be redirected into activities more beneficial to the life of the group.

Creative Writing

In most religions, a homily, sermon, or other message from the worship leader is expected and delivered at least once a week. In some cases, two or more such original messages are the norm. Whether the speaker is accustomed to speaking from a full manuscript, or simply from notes, a written guide is generally followed.

The regularity of these messages greatly restricts the amount of time available to the speaker in preparing messages. The act of writing and rewriting one's text often has caused this preparation to be limited in iterations, even though the speaker may wish to continue to develop the message further. Computers have eliminated the need for such religious leaders to retype the entire text simply because a new idea was introduced or a new method of organization was desired. Word processing has opened up the possibilities for sermon and homily refinement, freeing the speaker to develop the message to a far greater degree. In many areas this has led to improved preaching in worship services.

FOUNDATION FOR FUTURE USE

Computer technology has contributed significantly to the life and mission of religious organizations. Computers have been accepted and embraced by religious leaders while enabling new ministries and programs to develop. Since the vast majority of ministries and programs occur at the local level, where computer installations are still minimal in number, this indicates that the computer's impact on religious bodies carries a considerable amount of unrealized potential. Continuing developments in computer technology, with the continuing decline in the cost of this technology, give religious groups an immense potential for new and exciting ministries and programs in the future.

For Further Reading

Johnson, W. R. 1984. Discipleship in a technological society. *The Interpreter Magazine*, October, pp. 4–6.

————. 1984. *Selecting the church computer.* Nashville, Tenn.: Abingdon Press.

————. 1985. *The pastor and the personal computer.* Nashville, Tenn.: Abingdon Press.

Al Fifhause
William R. Johnson

REMOTE WORK

Information technology makes it possible to free work from the constraints of location and time. It is no longer necessary to commute daily to a central office to perform one's work; one can telecommute or work remotely. *Remote work* refers to organizational work performed outside the normal organizational confines of space and time. *Telecommuting* or *telework* refers to the substitution of computer and telecommunications technologies for physical travel to a central work location. A related term, *electronic cottage*, was coined by Alvin Toffler in *The Third Wave*, characterizing remote work as a return of the cottage industries, in which work will be performed at home but on a new, electronic basis.

Remote work is often associated with *homework*, but the workplace of a remote worker can also be a *satellite office*, a *neighborhood work center*, or even a hotel room. A satellite office is a regional office of an organization that is based on the residential location of the employees. The satellite office is equipped with resources such as computers and communications equipment for the employees who live in the vicinity to work on. It is differentiated from a branch office or a decentralization of the functional unit of an organization. A neighborhood work center is a shared office space located in a residential area where employees from many different organizations share resources in a common facility. Workers go to the center nearest their place to work. The cost of maintaining the center is shared by the employers.

The term *telecommuting* was coined by Nilles et al. (1976) to designate the total or partial replacement of the daily commute by communication via a computer terminal. The initial interest in telecommuting focused mainly on the telecommunication–transport substitution as a means of energy conservation during the oil crisis years of the early 1970s. Today, telecommuting is seen as an attractive option for work that can save energy and improve the environment and the quality of life. Many well-known companies have initiated telecommuting programs; these include Blue Cross/Blue Shield, Aetna Life, and Control Data Corporation in the United States and Rank Xerox, F International, and ICL in the United Kingdom.

JOBS SUITABLE FOR REMOTE WORK

Working at home is not a new phenomenon. Artists, writers, music teachers, insurance agents, consultants, technical and professional people, and the self-employed have traditionally used the home as a workplace. With the availability of a computer link between the office and the home, organization-

al employees, previously needed to be located at the office or factory, can now do remote work as well.

Not all office tasks lend themselves to remote work, however. Inappropriate jobs include those that require frequent face-to-face interaction with clients or colleagues or handling of physical products. Jobs that are good candidates for telecommuting include those that can be done with relatively little face-to-face contact with other people and those that require concentration and large blocks of time when the employee works independently of others. Jobs that are project oriented, with each project resulting in defined deliverables; jobs with defined milestones; and jobs that can be performed without close supervision are also suitable for telecommuting (DeSanctis 1983).

NUMBER OF REMOTE WORKERS

Estimates of the number of telecommuters in the United States, United Kingdom, and Europe vary greatly because different estimation methods and different definitions of telecommuters are used (Pratt 1987). Although a large number of people work at home, only a small number are actually telecommuters whose work involves the use of information technology. A report from the U.S. Bureau of Labor Statistics concluded that in 1985, "only about 100,000 of the persons with home-based work in professional specialty occupations, which includes computer programming as a subset, worked entirely at home" (Olson 1989).

TECHNOLOGY

The computer and telecommunications technologies that are used to support telecommuting include personal computers with modems, telephones, telephone answering services and machines, voice mail, facsimile machines, and electronic communications such as electronic mail and bulletin boards.

Telework can be performed using a "dumb" terminal, a terminal with limited calculating, processing, and storage capabilities, that is connected by modem and telephone line to a mainframe computer that processes the work. Increasingly, remote work is performed and processed on a microcomputer, and the completed task is transmitted over telephone lines (uploaded) to the company's computer facilities. When remote terminals are connected to an organization's communications network, employees can use electronic mail and computer conferencing systems to call up electronic files or databases onto their screens and work on them. The results can be transmitted back to the office or to a supervisor or deposited into a computer file. Any number of people can be working remotely for an organization at the same time. With advanced information technology, it is possible for the remote worker to maintain contact with and control over projects elsewhere, to communicate with colleagues in other time zones, and to gain rapid access to urgently needed information regardless of the time of the day, the day of the week, or the weather conditions.

ADVANTAGES

A major impetus for organizational interest in remote work is the need to attract and retain qualified employees and reduce staff turnover. The resulting economic benefit is reduced costs of replacing an experienced employee, including recruitment costs, time spent training a novice, and loss of efficiency during training. Another main economic benefit is the potential for saving on overhead costs because less office space is required. Parking space requirements and office expenditures on furniture, heating, air conditioning, and stationery are also reduced.

Studies have shown that productivity among telecommuters often declines for a short period initially, but then increases after a period of adjustment. The most commonly cited reason is that there are fewer distractions at home. Telecommuters also tend to work harder and longer than do their office-bound counterparts, putting in additional hours beyond their daily stipulated quota or converting their commuting time saved by telecommuting to work.

Companies with successful telecommuting programs report increases in loyalty among their employees. Employees appreciate the opportunity to work at home, the flexibility that this gives them, and the trust their employers place in them.

For the employees, the benefits include reduced travel time and costs, reduced distraction and interruptions, avoidance of office politics, and elimination of stress caused by commuting. Many people dislike having to rush to work or being caught in traffic jams. For people living in remote areas, the time spent commuting to the workplace can be substantial. Employees also opt for remote work because of the need for flexibility, autonomy, and control over timing of work. For a few whose skills are in demand, remote work is a convenience and a privilege. For some people, such as the disabled, women with small children, and those with few skills that are in demand, remote work may be the only option.

As a form of work arrangement, remote work is of particular interest to working women because it enables working mothers to keep their jobs and take care of their children at the same time. Studies have shown that women who work at home tend to do so because of domestic responsibilities. Remote work can be seen as one way for women with family commitments to remain in the labor force while fulfilling their domestic responsibilities. These women would otherwise be lost from the labor pool.

At the societal level, remote work can help to reduce gasoline consumption, air pollution, and traffic congestion on the roads. A major potential of remote work is to bring job opportunities to social groups who find it practically difficult to gain access to conventional forms of employment. Women with preschool children, the disabled, people looking after the elderly or the infirm, and other groups of people who are unable or unwilling to travel to work present a potential pool of labor that can be tapped. This is particularly important in economies that are facing a shortage of labor.

DISADVANTAGES

The main disadvantages of remote work are the high initial startup costs, difficulty in supervising and evaluating the performance of remote workers, loss of face-to-face communication, and potential problems with security of data and equipment.

For the remote worker, the disadvantages include lack of social interaction and difficulty in communicating with colleagues, accessing materials in the office, and getting help in solving problems. It is also not easy to integrate work and home activities. Role conflict problems may arise. The problem is particularly acute for women who must strike a balance between two roles, mother and wage earner. Remote work may also have negative implications for career advancement. There is some concern that the telecommuters will become "second-class corporate citizens" (Christensen 1987).

CONCLUSION

Remote work can be seen as one facet of the broader trend toward flexible working and organizational form in the economy. The macroeconomic preconditions, in terms of labor market forces, demographic change, and transport bottlenecks, appear to be favorable to telecommuting in the 1990s. Companies are increasingly looking for greater labor productivity through flexible working arrangements, including increased self-employment and the move to buy-in services. A shortage of skilled workers in the Western economies has been predicted for the 1990s because of a fall in the number of young people entering the labor market (*OECD Employment Outlook*, July 1990). Added to this is the congested transport systems in many big cities. Thus, remote work has instant appeal as an energy-efficient, environment-friendly, time-saving, and people-oriented solution to the problem of a severely overloaded transport infrastructure and the problem of a labor-tight economy.

Present evidence does not support the contention that full-time telecommuting is likely to become a widespread work arrangement. Ramsower (1985) suggests that the population of potential full-time telecommuters will be limited to homebound individuals who have a strong need to work at

home; however, part-time telecommuting holds greater promise. Working at home part of the time provides workers with flexibility and control in jobs while not significantly reducing their presence at the office, hence ameliorating many problems arising from working at home full time. For example, Bailyn's (1989) study of a group of telecommuters at ICL in the United Kingdom concluded that "working from home with computers for part of the regular work week may, under the right conditions, provide the perfect workplace for highly skilled employees whose skills and energies are needed for a productive society, but who are unwilling to have their lives controlled by the organizations that employ them."

Although many workers in jobs involving manipulation of information will spend all or much of their work time at home, the utilization of electronic cottages, forecasted by many experts, will be very limited. Information technology has made it feasible for people to do remote work, but it is *not* the force driving the telecommuting movement. Organizational culture and economic and social concerns of both employers and employees will have a greater influence on the acceptance of telecommuting as an alternative work arrangement. Most people appear to prefer a multiple-option solution, as a part-time remote worker and only for certain periods to accommodate particular needs, rather than the more drastic change from full-time working in the office to full-time telecommuting.

References

Bailyn, L. 1989. Toward the perfect workplace? *Communications of the ACM* 32(4):460–71.

Christensen, K. E. 1987. Impacts of computer-mediated home-based work on women and their families. *Office: Technology and People* 3:211–30.

DeSanctis, G. 1983. A telecommuting primer. *Datamation*, Oct.:214–20.

Nilles, J. M., F. R. Carlson, P. Gray, and G. G. Hanneman. 1976. *The telecommunications-transportation tradeoff.* New York: Wiley.

Olson, M. H. 1989. Work at home for computer professionals: Current attitudes and future prospects. *ACM Transactions on Office Information Systems* 7(4):317–38.

Pratt, J. H. 1987. Methodological problems in surveying the home-based workforce. *Technological Forecasting and Social Change* 31:49–60.

Ramsower, R. M. 1985. *The organizational and behavioral effects of working at home.* Ann Arbor, Mich.: UMI Research Press.

Toffler, A. 1980. *The third wave.* New York: William Morrow.

For Further Reading

Allen, S., and C. Wolkowitz. 1987. *Homeworking: Myths and realities.* Hampshire: Macmillan Education Limited.

Atkinson, W. 1985. *Working at home: Is it for you?* Homewood, Ill.: Dow Jones–Irwin.

Boris, E., and C. R. Daniels, eds. 1989. *Homework: Historical and contemporary perspectives on paid labor at home.* Urbana: University of Illinois Press.

Cross, T. R., and M. Raizman. 1986. *Telecommuting: The future technology of work.* Homewood, Ill.: Dow Jones–Irwin.

Huws, U., W. B. Korte, and S. Robinson. 1990. *Telework: Towards the elusive office.* Chichester: Wiley.

International Labor Organization. Telework. *Conditions of Work Digest* (Geneva) 9(1).

Kinsman, F. 1987. *The telecommuters.* Chichester: Wiley.

Korte, W. B., S. Robinson, and W. J. Steinle, eds. 1988. *Telework: Present situation and future development of a new form of work organization.* Amsterdam: North-Holland.

Lozana, B. 1989. *The invisible work force: Transforming American business with outside and home-based workers.* New York: Free Press.

Newsweek. Escape from the office. *Newsweek,* 24 April 1989, pp. 58–60.

Olson, M. H. 1983. Remote office work: Changing work patterns in space and time. *Communications of the ACM* 26(3):182–87.

Salomon, I., and M. Salomon. 1984. Telecommuting: The employee's perspective. *Technological Forecasting and Social Change* 25:15–28.

Chee Sing Yap

REPORT GENERATORS

A report generator is a special type of database programming; it is a program designed to assist you in extracting from a database the information you seek, and to put it in the format you want.

Databases are large, usually complex lists of facts and information; they usually contain regular arrangements of text and numbers, but modern databases, especially on personal computers, can contain video images (still or moving), sounds, large bodies of text, or combinations of all these elements.

Simple databases abound; most reference publications, heretofore available only on paper, are now available on computers, and simple report generators allow you to choose your areas of interest from telephone directories, library card catalogs, airline flight guides, and bibliographic references as well as conventional databases containing accounting information, mailing lists, and the like.

You can still get many reference works in paper, or "hard copy" form, but locating the data in a large volume requires elaborate indices, which are both tedious and expensive to prepare and keep up-to-date.

A database on a computer, on the other hand, can easily be reindexed whenever the underlying data are changed. Many such computer databases contain information that changes so often that they have no permanent indices; they are reindexed each time an information request is made. Sometimes the indexing step is bypassed altogether, in favor of a simple sequential scan of the entire database.

The craft of data management dates back to the Greek philosopher Aristotle and the scheme of interlocking knowledge classifications he expounded in his *Physica.* Automated data storage and retrieval first appeared in the 1880s, when the Jacquard loom was developed; the loom could weave intricate patterns under the control of programs recorded on punched cards. The use of punched cards as a general-purpose data storage medium was further developed by Herman Hollerith, and his card-sorting device, a precursor to the modern report generator, was used in the 1890 Census.

Over the years, data storage has come a long way, from the Hollerith cards to magnetic tape (with the data usually still in Hollerith's format) to massive modern databases stored on disk. Many modern databases are huge and complex, but the data input and inquiry programs make it relatively simple to use the data in them without a great deal of computer knowledge. When you call an airline's reservations agent, a special type of report generator tells him or her what seats are available on what flights, and at what prices; can you imagine booking airline flights in the days before American Airlines' Sabre seat reservations system came on-line in 1964?

The four types of databases, their major characteristics, and some examples of each are as follows.

- Hierarchical. Each set of facts belongs to a larger category. The biological classification system (kingdom, phylum, class, order, family, genus, species) places living things in a hierarchical database.

- Relational. A rows-and-columns, or tabular, approach to the organization of facts. A typical list of animals, with their names in a column down the left margin of the page and various animal characteristics (habitat, range, diet) assigned to the other columns, is a relational database.

- Multiple-file relational. A linked group of relational databases, used where the data are too complex for a single file. In a public library book catalog and circulation system, for example, there might be separate but linked databases for book publishers, the books they publish, the books the library owns, the subjects those books cover, the library's patrons, and the location of the books and their circulation status.

- Unstructured or full-text. Unlike the other database forms, full-text databases have very little organization beyond the indexing of key words. Many newspapers' entire noncommercial contents are available in full-text databases, as are magazines, wire service reports, scholarly and professional research papers, press releases, and other forms of information. Some of these databases use the HyperText concept, wherein words in one article are linked to other articles; if this encyclopedia entry were linked that way, you could select the word "HyperText" in the body of the text, see a complete article explaining that concept, then return to this discussion on report generators.

Although it is occasionally helpful to know the organization of the subject database before attempting to generate reports from them, many modern report generators are sophisticated enough to produce many different types of reports from their databases without your having to know what type of database you're dealing with.

Although the exact nomenclature differs, databases can generally be thought of as being divided into records (the rows in the relational model above), with each record divided into fields (the columns in the relational model). Of course, something like a full-text database may have very long records (a complete magazine article, perhaps) that contain only one field: the whole record.

Report generators have many ways of accepting your requests, but generally they allow you to specify three characteristics of the data you wish to see:

- Selection. Which records do you wish to consider in your report? Although you might want a printout of all the entries in your little black book, a full report of all the data on every one of a credit bureau's 20 million creditholders might prove a little overwhelming. The selection process lets you restrict the report to those records in the database that fit a certain criterion—perhaps everyone you know in New York—or all the creditholders who have gone bankrupt in the past 90 days.

- Sort order. In what order do you want your report? For your little black book you might want alphabetical by last name, but the credit bureau might want to report those bankruptcies with the largest dollar amounts first, or by some other criterion. The more sophisticated report generators will allow you to specify more complex report ordering, perhaps reporting those bankruptcies by state, then by amount within each state.

- Presentation format. Would you like it on

paper, in a disk file, or just on the screen? Once you have selected which data you wish to see, and in what order, you usually get your choice of presentation methods, from very complete paper reports with page headers, subtotals, totals, and summaries; to data files suitable for use by other database programs; to on-screen, record-by-record browsers.

Most report generators can be used in two different ways:

- Permanent reports. Also called "programmed reports" or "regular reports," these are part of regular data processing for the database concerned; when an accounting system is implemented as a database, such reports will include the income statement, balance sheet, accounts payable, accounts receivable, etc. The specifications for these reports are part of the data processing software and need not be repeated each time the reports are run.
- Ad hoc reports. These "spur-of-the-moment reports" let you see your data in new and interesting ways ("all the sales in Cleveland in October versus all the sales in Pasadena in October") and allow you to focus your attention on data patterns that may not be apparent in the regular reports. The flexibility of the report generator lets you enter the specifications for these reports as and when needed.

There are several ways of specifying your selection, sort, and presentation criteria to a report generator:

- Statements, commands, or code in a programming language. Although clearly most suitable for permanent reports, specifying the report's selection, sort, and presentation criteria in one or more commands is very flexible. In addition, the commands can usually be saved on disk and reused in the future when the same or a similar report is required. IBM's Structured Query Language (SQL) has been adopted by many other companies for this purpose; there is even an ANSI standard so that the same SQL program can be used with several vendors' database software.

- Query by example (QBE). Some microcomputer database management systems (DBMSs), notably Symantec's Q&A, as well as DBMSs on other computers, allow users to build on the screen a form that is then used for reporting as well as data entry. The QBE on-screen form also specifies the way the reports should look, and at report time you fill in the blanks on the form with samples of the data you wish to match, such as GA in the "State" blank indicating that you want all the records for residents of Georgia. Some QBE front ends can also generate SQL code for use with other DBMSs.
- HyperText. Some full-text databases use the HyperText concept, wherein words in one article are linked to other articles, and highlighting or otherwise selecting a key word in one article automatically brings up another article explaining the selected word or concept. If this encyclopedia entry were linked that way, you could select the word "HyperText" in the body of the text, see a complete article explaining that concept, then return to this discussion on report generators. The HyperText paradigm, although not suited to printed reports or to all types of data, is very effective in interactive work with full-text databases, and full-text databases are increasing in number and in subject coverage.

For Further Reading

Shuster, H. L., and R. D. Dillion. 1988. *The financial manager's guide to microsoftware.* New York: Wiley.

Russ, W. 1991. *The secret guide to computers.* 14th ed. Somerville, Mass.: Russ Walter Publications.

Sheldon T. Hall

RETAILING, COMPUTER USE IN

Use of computers in the retail industry spans a broad range of businesses and applications. Functions that have been dramatically changed through application of computer technology include accounting, merchandising, point-of-sale transaction processing, merchandise handling and distribution, store operations, company organization and job composition, and management information systems. New business formats have been developed, a broader geographic dispersion of retail outlets for chain stores has been facilitated, and the flexibility of company organizations and decision-making structures has been enhanced. Computer use has contributed to improved profits through speed of information availability, information analysis capability, automated actions and follow-ups, improved inventory management, increases in productivity, and more effective expense control. Many key retail executives have stated that the effective use of computer technology will be essential for business survival in a highly competitive retail environment.

The many types of business in the retail industry include department stores, discount stores, specialty stores, wholesale clubs, grocery stores, drugstores, hardware/home centers, general merchandise/variety stores, and mail and telephone order retailers. Although the specific emphasis of computer use in a given company will vary by retail format, size of company, organizational structure, and merchandise carried, some characteristics are general enough to be considered typical of the industry. The retail industry is a transaction-oriented business utilizing large files of data that experience limited activity on any given item on a daily basis. These files include inventory data, financial data, customer data, and employee data.

HISTORY AND TRENDS

One of the first comprehensive efforts in applying computers to retailing functions was the RCA Business Machines Project, undertaken with a group of volunteer stores belonging to the Associated Merchandising Corporation (AMC) during the mid-1950s. The project consisted of study teams of retailers charged with conceptualizing, programming, and testing the application of computers to major retail functions. A number of the department stores in the Federated department store and Dayton-Hudson department store groups participated in the project. The results of this project were very significant because they provided a framework for each of the participating companies to apply computer technology to the operation and growth of their own businesses.

Some of the key common computer-related retailing trends include:

- Use of on-line computer inquiry and analysis via cathode-ray tube (CRT) display terminals and exception reporting rather than printing lengthy reports for review.
- A strategic business focus to information systems planning rather than an individual application focus—accounts payable, accounts receivable, etc.
- Integration of systems, with multiple functional areas using common databases.
- Where possible, the capture of data as it is created, and flowing it through the computer processes without further human intervention.
- Expansion of distributed processing through on-line CRT use in functional user areas.
- Use of owned or shared satellite communication networks.
- Use of software packages rather than custom-developed software.
- Solidification and expansion in the use of industry coding standards for bar code, scanning, and electronic data interchange (EDI).
- Growing interest in "open systems"—industry standardization development to permit retailers to intermix the hardware and software of different vendors.

FUNCTIONS AND FEATURES

Although new applications are continuing to develop to cover the many facets of retailing, the predominant functions utilizing computers today involve the administration, processing, and management functions concerning store operations, inventory management, employee administration, financial management, and customer service and analysis.

Store Operations

Computer systems are used in a number of store planning and construction functions, including site selection models; computer-assisted design (CAD); simulations of alternative variations in floor layouts, fixture use, and merchandise mix; store remodeling and new store construction project schedules and progress tracking; and computerized plan-o-grams for both new and remodeled stores. A plan-o-gram is a specific layout of each merchandise fixture that indicates the exact location and amount of each type of merchandise that goes on the fixture.

Increases in the level of sophistication of point-of-sale systems and equipment have had an impact on credit administration, store layout, sales staff training, accounting and cash control, inventory management, and the manner in which customers are served. Features that enhance the importance of the point-of-sale functions include:

- Computer-programmed transaction control that provides a consistent transaction handling discipline and enforces company policy and procedures.
- A teaching machine concept used in point-of-sale terminals that leads the operator through the transaction steps, avoiding dependence on the operator's memory.
- Descriptive itemized receipt printing for improved customer service.
- Computer-controlled transaction monitoring to permit improvements in cash control, sales audit, and register balancing at the store level.
- On-line price look-up capability by individual item, which has reduced merchandise re-marking requirements and significantly tightened and simplified price change administration.
- On-line links to computers for credit authorization of company and third-party (bank) credit cards, which have reduced the retailer's risk concerning credit sales.
- Scanning of merchandise tickets and credit cards, which has increased the speed and accuracy of transaction processing and permitted a level of detail data capture that was not practical for high-transaction businesses prior to the availability of electronic processing.
- Capturing the data in machine-processible form, which permits electronic input of detailed transaction information to the inventory, finance, employee, and accounts receivable systems.

The availability of bar code and scanning technology has enabled some supermarkets to install self-checkout approaches in which the customer does the merchandise scanning and the store cashier concentrates on the payment. By combining the scanning with robotics, it is possible for retailers to use computer-driven, unmanned kiosks to sell and dispense merchandise. Some smaller stores have their point-of-sale terminals programmed to include items such as receipts of merchandise, transfers, special orders, and electronic mail as well.

A computerized price look-up system significantly simplifies retail price change administration. Merchandise identification numbers are keyed or scanned into a point-of-sale terminal; the computer looks up the current price and processes the sale. Scanning significantly enhances the speed and accuracy of the data capture compared to the keying alternative. Item-numbered or bar-coded tickets (see BAR CODE) are applied either by the manufacturer or by the retailer. Universal product code (UPC) marking has been extensively used in the grocery industry and is being expanded to other retail segments as manufacturers and retailers agree on standard coding technology and install the required equipment and systems. A computerized price look-up system also makes it unnecessary to re-mark merchandise physically before and after temporary sales.

Uses of computers in signing and merchandise presentation include electronic display, banner, or CRT signs; various forms of electronic sales aids utilizing computers linked with touch terminals and video; and electronic plan-o-grams. New plan-o-grams are generated any time there is a significant change in merchandise mix or store presentation to improve shelf productivity (seasonal changes, holidays, new product introduction, major sales promotions, etc.). Electronic shelves have the technology for electronic pricing, signing, and product information built into the fixture shelving.

Computerized staff scheduling utilizes the traffic tracking capability of the point-of-sale terminals by hour of day and day of week, and develops customer traffic models. These models are matched with sales plans, employee productivity, and employee availability information to match manpower with anticipated customer flow. Staff scheduling for nonselling activities uses a work-load forecast from the known truck schedules and anticipated receipts and matches it with staff availability and productivity information to develop the schedule.

Computer systems have improved work-load forecasting and productivity measurement capabilities, have provided more timely reporting of actual expense vs. budgets, and have provided the ability to analyze expenses by type and by responsibility. Computer systems are also used to control energy usage by monitoring and controlling switches on devices that utilize energy. Intracompany electronic mail has provided store management with the opportunity to reduce paper flow and improve communication and turnaround time on critical issues with other parts of the company.

Inventory Management

Retailers segment merchandise by department, class, subclass, and stock keeping unit (SKU) to monitor their businesses. The SKU is the unique item that the customer purchases, including style, color, and size. Information used for inventory management consists of units and dollars sold, on hand, and on order by the various segments. Margins (the difference between cost and retail prices) are monitored by the same segments.

The use of computers and the development of industry standards for purchase orders, invoices, and other shipping documents have enabled retailers and manufacturers to work together toward the concept of "quick response" inventory management to manage merchandise flow better. This is similar to "just in time" inventory management in manufacturing. It involves

computerized monitoring of rate of sale, computerized generation of purchase orders, and transmission of electronic purchase orders to vendors through ELECTRONIC DATA INTERCHANGE (EDI). EDI is also used among vendors, transportation carriers, and retailers to communicate merchandise shipment notification, invoices, and electronic payment transfers. Many retailers do not have the vendor link in place but are using computers for the internal processing of merchandise, such as on-line receiving of merchandise, including computerized matching of purchase order, receipt, and invoice information; computerized breakouts of merchandise quantities to be shipped to individual stores; computerized put-away locations for incoming merchandise; and computerized pick lists for outgoing shipments to stores.

Using computers in scanning, UPC coding, warehouse reserve stock management, merchandise flow tracking, and warehouse cube management has provided retailers with the opportunity for significant improvements in merchandise processing and productivity. By effectively managing the "merchandise flow pipeline" (from purchase order to retail customer purchase), inventory turnover is improved. Computerized monitoring and processing of return-to-vendor merchandise also helps to minimize inactive inventory dollars.

By applying a number of statistical techniques to the perpetual stock and sales history of an item, retailers forecast rates of sale, project out-of-stock conditions, and use the computer to reorder basic types of merchandise automatically. Using various decision rules, merchandise management can take advantage of the analytical and exception reporting capabilities of the computer to identify those items for potential action to improve sales and profit. These include early recognition of best-selling and slow-selling items, identification of items for assortment mix modification, margin contribution analysis, trends in fashion features, and direct product profitability. Planning simulation of the potential profit impact of various alternative merchandise mix modifications is also of value. Computerized perpetual inventories by location provide the retailer with sales and stock performance by store, the ability to develop individualized store inventory mix profiles to match local customer demand profiles (micromarketing), and the capability of balancing inventories by location.

Employee Management and Administration

Although computerized payroll processing is not a profit-producing application for a retailer, it does involve using computer power to handle one of the more complex administrative areas of the business. It includes complying with federal and multiple state laws, direct deposits to banks, various types of withholding record keeping, production of payroll checks, company and individual tax record keeping, and interfaces with employee benefit and performance evaluation systems. Without the computer, administration of employee records can be very paper-intensive. Employee benefit programs are a significant expense to retailers. Using a computer to maintain and track program offerings, employee eligibility, employee usage, and program costs is a real asset. In some cases it is necessary to interface with third-party providers of programs or insurance. Eligibility for certain benefits is sometimes linked to compensation. Compensation is increasingly linked to individual performance/productivity evaluation. As a result, it is necessary to maintain records concerning commissions and incentive bonuses/rewards as well as to identify people requiring additional training—all based on individual performance reviews. Computerized skills inventories are used in performance reviews, promotional opportunities, and manpower planning functions. Computerized staff scheduling utilizes a mix of information, including work-load projections, individual productivity performance, and individual schedule availability. Use of the skills inventory also provides the opportunity to use cross-trained people in multiple functions.

The growth in the number of electronic terminals in user areas throughout retail organizations necessitates some computer/terminal training for most retail jobs, particularly selling, clerical, and management positions. In some cases this training is handled through job simulation in a classroom environment. In others, a computer-assisted on-the-job training approach is used.

Financial Management

For a retailer, managing the credit function is a balance between risk assessment and using credit to promote merchandise sales. Automated accounts receivable systems provide management with valuable assistance in both of these efforts and in overall accounts receivable administration. Included are account promotion and instant credit programs; use of point-scoring techniques for credit granting; credit card production and distribution; on-line credit authorization; automatic finance charge calculation; automated billing; account aging analysis; automated dunning of slow-paying accounts; and collector management systems. In addition, those retailers using third-party credit cards, such as Visa and MasterCard, can be tied on-line to the bank service provider for credit authorization and for company-to-company transmission of bank card charges and electronic funds transfer (EFT).

By utilizing various formulas and the related computer systems, financial management has initiated automated expense allocations to work centers for improved profit responsibility reporting—that is, allocation of transaction-related expenses based on numbers of transactions processed by a given work center, etc. Also, the timely availability of actual expense performance information versus budget, last-year, and various productivity benchmarks by type of expense (payroll, supplies, etc.) and by manager responsible has enhanced management's ability to take more timely corrective action.

Cash flow is one of the key barometers of the financial health of a retail business. Computer systems are tools that management uses to plan, track, and enhance the ongoing cash flow of the business. Examples of specific applications include scanning for customer payment processing, electronic funds transfer (EFT) for more rapid bank deposits, automatic check printing to optimize the use of the trade discounts and deferred payments versus the need for cash, administering the accounting for vendor co-operative advertising, and deducting debit balances owed by vendors prior to making merchandise payments to those vendors. Computer systems tools used in attempting to improve vendor performance include debit balance monitoring; vendor compliance monitoring of price, shipping terms, timing of shipments, paperwork accuracy, terms, etc.; and vendor profitability analysis. These tools are used in vendor negotiation, to charge noncompliance fees to vendors, and to build relationships with positive-performing vendors.

Customer Considerations

Anticipating and responding to customer desires is critical to sustain growth in the retail industry. Use of computer technology is providing new insights into customer behavior through buying pattern analysis, customer traffic tracking through a store, and eye movement monitoring to determine the impact of merchandise, displays, and signing. Computerized targeted marketing approaches include selective mailings by Zip code, demographics, buying history, etc.; automatic customer follow-up triggering based on an elapsed time from a prior purchase of a related product or service; automatic coupon dispensing at point of sale (particularly in supermarkets); and computer-to-person telemarketing.

Computers have contributed to improved customer service in a number of ways, including faster point-of-sale and credit authorization transaction processing; more accurate and detailed receipts and billing; use of EFT to pay bills; cash machine availability; bridal and baby registry programs; on-line instructional point-of-sale displays; and personalized selling approaches such as cosmetic color profiles, personal wardrobe profiles, and frequent purchaser programs.

Administrative Assistance

Computers have been an integral part of substantial improvements in communications capability within the retail industry. Company and shared satellite networks have been installed. Electronic mail has replaced paper communication in many companies. The ability to combine voice, data, and video is providing retailers with new opportunities in training, communication with remote sites, and marketing techniques.

The ability of the computer to review large quantities of data and use decision rules for exception reporting and trend analysis provides retailers with time savings and the opportunity to develop more sophisticated "expert" systems and "decision support" systems.

Computer use has enhanced the planning process substantially through use of simulation of alternatives, model building, trend tracking and projections, advertising and promotional planning and production scheduling, on-line versus paper plans, and computerized explosion of general plans to detailed plans based on decision rules.

In total, the use of integrated computerized information systems (see Figure 1) has provided the retail industry with a new threshold of planning, organizational structure, performance, and opportunities for the achievement of new levels of sophistication and profitability.

For Further Reading

Because of the lack of books concerning computer use in retailing, the best published sources of information on the subject are in periodic trade publications. These include:

- *Retail Information Systems (RIS) News*—Edgell Corporation
- *Point-of-Sale (POS) News*—Faulkner and Gray
- *STORES Magazine*—NRMA Enterprises Division of the National Retail Federation
- *Retail Control*—Financial Executives Division of the National Retail Federation
- *Chain Store Age Executive*—Lebhar Friedman
- *Women's Wear Daily*—Fairchild Publications
- *Drug Store News*—Lebhar Friedman
- *ID Systems*—Helmers Publishing Company
- *Discount Merchandiser*—Schwartz Publications

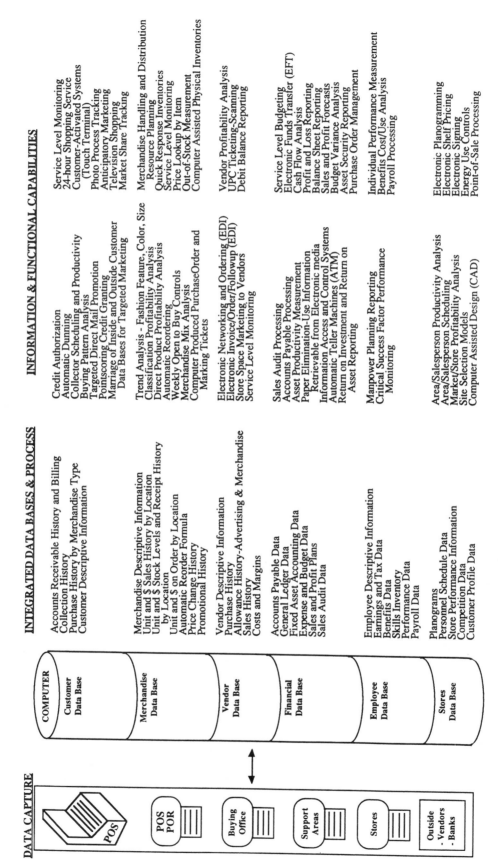

FIGURE 1. Integrated retail information systems.

• *Progressive Grocer*—Progressive Grocer Division of MacLean Hunter Media, Inc.

Additional information may be available through direct contact with major computer hardware and software vendors; major retail companies; the Information Systems Division of the National Retail Federation; the International Mass Retailers' Association; and major consulting firms possessing a retail industry focus.

Roy B. Burns

ROBOTICS

The word "robot" was first introduced in 1920, by playwright Karel Capek in his play *R.U.R.*, which stood for "Rossum's Universal Robots." In this play an Englishman named Rossum mass-produced robots (then called automata) to do all the work for human beings. But in the end, the robots rebelled, wiped out humanity, and created a new race of intelligent beings. The word "robot" came from the Czech word *robota*, meaning undesirable or unpleasant hard work. The popularity of this play resulted in the introduction of the term "robot" in every language to mean any artificial device that performs functions ordinarily thought to be appropriate for human beings. The term "robotics" (coined by the science fiction writer Isaac Asimov) refers to the science of designing, programming, and analysis of robots.

A British inventor named Cyril Walter Kenward and an American inventor, George C. Devol, are credited with development of the first programmable manipulator. Kenward obtained a British patent on a robotic device in 1957, and Devol obtained a U.S. patent for his device called a "Programmed Article Transfer" in 1961. Devol's work established the foundation for modern industrial robots. Later the joint efforts of Devol and Joseph F. Engelberger led to the development of the first industrial robot, called Unimate, which was introduced by Unimation, Inc., in 1962. The first Unimate robot was installed at the Ford Motor Company, for unloading a die-casting machine.

Since 1962 there have been many worthwhile achievements in the field of robotics, mainly due to advances in artificial intelligence (AI). Advances in robotics include use of sensory feedback to enable robots to be more flexible and intelligent, introduction of a number of robot programming languages, application of robots in a variety of applications and in industrial automation, introduction of multirobot systems technology, and development of mobile and walking robots. A number of commercial robot manufacturing companies also have evolved over the past 20 years. Currently industrial robots are primarily used in rather simple tasks such as material transfer, painting, welding, and machine tending. There is a growing trend to use industrial robots in applications such as assembly tasks that require sensory capabilities and higher precision. Robotic systems with multiple arms are also commercially available.

DEFINITION

Webster's Third New International Dictionary defines robot, in part, as "an automatic apparatus or device that performs functions ordinarily ascribed to human beings." According to this definition, a dishwashing machine can be considered a robot. Scientifically, a robot is considered to be a computer-controlled human armlike mechanical mechanism capable of manipulating and moving materials. Such robots are also called industrial robots or manipulators. A commonly accepted definition of industrial robots is due to the Robotic Industries Association (RIA), which was formerly known as the Robot Institute of America: "A robot is a reprogrammable, multifunctional manipulator designed to move material, parts, tools, or specialized devices, through variable programmed motion for performance of a variety of tasks." The key words here are "reprogrammable" and "multifunctional," because they indicate that a robot must possess intelligence. This property of a robot is normally due to built-in computer control and sensing systems. In other words, a robot is a reprogrammable general-purpose manipulator that can perform a variety of material-handling and as-

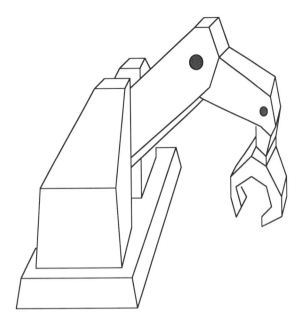

FIGURE 1. A characteristic manipulator.

sembly tasks. Recently, the design and analysis of walking machines and mobile robots have also become part of the field of robotics.

ROBOT ANATOMY

Most commercially available robots consist of several rigid links connected in a chain by joints. The motion of joints causes the relative motion of links. Two types of joint are commonly used: rotary or revolute joints, and sliding or prismatic joints. The relative displacement of the neighboring links in the case of revolute joints is called joint angle. The relative displacements between neighboring links of a prismatic joint is a translation (also called joint offset). There are motors at the joints between adjacent links that can set the joint to any value in its range. One end of the chain of links, called the body, is attached to the supporting base. Attached to the body is the arm subassembly, and at the end of the arm is the wrist subassembly. An end effector or tool is attached to the wrist subassembly. The wrist subassembly and hence the end effector can be oriented in a variety of positions. For each robot, a fixed number of independent position variables must be specified to locate all its parts. The number of independent variables is called

the degree of freedom. The arm subassembly generally can move with three degrees of freedom, which enables the positioning of the wrist unit at the desired location. The wrist subassembly usually has three permissible rotary motions, called pitch, yaw, and roll, which are used to orient the tool or end effector properly.

Most of the available robots fall into one of four basic configurations: (1) polar, (2) cylindrical, (3) Cartesian, and (4) revolute. The polar configuration (also called the spherical configuration) consists of a horizontal pivot mounted on a rotating base. Attached to the pivot is a telescoping arm that can be lowered or raised. Examples of commercial robots having a polar configuration include the Unimate 2000 series of Unimation, Inc., and MAKER 110 of United States Robot. The cylindrical configuration consists of a slide that can be moved up and down along a vertical. The robot arm is attached to the slide so it can be moved radially with respect to the vertical column. The GMF model M1A robot and the Versatran 600 robot of Prab are examples of cylindrical configuration. The Cartesian (also called xyz) configuration consists of three perpendicular slides that move to construct the x, y, and z axes. Examples of commercial robots with this configuration include the IBM RS-1 robot, and the Sigma robot of Olivetti. The revolute (also called the jointed arm) configuration has a structure similar to that of the human arm and consists of rotary joints. Examples of this configuration include the PUMA robots from Unimation, Inc., and the T3 robot from Cincinnati Milacron. The configuration, the sizes of the body, arm, and wrist components, and the limitations on joint movements determine the work volume of a robot. (Work volume refers to the space within which the robot can manipulate its wrist subassembly.)

ROBOT PLANNING AND CONTROL

The key steps involved in performing a given task by robot include planning motions, executing planned motions, and controlling the robot to ensure that the planned motions are followed. A basic problem in planning and control of robots, called kinematics, is to compute the position, velocity, and acceleration relationships between the joints and the end effector. There are two types of kinematics analysis: forward kinematics and inverse kinematics. The problem of forward kinematics deals with the computation of the position (velocity and acceleration) of the end effector when the position (velocity and acceleration) of every joint is specified. The problem of calculating the set of joint positions (velocity and acceleration), given the position and orientation of the end effector, is called the inverse kinematics problem. A manipulator is moved from one position to another in a smooth and controlled fashion by causing each joint to move as specified by a motion function. A motion function specifies a trajectory, which is the time history of position, velocity, and acceleration of a joint. The task of computing these motion functions or dynamic equations is called trajectory planning. Trajectory planning also involves avoiding collisions with objects in the workspace. The motion of a robot according to a specified trajectory is caused by exerting proper forces at the joints. The computation of joint forces required to obtain the desired motion is called dynamics. In general, because of inaccuracies caused by computational devices, modeling, friction, vibration, etc., the force command sequences for individual joints specified by a given set of dynamic equations of motion fail to produce the desired dynamic behavior of the robot. Therefore, a control system is used to maintain the robot dynamic response within a prespecified performance criterion. Control systems employ some sensors such as position and velocity sensors as feedback devices. The positions and velocities of the robot joints measured by these sensors are used to compensate automatically for the deviations from the desired trajectory. The control of grasping and material manipulation tasks requires use of force and torque sensors as feedback devices.

ROBOT SENSING

External sensors are used by robots to obtain useful information about the environment in which they are expected to function. These sensors enable a robot to interact intelligently with its environment and to adapt to a variety of complex situations and tasks. The two main classes of sensors used by robots are touch and nontouch sensors.

Contact sensors (also called touch sensors) detect information associated with the physical contacts between a robot and an object. Industrial robots usually employ touching sensors capable of detecting the presence or absence of an object, slippage, or forces exerted on the surface of the sensing device. There are two types of touch sensors: binary and analog. Binary touch sensors are simply microswitches that are turned on or off when touched by an object. Analog touch sensors produce output proportional to the local forces. Commercial analog touch sensors capable of detecting touch data at a single point of contact or generating a vector of touch data due to a contact over a wide area are available. Touch sensing data are mainly used to locate and identify an object and to control force required to be exerted by the end effector to grasp or move an object.

Nontouch sensors detect information based on the responses of the environment to light, acoustic, or electromagnetic signals. This type of sensing is used for (1) proximity sensing, detection of the presence of an object within a specified distance, and (2) range sensing, estimation of the distances between the sensor and the objects in the field of sensors. There are two classes of proximity sensors: (1) sensors based on the change of inductance or capacitance due to the presence of an object near the sensing device, and (2) sensors based on the influence of an object on an acoustic or an optical signal. The response of the first class of sensors strongly depends on the material being sensed. Range sensing devices utilize one of the three basic approaches: triangulation, structured light approach, and time-of-flight approach. To measure range through the triangulation approach, the object surface is illuminated by a narrow beam of light that is swept over the surface, and a detector is focused on a small portion of the surface to detect the light spot. When the detector detects the spot of light, its distance from the illuminated portion of the surface is D tan α, where D is the distance between the light source and the detector and α is the angle between the source-surface line and the source-detector line. The structured light approach involves projecting a light pattern onto the scene and calculating the range information based on the distortions of the light pattern by the objects. The time-of-flight approach computes distance based on the time elapsed between the transmission and return of a light or sonic signal. Vision sensors, similar to ordinary cameras, are also employed to give a robot the ability to see.

ROBOT PROGRAMMING

Robot programming techniques are used for communication between users and robots. The two basic modes of communication are the lead-through method and the use of high-level programming languages. The lead-through method of communication in-

volves teaching the robot the sequence of motions or actions required to accomplish a task by actually leading the robot through those motions and recording them, using a teach pendant (a hand-held button box that allows manual control of each manipulator joint). After the teaching phase the robot can be instructed to perform the taught motion sequence repeatedly at an appropriate speed.

High-level programming languages provide a more general form of human–robot communication. Robot programming by this method involves using a program—a set of commands of a programming language—to instruct the robot to perform a sequence of actions to accomplish a desired task. There are two types of robot programming languages: robot-oriented languages and task-level languages. The programs in a robot-oriented language specify a sequence of actions, whereas the programs in a task-level language specify only the desired subtasks. AML, AL, and VAL are commonly used robot-oriented programming languages. A

FIGURE 2. The robots are spot-welding automobile frames. *Courtesy Robotic Industries Association.*

truly task-level programming language is not yet commercially available.

APPLICATIONS

Robots are being used in a number of industrial applications to increase productivity, decrease manufacturing costs, improve product quality, and relieve humans of monotonous and/or hazardous tasks. In factories, industrial robots perform tasks such as welding, material handling, machine loading and unloading, assembly, spray painting, and machining. Robots spot-welding automobile frames are shown in Figure 2. In hazardous environments such as nuclear power plants and chemical plants, where radiation and/or toxic chemicals are hazardous to humans, remotely controlled robots are used for maintenance, repair, waste removal, and cleanup. Similar robots are used in undersea salvage and exploration and in space exploration. With the advent of machine vision technology, robots are gradually becoming smart or intelligent because they are able to sense and analyze their environment and act accordingly. At present, the majority of industrial robots in use are not intelligent.

For Further Reading

Craig, J. J. 1989. *Introduction to robotics mechanics and control.* 2nd ed. Reading, Mass.: Addison-Wesley.

Critchlow, A. 1985. *Introduction to robotics.* New York: Macmillan.

Dorf, R., and S. Nof. 1988. *The international encyclopedia of robotics.* New York: Wiley.

Fu, K. S., R. C. Gonzalez, and C. S. G. Lee. 1987. *Robotics control, sensing, vision, and intelligence.* New York: McGraw-Hill.

Groover, M. P., M. Weiss, R. N. Nagel, and N. G. Odrey. 1986. *Industrial robotics technology, programming, and applications.* New York: McGraw-Hill.

Smith, D., and P. Heytler. 1985. *Industrial robots forecast and trends, Delphi study.* 2nd ed. Dearborn, Mich.: Society of Manufacturing Engineers.

Wolovich, W. 1987. *Robotics: Basic analysis and design.* New York: Holt, Rinehart and Winston.

Rajiv Mehrotra

RPG

RPG (Report Program Generator) was introduced in 1961 and used initially on the IBM 1401. It was developed as an end-user tool, a way for programmers familiar with wiring plugboards to produce reports. Instead of plugging wires into hubs, the user would position the required numbers or letters in designated positions on each instruction line.

RPG was originally developed in Europe, and IBM eventually brought it across the ocean for use in the United States. RPG provided a relatively simple and compact compiler exclusive of the report writer specs contained in the earlier COBOL (though copying many of its concepts). RPG offered a nice way to write programs that looked like the flowcharts used with the older unit-record systems (more primitive card-handling devices). It served as a way to do the plugboard wiring on another sheet, which, instead of involving actual wiring diagrams, was keypunched and fed into the machine to perform the desired function.

The initial designers of RPG did not set out to develop a language that would compete with existing programming languages. They simply wanted to support the needs of businesspeople who had no programming experience. So it retains its initial purpose: designing application programs capable of producing commonly needed data processing reports.

A POWERFUL APPLICATIONS LANGUAGE

Though the concepts required to program RPG and the unit-record machines were very similar, RPG was much more convenient to work with and considerably more flexible.

Even so, some people would not classify it as a programming language, but simply, as its name implies, a report program generator. As users demanded more sophisticated features, RPG began to evolve into what might be considered a powerful applications language.

In the late 1960s, IBM announced the System/3 line. Its first two machines, the S/3 Model 6 and Model 10, both supported RPG II. So, criticism notwithstanding, RPG was elevated to "language" status in 1974, when RPG II was considered the primary programming language for the S/3 line. Though it closely resembled its predecessor, RPG II was theoretically a viable replacement for COBOL, in the sense that it offered essentially the same capabilities and would run on much smaller, cheaper machines.

The IBM S/3, S/34, and S/36 created a more affordable computer market for small businesses. The older machines were generally prohibitively expensive. Coupled with the lower prices, RPG itself made the new line of machines appealing. It may have been the first heavily productive language that could be compiled on as small a box as the early S/360 Model 20. (Though COBOLs may have been able to create object codes that would run on such tiny boxes, the compilers required what was then a tremendous memory to run, about 30K; they were also quite expensive.)

USE IN THE 1990s

RPG was originally best at general business applications—payrolls, accounts receivable, accounts payable, and so on. It lacked the power for the heavier computational needs of later applications.

With the development of high-level languages such as C and of many commercial report writer packages, RPG may not be as familiar to the new generation of programmers; however, it is still used by designers for the IBM S/34, S/36, S/38, and AS/400 (RPG III, in fact, is beginning to be referred to as RPG/400).

Personal computer (PC) versions of RPG are also available, and, as PCs become more powerful, RPG applications developed on the midrange machines may move down to PC local area networks.

ADVANTAGES OF RPG ON THE PC

As the 1990s begin, the personal computer is taking over many of the applications that were previously in the realm of the midrange machines. RPG is growing along with this segment of technology, offering many advantages.

First, many users perceive the PC to be a friendlier environment. The same genres of software can be easier to operate on the PC, and are often used more effectively. RPG appeals to PC programmers simply because the environment is more inviting.

Software can also be programmed, compiled, tested, and edited faster on the PC than, say, the S/36. Offloading development tasks can conserve system resources. And companies that have invested development time and programming skills in RPG applications on midrange machines are happy not to lose that investment when PCs are installed.

Conversely, companies that plan an upgrade path from their PCs to a minicomputer may start with RPG on the PCs and work up. Other companies that already have a minicomputer but do overflow work on PCs can use the same language on both.

NOT DIFFICULT TO LEARN

RPG is not a difficult language to learn, even for nonprogrammers. The most common growth path for an RPG programmer might be that of someone in an accounting department who takes a very basic course in the language so he or she can generate simple reports. RPG, though, has enough depth that a user could become very proficient on a more advanced level.

RPG also allows people to be productive quickly, and can grow along with the user's skill level.

```
H*************************************************************
H*                                                          *
H*   PROGRAMMER: STEVEN SULLIVAN     LATTICE, INC    01/89   *
H*                                                          *
H*   PROGRAM PROCESSES SOURCE FILES FOR RPG SCREENS TO      *
H*   TO CALCULATE THE MEMORY USAGE FOR EACH SCREEN.         *
H*                                                          *
H*************************************************************
FINP      IP   V      96              DISK
FOUTF      O   V      79              CRT
IINP      NS   01    6 CS   7NC*
I                                         7  14 NAME   L1
IINP      NS   02    6 CD   7NC*
I                                        15  18 FLEN
I                                        80  80 X
IINP      NS   03
C    01                 ADD  74        TOTAL    50
C    02N99              EXSR ADD
C    99                 SETOF                        99
C         X             COMP *BLANK                  99
CL1                     EXSR TOTAL
C* TOTAL SUBROUTINE
C          TOTAL        BEGSR
C                       ADD  TOTAL     TOTFMT   70
C          TOTAL        IFGT LTOT
C                       Z-ADDTOTAL     LTOT     50
C                       MOVELNAME      LNAME     8
C                       END
C                       Z-ADDTOTAL     SCR      50
C                       Z-ADD0         TOTAL
C                       ADD  1         SCRNO    20
C                       ENDSR
C* ADD SUBROUTINE
C          ADD          BEGSR
C                       MOVE FLEN      LEN      40
C                       ADD  26        TOTAL
C                       ADD  LEN       TOTAL
C                       ENDSR
OOUTF      T       L1
O                                      20 'SCREEN FORMAT: '
O                            NAME      30
O                                      50 'ESTIMATED USAGE:'
O                            SCR    Z  56
O                                      62 'BYTES'
O          T       LR
O                                      20 'NUMBER OF FORMATS: '
O                            SCRNO  Z  23
O                                      50 'LARGEST FORMAT: '
O                            LNAME     58
O                            LTOT   Z  65
O                                      71 'BYTES'
```

FIGURE 1. A sample program in RPG. *Courtesy Steven Sullivan, Lattice Inc.*

HOW DOES IT WORK?

Unlike other programming languages that require the user to write statements or paragraphs to tell the computer what to do, RPG uses a telegraphic notation form; an entry's position on a line determines its function. RPG logic is built around two-character codes called *indicators*, electronic switches that can be set on or off and tested. In calculations and output, the programmer can use indicators as short-term memory devices that tell the program what to do with tests performed in calculation and whether or not to print, punch, or display something.

Many computer languages require the programmer to break down each instruction into a set of smaller steps. In human terms, a simple command like "answer the phone" would be broken down into increments: "Move the muscles in your neck so that your head swivels in the direction of the phone. Focus your eyes on it. Start lifting your right arm and reaching your fingers out toward the handset. Curl the fingers of your hand around it and hold on. Lift the receiver."

RPG, in contrast, operates in cycles. These are embedded versions of three standard steps contained in all computer programs: read record, calculate, and write output. Programs are basically coded the same way. First, one defines the files and fields one wants to read from the record. Next, one defines the calculations one wants to perform and, finally, the form and location of the output wanted. By automatically performing some of these low-level commands, RPG saves the programmer steps and time. (Some programmers take a long time to get the cycle concept straight, because it is hard to see how something on page 2 will affect something on page 5. Often, they end up making paper listings of anything longer than a few pages.)

The mechanics of coding can be difficult, as RPG is heavily dependent on precise columnar orientation. This means that each of the "IF X IS GREATER THAN Y" lines must have a "C" in column 6 of the coding sheet; the X value must start in column 18; the operation code (COMP) must start in column 28; and the Y must be in column 33. The appropriate indicator starts in column 54, 56, or 58, depending on what kind of result (greater than, less than, equals) is desired.

THREE DRAWBACKS

An RPG code that is uncommented is almost as hard to read as Assembler or C; it is sometimes easier to rewrite something than to try to fix it if the original programmer did not leave complete enough comments. (Variable names only six characters long do not help. Array names are usually even shorter because there are only six or eight spaces in which to include the array name, a comma, and an index literal or variable.)

A second, and relatively unimportant, drawback is that most RPG implementations are totally divorced from the hardware, so one cannot PEEK or POKE, as one can with various forms of BASIC. (One can, within limits, do this with Assembler subroutines, but they are machine specific, and S/3X Assembler skills are rather rare.)

Finally, RPG II considers display screens to be simple buffers, a page (or screenful) at a time. Screens are essentially distinct programs, compiled separately. The programmer, then, has to match her or his program to the screen program to turn on specific indicators that cause a field to become underlined, locked out, or reversed, for example. The coupling between the two is very loose, but the interaction has to be tightly controlled. This can be problematic in complex programs with multiple screens.

MAINTENANCE MAY BE DIFFICULT

Maintenance of screen-oriented programs is difficult, as even minor changes to the screen may involve redoing hundreds of lines of code. Screen design aids can help here. One public domain program for PC RPGs permits a significant relaxation of the fixed format rules for creating RPG programs and offers other features to help the maintenance programmer.

RPG APPLICATIONS

Programmers should not expect to write flashy programs using RPG, and the complexity of creating on-line transactional programs (i.e., programs making extensive use of screens) may discourage users from that kind of application. It lacks the ability to deal conveniently with very large or very small numbers, particularly in combination with each other. It is also very weak in text handling, almost on a par with the early FORTRANs, and is not recommended for heavy scientific computation.

RPG, though, offers an excellent way to do batch-type processing. RPG is well suited to grabbing data records, totaling calculations, and printing checks and invoices. Its strength is in data processing and report generation. Some data processing applications that would take a lot of time and coding in C, for example, might take six lines and 5 minutes in RPG. One can develop a fairly small program to get the majority of what might be needed in a report.

Although a variety of commercial report writers have become available since the introduction of RPG, programming using RPG is still an attractive alternative because it generally offers more options than the commercial packages.

For Further Reading

Mini Magazine. RPG: Directions today and tomorrow. *Mini Magazine,* October 1987, pp. 6, 8, 10.

News 34/38 Magazine (Loveland, Colorado). RPG: A beginning. *News 34/38 Magazine,* November 1987.

Kathy Yakal

S

SCIENTIFIC APPLICATIONS, COMPUTER TECHNOLOGY IN

There are as many uses of computer technology in science as there are scientific disciplines; however, just as mathematics is the science that underlies all the sciences, and computer technology is largely a means of efficiently using mathematical tools, there are general areas of use that are common to most disciplines. Some implementations, such as database operations and statistical procedures, overlap with the realm of business applications. Others, such as computer visualization, are specialized applications developed specifically for scientific research.

Much slower to accept and exploit computer technology than the world of business, scientific endeavor has now embraced it, and scientific computer applications are often on the cutting edge of developments in software and hardware peripherals.

HARDWARE AND THE HISTORY OF SCIENTIFIC COMPUTING

Computers come in a variety of sizes and operating capacities, which have all been used in scientific research over time. The first very large computers were largely devoted to scientific projects, though these were projects of small scope, compared with present-day projects. As computers came into wider use, it became feasible to use them for general business procedures, and business largely preempted science as the principal use area of computer technology.

For a period of nearly 30 years, from the 1950s to the early 1980s, any scientific work requiring a computer had to be done on a mainframe computer or, beginning in the late 1960s, one of the new "minicomputers," such as a VAX or PRIME system (Data General, Hewlett-Packard, Tektronix, and Digital Equipment Corporation also manufacture minicomputers). Both mainframes and minicomputers were expensive to install and maintain, needed custom-written programs for each project done, and required the intermediary services of technicians to get raw data in and reports and analyses out. Consequently, the use of computers in science was not widespread; only projects using very large amounts of data, which absolutely required automatic computation, or those exploratory projects with outside funding were economically feasible to perform on a large computer.

Most individual scientists were not computer literate. Many, in fact, did not even consider using more computational power than was available in a hand-held calculator and the brain of a graduate student. Those scientists with access to a mainframe computer were compelled to "time-share" with other users, which meant that while an individual job could take only a few minutes to run on the computer, it might take hours or days for the job to get its turn to run.

Minicomputers

Midsized computers or minicomputers have been useful workhorses for scientific applications since the 1960s. For some time, these minisystems, the size of a refrigerator, with a 32-bit data bus (as compared with an 8- or 16-bit data bus for most personal computers) and multiple microprocessors, were the most popular computer systems for scientific applications. A mainframe system might cost several million dollars, whereas a minicomputer might cost $1 million, complete with tape drive units, peripheral hardware, operating system, and other software.

Much less expensive than the large mainframe computers, but still offering considerable power and memory capacity, a VAX or PRIME system could be dedicated to the projects of a single research group, lessening the difficulties associated with time sharing on a mainframe computer. Still, as with mainframes, software would generally have to be written for each individual job, which made complex problems time consuming and expensive to solve.

Although advances in manufacturing technology have made microcomputers available to individual researchers for small jobs, and workstations now provide sophisticated graphics and software support for more complex projects, many minicomputers are still in use, and are likely to remain so for several years. They are reliable, powerful, and simply too useful to throw away, even though workstation computers are likely eventually to replace most minicomputers as they wear out. Once software has been developed for a particular application, the cost of computer use drops dramatically. The minicomputers have now been around long enough that there are "libraries" of developed programs and routines that will run on them, whereas the scientific and technical software available for workstation computers still lags far behind the business applications.

Workstations

Workstations are the logical successor to the minicomputer. Much smaller in size—most workstations are little more than twice the size of a microcomputer—they offer similar speed of processing, with 32-bit data buses and up to 28 mips (million instructions per second), and have tremendously improved graphics capabilities. Resolution on a workstation monitor can reach 1,280 × 1,024 pixels, as compared with the 640 × 320 pixels available on a regular monitor used by a minicomputer or personal computer. Part of the increased sophistication in graphics is built into the hardware of the machine.

Workstations also cost substantially less than do minicomputers—perhaps $35,000 to $50,000 for a fully equipped workstation with peripherals and software, compared with $250,000 for a bare-bones minicomputer. On the other hand, although workstations are capable of multitasking (running several jobs simultaneously), they do not have multiple processors, as do minicomputers. This means that although workstations are suitable for individual researchers, or very small groups, they will not support nearly as many users (twenty to thirty) as can be supported on a minicomputer.

Still, the line between minicomputers and workstations is blurring, with increasing sophistication in workstation hardware and operating systems and with the increase in available software.

Workstations use "canned" software, obviating the need for developing expensive custom software for each job. Although the number of software packages available for workstations is very small compared with the software available for personal computers, enough powerful programs are available that very complex problems can be solved without the necessity for writing a great deal of special software.

Personal Computers

In the 1980s, the microcomputer revolution swept the world. Computers shrank dramatically, software applications boomed in number, and the business community eagerly adopted computer technology. The microcomputer (or "personal computer") revolution grew much more slowly in the sciences, because the relatively small size of the market meant that relatively few specialized software packages were available for scientific problem solving; however, scientific researchers soon realized that a number of general-purpose business packages, such as programmable database and statistical applications, could be adapted for scientific use at a fairly small cost in time and effort. As the potential for use increased, so did the number of personal computers in laboratories and university offices. And, as the number of computers increased, the market for more specialized scientific software grew as well, resulting in a steadily increasing number of such applications. Today, almost 10 years later, although the number of scientific computer applications is still much smaller than the number of business applications, the field of scientific computation is one of the healthiest and most diversified areas in computer technology.

Supercomputers

At the other end of the size range are the supercomputers, extremely large machines using parallel processing and vector hardware to achieve speeds far in excess of smaller computer systems. Although personal computers have carried computer technology into the lab and placed it within the reach of the individual scientist, supercomputers take advantage of the latest in computer innovation to solve problems that would have been inconceivable 10 years ago.

Because of their novel internal architecture, these machines are capable of handling several billion floating-point operations per second, in contrast to the few thousand instructions per second that a personal computer can manage.

The increase in speed possible with a supercomputer is achieved by use of parallel central processing units (CPUs)—numerous smaller processors working on the same task simultaneously, each taking a portion of the instructions and correlating their activities—and by use of vector hardware. Vector hardware is an innovation that allows the hardware of the supercomputer to handle iterative functions such as DO loops that are normally handled by software programs in smaller machines. Elimination of DO loop "overhead" from the processing of operating instructions results in a tremendous increase in speed. The single components, or CPUs, of a supercomputer are very fast in themselves, achieving speeds of up to 250 MHz, as opposed to the 8-MHz "clock speed" characteristic of the standard personal computer.

In addition to increased component speed and internal architectural innovations, supercomputers also have greatly increased memory capacity, which enables them to store vast amounts of data, with very fast data retrieval and fast input/output (I/O) operations. The speed and power of a supercomputer depend on a finely tuned balancing of powerful components working in unison.

The ability to handle a great deal of information at very fast speeds means that supercomputers can be used for very large, complex problems. In the scientific field at large, such problems frequently involve modeling, the construction of simulations of natural phenomena, in the hope of predicting or controlling changes in the natural system modeled. The kinds of projects suitable for supercomputer applications include atmospheric chemists modeling global climate systems to test for the effects of global warming or ozone layer depletion, geneticists and bioengineers conducting DNA analyses, and ecologists modeling biogeochemical cycling in various ecosystems.

Only a few companies make supercomputers, among them Cray, NEC, Fujitsu, and Hitashi. Supercomputers may cost from $3 million to $30 million to install, owing to the complexity of their internal architecture. Still, despite the high initial price, the cost of maintenance is not usually more than that for a standard mainframe computer. Consequently, these very large machines are beginning to be found much more commonly in scientific institutions than was the case even 2 or 3 years ago; more than 300 Cray supercomputers have been installed worldwide.

PERIPHERAL HARDWARE

Beyond the computers themselves, scientific use of computer technology has spawned a number of other electronic hardware devices, including digitizers and scanners for entering data; a variety of transducers and connectors for acquiring data directly from an experimental apparatus; and plotters and printers for producing the results of data analysis.

With the increasing sophistication of computer graphics, and the development of scientific visualization as an important field of application, there has been increased demand for a method of replicating and storing the images produced by computer graphics. Consequently, there has been an increase in the development of optical disks and compact-disk read-only memory (CD-ROM) technology for storage, and several systems for reproducing slides or videotape imagery directly from computer-generated images.

FOCI OF SCIENTIFIC COMPUTING: DISCIPLINES AND APPLICATIONS AREAS

Computer technology is not applied equally across all scientific disciplines. Some areas of scientific research depend extensively on computer technology, in particular, disciplines that require visualization techniques, such as the biomedical and chemical disciplines, and those that produce very large quantities of data or that require time-consuming methods of analysis.

Some fields of study, such as the social sciences, currently use computer technology only for educational simulations and for the relatively minor data processing and statistical analysis tasks associated with processing the results of surveys. Likewise, computer use tends to be limited in ecological and behavioral fields, where datasets tend to be small and research depends more on description and painstaking observation than on the analysis of large datasets, and statistical analyses tend to be of relatively common and uncomplicated form. By this, we do not imply that computers are not used extensively in support of these disciplines, but rather that the hardware and software so used do not differ substantially from those in use for more general applications.

Other scientific disciplines, such as bioengineering, molecular design, and some other fields of chemistry, literally would not exist in their present form without the assistance of computer technology.

Biotechnology applications depend on the ability of computers to gather and analyze data to conduct DNA sequencing and the other nucleic acid research that is at the root of biotechnological work. Molecular design depends on computer-generated images, using the data from large embedded

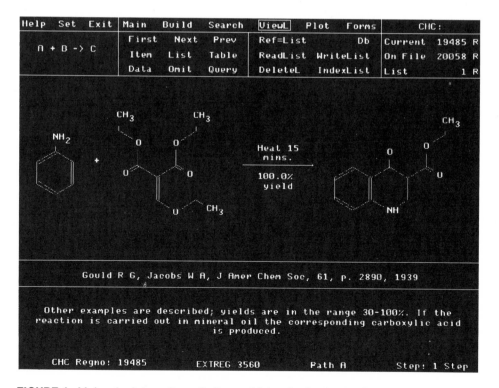

FIGURE 1. Molecular interactions. *Software: Molecular Design by ChemText.*

databases on molecular structure and interaction.

Scientific visualization refers to the ability of computer-generated graphics to produce a visual image of a process that is not generally visible or accessible by physical means. Computer-controlled visualization includes computed axial tomography scans, nuclear magnetic resonance and magnetic resonance imaging in medicine, molecular design and interaction in chemistry, and more generalized modeling and simulations in a great variety of fields, including biological, chemical, and physical systems. Modeling and the graphic visualization of atomic and subatomic interactions are two of the important applications of computer technology in physics.

In most scientific disciplines, computer-assisted instruction is a common and growing use of computer technology. The ability to construct and test simulations on a computer means a savings in laboratory space, less use of animal resources for standard educational exercises, and greatly increased flexibility for the instructor, who can modify exercises according to the needs of the students.

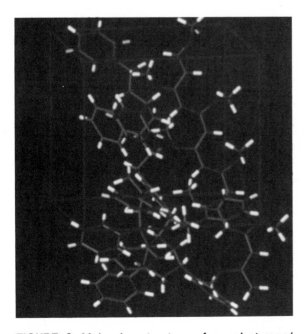

FIGURE 2. Molecular structure of a polystyrene/polymethylvinylether blend visualized in three dimensions. *Software by Molecular Simulations, Inc.*

SCIENTIFIC SOFTWARE DEVELOPMENTS

Laboratory Information Management Systems

One important type of specialized scientific software is the laboratory information management system (LIMS). This software package includes database functions with a system of tracking and record keeping that enables a laboratory manager to create documentation for all the procedures a lab carries out.

A LIMS may include peripherals such as bar code readers, "smart" instrumentation, and other types of laboratory automation, as well as the central computer that hosts the database functions.

Equation Processors

Although most software used in scientific applications, like database technology, was developed originally for business purposes, equation processors are an application developed specifically for scientific use and have limited use outside of scientific applications. Several of these mathematical tools are currently on the market (Universal Technical System's TK!Solver and MathSoft's MathCAD are two popular equation solvers), in use in a range of scientific applications, from education to laboratory use.

An equation processor essentially allows the user to perform a free-form series of mathematical manipulations, with the option of graphic representation, while exploring the shape and possibilities of a given set of data.

Graphics Software

Graphics software has made immense strides in sophistication and complexity within the last few years, reaching a level that makes possible the imaging of molecular interactions, the internal structures of the human body, computer representations of mathematically based models in pictorial form, and other systems and structures that cannot be viewed directly.

Graphics software seldom occurs as single-function software in scientific applications; it is more often included as part of a software package that also performs data storage, retrieval, and analysis.

Data and Number Crunching

The most widespread function of computer technology in scientific research continues to be "number crunching," the processing of large quantities of data. Database software to handle such functions does not differ fundamentally from that used in business applications; however, a number of specialized applications packages have been developed in recent years that cater to specifically scientific needs by combining several functions: data acquisition, storage and retrieval, and statistical analysis. In addition, such "integrated software" may include powerful graphics and report-generating capabilities. In principle, all the procedures that an individual or a laboratory requires can be performed using one large software program that will manage

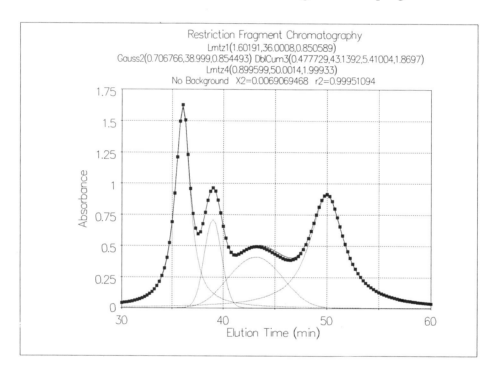

```
Restriction Fragment Chromatography          Nov 5,1990 5:03 PM
121 Active X-Y Points
X: Elution Time (min)     Mean: 45            SD: 8.768432965
Y: Absorbance             Mean: 0.43557156    SD: 0.343059327

Curve-Fit Std Error= 0.00799707518     r2= 0.999510935

Curve-Fit Coefficients
```

Peak#	Type	Ampl	Ctr	Wid1	Wid2	Wid3
1	Lorentzian	1.60191	36.00077	0.850589		
2	Gaussian	0.706766	38.99896	0.854493		
3	DblCum	0.477729	43.13923	5.410043	1.869705	
4	Lorentzian	0.899599	50.0014	1.999328		

```
Measured Values
```

Peak#	Type	PkAmpl	PkCtr	Wid@HM	Area
1	Lorentzian	1.60191	36.00077	1.701174	4.040507
2	Gaussian	0.706766	38.99896	2.012174	1.513821
3	DblCum	0.409658	43.13924	6.077085	2.594004
4	Lorentzian	0.899599	50.0014	3.998651	5.116295

FIGURE 3. Peak analysis and graph plotting. *Software: PeakFit by Jandel Scientific.*

everything from data acquisition to writing the final report.

In practice, many such packages (ASYST and LabTech NOTEBOOK are two of the most popular) are in use and have proven to be satisfactory. Many other individuals or laboratories choose instead to use smaller, separate packages, preferring either the lower cost or the increased flexibility and choice of function available with this option.

Laboratory Automation

One of the important applications of computer technology to scientific research has been in the field of laboratory automation and robotics. Laboratories handling large numbers of samples may now have sample handling, analysis, tracking, and recording all done automatically. Robotics, a specialized branch of computer technology, has given laboratories the capacity to automate the mechanical procedures such as aliquot handling, bar code reading, and reagent mixing with a much reduced possibility for error over that of purely human-controlled procedures.

Beyond the simple mechanics of carry-

ing out experimental procedures, one of the important uses of computer technology is now in data acquisition. By connecting the experimental apparatus to the computer, through some type of electronic transducer, experimental results can be transferred directly into the computer, eliminating the tedious and often error-ridden step of manual data entry.

Many software packages that perform data acquisition also include sophisticated analysis and report-generation procedures, so that data may be simultaneously viewed in "real time" (as results actually occur) and transformed by one or more mathematical procedures (Fourier transforms, for example) designed to indicate or emphasize underlying patterns that may occur in the data.

Word Processing

Although words are words, no matter what field they describe, scientific word processing presents special problems. Often, it is necessary to embed scientific equations in the text of an article, or to include graphic images as illustrative figures in a scientific paper or

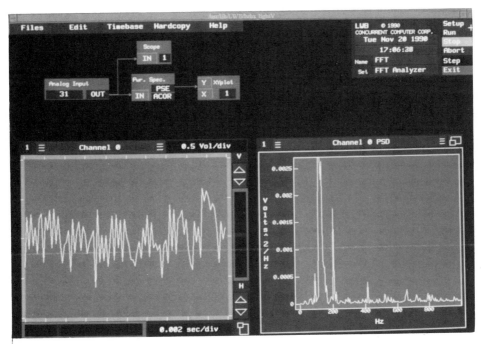

FIGURE 4. Data acquisition and analysis. *Software: Laboratory Workbench by Concurrent Computer Corporation.*

report. In the past, equations were carefully inked in by hand, and figures were cut out and pasted in, also by hand. Now, some general-market word processors include the ability to generate, manipulate, and print Greek letters, mathematical symbols, and logical symbols and to import graphic images as part of a document.

In addition to powerful popular packages such as Word and WordPerfect that include such capabilities, there are small "add-on" packages that can be used to generate equations and figures for inclusion in a document originally generated by a simple, general-purpose word processor.

Some mathematical packages that include equation processing capabilities (Theorist by Prescience, Inc.), as well as most of the large integrated database/analysis packages, also provide report-writing capabilities. Although the overall word processing functions of these packages are usually less extensive than those of large general-purpose word processors, they are specifically designed to include the functions, such as writing equations, desirable in preparing a scientific document.

The U.S. Office of Scientific Manpower estimates the number of scientists and engineers in the United States to be slightly in excess of seven million. Estimates of how many of these individuals directly use computer technology in their work varies. Five years ago, perhaps 10 percent of all scientists and engineers owned and used a personal computer. That number may easily have tripled by now, and will without doubt increase in the future. Now that software developments have increased the scope of problems that can be approached, and decreasing hardware costs have made it possible for individuals to have access to considerable computing power, computer technology is simply too useful for scientists to ignore, no matter what their field.

[*See also:* Astronomy, Computers in; Biological Use of Computers; Chemical Industry, Use of Computers in; Geology, Computers in; Laboratory Information Management Systems; Medical Imaging, Computer-Assisted; Meteorological Use of Computers.]

For Further Reading

Bryant, T. N., and J. W. T. Wimpenny, eds. 1989. *Computers in microbiology, a practical approach.* London: Oxford University Press (IRL Press).

Gjertsen, M. 1991. 1991 directory of physics courseware. *Computations in Physics* 5(1):71(56).

Orvis, W. J. 1989. *1-2-3 for scientists and engineers.* San Francisco: Sybex.

Smith, C. 1991. *The Mathematica graphics guidebook.* Reading, Mass.: Addison-Wesley.

Wilson, S. 1989. Chemistry by computer: An overview of the applications of computers in chemistry. *Journal of Chemical Information and Computer Sciences* 29:43.

Diana J. Gabaldon

SECURITIES INDUSTRY, COMPUTER USE IN

See Financial Services, Computer Use in

SECURITY, INFORMATION SYSTEMS

The information stored in computers is subject to loss, modification, or damage by intentional and unintentional acts. Intentional acts are known variously as computer fraud, computer crime, and computer abuse; unintentional acts are simply termed disasters. Information systems security is the set of actions organizations take to protect themselves from both computer abuse and disasters.

RISKS FROM ACCIDENTS AND NATURAL DISASTERS

Natural disasters such as flood, wind, or earthquake, and accidents such as fire, power failure, and breakdown of electrical, plumbing, and cooling systems pose threats to the continuous operation and integrity of organizational computing. The best organizations can do is to be prepared to recover from such catastrophes as quickly as possible, and with the minimal loss of data and functionality. Good contingency or disaster recovery planning will include (1) complete and secure backups of software and data stored at an off-site location and (2) off-site computer facilities for rapid recovery of operational capabilities. The following are the most common off-site facility arrangements.

Hot backup. An additional installation operates in parallel to the main installation and takes over immediately when the main site is damaged.

Warm backup. An additional installation is ready to become operational in a matter of hours.

Split site. Organizational computing is divided between two physical sites. One site can take over critical applications if the other is damaged.

Cold backup. An empty computing facility is ready for the immediate installation of new hardware.

Mutual backup: An agreement is made between two or more organizations to assist each other in case of damage to one organization's facilities.

Pooling. An arrangement is made among several organizations to maintain a "cold" or "warm" site ready for use by any member whose computing operations have been interrupted.

Insurance against losses. Although available to organizations, insurance is often insufficient to compensate for lost customers, contracts, or long-term consequences such as bankruptcy. Minimizing the risks of lost computer services through physical protection is often preferred to insurance arrangements.

RISKS FROM INTENTIONAL ACTS

The terms *computer fraud* and *computer crime* are often used interchangeably to mean the misuse of computer system assets to deceive intentionally, usually in violation of legal statutes or organizational rules. The category of computer fraud or computer crime does not include acts of sabotage, which do not necessarily involve deception and may not necessarily be illegal, but which do pose threats to operation of organizational information systems. *Computer abuse* is a more inclusive term used to refer to all types of security threats to organizational information systems.

Computer abuse is defined as the unauthorized, deliberate, and internally recognizable misuse of assets of the local organizational information system by individuals (Straub 1990), including violations against

1. hardware and other physical assets associated with computers (such as theft or damage to terminals, central processing units, disk drives, and printers);
2. programs (such as theft or modification of programs);
3. data (such as illegal copying or modification of data);
4. computer service (such as unauthorized use of service or purposeful interruption of service).

EXTENT OF THE SECURITY THREAT

To know accurately how much computer abuse really occurs is difficult. Various studies report a wide range of losses for organizations (American Institute of Certified Public Accountants [AICPA] 1984; Colton et al. 1982; Straub 1987). LaPlante (1987) cites an Ernst and Whinney study that reports a large percentage of major firms are uncovering one or more serious incidents of abuse each year, with 50 to 90 percent of the victims experiencing dollar losses.

There is also an important distinction between the computer abuse that occurs, abuse that has been discovered, and abuse that has been reported to the police. Discovered abuses are acts discovered by an organization but not necessarily reported to the media or police. Reported abuses are those acts reported to the police or media. Taken together, discovered and reported abuses are very likely only a portion of all the abuse that occurs.

HIGH RISK FACTOR FROM COMPUTER ABUSE

Although computer abuse is similar in nature to abuse of "manual" information systems, the nature of computerized information systems distinguishes them from their manual counterparts in several important ways.

High vulnerability. The high physical concentration of electronically stored information contributes to the risk that sensitive data can be destroyed, altered, or stolen. The equivalent of a file cabinet full of sensitive information can be copied to a diskette and carried out of the organization in a coat pocket or altered or destroyed with a single command.

Violation of the principle of separation of duties. The principle of separation of duties states that at least two independent processes involving separate persons should control each phase of a transaction. But with computers, various organizational groups process their information through a single processor and store it in a common working memory area or on a common set of storage devices. Checks and balances provided for by separate transactional controls may be invalidated in such a system.

Easy exploitation of system vulnerabilities. Once a system vulnerability is recognized, its exploitation can be programmed to occur in the absence of any human agent, at a time when the system is operating normally, and in ways that cover the audit trail and make detection or discovery extremely difficult.

Easy manipulation of large amounts of data. Fraudulent activities that require manipulation of large amounts of data and, therefore, are not possible under manual systems be-

come achievable with computer-based systems. In this respect computer technology makes new types of fraud possible.

Impersonal nature of systems. Because computer abuse is carried out against an impersonal machine and against what is often perceived to be an impersonal organization, perpetrators often rationalize their actions as not harming anyone.

In addition, END-USER COMPUTING increases the number of users accessing organizational data and hence increases the risk of abuse. User-developed applications may not be subject to the controlled development process used by professional systems developers. The lack of rigorous testing and integrity checking threatens data integrity and data security. Worldwide telecommunications networks represent a gateway to an organization's computing resources through which computer abuse may be perpetrated by both organization members and outsiders. Abuses carried out in this way can be very difficult to detect and trace. Organizational norms do not apply to persons outside the organization.

RISKS FROM INTENTIONAL ABUSE

In many ways, computer abuse is a typical amateur, white-collar crime or antisocial behavior and as such is perpetrated by persons who, in the pursuit of their occupations, normally abide by organizational policies and society's laws. Sanctions, therefore, may be able to reduce abuse significantly. Motivated by ignorance, a desire for pecuniary gain, or a wrong-headed playfulness, most abusers are willing to violate social norms, but are not so strongly motivated that either deterrent or preventive measures cannot inhibit them. In addition, the incidence of abuse as a result of misunderstanding between management and employees is undoubtedly very high.

The intentional abuse of organizational computer systems can best be understood by examining the different motivations of computer abusers. Criminologists have argued that motivation has a bearing on how to control antisocial behaviors. Straub and Widom (1984) developed a framework for linking motives to controls, thus allowing the determination of responses to particular motivational types.

Ethical ignorance. Although not a motivation for abuse, ethical ignorance characterizes abusers who, acting within their professional capacities, lack knowledge that their use of the computer is not acceptable to the owner of the information asset.

Personal gain. Abusers motivated by personal gain are aware that what they are doing is wrong or illegal but continue in spite of this knowledge. Amateur criminals, white-collar criminals, and embezzlers are examples of abusers motivated by personal gain.

Antisocial values. Abusers motivated by antisocial values are aware that their activity is socially unacceptable but proceed in spite of all sanctions. These persons may actually be reinforced by the antisocial values of their particular subculture. Career criminals and system crashers (see HACKING) belong to this motivational group.

Maliciousness. Abusers motivated by maliciousness have a clear sense of wrongdoing but believe they will escape the consequences of their actions by their mastery of the situation. Corrupt persons in high positions can dictate terms to lower ranking members of their organizations, thereby making prevention of malicious abuse almost impossible.

All of these motives will be present at one time or another in most organizational environments. In one study, Straub (1987) found that offenders were motivated first by desire for personal gain (30 percent), second by ignorance of proper professional conduct (26 percent), third by misguided playfulness (24 percent), and fourth by maliciousness (10 percent).

In protecting the organization against intentional abuse, the primary objective of computer security is to minimize undiscovered abuse through a combination of deterrent, preventive, and detection activities. Many potential perpetrators are deterred by administrative policies, employee training, and visible security functions. Some abusers are not deterred, though, and their attempted abuse must be thwarted by preventives such as passwords and other, more sophisticated access control mechanisms. If the preventives work, the attempt is foiled. If the preventives fail, however, detection through regular system audits may be the last avenue in attempting to uncover abuses.

Straub and Widom (1984) argue that deterrence by policy information is the most appropriate security measure to reduce abuses stemming from ethical ignorance. Deterrence by punishing cases of abuse and by maintaining a visible security presence is most effective for combatting abuse motivated by personal gain. Instituting effective access control is an appropriate measure for preventing abuse motivated by antisocial values. Abuses motivated by maliciousness are likely to be much more resistant to the rational deterrents and preventives available to systems security administrators. Detection through surveillance and monitoring of system activities may be the only appropriate measure for reducing malicious abuse.

These measures constitute the set of responses organizations may employ to combat computer abuse. Societal responses to computer abuse provide the legal framework within which detected computer abuse may be prosecuted.

FEDERAL LEGISLATION

Three major pieces of U.S. federal legislation are relevant to prosecuting computer abusers. The Counterfeit Access Device and Computer Fraud and Abuse Act of 1984 (contained within PL 98-473, 1984, Comprehensive Crime Control Act of 1984) addresses counterfeit access, such as credit card fraud, and computer fraud. These two components were separated in 1986 and the latter was subsumed under the Computer Fraud and Abuse Act of 1986 (PL 99-474, 1986). The importance of the 1986 law is that it defines certain aspects of computer abuse, such as access and data modification, that had not previously been defined as illegal and provides for severe penalties for violators.

The Computer Security Act of 1987 (PL 100-235, 1987) requires that security standards be developed for classified and unclassified federal data, and mandates that security plans and periodic security training be implemented on federal computer systems containing sensitive information.

The weakness of these three statutes is that they apply to *federal interest computers* only. A federal interest computer is a computer for the use of a financial institution or the U.S. government, or is one of two or more computers, used to commit an offense, that are not located in the same state (18 U.S.C. §1030). When federal interest is not present, definitions, prohibitions, and punishments are left to the discretion of individual states.

STATE LAW

State laws against computer misuse, which have been passed by forty-nine of the fifty states, vary widely and change rapidly. The National Center for Computer Crime Data reports the current status of state computer abuse laws. In the next decade, as society becomes more cognizant of the need to protect organizational information resources, clearer legal definitions and more comprehensive and consistent laws at both the state and federal levels are likely to come into effect.

PROTECTING INDIVIDUAL RIGHTS TO PRIVACY

Although computer abuse generally refers to the actions of individuals against organizational information resources, there are cases where information about individuals is misused and the organization itself is liable. Mason (1987) identified the basic information rights of individuals as (1) an individual's right to keep data about him or herself private, (2) an individual's right to ensure that data kept about him or her are accurate, (3) an individual's right to maintain owner-

ship of these data, and (4) an individual's right to have access to these data.

The Privacy Act of 1974 is intended to protect the privacy rights of individuals. This legislation, however, addresses only abuse by agencies of the federal government and does not cover abuse by state government agencies or in the private sector. A thorough review of key information liability issues facing organizations, including the protection of individual privacy rights, can be found in Straub and Collins (1990).

References

American Institute of Certified Public Accountants (AICPA). 1984. *Report on the study of EDP-related fraud in the banking and insurance industries*, pamphlet. New York: AICPA.

Colton, K. W., J. M. Tien, S. Tvedt Davis, B. Dunn, and A. I. Barnett. 1982. *Computer crime: Electronic fund transfer systems and crime.* Washington, D.C.: U.S. Department of Justice, Bureau of Justice Statistics.

LaPlante, A. 1987. Computer fraud and threat increasing, study says. *Infoworld*, 18 May 1987, p. 47.

Mason, R. O. 1987. Four ethical issues of the information age. *MIS Quarterly* 10(1):5–12.

Straub, D. W. 1987. Controlling computer abuse: An empirical study of effective security countermeasures. In *Proceedings of the Eighth International Conference on Information Systems, December 6–9, Pittsburgh, Pa.*

Straub, D. W., and R. Webb Collins. 1990. Key information liability issues facing managers: Software privacy, proprietary databases, and individual rights to privacy. *MIS Quarterly* 14(2):143–46.

Straub, D. W., and C. Spatz Widom. 1984. Deviancy by bits and bytes: Computer abusers and control measures. In J. H. Finch and E. G. Dougall, eds. *Computer security: A global challenge*, pp. 91–102. Amsterdam: Elsevier and IFIP.

For Further Reading

Parker, D. B. 1976. *Crime by computer.* New York: Scribner's.

———. 1981. *Computer security management.* Reston, Va.: Reston.

Straub, D. W. 1990. Effective IS security: An empirical study. *Information Systems Research* 1(3):255–76.

Michael D. Wybo
Detmar W. Straub

SIMULATION

Computer simulation is a very broad term encompassing many different kinds of problems, activities, and methods. Generally, though, it refers to a method of imitating, via a computer program of some sort, the behavior of a real system or process.

Studying a system or process often begins by building a logical/mathematical model of it. If the system or process is simple enough that a valid model of it is itself relatively simple, one may be able to use exact mathematical methods to study it. For instance, suppose one would like to understand how long customers in a fast-food restaurant are likely to have to wait in line. If the restaurant operates on a first-come, first-served queuing (waiting line) system, it could be modeled as a simple multiple-server queue with particular probability distributions to represent the times between successive customer arrivals and how long it takes to serve them. In this case, one might be able to get the answers (such as the average amount of time a customer stands in line or the average length of the line) from queuing theory. In such a case there is no need for simulation; in fact, simulation should not be used at all.

Suppose, however, that the restaurant actually operates in a more complicated way, and one wishes to incorporate these complications to get a realistic idea of how things will work. For example, customers may go away if the line is too long, or the number of servers may be adjusted in response to the arrival pattern or time of day. This results in a more realistic model, but also a more complicated one for which the mathematics of queuing theory fail us. In such cases, we turn to simulation as an alternative tool.

A *queuing* simulation can be used to model a wide variety of systems such as manufacturing lines, computer installations, communications systems, and transportation networks. Typically, these are very complicated queuing models, and simulation is the only real option in terms of studying them. Inventory systems can also be simulated to study issues such as the reorder policy. Both queuing and inventory simulations are *dynamic*, that is, are concerned with models in which conditions change through time.

Other simulations, though, do not have a time element; they are called *static*. For instance, a detailed financial model could be built and expressed with an electronic spreadsheet. One could then study what would happen to various key financial performance measures if interest rates were to rise or a supplier were to raise prices.

Another dimension along which simulations are classified is according to whether they contain random components. In a queuing simulation, for example, we generally model service times as being observations on some random variable whose probability distribution expresses the behavior of the real service times in terms of their mean, dispersion, and so forth. These are called *stochastic* simulations, and an important characteristic of them is that their results must be regarded as random as well, that is, not exact. On the other hand, a *deterministic* simulation does not contain any random inputs; its outputs, then, are also nonrandom and can be regarded as exact.

How one actually carries out a simulation depends heavily on the type of simulation involved. Dynamic simulation models can be coded in general-purpose languages like C or FORTRAN, but are more typically written in a special-purpose simulation language. Static simulations can often be coded in a general-purpose language or even in an electronic spreadsheet.

Once a simulation model is built and coded, one must ask whether the model is a valid representation of the real system; this is called *validation*. Furthermore, one must be sure that the model's expression in the computer code is correct; this is called *verification*.

Validation and verification in simulation can follow the same principles used for computer programs in general, but there are opportunities in simulation to do some special checks. For instance, most languages for dynamic simulation can create a *trace,* a detailed, step-by-step history of the model. This can be examined to look for errors and inconsistencies.

The difficulty in carrying out a simulation is roughly proportional to the complexity of the system to be modeled; however, there are very good software products to ease the task. (In fact, one must be careful in using a high-level product to make sure that it has the flexibility and capability to express the desired model.)

Perhaps the most important limitation of simulation (and one that is often overlooked) is that, in the case of a stochastic simulation, we do not get "exact" answers to our questions. Returning to the restaurant example, a queuing model could tell us that the expected time a customer has to stand in line is 3.6 minutes; this is exact. A simulation, however, might produce an observed average time in queue of 3.2 minutes on one run and 4.7 minutes on the next. Just as the restaurant itself does not operate in the same way every day, a simulation of it does not produce the same results every time. For this reason, it is essential to recognize that a stochastic simulation is an experiment, and its results must be regarded as random. Appropriate statistical tools must be used to interpret simulation output data.

The appeal and power of simulation is that it can be used to study extraordinarily complex systems for which exact mathematical analyses are virtually impossible. Thus, it provides a method of asking difficult questions about complex situations to gain insight at a fraction of the cost of studying the real system physically.

For Further Reading

Law, A. M., and W. D. Kelton. 1991. *Simulation modeling and analysis.* 2nd ed. New York: McGraw-Hill.

Morgan, B. J. T. 1984. *Elements of simulation.* London: Chapman and Hall.

Pritsker, A. A. B. 1986. *Introduction to simulation and SLAM II.* New York: Halsted Press (Wiley).

Schriber, T. J. 1991. *An introduction to simulation using GPSS/H.* New York: Wiley.

W. David Kelton

SIMULATION LANGUAGES

The design of complex computer-based systems will depend ever more heavily on simulation studies of realistic models. By computer-based systems we mean systems where computerization plays an essential role in almost all aspects of operation. Examples of computer-based systems are computer-integrated and flexible manufacturing, automation and robotics, large communication networks, and computerized process control. Powerful languages and workstations have been developed for modeling and simulation of such complex systems (see Garzia et al. 1986 for a general review). Although model building can be traced back at least as far as Newton, it received a tremendous impetus with the advent of the electronic computer. There are at least two main sources of approach and technique—from physical science and operations research.

Physical scientists, especially in the applied and engineering branches, are faced with increasingly complex equations—combinations of general laws and empirical relations—for which analytic solutions are of limited use. In response, automatic solvers of differential equations were developed, whose operation is based on an isomorphy (exact analogy) between the model's behavior and that of some particular natural medium such as mechanical motion of gears or flow of electrical currents. For example, an electronic analog computer uses the fact that circuits of resistors and capacitors can be readily created that are described by differential equations identical with those of diverse systems such as heat flow in a building, growth of populations, orbiting satellites, and so on. Electronic analog computers saw heavy use in the chemical and aerospace industries, among others.

Limitations on problem size and on stability and accuracy of analog computation led to harnessing of the emerging electronic digital computers to achieve equivalent capabilities. The latter perform integration numerically, using principles that originated with long-known manual approximation methods (Hamming 1973); however, what gave digital computers eventual primacy was their information processing abilities: simulation programming languages could be designed that would provide for convenient specification, processing, and manipulation of differential equation models (Forrester 1973, Pugh 1972, Chu 1969, Korn 1989, Cellier 1990). Analog computation survives today in the form of hybrid computers that place analog-based behavior generation under the control of digital information processing.

The second source of approach and technique lay in operations research with its desire to ameliorate industrial processing networks plagued by congestion, unproductive delays, and underutilization of resources. New concepts of discrete event systems were developed that (in the beginning) had little to do with the classic modeling concepts. An associated development was the use of random numbers to include the effects of chance in outcomes within the computation, originally known as Monte-Carlo methods.

As the field matures, the emphasis is shifting from simulation, as a set of computational techniques, to modeling, whether it be in a continuous or a discrete form (or in forms that combine the two) (Ören 1987). Indeed, simulation is best viewed as experimentation with models (Korn 1989). Shannon (1975) emphasizes the experimental orientation of simulation techniques but widens the term *simulation* to include modeling and design activities. Other definitions try to characterize simulation narrowly to distinguish it from other computational techniques (Pritsker 1979). This distinction lies in the fact that simulation tools make it possible to develop a (hypothetical) description of the internal structure of a real system to the level of detail that the modeler perceives in reality. This power of representation distinguishes simulation from analytical techniques; however, it also places responsibilities on the modeler, such as the choice of the level of detail compatible with the objectives of the modeling effort, the real-system data available, and the computational and human resources at one's disposal. To write a detailed description of a system (i.e., a model) is one thing; to verify that it reflects one's intentions and then to validate it as a true description of the real system is another.

FRAMEWORK FOR SIMULATION MODELING

Simulation modeling provides a means of specifying a mathematical object called a system (Zeigler 1976). Basically, a system has a time base, inputs, states, and outputs, and functions for determining next states and outputs given current states and inputs. Discrete event systems represent certain constellations of such parameters just as continuous systems do. For example, the inputs in discrete event systems occur at arbitrarily spaced moments, whereas those in continuous systems are piecewise continuous functions of time.

Figure 1 depicts a conceptual framework for a modeling and simulation enterprise. It concerns three basic objects (Zeigler 1976):

- The *real system*, in existence or proposed, which is regarded as fundamentally a source of data.

- The *model*, which is a set of instructions for generating data comparable to those ob-

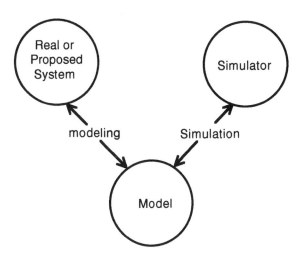

FIGURE 1. Entities and relations in simulation.

servable in the real system. The structure of the model is its set of instructions. The behavior of the model is the set of all possible data that can be generated by faithfully executing the model instructions.

- The *simulator*, which exercises the model's instructions to actually generate its behavior.

The basic objects are related by two relations:

- The *modeling relation*, linking real system and model, defines how well the model represents the system or entity being modeled. In general terms, a model can be considered valid if the data generated by the model agree with the data produced by the real system in an experimental frame of interest.
- The *simulation relation*, linking model and simulator, represents how faithfully the simulator is able to carry out the instructions of the model.

A crucial element must be brought into this picture—the experimental frame. This captures how the modeler's objectives impact on model construction, experimentation, and validation. An experimental frame specifies such items as the input stimuli to be fed to the model, including the generation of random variables, the outputs to observed and the associated collection of statistics, and the conditions under which experimentation should start, continue, and be terminated.

The basic items of data produced by a system or model are *time segments*. These time segments are mappings from intervals defined over a specified time base to values in the ranges of one or more variables. The variables can either be observed or measured.

TRADITIONAL SIMULATION LANGUAGES

Simscript II (Kiviat et al. 1968), Simula (Dahl and Nygaard 1966), GASP II (Pritsker and Kiviat 1969), GPSS (Schriber 1974), and SIMAN (Pedgen 1983) are popular languages for discrete event simulation. CSMP (Chu 1969), Dynamo (Pugh 1972), DESIRE (Korn 1989), and ACSL (Cellier 1990) are counterparts for continuous models. Such languages provide facilities for model and experimental frame specification.

Discrete event simulation languages focus on discrete changes of variable values and generate time segments that are piecewise constant. Thus, an event is a change in a variable value that occurs instantaneously. We distinguish events, which are changes in value, from event-generating mechanisms. The latter are simulation constructs (often called event routines) that at certain (scheduled) times determine whether an event actually occurs and what new values for variables are established. In essence a discrete event model tells how to generate new values for variables and the times the new values should take effect. An important aspect of discrete event simulation is that the time intervals between event occurrences are variable (in constrast to discrete time where the time step is a fixed number).

The three standard so-called "world views" for discrete event model specification —event scheduling, activity scanning, and process interaction—provide alternative means of model representation (Kiviat 1971). Zeigler (1984) showed that all world views have the same ability to express model behaviors. Thus, any advantage a particular world view has lies in the ease with which modelers can develop a match to the real world system they wish to represent.

Event scheduling languages provide means for scheduling events. The underlying world view of these languages may be characterized as event driven. That is, it is event routines that make things happen to objects but the events need not be directly linked to actions of objects. A simulation of chemical reactions at the molecular level provides an example. Here vast numbers of collisions are the events that trigger changes in states of colliding molecules. In writing such a model, one concentrates on how collisions schedule other collisions to occur, thus advancing the model through time.

Activity scanning languages view a system as consisting of a concurrent set of activities, each with its own conditions for activation and its own working time. An example is that of a shipping port in which boats and machines are involved in a number of activities including docking and undocking, loading and unloading, entering and leaving the port, and so on. Events in such models are directly associated with objects; indeed, the initiation and termination of activities would be characterized by events in the event scheduling approach.

Process interaction languages (Franta 1977) view a system as composed of processes, which are sequences, or cycles, of activities carried out by objects. This view would treat the shipping port as containing a collection of ships that each engage in a process, or sequence of activities, such as entering the port, docking, unloading the cargo, loading new cargo, and leaving the port.

OBJECT-ORIENTED SIMULATION

A variety of *object-oriented programming languages* have been developed: Smalltalk (Goldberg and David 1983), LOOPS (Bobrow and Stefik 1983), Flavors (Weinreb et al. 1983), C++, and CLOS (Keene 1988). Interestingly, the connection between discrete event simulation and object-oriented programming is quite old. The discrete event simulation language Simula (Dahl and Nygaard 1966) introduced class inheritance and association of both procedures and data structures with class instances. Simula allowed real-world objects to be directly represented by model counterparts whose behavior could be described by processes of activities. New languages have emerged for object-oriented simulation (Klahr 1986, Middleton and Zanconato 1986, Ruiz-Mier and Talavage 1989, Bryan 1989, Lomow and Baezner 1989); however, more than just a simulation tool, the object-oriented perspective also lends itself to the higher level of systems design in which complex processes and systems may be usefully encapsulated in objects (Zeigler 1990).

HIERARCHICAL, MODULAR SIMULATION

New simulation languages are being designed that enable real-world objects to be modeled in a systems framework. For exam-ple the DEVS-Scheme environment (Zeigler 1990) is an implementation of the DEVS formalism in Scheme (a LISP dialect), which enables the modeler to specify models directly as systems. DEVS-Scheme supports building models in a hierarchical, modular manner. This is a systems-oriented approach not possible in the popular commercial simulation languages discussed above. Hierarchical, modular system specifications have the following properties:

- **Modularity:** Model specifications are self-contained and have input and output ports through which all interaction with the external world must take place. Ports provide a level of delayed binding that needs to be resolved only when models are coupled together.

- **Closure under coupling:** Models may be connected together by coupling of input and output ports to create larger, coupled models, having the same interface properties as the components.

- **Hierarchical construction:** This follows as a consequence of modularity and closure under coupling; successively more complex models can be built by using as building blocks the coupled models already constructed.

- **Standalone and bottom-up testability:** Because of input/output modularity, models are independently verifiable at every stage of hierarchical construction. This fosters secure and incremental bottom-up synthesis of complex models.

- **Experimental frame model separation:** Experimental frames are independently realized as models of special kinds—generators, transducers, acceptors. Having input/output ports, they can be coupled to models to which they are applicable.

For further information you may read the books by Delaney and Vaccari (1989) on both discrete and continuous simulation, Cellier (1990) on continuous modeling and simulation, and Zeigler (1976, 1984, 1990) on systems and discrete event modeling.

[Research on this topic was supported by NASA and by McDonnell Douglas Space Systems.]

References

Bobrow, D. G., and M. J. Stefik. 1983. *The LOOPS manual.* Palo Alto, Calif.: Xerox Corporation.

Bryan, O. F. 1989. MODSIM II—an object-oriented simulation language for sequential and parallel processors. In *Proceedings of the Winter Simulation Conference,* pp. 205–10. La Jolla, Calif.: Soc. for Computer Simulation.

Cellier, F. E. 1990. *Continuous modelling and simulation.* Berlin: Springer-Verlag.

Chu, Y. 1969. *Digital simulation of continuous systems.* New York: McGraw-Hill.

Dahl, O. J. and K. Nygaard. 1966. Simula: An Algol-based simulation language. *Communications of the ACM* 9:671–88.

Delaney, W., and E. Vaccari. 1989. *Dynamic models and discrete event simulation.* New York: Marcel Dekker.

Forrester, J. W. 1973. *World dynamics.* Cambridge, Mass.: Wright-Allen Press.

Franta, W. R. 1977. *The process view of simulation.* Amsterdam: North-Holland.

Garzia, R. F., M. R. Garzia, and B. P. Zeigler. 1986. Discrete event simulation. *IEEE Spectrum,* Dec., pp. 32–36.

Goldberg, A., and R. David. 1983. *Smalltalk-80: The language and its application.* Reading, Mass.: Addison-Wesley.

Hamming, R. W. 1973. *Numerical methods for scientists and engineers.* New York: McGraw-Hill.

Keene, S. E. 1988. *Programming in common LISP object-oriented system.* Reading, Mass.: Addison-Wesley.

Kiviat, P. J. 1971. Simulation languages. In T. H. Naylor, ed. *Computer simulation experiments with models of economic systems.* New York: Wiley.

Kiviat, P. J., R. Villaneuva, and H. M. Markowitz. 1968. *The Simscript II programming language.* Englewood Cliffs, N.J.: Prentice-Hall.

Klahr, P. 1986. Expressibility in ROSS, an object-oriented simulation system. In G. C. Vansteenkiste, E. J. H. Kerckhoffs, and B. P. Zeigler, eds. *Artificial intelligence in simulation.* San Diego, Calif.: SCS Publications.

Korn, G. A. 1989. *Interactive dynamic system simulation.* New York: McGraw-Hill.

Lomow, G., and D. Baezner. 1989. A tutorial introduction to object-oriented simulation and SIM++. In *Proceedings of the Winter Simulation Conference,* pp. 140–46. La Jolla, Calif.: Soc. For Computer Simulation.

Middleton, S., and R. Zanconato. 1986. BLOBS: An object-oriented language for simulation and reasoning. In G. C. Vansteenkiste, E. J. H. Kerckhoffs, and B. P. Zeigler, eds. *Artificial intelligence in simulation,* pp. 130–35. San Diego, Calif.: SCS Publications.

Ören, T. I. 1987. Taxonomy of simulation model processing. In M. Singh, ed. *Encyclopedia of systems and control.* Elmsford, N.Y.: Pergamon Press.

Pedgen, C. D. 1983. *Introduction to SIMAN.* Proceedings, Winter Simulation Conference. San Diego, Calif.: SCS Publications.

Pritsker, A. A. B. 1979. Compilation of definitions of simulation. *Simulation* 33:61–63.

Pritsker, A. A. B., and P. J. Kiviat. 1969. *Simulation with GASP II.* Englewood Cliffs, N.J.: Prentice-Hall.

Pugh, A. L. 1972. *DYNAMO II user's manual.* Cambridge, Mass.: MIT Press.

Ruiz-Mier, S., and J. Talavage. 1989. A Hybrid Paradigm for Modeling of Complex Systems. In L. A. Widman, K. A. Loparo, and N. Nielsen, eds. *Artificial intelligence, simulation and modelling,* pp. 381–95. New York: Wiley.

Schriber, T. J. 1974. *Simulation using GPSS.* New York: Wiley.

Shannon, R. E. 1975. *Systems simulation: The art and the science.* Englewood Cliffs, N.J.: Prentice-Hall.

Weinreb, D., D. Moon, and R. Stallman. 1983. *Lisp machine manual.* Cambridge, Mass.: MIT.

Zeigler, B. P. 1976. *Theory of modelling and simulation.* New York: Wiley (reissued by Krieger Pub. Co., Malabar, Fla., 1985).

———. 1984. *Multifacetted modelling and discrete event simulation.* London/Orlando, Fla.: Academic Press.

———. 1990. *Object-oriented simulation with hierarchical modular models: Intelligent agents and endomorphic systems.* Boston: Academic Press.

Bernard P. Zeigler

SMALLTALK

See Object-Oriented Programming

SOCIAL IMPACTS OF COMPUTING

Macroergonomics (or social factors) is the study of the social impacts of computing. Computers change relationships among individuals by altering the way they communicate and make decisions. Computers influence cultural beliefs and values by giving us new concepts of ourselves and the world. Computerization changes the structure of business and government organizations and affects social institutions such as education, the family, and the military. It alters the political, economic, and legal arrangements of society, and has an impact on international relations. Because of the great flexibility in computer application design, social impacts are not easy to predict. One goal of macroergonomics is to help us make choices that avoid negative social impacts and promote desirable ones. This article discusses only a few of the impacts of computing. They occur in virtually every aspect of social life.

COMMUNICATION AND SOCIAL INTERACTION

Computer-mediated communication (e.g., electronic mail and computer conferencing systems) changes the rules of conversation by removing elements of emotion and social control. Studies of interruption patterns in conversations show that men in the United States interrupt women over 80% of the time. Similar patterns occur between high- and low-status people. Computer-mediated communication eliminates some inequality in conversation, because we cannot see the physical characteristics that give higher-ranking or verbally aggressive people an advantage in face-to-face speech. Computer designs to support cooperative work create opportunities for participation and group decision making. Designs for the physically

disabled, now required by law in U.S. workplaces, open up new possibilities for those whose activities have been severely restricted. But computer-mediated communication can reinforce unequal participation, as in workplace surveillance. Computer interfaces are a more subtle case of inequality. Because interfaces appear to many computer users as things to which they must adapt, designers' choices have the power to control users' behavior.

In some computer-mediated communication it is difficult to tell with whom we are conversing. If we think of ourselves as engaged in conversation with an anonymous network, we lose sight of the humans whose programs and messages we are using. Research shows that network users do focus more on the message and less on the person who sent it. This tendency to focus on statements of fact rather than emotional evaluations can be a positive social impact. Delegates to the International Law of the Sea Conference solved the problem of how to divide the costs and benefits of seabed mining in international waters by using a computer model to evaluate their individual proposals. Delegates were able to distance themselves from feelings of national pride and suspicion of other nations' intentions. Other studies of computer-mediated communication report a reduction in cooperation and a lengthening of decision-making time, as well as an increase in participants' willingness to change their opinions. Slow typing speeds explain much of the increased decision-making time. Participants in computer-mediated decision making often seem "out of control" because the visual expressions of approval or disapproval we ordinarily use to exert social control are missing. Unconventional decisions are more likely in computer-mediated communication, which is a negative impact when conservative judgment is needed and a positive impact when innovative solutions are sought.

The negative effects of computer-based communication—loss of face-to-face contact, strains on trust, and reduction in social control—are balanced by the possibilities for formation of new communities around electronic networks. Unlike most electronic mail systems, bulletin boards are designed to support conversations among many participants. Problems reported by bulletin board operators include the exchange of pirated software, the use of inflammatory language, and vandalism by hackers. Social control has not been well established in the culture of most electronic communities.

CULTURE AND SOCIAL CONTROL

Culture is the entire way of life shared by a people. It includes both their material possessions and their shared beliefs, values, and patterns of behavior. Culture controls people's behavior in the sense that it gives them models of appropriate conduct. Computerization can contribute to changing beliefs, as when computer models of global warming increase people's concern for environmental protection. Computer use can change what people value. For example, some expert skills become devalued when a nonexpert using a computer can accomplish the same task or the task can be performed by a fully automatic system. Critics of artificial intelligence fear that human judgment will be replaced by calculation or that rational thought will become devalued when it is seen as a characteristic of machines. As computers become important in a culture, a higher social value is placed on the ability to understand and use them. Having control over computer resources increases a person's status, as does having power over others by means of a computer.

The cultural values of privacy and property are being transformed as computerization makes information about individuals and computer-based intellectual property easier to collect and access. Some kinds of intellectual property, like commercial mailing lists, are both property and information about individuals. Other proprietary databases contain public information (e.g., data gathered at taxpayer expense) that has become the private property. It is not yet clear how we will balance the values of privacy, property, and public information in a computerized society.

Communities within a society create subcultures. Organizations have different corporate cultures that define how people are to behave at work. Computer-aided white-collar crime is a growing problem in companies whose corporate cultures are ineffective at deterring illegal and unethical behavior. Subcultures often develop among users of special-interest computer networks. Hackers, although a small group, have a subculture that is particularly disturbing in a computerized society. Their existence reminds people of the vulnerability of computers. Like other deviant subcultures, hackers often serve as scapegoats, receiving the blame for computer malfunctions or crime committed within organizations by authorized computer users. Most cultures find it easier to blame outsiders than to take a serious look at their own internal problems. The social impulse to control hackers and white-collar criminals by restricting access to computerized data and by using computer technology for surveillance of employees and citizens interferes with the advantages of computers for communication, information sharing, group decision making, and efficient organizational function.

Although widely shared ethical values are the most effective means of protecting society from computer abuses, many people look to laws and law enforcement for the solution of computer problems. Although the control of crime is the most widely publicized legal issue in computing, intellectual property has presented the legal system with some of its greatest challenges. If computer-based information is property, it will be taxed and regulated as are other products, and it will be subject to product liability law. This means that courts must find a way to allocate responsibility for any damage done by computer software. In the case of expert systems and other artificial intelligence programs, it is difficult to decide which individuals and corporations to hold responsible for the social costs of computer errors. If computer data transmission is speech, it falls under the protection of the First Amendment of the U.S. Constitution. Because the technologies for television and radio broadcasting are now merging with those for cable and telephone transmission, laws regulating information are becoming increasingly unable to distinguish between the electronic transmissions of speech and property. Some analysts believe that speech will prevail in our cultural definition of computer-based information, with a resulting decline in copyright protections. Others see an expansion of copyright and patent protections for intellectual property that threatens First Amendment rights.

COMPUTERIZED WORK AND ORGANIZATIONAL DECISIONS

Computerization does not have a simple impact on work. Fast food restaurant systems can be designed for employees who push buttons with pictures of french fries. These low-paid workers develop few skills enabling them to move into better jobs. Computer-aided design for engineers speeds up time-consuming drafting and calculating, freeing skilled employees for more creative problem-solving tasks. Computer-aided engineering also has a tendency to eliminate jobs as drafting becomes part of the engineer's work. Both fast food workers and engineers are more productive using computers. But the two styles of computerization have very different impacts on working conditions and on job opportunities in society. Although it is too soon to see the overall impact of computerized work, some analysts see a "declining middle," with fewer jobs for middle-skill levels and two emerging classes of computerized worker.

When work depends on a group of individuals coordinating their efforts, computerization can reduce productivity if it interferes with people's ability to communicate and discuss common problems and tasks. Organizational interfaces are the parts of a computer system that connect human users to one another. Other kinds of organizational interfaces are management tools for keeping track of resources and tasks. The design choices for such interfaces incorporate choices about whether power and decision-making authority should be widely distributed or centralized in hierarchical structures. If organizational interfaces are designed primarily to monitor activities and allocate tasks to people, they become the instruments of managerial control to super-

vise and coordinate individual activities without providing the social interactions necessary for cooperative work. Effective designs for cooperative work include such features as video conferencing and mixed voice, image, and text exchanges. One test of a cooperative work design is the speed with which a group of geographically scattered workers can use the system to order a pizza with a selection of toppings. This familiar group decision-making process illustrates what sort of social interactions occur during more serious examples of cooperative work. For managers, the dilemma of computerized work lies in achieving a balance between controlling employee activities and giving them enough access to the computer and to one another to perform their jobs well. When managers choose to maximize control, the work tends to become bureaucratic, less productive, and unsatisfying for both employees and their clients or customers. When people have more autonomy, they tend to be more committed to and satisfied with their jobs.

With computer-based data and models, organizational decision makers can find out what is happening sooner and respond more quickly and on the basis of better information. Although computer use can reduce the risks of making decisions based on uncertain information, the actual risks of failure may be inadvertently increased. More rapid response time can even be a problem, as when the computerization of stock market trading destabilized the market. When complex organizations computerize their information gathering and some of their actual decision making, disastrous systems accidents can occur. Why? Perhaps the computer models being used do not represent the underlying reality, or maybe truly complex computer software can never be completely tested to remove bugs. Organizational decision makers often use computer information to justify their decisions, especially when they are involved in conflicts with those who do not have access to the data. They also have a tendency to blame computers, programmers, and computer operators for their own decision errors.

Military decision making, which tends to be hierarchical, has influenced the entire history of U.S. computing. Since World War

II, the military has been the main funding source for computer research. Military needs have created much of the demand for computer hardware and software. The Strategic Defense Initiative (SDI, or Star Wars) was a controversial effort to defend the United States against nuclear war by building an automated antiballistic missile system. The controversy was whether a huge, untestable computer program could be trusted not to malfunction. The great majority of computer professionals believed that SDI would not work, but often found that their opportunities for employment or research were SDI related. With the political transformation of the Soviet Union and the Gulf War, military interest has been focused on computer applications to conventional warfare. Smart weapons such as the Patriot Missile may actually increase the risk of war by convincing the public that warfare can spare civilians and avoid casualties on the side with the best weapons. A nuclear war was publicly unthinkable. Small wars shown on television with video game imagery may become acceptable elements of U.S. international relations. With the growth of Japanese and Western European computer industries aided by their governments and aimed at civilian applications, some analysts question the wisdom of continuing to link U.S. expenditures on defense and computer development. They believe that more government support for commercial developments would be the best way to make the U.S. computer industry internationally competitive.

COMPUTER CHOICES

Computer applications can be designed for communications or surveillance, for cooperative problem solving or for hierarchical control, for military weapons or for consumer products and services. The social impacts of computing depend on the choices a society makes as it computerizes. The power to make these choices is not evenly distributed, even in a democracy. So far, business, political, and military decision makers have determined the majority of society's computer choices. If this continues, we may expect to see more protection of intellectual property at the expense of individual privacy and public information, more value placed on hierarchical control than on citizen and employee empowerment, and more sophistication in weapons than in consumer products and services.

[See also: Ethics and Computers.]

For Further Reading

Beniger, J. 1986. *The control revolution: Technological and economic origins of the information society.* Cambridge, Mass.: Harvard University Press.

Burnham, D. 1983. *The rise of the computer state.* New York: Random House.

Dertouzos, M., and J. Moses, eds. 1980. *The computer age: A twenty-year view.* Cambridge, Mass.: MIT Press.

Dreyfus, H., and S. Dreyfus. 1986. *Mind over machine: The power of human intuition and expertise in the era of the computer.* New York: Free Press.

Dunlop, C., and R. Kling, eds. 1991. *Computers and controversy: Value conflicts and social choices.* Boston: Academic Press.

Fletcher, J. C. 1984. *Report of the study on eliminating the threat posed by nuclear ballistic missiles.* Washington, D.C.: Department of Defense Technologies Study Team.

Goldkind, S. *Machines and intelligence: A critique of arguments against the possibility of artificial intelligence.* Westport, Conn.: Greenwood Press.

Grief, I., ed. 1988. *Computer-supported cooperative work: A book of readings.* San Mateo, Calif.: Morgan Kaufmann.

Hartman, H., R. E. Kraut, and L. A. Tilly, eds. 1986. *Computer chips and paper clips: Technology and women's employment.* Washington, D.C.: National Academy Press.

Johnson, D. G., and J. W. Snapper, eds. 1983. *Ethical issues in the use of computers.* Belmont, Calif.: Wadsworth.

Kraemer, K. L., S. Dickhoven, S. Fallows Tierney, and J. King. 1987. *Datawars: The politics of federal policymaking.* New York: Columbia University Press.

Kraut, R. E. 1987. *Technology and the transformation of white-collar work.* Hillsdale, N.J.: Lawrence Erlbaum.

Laudon, K. C. 1986. *Dossier society: Value choices in the design of national information* systems. New York: Columbia University Press.

Levy, S. 1984. *Hackers: Heroes of the computer revolution.* Garden City, N.Y.: Anchor/Doubleday.

Perrolle, J. A. 1987. *Computers and social change: Information, property, and power.* Belmont, Calif.: Wadsworth.

Pool, Ithiel de Sola. 1986. *Technologies of freedom.* Cambridge, Mass.: MIT Press.

Tirman, J., ed. 1986. *Empty promise: The growing case against Star Wars.* Boston: Beacon Press.

Turkle, S. 1984. *The second self: Computers and the human spirit.* New York: Simon and Schuster.

U.S. Congress, Office of Technology Assessment. 1986. *Intellectual property rights in an age of electronics and information.* Washington, D.C.: U.S. Government Printing Office.

————. 1987. *The electronic supervisor: New technology, new tension.* Washington, D.C.: U.S. Government Printing Office.

U.S. National Institute on Disability and Rehabilitation Research. 1987. *Access to information technology by users with disabilities: Initial guidelines.* Washington, D.C.: Federal Information Resources Management, General Services Administration.

Weizenbaum, J. 1976. *Computer power and human reason: From judgment to calculation.* San Francisco: Freeman.

Wiener, N. 1967. *The human use of human beings.* New York: Avon Books.

Zuboff, S. 1988. *In the age of the smart machine: The future of work and power.* New York: Basic Books.

Judith A. Perrolle

SOCIAL SCIENCE APPLICATIONS OF COMPUTERS

Although quantitative approaches to social science can be traced back to the work of Harold Lasswell and the public opinion research of Stouffer and others in the 1930s and 1940s, and to the rise of behavioral approaches to social science in the 1950s, social science computing became widespread only after IBM's release of the System 360 series of computers in 1964. The development of the Statistical Package for Social Science (SPSS) by Norman Nie and others followed, leading to an era in which knowledge of SPSS became required of most graduate students. Although BMDP and SAS statistical packages also became popular in the social sciences, social science computing in the mainframe era (1964–1980) was equated with statistical processing and data management associated with it. The Inter-University Consortium for Political and Social Research (ICPSR) at the University of Michigan arose as the dominant data management and distribution service for the social sciences.

When microcomputing became popular in social science after IBM's introduction of the PC in 1980, however, social science computing quickly came to mean much more than statistics. Among the most popular application areas have been data management, word processing and text management, mapping, and instruction, but dozens of specialized application areas exist. By the 1990s, much of social science research and instruction had shifted from mainframe to microcomputer platforms, though the large datasets (e.g., U.S. Census) associated with social science have preserved a strong role for mainframe applications. Microcomputer usage in social science is overwhelmingly based on MS-DOS (as of 1991), though Macintosh systems have made significant inroads in psychology, which sometimes also still uses Apple II systems for instrument control.

APPLICATIONS IN SOCIAL SCIENCE

Statistical Analysis

Statistical analysis is the mainstay of social science computing. The leader is still SPSS-X (SPSS Inc.) for the mainframe and SPSS/PC+ for PCs, also now available for the OS/2 operating system, featuring all the power of the mainframe version with no data limitations. In economics, SAS (SAS Institute) is probably more widespread, because of its superior data management and business graphics features. SAS is also available for PCs and for the OS/2 operating system. BMDP has been popular in psychology because of its biomedical associations. Systat (Systat, Inc.) is the newest of the top four statistics packages, now featuring a user-friendly menu system and superior graphics, including three-dimensional data rotation. Figure 1 illustrates typical Systat output, in this case a scatterplot matrix. Scatterplot matrices are used for multivariate visual analysis of the interactions of three variables, in this case cigarette pricing, consumption, and year.

Survey research is a related domain that has become heavily computerized in recent years. Computer-assisted telephone interviewing (CATI), although available since the 1970s (Fink 1983), has become popular as a convenient, cost-efficient survey method. Computerized survey instruments have been shown to have greater stability, require less time, and elicit more honest responses (Vasu and Garson 1990). Disk-by-mail surveys are also increasing in use, as is the use of bar code technology. No one software package dominates survey research. QPL (Questionnaire Programming Language), which is

available from the National Technical Information Service, is widely used in government. Other popular packages are ParSurvey (Economics Research Inc.), Ci2 (Sawtooth Software), and the Microcase Aggregate Analysis Program (Cognitive Development).

Data Management

There are almost innumerable computerized datasets directly of interest to social scientists. The most common format is still the standard data file (SDF, also called column-aligned ASCII) because of its compatibility with many mainframe packages. Other common formats are dBASE DBF, Lotus WK1, SPSS SYS, DIF data interchange format, and comma-delimited ASCII. Many databases are available through the ICPSR, noted earlier, and others can be found on-line in Computer-Readable Databases (CRDB), File 230 on DIALOG, which had more than 6,000 listings as of 1990.

The Bureau of the Census makes available many datasets used by social scientists. These include not only the TIGER files from the population census, but also County Statistics on compact-disk read-only memory (CD-ROM), with more than 1,000 variables on all counties, and *County and City Data Book 1988* on CD-ROM.

The United Nations and foreign governments also release datasets used by social scientists. An example is the *United Nations Disability Statistics Data Base, 1975–1985: Technical Manual*, now available on microcomputer diskette.

Other social science datasets include the Time Series Library (CoWorks), which is a menu-driven package for accessing and displaying data series on social indicators (crime, education, politics), economics, demographics, and other data for the world, a continent, or a nation. Some series go back to the late nineteenth century.

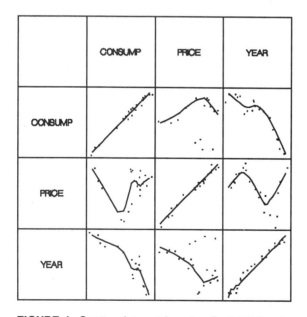

FIGURE 1. Scatterplot matrix using Systat 5.0 software.

Word Processing and Text Management

Social science echoes other domains in the widespread use of word processing, often through the WordPerfect package. Word processing features of special interest to social scientists are footnoting, indexing, importation of spreadsheet and database information, use of the equation editor to display complex formulas, use of graphics features to incorporate charts and maps, and bibliographic management features. Mail merge has a special social science use in survey research, which is now a heavily computerized subfield.

Content analysis is a special social science interest as social science data are often in the form of text archives, not numeric tables. Computerized analysis of text content is based on word counts. For instance, content analysis can be used to analyze media imagery with regard to a particular public policy. The techniques are described by Robert Philip Weber of Harvard University (Weber 1990). Many content analysis procedures discussed are implemented in TEXTPACK V, a comprehensive text analysis system available at nominal cost from the Computer Department, ZUMA, The Center for Surveys, Methods, and Analysis, B2, 1, D-6800 Mannheim 1, Germany. Microcomputer, workstation, minicomputer, and mainframe versions are available. ZUMA also makes available the General Inquirer III package, which classifies words into content categories using a content analysis dictionary such as the *Lasswell Value Dictionary* or the *Harvard Psychosociological Dictionary*, as discussed in Zuell et al. (1989). Other pertinent software includes the Oxford Concordance Program, available from OCP, Oxford University Computing Service, 13 Banbury Road, Oxford, UK. Micro-OCP is also available for microcomputers.

Text management is used extensively by social scientists apart from content analysis. It is used, for instance, to manage field notes, systematic social observations, responses to open-ended items in questionnaires, newswire accounts, court transcripts, and more. The search functions in word processors like WordPerfect are slow and limited compared with text information management systems (TIMS) software designed for the purpose. Good TIMS software is much faster and allows more complex search patterns. For example, a good TIMS package may have relevance index searching. This alternative to Boolean And/Or/Not searching has the user type in as many words or phrases as wanted, then optionally attach weights to each to indicate the most important ones (or negative weights for ones that should not be in the file). TIMS packages then return a list of relevant files, listed in the order of relevance as reflected in the relevance index. As a second example, TIMS software usually allows one to retrieve a user-defined text chunk around the search word (e.g., 15 lines before and after), often much more convenient than WordPerfect, which is limited merely to returning the file names from Find successes.

For microcomputers, ZyINDEX (ZyLAB Corp.) was one of the first text management leaders, known for rapid searching of large text bases without requiring special text preparation. It indexes all text files on all words (except certain trivial common words) and does not involve keyword coding. For microcomputers operating under OS/2, a TIMS package is Topic (Verity, Inc.). This powerful system is used in the intelligence community, for instance, because of its support for image as well as text searching and retrieval. For more powerful workstations, Metamorph (Thunderstone Software) is a text retrieval package for MS-DOS, UNIX, and MVS platforms. Metamorph accepts natural language queries and searches files without preprocessing. For mainframe computers, BASISplus (Information Dimensions Inc.) is an example of TIMS software. Used by thirty-five of the top forty American companies to allow organizationwide network access to massive electronic files of organization documents, it uses a graphical user interface. One enters any relevant word, phrase, or concept to retrieve all pertinent documents in seconds, displaying even compound documents in their true form as used within the organization. BASISplus also works on minicomputers such as the DEC VAX and UNIX workstations.

Mapping

Mapping is important in social science not only because many fields (e.g., public administration, demographics) involve geographic databases, but also because geographic distribution of social variables is important in studying cultural correlations, diffusion patterns, and other phenomena. The National Center for Geographic Information Systems and Analysis has released a model core curriculum on geographic information systems (GIS). Atlas*Graphics (Strategic Mapping) is one of the most popular microcomputer GIS packages in social science, combining ease of use with power and flexibility. There are, however, numerous competing products. For instruction, sociologist Kenneth Hinze (Louisiana State University at Shreveport) has created Electronic Atlas, a set of programs for displaying national or state data on maps or for creating one's own maps, and his PC Datagraphics package allows three-dimensional fishnet and other maps as well as the standard choropleth style (both from National Collegiate Software, Duke University Press).

Other Specialized Application Areas

On-line searching of bibliographic and other databases is a major social science computing activity. DIALOG Information Services, Inc., has designated seventeen of its hundreds of online databases within the "SOC-SCI" category. These include on-line versions of Sociological Abstracts, PAIS International, PsycINFO, and SOCIAL SCISEARCH; however, many of its other databases, such as the Economic Literature Index, are also directly relevant to social science. Current Contents on Diskette/Social and Behavioral Sciences (Institute for Scientific Information) gives weekly access to the latest contents from 1,300 leading social and behavioral science journals, on diskette.

Among the newest and most important on-line database sources for social scientists is POLL, also on DIALOG. POLL contains the public opinion item library maintained by the Roper Center at the University of Connecticut, including Gallup, Roper, ABC, NBC, CBS, *New York Times*, and many other surveys. Other on-line databases on DIALOG pertinent to social science are CENDATA from the U.S. Census and Econbase: Time Series and Forecasts.

COMPUTING IN SOCIAL SCIENCE

Anthropology

Among specialized anthropology software is Anthropac, developed by Steven Borgatti (University of South Carolina) to implement several algorithms useful in cultural anthropology. Ethnograph (Qualis Research Associates) is designed to allow conceptual coding of observational and other studies, and Ethno (National Collegiate Software, Duke University Press) constructs and tests graphic action grammars to interpret narratives and other textual material. The Archaeological Database Analysis Package (ADAPt), to take another example, is used at Indiana University to allow on-site examination of data, giving clues as to where to dig next; however, anthropologists more often use generic tools like spreadsheets, databases, computer-assisted design (CAD), and statistics packages to accomplish research objectives (Read 1990).

Perhaps the leading computerized anthropology database is the Cross-Cultural CD (SilverPlatter, Inc.), a CD-ROM of the full text files extracted from the Human Relations Area Files, containing extracts of more than 500 anthropological, sociological, and psychological monographs in sixty societies in the nineteenth and twentieth centuries. This makes convenient for computer analysis much of the Human Relations Area Files at Yale. National Collegiate Software (Duke University Press) also distributes several anthropology databases on disk, including Ethnographic Atlas by Douglas White (University of California at Irvine).

Economics

Although economists use generic tools like the SAS statistical package extensively, specialized econometric and time series packages also play an important role. SORITEC (Sorites Group), a leading econometrics package, has been adopted as a standard by the World Bank and the Organization for Economic Cooperation and Development (OECD). RATS (VAR Econometrics) is another leading econometric package for the PC and Macintosh. Needless to say, spreadsheet applications are commonplace in economics (Yohe 1989).

Computers are used extensively in economics research. Recent work includes computerized general equilibrium models, experimental economics applications, Bayesian Monte Carlo integration, nonlinear stochastic growth models, and applications of chaos theory (Yohe 1990). Instructional examples include the award-winning Econolab by Michael Lovell (Wesleyan University), the Simulating the U.S. Economy series by William Yohe (Duke University), and MACMOD: General Macromodeling Framework Program by Peter Taylor (University of Bristol, UK), all from National Collegiate Software, Duke University Press.

Numerous computerized databases serve economics. The OECD Main Economic Indicators (Doan Associates) database, for instance, provides macroeconomic data on twenty-five nations, including Western Europe, the United States, Canada, Japan, and some others, covering more than 100 time series since 1960. Citibase is the U.S. macroeconomic database of 6,000 time series from Citicorp Database Services. Both are available in RATS format as well as other formats.

Political Science

Computerized databases frequently used by political scientists include PAIS, U.S. Political Science Abstracts, Federal News Service, and LEXIS for legal research. The first three are available on DIALOG, while LEXIS is available from Mead Data Central. Instructional software is illustrated by packages like Presidential Campaign! (National Collegiate Software, Duke University Press) and American Politics Showcase (Cognitive Development).

International relations has been a traditional bastion of computer applications in political science (Bremer 1989), dating from early work on the Inter-Nation Simulation by Harold Guetzkow (INS4 is now published by National Collegiate Software, Duke University Press). The World Game Institute is dedicated to creating the world's most comprehensive database on global statistics (re-

sources, production, human needs, trends), computer software to access this database, and instructional software for global problem solving. They produce Global Recall, a Macintosh HyperCard-based interactive atlas (over 200 maps) and global informational package showing, for instance, the extent of deforestation in any country, the number of illiterate people, nuclear capabilities by nation, and more than 100 other topics on 166 countries ($85).

Psychology

Computer simulation of psychological experiments is now commonplace (for a review of computer simulation in social science, see Crookall 1988, Garson 1987, and Slotnick 1990). Among illustrative software is the Illusions Pack (IBM and Apple II, from PSI and EYE), covering experiments on perception, psychophysics, and individual differences, including operant chamber experiments. The Active Eye Stack (Macintosh, Erlbaum Associates) has some fifty animated demonstrations pertaining to event perception phenomena keyed to William Schiff's well-known text on perception. Explorations in Cognitive Psychology (Wisc-Ware) is a "tool box" for experiments in basic cognitive psychology, including Sperling Memory Task, Stroop Interference Effect, Lexical Decision-Making, Serian Position Curve in Long-Term Memory, and Meyer-Schaneveldt Semantic Priming Task. Experiments in Cognitive Psychology (Stanford University) is award-winning Macintosh software for similar purposes and MacLaboratory for Psychology (McGraw-Hill) is award-winning software for Macintosh stations. FIRM (CONDUIT) is an authoring package for creating simulations in psychology and other fields. In addition to simulation, computers are used extensively in psychology to control equipment and record data in actual experiments, both animal and human.

A number of on-line services are germane to psychology. PsycLIT on DIALOG is undoubtedly the main one used. ComPsych provides an on-line catalog of more than a thousand psychology-related computer applications, as well as a forum for professional communication (Anderson et al. 1988). Another service is Psycholoquy, an on-line juried publication directed by Stevan Harnad, Princeton University.

Sociology

Sociologists, like other social scientists, are more apt to use generic software tools like statistical packages, such as SAS and SPSS-X for general research, or specialized packages, such as LISREL (LISREL, Inc.) for more sophisticated models (Brent and Anderson 1990). Edward Brent (University of Missouri) has systematized several research methodology subfields (research design, measurement and scaling, significance testing, and others) in a series of expert systems such as Methodologist's Toolkit (IdeaWorks). For instruction, Harvard sociologist James Davis has created Chipendale (TrueBASIC) and related software to simplify research methods teaching in sociology.

To a more limited extent, computer simulation and other tools are also used in sociology. An example is William Feinberg's work on modeling affirmative action (Feinberg 1988). Siminteract (National Collegiate Software, Duke University Press), by Donal Muir (University of Alabama), is a system for creating experimental research simulations in sociology. To take an instructional example, Starr Roxanne Hiltz has been part of a team at the New Jersey Institute of Technology that has implemented the teaching of sociology through a "virtual classroom" system based on interactive telecommunications with students at remote locations. Demography is a particular computer-intensive subfield; examples are Popshow, Popsim, and Future Pop (all from National Collegiate Software, Duke University Press).

Many computerized databases are directly pertinent to sociology. POPLINE (SilverPlatter, Inc.) is a CD-ROM containing 150,000 citations since 1827 on population, family planning, law, and policy, for instance. Drugs & Crime CD-ROM (Bureau of Electronic Publishing) is a collection of books, reports, articles, datasets, abstracts, and images on drugs and crime, including National Institute of Justice and other government publications. *Demometrics Newsletter* from the National Planning Data Corporation covers demographic data products and their use.

References

Anderson, M., P. Hornby, and D. Bozak. 1988. ComPsych: A computerized software information system. *Behavior Research Methods, Instruments, and Computers* 20(3):243–45.

Bremer, S. A. 1989. Computer modeling in global and international relations: The state of the art. *Social Science Computer Review* 7(4):459–78.

Brent, E. E., Jr., and R. E. Anderson. 1990. *Computer applications in the social sciences.* New York: McGraw-Hill.

Crookall, D., ed. 1988. Special issue on computerized simulation in the social sciences. *Social Science Computer Review* 6(1).

Feinberg, E. E. 1988. When a model needs a model: Convincing skeptics of counterintuitive results—An example of affirmative action modeling. *Social Science Computer Review* 6(1):66–74.

Fink, J. C. 1983. CATI's first decade: The Chilton experience. *Sociological Methods and Research* 12(2):152–68.

Garson, G. D. 1987. *Academic microcomputing,* chap. 5. Newbury Park, Calif.: Sage.

Read, D. W. 1990. Anthropology and computers: Promise and potential. *Social Science Computer Review* 8(4):503–19.

Slotnick, R. S. 1990. Academic computing in psychology: Trends and issues. *Social Science Computer Review* 8(4):558–91.

Vasu, M. S., and G. D. Garson. 1990. Computer-assisted survey research and continuous audience response technology for the political and social sciences. *Social Science Computer Review* 8(4):535–57.

Weber, R. P. 1990. *Basic content analysis.* 2nd ed. Newbury Park, Calif.: Sage.

Yohe, W. P. 1989. Spreadsheets in teaching economics. *Social Science Computer Review* 7(4):431–45.

———, ed. 1990. Computer-based research

advances in economics. *Social Science Computer Review* 8(4):515–34.

Zuell, C., R. P. Weber, and P. P. Mohler. 1989. *Computer-assisted text analysis for the social sciences: The General Inquirer III.* Mannheim: ZUMA.

G. David Garson

SOFTWARE ENGINEERING

In the 1950s and early 1960s, programming was an art form in which each programmer created software in ad hoc fashion. As computer-based systems have become more complex, the demand placed on software has increased dramatically. The need for systematic approaches to development and maintenance of software systems became apparent in the late 1960s. During that decade, third-generation computers were invented, and the techniques of multiprogramming and time sharing were developed. New applications of computers based on the new technology included systems for airline reservations, navigational guidance, and military command and control. Initial experience in developing large software systems showed that existing methods of software development were inadequate. A number of software systems were subject to cost overruns, late delivery, lack of reliability, inefficiency, and lack of user acceptance. Software development was in a crisis. There was an urgent need for new techniques and methods to manage the inherent complexity of large software systems.

The term *software engineering* was first introduced at the 1968 NATO Software Engineering Conference held to discuss the software crisis. The aim of software engineering is the production of quality software that is delivered on time and within budget and that satisfies all software requirements. Software engineering is concerned with large software systems, developed by teams rather than individual programmers, and uses engi-neering methods in the development of these systems.

Software engineering and traditional engineering disciplines share the pragmatic approach to development and maintenance of technological artifacts. There are, however, significant differences between software engineering and traditional engineering (Pressman 1987).

1. *Software is intangible.* It has no mass, no volume, no color—no physical properties. When hardware is built, the human creative process is ultimately translated into physical form. Software is a logical rather than a physical system element.

2. Software is developed or engineered; it is not manufactured in a classical sense. Although some similarities exist between software development and hardware manufacturing, the two activities are fundamentally different. For example, the manufacturing phase for hardware can introduce quality problems that are nonexistent or easily corrected for software. Software costs are concentrated in engineering whereas hardware costs are concentrated in manufacturing.

3. Software does not wear out. Software does not degrade with time as hardware does. When a hardware component wears out, it is replaced by a spare part. There are no software "spare parts." Software failures are caused by design and implementation errors, not by degradation.

Software engineering is a labor-intensive activity and requires both technical skill and managerial control. Software engineering encompasses three basic elements: *methods, tools,* and *procedures.* Software engineering methods encompass a broad array of tasks, including project planning and estimation, software requirements analysis, design, implementation, testing, and maintenance. Software engineering tools provide automated or semiautomated support for methods. Software engineering procedures define the sequence in which methods will be applied, the "deliverables" (documents, reports) required, and the controls that help software engineers to assure quality and assess progress. Procedures are the glue that holds the methods and tools together and enables timely and rational development of software systems.

SOFTWARE MANAGEMENT

A large software system takes time and resources to develop. *Software management* deals with three main components: the work to be done, the resources with which to do it, and the money to pay for it all. *Software project planning* and *software cost estimation* are the major management activities in software management.

Software Project Planning

Planning provides a road map for software development. As in any large engineering project, careful planning is perhaps one of the most important factors in software development. During planning, the scope of the software effort is established, and resources, cost, and schedule are estimated. Estimation is accomplished with techniques that rely on historical productivity data for previous software development. *Project scheduling* is one of the most difficult tasks of software management. Unless the project being scheduled is similar to a previous project, previous experience is of limited relevance. Different projects use different programming languages and methods, which further complicates the task of project scheduling. Scheduling is an iterative process. An initial schedule is estimated but is not considered inviolate. As the project progresses, information is fed back to the scheduler and the initial schedule is modified.

Software Cost Estimation

One of the major goals of software management is to control the costs of a software project. Software cost estimation is important for making good management decisions in a software project. Estimating the cost of a software system is one of the most error-prone tasks in software engineering, because of the large number of factors that influence the cost of software systems. The primary cost factors are the complexity of the software system, the size of the system, the available time, the required level of availability, the abilities of individual software engineers, and their familiarity with the application area. Software cost estimation techniques strive to provide the highest degree of reliability, that is, the lowest risk of major cost estimation error.

SOFTWARE LIFE CYCLE

The *software life cycle* is the series of phases, from requirements analysis to maintenance and, finally, retirement, that a software system undergoes. A number of different software life cycle models have been developed. The oldest and the most widely used software life cycle model is called the *waterfall model*. This model demands a systematic, sequential approach to software development that begins at the system level and progresses through analysis, design, implementation, testing, and maintenance. Patterned on the conventional engineering cycle, the waterfall model encompasses the following activities.

Requirements analysis. The first step in system development is to analyze, understand, and record the problem the user is trying to solve. The functions, goals, and constraints on the proposed software system must be precisely specified.

Design. The design phase involves creating a solution that meets the specifications outlined in the requirements analysis.

Implementation. The major product of the implementation phase is the source code for the software system.

Testing. The major goal of testing is to make sure that the implemented software system meets the requirements set forth in the requirements analysis.

Maintenance. Software maintenance involves changing the software system after it has been delivered and is in operation.

REQUIREMENTS ANALYSIS

Before a software system can be built it is necessary to draw up a *requirements specification,* that is, a document that states what the software system must do. Because software is always part of a larger system, requirements for all system elements are established first; some of these requirements are then allocated to software. This is essential when software must interface with other elements such as hardware, people, and databases. Next, the requirements-gathering process is intensified and focuses specifically on software. During requirements analysis, software engineers interact with users to specify software functions and performance, determine software's interface with other system elements, and establish constraints that the software must meet. A complete and unambiguous specification of software requirements is essential to the success of a software development effort.

Various notations for writing requirements specifications exist and span the entire spectrum from formal mathematical notations to informal descriptions in natural language. Somewhere between these two extremes are notations that use diagrams or tables. Depending on software project objectives, some notations are more appropriate than others. Some cover all steps and activities of developing requirements specifications, others only a specific aspect. Notations based on natural language, supplemented by diagrams and tables, are very often used for expressing requirements specifications because they are understood by users who have not been trained in the use of specialized notations.

Often a requirements specification cannot be developed completely at an early stage. *Prototyping* offers an alternative approach that results in an executable model of the software system from which requirements can be refined. A prototype is a mock-up or a model of the software system that exhibits limited functional capabilities and inefficient performance. Prototyping is a valuable mechanism for explaining various processing options to the user and for gaining better understanding of the user's needs. When a prototype is built, the user can interact and experiment with it. Once the user is satisfied that the prototype does what is required, the software engineer can complete the requirements specification, knowing the user's real needs.

SOFTWARE DESIGN

Whereas the requirements analysis concentrates on what the software system will do, the design describes how the software system will be implemented. The design phase involves creating a solution that meets the requirements specification outlined in the requirements analysis. Design is a complex process and is often divided into two phases. In the first phase, or *architectural design* phase, the software system as a whole is broken down into components called modules. In the second, or the *detailed design* phase, each module, in turn, is designed.

Architectural Design

Architectural design is the process of partitioning a software system into smaller parts, that is, subsystems and modules. The primary objective is to develop a modular structure of a software system and represent the control relationships between modules. The result of architectural design is a software system structure, definition of modules, and their interfaces. Many different notations are used to represent software system structure. The most common is the treelike diagram shown in Figure 1. The diagram implies that a module M invokes modules M_1, M_2, and M_3. Data items may be passed between M and M_1, M_2, and M_3. Similarly, module M_1 invokes modules M_4 and M_5, and so on.

A central technique in architectural design is a hierarchical *decomposition:* the system is partitioned into subsystems, the sub-

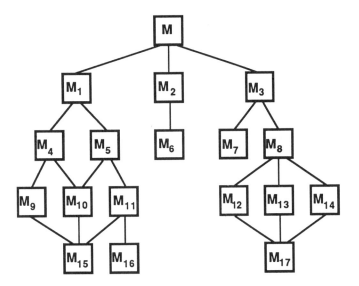

FIGURE 1. Software system structure.

systems partitioned in turn, and so on. The process is repeated recursively until the whole software system is expressed in terms of a well-formed structure of manageable modules. Several different criteria are available to guide hierarchical decomposition of a software system. They are used as objectives for achieving good software design. The most important are *cohesion and coupling* and *information hiding.*

Cohesion and coupling. Cohesion is a measure of the relative functional strength of a module. A cohesive module performs a single task requiring little interaction with modules in other parts of a system. Coupling is a measure of interconnection among modules in a software system. Coupling depends on the interface complexity among modules. In software design, the simplest connectivity among modules is most desirable.

Information hiding. Information hiding is a fundamental concept of software design. The principle of information hiding was formulated by Parnas (1971). When a software system is designed using information hiding, each module in the system hides the internal details of its processing activities and modules communicate only through well-defined interfaces. The use of information hiding

provides its greatest benefits when modifications are required during testing and software maintenance.

Detailed design

In the detailed design phase, the internal design of modules is determined. This includes the design of algorithms for each module (i.e., how the module will accomplish its task) and the design of concrete data representations for those modules. An important design technique used in detailed design is *stepwise refinement,* which was first introduced by Wirth (1971). Stepwise refinement is a design strategy in which the design of a program is developed by successively refining levels of procedural detail. A hierarchy is developed by decomposing a general statement of function. An overview of the concept is provided by Wirth:

> In each step of the refinement, one or several instructions of the given program are decomposed into more detailed instructions. This successive decomposition or refinement of specifications terminates when all instructions are expressed in terms of any underlying computer or programming language. . . . As tasks are refined, so the data may have to be refined, decomposed, or structured. . . .

The power of stepwise refinement is that it helps the software engineer concentrate on the relevant aspects of the current development phase and ignore details that need not be considered.

IMPLEMENTATION

The main activity of the implementation phase is to translate detailed design into *source code,* that is, programming language representation. The translation process continues when a compiler accepts source code as input and produces *machine code* as output, that is, computer-executable instructions. The primary goal of implementation is production of source code that is simple, readable, and well documented. Clarity of source code eases testing, debugging, and modification. Source code clarity is enhanced by features provided in programming languages and good coding style. Programming language characteristics have an impact on the quality and efficiency of translation. Selection of a programming language is one of the most important decisions made during the implementation phase. Recently, much attention has been focused on coding style. Good coding style can significantly improve simplicity and clarity of source code. A number of guidelines related to good coding style have been developed, for example, guidelines for commenting on the source code.

SOFTWARE TESTING

Once the software system is implemented, it is tested. Software testing is a critical element of software development and represents the ultimate review of specification, design, and implementation. It is the process of feeding input data into a software system, executing it, and inspecting the output for correctness. The primary objective for testing is to derive a set of tests that have a high likelihood of uncovering errors in the software system. To accomplish this objective, two different categories of testing techniques are used: *structural testing* and *functional testing*. Structural testing focuses on the software structure. Tests are derived to assure, for example, that all statements have been executed at least once during testing and that all logical conditions have been exercised. Functional testing enables the software engineer to derive tests that will exercise all functional requirements for a software system. Functional testing disregards the software structure, and attention is focused on the functions of the software system.

In development of large software systems, testing comprises several stages. First, each module is tested, isolated from the other modules in the system. Such testing, known as *module testing*, verifies that each module functions properly. The next step is to combine the modules into a single software system. The assembled modules are tested to see whether they function properly when put together. This type of testing is called *system integration testing* and focuses on testing the interfaces and interdependencies of the modules. The last testing stage includes *acceptance testing* to demonstrate to the user the capabilities of the completed software system.

Debugging. Debugging starts when testing has uncovered an error. Although testing and debugging are closely related, they are distinct processes. Debugging involves locating the source of the error and correcting it. Testing must then be repeated to ensure that the change has been made correctly. A simple coding error is usually fairly easy to correct. On the other hand, if the error is a design error or involves a misunderstanding of system requirements, correction may be difficult. It may be necessary to redesign part of the software system and consequently retest the whole system.

Correctness of programs. A software system is correct if it satisfies its specifications when operated under permitted conditions. In other words, if input data satisfying the input specifications are provided, the software system is correct if the output produced by the system satisfies the output specifications. Software testing can be used successfully to uncover errors, but it cannot be used to demonstrate software correctness. As Dijkstra put it, "Software can show the presence, but never the absence of errors in software" (1972). By using mathematical techniques, it is possible to demonstrate software correctness. A *correctness proof* is a formal mathematical verification that a software system is correct without executing the software system. The correctness proof is currently limited to relatively small software systems, and much work remains to be done before it can be practically applied to large-scale software.

SOFTWARE MAINTENANCE

System development is complete when a software system has been delivered and is in use. Software systems undergo changes after they are delivered. Changes occur because errors have been encountered, because the software must be adopted to its changing external environment (e.g., a change in software system is required because of a new operating system), or because functional or performance enhancements are required.

The term *software maintenance* is used to describe the software engineering activities that involve making changes to a software system after it is in operation. Software maintenance cannot be viewed in the same way as hardware maintenance, which means repair or prevention of broken or improperly working parts. Software does not degrade with time as hardware does. Software maintenance activities only involve making changes to software systems. These activities are similar to those of software development: analysis, design, implementation, and testing. Analysis activities involve understanding the scope and effect of a desired change, as well the constraints on making the change. Design during maintenance involves redesigning the software system to incorporate the desired changes. The changes are then implemented by updating the source code. During testing, new tests are designed to assess the adequacy of the modification. Software maintenance activities consume a large portion of the total software system budget over the lifetime of the system, commonly accounting for 70 percent of total software system costs (with development requiring 30 percent).

[*See also:* Computer-Aided Software Engineering; Programming Language Design; Systems Development Life Cycle.]

References

Dijkstra, E. W. 1972. The humble programmer. *Communications of the ACM* 15(10):859–66.

Parnas, D. 1971. Information distribution aspects of design methodology. In IFIP Congress Proceedings, Ljubljana, Yugoslavia.

Pressman, R. S. 1987. *Software engineering: A practitioner's approach.* New York: McGraw-Hill.

Wirth, N. 1971. Program development by stepwise refinement. *Communications of the ACM* 14(4):221–27.

For Further Reading

Beizer, B. 1990. *Software testing techniques.* 2nd ed. New York: Van Nostrand Reinhold.

Fairley, R. E. 1985. *Software engineering concepts.* New York: McGraw-Hill.

Mayrhauser, Anneliese von. 1990. *Software engineering: Methods and management.* San Diego: Academic Press.

Pfleeger, S. L. 1987. *Software engineering: The production of quality software.* New York: Macmillan.

Schach, S. R. 1990. *Software engineering.* Homewood, Ill.: Aksen Associates.

Sommerville, I. 1989. *Software engineering.* Reading, Mass: Addison-Wesley.

Bogdan Korel

SOLID MODELING AND FINITE ELEMENT ANALYSIS

Traditionally engineers have used a drafting language to describe three-dimensional objects. The edges of these objects are projected on mutually perpendicular planes, as suggested in Figure 1. This drafting language required great skill by the engineer or drafter when complicated parts were involved. It also required skill by the machinist or fabricator who had to read the drawing. Sometimes distinctly different parts could be made from the same drawing by two different machinists because of ambiguity or unspecified detail.

Computer-based graphics, which began to be used in the 1960s, at first directly imitated traditional drafting language. They reduced the three-dimensional design to a series of two-dimensional views. These views were an electronic substitute for pencil lead and paper, and people trained in the old method could rapidly switch to the compu-

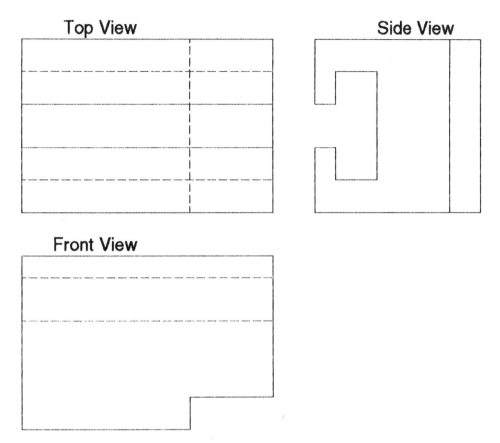

FIGURE 1. Three views of a machined part. Dashed lines indicate that they are behind a surface.

ter-based method. However, people began to realize that there were more efficient ways to work. An evolution followed that did the following:

1. It replaced the mutually perpendicular views by a single wireframe representation of the edges of the part. This wireframe could be manipulated to be shown from any point of view.
2. It added explicit description of the surfaces that lay between the edges. This permitted a realistic portrayal of the object, using shaded surface representation. (See Figure 2.) Edges or surfaces hidden by surfaces that lay in front of them could be removed by logical procedures or algorithms. The calculation and display of surface intersections, formerly a difficult and time-consuming procedure, became a trivial task.
3. It added logic, which permitted a knowledge of the inside from the outside of the object. Now the object could be completely and unambiguously defined. Techniques were developed to allow the user to add, subtract, or intersect solids, as shown in Figure 3. These techniques are known as Boolean operations.

Thus an evolution was completed from a specialized drawing language to a computer representation so realistic that a photograph of a computer representation could be indistinguishable from a photograph of the real object. Furthermore, enough information was contained in the solid model that its volume, weight, and mass moment of inertia (resistance to rotational acceleration) could be automatically calculated.

Improvements were also being made in computer graphics devices and techniques.

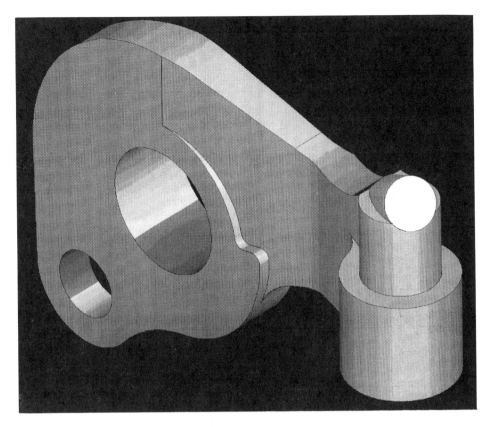

FIGURE 2. Surface model of automotive rocker arm.

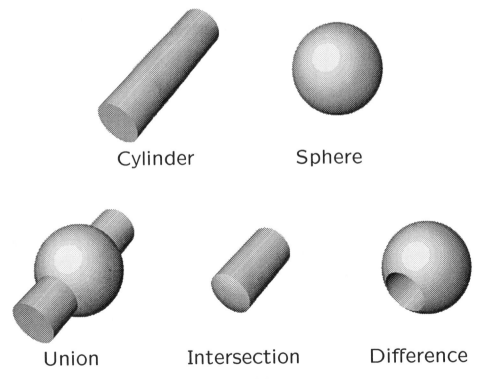

FIGURE 3. Boolean operations to combine solids.

Surfaces could be represented with color, shadow, and texture. "Ray tracing" algorithms were developed to simulate the reflections observed in a highly polished mirror-like surface. Imaging techniques were developed that permitted the observer, while wearing a special pair of glasses, to observe an object or assembly in stereoscopic three-dimensional form.

At the same time, important developments initiated in the late 1950s were being made with regard to computer-aided analyses of stress, vibration, and heat transfer. Historically, parts of complex shape were approximated by parts of simpler shape. Solutions for the behavior of these simpler shapes could be calculated or found in handbooks. The new computer-based developments centered on the fact that an object of complex geometry could be subdivided into elements of specific shapes of small but finite size. (The word "finite" is used here to distinguish from the infinitesimal size used in the mathematics of calculus.) The mechanical stiffness or heat-conductive proper-ties of each of these elements could be computed and their values assembled and analyzed by matrix methods. These techniques came to be known as finite element methods.

Figure 4 illustrates the solid model of a connecting rod used in an automotive engine. Figure 5 shows one possible breakdown of that rod into finite elements. The faces of the rod are covered in a triangular pattern. The elements themselves are tetrahedral—that is, pyramidal solids bounded by four triangular faces. Other specific shapes used in finite elements are pentahedral and hexahedral—that is, solids with five and six faces, respectively. Each element is of simple enough shape that its interior behavior can be interpolated from the behavior of the vertices or nodes. ("Behavior" here refers to a displacement in a stress problem, a motion in a vibration problem, or a temperature in a heat transfer problem.) Note that interpolation is not usually an exact process.

Solutions found by finite element methods are rarely exact but require judgment

FIGURE 4. Solid model of half of a connecting rod.

FIGURE 5. Finite element of half of a connecting rod.

and experience by the engineer. More nearly exact answers can be found by using more rather than fewer finite elements. However, increasing the number of elements in the finite element model increases the computer time required to produce an answer. The time requirements often vary as the square or cube of the problem size, so that doubling the number of elements in the model can increase time requirements from four to eight times that of the smaller model. Computer time costs money! Worse than that, a problem can outgrow the size of the available computer. Large problems, such as simulation of an entire automobile, can occupy a multimillion-dollar computer for days at a time.

Due in part to the progress in solid modeling and especially finite elements, engineers have been able to design and analyze aerospace, automotive, and other types of structures more quickly. Automotive engines, for example, have become lighter, quieter, smoother, more fuel-efficient, and less polluting than engines of decades past.

For Further Reading

Brauer, J. R., ed. 1988. *What every engineer should know about finite element analysis.* New York: Marcel Dekker.

Computer Graphics & Applications (journal). New York: IEEE. See especially vol. 5, no. 2, Feb. 1985, pp. 45–56, and vol. 7, no. 1, Jan. 1987, pp. 8–19, 33–43, and 44–55, for material on solid modeling.

Cook, R. D., D. S. Malkus, and M. E. Plesha. 1989. *Concepts and applications of finite element analysis.* New York: Wiley.

Huebner, K. H., and E. A. Thornton. 1983. *The finite element method for engineers.* 2nd ed. New York: Wiley.

Donald L. Dewhirst

SOUND, COMPUTERS AND

Interest in replicating natural sounds, particularly those of musical instruments and the human voice, with a computer began in the 1950s. However, through the 1970s, computers did not have the computing power to imitate natural sounds accurately. Sound generation by computer was based on software and small speakers. The central processing units could not make computations fast enough and the computers did not have enough memory to store the complex characteristics necessary for natural sounds. In the 1980s, special hardware became popularly available to assist the computer in sound generation. At the same time, special functions were added to high-level languages to aid in the production of sound. Computer-generated sound is used in computer music, voice mail, computer-aided instruction, and as output for people who cannot use a visual terminal.

CHARACTERISTICS OF SOUND

Nature produces sounds by compressing molecules into pressure waves that then cause the eardrum to vibrate. This is how humans perceive sound. The shape of these compression waves is smooth in that the transition from the peak of a wave to the decline of the wave is virtually undetectable. Sounds have three basic characteristics: loudness, pitch, and timbre. The size of a tone's wave (its amplitude) determines how loud the tone will be. We can measure the waves for simple tones by counting the number of vibrations per second, known as hertz (Hz). Humans can optimally detect sounds from 20 Hz to 20,000 Hz (20 kilohertz, kHz). A tone's pitch (frequency) is the number of hertz necessary to produce it. Frequency gives a sound its quality of "high" or "low" pitch. There is an additional quality to sound that allows humans to distinguish one sound from another even if the sounds occur at the same loudness and pitch. This quality is called timbre. Timbre is often called tonal "color." Two components of timbre are how quickly the sound starts (its attack) and how quickly the sound fades (its decay). In nature, timbre is also produced by the presence of complex waves. Complex waves exist when two or more simple waves combine to produce one new wave. Some parts of complex waves are known as overtones, where certain

higher-pitched tones combine with the primary tone. Overtones may start at the same time as the primary tone or, as in the sounds produced by woodwinds and pipe organs, may start before the primary tone. Additionally, some tones gain more overtones as the sound gets louder, like those of a trumpet.

REPRESENTING SOUNDS IN A COMPUTER

To reproduce sounds accurately, it is necessary to understand how natural sounds are formed and their specific characteristics. Once a sound is understood, a mathematical representation needs to be developed so that the computer can reproduce the sound. Because most sounds in nature are complex compression waves, it has not been possible to map, or analyze, very many sounds. The complexity of the compression waves found in nature means that the mathematics needed to model these sounds is also complex. Most of the in-depth analysis of sound has focused on musical instruments. One reason it hasn't been possible to map nature's sounds completely is that each sound has a large number of different tonal characteristics. To produce these sounds accurately, the computer would have to be able to reproduce all these complex characteristics. If any characteristics were omitted, the computer-generated sound would seem incomplete.

PRODUCING SOUND WITH A COMPUTER'S SPEAKER

To produce sound, a computer needs some mechanism to produce compression waves. Most computer systems come with a small speaker for this purpose. Even terminals connected to large computers have a small speaker. A computer speaker contains a membrane that vibrates in and out, resulting in compression waves and, therefore, sound. These speakers were designed primarily to produce obnoxious beeps to notify the computer user of a special condition, such as an error. The speakers found in most computer systems are small and have limited capability; however, the primary cause for the computer's inability to produce natural sounds is how the speaker forms the compression waves. In contrast to the smooth waves found in nature, most computers are digital, meaning that they work in a manner that is either on or off. If we could see natural waves, they would look smooth from the peak of one wave to the peak of the next wave. The computer-generated waves would look like three-sided boxes. The best that a computer can do is to have the wave composed of very small changes so that the wave looks like stair steps. Even if the waves are made smoother with small changes, sounds produced by computers still remind one of stereotypical invaders from space, lacking emphasis and complexity, low in tone quality, and lacking resonation. The computer cannot easily control the attack or the decay of a tone. When the computer instructs the speaker to vibrate, the amount of vibration is limited to the amount that can be controlled by the computer. In addition, the waves that are easily formed by the computer are not as complex as the waves found in nature.

The computer controls the speaker by magnetically pushing the speaker's membrane out to produce a compression wave or pulling it in to prepare for the next wave. Because the computer causes this vibration, the waves occur digitally, forming a square wave pattern. By vibrating the speaker's membrane at different rates, the computer can produce tones of different pitches. The faster the membrane vibrates, the higher the pitch of the tone. Some computers rely on the central processing unit (CPU) to control the vibrations. Software produced for these computers must be used on other computers with the same type of CPU and equivalent processing speed. If the sounds are produced on computers with a faster processor, the sounds will be pitched higher and otherwise distorted. Other types of computers use a timer chip, which produces pulses in absolute time (as opposed to relying on the relative speed of the CPU). This technique allows software to produce the same tones on another computer with the same type of CPU running at any speed. Small computers usually control the speaker by referencing a specific address in primary memory or a port

designated for the speaker. When the address or port is referenced, the speaker changes state, the membrane is pushed out if it is in or pulled in if it is out. This either compresses the air in front of the speaker or pulls back to get ready for the next wave. The algorithm to produce a tone depends on the frequency of the tone (how many waves per second) and the amount of time it needs to produce one vibration. By use of a timing loop where the speaker changes state in the body of the loop, a scale of simple tones can be produced. It is obvious from this simple discussion that complex waves would not be easy to produce. The complex waves would have to be controlled by the software. Instead of just calculating how many waves per second, the programmer would have to change the frequency of the tone many times during a second. Another implication of this algorithm is that attack and decay cannot be controlled. They can be emulated by inserting short spaces (milliseconds) of silence when producing the tone. The result, however, is far from natural.

The above algorithms depend on the ability to access specific memory addresses. This means that assembler language is the obvious choice to write such programs. At the very least, assembler routines that may be incorporated into a high-level programming language would be needed. The programming language C also allows direct manipulation of memory addresses. Most new commercial sound-producing software packages are written in C. Some high-level languages, such as BASIC, Logo, and some versions of Pascal, allow the programmer to produce simple tones easily. These languages have a command (usually a subprocedure) that accepts the frequency and duration as parameters and then produces a tone; however, these languages do not usually have the capability to produce complex sounds.

COMPUTER-COMPOSED SOUND

A computer program can also be used to select how the sounds will be produced. For example, a program can use existing data values to determine the pitch (or whether the tone is higher or lower than the previous tone) and the duration. This is called computer composition. Most of the work in this area has focused on computer music composition. Early attempts at computer composition used random numbers to decide pitch and duration. The results were as one would expect: computer noise. Some programmers found that if they restricted the random selection to a known statistical distribution, arguably pleasing sounds could be produced. The pentatonic (five-tone) scale proved to be very adaptive to this type of composition. Music has also been produced by the computer on the basis of fractal geometry and artificial neural networks. Computer composition can also be used in seismology to produce sounds much like that of an earthquake. Jet engines and other types of machinery vibrate and produce sound. The computer has the ability to model these vibrations and can produce sounds of engines and other machinery in various states of operation or malfunction. Technicians may then train on computers using the computer-generated vibrations. Computers also have the capability to make subtle changes when reproducing animal noises. This allows scientists to develop theories on regional vocalization and look for similar patterns among different species.

COMBINING SPECIAL HARDWARE AND SOFTWARE TO PRODUCE SOUND

Without special hardware, sound generation is not a simple task. Two different methods have evolved in the production of sounds by computer. One method uses software models to create the waveform for a particular sound. These models are mathematical representations of the waveform for that sound. The other method records, or "samples," sounds and saves them in a form the computer could use. Both forms are in popular use for producing complex sounds with a computer. Modern specialized hardware and software include the algorithms that produce tones of specific musical instruments to enable the computer to act as an entire orches-

tra. Each instrument should be sampled at different parts of the scale because the waveform for an instrument changes as the pitch changes. Additional algorithms and specialized hardware have been developed to produce parts of human speech called phonemes. By using these phonemes, the computer can produce a primitive approximation of speech with the small speaker available on most small computers. Voice mail systems are commercially available that allow a person to leave a message on a computer system much the same way a message is left on tape answering machines. The entertainment industry has found that impressive special effects may be obtained by combining the two systems. A sound can be sampled into a computer's memory and then modified to produce a new sound not found in nature. A sound can be produced that is very close to a natural sound but with components of the wave modified (the new voices of invaders from space). Sampling also allows a user to store other sounds on secondary storage for later retrieval. Examples of this would be animal sounds, speeches or lectures, computer-assisted instructional material, and machinery to be analyzed by sound. Because the sound is stored on the computer's secondary storage and can be transferred to the computer's primary memory, the user can employ traditional database functions. The user has the ability to skip forward to a specific sound segment, erase selected sounds or characteristics of certain sounds, archive sounds on semipermanent media, and even search for segments containing certain key sound characteristics.

The computer has the capacity to store, produce, and analyze sounds. This capability has allowed computer scientists and musicologists to further analyze music. This has led to additional discoveries of music's underlying concepts. Other sounds can be stored and analyzed. One example is the study of bird songs from one region to another to examine the change these songs undergo. Computers are used to study the sounds created by the movements of the Earth. By analysis of these sounds, it may be possible to predict the time and location of future earthquakes. Computers are also being used in military applications to analyze ocean sounds to detect manmade objects underwater. By reproducing underwater sounds, the computer can provide a cloaking mechanism to hide manmade sounds in varying conditions. Computers can serve an additional purpose in each of these fields by acting as an educational tool. The computer can produce these sounds with small, controlled variations for students to identify.

Other than music, the most popular use of computer-generated sound is voice synthesis. Early attempts at computer speech involved algorithms for simple phonemes. Phonemes do not have a direct relationship with alphabetic letters. Rather, they are representations of the individual sounds of speech. For example, the word "all" is represented in phonemes by "au-l" or "aw-l." This method requires the computer to have the algorithms to produce a small number of phonemes but be able to produce a large number of word combinations. Current research is focused on creating the algorithms for phonemes of different languages and cultures. With an accurate set of phonemes, the computer can produce speech that has a Southern accent, intones pitch changes as at the end of a question, or produces speech that is characteristically male or female.

Special hardware is able to form complex waves so that the computer sounds have a more natural quality. Several computer manufacturers have delivered systems with special hardware for sound as an integral part of the basic computer system. The primary part of this hardware changes the digital signal produced by a computer to an analog signal like that of natural sounds. This is called a digital-to-analog (D/A) converter. The D/A converter produces compression waves that are very similar to the waves found in nature. These computers also include specialized software to control the D/A converter. The languages available for these computers have special functions and procedures that allow manipulation of sound production. Sounds that can be easily produced are music, voice, and special effects.

APPLICATIONS

New or enhanced applications are available on these systems. Voice mail is standard, with computer workstations having special sound-producing hardware. A user simply chooses a record icon and speaks into a microphone. Sound from the microphone is changed from the analog waveform of natural sound to a digital form, which can be stored by the computer. This hardware is called an analog-to-digital (A/D) converter. When the message is saved to disk, the user may now include the voice message in a text message, a program, or other file. It is possible for the user to edit the voice message by viewing the wave patterns representing the message and changing the selected message part with a sound editor. The computer system will play designated parts of the message to verify that the user has selected the right message segment. If the user made a mistake in the original message or wants to modify the message, the edit capability makes this task easy. Often, the user would like to modify selected characteristics of the sound file. Most computer systems that allow voice mail allow the user to change the shape of the compression waveform. This capability allows the user to create new sounds or emphasize certain passages in the sound file.

Voice mail is only one application that takes advantage of the computer's ability to produce and manipulate sound. Some computer game manufacturers have started allowing the games to take advantage of any available special hardware for sounds. The Apple II computers had games that used phonemes with the system speaker but the newer computers have the capability to produce other natural sounds. Research is also underway to use the sound production capabilities of computers to implement multimodal systems. These systems give output by screen and speaker. By using this system, the user is more aware of critical conditions that might be overlooked in the complex multiwindowed interfaces of today. The primary disadvantage of this arrangement is that when more than one of these systems is used in one room, the noise is distractive and users can get confused.

Computer-synthesized speech has allowed people who are blind or have poor eyesight to receive computer output. Output can be sent to a speech synthesizer instead of a video screen. This has necessitated a change in the way computers present information. On a typical computer system, information scrolls down the screen. When we read a computer screen, we tend to scan forward and periodically back up to reread a section of text. Most modern computers show a screen of text and wait until the user has read the screen before continuing. This is not possible with auditory output. With an auditory monitor (output by sound), less information should be presented at one time. Screens of text no longer have any meaning; therefore, a new unit of output such as paragraph or block must be used. Also, different fonts cannot be duplicated aurally but verbal emphasis can be included in the output. The speaker that comes with most small computers does not have the quality of sound to function effectively as an auditory monitor so most auditory monitors have special hardware to produce more human-like speech.

[See also: Speech Synthesis and Recognition.]

For Further Reading

Most PC assembler books have a chapter on making noises with the computer. For more technical references, consult any digital signal processing text.

Baecker, R. M., and W. A. S. Buxton. 1987. *Readings in human–computer interaction: A multidisciplinary approach.* San Mateo, Calif.: Morgan Kaufman. Several sections of this text refer to topics presented in this article.

Newquist, H. P. 1989. *Music & technology.* New York: Billboard Books. This is a very informative and easy-to-read book on MIDI (Musical Instrument Digital Interface), a widely used protocol for communication between computers and synthesizers.

Saffari, B. 1989. Putting DSPs to work. *Byte* 14(13):259–72.

F. Layne Wallace

SPEECH SYNTHESIS AND RECOGNITION

The most common form of communication involves speech, in which one person generates a speech waveform or signal via vocal tract manipulations and another interprets this signal via the auditory system. The speech signal consists of variations in pressure usually coming from the speaker's mouth, but computers can generate synthetic versions of intelligible speech, given a text as input. Similarly, the role of the listener can also be taken by a computer, in automatic speech or speaker recognition, where an algorithm deciphers a speech signal into either the underlying textual message or the speaker's identity.

Basic understanding of how humans produce speech has existed for hundreds of years (some mechanical speech synthesizers existed in the 1700s), but modern speech synthesis and recognition started in the 1940s, with the invention of the sound spectrograph, which displays patterns of speech energy as a function of time and frequency. The basic methods of modern synthesis and recognition were established in the early 1970s, as the power of computers rapidly increased and our understanding of the human processes of speech production and perception also matured. Today's systems fit easily on printed circuit boards, or even on single chips in the case of simple synthesizers. They are capable of synthesizing intelligible (albeit not completely natural) speech in several languages and of understanding human speech (with some restrictions on vocabulary size and style of speaking).

AUTOMATIC SPEECH SYNTHESIS

Speech synthesis is the automatic generation by computer of speech signals, either from stored speech representations directly (*voice response*) or from rules based on phonetics (*text-to-speech*). There are conflicting demands of maximizing the output speech quality while minimizing the memory space that the computer program occupies, the complexity of the program, and its computation time. Memory size often grows with the vocabulary of the synthesizer. The simplest methods to store speech require rates up to 100,000 bits per second, which permit only very small vocabularies even with the rapidly decreasing cost of memory, when one considers the immense number of possible speech utterances. Large-vocabulary synthesizers require sacrifices such as simplistic modeling of the spectral dynamics of the vocal tract and its excitation, and of intonation, with the result that output quality is limited.

Speech is synthesized by concatenating either stored speech units directly in voice response systems (as in talking toys or cars) or more abstract spectral representations of speech for text-to-speech applications (where the vocabulary can be large). Large speech units (e.g., phrases or sentences) can give high-quality output speech but require much memory. Text-to-speech uses small units and extensive linguistic processing, to transform each input text into a form having syntactic, semantic, and phonetic codes, suitable to drive the synthesis algorithm.

The difficulty with simply linking stored words to create new utterances is that each word's timing, intonation, and phonetics in natural speech vary with the context. Merely concatenating words originally spoken in isolation usually leads to degraded intelligibility and naturalness. For synthesis of unrestricted text, speech is generated from sequences of basic sounds called phonemes, which substantially reduces memory as most languages have only thirty to forty phonemes; however, the spectral features of these short sounds (0.03 to 0.3 second each) must be smoothed at their boundaries to avoid jumpy, discontinuous speech. Some commercial systems link diphone units of speech, which are obtained by dividing speech into phoneme-sized units, but with the cuts in the middle of each phoneme (to preserve the transition between adjacent phonemes). Diphone concatenation yields smooth speech because the merged sounds at boundaries are spectrally similar. Coding each of about 1200 diphones in English with two to three frames of parameters (to represent each transition) requires about 200K of speech storage. More popular are phoneme synthesizers, where one or two sets of amplitude and spectral parameters for each phoneme require as few as 2 kilobits; for such a method, however, many complex rules are needed to properly simulate the spectral results of vocal tract movements (so-called coarticulation).

Synthesizing speech from unrestricted text requires a set of language-dependent rules to convert letters into phonemes. English needs hundreds of such rules, which examine the context of each letter; for example, the letter *p* is pronounced with lip closure, except before the letter *h*, as in *telephone*. Many common words (e.g., *of*, *the*) violate basic pronunciation rules; thus, lists of exception words are needed. Sometimes, a word decomposition algorithm tries to strip prefixes and suffixes from each word, which affects pronunciation (e.g., *algebra* versus *algebraic*). Use of a pronunciation dictionary can handle exception words and provide syntactic part-of-speech information, to help in parsing each input text. The syntactic structure of a text has a large impact on its intonation; poor handling of intonation is a major reason why much unlimited text synthesis sounds unnatural.

Text-to-speech employs a model of the vocal tract that simulates human speech production, where movements of the tract result in a time-varying filter that is activated by either a periodic source at the glottis or a noisy excitation at a narrow constriction caused by the tongue or lips. Different sounds are characterized by the shape of the tract (which results in spectra with resonance peaks at varying frequencies) and by the type of excitation. In synthesis, the vocal tract is often modeled as a cascade of second-order digital resonators, because the ear is most sensitive to the presence of spectral peaks. The excitation is usually a periodic set of impulses, pseudorandom noise, or periodically shaped noise. This simple excitation model yields periodic vowels, which sound unnatural because humans are incapable of any purely periodic activity.

AUTOMATIC SPEECH RECOGNITION

The other aspect of vocal communication between people and computers involves automatic speech recognition (see SPEECH TO PRINT). Algorithms to perform recognition have been less successful than those for synthesis because of asymmetries in producing and interpreting speech. Recognition products often limit the number of speakers they accept as well as the words and syntactic structures that can be used, and often require speakers to pause after each word. To illustrate the difficulty of recognition, consider the problems of segmentation and adaptation. For both synthesis and recognition, the input is often partitioned for efficient processing, typically into segments of some linguistic relevance. In synthesis, the input text is easily divided into words and letters, whereas the speech signal provides only tentative indications of phoneme boundaries. Sudden large changes in speech spectrum or amplitude are often used to estimate boundaries, which are nevertheless unreliable because of coarticulation and highly variable phoneme durations. Boundaries corresponding to words are very difficult to locate except when the speaker pauses. Many commercial recognizers require speakers to pause briefly after each word to facilitate segmentation. Continuous speech recognition allows natural conversational speech, but is more difficult to recognize by algorithm.

Human listeners adapt to synthetic speech and usually accept it as if from a strange dialect. For recognition, the computer instead must adapt to different voices. Most systems are speaker dependent, requiring people to train the system beforehand by entering their speech patterns into the recognizer memory. As memory in such systems grows linearly with the number of speakers, less accurate speaker-independent recognizers (trained by many speakers) are useful if a large population must be served. In speech-understanding systems, the output is not a text but an action, where some errors can be tolerated if they do not block understanding. Some systems operate on a word-spotting principle: the user may say any-thing, but only stressed words found in the system vocabulary cause action to be taken.

Speech recognition is a pattern recognition task, requiring a mapping between each speech wave form and its corresponding text. The focus of recognition is often a comparison between templates of parameter or feature representations of both an unknown test speech signal and a reference signal. This involves training and recognition steps. Training (which can be automatic or manual) establishes a reference memory (dictionary) of speech patterns, each assigned a text label. The automatic recognition phase tries to assign a label to each unknown input. The key to speech recognition is proper information reduction, converting a speech signal (many thousands of bits per second) into a text of perhaps 60 bits per second (about 12 phonemes per second × 5 bits per phoneme).

One can view speech recognition from either an expert system or statistical perspective. In the former, relationships between speech and its corresponding text messages are observed, and rules are established by researchers to explain the phenomena. Capturing all the complex interrelationships of speech redundancies in one comprehensive structural model, however, is very difficult. In the statistical approach, speech properties are exploited as part of a general framework (often using networks), to maximize the likelihood of choosing the correct symbols (e.g., text) corresponding to an input signal. The models are trained on large amounts of speech and often use general comparison techniques involving templates and standard speech spectral distance measures. The statistical method has had more commercial success than the cognitive approach.

For Further Reading

Klatt, D. 1980. Software for a cascade/parallel formant synthesizer. *Journal of the Acoustical Society of America* 67:971–95.

O'Shaughnessy, D. 1987. *Speech communication: Human and machine.* Reading, Mass.: Addison-Wesley.

Special issue on Man–Machine Speech

Communication. 1985. *Proceedings of the IEEE* 73:1539–1676.

Special issue on Speech Processing and Applications. 1990. *IEEE Communications Magazine* 28(1):28–41.

Douglas O'Shaughnessy

SPEECH TO PRINT

An important application of speech-recognition technology is the ability to perform word processing without the use of a keyboard. Large-vocabulary speech-recognition systems have been available since the early 1980s. Currently available speech-recognition systems similar to that described here are based on the assumption that all of the necessary information needed for recognizing the spoken words is available in the speech signal itself. The most successful form of transformation used to minimize the effect of variability has been that of dynamic time warping, first introduced by Sakoe and Chiba in 1971 and refined in many ways to provide for efficient utilization (see SPEECH RECOGNITION AND SYNTHESIS).

The speech-to-print process typically begins with a digital signal processor that breaks speech into different frequency bands—a function like that performed by the cochlea of the human ear, which has different regions sensitive to different pitches. This information is then analyzed by expert-system software embodying the judgment of linguists. The computer processes the frequency bands to identify sound segments called phonemes. More information is needed in order to identify combinations of phonemes as words. One approach is to form and test hypotheses about the phrase in which the word occurs. A specialized software module is used to parse the phrase, that is, to label each word and identify the role it plays in the sentence. This creates a context from which the words themselves can be deduced.

Current commercial systems may have vocabularies as large as 30,000 words. Early versions required a speaker to repeat every word in an application into the system beforehand, so that the system could recognize that speaker's particular inflections, accent, and pronunciation. Speaker-independent systems, with vocabularies of over 5,000 words, followed. Both require the speaker to pause slightly between words.

Speech-to-print technology has found its widest acceptance so far in the area of medical reporting. Voice recognition allows physicians to compile reports quickly without stopping to write with a pen; it also guards against serious errors and resulting malpractice suits. The systems also enable hospitals to save on the costs of transcription, which often run into hundreds of thousands of dollars. By 1991 more than 600 systems had been installed at hospitals and clinics, where they are used by more than 3,000 doctors to enter patient information into hospital and office computers.

Commercial speech recognition systems in languages other than English are in the course of development. Several companies have focused in particular on adapting the technology to the Japanese language. Japan may become a significant market for such products because Japanese-language keyboards are difficult to use. Keyboards based on the kanji system of more than 7,000 characters resemble the console of a church organ in complexity; newer keyboards use hiragana, a simpler system of syllabic writing, but their output must then be translated into kanji characters. As a result, it has been estimated that only 4 percent of Japan's population uses personal computers, compared with more than 12 percent of the U.S. population.

Proponents of speech recognition technology predict that it will be crucial in making personal computers fully available to Japanese users. A potential obstacle is the lack of space in many Japanese offices: because of crowded conditions, more than half of the 6 million personal computers in Japan are laptops, whereas speech recognition systems now in development will need to run on workstations or powerful personal computers. Pen-based handwriting recognition

HOW A COMPUTER RECOGNIZES THE SPOKEN WORD

Figure 1 shows how a phrase, "I can see my words as I say them," is transformed from sound waves spoken by the user to a personal computer (upper left) into word-processed digital code that is displayed on the computer terminal, or printed out, faxed, or stored in memory (lower right).

The beginning and end stages of the speech recognition process involve powerful but standard hardware (a microphone and a digital signal-processing chip at the beginning; a fax machine, a printer, and a storage system at the end). But the main functions of the process depend on a series of very specialized and extremely sophisticated software modules.

One of the most complex software procedures occurs after the system has produced an intermediate list of possible acoustic or phonetic recognitions of the word or phrase the user has uttered (see lower left of figure). Suppose the possible recognitions for the fourth word, *my*, in "I can see my words as I say them," are three: *by*, *my*, and *fry*. Now, a grammar expert considers the suggestions, assigning a high score to the possessive adjective *my*, because, among other things, it agrees in person and number with the subject of the sentence, *I*. It is also a likely first part of a noun phrase ("my words") that will be the direct object of the verb, "see." On the other hand, a low score is assigned by grammar and syntax experts to the possible recognitions *by* and *fry* because they would not create sentences or are statistically unlikely from the point of view of standard English syntax at that point in the sentence.

In speech-recognition systems for a specific application, such as emergency-medicine patient reporting, knowledge "experts" —actually, computer algorithms that store the knowledge and language, including common words and phrases, for a particular domain of human activity—play a crucial role in sorting out competing possible recognitions. For example, in VoiceEM, a commer-

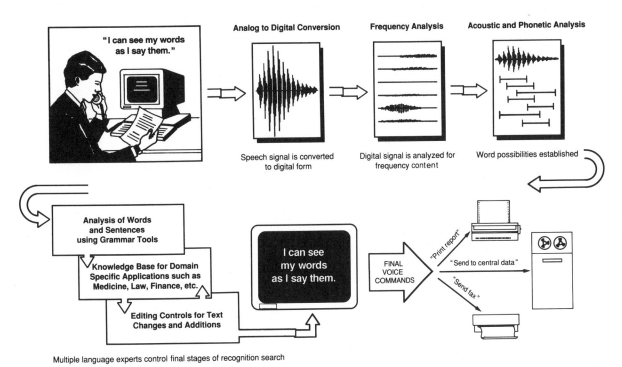

FIGURE 1. Automated speech recognition for large vocabularies. *Figure by Martin L. Schneider - Ryan.*

cial system for speech-controlled emergency-medicine reporting, a high score would be given to the word *fracture*, since it occurs frequently in emergency-medicine discourse. In contrast, low scores would be given to the words *rapture* and *actor*, which do not.

The domain-specific aspect of the software, in effect, makes it possible for a physician or any specialist to talk to the expert computer as if it were another person specifically trained in this particular field. Thus, descriptions of patient conditions—including standard terms, phrases, even entire paragraphs of text—are actually anticipated by the computer as the physician speaks. All of the experts—both for English-language grammar and syntax and for application-specific knowledge bases—and all other parts of the speech-recognition process work together in real time.

For Further Reading

Allen, J. 1987. Speech recognition. In S. C. Shapiro, ed. *Encyclopedia of artificial intelligence*, pp. 1065–70. New York: Wiley.

Fallside, F., and W. A. Woods. 1985. *Computer speech processing.* Englewood Cliffs, N. J.: Prentice-Hall.

Online Conferences, Ltd. 1985. *Voice processing: Technology and opportunity in the office.* Pinner, U.K.: Online.

Reddy, D. R., ed. 1975. *Speech Recognition.* New York: Academic Press.

Sakoe, H., and S. Chiba. 1971. A dynamic programming approach to continuous speech recognition. *Proceedings of the International Congress of Acoustics,* Budapest, Hungary, Paper 20C-13.

Tetschner, W. 1991. *Voice processing.* Boston: Artech.

Glenn Rifkin

SPORTS, COMPUTER APPLICATIONS IN

From the press box to the dugout to the training room to the recreational park, the increase in the use of computers has had and will continue to have a strong influence on coaches, players, fans, trainers, and administrators. Terminology and job positions unheard of two decades ago are now becoming common in our society. This article will focus on five areas of the use of computers in sports: historical development; typical hardware and software requirements; difficulties in implementation; advantages of computer use in sports; and computer applications in body fitness.

HISTORICAL DEVELOPMENT

The early 1970s ushered in the earliest stages of the use of computers in sports. With a limited foundation, computers of this vintage were large in size and unwieldy. Most of the time, users found themselves in a perplexed state while trying to employ the machines. Since each type of computer had its own individual semantics, programming was a delicate point to attempt. Applications were few for the general user. Effort was lacking on programs designed for individuals interested in an aspect of sports that could be utilized on a computer (Francis 1989).

In time, innovations in technology resulted in a mushrooming of more efficient programmable hardware. The unfolding of these recent developments has led to a computer that can be geared to an individual's interests, objectives, and goals pertaining to many facets of sports (Francis 1989).

TYPICAL HARDWARE AND SOFTWARE REQUIREMENTS

The ability to expand the proficiency of the computer with supplementary devices is an option worth considering in assessing the requirements for hardware. The user may wish to go beyond the convenience of a printer. One possibility is the utilization of a modem, which enables information to be received or displaced via telephone lines. Another alternative is to interface the computer with various pieces of fitness equipment. Exercise bicycles, treadmills, and other machines used to measure muscular strength are examples of this type of interfacing.

A problem often encountered is the erroneous purchasing of software. To avoid this pitfall, a knowledge of the traits of hardware is of the essence in the use of the software. Software must be harmonious with the computer; what is intended to run on one brand of computer will not run on an incompatible brand. The user must, therefore, purchase only software programs compatible with the hardware used. A knowledge of memory and storage required by the software package is also vital. Computer memory now ranges from 256K to several million bytes of storage, while many computer systems utilize a floppy or hard disk providing 640K to 30 megabytes. Therefore, as with the compatibility of the software package to the hardware being used, the user should be careful not to purchase software requiring a higher degree of memory than is available on the user's hardware.

A critical aspect to consider concerning requirements for software should be the ease with which data may be added or updated. With the use of a relational database program, new data may be augmented to files already in existence (Chatfield et al. 1990). A program designed with this important feature makes tasks such as inventory and/or record keeping much simpler and easier to maintain.

the grammar correct, and are the words spelled correctly? These points may seem trivial, but this could be an indication of the efforts needed to deliver workable programming (Stroot and Bumgarner 1989).

When choosing a software system, those in administrative positions must decide between in-house development or the support of an outside adviser. Regardless of the decision, users should be properly instructed in the operation of commercially developed software programs. If problems of this nature persist, the administrator may wish to consider hiring a consultant (Chatfield et al. 1990).

Every effort must be attempted to ascertain computer needs prior to purchasing hardware and software. The initial cost can be high, and these items need to be updated periodically. Training and security must also be provided, and space will probably be taken from other functions (McLellan et al. 1988). While difficulties in implementation may occur in any setting, they probably most generally occur within small departments or with the individual user. Large organizations can and do, of course, hire professional computer consultants to implement their computer system and train those hired to maintain them.

DIFFICULTIES IN IMPLEMENTATION

When setting up a new computer system a certain fascination often develops in the would-be user. Within a short time of implementation, however, the fascination may wear thin, and the system may not be used to its full potential. The task of setting up and learning the operation of a new computer system can take its toll on those individuals for whom the computer was purchased. Creative benefits realized as a result of the implementation of the system can be quickly forgotten through misuse and frustration.

Technical considerations also need to be taken into account when selecting software. Some questions that can be asked are: (1) Could the user be "caught" in a program, or have to exit a program in the middle due to programming that is not quality work? (2) Is

ADVANTAGES OF COMPUTER USE IN SPORTS

The advantages of using computers in sports appear endless. For the sports administrator, problems in day-to-day operations are eased considerably. For example, an intramural soccer coach wanting to know how many of the fields in the area have lights may find this information provided with a small number of strokes on the keyboard. Answers to questions that in the past could take several minutes or even hours to determine are now presented in a matter of seconds. For instance, maps can be displayed indicating where a city's racquetball courts are located. A table may then show the names of the facilities, addresses, and the number of racquetball courts available. Such tasks as inventory, maintenance, and salary schedules are less demanding when the necessary information is placed in a database. A properly installed computerized management system can precisely reveal how satisfied residents are concerning standards of recreation.

Perhaps the team sport most influenced by the use of computers has been baseball. It is, after all, a game of numbers—thousands of numbers generated each season: batting averages, earned-run averages, slugging percentages, on-base percentages, errors per game, runs per season, and miles per hour. In an attempt to gain every conceivable advantage, staffs of teams consisting of the manager, coaches, scouts, and other personnel are poring over these numbers with more zeal than was ever imagined three decades ago. With this heightened interest, a new term has entered the vocabulary of the sports enthusiast: *sabermetrician* (Cipher 1987). This term was coined from the initials of the Society of American Baseball Research. Founded in 1971, this organization has as its mission the promotion of the historical and statistical study of baseball. Devices used by sabermetricians include computers, modern statistical formulas, and a thorough knowledge of the game. Index cards used by earlier analysts of baseball have been succeeded by microchips.

Corporations such as the Elias Sports Bureau supply statistics prepared by a computer to major league baseball and the media (Cipher 1987). This information can be either specific or general. Specific information would be, for instance, a particular player's on-base percentage during a week of the season. Other information provided could indicate how a player performs under certain situations. Using this information, teams can ascertain many variables. An example would be the type of pitch a batter is likely to hit to a specific location on the playing field. Defensive strategy can also be improved with this type of data. A manager can change the defensive positioning of individual players using the given information.

By devising formulas that incorporate batting averages, on-base averages, and slugging percentages, sabermetricians assist clubs in offensive improvement. These formulas measure how well a player assists in run production. According to Cipher (1987) this may be the most accurate measure of run production yet developed.

Football and hockey teams have also benefited from the use of computers. Computerized offensive play selection, defensive alignments, game statistics, and individualized conditioning programs used during the season and in the off-season have been developed. Coaches and other staff personnel such as trainers are able to take a more creative approach to their specific responsibilities.

For the basketball enthusiast, computer systems have created yet another abbreviation, PPP (points per possession). This term was coined by Mikes (1987). To determine a team's PPP, a grid indicates the team on offense, lineups, substitutions, how the ball was acquired, type of offense/defense played, the individual offensive move completing the possession, the play result, the passer or the direction of the offensive move, the area in which the ball was acquired, and the pressure on the key offensive player. This information is then entered into a specific analysis program. From the information provided by several teams the following conclusions can be drawn according to Mikes (1987): Fast-break basketball (1.05 PPP) is more effective than set offenses (0.83 PPP); press defenses give up the same points per possession (0.83) as set defenses; of the four set defenses, the combination sets (box-and-one, triangle-and-two, etc.) allow the lowest points per possession figure (0.79), while the matchups allow the highest (1.11). Results of this study overturned the commonly held belief that shots attempted closest to the basket generated a higher percentage of scoring. With this and other types of information available, coaches and staff members at all levels of competition can do a more successful job of winning with the level of talent at their disposal. Playing percentage basketball can raise individual players and their teams to new plateaus of success.

Another area of sports that has developed into a refined science is sports medicine. Trainers and physical therapists are more accurately able to assess injuries caused by participation in athletic activities. As a result of computer technology, coaches can now be more confident in returning an injured player to action.

The assessment of athletic potential is another result of the greater usage of computers in sports. According to DaSilva (1987) a device known as the Vermeil Time Machine can recognize and evaluate talent. To carry out this task, baseline data are confirmed by specific criteria tests. Progress can be checked closely. Training can be compensated according to results of repeated tests. Prompt feedback is a tool of motivation that cannot be overemphasized. In an attempt to attain higher levels of play, an athlete can make the necessary alterations to a specific technique. The steps needed to reach these new levels are more fulfilling to the athlete as a result of the utilization of equipment such as the Vermeil Time Machine.

For those people who no longer participate or who never have participated in team sports, computers have enabled their activities to be more enjoyable and beneficial. Spending time on an exercise bike no longer has to be compared to a trip to the dentist's office. In the past, when using an exercise bike in time to music, there was no way to change the speed of the bike without then being offbeat with the music. According to Mertesdorf (1989), this no longer has to be the case. Results of this research reveal a means of synchronizing music with the rotation of the bike pedal. Electrical pulses are produced while the pedal is being rotated. This motion then controls transmission to a synthesizer of note codes for songs stored in a computer. One can keep time when the rate is altered without having to concentrate on doing so. This process can lessen the effect of unconscious mental fatigue, which can drain the supply of desire from the individual. Due to this drain, the enthusiastic start of a fitness program can terminate in frustration and a return to previous levels of such unwanted health threats as stress and excess poundage. By receiving more satisfaction from exercise, an individual can experience such positive attributes as healthier self-esteem and personal appearance. Other exercise equipment that may include computerized features include rowing machines and treadmills.

COMPUTER APPLICATIONS IN BODY FITNESS

Since 1983, a sufficient number of software programs have been produced to administer data pertaining to physical fitness (Stroot and Bumgarner 1989). Combining the expertise and efforts in physical fitness, instructional design, and computer programming, many excellent software programs have been developed. This new generation of computer-interfaced devices enables a measurement of strength of muscles for exercises that include whole body motions. For example, a computerized dynamometer has been used to determine reliability of multijoint upper and lower body muscular performance (Hortobagyi and Katch 1990). With proper training, these software programs can be effectively used without a great deal of difficulty or problems, either short- or long-term in nature.

These software programs can provide the user with such material as a fitness profile, a prescription of exercise determined by individual needs based on an in-depth assessment prior to the commencement of the program, and an ongoing and total record of the results of the tests. All of this information can provide the individual with a means of maintaining a proper level of motivation to reach attainable, desired goals (Stroot and Bumgarner 1989).

References

Chatfield, D., C. B. Deans, Jr., and D. B. Freshwater. 1990. Computerizing parks and recreation. *Parks and Recreation* 25(6): 54–59.

Cipher, B. 1987. Square root, root, root, for the home team. *Discover* 8(10):87–88, 90–92.

DaSilva, D. 1987. Vermeil's Time Machine. *National Strength and Conditioning Association Journal* 9(6):57–59.

Francis, K. 1989. Normalization of weight-lifting performances. *National Strength and Conditioning Association Journal* 11(6):45–47.

Hortobagyi, T., and F. I. Katch. 1990. Reliability of muscle mechanical characteristics for isokinetic and isotonic squat and bench press exercise using a multifunction computerized dynamometer. *Research Quarterly for Exercise and Sport* 61(2):191–95.

McLellan, G. K., J. H. Syme, and M. Uysal. 1988. A multiuse computer training lab. *Journal of Physical Education, Recreation, and Dance* 59(9):53–55.

Mertesdorf, F. L. 1989. A device for using an exercise cycle in time with music. *Perceptual and Motor Skills* 69(2):475–80.

Mikes, J. 1987. A computer breakdown of percentage basketball. *Scholastic Coach* 57 (4):52–55.

Stroot, S., and S. Bumgarner. 1989. Fitness assessment—Putting computers to work. *Journal of Physical Education, Recreation, and Dance* 60(6):44–49.

For Further Reading

Mikes, J. 1988. Percentage basketball, #3. *Scholastic Coach* 57(6):52–55.

Kenny O. McDougle

SPREADSHEETS

In 1979 a program called VisiCalc, the first electronic spreadsheet program, was introduced for the Apple II microcomputer. Little did anyone suspect that the spreadsheet would almost create the microcomputer industry through its amazing ability to answer "What if?" questions. Essentially, VisiCalc (an abbreviation for *visi*ble *calc*ulator) was an electronic substitute for the columnar pad, pencil, and calculator that permitted mathematical and financial modeling. Microcomputer users now take the spreadsheet and related software for granted, but before VisiCalc there was no easy way to plan, calculate, revise, and recalculate a set of numbers.

VisiCalc was the creation of two business students, Dan BRICKLIN and Bob Frankston, who sensed a need to be able to "word-process" numbers. After writing prototypes, the authors developed a commercial version in 6502 assembly language to run on a 32K-byte Apple II. The reaction was beyond anyone's expectation, and soon cus-

tomers were purchasing computers just to run VisiCalc. It was converted to run on other machines such as the TRS-80 Model I, Commodore PET, Atari 800, Apple III, Hewlett-Packard, and IBM PC. By 1985, over 800,000 copies of VisiCalc had been sold. Companion programs, VisiTrend and VisiFile, for graphics and file management, respectively, using the existing spreadsheet computer file, also appeared and gained popularity during the early 1980s.

In 1983, VisiCalc's position on the bestseller list was overtaken by Lotus 1-2-3, a Lotus Development Corporation product that was similar to VisiCalc and other spreadsheets. The important distinction was that Lotus combined presentation graphics features (bar graphs, pie charts, and line graphs) and database management capabilities (sorting, searching, and extracting) with the spreadsheet functions. Since its introduction, Lotus 1-2-3 has been the major force in the spreadsheet industry. Today it has an installed base of over 7 million users.

The packaging of several features became known as "integrated systems" or "integrated software packages." Since the advent of Lotus, many other integrated spreadsheet systems have appeared, such as SuperCalc, Multiplan, Microsoft Excel, Quattro, VP Planner, and Symphony. Today the spreadsheet industry is among the most competitive in the entire microcomputer industry.

SPREADSHEET CONCEPTS

As mentioned above, most modern productivity software packages such as Lotus 1-2-3 combine the spreadsheet with other functions such as graphics and database management. This section will address the spreadsheet function only.

The simplest way to describe a spreadsheet is to imagine a grid or array with rows and columns. Rows are numbered (1, 2, 3, 4 . . .) and columns are denoted by letters (A, B, C, D . . .). The intersection of a row and a column forms a "cell." Each cell is given a location or address using the row and column in which it is located. The cell in the upper left corner of the matrix would, therefore, have location A1. The cell to its immediate right would be location B1, since it resides in row 1 and column B. The cell below A1 would be location A2, and so on. The contents of the respective cells can be values (numbers that can be used in numerical calculations), labels (text, letters, numbers, and special characters that cannot be used in mathematical manipulations), or formulas (either user-defined mathematical calculations or predefined formulas). The number of possible cells is a function of the specific spreadsheet software, the type of microcomputer, and the amount of available computer memory.

As an illustration of a spreadsheet, consider the following simple example. A person is developing a household budget for three months: January, February, and March. This example includes four objects of expense only: food, rent, utilities, and entertainment. A layout or spreadsheet of the household budget form might resemble Figure 1. This example includes three possible cell contents. In cells A1 through A6 and B1 through E1 are labels (text or words). In cells B2 through D5 are numbers (values), the estimates of the monthly expenses by category. Even though numbers appear in cells B6 through E6 and E2 through E5 (the totals by month and by category), the cell contents are really formulas. The displayed numbers are the answers to the calculations of the formulas. In cell B6 would be a formula such as @SUM(B2 . . . B5). The exact format and

formula syntax depend on the specific spreadsheet. This notation indicates that the number displayed in cell B6 will reflect the sum of cells B2+B3+B4+B5. In a similar manner, the formula in cell E2 would be @SUM(B2 . . . D2). This will cause the contents of cells B2, C2, and D2 to be added and this sum to be shown in cell E2.

The "@SUM" is an example of a built-in function. Most modern spreadsheets will contain dozens of built-in formulas and functions for statistics and for financial and mathematical calculations. Even though many of these functions may perform rather complex calculations, they are easily entered and will execute almost instantly. Other common built-in functions include square roots, rounding of numbers, random numbers, logarithms, exponential functions, trigonometric functions, statistics (mean, standard deviation, and variance), financial and accounting functions (investment returns, loan payments, present value, future value, depreciation, etc.), logical conditions, and many others. Because the cells "interact," any change in an expense estimate will be immediately reflected in the row and column totals. For this reason, the budget can be used to answer "What if?" What if, for instance, the entertainment estimate in March were increased from $50 to $100? The revised spreadsheet, which would be instantly recalculated, is shown in Figure 2. Not one but four cells are affected—D5 (the March entertainment estimate), E5 (total entertain-

	A	B	C	D	E
1	Expense	January	February	March	TOTAL
2	Food	$200	$200	$200	$600
3	Rent	$250	$250	$275	$775
4	Utilities	$100	$100	$ 75	$275
5	Entertainment	$ 50	$ 75	$ 50	$175
6	TOTAL	$600	$625	$600	$1825

FIGURE 1

	A	B	C	D	E
1	Expense	January	February	March	TOTAL
2	Food	$200	$200	$200	$600
3	Rent	$250	$250	$275	$775
4	Utilities	$100	$100	$ 75	$275
5	Entertainment	$ 50	$ 75	$100	$225
6	TOTAL	$600	$625	$650	$1875

FIGURE 2

ment), D6 (total expenses for the month of March), and E6 (the grand total).

The capabilities of a spreadsheet are now examined in a slightly more complicated application. In this example a teacher/class sponsor is developing a budget for the prom. The teacher anticipates revenue (income) from three sources—car washes, bake sales, and admission tickets. Some expenses will be associated with each of these fund-raising activities. The prom will require funds for five items—decorations, food, the band, security, and a custodian. Anyone who has ever prepared a budget knows that the initial stages represent a "What if?" situation. The teacher has projected $500 in revenues from the car washes and $550 from the bake sale. She also expects to sell 1,000 tickets at $2 per ticket. The band has agreed to play for a guarantee of $500 plus one-half of the paid admissions. Other expenses are for decorations and food. Figure 3 shows

```
            A              B              C              D              E
 1                   PROM INCOME
 2   # OF TICKETS                1000
 3   ***************************************************************************
 4   SOURCE        CAR WASHES     BAKE SALE      DOOR @$2       TOTALS
 5   - - - - -     - - - - - - -  - - - - - -    - - - - - -    - - - - -
 6   INCOME           500.00         550.00        2000.00        3050.00
 7   EXPENSES          50.00          20.00          10.00          80.00
 8   NET PROCEEDS     450.00         530.00        1990.00        2970.00
 9
10   ***************************************************************************
11                   PROM EXPENSE
12   ITEM
13   - - - -
14   DECORATIONS      325.00
15   FOOD             225.00
16   BAND            1500.00
17   SECURITY         100.00
18   CUSTODIAN         50.00
19                    - - - - -
20   TOTAL EXP       2200.00
21
22   TOTAL INC       2970.00
23
24   NET DIFF         770.00  (INC–EXP)
```

FIGURE 3

how the prom budget might look if presented as a spreadsheet. The net difference of income minus expenses is $770. More importantly, in a spreadsheet form the question "What if?" can now be easily answered. What if only 700 tickets are sold and the car wash nets only $250? Income minus expenses (NET DIFF.) equals only $40. Figure 4 illustrates this spreadsheet. What if 600 tickets were sold, the car washes net $200, and the bake sale provides only $300? Now the net difference is a loss of $110, since expenses exceed revenue. Figure 5 presents this scenario.

USES OF SPREADSHEETS

As can be seen from the previous two examples, spreadsheets can be used for almost any application in which data and text are presented in rows and columns. Planning, estimating, budgeting, and decision making account for the majority of spreadsheet usage. Most business budget applications involve calculation of anticipated revenues and expenses from multiple sources. Because of the uncertainty of the data projections, users may wish to examine multiple scenarios based on different estimates.

In addition, spreadsheets can be used for business applications, such as:

- investment analysis (e.g., determination of lease versus purchase arrangements or examination of real-estate return potential)
- financial statement preparation
- personnel records and payroll
- expense calculation and reporting
- data entry (including data export to other software)
- statistical analysis
- tax records and calculation
- sales reporting and analysis
- depreciation schedules
- amortization tables
- balance sheets
- cash flow analysis
- loan management
- accounts payable/receivable management
- income statements
- cost-benefit analysis
- production scheduling

	A	B	C	D	E
1		PROM INCOME			
2	# OF TICKETS	700			
3	***				
4	SOURCE	CAR WASHES	BAKE SALE	DOOR @$2	TOTALS
5	– – – –	– – – – – – –	– – – – – –	– – – – – –	– – – – –
6	INCOME	300.00	320.00	1400.00	2020.00
7	EXPENSES	50.00	20.00	10.00	80.00
8	NET PROCEEDS	250.00	300.00	1390.00	1940.00
9					
10	***				
11		PROM EXPENSE			
12	ITEM				
13	– – – –				
14	DECORATIONS	325.00			
15	FOOD	225.00			
16	BAND	1200.00			
17	SECURITY	100.00			
18	CUSTODIAN	50.00			
19		– – – – –			
20	TOTAL EXP	1900.00			
21					
22	TOTAL INC	1940.00			
23					
24	NET DIFF	40.00	(INC–EXP)		

FIGURE 4

```
            A              B            C            D            E
 1                   PROM INCOME
 2      # OF TICKETS                  600
 3      *******************************************************************
 4      SOURCE      CAR WASHES    BAKE SALE    DOOR @$2      TOTALS
 5      -----       ---------     -------      -------       -----
 6      INCOME         250.00       320.00      1200.00      1770.00
 7      EXPENSES        50.00        20.00        10.00        80.00
 8      NET PROCEEDS   200.00       300.00      1190.00      1690.00
 9
10      *******************************************************************
11                   PROM EXPENSE
12      ITEM
13      ----
14      DECORATIONS    325.00
15      FOOD           225.00
16      BAND          1100.00
17      SECURITY       100.00
18      CUSTODIAN       50.00
19                     -----
20      TOTAL EXP     1800.00
21
22      TOTAL INC     1690.00
23
24      NET DIFF      -110.00  (INC-EXP)
```

FIGURE 5

- strategic marketing
- determination of personnel requirements
- almost any financial or mathematical model

Personal uses of spreadsheets can be as equally productive and time-saving as business applications. Uses include home budgets, checkbook registers, income-tax records calculation and preparation, loan analysis, financial statements, home mortgage amortization schedules and analysis, small business finanical records and accounting, schedules, investment evaluation, mailing lists, and numerous other possible applications.

FEATURES OF SPREADSHEETS

Almost all modern spreadsheet software packages include provision for certain functions or features: (1) creating the spreadsheet; (2) revising; (3) formatting; (4) printing; and (5) file management. Additionally, integrated software includes presentation graphics and database management. Creation of the spreadsheet involves initial entry of text, numbers, and formulas into the respective cells. Revision refers to the modification (deletion, insertion, replacement) of the content of the various cells. Formatting indicates the change of appearance of cell entries (e.g., numbers may be formatted as currency, as integers, or in scientific notation). Printing can refer to output as hard copy (paper) or as a disk file. File management includes saving the spreadsheet as a disk file, replacement, or deletion or combining of files.

Popular commercial spreadsheets for microcomputers offer the advantage of being menu-driven systems. Once the user has a basic understanding of the spreadsheet software, commands can be selected from menus on the screen.

When spreadsheet software is executed, the program is read or loaded into the random-access memory (RAM) of the computer. There it resides along with the disk operating systems (DOS) and any other program that may be resident. Once the spreadsheet program is executed or run, the user is presented with an essentially blank screen similar to the one illustrated in Figure 6. As discussed above, the cells are addressed according to

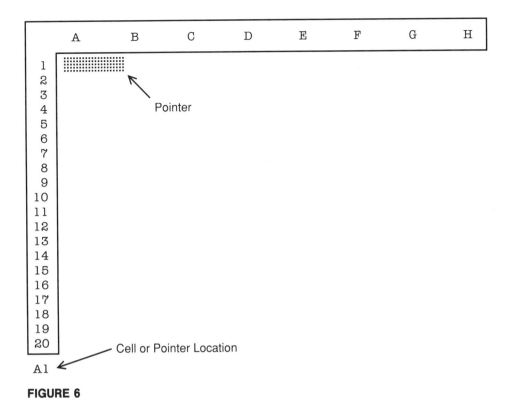

FIGURE 6

the row numbers and column letters displayed on the screen. The current location of the spreadsheet pointer is shown in the bottom left corner. Once the user has accessed this screen, contents of cells (text, numbers, or formulas) can be entered. When a calculation occurs in a given cell, the results of that calculation (e.g., a sum or average)—not the formula itself—are displayed on the spreadsheet. The formula, which is the real cell content, will be displayed at the bottom or top of the screen.

Spreadsheet usage involves data entry (entering contents into the respective cells) or command entry. This is a fundamental and important point. Various commands can then be selected. As data and commands are entered, they reside in the memory of the computer. Once the user has completed entry, or even during the entry process, the spreadsheet data can be saved to a disk file by using the appropriate command from a menu.

In summary, the impact of the electronic spreadsheet on the microcomputer industry cannot be overstated. The spreadsheet has, in fact, been the principal impetus for the success and acceptance of microcomputer technology. One would be hard pressed to find a successful corporation, business, government office, or industry of almost any size that did not use spreadsheets productively. Students at most colleges and universities now find themselves routinely working with spreadsheets in their studies. Users of spreadsheets report that they are almost indispensable. The future of the spreadsheet appears promising with regard to power, efficiency, and features. The intense competition among the major producers (Lotus Corporation, Microsoft Corporation, Borland International, Paperback Software, Computer Associates, and others) will benefit the entire microcomputer market and industry. With the advent of increasingly powerful operating systems, faster microprocessors, and large amounts of addressable memory, there will be numerous enhancements. Already these improvements include three-dimensional worksheets, multiple sheets on screen, enhanced graphics, access to external files, file linking, pull-down menus, and faster calculation speeds. No doubt these and other features will make the spreadsheet both a more productive microcomputer tool and more enjoyable to use.

For Further Reading

Hallam, T., S. F. Hallam, and J. Hallam. 1985. *Microcomputer use.* Orlando, Fla.: Academic Press.

Ingalsbe, L. 1989. *Using computers and applications software.* Columbus, Ohio: Merrill.

Loebbecke, J. K., and M. A. Vasarhelyi. 1986. *Microcomputers.* Homewood, Ill.: Richard D. Irwin.

Perry, C. S. 1988. *Productivity software guide.* New York: Holt, Rinehart, and Winston.

Que Corporation. 1989. *Using 1-2-3.* Carmel, Ind.: Que Corporation.

Vinsonhaler, J. F., C. C. Wagner, and C. G. Gantry. 1989. *People and computers.* St. Paul, Minn.: West.

William C. Bozeman

STATISTICAL APPLICATIONS OF COMPUTERS

The computer has fostered the application of statistics and revolutionized its practice. It has furthered the spread of quality control and facilitated ever larger and more frequent experimental studies, clinical trials, opinion polls, and surveys. While it has provided the professional statistician with new and more powerful statistical tools, it has also given the nonstatistician access to techniques that were formerly the exclusive domain of the professional. Three new statistical methodologies have arisen in response to the computer's use: subsampling techniques, statistical computing, and statistical graphics.

STATISTICAL SOFTWARE

The spread of statistical applications in every branch of science, government, and industry has been fostered by the ready availability of statistical software. Today, computers perform every aspect of the statistical process from the design of an experiment through the collection, maintenance, and analysis of data. Users range from the executive to the scientist, from the professional statistician to those with little or no knowledge of statistics.

Statistical software may be subdivided into five categories: general-purpose, experimental design, forecasting, quality control, and other, special-purpose statistical software.

General-purpose statistics packages are available for virtually all models of computer from the smallest microcomputer to the largest mainframe computer. These perform a wide range of statistical procedures from descriptive statistics—means, variances, and frequency distributions—through analysis of variance and covariance, regression, and discriminant analysis.

The choice of general-purpose packages is limited on the mainframe: SPSS and SAS are the two chief competitors, though the NAG and IMSL statistical subroutine libraries are in common use as supplements to standard computer languages. On the other hand, there are about fifty commercially available general-purpose statistics packages for MS-DOS-based computers and more than ten packages for UNIX-based workstations and multiuser systems (*Annual Report on Statistical Software,* 6th ed.).

The minimal computer system for statistics applications, an Apple II, consists of an 8-bit processor, 48K of memory, and a floppy disk for mass storage. For the repeated analysis of large datasets, a mathematics (floating point) coprocessor, an array processor, a hard disk, a high-resolution graphics device, and extra memory are desirable.

Ease of use varies dramatically from program to program. Some statistics packages are mere collections of isolated routines; others are built around an arcane command language with a database manager as a central core; still others, the best for the average user, incorporate pull-down point-and-click menus, icons, defaults, prompts, context-sensitive help, hypertext, and expert systems.

Though the nominal objects of a statistics program are the statistics, the entry and management of data and the reporting of results constitute at least 95 percent of the computing and personnel effort. Thus, the ideal general-purpose statistics package (1) provides for data verification at the time of data entry; (2) converts and uses data from other computer programs (both microcomputer and mainframe computer); (3) maintains a single, integrated database; (4) merges two files into a single file correctly on the basis of a common matching variable; (5) provides the needed statistical routines for at least 95 percent of statistical applications; (6) saves command (macro) files for reuse; and (7) produces reports—graphics and text—that can be passed on directly to others.

This ideal is seldom realized in practice and most statistics users today must rely on a wide variety of other computer software including spreadsheets, database management systems, report generators, and graphics packages. As a result, one of the best-selling programs for the IBM personal computer is DBMS-Copy, which can exchange data among thirty-two different statistics packages and databases.

EXPERIMENTAL DESIGN

Experimental design programs help scientists and engineers determine the optimal number of observations and factor levels for use at each stage in a series of experiments. These programs divide between relatively simple software for use in designing surveys and single-factor experiments and more complex programs for use in response surface analysis. In the future, computer software may also be expected to help in the design of multistage and sequential experiments.

Off-the-shelf experimental design programs are available for only a few models of computer, such as MS-DOS- and UNIX-based workstations.

FORECASTS

Forecasting software is in common use for projecting the demand for products and resources, manpower requirements, and opportunities for new products and services.

In the early 1980s, only large corporations and big government could afford the trained personnel and computer time needed to make accurate forecasts. Today, inexpensive personal computers coupled with easy-to-use forecasting software put accurate forecasts within the reach of every business.

The ideal forecasting program can process data from a variety of sources (spreadsheets and economic projections, as well as data entered at the keyboard), perform an exploratory analysis, "recommend" appropriate transformations and analyses, perform all three of the principal forecasting algorithms (exponential smoothing, multivariate regression, and Box-Jenkins), and provide forecasts and confidence intervals in graph as well as tabular form.

QUALITY CONTROL

The computer, long acknowledged as responsible for major improvements in industrial productivity, is also responsible today for improvements in product quality. Manufacturers, small and large, along with clinical and testing laboratories, use quality-control software to track and control the quality of their products.

The ideal quality-control program integrates real-time data acquisition, database management, real-time display, statistics, and graphics in a single package. The challenge lies in adapting these capabilities for use by workers with little or no statistics background.

A dedicated minicomputer or a network of MS-DOS-based computers is commonly used for quality-control purposes. Quality-control programs range in complexity from a set of templates for use with a spreadsheet to a series of modules built around a single integrated database.

As one example, the MS-DOS-based personal computer program MetriStat allows users to enter and track the date and time of day of each reading, the machine, the operator, the supplier, the lot number, up to five measurements per reading, and the nature and number of defects. Data may be acquired directly from the keyboard or a variety of different computerized gauges.

This program is completely menu-driven to facilitate its use by less-motivated personnel. The output of the program, designed to facilitate rapid decision making, includes charts of fraction defective, nonconformities, X-bar, range and runs, and Pareto diagrams as well as cause-and-effect, acceptance sampling, and tool wear analyses.

TRENDS

Statistical applications have benefited from recent hardware advances in parallel and array processing, increased processor speed and addressing capability, and higher-speed memory and mass storage devices. Corresponding trends in statistical software include modifications to support parallel processing, additional data entry and reporting routines, high-resolution graphics and hypertext, and built-in expert systems.

Direct data entry from computerized instruments and voice recognition devices is eliminating the errors associated with time-consuming keyboard entry. High-resolution graphics displays and laser printers are replacing character-by-character line-printer graphics, facilitating the presentation of results and stimulating new insights.

The wide availability of inexpensive statistical software has had both pluses and minuses. On the one hand, it has freed many workers in the sciences and engineering from dependence on the statistician. On the other, the inappropriate and improper use of statistics is more and more in evidence. One solution to the misuse of statistics lies with expert systems that guide the novice to the correct statistic. Recent personal computer programs that incorporate expert systems include the Scientific Wheel, Design Ease, and Forecast Pro. The trend toward smarter software is expected to continue.

REVOLUTION IN STATISTICS

The plethora of readily available software tools has seen a shift in the focus of the professional statistician from calculation to model building and model verification. Three new and not-so-new statistical disciplines have arisen: subsampling techniques, statistical computing, and statistical graphics.

SUBSAMPLING TESTS

The permutation tests credited to Pitman (1937/1938) were among the first statistical tests to be developed. Computational complexity made their use impractical initially because of the limited computing power available in the 1930s. Much of the statistical theory developed in the 1940s and 1950s represents an attempt to get around this restriction through the use of asymptotic or large-sample approximations. The permutation test's revival in popularity parallels the increased availability of high-speed computers. The first- and second-generation computers of the 1950s and 1960s gave rise to the field of nonparametric statistics, that is, permutation methods applied to ranks (Bradley 1968); the third- and fourth-generation computers of the 1970s and 1980s have seen increased use of the observations themselves (Howard 1981, Maritz 1981).

The second category of subsampling method, the bootstrap, also would be inconceivable without the ready availability of inexpensive high-speed desktop computers. The bootstrap, introduced by Efron (1979) and Hartigan (1969), entails repeated random sampling with replacement from the original observations (or a suitable transformation thereof); the permutation test requires methodical sampling without replacement until all combinations of the original observations (or a relevant random sample thereof) have been examined.

The value of the two types of subsampling test lies in their wide range of applications. They can be applied to continuous, discrete, or categorical data; normal, almost normal, or nonnormal data; and homogeneous (textbook) or heterogeneous (real-life) data. Missing or censored data may affect the power of a resampling test but not its existence or exactness. A most powerful bootstrap and/or a most powerful unbiased permutation test often exists in cases where a most powerful parametric test fails for lack of knowledge of some yet unknown nuisance parameter (Lehmann 1986).

STATISTICAL COMPUTING

Computers can create as many problems as they resolve. A classic example is the rounding errors that can arise in the computation of a sample variance. A well-known computational shortcut entails subtracting the square of the sum of the observations from the sum of the squares. This method of computing the sample variance requires only a single pass through the data. This method works well with pencil and paper, but on a computer, the errors resulting from rounding may equal or exceed the variance itself. One time-consuming solution is to perform two passes through the observations: one pass to sum the observations and compute the mean, and a second pass to compute the sum of the squares of the deviations about the mean. A more modern method makes use of a moving average so that the calculations may again be completed in a single pass through the data.

The development of this and similar algorithms that increase both the speed and the accuracy of statistical calculations is the substance of a new mathematical discipline called statistical computing.

STATISTICAL GRAPHICS

Sometimes, how results are reported can be as important as the results themselves, or more so. An effective graphics display can jog the intuition and provide additional insight into the data. New computer-aided graphics include rotating three-dimensional displays, which help the user to discern patterns, and hypertext, which allows the user to gain information quickly about typical or outlying values. The study of new and faster methods for retrieving and displaying data is the substance of a new field called statistical graphics (Tufte 1983).

References

Annual report on statistical software. 6th ed. P. Good, ed. Huntington Beach, Calif.: Information Research.

Bradley, J. V. 1968. *Distribution-free statistical tests.* Englewood Cliffs, N.J.: Prentice-Hall.

Efron, B. 1979. Bootstrap methods: Another look at the jacknife. *Annals of Statistics* 7:1–26.

Hartigan, J. A. 1969. Using subsample values as typical values. *Journal of the American Statistical Association* 64:1303–17.

Howard, M. [Good, P.]. 1981. Randomization in the analysis of experiments and clinical trials. *American Laboratory* 13:98–102.

Lehmann, E. L. 1986. *Testing statistical hypotheses.* New York: Wiley.

Maritz, J. S. 1981. *Distribution-free statistical methods.* London: Chapman and Hall.

Pitman, E. J. G. 1937/1938. Significance tests which may be applied to samples from any population. *Royal Statistical Society Supplement* 4:119–30, 225–32. *Biometrika* 29:322–35.

Tufte, E. R. 1983. *The visual display of quantitative information.* Cheshire, Conn. Graphics Press.

For Further Reading

New Developments in Statistical Computing, American Statistician. Monthly. Alexandria, Va.: American Statistical Association.

Software Design Section, *Journal of Statistical Computing and Simulation.* London: Gordon and Breach.

Statistical Computing and Statistical Graphics Newsletter. Alexandria, Va.: American Statistical Association.

Phillip I. Good

STATISTICAL DATABASES

See Access Control

STRATEGIC APPLICATIONS OF INFORMATION TECHNOLOGY

Strategic uses or applications of information technology (IT) are usually designed to provide an organization with a distinct advantage over competitors. The strategic applications of a competitor may motivate investment in such systems to help meet the competitive challenge. A competitive advantage results in such benefits as greater sales, improved profits, greater customer retention, and improved pricing.

TYPES OF STRATEGIC USE

Major types of strategic applications of information technology are IT-based products or services, control of a distribution channel, interorganizational systems, personalization of products or services, and leveraging of scarce resources.

An example of an IT-based product or service is the Merrill Lynch Cash Management Account (CMA), developed in 1978. The service provided an interest-bearing alternative to a traditional checking account, with a single statement summarizing securities held in the account. The CMA allowed a variety of services. By 1985 the sophisticated IT-based product had attracted a dominant share of the U.S. market for this type of account.

Control of a distribution channel is illustrated by Benjamin Moore Paints. This corporation provides independent home decoration centers that distribute its product with a computer system that can exactly match a sample of paint brought in by a customer. For a typical store, the computer system increased by 5 to 10 percent the sales of Moore's paint as a proportion of the sales of competitors' products.

Interorganizational systems achieve strategic advantage by working with two or more cooperating organizations. Citibank POS, for instance, established electronic connections with grocery chains throughout the United States. At Tom Thumb stores in Texas, customers who purchased groceries with their magnetically encoded card received discounts on some items and rebate certificates at the end of the month. Each night, Citibank POS accessed the detailed purchase data in the stores' computers. After demographic information on shoppers was appended, the purchase behavior database was available for sale to consumer foods manufacturers to track the effectiveness of a new advertising campaign or for other marketing uses.

Strategically advantageous interorganizational linkages are most commonly between the firm and its customers. They often represent extensions of systems developed initially for the firm's own internal use. For instance, an order entry system used by salespeople may be made available to customer purchasing agents. Firms have also gained strategic advantage through interorganizational systems linking them with suppliers, dealers, government agencies, or even competitors.

Advantage can also be achieved by personalizing the service or product to meet the unique needs of a specific customer. For instance, the Marine Division of International Paints developed an information system that provided its customers, the managers of large fleets of oceangoing vessels, with information on the painting requirements for each ship within the customer's fleet. The information was captured by the Marine Division's worldwide network of dealers. As a ship tied up at port, the company's representative carefully categorized the condition of the ship's paint. The information was then sent back to headquarters where it was available for use by sales, marketing, and product development personnel.

Often significant cost advantages can be achieved by leveraging scarce expertise or by electronically moving work to sources of low-cost labor. For instance, the foreign division of a large engineering company uses videoconferencing technology to augment its small Asian staff with electronic "visits" by specialized engineers from its European headquarters. Customers participating in such conferences are assured that they are dealing with a global firm capable of providing service on a worldwide basis. By use of a central engineering database, common computer-aided engineering tools, and electronic and voice mail, the engineering firm is able to move design work instantly from engineering centers in one part of the globe to another.

SUSTAINING COMPETITIVE ADVANTAGE

Since strategic uses usually draw their justification from anticipated increases in revenues and market share, management needs to consider carefully the likely sustainability of the proposed application—that is, for how long can the firm expect to achieve these advantages before one or more competitors effectively respond? Sustainability usually depends on three questions: how long to copy, who can copy, and whether it will help to copy.

How Long to Copy?

Some strategic applications can be quickly copied by competitors. The technology may be available for purchase, customers or others may have a good understanding of how the system operates, or the firm's own personnel may be hired away by a competitor to produce a similar system. On the other hand, some systems may be protected by patents, copyright, secrecy, the inherent complexity of the application, or the unwillingness of a competitor to respond quickly.

Who Can Copy?

Firms competing in the same industry often use quite different strategies and technologies. If a strategic application of information technology builds on the organization's existing unique characteristics, it may prove virtually impossible for a competitor to duplicate it. For instance, Wingtip Courier, a Dallas-based local package delivery service, installed radio-communicating computer terminals in all its delivery vehicles. The dispatch system they developed for the terminals permitted Wingtip to provide higher-quality service to the professional firms they served. It was an advantage that Wingtip's competitors found difficult to match because competitors operated in a different way. Wingtip owned its own vehicles and paid its drivers a wage, but most competitors contracted with independent drivers who worked for commission. Placing expensive computer systems in independent vehicles and training independent drivers was a near-ly insurmountable barrier to competitive response.

Will It Help to Copy?

Being first with a strategic system may preclude competitive response because one system is sufficient or switching costs are very high. For instance, in the case of the Benjamin Moore paint-matching computer, there was little incentive for a paint dealer to have more than one such system installed, though the Benjamin Moore System could only be used with Moore's paints. Likewise, a customer of Merrill Lynch's CMA probably has no real need for a second such account and little incentive to switch from a satisfactory system to a competitor.

For Further Reading

Cash, J. I., and B. Kosynski. 1985. IS redraws competitive boundaries. *Harvard Business Review* 63(2):134–42.

Feeny, D. F., and B. Ives. 1990. In search of sustainability: reaping long-term advantage from investments in information technology. *Journal of Management Information Systems* 7(1):27–46.

McFarlan, F. W. 1984. Information technology changes the way you compete. *Harvard Business Review* 62(3):98–108.

Porter, M., and V. E. Millar. 1985. How information gives you competitive advantage. *Harvard Business Review* 63(4):149–60.

Vitale, M. R. 1986. The growing risks of information systems success. *MIS Quarterly* 10(4):327–34.

Wiseman, C. 1985. *Strategy and computers: Information systems as competitive weapons.* Homewood, Ill.: Dow Jones–Irwin.

Blake Ives

SUPERCOMPUTERS

A computer is called a *supercomputer* if it is among the fastest numerical processors in the world. It must also have sufficient memory, input/output (I/O) bandwidth, and software support to be usable for large-scale scientific calculation. Supercomputers are large computers, typically costing tens of millions of dollars. Only a few companies manufacture them, most notably Cray Research and Thinking Machines (of the United States) and Fujitsu, NEC, and Hitachi (of Japan).

The essence of supercomputing is the ability to deliver high-performance computer resources to many users simultaneously. This requires a combination of the fastest available central processing units (CPUs), large memories, high-speed secondary storage, and high-bandwidth network connections. Software requirements include highly *optimizing compilers*, extensive mathematical and scientific libraries, and multiuser operating systems.

Supercomputers are used for modeling a variety of physical and mathematical systems and for large-scale data analysis. Engineers employ supercomputers for finite element analysis and fluid dynamics. Physicists utilize them for development and analysis of physical theories, design of experimental apparatus, and analysis of experimental data. Geologists model oil reservoirs and analyze seismic data.

The development of supercomputers is driven forward by the increasing demand from scientists for computer resources. The newest experimental devices such as the Hubble Telescope and the Superconducting Supercollider will generate many times more data than any previous devices. Climate models and weather forecasting are limited in their accuracy and timeliness by available computers. The need for supercomputers is increasing, and the architecture of supercomputers will continue to change to address those needs.

The U.S. government has identified a need for computers that can perform 1 trillion operations per second (1 teraflop) with 1 trillion bytes of high-speed storage (1 terabyte). This is at least 100 times faster and larger than for existing supercomputers. Major manufacturers and research consortiums are proposing methods of achieving this goal. All feasible alternatives require the exploitation of massive amounts of parallelism.

CHARACTERISTICS OF SUPERCOMPUTER COMPUTATIONS

Supercomputer computations are characterized by a combination of a large number of data points and a large amount of calculation per data point. There is usually a regularity in the computation that allows highly parallel execution. A typical numerical simulation has a discrete grid of data points that represents an approximation to some physical system. The identical calculation steps are applied to every data point.

In the case of a weather model, the atmosphere is represented as a collection of physical quantities such as pressure, temperature, wind velocity, and density. The computer model consists of a value for each quantity at a discrete, finite set of points. The simulation proceeds by calculating values for each data point at time $t + 1$ from those of its neighbors at time t. After each time step, the data values are copied to secondary storage, to be saved for visualization and further analysis.

A supercomputer provides the advantages of larger models, more complex and more accurate algorithms, and fast production of data for visualization. The major weather forecasting centers depend on a large collection of supercomputers for their calculations. An increase in supercomputer performance produces a direct improvement in the accuracy of forecasts.

CHARACTERISTICS OF SUPERCOMPUTER ARCHITECTURE

Most supercomputer architectures include *pipelined instruction execution, pipelined arithmetic units,* and *interleaved memory access.* The peak performance is achieved by utilizing these components in parallel. A program that does not employ these parallel capabilities will execute many times slower than one that has been carefully adapted to the architecture.

The Cray Y-MP produced by Cray Research, Inc., is an excellent example of current supercomputer technology. As shown in Figure 1, the system supports up to eight CPUs, each with four parallel memory ports, large instruction cache, multiple pipelined arithmetic units, and 512 vector registers. All CPUs share a *multiported memory* with 32 million 64-bit words in 256 banks. The pipelined arithmetic and memory access units allow a single operation to specify a vector for each of its operands. Hence, a vector register load can read sixty-four operands from memory and a vector multiply can multiply sixty-four pairs of operands and produce sixty-four results. Each vector operation yields a single result in each clock cycle. The high performance of the Y-MP is achieved by exploiting all of the CPU components in parallel. For example, during a single clock cycle of 6 nanoseconds, the CPU

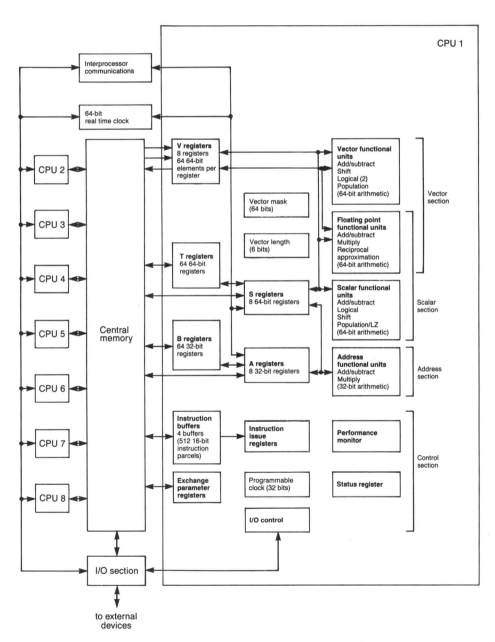

FIGURE 1. Cray Y-MP system organization. *Courtesy Cray Research, Inc.*

can load two data values into registers, store a third data value from register to memory, complete an operation on every vector unit, and execute a scalar instruction. This results in a sustainable computation rate of over 2 billion floating-point operations per second (gigaflops) for an eight-CPU system.

There is a high-speed secondary memory of up to 512 million words, called the Solid-state Storage Device (SSD), used for large intermediate files. Transfer rates of 100 to 1,000 megabytes per second and access times of less than 25 milliseconds can be achieved between the Cray mainframe and the SSD. I/O is performed by one or two I/O subsystems, each with four I/O processors. Each I/O processor has local memory and up to four parallel data streams per disk control unit. Network connections are supported at up to 100 megabytes per second. Disk performance has been enhanced by using parallel disk farms. Eight standard 1-gigabyte disks are connected to a single controller, which reads or writes a full track on each disk in parallel. This results in a physical record size of eight tracks and a transfer rate eight times that of an individual disk.

The Japanese supercomputer manufacturers Fujitsu, NEC, and Hitachi have chosen to increase the parallelism within the CPU by adding more arithmetic pipelines and more vector registers. The NEC SX-X, for example, has 18,432 vector registers and sixteen vector arithmetic units. This organization yields a higher peak calculation rate than that of a Cray YM-P and also requires better compilers and more parallelism in programs to achieve this high performance. The availability of *multiprocessor computers* with this organization will challenge Cray's dominance of this market.

SUPERCOMPUTER PROGRAMMING

The parallel processing capabilities of supercomputers must be matched by parallel programs. The single-instruction, multiple-data (SIMD) program structure is most suited to efficient execution. In this style, a single operation such as a floating point add is applied, pairwise, to the elements of two operand arrays. The result is an array the same shape as the operands.

The Cray Y-MP is supported by highly optimizing compilers that translate standard scalar algorithms into SIMD programs. There are also a variety of programming languages for explicitly representing the parallel structure of algorithms. The recommended style of Cray programming is to use standard FORTRAN-77, Pascal, or C programs. The Cray *vectorizer* translates iterative loops into SIMD code. The optimizer will rearrange that code to produce the best performance. In many cases the scalar code cannot be vectorized very well. Such a program must be rewritten, often with different algorithms, to achieve efficient execution. The vectorizer identifies those parts of programs that cannot be changed to SIMD form, and the programmer may attempt to improve those parts. Many programmers prefer to express programs in an SIMD style, such as that provided by the FORTRAN-90 *array programming* constructs. This adds an array assignment statement and array expressions that describe each element of an array in parallel. The Cray Y-MP also has an *automatic parallelizer*, which can generate programs that will execute on *multiple processors* in parallel. The *shared memory architecture* allows this to work efficiently, even on moderate-size datasets.

MASSIVELY PARALLEL COMPUTERS, THE FUTURE OF SUPERCOMPUTING

The development of current supercomputers has centered around the use of parallel computer structures within a small number of CPUs. The emerging trend is to use a large number of processing units in parallel. The processing units range from the 1-bit units of the Connection Machine (CM-2) to the vector processor microcomputers in the Intel iPSC-860.

Thinking Machines Corporation's CM-2 provides supercomputer performance through use of 65,536 processing elements, all executing a single program in the SIMD style. *Floating-point processing* is carried out by 2,048 *vector arithmetic* processors. A parallel connection to thirty-two disk drives provides high-speed access to secondary storage. A hypercube interconnection structure allows parallel exchange of information between the individual processors. Parallelizing compilers have been developed that allow the automatic translation of sequential programs for execution in the massively parallel SIMD style. Execution speeds of over 14 billion floating-point operations per second have been measured for some applications on the CM-2.

Intel Corporation's iPSC-860 provides up to 128 microcomputers linked by a very fast *hypercube interconnection network.* Each processor has a vector arithmetic unit with a large local memory, and each may have its own secondary storage and network connections. The performance of the Intel iPSC-860 meets or exceeds that of an eight-processor Cray Y-MP in numerical computation and in the bandwidth and capacity of memory, secondary storage, and networks. Intel has recently announced the Delta System, which is a modified iPSC-860, using over 500 processors and a *mesh interconnection* structure. This system can perform over 25 billion floating-point operations per second.

BBN Systems has anounced the Monarch computer, which will support up to 65,536 processors with shared access to 32,768 memory modules of 2 megabytes. The peak *floating-point calculation* rate is estimated at over 100 billion operations per second. The network that interconnects processors and memory modules has a capacity of 500 billion bytes per second.

The future of supercomputing is in massively parallel systems. They will include *multiprocessor vector* computers; large, high-speed networks of computers; and massively parallel computers. The development and availability of parallelizing compilers and parallel programming languages will make these machines more usable to scientists.

DESKTOP SUPERCOMPUTING

The processing capability that has been available only through large mainframe computers is becoming available in smaller and less expensive computers. As an example, the IBM RS-6000 microcomputer has been measured at speeds approaching those of the Cray 1, which was the world's first supercomputer in 1976. The RS-6000 is small enough to fit under a desk, and the RS-6000's cost is a small fraction of that of a supercomputer. This microcomputer has many of the parallel processing characteristics of supercomputers, such as multiple pipelined arithmetic units and interleaved memory banks. For many users, this is a very cost-effective way to achieve supercomputer performance.

An alternative view of desktop supercomputing is provided by *high-speed network access* to traditional supercomputers. A *graphics computer* may use a remote supercomputer to execute large applications, with the user interface provided locally. Systems such as X-windows make this possible in a transparent style.

[*See also:* Appendix: Supercomputer Manufacturers.]

For Further Reading

August, M. C., G. M. Brost, C. C. Hsiung, and A. J. Schiffleger. 1989. Cray X-MP: The birth of a supercomputer. *Computer* 22(1): 45–52.

Bromley, M., S. Heller, T. McNerney, and G. L. Steele, Jr. 1991. Fortran at ten gigaflops: The Connection Machine convolution compiler. In *Proceedings of the ACM SIGPLAN '91 Conference on Programming Language Design and Implementation,* pp. 145–56. New York: ACM Press.

Cheng, H. 1989. Vector pipelining, chaining, and speed on the IBM 3090 and Cray X-MP. *Computer* 22(9):31–46.

Mangione-Smith, W., S. G. Agraham, and E. S. Davidson. 1991. A performance comparison of the IBM RS/6000 and the Astronautics ZS-1. *Computer* 24(1):39–46.

Stone, H. S. 1990. *High–performance computer architecture.* 2nd ed. Reading, Mass.: Addison-Wesley.

Gregory A. Riccardi

SWITCHING THEORY

See: Hardware: Computer Design

SYMBOLIC COMPUTATION

We often use the term "symbolic computation" as a synonym for "algebraic manipulation," and both terms are implied when we talk about "computer algebra." By all these terms we mean the capability of computers to manipulate mathematical expressions in a symbolic rather than numerical way (much as we do algebra with pencil and paper) and to handle exact numbers (i.e., employing appropriate data structures, we can perform arithmetic operations on "infinite" precision integers and rational numbers). For example, using any of the available symbolic computation software packages, we can easily expand the expression $(a + b)^{15}$ (where a and b are treated as symbols) as well as compute the number 100! (the product $1 \cdot 2 \cdot 3 \cdots 100$). The need for such software packages arose in the early 1960s when scientists realized that by symbolic transformations they can gain more insight into the various problems under consideration (to quote R. W. Hamming, "the purpose of computing is insight, not numbers") and that they can free themselves from the painstaking concern for numerical errors (truncation and round-off).

In symbolic computation, with the help of appropriate data structures, we use only symbols and integers of arbitrary precision; this results in error-free computations that are executed somewhat slowly because the arithmetic operations have to be software-implemented (i.e., the computer has to use special programs to perform arithmetic operations on long integers). Moreover, due to the sometimes explosive growth of intermediate expressions while executing various algorithms, there is great demand for memory space; therefore, symbolic computation packages run on computers with ample memory. In short, symbolic computation complements numerical analysis (which was

developed first), and there is little if any overlap in the treatment of topics between them.

Publications in this area usually appear in the quarterly *Journal of Symbolic Computation* (earlier works were published in a variety of journals). Additional information, conference announcements, etc., appear in the quarterly *SIGSAM* bulletin of the ACM (Special Interest Group on Symbolic and Algebraic Manipulation of the Association for Computing Machinery). The relatively few books (at the time of this writing) available in this area are listed in the Reference and For Further Reading sections.

WHAT IS SYMBOLIC COMPUTATION?

The material that follows is divided into three sections (following Akritas 1989). In the first section we make clear the difference between symbolic computation and numerical analysis; in the second section we briefly describe how long integers and polynomials can be represented inside the computer; finally, in the third section we list several of the most widely used software packages for symbolic computation.

Symbolic Computation Versus Numerical Analysis

To understand the need for exact integer arithmetic better, let us look more closely at the inherent limitations of numerical computations using computers. These limitations are due to the fact that a computer is a machine with a finite memory composed of words having finite length; 16 or 32 bits are common lengths of computer words, in which case the maximum integer that can be stored in them is $2^{16} - 1$ or $2^{32} - 1$, corresponding to a five- or ten-digit number (to base 10), respectively.

Therefore, in performing numerical computations on a computer, we are faced with the problem of representing the *infinite* set of real numbers within a computer of finite memory and of given word length. The most widely implemented solution in numerical analysis is to approximate the real numbers using the *finite* set of floating point numbers. A set F of floating-point numbers is characterized by a number base β, a precision t, and an exponent range $[L,U]$, where the parameters β, t, L, and U clearly depend on the computer. Each floating-point number f in F can be represented as

$$f = \pm (d_1/\beta + d_2/\beta^2 + \ldots + d_t/\beta^t) \beta^e$$

where the integers d_i, $i = 1, 2, \ldots, t$ satisfy the inequality $0 \le d_i \le \beta-1$ and $L \le e \le U$; if we require $d_1 \ne 0$ for all f in F, $f \ne 0$, we have the *normalized* floating-point numbers.

Using floating-point numbers (or integers that can be stored in one computer word), the arithmetic operations $+$, $*$, etc., are executed very fast. This is due to the fact that the computer circuitry performs these operations instead of having a software routine do the job; therefore we say that the arithmetic operators $+$, $*$, etc., are *hardware-implemented*.

Let us now look at the kind of problems that arise from this approximation of the reals by the floating-point numbers. First, the set F is not continuous or even an infinite set. There are exactly $2(\beta - 1)\beta^{t-1} (U - L + 1) + 1$ normalized floating-point numbers (including 0) in F; moreover, these numbers are not equally spaced throughout their range but only between successive powers of β. As an example, consider the 33-point set F with $\beta = 2$, $t = 3$, $L = -1$, and $U = 2$, whose positive points are 4/16, 5/16, 6/16, 7/16, 8/16, 10/16, 12/16, 14/16, 16/16, 20/16, 24/16, 28/16, 32/16, 40/16, 48/16, and 56/16.

Because of the above, it is possible that given f_1 and f_2 in F their sum (or product) will *not* be in F and will have to be approximated by the closest floating-point number. This difference between the true and the approximated sum (or product) is the *round-off* error. It should also be noticed that the operations of addition and multiplication in F are not associative and that the distributive law also fails. Consider, for example, in our toy 33-point set F, the expression $5/4 + (3/8 + 3/8) = 2$, where 5/4, 3/8, and 2 belong to F. In this expression, though, $(5/4 + 3/8) + 3/8 \ne 2$ because the sum $(5/4 + 3/8)$ does not belong to F and has to be approximated by

either 3/2 ($= 24/16$) or 7/4 ($= 28/16$). Round-off errors do not only occur while using floating-point numbers; they may also appear when one is dealing with integers, as, for example, when one wants to calculate the product of, say, two s-digit numbers in a computer that cannot handle numbers having more than s digits.

We see, therefore, that in numerical analysis one has to estimate carefully (and compute bounds of) the round-off errors performed by each algorithm instead of only focusing attention on the algorithms themselves and their efficiency. This, combined with the fact that mathematical expressions can only be stored and manipulated numerically, points to the need for software systems that can manipulate expressions symbolically and perform error-free computations. This is how symbolic computation was "born."

Exact Integer and Polynomial Arithmetic

To be able to store inside a computer integers of arbitrary precision and to do exact arithmetic, we represent them as lists. (Of course, we can represent them using arrays, but the latter are not "dynamic" data structures.) In this way, though, we lose the ability to perform on these integers the hardware-implemented operators $+$, $*$, etc.; instead, as we will see below, we have to develop special software routines that will do the job. Therefore, we now say that the arithmetic operators $+$, $*$, etc., are software-implemented and that they are slower than their hardware-implemented counterparts.

For example, suppose that a word of our fictitious computer can hold only three digits (to base 10) and that we want to store the integer $i = +23456789$; this can be accomplished as shown in Figure 1. The arrows indicate that a node or cell (which is made up of one or more computer words) is linked to the next one; the whole structure is addressed by the variable i. When dealing with

FIGURE 1

linked structures, the first thing that needs to be taken care of is how to construct the nodes—that is, how many computer words per node we use, how many data fields per node we are going to have, and what the size of these fields will be. We will not address these issues here.

Suppose, now, that we want to compute the sum of two long integers i_1 and i_2 represented as shown above. From the programming point of view we can follow one of two approaches:

1. Write a procedure—call it ISUM for integer summation—that will accept i_1 and i_2 as inputs and will return their sum s as output, or
2. "Overload" the + operator; that is, when the + operator is encountered, the type of the surrounding variables is checked, and when long integers are discovered, there is a branch to the procedure ISUM. (We call this a "user-friendlier" approach because, in this case, we do not have to memorize the name of any procedure that needs to be invoked.)

The output $s = i_1 + i_2$ is another list that is derived by simultaneously scanning (advancing through) the lists i_1 and i_2 and adding the small (single-precision) integers of the corresponding nodes (using the hardware-implemented +), as well as propagating, of course, any carry. (For ease of operation, the least significant node appears first in the list representation of an integer shown above.) For the other operations we proceed in a similar manner.

We next consider polynomials with integer coefficients. There are two ways to list-represent a univariate polynomial $p(x)$ of degree n (and the equation $p(x) = 0$) inside the computer. The first way is to represent it by the ordered list $p = (x, c_r, e_r, c_{r-1}, e_{r-1}, \ldots, c_1, e_1)$, $r \geq 1$, where each integer coefficient c_i is $\neq 0$ and is also represented by a list; the exponents e_i are in decreasing order $e_r > e_{r-1} > \ldots > e_1$; the degree of $p(x)$ is $n = e_r$. The second way is to use the list $p = (x, n, c_n, c_{n-1}, \ldots, c_0)$, where zero coefficients are included. Each approach has its advantages and disad-

vantages. Once we have chosen the representation we can then easily develop the algorithms for polynomial arithmetic, as known from algebra.

The empty list represents the polynomial $p(x) = 0$. Multivariate polynomials over the integers can be represented in recursive canonical form—that is, a polynomial in v variables $x_1, x_2, \ldots, x_v$ is considered to be a polynomial in one variable, x_v, with coefficients c_i, which are polynomials in $v-1$ variables $x_1, x_2, \ldots, x_{v-1}$.

Symbolic Computation Software Packages
Computer algebra systems exhibit great sophistication and diversity of design and can be classified into two main groups that reflect their development.

The systems in the first group can be looked on as *special-purpose* programs—that is, they were designed to solve specific problems in various fields such as mathematics, theoretical physics, and chemistry. All these systems can operate at relatively high speeds because a special-purpose program can be tuned for the kind of input expected. The following list is a sample of such systems: **camal,** a British system for lunar theory and general relativity; **schoonship** for high-energy physics; **altran, sac-1,** and **sac-2** for polynomial arithmetic; and **caley** for group theory.

The systems in the second group are *general-purpose* programs that provide the user with as many mathematical capabilities as possible. Most of them are available for various types of personal computers (with ample memory space). Major representatives of this group are **macsyma, reduce, scratch-pad, maple** (a Canadian system), and **mathematica.**

maple and **mathematica** are the newest and by far the best computer algebra systems to use. Both were developed in the 1980s and incorporate the best features of the other systems, which were developed in the late 1960s. For users there is a high-level language with modern syntax more suitable for describing algebraic algorithms.

General-purpose computer algebra systems have also been developed for personal computers with "small" memories but generally are slower and less comprehensive than their counterparts designed for large-memory computers; the most widely available such system is μ-**math** (mu-math) and its successor **derive** (a pleasure to use).

We conclude with some examples using the **maple** system: To compute the product of 20! times 30! we enter

>(20!)*(30!);

and we obtain the answer

645, 334, 215, 311, 676, 394, 593, 146,
071, 296, 945, 369, 907, 200, 000, 000, 000

To factor the polynomial $x^5 + x + 1$ we type

>factor($x^5 + x + 1$);

and we obtain the answer

$(1 + x + x^2)(x^3 - x^2 + 1)$

The command

> expand(");

will multiply out the two factors above and will yield the polynomial we started with, namely,

$x^5 + x + 1$

To integrate $\tan(x)$ we type

>int[tan(x),x];

and we obtain

$-\ln[\cos(x)]$

which we can differentiate by

>diff(",x);

to obtain back

$\sin(x)/\cos(x)$

Finally, to compute the greatest common divisor of the polynomials $x^5 + x + 1$ and $x^3 - x^2 + 1$ we type

>gcd($x^5 + x + 1$, $x^3 - x^2 + 1$);

to obtain

$x^3 - x^2 + 1$

and

> quit;

will terminate our session. **mathematica** works in a similar way (see Figure 2 for a sample screen).

Among others, **maple** includes packages for linear algebra, number theory, power series, linear optimization, statistics, and calculus.

```
In[1]:=
    (20!)*(30!)
Out[1]
    645334215311676394593146071296945369907200000000000
In[2]:=
    Factor[x^5+x+1]
Out[2]
                 2        2    3
    (1 + x + x ) (1 - x  + x )
In[3]:=
    Expand[%]
Out[3]
             5
    1 + x + x
In[4]:=
    Integrate[tan(x),x]
Out[4]
         2
    tan x
    ------
       2
In[5]:=
    D[%,x]
Out[5]
    tan x
In[6]:=
    GCD[x^5+x+1,x^3-x^2+1]
Out[6]
         2    3
    1 - x  + x
```

FIGURE 2. A sample screen from the symbolic computation software package **mathematica**.

Reference

Akritas, A. G. 1989. *Elements of computer algebra with applications.* New York: Wiley. The textbook in the area.

For Further Reading

Buchberger, B., G. E. Collins, and R. Loos, eds. 1982. *Symbolic and algebraic computation,* Computing Supplement 4. New York: Springer-Verlag. A collection of articles on many different topics.

Davenport, J. H., Y. Siret, and E. Tournier. 1988. *Computer algebra, systems and algorithms for algebraic computation.* New York: Academic Press. Handy descriptions of the **macsyma** and **reduce** systems.

Mignotte, M. 1989. *Mathématiques pour le calcul formel.* Paris: Presses Universitaires de France.

Pankrat'ev, E. B. 1988. *Computer algebra-factorization of polynomials* (in Russian). Moscow: Moscow State University. Thorough treatment of the subject.

Alkiviadis G. Akritas

SYSTEM RELIABILITY

Reliability of computer systems has gained considerable importance because of the large-scale applications of computers at present times, particularly when they are used in critical applications, for example, in military, communication, and aerospace, where failures can cause significant losses. In a computer, failure can occur in its hardware (the electronic, electrical, and mechanical components) or in its software (the programs run on the machine). Hardware failures can occur because of incorrectness in design and manufacturing, inadequate quality of components, environments (temperature, humidity, dust, etc.), and so on. Software failures can occur because of incorrect design and/or data structure, loss of data, and so on. In a reliable computer system, there are mechanisms to determine if any error has occurred. In its simplest form such a system produces warnings if errors are found and accordingly an off-line repair process should start. Such a system is not suitable for critical applications where taking the system off-line is either impossible (e.g., when a control computer in an aircraft about to land is controlling the landing gear) or is expensive (e.g., when a computer is used to switch long-distance trunk lines). A more sophisticated reliable machine continues to extract the correct computational results even when some failures have occurred by properly masking (or hiding) the incorrect results. For such a system, the fault still persists and might not be detected but its effect is masked out (or hidden) so that correct results are still available and as such no warning is created. Evidently such a system uses redundancy in its computation so that correct results can be determined. Another category of reliable machines is designed to carry out on-line repair once some failures have been detected. This on-line repair is usually done by reconfiguration of the system to replace the faulty unit or component with some similar spare component. Alternatively the faulty unit might be cut off from the system, causing some degradation or deterioration in the system performance, commonly referred to as graceful degradation.

To enhance the reliability of a system, the system is usually designed to reduce the possibility of fault occurrences. Faults can occur because of variation of the performances of some of the components, loss of electrical signals because of noise or radiation, generation of heat because of too much flow of electrical currents (performance of electronic components is susceptible to temperature), and so on. Possibility of faults can be reduced by using more reliable components, reducing noises, shielding to avoid external interfering signals, controlling the amount of current flow (to reduce heat generation), and so on. Generation of heat is a major factor in faulty behavior not only because of change in the performance of electronic components but also because of increase in noise signals. To avoid heat generation, sometimes systems are enclosed in a cold environment. In general, reducing the possibility of fault occurrence is not good enough to achieve the adequate reliability of the system. Systems are generally made fault tolerant to achieve proper reliability. A fault-tolerant system might be designed using the fault-masking technique mentioned before or by detecting faults and performing a reconfiguration to avoid the faulty parts of the system.

FAULT DETECTION METHODS

There are several methods of detecting faults. One simple method is by duplication of computation and comparison of results, whereby a fault is detected whenever non-identical results are produced. Evidently significant redundancy is needed for duplicating the computation and additional components for comparison. Also, detecting faults by duplication assumes more reliance on the comparator. Usually the comparison components are made more reliable by using some of the methods discussed later. Note that duplication of computational modules does not necessarily imply that only the comparison of module outputs is made. For example, in the Bell ESS-1 system, even though duplications are used at the system level, comparisons are made at lower levels of the modules. Other commonly used techniques include the application of error-detecting codes, watchdog timers, and so on. The principle of error-detecting codes is primarily to add redundancy in representing information. For every string of information bits suitable redundant bits are added to represent the coded information so that in case of some error the coded information becomes an invalid code and hence an error can be detected. How to add the redundant bits and how many to add depend on the kind of error to be detected. For some applications, the errors might be random (i.e., the bits of the coded information might get corrupted in an arbitrary way: some of the 1 bits change to 0 and some other 0 bits might change to 1); in some other application, the errors might be unidirectional (i.e., some of the 1 bits change to 0 or some of the 0 bits change to 1, but not both in the same coded information). Accordingly, different coding schemes are used. These coding schemes also depend

on how many bit errors in the information are expected to be detected. Error-detecting codes (for random and unidirectional errors), check summing codes, totally self-checking codes, partially self-checking codes, and arithmetic codes are some of the codes used for detecting errors in information for memory access or arithmetic and/or logical computations.

Watchdog timers are used to detect errors at the task level. The principle is primarily to maintain a timer that is expected to be reset in normal operation before it expires. If it is not reset, then some failure in the task is assumed. To ensure that a failed task is not able to reset the timer the tested task should do significant computation to reset the timer. Some systems like the VAX 11/780, ESS-2, and PLURIBUS use watchdog timers.

FAULT-MASKING TECHNIQUES

The basic principle of the masking technique is to mask or hide the faulty behavior of the components and produce the normal or fault-free results. Among the different fault-masking techniques, error-correcting codes and voting with modular redundancy are commonly used. The principle of the error-correcting code is similar to that of error-detecting codes discussed before. Redundant bits are added to the information bits so that, in the case of error occurrence, the erroneous bits can be identified. For example, to correct a single-bit error, suppose the redundant bits are so added that at least three bits of coded information have to be changed to produce another coded information. Then, in the case of a single-bit error, the valid code closest to the erroneous code is the correct code. These are usually called single-error-correcting (SEC) Hamming codes. In general, to correct any error not exceeding t bit errors, a code with a Hamming distance $2t + 1$ is sufficient (the Hamming distance of a code is the minimum number of bits that must be changed to produce a valid code from another valid code). Obviously, more redundancy is needed to correct more errors. Use of error-correcting codes requires additional components (usually hardware components) to encode and to decode the information bits. During the decoding process, if an erroneous code is found, the decoder finds the correct information bits, and hence to the external world, the effect of the error is kept hidden.

Voting with modular redundancy uses replication of the modules, and some voting of the outputs of the modules is done to get the correct result. For example, to mask the error in a single module, a simple technique would be to use three identical copies of the same module and run them in parallel. Taking the majority voting of the three outputs of the modules will ensure the correct result so long as at most one module is faulty. This technique is usually called triple modular redundancy (TMR) for masking single failure. Extending the same idea to N modular redundancy (NMR), where N is odd to avoid a possible tie, can be used to mask a larger number of module failures. The cost of an NMR system is N times the basic module cost plus the cost of the voting hardware. Voting with modular redundancy technique is used in the FTMP system and the SIFT system (using software voting; see below).

RECONFIGURATION

From the previous discussion, it follows that only fault detection cannot increase the reliability of a system. Once a fault has been detected, some diagnostic procedure is carried out to identify the faulty module. The system is then reconfigured to avoid the faulty module by switching it out of the system and replacing it with a spare or by allowing the system to run (if possible) in the absence of the module with a degraded performance. In a reconfigurable duplicated system (such as the ESS-2 system), two modules (e.g., processors) are run together. When an error is detected by an observed mismatch in their outputs, one processor called the active processor runs a diagnostic test that if failed causes a transfer of control to the standby processor, and the faulty processor is switched off from the system and repaired. In a system using voting in modular redundancy, usually the modules in the minority are considered to be faulty and are replaced by spares to ensure that voting continues to

give correct results even with occurrences of more faults. In the above reconfiguration techniques, the faulty components should be replaced by fault-free spares. In some commercial systems, the presence of an error is flagged as a warning and the system continues to run with degraded performance unless the error is fatal. Typically, errors in some segments of memory mark the concerned segments inaccessible and the system continues to function with the remaining segments. A similar case occurs when some tracks of a disk are faulty. In these cases the system is designed to perform with graceful degradation in the presence of faults.

OVERVIEW OF SOME FAULT-TOLERANT MACHINES

STAR (Self-Testing and Repairing) Computer
The STAR system, developed at the Jet Propulsion Laboratory, uses standby spares to replace the faulty functional units. The faulty functional units are removed from the system by switching their power off. The system is designed as an interconnection of replaceable functional units and errors are detected using error-detecting codes. There is a special-purpose processor for testing and repair called TARP. The TARP monitors the data communicated over the buses between the functional units as well as the status of the different functional units. One part of TARP does the fault location and the other part takes care of the recovery process when errors are detected. Three copies of TARP are used simultaneously to protect against an error in TARP itself. In the case of an error in TARP, the erroneous TARP enters the recovery status. If it cannot recover, a standby TARP is switched into the system, removing the erroneous one.

SIFT (Software Implemented Fault Tolerance) System
The SIFT system, developed at SRI International, achieves fault tolerance as far as possible through programs instead of hardware. The system was designed primarily for com-

putation needed in the control of commercial aircrafts. The system has several processing modules; each module has a processor and its associated memory. The processing modules communicate through multiple buses. For processing, each module might use data from several other modules, but to store the result, each module can store only in its own memory element. This restriction ensures that in case of any error in a module, if incorrect data are produced, the incorrect data never reside in an error-free module; however, a fault-free module might receive incorrect data from a faulty module. To ensure that incorrect data are not used by a fault-free module, each module receives several copies of the same data from different memory units through different buses and uses majority voting to extract the correct data. The design goal of SIFT was achievement of a failure rate of 10^{-9} per hour in a 10-hour period.

FTMP (Fault-Tolerant Multiprocessor) System

The FTMP system, developed at the Draper Laboratory, achieves fault tolerance using TMR technique. The system consists of several processors sharing a common memory. Each processor has its own cache. All activities, computations or data transfers, are carried out by triplets of modules and buses. All the spares form a common pool from which modules or buses are selected to form a triplet. The active buses in a triplet carry three versions of data generated independently by the different members of a triplet. Additional modules called *guardians* are responsible for maintaining the status of the relevant modules. If a processor fails, it is removed from the triplet, issuing a suitable command to the relevant guardian, and a spare, if available, replaces the faulty processor by connecting to the proper bus. If no spare is available, the two remaining fault-free processors are treated as spares for any other triplet. FTMP was designed to achieve a failure rate of the same order as in SIFT. Figure 1 is a schematic diagram of the FTMP system. There are several such memory modules and processor modules sharing the buses, with associated bus guardians and bus isolation blocks. In a similar manner, processors and input/output interface units also share another set of buses under separate bus guardians.

For Further Reading

Pradhan, D. K., ed. 1986. *Fault tolerant computing: Theory and techniques.* Englewood Cliffs, N.J.: Prentice Hall.

Proceedings of International Symposium on Fault-Tolerant Computing (annual symposium since 1971). New York: IEEE Press.

Siewiorek, D. P., and R. S. Swarz. 1982. *The theory and practice of reliable system design.* Bedford, Mass.: Digital Press.

A. Sengupta

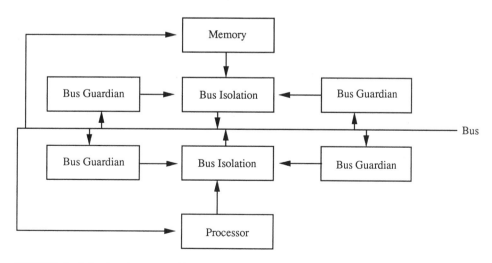

FIGURE 1. A fault-tolerant multiprocessor system.

SYSTEMS DEVELOPMENT LIFE CYCLE

In a broad perspective, the system life cycle is the evolution of an information system from creation to installation, through months or years of production use and adaptations, until it is discarded or replaced by another system. The cycle may last a few months or a few decades.

The life cycle of an information system has two phases: development and production. In the development phase, the information system is created or revised. In the production phase, the system is part of the ongoing process of the organization in which it is used; data items are entered and reports are produced as required by the organization's operations. The point at which a system moves from the development phase into the production phase is called changeover. At changeover, the primary responsibility for the system shifts from the information systems staff, that is, the developers, to the production staff, that is, the operators and users.

As illustrated in Figure 1, viewing an information system's lifetime as a recurring cycle emphasizes its evolutionary nature: an

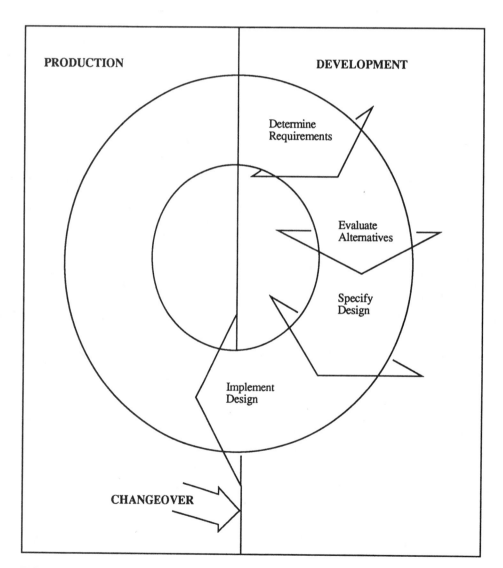

FIGURE 1. Systems development life cycle. *Adapted with permission from Jordan and Machesky 1990.*

information system evolves as the organization in which it is used changes. A system, once put into production, will need to be adapted to the changing requirements of its users. Thus, periods of development and production alternate as long as the system is used by the organization. This article focuses on the development portion of the system life cycle. This systems development life cycle (SDLC) is the subject of basic, comprehensive texts, for example, those by Flaatten et al. (1989), Jordan and Machesky (1990), and Whitten et al. (1989).

STAGES OF SYSTEMS DEVELOPMENT

The development phase is divided into several stages that have been assigned various labels; one common model groups activities into four stages: (1) requirements determination, (2) evaluation of alternative solutions, (3) design specification, (4) implementation. These four stages are labeled in Figure 1.

Requirements Determination Stage

Requirements determination is the set of activities performed to gain an understanding of a problem. It provides a systematic way of structuring a definition of the current and required systems and identifying the objectives of and constraints on development. The basic goal of this stage is to identify a solution that meets the users' requirements. As illustrated in Figure 2, the fit between requirements and solution is seldom perfect; solving the wrong problem (A), solving only part of the problem (B), or providing more capability than required (C) all too commonly waste organizational resources. The most realistic fit (D) is to address 80 percent of the requirements at 50 or even 20 percent of the cost of fine-tuning the system to meet every requirement.

During this first stage of systems development, the system boundary, or scope, is defined and its requirements investigated. To define the system boundary, developers work with users to determine system objectives and constraints. System objectives are the goals that the production system should meet. For example, systems are developed to

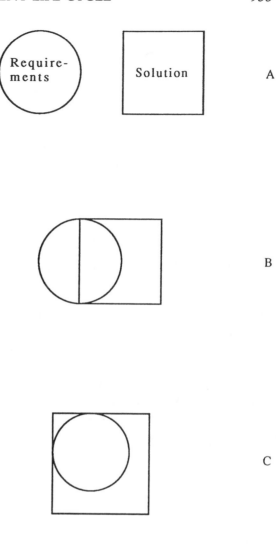

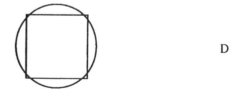

FIGURE 2. Examples of requirements–solution boundaries: A, no correspondence between requirements and solution; B, partial solution; C, megasolution; D, 80/20 solution. *Courtesy Thomas O. Meadows, Syscorp International.*

reduce labor costs, to improve customer service, to increase accuracy, or to provide more timely reports. These objectives should state realistic goals and define measurable standards for the project. System constraints are limits on the resources available for development and production. Every organization has limited time, money, and personnel, and thus must invest these resources wisely. Examples of constraints include using existing hardware and personnel, completing the system within six weeks, and incurring production costs of not more than $750 per week.

On the basis of these objectives and constraints, developers determine system requirements: the features of the system necessary to achieve the objectives within the given constraints. Requirements are sometimes called functional requirements because they state what the system must do and what functions it must perform. For example, the system must

- Allow users to access customer account records and display them on the monitor.
- Produce a summary report of sales activity at the end of each day.
- Generate a purchase order for an inventory item when its in-stock level falls below a prespecified level.

The task of determining requirements can be very easy if the system is a common one that users understand well, for example, the typical payroll system; this task can also be very difficult, especially if the system performs complex functions or spans several organizational units or sites.

The requirements determination activities culminate in the requirements document and user review. The requirements document is a formal written report that brings together the developers' findings about the current system and the requirements of the proposed system. At a minimum, this document should clearly identify the acceptance criteria for the new system: those features and attributes the system must attain to be accepted for production use. Parts of this report are usually presented during the user review, a meeting at which developers verify their understanding of the problem and the requirements with a representative group of users. The approved requirements document then becomes the foundation of the evaluation, design, and implementation stages.

Evaluation Stage

Evaluation refers to the activities leading to the choice of a system solution from a range of alternatives. During the evaluation stage, developers identify alternative systems that meet the system objectives, constraints, and requirements. As alternatives are generated, solutions will tend to be "driven" by the system component whose alternatives are generated first. For example, the selection of a software source (e.g., purchased, custom developed by end users, or custom developed by developers) may constrain hardware options, data storage, procedures, and personnel. Typically, alternatives generation is driven by one of two system components: hardware or people. In the hardware-driven approach, the possible alternatives for data, software, procedures, and people are limited by deciding in advance to use existing hardware or a particular computer system. This choice constraints the selection of a software source and may require special user training or the hiring of additional staff. The hardware-driven approach is contrasted by Jordan and Machesky (1990, pp. 364–69) with the user-driven approach. The needs of the primary system users determine the characteristics of the other components in a user-driven approach. People-driven solutions emphasize what the users need, not what the hardware can do. Such a user-driven approach is often a key to successful systems development; the term *sociotechnical development* is also sometimes used to describe this socially oriented approach to systems development, as explained in a two-part article by Bostrom and Heinen (1977).

The alternatives are then analyzed in terms of their feasibility and compared in terms of their costs and benefits to decide which alternative best satisfies the system objectives. The feasibility study addresses five broad questions:

1. Can the system be implemented with existing technology? (technical feasibility)
2. Do the system's benefits outweigh its costs? (economic feasibility)
3. Can the system be completed in a timely manner? (schedule feasibility)
4. Is the organization committed to the proj-

ect? Will it provide the resources needed to develop the system? (motivational feasibility)

5. Will the system be accepted by users when installed? (operational feasibility)

Before analyzing costs and benefits, developers consult with users to identify the evaluation criteria: the most important system attributes based on the system objectives. These criteria, which are usually similar to the acceptance criteria identified during the requirements determination stage, will vary from project to project; for example, response time may be a very important attribute in one system but not in another.

The project team presents its findings about each alternative's feasibility and ratings on the evaluation criteria in an evaluation document and/or at a user review. Users then decide the next step: (1) accept one of the proposed solutions and proceed with the development project, (2) request that the development team perform further evaluation based on different criteria or in consideration of a different set of constraints, or (3) determine that no solution is feasible at this time and therefore decide to abandon the development effort. If the users accept one of the proposed solutions, the project enters the design specification stage.

Design Specification Stage

Design is the process of creating the specification, or blueprint, used to implement an information system. The purpose of systems design is to specify how the system requirements will be met, that is, what combination of people, procedures, data, software, and hardware will be included in the system. Often one or more of these components will be emphasized; for example, design of multiple-user systems will generally require more attention to procedures and data than will design of single-user systems. The input for the design stage is the requirements specification for the alternative chosen in the evaluation stage. The major output, or deliverable, of this stage is a design specification approved by the users of the system.

Design specification generally proceeds in two phases. First the logical design of the system is specified; the logical system design identifies the inputs, outputs, files, databases, and procedures of the new system. During the physical system design phase, the developers translate the logical design specifications into specifications for the automated solution by writing the program specifications, designing the file structures and databases, indicating the personnel responsible for each procedure, and specifying the equipment used to input data (e.g., keyboard or magnetic character reader) and output reports (e.g., monitor or printer). The classic explication of logical design and physical design has been written by DeMarco (1979), who also presents arguments about why these phases should be separate and distinct activities.

Design specification encompasses six major activities: (1) designing the user interface, (2) designing the database, (3) designing the programs, (4) designing the procedures, (5) negotiating hardware and software contracts, and (6) obtaining user approval of the design. More specifically, program design is the process of packaging the interface, procedure, and database specifications into specifications that will guide programmers in constructing the software for the system. Its objective is to specify programs that are adaptable and easy to maintain. Procedure design involves describing the flow of work for the new system. Normal and failure recovery procedures must be designed for both end users and operators.

Design activities tend to be iterative because altering the specification of one system component affects the specifications of the other components. For example, a change in database configuration necessitates a change in program specification. Design activities are also interdependent; for example, the programs cannot be designed until the interfaces have been identified and specified. The end products of these activities are a detailed plan and blueprint for implementing the new system.

Implementation Stage

Implementation is the completion stage of the systems development project. Its activities transform plans on paper into a functioning system. Depending on the complexity of the software and data components, implementation time varies greatly. A new system that uses existing software and that requires no major data conversion will be much more readily implemented than one that requires a dozen new programs and the conversion of all of a functional area's files.

Creating a production system from the design specifications requires three basic activities: construction, testing, and installation. System construction is the process of building the components to meet the specifications defined during the design stage. Construction activities include coding programs, preparing the hardware facility, writing user and system documentation, and building data files. As the system is constructed, individual components are tested to ensure that the users understand the procedures, that the hardware operates correctly, and that the software produces the correct output. Testing is an important systems development activity that is too often omitted or performed haphazardly. Yet it is critical to system success in that it uncovers unforeseen requirements, design limitations, coding errors, faulty procedures, and more. Testing is an iterative activity whose primary goal is to ensure that system errors are located and corrected *before* installation.

Installation is the process of putting the system into production use; during this phase, all affected components of the old system are replaced by those of the new system. The transition from the old system to the new system can be achieved in several ways: immediate replacement, parallel operation, or phased installation. The best approach depends on the nature of the system to be installed. Immediate replacement is a viable approach when the installation is simple and straightforward or when no other strategy is feasible. In this low-cost, high-risk strategy, the old system is dismantled and the new system is put into operation simultaneously. The parallel operation installation strategy offers a more cautious approach; here the old and new systems run in parallel until the accuracy and reliability of the new system can be verified. However, this low-risk strategy incurs high costs. An installation strategy that achieves a happy medium on the cost and risk scales is phased installation, in which the system is installed in phases by functional area, geographic area, or subsystem.

The implementation stage concludes with an acceptance review and postimplementation evaluation. During the acceptance review, the users test the system under routine and exceptional conditions to determine whether it satisfies the acceptance criteria established during requirements determination. Changeover is achieved if the users sign off on the acceptance criteria and accept responsibility for the new system. At this point, the system enters its production phase, but the developers' job is not finished until they have completed the postimplementation evaluation. After the system has been in production for a few months, the developers evaluate the development project. The purpose of this evaluation is to investigate the results of the project and to alert developers to ways in which future projects can be improved. It also provides feedback on how well the system met its objectives and whether the project was completed within its budget and time constraints. As a reference for future projects, the postimplementation evaluation report is an invaluable sourcebook for estimating and managing projects, deriving technical solutions, and improving user–developer relations.

SYSTEM MAINTENANCE

The life cycle of a system is a series of development and production phases. These periods alternate, with total development costs accumulating over the life cycle of the system. The common term for subsequent development phases is maintenance. Numerous studies, including a major software economics study by Boehm (1981), have shown that maintenance typically accounts for 60 to 80 percent of a system's total development costs; that is, if a system is an integral part of an organization and is used for 10 or more years, its initial development incurs only 20 to 40 percent of its total life cycle development costs. The reasons for returning a production system to the development phase for maintenance, according to an extensive survey by Lientz and Swanson (1980), include improving system efficiency, revising to incorporate new hardware or data requirements, and providing user enhancements, for example, generating new reports, the single greatest reason for maintenance.

Because maintenance incurs a major portion of a system's development costs, managing change is an important factor in increasing system productivity. The need for compatibility revisions can be reduced by designing and implementing systems that operate well in various environments with various equipment and that ensure program-data independence. The need for efficiency and enhancement revisions can be reduced by training users well, by involving them in the design of the system, and by encouraging them to project their future needs during requirements determination. Involving users in every stage of the development project increases the likelihood that the system will meet their expectations and will provide the functionality they need. Finally, as some maintenance is inevitable, developers should use structured techniques to document the system, thereby reducing the time and effort required for maintenance.

VARIATIONS IN THE LIFE CYCLE

The traditional systems development life cycle is a linear sequence of stages—requirements determination, evaluation of alternatives, design, and implementation—as shown in Figure 1. In structured systems development, the focus is on creating and revising graphical specifications, beginning with data flow diagrams of the system requirements, evolving to structure charts detailing the program specifications, and finally yielding structured programs that are easier to maintain than unstructured programs. Although the user is shown requirements documents, evaluation tables, and design specifications throughout the development phase for both the traditional and the structured systems development approaches, the system itself is neither constructed nor viewed

by users until the final implementation stage of the life cycle. For large systems, implementation may occur months or years after the project was initiated. Such a long lag time from the beginning of a project until its first viewing by users increases the risk of major misunderstandings between the users and the developers and may jeopardize system success.

The traditional and structured development approaches were created to develop systems that used third-generation languages such as COBOL and FORTRAN. With the introduction of database management systems, fourth-generation languages, and computer-aided system engineering (CASE) tools, it is feasible to develop systems following an iterative approach in which system versions are created, viewed by the users, revised, and again viewed by the users in a rapid repetition of definition, design, and construction activities. Using this approach involves a series of development cycles that are repeated until the users are satisfied. At that time the system is fully tested and refined before completing the final implementation activities, that is, the final user acceptance review, installation, and postimplementation review. This iterative approach is sometimes called heuristic development, because of its trial-and-error nature, or prototyping, because of the analogy with building a model or prototype of the system. When the best development tools are used to prototype a system, however, the model is not discarded, but is refined to become the production system.

A major advantage of the iterative development approach is increased feedback from users. Maintenance time is reduced because users can respond to a functioning system as it develops, rather than to ideas on paper. Another variation that further speeds both initial development and maintenance activities is user development. This strategy, like iterative development, has become possible only recently as easy-to-learn systems development tools, such as fourth-generation languages, spreadsheets, and CASE tools, have become available. Development effort is significantly reduced by eliminating the need for developers to learn the users' requirements during initial development and then again during all subsequent maintenance of the system.

An even more dramatic reduction in development effort can be achieved by purchasing existing software that has been designed, coded, documented, and tested by organizations with similar requirements. The activities of the traditional systems development life cycle must still be followed, but, when purchased software is used, the key activities will be defining requirements and evaluating alternatives, as design and implementation expertise will be purchased. When a system is developed using existing software, the 80/20 compromise in requirements–solution fit, shown in Figure 2, becomes especially critical because it is unlikely that existing software can meet all the users' requirements.

Increasingly, the development approaches classified here as "variations" of the traditional systems development life cycle are becoming commonplace. For large systems that must address unique needs, information systems professionals will continue to carry the major development responsibility and to follow the iterative development strategy. For smaller systems requiring custom development, end users will adopt a traditional or structured approach to create the system in a linear sequence of requirements determination, evaluation, design, and implementation. For systems that must meet routine requirements, software and documentation will be purchased, drastically compacting the initial development phase of the life cycle. With the growing variety of prepackaged systems available on the market, the life cycle itself will be compressed as it becomes economical to replace an existing system by purchasing a new system that reflects current advances in functional expertise and system design.

References

Boehm, B. W. 1981. *Software engineering economics.* Englewood Cliffs, N.J.: Prentice-Hall.

Bostrom, R. P., and J. S. Heinen. 1977. MIS problems and failures: A socio-technical perspective. *MIS Quarterly* 1(3):17–31; 1(4):11–28.

DeMarco, T. 1979. *Structured analysis and system specification.* Englewood Cliffs, N.J.: Prentice-Hall.

Flaatten, P. O., D. J. McCubbrey, P. D. O'Riordan, and K. Burgess. 1989. *Foundations of business systems.* Hinsdale, Ill.: Dryden Press.

Jordan, E. W., and J. J. Machesky. 1990. *Systems development: Requirements, evaluation, design, and implementation.* Boston: PWS-Kent.

Lientz, B. P., and E. B. Swanson. 1980. *Software maintenance management.* Reading, Mass.: Addison-Wesley.

Whitten, J. L., L. D. Bentley, and V. M. Barlow. 1989. *Systems analysis and design methods.* 2nd ed. Homewood, Ill.: Irwin.

Sandra Dewitz
Eleanor Jordan

T

TEACHING

See Education, Computers in

TEXT EDITORS

See Authoring Languages, Systems, and Environments; Word Processing

THROUGHPUT

See Performance Evaluation

TRADING, COMPUTER USE IN

Trading in stocks, bonds, commodities, and foreign exchange is performed both by individuals at trading desks of brokerage firms and by individuals who trade only for their own account. A key characteristic of trading is the need to process information quickly and accurately in order to make quick decisions. Because of the amount of information that is available, it is often important to have computers process it and present data in a manner that facilitates trading decisions. This is especially vital in the case of trading complex products such as options to buy or sell foreign exchange.

Although computers are used to support bookkeeping functions in connection with trading, the computer support activities most vital to trading are providing market data and manipulating market data to support decisions.

DIGITAL VS. VIDEO MARKET DATA

Market data vendors provide real-time price and rate information to the financial community in both video and digital form (examples are Telerate and Reuters). A video controller provided by the vendor passes on the market data to a trader's monitor in a video format (analog signal). When data from a market data vendor arrive in video format (through a video controller), the trader can look at but not manipulate the market data. Digital data are provided by the same vendors. A feature of a digital market data system is that the trader can manipulate the incoming digital market data using computers.

A financial markets business needs to link the market data vendor–provided video controllers into the trading floor system vendor–provided video switch, as shown in Figure 1. The X path in Figure 1 represents a video market data feed coming from a video controller into the video switch prior to entering monitor A. The trader uses these market data to guide his or her trading decisions. Focus next on the path marked Z in Figure 1. The digital market data side of the system that generates digital market data is shown in the box labeled "digital generation."

Digital market data are provided by the market data vendors using proprietary protocols. For example, Telerate provides digital market data in a protocol called the Standard Operating Protocol (SOP), which is some-

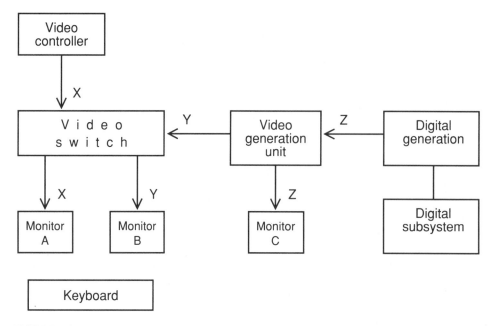

FIGURE 1. Video switch and digital data delivery system.

times referred to as Telerate's Digital Page Feed (TDPF).

The digital data from path Z pass through a video generation unit (often referred to as a VGU), which transforms the digital market data into a video format. The video format next passes through the video switch after entering the VGU, as shown in the Y path. Traders can arrange monitors, such as monitor B, to display data from both a digital and a video source, whereas monitor A can be set to show only video data. Not all digital market data need to pass through the video switch. In other words, after the digital market data enter the VGU, they can go directly into monitor C and do not need to go through the video switch. Unswitched digital market data would be displayed using path Z. In this configuration, monitor B is the only one of three monitors that gets both digital and video market data. One advantage of passing digital market data into the video switch prior to displaying it on monitor B is that several traders can share the same information at a small incremental cost. The video switch expects to see a video signal. The video switch is essentially a device that allows one television screen filled with video market data to be shared simultaneously by different traders. A composite cabling scheme links the video and digital systems as

represented in the X, Y, and Z paths of Figure 1.

DIGITAL SUBSYSTEM

The digital subsystem resides outside the vendor-provided trading floor system. The digital subsystem receives digital market data from the trading floor system vendor. The trading floor system facilitates entry of the data into the digital subsystem, but the trading company needs to develop its own application software to manipulate the digital market data. To appreciate the potential of digital subsystem software to create and evaluate investments, it is necessary to understand the three page types: standard, composite, and derived pages.

Standard Page

Figure 2 shows a typical standard page such as Telerate page 5. The page format can be viewed through either the video or digital side, since it is available on both video and digital services. A trader might use Telerate's page 5 to look at the fed funds rate, T-bill rate, Euro deposit rate, and so on. This basic information is provided in a standardized format.

```
14:43 EST                          (U.S. TREASURY AND MONEY MARKETS)                    PAGE 5
FEDERAL FUNDS  14:42    | T–BILL   14:42      YIELD  | EURO$   DEP 14:35  | GOV  RP    13:23
BID  6 1/2  OPN   6 1/2 | * 3M  5/78–76 – .10  5.943 | 7    3/8    –  1/2  | O/N      6.30 – 20
ASK  6 1/2  HIGH  6 1/2 | * 6M  6.27–25 – .02  6.561 | 7   7/16    –  9/16 | 1 WK     6.65 – 45
LST  6 1/2  LOW   6 1/4 | 1 YR  6/54–52 – .04  6.956 | 7  13/16    – 15/16 | 2 WK     6.65 – 45
FUNDS SOURCE:  G. GUYBUTLER | *CHANGE FROM AUCTION   |                    | 1 MO     6.70 – 60
-------------------------------------------------------------------------------------------
TREAS  CPNS  NY EST   14:42       YIELDS:CD–BID        14:40      BAS–BID         14:40
7.875  10/89  100/08  –12  +01  7.660  |     | EARLY | LATE  | EARLY | LATE
8.000  10/90   90.31  –03  UNC  7.964  |DEC | 6.82 –03 | 6.82 –03 | 6.75 –05 | 6.75 –05
8.125  09/91  102.29  –01  UNC  8.192  |JAN | 7.20 –10 | 7.20 –10 | 7.10 –02 | 7.10 –02
8.375  11/92   99.31  –03  UNC  8.351  |FEB | 7.20 –05 | 7.20 –05 | 7.10 –02 | 7.10 –02
8.500  10/94  104.08  –12  +04  8.643  |MAR | 7.25 –10 | 7.25 –10 | 7.10 –05 | 7.10 –05
8.875  11/97  100.06  –10  +01  8.827  |APR | 7.30 –10 | 7.30 –10 | 7.10 –05 | 7.10 –05
9.375  02/06  102.16  –20  –03  9.075  |MAY | 7.30 –15 | 7.30 –15 | 7.10 –02 | 7.10 –02
9.250  02/16  102.08  –12  –04  9.014  |DEALER COMML PAPER OFFER 12.05  |BANK RATES
8.750  05/17   97.15  –19  –03  8.984  |  30  6.74  90  7.12 180   7.12  |PRIME   8.75
8.875  08/17   99.10  –14  –01  8.922  |  60  7.09 120  7.12 240   7.12  |BROKER  8.00
```

FIGURE 2. Telerate page 5.

Composite Page

A composite page is formed by electronically cutting and pasting pieces from more than one standard page. For example, if the trader wants to cut and paste electronically two different subsections of Reuters pages called USFX and USFY on one page, then the trader enters a code into his or her preset composite page directory, and sections of both pages appear on one screen. The trader can also take sections of pages from two different market data vendors, such as Telerate and Reuters, and put them onto one page. Composite pages accept real-time updates from specified subsections of other pages, since a digital trading system can manipulate digital data instantly.

Derived Page

Derived pages process information from standard pages through special trader-created formulas to create value-added information. For example, suppose a trader wants to create a real-time options pricing page. An option gives the right but not the obligation to purchase or sell a security at a fixed price called the strike price for a preset period of time. A call option gives the right to purchase the underlying security within a given time period, whereas a put option gives the right to sell the underlying security within a given time period. The derived page is created by having the trader's in-house–developed option pricing software manipulate the digital market data from a standard page to price an option fairly. The capability to produce fair option prices enables traders to create a competitive options pricing business as well as to evaluate the real-time profitability of their investments. In the option pricing example, the trader needs to access elements from standard pages such as foreign exchange spot rates from Telerate page 261 and a risk-free interest rate from Telerate page 5. These basic input data are then channeled directly into an option pricing formula. As shown in Figure 3, four panels then show various fair-valued call and put foreign-exchange option prices.

The foreign-exchange options pricing formula in this example contains basic mathematical computations, such as calculating the value of a cumulative normal probability density function. The trader puts the real-time fair value of the option on a derived page after the digital data have been input into the formula. The fair value can then be compared with actual values to help traders evaluate investment decisions and track performance. On top of the derived page shown in Figure 3, the raw input includes the live foreign-exchange spot rate as well as the live domestic and foreign interest rates. Below

OPTION 1		OPTION 2		OPTION 3		OPTION 4	
INSTRUMENT UK		INSTRUMENT YEN		INSTRUMENT FFR		INSTRUMENT SWF	
SPOT RATE	177.3500	SPOT RATE	73.9372	SPOT RATE	17.5055	SPOT RATE	72.3851
STRIKE PR	180.0000	STRIKE PR	75.0000	STRIKE PR	15.0000	STRIKE PR	65.0000
DOM INT	5.7800	DOM INT	5.7800	DOM INT	5.7800	DOM INT	5.7800
FOR INT	9.0000	FOR INT	3.9000	FOR INT	9.0000	FOR INT	4.0000
DAYS TO EXP	90	DAYS TO EXP	90	DAYS TO EXP	90	DAYS TO EXP	90
VOLATILITY	0.1300	VOLATILITY	0.1200	VOLATILITY	0.1380	VOLATILITY	0.1380
---------------		---------------		---------------		---------------	
CALL PRICE	2.7982	CALL PRICE	1.4172	CALL PRICE	2.3379	CALL PRICE	7.6939
PUT PRICE	6.7934	PUT PRICE	2.1264	PUT PRICE	0.0434	PUT PRICE	0.0994

FIGURE 3. Real-time foreign-exchange option pricing derived page.

the dotted lines are the real-time call and put prices.

In summary, a trading company can use its own software, such as the option pricing software, to create a derived page, which creates new information. The example shown above consists of four panels. An unlimited variety of output formats can be used.

POSSIBLE PRODUCTION CONFIGURATION

A financial markets firm will link a variety of computers such as computation engines (large computers), database servers, and dealer workstations to its trading floor system. The firm might also want to link its back office computers with the vendor-provided digital distribution system. The business strategy will dictate the required equipment composition. The vendor-provided digital generation system is shown above the dotted line in Figure 4. The detail of the digital subsystem architecture, starting with the advanced workstation software (AWS), which resides in a gateway computer, is shown below the dotted line. At the top of Figure 4 are rectangular boxes that represent service access units (SAUs). The SAUs take in the market data vendor digital feeds and broadcast the digital market data over a proprietary in-house trading floor system using a vendor-provided local area network (LAN).

The digital market data, in page format,

are then moved down below the dotted line through a gateway that contains AWS software. The AWS software, developed by the vendor, takes the digital data and passes them into the in-house LAN, which links diverse hardware. The LAN allows data to be moved through the gateway to the back office. A trader can dial into the trading system from a remote personal computer to obtain market data. At the top right-hand side of the figure is a composite page unit in a rectangular box. (As explained earlier, the composite page unit gives the capability to cut and paste together electronically information from different standard digital pages.)

The architectures of various trading floor systems being provided by major vendors facilitate digital data manipulation. The digital subsystem includes the financial market firm's series of intelligent workstations and computation engines for "number crunching." The AWS software pulls the digital data out of the vendor-provided system. The VGU is the path from the digital subsystem to the video switch. The firm needs to consider the degree to which it wants to standardize the architecture. Standardization is particularly important when the firm wants to have a common global network spanning disparate organizations.

Intelligent workstations hooked into the network contribute analytics throughout the network. These analytics are used to create, trade, and market financial instruments.

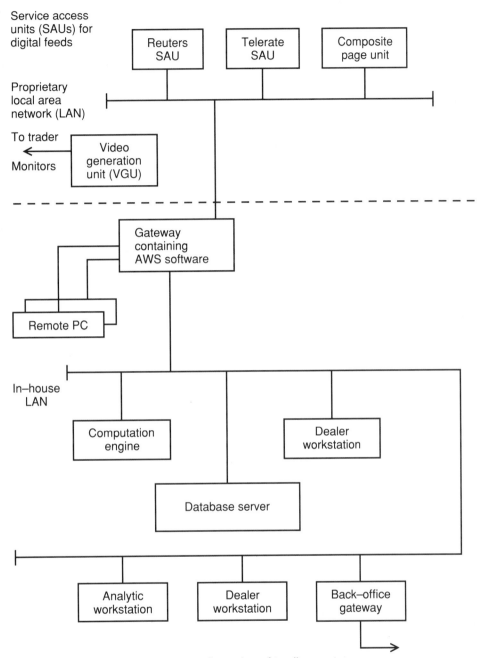

FIGURE 4. Possible production configuration of trading system.

Computer vendors have developed industry-wide information transfer standards that enable transparent file system access among intelligent workstations on the LAN. Personal computers along the network can also have transparent access to disk space. In a larger sense, distributed network resources are available to personal computers on the network through a variety of network facilities. In addition, personal computers along the network can be linked to relational database software through facilities within the software. A series of features and facilities are normally built into a workstation environment. The communication resources that can be shared by personal computers and workstations on a network include modems and other serial line devices. The workstation environment allows for high modularity, smooth hardware, and operating system growth paths as well as hardware and software standards to incorporate artificial intelligence (AI) and expert system developments.

The vendor-provided architecture is open to external access through the AWS interface. Workstations can be connected to the vendor-provided system computers and networks through standard bridges and protocols. Trader software will fall into three or four major categories: data acquisition, database service, background analytics, and actual user applications. The AWS interface allows data acquisition access to page-oriented market data vendors. Feeds from other market data vendors (such as Lotus Signal) supply ticker-oriented feeds and require different data acquisition software to interface with them. Additional data acquisition software can perform field extraction from pages, sort and classify data types as they are received, and create market data streams. Some database interface software will make contributions to the database, and some will access the database to feed applications with the database software itself in the middle. The database access software is the base for background analytic routines and user applications such as modeling, data manipulation, graphic representations, and composite paging.

[*See also:* Financial Services, Computer Use in.]

For Further Reading

Binder, B., and R. Mark. 1989. Technical ALCO in the new marketplace, Chapter 3 in *Banker's treasury management handbook*. Boston: Warren Gorham and Lamont.

Lucas, H. C., Jr., and R. A. Schwartz. 1989. *The challenge of information technology for the security markets: Liquidity, volatility and global trading.* Homewood, Ill.: Dow Jones-Irwin.

Steiner, T., and D. Teixera. 1990. *Technology in banking: Creating value and destroying profits.* Homewood, Ill.: Dow Jones-Irwin.

Walton, R. E. 1990. *Up and running: Integrating information technology and the organization.* Boston: Harvard Business School Press.

Robert M. Mark

TREASURY MANAGEMENT

See Financial Services, Computer Use in

TURING, ALAN MATHISON

Alan Mathison Turing was born at Warrington Crescent in London, England, on June 23, 1912, of upper-middle-class, well-educated parents. Turing showed his brilliance early. Around his third birthday, his mother wrote to his father, who was frequently away from home on business, that Alan was "a very clever child, I should say, with a wonderful memory for new words. Alan generally speaks correctly and well. He has rather a delightful phrase, 'for so many morrows,' which we think means 'for a long time,' and is used with reference to past or future."

When Turing was 6 years old, he found a copy of *Reading without Tears,* and taught himself the rudiments of reading in about 3 weeks. At the age of 9 he is said to have startled his mother, out of the blue, with the question, "Mother, what makes the oxygen fit so tightly into the hydrogen to produce water?"

In preparatory school, Turing looked on sports as a waste of time, although years later he would become a first-class marathon runner. His mathematics teacher claimed that Turing was "a mathematician, I think." Not yet 15 years of age, he had already evolved the calculus term "$\tan^{-1} x$," without any knowledge of calculus.

From his early days at school, Turing cared only about mathematics and science. He was conscious of his own scientific genius at an early age, and was sufficiently aware of it to write to his mother from school: "I always seem to want to make things from the thing that is commonest in nature and with the least waste of energy." He left the Sherborne School loaded with mathematics prizes and a scholarship to King's College, Cambridge.

He went to King's College in 1931. In 1935 he began work in mathematical logic and started on his best-known investigation on computable numbers. In 1937, Turing published his famous paper, "On Computable Numbers with an Application to the Entscheidungsproblem." In that paper, he envisioned the Turing machine, which could be fed instructions from punched paper tape. Two years after being graduated from King's College, Turing was invited to Princeton University, where he earned his doctorate in 1938. Turing contemplated staying in the United States and was offered a post as assistant to John VON NEUMANN, but in 1938 he decided to return to Cambridge. Shortly after he returned to Cambridge, the war broke out and he spent the next 6 years with the Foreign Office.

During World War II, Turing was one of a team of British scientists sequestered at the Bletchley Park estate and ordered to develop machinery that could decipher codes from Germany's Enigma encoding machines. The results of these efforts, often credited with a decisive role in winning the war, were several electromechanical machines. The successor to these machines, the Colossus codebreaking computer, is now accepted as the first operational electronic computer.

In 1945, he joined the staff of the National Physical Laboratory to work on the design, construction, and use of a large automatic computer that he named the Automatic Computing Engine (ACE). About 1949 he became deputy director of the Computing Laboratory at the University of Manchester where the Manchester Automatic Digital Machine (MADM), the computer with the largest memory capacity in the world at that time, was being built. His efforts in the construction of early computers and the development of early programming techniques were of prime importance.

Turing spent a major part of his life trying to answer the question, Can a machine think? His interest in this problem was stimulated by talks with Norbert Wiener, the founder of cybernetics, whom Turing first met on visits to America. Wiener, applying the mechanism of computers to human behavior, believed that mental disorders are primarily diseases of the memory. The question of thinking machines and their possibilities is frightening. If machines think, then is human thinking just a mechanical activity? If so, then where does one's potential lie? As greater machines develop where will their capacities end?

Turing believed that machines do think and explained his position in an article, "Can a Machine Think?" As a practical demonstration he designed a machine that simulated human thinking by playing off a single move in a chess game. He succeeded in proving that machines can perform deductive analysis by solving mathematical equations and making logical decisions.

At the peak of his career and in the prime of life, Alan Turing was found dead in bed, on June 8, 1954, at the age of 42. His death was caused by poisoning from potassium cyanide, ruled at the inquest to have been self-administered.

The Association for Computing Machinery (ACM) has annually given its highest award, the Turing Award, for technical contributions to the computing community. Alan Turing's name and influence live on. His work remains relevant even in today's world of advanced research.

For Further Reading

Harmon, M. 1975. *Stretching man's mind: A history of data processing.* New York: Mason/Charter.
Williams, M. 1985. *A history of computing technology.* Englewood Cliffs, N.J.: Prentice-Hall.

Donald D. Spencer

TYPESETTING

The setting of type for printing is a process that has become all but unthinkable without the use of computers. They are essential at all levels of typesetting, from the dedicated minicomputers used by full-service compositors (or as in-house systems for newspapers and magazines) to the microcomputer that enables a single person to put out a newsletter of professional appearance. This article focuses on the typographical aspects of personal computer–based publishing, also known as desktop publishing (DTP).

THE SOFTWARE

With a DTP package, the user sees on the monitor screen something that closely resembles the eventual printer output. It is not exact because the screen resolution is considerably less fine than that of any laser printer. But a page can be laid out on the screen and modified without being printed. This is referred to as "what you see is what you get" (WYSIWYG) and is a necessary component of any DTP package.

The first two widely known DTP software packages are still probably the best for most uses. Although dozens of others have entered the field, they have tried mostly to reduce costs and, therefore, are able to do only some of what Aldus Pagemaker and Ventura Publisher are capable of. Both of these leaders have recently issued new, enhanced versions of their programs. Each has certain strengths when compared with the other. Pagemaker is usually viewed as an "advertiser's" program. It seems especially well suited, as its name implies, to single-sheet projects that carry a lot of graphics and design. Publisher, on the other hand, is often used to create books, magazines, and pamphlets where design elements are likely to carry over from page to page. Each package, however, is fully capable of doing either sort of work.

Neither program, nor any currently available DTP package, allows the very finely controlled typography that can be achieved by a professional typesetting system. They are simply not complex enough nor do they produce the proper control codes, proprietary to each system manufacturer, to properly control such systems. However, the PostScript page description language is powerful enough for most purposes and many type-setting shops can now accept PostScript files for direct transfer to photographic plates.

Although most DTP programs can be used as word processors (all allow text entry and some even have spellcheckers), they are primarily layout and design tools. Most DTP users find it much easier to use a true word processor for text entry and then import the resulting file into the DTP program. Most DTP programs allow direct importation of the more popular word processing formats: WordPerfect, XYWrite, AMI Pro, WordStar, MS Word, and so on.

Few DTP programs allow any but the most elementary manipulation of graphic images but drawings and photographs can be imported after they are created elsewhere. Aldus Freehand and Adobe Illustrator are two very high quality graphics programs. Each uses PostScript and each can output both black and white halftones and color separations.

THE HARDWARE

The Macintosh computer, specifically designed for graphical work, had a big head start in the DTP field. When it was first introduced, it came with two programs that could produce acceptable, if limited, printed work. MacWrite and MacDraw were immediately thrown into service for DTP, though neither was especially well suited. The reason? No other DTP package was available for the microcomputer user. Once developers realized the demand was great, the situation changed quickly. Desktop publishing packages appeared for the Mac and for MS-DOS machines. Now, the real considerations for choice of a computing platform are cost, convenience, and adaptability.

The real heart of a DTP system is the printer. A laser printer is essential and two main kinds are available: PostScript or PostScript compatible and Hewlett-Packard compatible. The difference is primarily in the way the printers are controlled. PostScript is a page description language (PDL) that allows a DTP program to be essentially device independent. A user can run "roughs" from a laser printer until everything is right, then take a disk with a PostScript output file to a service bureau for high-resolution photographic output on a Linotronic or similar device. Hewlett-Packard-compatible printers are usually less expensive but also less versatile.

Laser printer output has gotten so good in recent years that, for many projects, it is "camera ready." The 300-dots/inch resolution of a laser printer is not good enough for slick magazine production but is often fine for short-run newsletters, particularly those that are "printed" on a high-quality copy machine.

Desktop publishing and drawing programs have begun to make impressive use of color, and the Macintosh computer, in particular, can be matched with very good color monitors. Good color monitors are available for MS-DOS computers as well. Whether or not color is chosen, the monitor screen should be quite large when compared with a "normal" monitor. The user wants to be able to see a full 8 ½ × 11-inch sheet as close as possible to full size. Some monitors are capable of showing 16 × 11 inches at full size.

TYPEFACES AND SETTING TYPE

It is not sufficient, in designing a well-turned page, to simply throw down a typeface and let it lie there. Desktop publishing systems must be capable of manipulating the type for best looks and readability. The space between lines (called leading [led-ing] from the strips of lead that were used as spacers way back in the old days of typesetting) should be adjustable. Leading is important; it affects the texture of the copy, the readability, and the amount of copy that can be put on a page.

Justification, the ability to set the type with flush margins on both sides, is important. This effect is achieved by increasing or diminishing the spaces between words and letters on a line. Few microcomputer-based DTP packages do a really good job of justification. They do not have fine enough controls to adjust spacing adequately. Many lack entirely the ability to adjust spacing between letters. For this reason, many DTP projects are designed with "ragged right" margins, to

improve the texture and readability of the page.

Hundreds of typefaces are available. All but a few are suitable only for headlines and subheads. The most readable typefaces are those with serifs, the little "feet" on the letters. The most widely used serif face is "Times Roman," developed for the *New York Times* to be easily readable even in very small point sizes. It is possible (though difficult) to read 2-point Times Roman without a magnifying glass. Other serif faces suitable for DTP text use include Century Schoolbook, Palatino, and Garamond.

Typeface designers have focused a great deal of attention on the issue of "kerning." In the old days of hand-set metal type, certain letter pairs were cast as single units to ensure pleasing relationships. An example is the "w" and "o" of "word," where the "o" is slightly tucked under the slant of the "w" to preserve the texture of the typeface. If the two were to be spaced "normally" the eye would perceive too much white and the letters would seem to be too far apart. Another good example of effective kerning is the word "offset." Note how the two "f"'s nearly touch and how the "s" is tucked tightly under the downsweep of its neighbor "f." A DTP program that does not have adequate kerning controls (some have none at all) will produce ugly typesetting. The best programs do not require any intervention by the user. They have "kerning tables" that automatically check for the problem relationships. When found, the program automatically kerns the pair. It is almost as good as the old cast pairs method.

CHARACTER GENERATION

The two main printer types differ widely in how they treat typefaces. A PostScript printer has, in its memory, a mathematical template that yields a 1-point version of each character in a typeface. A point is one seventy-second of an inch. When a typeface is selected and sized, PostScript simply expands the template by the point value desired.

One of the subtleties of type design is that the relative weights of the thick and thin strokes sometimes vary from point size to point size. An outline-generated typeface, by its nature, carries the same line weights throughout the range of sizes. The effects are not usually noticeable in the smaller point sizes, but at around 10 to 12 points, some PostScript typefaces begin to look noticeably "fat." Often, a designer tries to compensate for the effect, with marginal success, by increasing the leading.

The outline method of PostScript allows a comparatively large number of typefaces to be held in a printer's read-only memory (ROM), with the major disadvantage noted above, and allows greater freedom in manipulation of the typeface than does the Hewlett-Packard bit-map technique. In bit-mapping, imagine a grid, with squares 1/300th of an inch on a side, that covers the entire character with space all around to account for letter spacing and leading. Each square in the grid is assigned a coordinate and each is designated "black or "white." This means that, for each typeface, size, and style (italic, bold, thin, etc.) desired, the full character set must be available for downloading into the printer memory. A Hewlett-Packard-compatible printer has only a few typefaces and styles in its ROM. More are available in ROM cartridges that plug into the printer as needed. Fonts can also be downloaded to the printer from disk storage, if desired.

The primary advantages of the bit-map technique are an initially lower cost and generally high quality. Because the characters always remain as they are mapped, the designers can be more faithful to the original typeface design, including those subtle variations resulting from size expansion. Furthermore, kerned pairs can be mapped for use as needed, almost as if they were cast in metal. PostScript uses kerning algorithms to accomplish the purpose so its kerned pairs are generated "on the fly."

In both methods of character generation, the alphabets are stored in the printer's random-access memory when in use and must be rebuilt or reloaded for each printing session, so the size of the printer's memory is an important consideration. The minimum amount to print a full page of text and graphics is 1.5 megabytes. A capacity of 2 megabytes allows the printer to operate more quickly.

MUSIC AUTOGRAPHY

Until very recently, the publishing of music scores was a costly, time-consuming process, dominated by a few large publishers with expensive equipment. The versatility of computers has changed that, as it has so much else. It is now possible to create a complete orchestral score and all the separate parts on computer in far less time. A composer can easily transpose a score to any key in seconds. The quality of the programs available varies widely, however, and few have every feature a composer might wish for.

Music desktop publishing occurs in the same three stages of ordinary DTP: data entry, editing, and printing. By use of a MIDI interface, the notations can be automatically generated simply by playing a keyboard instrument to accomplish the data entry. Sequencing software converts the digital information into on-screen musical notation. This is then edited, in much the same way text is edited, to change the notation from a rough draft to a finished score. During editing, a composer can check the work by having the computer play the score back. After the score is completed, it is printed out using the graphic capabilities of a laser printer.

Music notation is considerably more complex than alphanumeric data yet many music publishing programs are, for the experienced musician, extremely easy to use. Most difficulties have to do with the nature of music notation, its hundreds of symbols and myriad rules. Choosing a music notation program can be a difficult task, compounded by the fact that few computer stores carry MIDI keyboards that might allow adequate testing and few music stores carry computers and software. The last statement may soon become untrue as computers become more and more a part of musical performance and recording. (See also MUSIC, COMPUTER APPLICATIONS IN.)

SUMMARY

Even though desktop publishing is different from "traditional" pasteup methods (which, themselves, are less than 30 years old), most of the process is essentially similar. The tools are different, keyboards and mice rather than

X-acto knives and drawing boards, but the results desired are the same: effective communications using good design principles combined with creative sensibility.

It is often the case that the microcomputer does not speed up work. But it does allow much more care to be taken in the same amount of time, thereby improving the quality of the work. By reducing the amount of time spent on routine tasks, desktop publishing allows designers, artists, and writers the freedom to discover new creative relationships. Desktop publishing allows nearly anyone to have true "freedom of the press" with some assurance that the printed product will be attractive enough to be read.

[*See also:* Desktop Publishing.]

For Further Reading

Beach, M., S. Scepro, and K. Russon. 1986. *Getting it printed.* Portland, Ore.: Coast to Coast Books. Very complete print-production how-to. Begins at beginning.

Chappell, W. 1970. *A short history of the printed word.* New York: Alfred A. Knopf. Written by a type designer who shows his love of the craft.

Craig, J. 1978. *Phototypesetting: A design manual.* New York: Watson-Guptill. Covers design issues very well; discusses high-end typesetting systems in detail.

Parker, R. C. 1988. *Desktop publishing with WordPerfect.* Chapel Hill, N.C.: Ventan Press. Use of a high-end word processing program to do simple DTP work. Good primer on overall technique.

Stockford, J., ed. 1987. *Desktop publishing Bible.* Indianapolis, Ind.: Howard W. Sams. Gives the beginner an excellent stepping-off point and a good grasp of concepts.

Walter Hawn

U

USER DOCUMENTATION

User software manuals are written for a person using a software product—a manager, writer, student, or programmer. Even though a user may be experienced in working with computers, the emphasis in user manuals is on what the software can do for the user, not on a technical discussion of how the software operates. A user manual describes how someone can accomplish tasks with the software.

Although manuals are usually printed as books, they may also be available on-line as "help" screens or interactive tutorials. This article emphasizes the printed version; however, many of the same principles apply to either format.

The working conditions and requirements affecting a technical writer writing a user manual will vary with each software development company's practices and procedures. The following guidelines can be adapted to a variety of situations.

ESTABLISHING A PLAN

The first step in writing a user manual is to make contact with the programming team as soon as possible. The earlier you are involved with the team's software design, writing, and testing, the more time and opportunity you will have to produce an accurate manual. Start by gathering information on the software project.

Who are the software's and manual's intended users: novices or experienced users? The answer will help you visualize your audience and write the manual at the appropriate level.

What will the software do? This should be described in terms of what tasks a user can do, not the internal program features that a user may never notice.

What manuals are required? There may be one manual with tutorial and reference material combined or several manuals.

When should the software and, therefore, the manual be complete? The programmers will have a schedule that outlines the steps needed to produce the required software and due dates to complete each step. Even though software development practices vary, producing the manual will roughly follow these stages: software design (outline/rough drafts of the manual), writing the software (writing more complete versions of the manual), and testing the software (using the manual with the software to determine if the two match).

When you have answered the preceding questions, you are ready to make your schedule for writing and testing the manual. Your schedule is dependent on that of the programming team and should list what you need to do, what you need from the programmers at each step, and the length of time needed to complete each step. These estimates are based on your prior experience, the programming team's schedule, the proposed length of the manual, the number of software and manual tests, the number of drafts to be reviewed, and the number of reviewers who must read them. Discuss your schedule with the programming team and your supervisor, negotiate dates if necessary, and keep project participants informed of your progress or delays during the project. Be aware that the completion date as well as the other dates in the programming and writing schedules may change because of events beyond your control.

PREPARING TO WRITE

Writers have their favorite methods for starting a project but it is a good idea to have a map to see where you are going. You may favor the traditional outline or a list of topics. Why not start with a table of contents for the manual? You will have a ready-made outline and will not be tempted to compile the table of contents as an afterthought during the last-minute rush of producing the manual. A main table of contents covers the entire manual, but tables appearing at the beginning of sections and chapters provide immediate descriptions of portions of the manual for those users who flip through.

You should take every opportunity to collect information on the software from the design stage through testing. You will probably start by not understanding the project; this is an advantage. Not only are you writing a manual; you are representing the user who also starts as a novice when using the software. Experiencing the same unfamiliarity and frustrations as the user helps you explain the software more clearly.

Talk to the programmers, the marketing department, test sites. Attend project meetings held by the programming team. Compile a list of questions so you do not waste your informant's time or your own. Take detailed notes or tape record interviews. Collection of data continues throughout the project as the software changes and your understanding of it changes. After an interview or meeting, write a description of the information you have gathered while it is still fresh. Writing will help you uncover gaps in your knowledge: if you cannot explain it to yourself, ask someone to explain it to you again and rewrite. Revision is continuous and writing manuals is an incremental process.

As you write, the software development/testing schedule will probably change several times for various reasons. This means your schedule will also change and you may have less time than anticipated. Although there is little you can do to avoid this situation, you can keep project participants informed of how your schedule and work are affected and negotiate changes to your schedule.

Writing a Tutorial

A tutorial provides step-by-step instructions on how to perform specific tasks: printing mailing labels, producing a parts inventory report, cutting and pasting text in a word processor document, starting and stopping the software. As you write a tutorial, imagine that you are standing over the user's shoulder, teaching the user how to do something. This is not the place to comprehensively explain every aspect of the software; that is information for the reference section of the manual.

Each chapter in the tutorial manual should cover one task. Start the chapter with a brief description of the task and a list of skills that the user will acquire after learning to perform the task. Then explain how to do the task step-by-step, numbering each step. Include graphics of the screen to show what the user should see at each step. Include samples of printed reports if appropriate. Try to anticipate user problems such as making the wrong choice on a menu or pressing the wrong key and describe ways of correcting the problems.

Include several ways of finding information in the tutorial: a table of contents, an index, a glossary, and section and chapter overviews. Users will look for information in different ways; try to provide as many access points as possible.

Writing Reference Material

The reference section of a manual is comprehensive; it covers anything the user can do with the software. It is a source of information on how to perform tasks but does not use the step-by-step format of the tutorial. The reference section describes tasks the software performs; terms used in software; functions (delete, copy, save); messages and how the user can respond to them; exceptional situations when software can malfunction and how to correct them; and reports produced by the software.

The reference section is usually organized around functions that can be grouped alphabetically or by similarity of purpose. Software messages and tips on troubleshooting problems are also included, often in appendixes. Tables or lists of functions and messages are also useful for quick reference. Whenever possible, use graphics of screens, menus, and reports to illustrate functions.

CHOOSING A STYLE AND APPEARANCE

Writing styles for user manuals tend toward informality, directly addressing the user ("Before you select . . ."); using brief explanations and lists surrounded by white space to focus the user's attention; using graphics to demonstrate what to do rather than relying on dense paragraphs of explanation; and using active verbs ("Select the Paste icon . . .") rather than passive verbs ("When the Paste icon is selected . . ."). However, follow the company style guide if one exists.

Depending on your company's work environment, you may be collaborating with an editor and a graphic artist. The editor will check grammar, punctuation, consistency, spelling, and style for conformance to the company's style guide. If you are on your own, rely on a style manual such as *The Chicago Manual of Style* and use a spell checker and similar software tools to spot errors. A graphic artist can suggest useful devices to highlight information such as marginal notes, color, and typefaces. You should also define typographical conventions used in the manual to indicate how the user enters information (highlighting to indicate clicking on an icon or printing typed commands in capital letters). Large companies producing many software products will usually have a style guide for graphics; it provides continuity in presentation for users who have bought several products from the same company.

TESTING

You will eventually need versions of the software to expand the material you have written using preliminary information such as project descriptions. Like the software, the manual will probably have an alpha test version, a beta test version, and a final version. Whenever possible, use the software as soon as it becomes available from the pro-

gramming team. You can then compare it with what you have written, take note of discrepancies, ask questions about anything you do not understand, and rewrite if it is your misunderstanding. Your tests can help the programmers uncover software errors (even if they do not want to hear about them).

Ask others (other writers, users at test sites) to operate the software using the manual. Make arrangements if possible to observe the testers using the manual and take notes of their questions, problems, and reactions. Incorporate changes based on the tests and test again until the manual is correct and clear.

WRAPPING IT UP

Final approval of the manual depends on the company's procedures. The manual will go through several levels of editorial checking and tests, and be signed off at each stage before proceeding to the next.

After initial release software typically goes through several revisions to correct errors or add a few changes. Later, it may be released as a new level, indicating that major changes have been made. A file of corrections and possible changes should be maintained for the next version.

For Further Reading

Price, J. 1984. *How to write a computer manual: A handbook of software documentation.* Benjamin/Cummings.

The Chicago manual of style, 13th ed. 1982. Chicago: University of Chicago Press.

Weiss, E. H. 1985. *How to write a usable user manual.* Philadelphia: ISI Press.

Lisa M. Lehman

USER GROUPS

See Appendix

V

VIDEODISCS

Interactivity is an attempt to provide the viewer with some control over the content and duration of the information viewed. The interactive video industry began simply enough, permitting the viewer to stop and start video segments. Slide and filmstrip projectors allowed the viewer to stop on particular slides but the content was predetermined and accessing different materials required moving through the entire collection.

Videotape players allowed audio and video segments to be combined. The viewer, with a hand-held remote control, was able to fast-forward, rewind, or pause on a particular image. Still the viewer had to search through the entire videotape to locate desired segments. The videotape medium was advanced as an appropriate medium for education, training, or information delivery because of this simulated "interactivity" capability and because it was less expensive to duplicate than film.

Videotape applications in education and training continued to be the dominant delivery system of the 1970s. The videotape player/recorder has been successful as a consumer appliance but training and education found two major disadvantages: (1) the time required to move from a video image in one part of the tape to another part of the tape was unacceptable; (2) videotape, like film, wore out. This problem accelerated as the tape stretched from constant starting and stopping. Later addition of computer control devices would minimize the search process and increase interactivity but still at a minimal level. A computer program could be written that caused the video program to play a specified segment of the videotape based on viewer responses to questions or directions; however, the addition of a computer control did not eliminate the disadvantages inherent in interactive videotape systems.

The first visual storage media—disk, magnetic tape, and film—all began about 1927. At that time James Baird stored television images on waxed phonograph discs (Sigel et al. 1980). In 1961, 3M teamed with Stanford Research Institute to develop an optical disk medium that could store video programs for inexpensive home video systems. By the time the research had produced a prototype, other approaches to optical disk storage had been developed and the 3M approach was temporarily halted. In 1965, P. M. G. Toulon received a patent for a visual disk that recorded minute images on a photographic plate (Rice and Dubbe 1982). Also in 1965, Magnetic Video Recording offered a magnetic disk with stop action and instant replay. This was the beginning of the "instant replay" for American football broadcasting.

By the early 1970s it was agreed that disk storage devices were practical for multiple uses. The disk was an 8- or 12-inch platter on which up to 54,000 still images or 30 minutes of linear video (motion) could be imprinted. The information is stored on the disk as microscopic three-dimensional pits. The images and one or two audio tracks for stereo, or two separate mono tracks, were imprinted on the laser disk in concentric circles much like the traditional phonograph. Otherwise there is no standard in the laser disk industry. Different systems were being developed that used different methods of creating the disk, different methods of duplicating the disk, and different methods of reading the disk. There were two basic formats for the disk imprinting: "pressing" and playback. Mechanical storage and/or playback were represented by TelDec's TeD system, JVC's Video High Density system, and RCA's Selectavision Videodisc system. Information was recorded on these disks either using a mechanical cutting device, much like creating a phonograph record or using a laser to implant the information. The playback systems employed either a mechanical stylus or a laser for reading the information. RCA and JVC used a technique called a capacitive system for reading stored information. The disk served as one plate and the stylus as the second. Information was retrieved as electrical charges moved between these two plates. This system was called CED for capacitance electronic disk.

Optical laser disks were recorded and read using a laser. Representatives of this technology were Magnavox (Philips), Pioneer, Discovision Associates, and Thompson-CSF. The laser technology was more durable as minor scratches and dust had no effect on the quality of the transmission and therefore less protection was needed. A disk using the laser playback system would last longer (estimated at more than 10,000 playings) because there was no mechanical contact or wear on the disk. Duplicates of either type of disk were simply pressed using basically the same technology that the audio industry employed for phonograph records. Playing time ranged from 30 to 60 minutes depending on the revolutions per minute (rpm) the disk required to play the information. Optical videodiscs employed either constant linear velocity (CLV) or constant angular velocity (CAV) as a format. Constant angular velocity requires the disk to rotate at a constant speed, usually 1,800 rpm or 30 frames per second. As information is recorded on tracks that encompass the disk, a track at the center of the disk is shorter and requires less time to read than a track at the circumference of the disk, but the disk maintains the same rpm. Constant angular velocity disks store information by segment on each track. This permits exact addressing of the information and increases the interactivity potential. Constant linear velocity is de-

pendent on a specific length of track, or segment, passing the reading light beam in 1 second, about 31 feet per second. The motor slows down as the tracks at the center of the disk are being read and speeds up at the circumference. With this format twice as much information can be stored on a disk, but at the expense of slow motion and freeze-frame capability, as the information can be accessed only by stops that separate each of the segments (Schneider and Bennion 1981, Lehman 1986).

It was anticipated that the videodisc industry would create a video/audio delivery system that would eclipse the growing videotape industry. It was believed that consumers would purchase a system that provided large storage capacity of nondegenerating, high-quality audio/visual information at a cost per disk that would be less than videotape. Although the playback system was still more expensive than videotape players it was felt that mass production would reduce this price and the quality of the recording would attract the consumer. Predictions were only partially accurate. The consumers did appreciate the higher quality that was available from the laser disk but they insisted on being able to record their own material. As laser disk was a read-only delivery the demand for the playback units never grew to the point of reducing the cost. The major consumers of videodisc technology have been the military, industry, and, to a lesser degree, education. This technology allows the creation of instructional materials that are truly interactive. Varied outcomes are possible with quick, if not, instantaneous response to user input. Random access becomes possible because the videodisc can access any information, by address (either frame number or disk location), without searching through all of the material on the disk (Iuppa 1984).

By 1978 the videodisc industry was ready to offer something to the public, but the fledgling industry still had problems. Both mastering and replicating a videodisc involved technological problems. The major obstacle seemed to be the inability to produce a "clean room" (common in modern production of microchips) and as much as 95% of the content on the videodisc was affected. Thompson-CSF, a French company, offered the TTV3620 to industrial users that sold for $3,000. This optical laser disk system used a transmissive optical disk, a flexible, translucent disk with the light source and the detector on opposite sides of the disk. The player could read either side of the disk simply by changing the focal point of the light (Sigel et al. 1980). Magnavox (Philips subsidiary) and MCA (Music Corporation of America) introduced DiscoVision, in this same year, as a consumer model to show movies from MCA's Universal studios (Gray 1978). The Magnavox 8000 sold for almost $800 (Schneider and Bennion 1981). Disco-Vision was also an optical laser disk, but it used the reflective system to read information. The player could read only one side of the disk at a time; it had to be turned over to access the second side. The laser light was reflected off the disk itself and was directed to the detector. This type of disk was rigid and more durable than the transmissive type. The rigid optical disk has become the most popular type and is used in the majority of videodisc productions.

In 1979 IBM joined with MCA and Philips to help solve the mastering and duplication problems and DiscoVision Associates was created. That year DiscoVision produced their own player, the PR 7820, which was directed toward the educational/industrial market and sold for $3,000. Industrial laser disk systems included 1 to 7 kilobytes of memory in a microprocessor in the player and made possible greater interactivity. In 1980 the first Videodisk conference was held at the University of Nebraska by the Nebraska Videodisk Production Group and the Society for Applied Technology. At that conference, attended by groups and individuals interested in application of the videodisc technology to training and education, the concept of levels of interactivity was introduced.

Level I interactivity uses a videodisc player capable of individual frame accessing, freeze frame, and playback. The user manually operates the controls. The system is relatively inexpensive, costing several hundred dollars. A Level II system uses a player with a built-in microprocessor that has a limited amount of memory. The player reads a digital program encoded on the disk and allows the user to interact with the player and branch to different parts of the disk. Such systems cost over $1,000. Level III systems are fully interactive. They feature the storage capability of the videodisc with the managerial capability of the computer. Using a computer to manage the interaction allows additional memory, graphic resolution and additional input/output devices to be integrated. This system will cost between $2,000 and $10,000. Level IV systems return the program control information to the disk. Hardware used in Level III and IV systems are RGB video and keyboard/mouse/touch screen. Level I and II systems use composite video and a keypad (Magel 1990).

In 1981 RCA introduced their videodisc system, Selectavision. This mechanical player was targeted to the consumer who, it was hoped, would want a simple machine for high-quality playback of movies. The system sold for $500, but even the modest cost was not enough to make the videodisc player competitive. Videocassette recorders continued to decrease in cost and consumers found the different videodisc systems confusing and incompatible. RCA retired from the videodisc market in 1984 (Graham 1986). The JVC videodisc system JVC-VHD, also introduced in 1981, also sold for $500. It was similar to the RCA system except that it used a "grooveless" disk instead of the grooved version that RCA developed. Pioneer also introduced the Laserdisc VP-1000 for the consumer market and sold it for $750. One unique feature of the VP-1000 was the inclusion of a communication port that permitted the player to interface with a microcomputer. By this time, 3M had begun mastering disks for Thompson and was now processing reflective disks. 3M has continued to be a major producer of optical laser disks.

APPLICATIONS OF INTERACTIVE VIDEO

Military and industry users were the first to recognize the value of laser disk technology in training. In 1979, General Motors ordered 11,500 videodisc players to be sent to their dealers for training mechanics and sales personnel and for systems that would be available to illustrate product characteristics to customers. Ford and Chrysler followed GM in implementing laser disk training and sales in their dealerships.

WICAT received a grant from the National Science Foundation to design, build, and evaluate an intelligent videodisc system. To implement an intelligent videodisc system a small computer was required. In fact, the key components of an intelligent interactive videodisc system are the interface and the software to control the interface. The standard configuration would consist of a computer, a laser disk player, a monitor and internal or external interface device, and appropriate cables. (Early systems often took several people to transport the equipment and several hours to set up because of the number of cables that had to be connected to the correct sources.) Although many systems use a standard RS-232C interface there is no real industry standard (Lehman 1986). (See Lehman 1986 for a list of interface producers.)

WICAT built their intelligent system using a biology disk they developed in 1977 for McGraw-Hill. About the same time, several companies introduced videodisc players with communication ports (Sony LDP-1000, DVA PR-7820, Pioneer VP-1000).

Once laser disk players with microprocessor and computer interfaces were available, multiple applications were developed. In 1981 David Hon produced a training program on cardiopulmonary resuscitation (CPR) for the American Heart Association. For this widely acclaimed production, he used a unique configuration of hardware. It consisted of an Apple computer with two control cards; the video card controlled a videodisc player and the audio card, from BCD Associates, interfaced with an audiotape player. Two monitors were used in such a way that they appeared to talk to each other. Using this configuration, Hon was able to overcome the audio limitations from the laser disk. The audio tracks on the laser disk often were the limiting factor in increased information storage and retrieval, as the audio was attached to the visual frames. To play 10 seconds of audio, 300 frames of visual storage were used because linear vid-

eo used 30 frames per second. This limitation was not serious as long as the information was done as a motion sequence. If, however, the information involved a still picture, that picture was shown over the 300 frames, a very inefficient use of storage space. A final piece of unique equipment consisted of a special mannequin. This mannequin had sensors embedded in it, and the computer monitored these sensors and provided visual and auditory feedback to the user. The computer was able to "show" the user when pressure or breathing was too great, too light, or in the wrong place.

As the equipment grew more sophisticated, others who had attended the Nebraska conference were able to build unique programs to take advantage of the technology to address specific training demands. The military was particularly interested in random access of motion and still video from the laser disk as a method of creating a paperless training program for the army, by the year 1990. Videodiscs to train military personnel on equipment repair, other specific tasks, and recruitment were being produced. With intelligent videodisc technology the military, and others, accelerated simulation programs in their training. For example, a Tank/Gunnery system is viewed from inside the tank. A vehicle maintenance program tours the inside of an engine. A map reading course allows the user to zoom in on areas of interest. A Bank of America program focuses on teller communication skills between coworkers and customers. The Aspen disk tours the city by car or plane, allowing the user to stop at various points of interest. A similar concept was used to reduce boredom in a stationary bicycle exercise program. The user views a scene on a monitor that changes to different locations and watches the scenery pass with different speeds depending on how fast the rider pedals.

Laser disk systems are used to teach human genetics, relaxation, jazzercise, belly dancing, cooking, and golf. One golf game allows the golfer to play famous holes on famous courses around the world. The player indicates the direction, force, and type of club to use and watches the ball land in specific locations on the course. The technology was readily applicable to retail/catalog stores to present and demonstrate products. Sears had a system that permitted a customer to browse through home products. (See Levin 1983 for a listing of organizations involved in developing laser disk systems.) Miles Pharmaceutical Laboratory donated laser disk players to hospitals and medical schools to facilitate the study of and diagnosis of various diseases and to study surgical techniques.

Educational disks are used to teach a variety of subjects. In 1985 the Texas Learning Technology Group embarked on a project to develop interactive videodisc high school science curriculums. The system used graphic interface computer boards that allowed computer-generated graphics to be mixed with the laser disk video. The delivery platform used was the recently introduced IBM InfoWindow. This technology employed a special touch-sensitive monitor as the presentation mode and user response mode. When asked a question the user responded by touching the screen. A whole semester curriculum for physical science, including teacher manuals, tests, and other support materials, was made available. Teachers were trained to use the system, either as a standalone instructional component or as an integrated component in the classroom.

RECENT AND FUTURE DEVELOPMENTS

The demand for better simulations by the military and other industrial users encouraged the interactive video industry to explore alternative hardware configurations. Videodisc information is stored in an analog format. Audio was restricted to the two tracks on the laser disk or to peripheral hardware that played audio to accompany the video images. Digital information storage, common in computers, was applied to optical disks. Compact disks (CDs) are optical disks on which information (i.e., music) is encoded digitally. This is a "read-only" memory format (CD-ROM) of large amounts of high-quality material. Seventy-four minutes of high-fidelity music can be stored on one

compact disk and the entire Encyclopedia Britannica, or 84 billion bits of information, could be stored digitally on one laser disk (Lehman 1986).

In 1986 Microsoft sponsored a conference in Seattle to develop standards for the industry that was growing up around digitized information. The intent of the conference was to establish production standards for CD-ROM. It was hoped that the mistakes made by the laser disk industry could be avoided. (The laser disk industry had two different processing methodologies, two incompatible playback formats, and three different types of code for controlling the laser disk.)

The conference never got the chance to establish standards for CD-ROM because new formats were already being developed that were even more appropriate for training implementations. In a relatively short period, 1986–1990, several new storage formats have been developed.

The following developments are presented in Christie (1989a, b) and Magel (1990):

1. The Pioneer LD-V8000 has a buffer that can hold individual video frames, from a CLV optical disk, while the disk continues to play. This technology permits one frame to be viewed on the screen while the laser disk continues to play the appropriate audio.

2. Pioneer's LV-ROM technology will supply analog audio and visual and digital audio on a CD-ROM format.

3. Philips has introduced a player that can decode both normal audio and video information as well as computer text.

4. Compact disk video (CDV) combines digital audio and analog video on the same disk.

5. DRAW disks can be locally recorded with a laser recorder, but not erased.

6. WORM (write-once/read-many memory) is a computer memory device that stores hundreds of megabytes.

7. Erasable optical data disks that use a laser to erase previous material are now available.

FIGURE 1. The Pioneer LD-V8000 videodisc player.

8. Compact Disk-Interactive (CD-I) provides graphics, digital data, audio, and motion on the same disk.

9. Digital video interactive (DVI) from Intel is a computer board for IBM-compatible computers that permits real-time compression and decompression of video for recording on any digital storage medium. Digital video interactive has the potential to produce real-time three-dimensional simulations of reality.

10. Panasonic's LQ-4000 is a rewritable videodisc recorder.

11. IBM has introduced motion video (MV) to replace the InfoWindow. This is a computer board that will integrate NTSC standard video with a VGA monitor.

Current development efforts continue to attempt to provide all of the advantages of digitized audio and video with full-motion, full-frame video. It is even postulated that holographic instructional environments will soon be possible.

References

Christie, K. 1989a. Interactive media primer. *AV Communications*, April, pp. 28–31.

———. 1989b. Media primer part two. *AV Communications*, May, pp. 21–22, 34–35.

Graham, M. W. 1986. *RCA and the videodisc: The business of research.* New York: Cambridge University Press.

Gray, R. A. 1978. Watch out for videodiscs in your future. *AudioVisual Instruction* 23(9):19.

Iuppa, N. V. 1984. *A practical guide to interactive video.* White Plains, N.Y.: Knowledge Industry Publications.

Lehman, J. D. 1986. Interactive video—A powerful new tool for science teaching. *Journal of Computers in Mathematics and Science Teaching* 5(3):24–29.

Levin, W. 1983. Interactive video: The state-of-the-art teaching machine. *The Computing Teacher* 11(2):11–17.

Magel, M. 1990. Striking a balance: Interactive media ups and downs. *AV Video,* June, pp. 56–61.

Rice, P., and R. Dubbe. 1982. Development of the first optical videodisc. *SMPTE Journal,* March, pp. 277–84.

Schneider, E. W., and J. L. Bennion. 1981. *The instructional media library: Videodiscs.* Englewood Cliffs, N.J.: Educational Technology Publications.

Sigel, E., M. Schubin, and P. F. Merrill. 1980. *Video discs.* White Plains, N.Y.: Knowledge Industry Publications.

For Further Reading

Clement, F. 1981. Oh dad, poor dad, mom's bought the wrong videodisc and I'm feelin' so sad. *Instructional Innovator* 26(2):12–15.

DeBloois, M. L. 1982. *Videodisc/microcomputer courseware design.* Englewood Cliffs, N.J.: Educational Technology Publications.

Floyd, S., and B. Floyd. 1982. *Handbook of interactive video.* White Plains, N.Y.: Knowledge Industry Publications.

Rothchild, E. 1983. Optical-memory media. *Byte* 8(3):86–106.

Jon Young

VIDEO GAMES

See Games, Computer

VIDEOTEX

The term *videotex* is sometimes used to describe any system delivering electronic information to the consumer market by way of a screen, as opposed to print or audiotext. More specifically, videotex has come to mean mass-market-oriented systems that interactively deliver information for personal use. Well-known examples of videotex are the French Minitel system, which delivers telephone directory information and other services to consumers in France, and Bell Canada's ALEX. Videotex services available in the United States include Comp-U-Card, CompuServe, GEnie, PC-Link, Prodigy, and Quantum.

The chief distinction between videotex and other on-line information retrieval services is that videotex is designed to serve the mass market (consumers) rather than professional or business users. Many videotex services place a major emphasis on games and other entertainment services; the concept of a database is not suitable in those environments and is therefore frequently hidden from the user. Other electronic information services falling into the realm of videotex include bulletin boards, chat services, and directories of local information.

Some user communities have readily taken to electronic information, whereas others continue to rely on their own intermediary services. In terms of numbers of potential users, the mass market is larger than the business market. Although the theoretical market (85 million households) is large, the actual market is much smaller. Business users of information recognize its value and are willing to pay for it; household consumers usually are not.

Despite the immense obstacles facing videotex providers, there does seem to be a market for their services, small though it may be. Service to even a small percentage of the 85 million U.S. households, not to mention those in other countries, can be a significant business.

THE VIDEOTEX GRAVEYARD

The 1980s were marked by several heavy investments in videotex trials that resulted in spectacular failures. The tombstones in the videotex graveyard contain well-known and respected names in American business: Times/Mirror, Knight-Ridder, American Express. Losses sustained by these firms have been significant; industry estimates are that Times/Mirror's Gateway lost approximately $30 million, Knight-Ridder's Viewtron service lost $50 million, and American Express's joint venture with Warner Communications to produce the Qube service lost $20 million. It is little wonder that many potential videotex sponsors have taken a skeptical attitude.

The most important lesson learned from the early videotex trials is that the information content determines the success of the service. Many videotex systems of the 1980s offered electronic access only to news, stock quotes, sports scores, and related items. These systems were doomed to failure because the information they delivered was available more cheaply and easily elsewhere. The cost of newspapers is extremely low compared with that of electronic information services, and network television is free to consumers. Both media deliver information to consumers with little or no additional effort on their part (newspapers can be delivered automatically, and the television needs only to be turned on).

Videotex has been portrayed as a social phenomenon and benefit to society because it would do the following:

- Give electronic mobility to customers
- Provide access to information for the hearing impaired
- Combat illiteracy
- Reduce pollution (particularly the problem of telephone directories accumulating in landfills)
- Reduce air pollution from cars by providing opportunities for teleshopping and telecommuting
- Bring nations together in an "information railroad" much as the railroads brought the United States together in the 1800s

WHAT DOES IT ALL MEAN?

Some systems designers and providers appear to have learned from the hard lessons of the 1980s. Entertainment content is important to attract consumers and convert them to a critical mass of users; experience has shown that entertainment applications often lead users to the more serious content on a system. Other applications include home transactions, information access, communications, and directories.

With the Prodigy service (Prodigy Services Co.), a new videotex service with over 750,000 passwords and nationwide access, and jointly owned by IBM and Sears, the user can peruse a diverse storehouse of information such as telephone directories, home shopping and banking, travel, finance, or products; play games (see GAMES, COMPUTER); make reservations for cultural or sporting events; or communicate with other users (Antonoff 1989). Advertisements appear on many Prodigy screens; users can place orders for merchandise while still on-line. A personal computer with a modem is required plus special software that can often be obtained free or at a reduced price. The advertisers (170 in 1990) pay a flat fee to have their ads displayed; if an on-line sale results, a commission is collected.

CONCLUSION

Technology has made great strides since the days of the early videotex trials. Personal computers are beginning to penetrate house-

holds significantly. LINK Resources, a market-research firm, estimates that 24 percent of the 85 million U.S. households now have a personal computer, with 1990 sales estimated to be up 11 percent over 1989 ("Home computers . . ." 1990), and new powerful, sophisticated, and cheaper models are appearing. Coincidently, systems that take advantage of these new personal computer capabilities are coming to the market. Although these trends are encouraging for videotex and portend brighter days ahead, there are still many hurdles to surmount before videotex systems become widely used.

References
Home computers: Will they sell this time? 1990. *Business Week*, September 10, pp. 64–74.
Antonoff, M. 1989. The Prodigy promise. *Personal Computing* 13(5):89–90.

For Further Reading
Hawkins, D. T. 1990. And you thought videotex was dead! *ONLINE*, November, pp. 113–15.
Hawkins, D. T. 1991. Lessons from the "Videotex school of hard knocks." *ONLINE*, January, pp. 87–89.
Hawkins, D. T. 1991. Videotex markets, applications, and systems. *ONLINE*, March, pp. 97–100.

This article was adapted with permission from material published in ONLINE magazine (ONLINE, Inc., Weston, Conn.).

Donald T. Hawkins

VIRUSES

A computer virus is a self-replicating program or segment of code that inserts copies of itself into other programs, thus "infecting" them. When an infected program is run, the hidden virus is activated and attempts to infect additional programs. This contagious process is compared to a biological virus spreading from cell to cell within an organism, where each infected cell can spawn viruses of its own. Also like its biological counterpart, a single computer virus can spread to any number of compatible computer systems if given a pathway for infection.

Viruses typically infect a system through the sharing of transportable media, such as an infected diskette, or through communication links such as local area networks or programs downloaded from remote systems via a modem.

In addition to their ability to infect, many viruses are programmed to attack or otherwise compromise the security of the host computer when a specific condition is met. Some typical triggering conditions are listed here:

- A certain calendar date and/or time
- A specific number of virus generations
- An entirely random process
- A certain number of system startups or program runs
- Presence of a specific type of file or user identification
- The privilege level of the host program or user
- A particular command entered at the keyboard

Typical destructive actions taken by viruses include deleting files, rendering entire drives unreadable, and interfering with communications. Other viruses cause noncatastrophic harassment such as displaying unusual messages, plotting text backward, or "melting" characters off the screen. Often the most difficult to diagnose are viruses that mimic intermittent problems with modems, printers, or other processes.

Only during the late 1980s did viruses become a serious computer security problem. Large organizations tend to suffer the most frequent virus infections because software and other computer resources are shared among a large number of users and computers, any one of which may intentionally or unintentionally introduce a virus into the system.

HOW DOES A VIRUS WORK?

Most viruses are written in assembler or machine code to remain fast and small, and thereby elusive; however, viruses can be written in any programming language that supports file manipulation; even batch and macro languages commonly used within spreadsheets and other software products can support viruslike activity.

Viruses usually attach themselves to other executable files or inside the operating system. As a virus must be run to do its work, one that resides in the operating system is usually a more serious threat because it can be continually active and watching for opportunities to infect or attack.

An executable file virus typically appends a copy of itself to the beginning of another program. When the program is run, the virus runs first, attempts to infect another program, and then passes control to the original program's logic. The computer user usually sees nothing wrong except possibly a slight hesitation when the program is first run—the time it takes the virus to infect another program.

An infected program can be visualized as in Figure 1. In some instances, a virus removal utility needs simply to strip the virus from the beginning of the file to restore the original program.

WHY ARE VIRUSES WRITTEN?

As the vast majority of virus authors are never caught, virus authorship and intentional infection carry very little risk to the perpetrator. It is therefore not surprising that viruses represent a potentially enticing concept to malcontents and subversives of all types.

Analyzing the motives of the few known

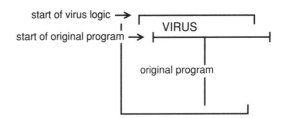

FIGURE 1

virus authors and clues held in the viruses themselves provides evidence of two major sources of viruses:

1. Many viruses are designed only to infect and contain no intentionally destructive logic. They appear to have been created out of curiosity, for the intellectual challenge, or even as instructor-authorized programming projects in school (an unwise exercise.) As they operate invisibly and can "live" forever on a diskette, many of these viruses end up being accidently released into the community, even where that may not have been the original intent. Others are released in what is seen as a "harmless" prank that nevertheless causes damage through programming errors or the tying up of victims' limited computer resources.

2. Some viruses are designed from the start as destructive weapons. Motives for their development and/or intentional introduction into a system may include thrill seeking; political aims; or revenge against an employer, co-worker, industry, government agency, or society as a whole. Similarities in programming style indicate that entire groups of destructive viruses are being written by a relatively small group of programmers.

Many viruses show evidence of having been "hacked" or modified by a number of different people over a period. In many cases, what was originally a harmless virus is turned into a dangerous virus.

WHY ARE VIRUSES A RECENT PHENOMENON?

Several factors have contributed to the recent emergence of computer viruses.

- *Increased numbers of computers and programmers:* In the past, computers were very costly and access to them was limited. Today's technology, however, has led to a huge base of inexpensive computers that are available to practically anyone. This has had a twofold effect. First, with an increase in the numbers of programmers comes a corresponding increase in those able and

motivated to write a virus. Second, once launched, a virus benefits greatly by the existence of a large number of target computer systems. These factors also explain why the more numerous microcomputers have a higher incidence of viruses than midrange and mainframe computers.

- *Increased adherence to industry standards.* Like a biological virus, a computer virus needs compatible hosts to infect. As the computer industry standardizes around specific operating systems and storage medium formats, virus authors are presented with large and well-understood targets. Thus, viruses can contain more and more sophistication and still be compatible with most of the computers they are likely to encounter.

- *Increased casual sharing of software via diskettes, local-area networks, and modems.* As computers play an ever-increasing role in business and society, more and more sharing of hardware and software resources occurs. Even in a business environment, these activities are often undertaken in an unguarded and careless manner, thus providing a means for viruses to spread.

The science of biology provides yet another analogy to the computer virus problem. A field of wheat is much more susceptible to a catastrophic viral outbreak than is a field of genetically mixed prairie grasses. Given the laws of statistical chance, human nature, operating system standardization, and an increasingly networked world, computer viruses appear to be a fact of computing life for the foreseeable future.

HISTORY

The possibility of self-replicating code was discussed among scientists as early as the 1960s, and the first known example was demonstrated at Xerox Corporation in 1974.

Dr. Frederick Cohen began research on actual computer viruses in 1983 at the University of Southern California, and subsequently published warnings concerning the potential of widespread virus epidemics. Other research efforts sprang up, including one at the University of California at Los

Angeles that received funding from IBM Corporation and the National Science Foundation.

A small volume of relatively minor virus infections occurred during the mid-1980s, primarily among lower-priced personal computers. In late 1987, a number of serious virus infections occurred in close succession. It was particularly troubling to many security analysts that a different virus was responsible in each case:

- Pakistani (also called Brain) virus at the University of Delaware
- Lehigh (also called COMMAND.COM) virus at Lehigh University
- Friday the 13th (also called April Fool) virus at Hebrew University in Jerusalem
- Christmas (also called Christmas Card or Christmas Tree) virus within the Bitnet network

The Pakistani, Lehigh, and Friday the 13th viruses spread primarily from infected computers that were shared within university libraries and computer labs. Many students unknowingly carried infected diskettes from the lab to their own computers and back again, causing campuswide epidemics that were very difficult to eradicate. The Friday the 13th virus spread from Hebrew University to computers all across Israel, and was estimated to have infected between 10,000 and 20,000 disks.

The Christmas Virus was actually an electronic chain letter that sent duplicates of itself through the worldwide Bitnet electronic mail system. From its origin in West Germany, this fast-multiplying "Merry Christmas" message spread over five continents, and within a few days had swamped the IBM electronic mail system.

In November of 1988, perhaps the most infamous virus attack to date occurred when approximately 6,000 computers were shut down by a virus entering through the Arpanet/Internet network. The Arpanet virus was widely covered in the press, and viruses began to be viewed as a very real threat by business and government organizations. Responding to this concern, a wide assortment of antivirus products and information sources began to appear.

COST TO SOCIETY

Because it is not in an organization's best interest to advertise a security weakness, virus infections are rarely publicized. Therefore, an exact measurement of the problem is difficult to gather.

One measurable example is the Arpanet virus, which, although it was very short-lived and had no intentional destructive ability, was estimated to have cost as much as $157 million in system down time and eradication costs. Typical estimates for worldwide virus-related losses and the cost of protective measures range from $100 million to $1 billion per year.

There are also indirect costs to consider. Society can benefit greatly through networking and the sharing of information, activities that computer security hazards have forced organizations and individuals to restrict.

VIRUS PREVENTION, DETECTION, AND REMOVAL

A number of precautions can be taken to reduce significantly the odds of a virus infection:

- Carefully review all new software on an isolated system first, particularly if it is to be installed for sharing on a local-area network or company bulletin board.
- Use particular caution when installing programs that do not come directly from a manufacturer. Do not run programs that come from unauthorized or unknown sources.
- Download software only from professionally run bulletin boards whose system operators check their software for viruses. Bulletin boards that charge money for access are typically safer because a more accurate record is maintained of users.
- Where possible, restrict access to system programs.
- When possible, write-protect executable files and use write-protected diskettes.
- Use a virus detection and removal utility regularly.

Additional policies can ease the process

of recovering from an infection, should one occur:

- Make backup copies of all original software as soon as the package is opened, and store these copies in a safe place.
- Make backup copies of important data (or, ideally, the entire system) on a regular basis.
- Develop and test a recovery plan, and make it known to all computer users in the organization.
- Keep a write-protected copy of the original system startup diskette(s) available.

A computer or program that exhibits suspicious behavior should be immediately disconnected from any local-area or modem network. If a virus is suspected, all users within the organization should be notified. Observable virus symptoms include programs loading slower than they used to, disk drive filling up for no apparent reason, system files or other programs changing size, drives accessed for no apparent reason, drive or other hardware ceasing to work, and strange messages displayed.

Anti-virus utilities, commonly called *vaccines,* are available that allow virus prevention, detection, and removal. The first commercially available product, Data Physician, was developed by Digital Dispatch, Inc. in 1985. The utilities included with this product illustrate the variety of current anti-virus techniques:

- VirHUNT is a virus *scanner* utility that searches drives and memory for specific, known viruses. If a virus is found, Vir-HUNT can completely remove it from the system, repairing any infected programs to their original form. VirHUNT can also store information called *file signatures* on each program, which allows the detection and removal of even previously unknown viruses.
- RESSCAN is a scanner resident in random-access memory (RAM) that automatically checks programs for infection as they are run, copied, or opened in any way. Its operation is invisible to the user unless a virus is detected. RESSCAN also protects

the user against booting from an infected disk.

- VirALERT is a virus *monitor* that resides in memory to intercept and warn the user about viruslike activity before it is allowed to occur. Suspicious activity includes any manipulation of executable and operating system files, attempted writes to the boot record, disk formatting attempts, and terminate-and-stay-resident (TSR) program installations.
- SAFEBOOT adds security logic inside the operating system files and boot record to prevent a virus from gaining control at this powerful vantage point.
- ANTIGEN installs virus protection directly on other programs. Each time the protected program is run, it checks itself for tampering and can remove an attached virus on its own.

Comparable vaccine products include Vi-Spy from RG Software Systems Inc., Viruscan from McAfee Associates, Mace Vaccine from Fifth Generation Systems, Panda Pro from Panda Systems, and Flu-Shot Plus from Software Concepts Design.

[*See also:* Hacking.]

For Further Reading

Associated Press. 1988. Electronic bug sickens Israeli computer system. January 8, 1988.

Burger, R. 1988. *Computer viruses: A high-tech disease.* Grand Rapids, Mich.: Abacus.

Cohen, F. 1985. Recent results in computer viruses. Paper presented at Conference on Information Sciences and Systems, Johns Hopkins University, March 1985.

Cohen, F. 1984. *Computer viruses—Theory and experiments.* Address to 7th Security Conference, DOS/NBS, September 1984.

Dembart, L. 1984. Attack of the computer virus. *Discover,* November 1984, pp. 90–92.

DiDio, L. 1988. Caution: Viruses at play. *Network World,* July 4, 1988, pp. 1–46.

Greenberg, R. M. 1989. Know thy viral enemy. *Byte,* June 1989, pp. 275–80.

Hafner, K. M. 1988. Is your computer secure? *Business Week,* August 1, 1988, pp. 64–72.

Markoff, J. 1987. Vandals hit computers with virus. *San Francisco Examiner*, December 20, 1987.

McLellan, V. 1988a. Computer systems under siege. *New York Times*, January 31, 1988.

McLellan, V. 1988b. Seeking an Rx for computer viruses. *The Boston Globe*, November 13, 1988.

Pozzo, M. M., and T. E. Grey. *Computer virus containment in untrusted computer environments*. Los Angeles: Computer Science Department, University of California.

Quraishi, J. 1990. Computer viruses: The Black Plague of the 1990s? *Computer Shopper*, March 1990, pp. 378–649.

Stover, D. 1989. Viruses, worms, Trojans, and bombs. *Popular Science*, September 1989, pp. 59–108.

Barbara Hansen
Scott J. Koltes

VISUALIZATION TECHNIQUES

The field of scientific visualization, although only recently formalized under a study conducted by the National Science Foundation, has been a part of the educational process for many years. Relationships between angles and sides of triangles are usually illustrated by drawing examples before formal proofs are attempted. Scientists can now use the computer to *visualize* events that haven't occurred in reality, places they haven't been to see, and the actual process of running their programs.

The advent of lower-cost, faster personal computers has allowed this visualization experience to become part of people's everyday lives. Modern medical diagnosis is assisted by visual interpretation of images such as those obtained from a computer-aided tomography (CAT) scan machine. These images, as well as being helpful for diagnosis, are oftentimes beautiful in their own right. There are a number of books recently published with a wide variety of pictures from the collaboration of artists and scientists using the techniques developed originally for scientific visualization (Friedhoff and Benzon 1989, Deken 1983, Pruett 1984). Research in the field of visualization is presented at the annual computer graphics conference called SIGGRAPH, sponsored by the Association for Computing Machinery (ACM) (Proceedings published as *ACM Computer Graphics*).

Visualization techniques can be broadly separated into three areas, with wide amounts of overlap among them. The first area uses computer graphics to generate realistic images that would be useful in such fields as architectural design. Two of the techniques used here are ray tracing and radiosity. The next area, called multivariate data analysis or volumetric rendering, uses some of these techniques to display and interact with large amounts of data that are the result of large scientific calculations such as those found in the modeling of global weather patterns. The last area, called algorithm animation, uses a different set of graphics tools to allow a scientist to watch his or her program execute.

RAY TRACING

Ray tracing is a technique used for generating realistic images that might include multiple light sources, and a wide variety of objects with surface material properties such as glossiness and transparency. A review of the basics of ray tracing can be found in the work edited by Glassner (1989). Early work on ray tracing includes that of Kay and Greenberg (1979) and Whitted (1980). These algorithms recursively trace rays from the viewer's eye through each pixel on the display onto the objects in the graphics database. New rays are spawned whenever a ray bounces off or passes through a transparent surface. Further work by Cook et al. (1984) on distributed ray tracing allowed the inclusion of such effects as depth of field and motion blur. Since the ray tracing process is so computationally expensive, often taking days of supercomputer time, recent work has centered on making the process faster. Generally this can be done if many computers are assigned to produce pieces of the final image. Numerous approaches can be found in the recent work edited by Dew et al. (1989). A ray-traced image of the space shuttle payload bay is shown in Figure 1.

RADIOSITY

Radiosity is an advanced rendering technique introduced by Cohen and Greenberg (1985) that uses the positions of objects in a scene to determine shading. The difficulty that ray tracing has with accurately modeling light that doesn't come from a single light source, called diffuse reflection within an environment, is addressed by radiosity. Radiosity algorithms are derived from heat transfer methods that explicitly calculate the energy received and transferred between all surfaces in a scene (Siegel and Howell 1981). As such, these algorithms can be run without knowing where the viewer is located. Adaptation of these algorithms for computer graphics was first done by Goral et al. (1984) and Nishita and Nakamae (1985).

Radiosity is defined as the rate at which energy leaves a surface, and it is composed of the rates of emission and reflection or transmission of energy from itself and other surfaces. Relationships between or among surfaces for transfer of energy is contained in the form factors, which are defined as the fraction of energy received by any surface patch from any other surface patch in the scene. Patch shape, orientation, and possible occlusion are all taken into account by the form factors. All of the intersurface interactions for a scene can be expressed as a set of simultaneous linear equations, which can be solved using any suitable technique, such as Gauss-Seidel iteration.

The number of linear equations that need to be solved in the radiosity calculation is equal to the number of patches in the environment, which may run into the tens and hundreds of thousands. This large a system would be computationally intractable. A progressive refinement technique has been introduced by Cohen et al. (1988). This method progressively calculates the radiosity by examining patches that emit the greatest amount of light first, with the contribution from each additional patch being added to the intermediate image. Recent work by Chen (1990) has centered on incremental techniques for radiosity in an animation environment such as that used in architectural studies where an individual can walk through a computer-generated building.

THREE-DIMENSIONAL DATASET VISUALIZATION

One of the techniques for the display and manipulation of three-dimensional datasets is called volumetric rendering. This method has been used for three-dimensional medical datasets such as CAT scans, where a serious of slices are generated, and for visualization of meteorological data (Papathomas et al. 1988). The volume enclosed by the dataset is first broken up into small boxes called voxels, which have a spatial extent that is not necessarily a cube. To view voxels that may be hidden from a particular viewpoint, a transparency or partial opacity is assigned to each voxel. This is in addition to the color assignment, which is usually based on material properties in the original dataset.

Images are formed by geometrically transforming the voxels to the image plane and then using a blending function to inte-

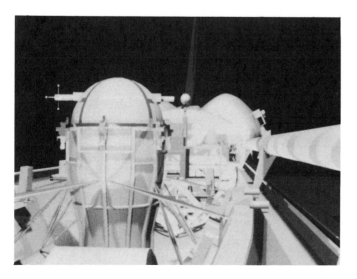

FIGURE 1. A ray-traced image of the space shuttle payload bay.

grate each slice of three-dimensional space with previous voxels that have been mapped. This technique was developed by Drebin et al. (1988) of the Pixar Corporation in San Rafael, California. Another method developed for display generation, by Levoy (1988), uses a ray tracing approach, where rays are shot into the volume enclosing the dataset.

An alternative method for the visualization of three-dimensional data is based on surfaces. In this case, the dataset is broken into slices along some axis, and polygons are fitted to a predefined contour on each slice. This method was pioneered by Fuchs et al. (1977). The quality of the display from this technique is dependent on the contour extracted from the data in each slice.

ALGORITHM ANIMATION

Algorithm animation is a method for graphically displaying either movement of data through the data structures in a program or the flow of program execution through the individual modules that make up a program. The BALSA system, developed by Brown and Sedgewick (1984), uses the spatial layout of the data structure as a row on the screen. As the algorithm progresses, the organization of the data in the structure is displayed on a new row. Color is used to indicate the movement of the data through intermediate data structures, such as the heap used in a heap sort. Another method employed in the BALSA system is that of multiple views on the same screen. The organization of the data is represented as a set of vertical bars called Sticks, whose height indicates the value of the element. The dynamics of the running algorithm are shown as labeled circles, with shading being used to indicate which pieces of information are being processed at any given time.

Algorithm animation is also being used to monitor the execution of parallel programs. These types of programs typically run on multiple processors, whose numbers can sometimes run into the tens of thousands. An example of this sort of system is the ParaGraph system developed by Heath

(1990) at the Oak Ridge National Laboratory. This system uses information about the execution of an algorithm, compiled during the running phase. Nine different types of displays are then used to monitor the program execution. A colored graph displays processor activity. Load balancing of processor use is shown using a Kiviat diagram, where each processor is presented as a spoke in a wheel and the processor utilization is shown as the spoke length. The outside of the wheel corresponds to a completely busy processor. Communication load is shown as a histogram, with total message size on the vertical axis and time on the horizontal axis. Other displays of the nine types include message lengths, Feynman diagrams, Gantt charts, message queues, and node statistics.

References

Brown, M. H., and R. Sedgewick. 1984. A system for algorithm animation. *ACM Computer Graphics* 18(3):177–86.

Chen, S. E. 1990. Incremental radiosity: An extension of progressive radiosity to an interactive image synthesis system. *ACM Computer Graphics* 24(4):135–44.

Cohen, M. F., S. E. Chen, J. R. Wallace, and D. P. Greenberg. 1988. A progressive refinement approach to fast radiosity image generation. *ACM Computer Graphics* 22(4):75–84.

Cohen, M. F., and D. P. Greenberg. 1985. The hemi-cube, a radiosity solution for complex environments. *ACM Computer Graphics* 19(3):31–40.

Cook, R. L., T. Porter, and L. Carpenter. 1984. Distributed ray tracing. *ACM Computer Graphics* 18(3):137–45.

Deken, J. 1983. *Computer images: State of the art.* New York: Stewart, Tabori and Chang.

Dew, P. M., T. R. Heywood, and R. A. Earnshaw, eds. 1989. *Parallel processing for computer vision and display.* Reading, Mass.: Addison-Wesley.

Drebin, R. A., L. Carpenter, and P. Hanrahan. 1988. Volume rendering. *ACM Computer Graphics* 22(4):65–74.

Friedhoff, R. M., and W. Benzon. 1989. *Visualization.* New York: Harry N. Abrams.

Fuchs, H., Z. M. Kedem, and S. P. Uselton.

1977. Optimal surface reconstruction from planar contours. *Communications of the ACM* 20(10):693–702.

Glassner, A., ed. 1989. *An introduction to ray tracing.* New York: Academic Press.

Goral, C. M., K. E. Torrance, D. P. Greenberg, and B. Battaile. 1984. Modeling the interaction of light between diffuse surfaces. *ACM Computer Graphics* 18(3):213–22.

Heath, M. T. 1990. Visual animation of parallel algorithms for matrix computations. In *Proceedings of the Fifth Distributed Memory Computing Conference (DMCC5)*, Charleston, S.C., April, pp. 1213–22.

Kay, D. S., and D. P. Greenberg. 1979. Transparency for computer synthesized images. *ACM Computer Graphics* 13(2):158–64.

Levoy, M. 1988. Display of surfaces from volume data. *IEEE Computer Graphics and Applications* 8(3):29–37.

Nishita, T., and E. Nakamae. 1985. Continuous tone representation of three-dimensional objects taking account of shadows and interreflection. *ACM Computer Graphics* 19(3):23–30.

Papathomas, T. V., J. A. Schiavone, and B. Julesz. 1988. Applications of computer graphics to the visualization of meteorological data. *ACM Computer Graphics* 22(4):327–34.

Pruett, M. L. 1984. *Art and the computer.* New York: McGraw-Hill.

Siegel, R., and J. R. Howell. 1981. *Thermal radiation heat transfer.* Washington, D.C.: Hemisphere.

Whitted, T. 1980. An improved illumination model for shaded display. *Communications of the ACM* 23(6):343–49.

Terry Huntsberger

VOICE MAIL

Voice mail, or voice messaging, is a new telecommunications technology used to store and transmit phone messages digitally.

Traditional forms of "telephone tag," in which people return each other's calls but never manage to have a conversation, are replaced by the transmission and receipt of verbal messages through a voice mail system using a touch-tone telephone. A telephone call is interactive; two or more parties are on the phone simultaneously. Voice mail is noninteractive, as messages are prerecorded, edited, and sent to one person or groups of people. The receiver can retrieve messages at any time. For people who regularly exchange information and are hard to reach, voice mail is a simple and effective solution.

Voice mail (V-mail) digitally stores voice messages. Through activation of special commands from a simple touch-tone telephone touchpad, voice messages can be prepared in advance to be broadcast to single users or telephone numbers or to large groups. A user can listen to messages, reply to them, send copies to others, erase the messages, or save them for future reference. A message can be recorded and prepared for delivery at a future date. Software controls the features and runs the system. Two-way messaging, call answering, out calls, future delivery, nondelivery notification, and group codes are some of the features of a V-mail system. A mailbox can be customized to scan messages. Personal greetings recorded by the user make the box unique. The custom greeting can be changed by the user any time. Telephone calls can be forwarded to a V-mail system for a more prompt connection to a user mailbox.

Some V-mail systems allow long-distance calls from their system; some, only local calls. Telephone switches use voice response units (VRUs) for "message waiting indication" (MWI) or message delivery notification with lamps on phones or activate pagers to notify users of receipt of a voice message. Some systems can integrate with electronic mail, leaving a written message that a V-mail message has arrived. Messages from outside callers and inside users are stored separately. An escape option or transfer to an operator is usually offered with the system. The caller can leave a message or press a number to be connected to a live operator or receptionist. Most functions require the caller to have a touch-tone phone, but a caller from a rotary phone can still leave a message in a V-mail box.

Users are guided through voice prompts and tones to activate features. With auto attendants or info-link, callers or users are greeted with general information and a directory of options with a list of numbers to dial for information. Some businesses offer this option in a simple form with one or two choices; others can route a caller. Examples of routing are registering for classes at a university, checking an account with a bank, and ordering a newspaper. Some systems offer on-line tutorials for users through the system. Lists of tutorials are available to the user to dial for the specific session or title. Most users need training to realize the full potential.

Voice mail systems (VMSs) can be incorporated into business by two basic methods. First, a private system can be installed with a telephone switch; second, a business can subscribe to an existing vendor. Voice mail systems range in cost from a few hundred dollars for a few users on a personal computer to $50,000 to $1 million for several thousand users on a large system. Subscribing usually involves a monthly fee for each telephone.

A simple telephone number or extension can identify a "mailbox," and a password for security is added by the user. Voice mail is accessed by dialing a phone number and entering a personal mailbox identification number (usually a user phone number) and password. All systems are usually open 24 hours a day, 7 days a week, thus making V-mail independent of office hours, time zones, busy receptionists, and human attendants. Voice mail systems can be accessed from other countries around the world using a touch-tone telephone.

A private V-mail system is installed to operate internally with a private telephone switch. The private switch system handles all internal calls but must be connected to the public phone system for incoming and outgoing calls. Voice lines or ports provide outside access to the system. These can be single line connections or trunk lines. Typical capacities of system accesses are 60 to 120 ports into the V-mail machine for 10,000 users.

Modems are used by remote access administrators for diagnostics and maintenance. Power sources and uninterrupted power supplies (UPSs) are basic requirements. There is separate backup storage of the operating system.

Storage or voice message compression of a system can vary. The compression method used to digitize voice can be traded for voice quality. Usually systems allow twenty-five to fifty messages per mailbox, with a 2- to 3-minute time limit for each message. The specific parameters of a system are set by the system administrator. Routine purges of saved messages, based on a date threshold, reduce excess storage by users.

Resource limits can be set with the class of service. System administrators set parameters for the defined use. Most privately owned systems set their own standards of use as there are no industry standards.

Some V-mail issues remain unresolved and are debated in the industry. These issues are related to privacy, intrusion, security, who owns the message, and how to network unlike voice message systems together.

[*See also:* Electronic Mail.]

For Further Reading

Fermazin, T., and M. Rosenblatt. 1988. How to manage a voice message system. *Business Communications Review*, November/December, pp. 33–37.

Rosenberg, A. M. 1989. Voice messaging—Hot but underutilized. *Business Communications Review*, June, pp. 73–75.

Rosenberg, A. M., and M. I. Rosenblatt. 1989. Configuration planning for voice messaging systems. *Business Communications Review*, April, pp. 70–74.

Sykes, D. 1988. Voice messaging: Brisk growth and critical issues. *Business Communications Review*, November/December, pp. 28–32.

Shahnaz Y. Coyer

VOICE TO PRINT

See Speech to Print

VON NEUMANN, JOHN

John von Neumann was born in Budapest, Hungary, on December 28, 1903. A child prodigy, he could read Latin and Greek at age 5. As a 6-year-old he could divide two eight-digit numbers in his head. At 8 years of age, he had mastered that difficult branch of mathematics known as calculus.

Von Neumann came out of an upper-class Hungarian background that produced other giants in mathematics and physics. His father, a Jewish banker named Max Neumann, earned sufficient respect to add the honorific "Margattai" to his family name (later changed, by John, to "von"). John was the eldest of three sons.

Even as a child, John loved mathematics and constantly sought to adapt its logic to the world at large. From 1911 to 1916, he attended the Lutheran gymnasium in Budapest, becoming its best mathematician. Though he enrolled in the University of Budapest in 1921, von Neumann acquired the bulk of his education at other institutions. Most of his time, especially from 1921 to 1923, was spent at the University of Berlin. There he listened to lectures by Albert Einstein. Von Neumann went on to the Swiss Federal Institute of Technology in Zurich, where he received a diploma in chemical engineering in 1925. In 1926, he received a doctoral degree in mathematics from the University of Budapest. Studying at the University of Göttingen in 1926 and 1927, von Neumann mixed with some of the most superb minds in mathematics.

Between 1927 and 1930 von Neumann was a lecturer in mathematics at the University of Berlin. Rarely had one so young held that post. During his first year there, he published five papers. Three of them, by setting out a mathematical framework for quantum theory, were of great importance to that field. A fourth paper was a pioneering

effort in game theory. The fifth dealt with the link between formal logic systems and the limits of mathematics. By the 1930s, von Neumann was recognized as one of the world's leading mathematicians.

In 1930, Princeton University invited him to be a visiting lecturer, an appointment he held for 3 years. In 1933, he received a permanent position at Princeton's newly created Institute for Advanced Study.

With the onset of World War II, von Neumann's knowledge of mathematical physics proved of great value to his adopted country. His contributions to supersonic wind tunnel development and solutions to nonlinear systems of equations and implosion were instrumental in advancing the Allied cause.

During and after the war, his main professional interest shifted from pure to applied mathematics.

Von Neumann did important work in many branches of advanced mathematics. For one thing, he made a thorough study of quantum mechanics and showed that Schrödinger's wave mechanics and Heisenberg's matrix mechanics were mathematically equivalent.

Even more important was his development of a new branch of mathematics called "game theory." He had written on the subject as early as 1928, but his complete book, *The Theory of Games and Economic Behavior*, did not appear until 1944. This branch of mathematics is called game theory because it works out the best strategies to follow in simple games, such as coin matching; however, the principles will apply to far more complicated games such as business and war, where an attempt is made to work out the best strategy to beat a competitor or an enemy.

Von Neumann early recognized the importance of computing devices. A major advance in computer design occurred in 1946 when he reintroduced the stored-program idea and revolutionized the technology of computing. Von Neumann suggested that programs (instructions for problem solutions) be stored in the computer's memory until needed. Prior to this time programs were contained on wired control panels or punched cards, both external to the computer. With the programs in the computer, instructions could be manipulated and modified by machine commands.

In 1947, von Neumann suggested a method for converting ENIAC, an early electronic computer, into a stored-program machine. His extraordinary skill in mathematical operations contributed to the development of the computer known as MANIAC (Mathematical Analyzer, Numerical Integrator and Computer). This computer enabled the United States to produce and test (first test, 1952) the world's first hydrogen bomb.

Von Neumann was a generalist among contemporary scientists. His clarity and precision of thought had a profound impact in many areas from which we will continue to benefit in the years ahead. He was one of the most respected scientists of his time.

For Further Reading

Goldstine, H. 1972. *The computer from Pascal to von Neumann.* Princeton, N.J.: Princeton University Press.

Heims, S. 1980. *John von Neumann and Norbert Wiener.* Cambridge, Mass.: MIT Press.

von Neumann, J. 1958. *The computer and the brain.* New Haven, Conn.: Yale University Press.

Donald D. Spencer

WARFARE

See Military Use of Computers

WATSON, THOMAS JOHN, SR.

Thomas John Watson was born on February 17, 1874, in a farmhouse in East Campbell, New York, a rural area southwest of the Finger Lakes. Watson's childhood was largely uneventful. Neither studious nor athletic, he reportedly was lively and assertive, with a quick temper that was to plague him all his life. He grew up in an ordinary but happy home where the means and wants were modest and the moral environment strict. The important values, as he learned them, were to do every job well, to treat all people with dignity and respect, to appear neatly dressed, to be clean, to be optimistic, and, above all, to be loyal.

His father, a tough lumberjack with little formal education himself, held high ambitions for his son and advised him to become a lawyer. Young Watson, however, was more interested in accounting and business. After a year at the Miller School of Commerce in Elmira, New York, studying accounting and business, Watson landed a job as a bookkeeper in a meat market. He was 18 years old and his salary was $6 a week.

He gave up his bookkeeping job to sell pianos, organs, sewing machines, and caskets with a friend, George Cornwell. Learning from Cornwell's easy manner, he developed skill in selling. This ability to observe others, focus on the good traits, and weave them into his own approach to people was to play a major role in his success.

In 1895, Watson took a selling job with National Cash Register (NCR), whose powerful president, John H. Patterson, was also to be a strong influence on his life. Four years later, he was promoted to manager in Rochester, New York. By 1907, Watson was in charge of the company's second-hand business. Now the third most powerful man at NCR, Watson was 33 years old.

Watson met Jeannett Kittredge, daughter of a successful Ohio businessman, in the spring of 1912. A year later they were married. They had four children: Thomas, Jr., Jane, Helen, and Arthur.

While at NCR, Watson originated his famous instruction, THINK. Framed placards with that one word appeared in the company's offices. The purpose was to inspire a dispirited NCR sales force. Later, when he took the helm at IBM, he reintroduced this motto.

He left NCR in 1913 to become president of the Computing-Tabulating-Recording (C-T-R) Company, a punched card equipment manufacturer. By introducing the selling methods successful with cash registers, he transformed C-T-R into the leading manufacturer of business machines. C-T-R had been created in 1911 by combining three separate companies, including Herman HOL-LERITH's Tabulating Machine Company established in 1896. Watson carried on a running battle with Hollerith, who was still involved in the company, feeling that Hollerith's technical genius was not matched by business genius. For the rest of his life, Watson favored salespeople over technical people. C-T-R was renamed International Business Machines (IBM) in 1924.

Watson guided the IBM Corporation, the

975

world's largest manufacturer of computers, throughout the rest of his life. He established a research and development group with a laboratory and a small staff of inventors. From this group came improved punched card tabulating equipment and, later, a large number of computer systems. Watson always placed heavy emphasis on education, research, and engineering to ensure the growth of the company. A great deal of Watson's success was due to his understanding of customers' needs, which resulted in steady improvements in IBM's products.

Watson demanded that his sales representatives not only sell the company's products, but come up with new ideas for their use. He also believed that they should always reflect IBM's principles: respect for the individual, service to the customer, and superior performance. Such a sales force gave IBM the reputation of being different. Its people were noticed; even on a service call, IBM employees wore suit jackets to the amazement of customers.

Watson created a corporate culture, an esprit de corps that is the envy of the business world to this day. The Watson way was also admired by President Franklin D. Roosevelt, who offered two prestigious posts to the patriotic IBM founder during World War II: Secretary of Commerce and Ambassador to Great Britain.

It was largely through Watson's efforts and funding that Howard Aiken's Mark I was built. Watson ordered his engineers to develop a new machine that could outperform the Mark I. The resultant IBM machine was the Selective Sequence Electronic Calculator (SSEC). When completed in 1947, it was far more powerful and flexible than anything previously built.

Following the Korean War, IBM designed the 701 computer. One-fourth the size of the SSEC, the 701 was twenty-five times as fast, performing 21,000 calculations a second. The IBM 650 computer was released in December 1954. It was a great success. Also in the same year, the IBM 704 scientific computer was introduced. Two new IBM computers followed in 1955 and 1956, the IBM 702 and the IBM 705. By now the IBM Corporation was on its way to becoming the leader in the computer industry. Watson

lived long enough to see the introduction of the 700 family of computers, IBM's first production computers.

On May 8, 1956, Watson turned over the post of chief executive officer of IBM to his eldest son, Thomas Watson, Jr. On June 19, just over a month later, Watson died of a heart attack at the age of 82. His two sons both held senior executive positions within IBM and both became U.S. ambassadors, Thomas John to Moscow and the younger son, Arthur Kittredge, to Paris.

For Further Reading

Rodgers, W. 1969. *Think: A biography of the Watsons and IBM*. New York: Stein and Day.

Donald D. Spencer

WIDE AREA NETWORKS

Computers process and manipulate data to provide us with useful information. This capability of computers is further enhanced when multiple computers are able to exchange data among themselves. Telecommunications networks provide for the transport of data among computers scattered all over the globe. In virtually all areas of modern society—banking, reservations, automated checkout in supermarkets, and electronic mail, to mention a few—we clearly see the role of computers and telecommunications.

A wide area network (WAN) is a network of computers covering a large geographical area, such as a country, a continent, or even the entire globe. The extent of coverage of a WAN influences its design and, consequently, its performance. Wide area networks operate quite differently from local area networks (LANs), which span a limited area. Two approaches are principally used to build a large network: (1) attaching computers to the endpoints of a *communications network*, and (2) interconnecting several smaller networks by *bridges, routers,* and/or *gateways*.

A communications network, also called a telecommunications network, provides communications services to its users. A communications network accessible to the public by subscription is also called a public data network (PDN). The company operating a PDN is often called a *common carrier*. The most familiar common carriers are the telephone companies.

As a communications network user, one merely needs to know two things: (1) the type of services, and their costs, provided by the network; (2) how to attach one's equipment to the network to use the desired services. The services offered by a communications network depend on its internal structure and the communications technology deployed. For a subscriber's equipment to attach to the endpoints of a communications network, it must follow a protocol that is understood by the endpoints. The basic purpose of communications software is to establish and maintain communications among remote communicating entities.

Communications networks provide two different types of services: *connection-oriented* and *connectionless.* In a connection-oriented service, the user sets up a connection with the remote system, transfers data over the connection, and terminates the connection after the completion of data transfer. A connection-oriented service is invariably packaged as a reliable service; that is, the messages sent are not lost, no duplication occurs, and they are delivered in proper sequence. A message-sequence-reliable, connection-oriented service, in addition to reliability, also preserves the message boundaries; that is, the messages are delivered in the same chunks as emitted for transmission. In a byte stream service, message boundaries are not preserved.

In a connectionless service, no connection is established before transmission. Each message contains the complete addresses of the sender and the receiver. The address information in the message is used for routing the message toward the destination. Unreliable connectionless service provides no guarantee or indication of delivery and is often called *datagram* service. In an *acknowledged datagram* service, an acknowledgment facility is provided to the sender to confirm the message delivery.

DATA COMMUNICATIONS NETWORKS

A data communications network interfaces with its subscribers through units called data circuit terminating equipment (DCE). A telephone jack is an example of DCE. The subscriber's computer, also referred to as the host or data terminating equipment (DTE), attaches to a DCE. Both DTE and DCE must follow an identical communications protocol to exchange data. In a PDN, it is impossible to provide a direct point-to-point link between all DCE units. In the absence of a point-to-point connection, a message from one DCE to another must pass through specialized processors, called *switches* or interface message processors (IMPs). The term *switching* refers to the manner in which the switches propagate messages. Major switching techniques are *circuit switching* and *packet switching.*

In circuit switching, a direct communication path is first established through the communications network between the communicating DTEs. This path is then exclusively used throughout the communications session. A circuit-switched data network (CSDN) is a data network that employs circuit switching in its operation. The public telephone network is a prime example of a CSDN.

Packet switching is an alternative to circuit switching and is designed specifically for communication of data. In contrast to circuit switching, no communication path is established in advance in packet switching. Each message to be transmitted is first divided into smaller chunks called packets. Each packet is then forwarded one hop at a time. When an intermediate processor receives a packet, it stores the packet and inspects it. If the processor is not the final intended receiver of this packet, the packet is forwarded to an adjacent (directly connected) processor. Eventually, after several hops the packet reaches the required destination. A data network employing packet switching in its operation is referred as a packet-switched data network (PSDN).

Circuit-Switched Data Networks

The most familiar communication link providers are voice telephone networks. The massive installed base of public telephone systems existed before the appearance of computer networks; in the United States alone, there are more than 120 million telephone lines. Even though public telephone networks were originally tailormade and designed to handle voice, they have also been useful in data communications. Real-time voice communication by telephones is mostly analog and of the circuit-switched type; certain data communications systems function on the same principle. Computer data must be converted from their native digital form to the analog form to be carried by the telephone network. At the receiving end, the data must be converted back to digital form. A *modem* (modulator/demodulator) is the device used for this purpose. Long-haul, voice-grade modems typically transmit at speeds ranging from 300 to 19,200 bits per second (bps).

Increasingly, digital transmission and switching facilities are being introduced into telephone networks. The bulk of telephone communications, however, is still analog. This limits the rate of transmission of data. Typical data transmission rates are 1,200 to 2,400 bps in a circuit-switched network. Higher transmission speeds are possible over private leased lines.

The introduction of digital transmission and switching led to development of the T1 system, which offers a transmission speed of 1.544 million bits per second (Mbps), and can handle twenty-four voice channels at 64,000 bps each. In an all-digital telephone network, it would be possible to transmit any kind of data, whether text, binary data, digital voice, or digital images. At present, however, telephone networks are only partly digital and do not provide an all-digital transmission.

Packet-Switched Data Networks

The packet switching technology evolved from several major developments. One such development was the setting up o dedica ted networks by various service companies to enable terminal users to access their host computers at a reasonably low cost. Two major public packet-switched networks in the United States thus evolved are TYMNET of Tymshare Inc. and TELENET of GTE. Computer manufacturers have been the major contributors toward packet switching in many ways. They developed special-purpose communication processors and software packages to handle communication tasks and were instrumental in developing the concept of layered communication architectures. Notable among these is SNA (Systems Network Architecture), developed by IBM.

Many fundamental concepts in packet switching came from the pioneering work in the ARPANET project funded by the Advanced Research Projects Agency of the U.S. Department of Defense. The ARPANET experiment led to the development of many similar networks worldwide; for example, GTE TELENET in the United States, Datapac in Canada, and Transpac in France all gained from the ARPANET experience. Another example is the worldwide university network called BITNET, which was started in 1981.

Internetworking

A set of networks interconnected by internetworking units (IWUs) is called an internet. A constituent network of an internet is called a subnetwork. From a user's point of view, an internet is just like a single network. Examples of IWUs are bridges and routers or gateways. A bridge is a device used to connect two or more LANs that follow identical LAN protocols. A router or a gateway is a device used to connect two networks that may or may not be similar.

The International Standards Organization (ISO) has standardized two general approaches for internetworking: connection mode and connectionless mode. In the connection mode operation, it is assumed that each subnetwork provides connection-oriented service. An IWU appears as the DTE to each of the subnetworks to which it is attached. An internetworkwide logical connection, made up of a sequence of logical connections across subnetworks, is set up between the communicating DTEs. From the point of view of network users, an internet-work logical connection has all the features of a logical connection across a single network and is, thus, indistinguishable from a single network connection. In connection mode operation, each message is treated independently and routed from source DTE to destination DTE through a series of networks and IWUs. All DTEs and IWUs follow a generic internet protocol (IP).

Communication Protocol Standards

A communication protocol is a set of rules that must be followed by communicating partners for proper communication. A message sent by a transmitter can be received correctly by a receiver only if the receiver follows the same protocol as the transmitter. To control the proliferation of dissimilar protocols, the ISO has proposed the ISO/OSI Reference Model for Open Systems Interconnection as a standard for describing and categorizing network components. The reference model consists of seven layers. The ISO/OSI standard includes service definitions and protocols for all seven layers. Other major institutions involved in the standardization efforts are the Institute of Electrical and Electronics Engineers (IEEE) and CCITT, a subgroup of the International Telecommunication Union. Several ISO standards are adopted from IEEE and CCITT standards. X.25 is a popular CCITT protocol for layer 3 of the ISO model. A collection of protocol standards for all layers in a network model is often called a protocol suite. Besides the OSI protocol suite, another widely popular set of protocols is the Internet protocol suite, which evolved from the ARPANET project. The Internet protocol suite is referred as the TCP/IP protocol suite; TCP (Transmission Control Protocol) and IP (Internet Protocol) are protocols at the transport layer and network layer, respectively. Many proprietary protocol suites have evolved over private vendors' networks.

COMMUNICATIONS SOFTWARE

The simplest types of commercially available communication software are the so-called telecommunications (or modem) programs.

A minimal communications program must follow the communications protocol understood by the modem or DCE. These programs, however, provide additional capabilities to simplify the communication-related activities of the user. Terminal emulation is one such capability that allows a microcomputer to pretend it is a computer terminal. File transfer is another common capability supported by communications packages. Some common file transfer protocols offered by communications programs include XON/XOFF, Xmodem, and Kermit. Yet another capability called remote log-in is needed when execution of a program from a remote computer is required.

Many other communication-based applications are in regular use today. Remote file access and electronic mail are two of the most common applications. Other important applications include directory services and remote information access.

For Further Reading

Comer, D. 1988. *Internetworking with TCP/IP: Principles, protocols, and architecture.* Englewood Cliffs, N.J.: Prentice-Hall.

Davidson, J. 1988. *An introduction to TCP/IP.* New York: Springer-Verlag.

Guruge, A. 1987. *SNA: Theory and practice.* Elmsford, N.Y.: Pergamon Press.

Halsall, F. 1988. *Data communications, computer networks and OSI.* 2nd ed. Reading, Mass.: Addison-Wesley.

Henshall, J., and S. Shaw. 1988. *OSI explained: End-to-end computer communication standards.* New York: Wiley.

Land, J. 1987. *The integrated services digital network (ISDN).* Manchester: National Computing Centre.

Martin, J., and K. Chapman. 1987. *SNA: IBM's networking solution.* Englewood Cliffs, N.J.: Prentice-Hall.

Stallings, W. 1990. *Handbook of computer-communications standards.* Vol. 1: *The open systems interconnection (OSI) model and OSI-related standards.* 2nd ed. Carmel, Ind.: Howard W. Sams.

———. 1990. *Handbook of computer-communications standards.* Vol. 3: *The TCP/IP protocol suite.* 2nd ed. Carmel, Ind.: Howard W. Sams.

Tanenbaum, A. 1988. *Computer networks*. 2nd ed. Englewood Cliffs, N.J.: Prentice-Hall.

S. P. Rana

WINDOWS

Windows is a software product developed by the Microsoft Corporation, Redmond, Washington. It is designed to bring the ease and simplicity of a graphical interface to microcomputers that function under the disk operating system (DOS). It operates in conjunction with DOS to facilitate the user's interaction with the computer.

The name of the product is very appropriate. It does, in fact, present the capabilities of the computer through a "window." The user need only "reach through the window" and initiate various actions by the computer. Another way of visualizing Windows is through the analogy of a desktop. The system causes the screen to be arranged in such a way that it presents an image of a desktop. On the desktop are various folders that must only be opened to perform some processing function. The product does, in fact, function that simply.

Windows has had a significant impact on the DOS world of microcomputers. This is evidenced by the fact that OS/2 (Operating System 2), the operating system that was expected to be adopted throughout the world of DOS small computers, has been very slow to gain the acceptance of users. Many believe that Windows is so powerful that they will not have to move to OS/2 for many months to come, if at all.

Windows was originally released in 1985 but, though there were periodic enhancements, did not reach its potential until release 3.0 became available in May of 1990.

GRAPHICAL INTERFACE

The advent of the Macintosh from Apple Computer in January 1984 made popular a whole new method of interacting with a computer. Instead of responding to prompts by entering a series of commands and codes, the user of the graphical interface of the Macintosh communicated with the computer through the use of icons, pull down menus, and a mouse.

The mouse is a small device, whose movement on a flat surface allows the user to control a pointer (arrow or flashing cursor-like symbol) that can be moved to any location on the screen. Icons (pictorial images) on the screen represent software available for execution or files or documents that can be manipulated. The person at the computer uses the mouse to move the pointer to the appropriate icon and clicks (depresses) a button on the mouse, and the software or file is automatically invoked for use.

Special actions, such as printing a draft of a document while using a particular package, are easily done through the use of pull down menus. Such menus are identified by key words across the top of the screen. When the user points and clicks on one of these words, the options available to the user are displayed in a column below the key word.

Users quickly found that this graphical interface was much easier than the character interface they had been using. The simple, intuitive nature of this approach significantly reduced the amount of training required. This simpler interface even enabled managers and others having little or no experience with computers to become very effective computer users.

The ease of use that the Macintosh offered attracted a great deal of attention. Consequently, Microsoft soon came up with a means of doing some of these things on a DOS-based microcomputer—through Windows. At its initial release, Windows was introduced as a package that would provide considerable benefits to personal computer (PC) users. Included among those benefits were a significantly reduced training requirement, higher user productivity, and lower overall costs. Needless to say, many DOS users adopted Windows as their main mode of operation. By the end of 1988, for example, 2.5 million copies of Windows had been sold.

WINDOWS 3.0

In May of 1990 Windows 3.0 was released. A quote from Bill Gates, the Chairman and CEO of Microsoft, illustrates that company's vision for the product: "There is nothing in this industry that Windows 3.0 isn't going to change."

Gates also revealed the reasons his company came up with the product and what they were trying to achieve. Their premise was that DOS-based computing was becoming quite complex. Though there are many fine character-based applications in use, the problems

> of setup and operation still abound, and the complicated command schemes and codes make them unfriendly. Other problems of the DOS world include the 640K memory limitation, file configurations that vary with each application, and the proliferation of drivers—for the network, the mouse, the printer, and so on—with every new application.
>
> Windows version 3.0 and Windows-based products are our best effort to eliminate these problems while maintaining the original plan for the PC—to give people a tool to make them more productive. One of our primary goals is to allow users to exploit powerful printers and access resources on networks easily, in essence, to make power more accessible while at the same time keeping the personal computer personal. (Gates 1990, p. 2)

Microsoft went to great lengths to make this new product both easier to learn and easier to install. The capability provided to users to organize their own files and screens and develop their own icons achieves the intended purpose of making the PC "friendlier." This ease-of-use factor will, in actuality, make the PC more competitive with the Macintosh.

WINDOWS 3.0 OPERATING MODES

The new version of Windows has three distinct operating modes: real, standard, and enhanced 386. The mode used is determined by the hardware available and the software to be executed. The *Microsoft Windows 3.0 User's Guide* (1990, p. ix) describes these modes as follows:

- *Real mode* is the operating mode that provides maximum compatibility with previous versions of Windows applications. For operation in *real mode*, a personal computer is required that has the Intel 8086 or 8088 processor (or higher) and 640K of conventional memory.
- *Standard mode* is the normal operating mode for running Windows. This mode provides access to extended memory and also lets you switch among non-Windows applications. To operate in *standard mode*, a personal computer is required that has the Intel 80286 processor (or higher) and 1 megabyte or more of memory (640K of conventional memory and 256K of extended memory).
- The *386 enhanced mode* provides access to the virtual memory capabilities of the Intel 80386 processor. Virtual memory capabilities let applications use more memory than is physically available. Enhanced mode also allows for multitasking of non-Windows applications. To operate in enhanced mode, a personal computer is required that has the Intel 80386 processor (or higher) and 2 megabytes (MB) or more of memory (640K of conventional memory and 1024K of extended memory).

WINDOWS 3.0 FEATURES

As might be expected of a product that has had the impact of Windows, there are many features that empower the user:

Enhanced memory management. Memory is much more effectively used; there are times when the user is able to make use of more memory than actually exists on his or her computer.

Network support. Unlike the earlier versions of Windows, which had almost no support for networks, 3.0 has many features that facilitate the use of networks and their resources.

Information transfer. There is an extensive capability for moving information from one application to another.

Multitasking. The user is able to execute two or more applications simultaneously.

Word processing. A word processing application called Write provides the capability for creating and printing routine documents.

Drawing. Paintbrush is an application that enables the user to create simple or elaborate color drawings.

Communications. An application called Terminal allows the user to connect his or her computer to other computers or networks via a modem.

Accessories. Windows comes with several programs that facilitate daily activities, such as an appointment calendar, a calculator, a clock, a card file, and a notepad.

Support. An owner of Windows is asked to complete a registration card and return it to Microsoft. He or she is then entitled to receive technical support from specialists on the product. They also receive notices of upgrades and information about new products that become available for Windows.

THE FUTURE

The future of Windows appears to be very bright. As indicated, it has already had an impact on the acceptance of OS/2, causing many to postpone, if not cancel, their movement to that operating system. The number of users in this category is likely to increase as more and more people are introduced to the enhanced capabilities of 3.0.

Some observers believe that the software market for packages that operate under Windows may explode. Considering that, at the time 3.0 was released, approximately thirty sellers of personal computers agreed to bundle Windows 3.0 with their sales, it would appear that there will be a sizable market for such software products. Reinforcing this view is the fact that some of those software publishers that had planned to develop only for OS/2 are now working on Windows versions of their products. This includes some of the largest software firms in the business: Ashton-Tate, WordPerfect, and Lotus.

In its development of Windows, Microsoft apparently kept the future in mind. Among the products that are expected to emerge for use with Windows are support for IBM 3270-type terminals and multimedia applications. This latter area will encourage developers to produce packages that employ animation, full-motion video, voice, and music.

SUMMARY

The character-based interface was long the standard for computer use. Apple's Macintosh, with its graphical interface, made many realize that the character-based interface was not so simple after all. Microsoft soon manufactured Windows as a means of bringing the easier-to-use graphical interface to the MS-DOS world. The initial reaction to Windows 3.0 suggests that this product will be very successful. It may, in fact, cause many personal computer users who previously planned to implement OS/2 to delay that move.

Windows has many features that empower the user. It is also a very robust product in that it seems to accommodate most of the basic needs and some of the more sophisticated needs of the typical computer user. Finally, it would appear that, in the future, its capabilities will be expanded substantially, making it an even more powerful resource.

References
Gates, B. 1990. Keeping personal computers personal. *One–to–One with Microsoft*, Issue 11, June, p. 2.
Microsoft Windows 3.0 User's Guide. 1990. Redmond, Wash.: Microsoft.

For Further Reading
Currid, C. 1990. Windows 3.0—Designed with networks in mind. *PC Week Special Report: Windows 3.0*, May 22, pp. 44, 46.
Curry, J. 1990. 3.0's power, promise catching developers' eyes. *PC Week Special Report: Windows 3.0*, May 22, pp. 39, 41.
Glitman, R. 1990. Windows 3.0: The realization of Bill Gates' grand plan. *PC Week*

Special Report: Windows 3.0, May 22, pp. 14–15.

Lovejoy, P. 1990. Graphical interface switches the focus for DOS diehards. *PC Week Special Report: Windows 3.0,* May 22, p. 22.

———. 1990. With Windows 3.0, users will experience a more human touch. *PC Week Special Report: Windows 3.0,* May 22, pp. 21–22.

Methvin, D. 1990. In managing memory, Windows 3.0 gains its strength from diversity. *PC Week Special Report: Windows 3.0,* May 22, pp. 31, 40.

Morse, S. 1990. First look: With Version 3.0, Windows realizes its full potential. *PC Week Special Report: Windows 3.0,* May 22, pp. 5, 12–13.

Nelson, R. 1990. Product reviews: Microsoft Windows Version 3.0. *Personal Computing,* July 27, pp. 117–21.

Scannell, E. 1989. Lotus designing 1-2-3 for Windows. *Infoworld,* December 18, pp. 1, 97.

Scannell, E., and L. Flynn. 1989. Windows' similarity to PM could undercut OS/2 sales. *Infoworld,* September 4, pp. 1, 81.

Scheier, R. L. 1990. Beta users applaud Windows' low memory usage. *PC Week Special Report: Windows 3.0,* May 22, p. 25.

Von Simson, C. 1990. Microsoft leads DOS revival. *Computerworld,* May 28, pp. 1, 116.

David Brittain

WIRTH, NIKLAUS

Niklaus Wirth entered the computing field in 1960. He received his doctoral degree from the University of California at Berkeley in 1963 and was assistant professor at Stanford University until 1967. He was a professor at the Swiss Federal Institute of Technology (ETH) in Zurich from 1968 to 1984. From 1982 to 1984 he was chairman of the division of computer science (Informatik) at ETH.

His first introduction to computers and programming was a course in numerical analysis at Laval University in Canada. Here, however, the Alvac IIIE computer was out of order most of the time, and exercises in programming remained on paper in the form of untested sequences of hexadecimal codes. His next attempt at using computers was with the Bendix G-15 computer. This machine required the user to allocate program instructions cleverly on the drum. If the user did not, the programs could well run slower by a factor of 100. It was obvious to Wirth that computers of the future had to be more effectively programmable. Wirth therefore gave up the idea of studying how to design hardware in favor of studying how to use it more elegantly.

He joined a research group that was engaged in the development of a compiler and its use on an IBM 704. The language was called NELIAC, a dialect of Algol 58. The benefits of such a "language" were quickly obvious, and the task of automatically translating programs into machine code posed challenging problems. The NELIAC compiler, itself written in NELIAC, was an intricate mess. Wirth felt that programs should be designed according to the same principles as electronic circuits, that is, clearly subdivided into parts with only a few wires going across the boundaries. Only by understanding one part at a time would there be hope of finally understanding the whole. Algol 60 was the first language defined with clarity; its syntax was even specified in a rigorous formalism. Could Algol's principles be condensed and crystallized even further?

Wirth then started his adventures in programming languages. The first experiment led to the development of EULER, an Algol-like programming language. This language created a basis for the systematic design of compilers. The next language developed by Wirth was Algol W. This language took Algol 60 as a starting point and attempted to rectify some of the ambiguities and deficiencies of the language.

In the fall of 1967, Wirth returned to Switzerland. A year later he was able to implement the language that later became known as PASCAL. After an extensive development phase, a Pascal compiler became operational in 1970. The development of Pascal was based on two principal aims. The first was to make available a language suitable to teach programming as a systematic discipline based on certain fundamental concepts clearly and naturally reflected by the language. The second was to develop implementations of the language that are both reliable and efficient on available computers. Pascal has become a very popular teaching language because it allows the teacher to concentrate more heavily on structures and concepts than features and peculiarities.

Wirth's ability in language design is complemented by an excellent writing ability. In 1971, Wirth published a paper on structured programming that recommended top-down structuring of programs (i.e., successively refining program stubs until the program is fully elaborated). Two later papers on real-time programming and notation speak to Wirth's consistent and dedicated search for an adequate language formalism.

As Pascal was gaining widespread recognition throughout the world, Wirth was investigating the subject of multiprogramming. The attempt to distill concrete rules for a multiprogramming discipline led Wirth to formulate them in terms of a small set of programming facilities. The result was the programming language MODULA-2. Although a Pascal-like language, Modula-2 provides two features lacking in Pascal: easy hardware access and separate compilation of program modules.

In 1980, Wirth blended the Pascal and Modula-2 languages to form the native language of LILITH, a workstation dedicated specifically to software design. The LILITH project proved that it is not only possible but advantageous to design a single-language system. Everything from device drivers to text and graphics editors is written in the same language. There is no distinction between modules belonging to the operating system and those belonging to the user's program.

The hallmarks of a programming language designed by Wirth are its simplicity, economy of design, and high-quality engineering, which result in a language whose notation appears to be a natural extension of algorithmic thinking rather than an extraneous formalism.

For Further Reading

Wirth, N. 1985. 1984 ACM A. M. Turing Award recipient. *Communications of the ACM* 28(2):159–64.

Donald D. Spencer

WORD PROCESSING

A need as old as the written word was finally met in the late 1960s by word processing programs. From the very first, once a thing was written, it inevitably had to be written again and again, often identically and sometimes with slight amendments. In early Mesopotamia, rooms full of slave clerks met the need, pressing reed styli into soft clay as a reader called out the words. Paper, pens, and ink were invented but the rooms full of clerks remained. The printing press cut down the number of clerks but had its limitations. The typewriter, especially when used with carbon paper, certainly helped ease the situation but business needed more and more copies and more slightly changed documents, so the rooms full of clerks remained, as typists in typing pools.

Oddly, even though the need was finally met by automation, the rooms full of clerks remain because the more documents it is possible to produce, the more documents business and government seem to need. The clerks are now called word processing technicians and they are organized into word processing departments.

A word processing program is any one of several dozen computer programs intended to manipulate written text. The material may be called from storage and modified or it may be newly composed. The essential functions of a word processing program are the ability to accept newly typed input and store it, and to edit, rearrange, and print out stored material without the need to manually retype it. The material being processed is displayed on a computer's monitor screen where an operator may, depending on the program in use, perform any number of formatting operations on it, from simple margin changes to specification of typefaces and inclusion of photographs, with captions.

HISTORY

IBM brought to the market the first machine that could be considered a word processor. At the beginning of 1964, every business letter, every report, every memo was typed, corrected, and retyped by hand. By the end of that year, the IBM Magnetic Tape Selectric Typewriter had become a fixture in literally hundreds of typing pools. It was called a text editor by some—the term *word processor* was still in the future—and could capture a typist's keystrokes on ordinary magnetic tape. Not only could the document be played back repeatedly but the operator could add or delete paragraphs and could make corrections to an original rough draft without retyping the whole document.

One of the first word processing programs for use on personal computers appeared in the late 1970s. Electric Pencil allowed a typist, for the time, incredible control. As characters were deleted or inserted, words wrapped up or down on the screen. Blocks of characters could be moved or copied to new positions in the document, any portion of the document could be displayed on-screen, and words and entire lines could be deleted with just two keystrokes. It was not perfect, though. The typist had to guess where the pages broke. The margins on the screen had no relation to the margins on the printed output. Formatting was primitive, to say the least.

The first widely accepted program to provide adequate formatting control was probably Perfect Writer, but the typist still had little idea of how the finished page would look until after the document was printed. In 1980 a new term was coined to describe the effect of a program called Word-Star. "What you see is what you get" (WYSIWYG) became the only word processing software worth buying. The typist had nearly absolute on-screen control of the final output. Margins, tabs, line spacing, and pagination could all be controlled and the effect tested before the printer was turned on.

Another of the dreams of business was quickly realized. It became possible to easily automate such things as billing and sales letters by coupling a word processing program with a data file. An operator had only to type one master document with special symbols included for the insertion of the variable information. Although the function is known as "mail merge" its versatility far transcends the handling of mailing lists. When first introduced, mail merge was considered an exotic option, but now only the most rudimentary word processing programs lack the feature.

INTEGRATED SOFTWARE

One of the complaints against personal computers is that the various programs do not always work well together. Keyboard commands vary from one application to another and many require pretty intensive training. Several approaches evolved to handle the problem. MicroPro, the publisher of Word-Star, used the same keystroke commands for similar functions in each of its family of applications: ReportStar, DataStar, and Calc-Star. Unfortunately, the companion programs were not up to the quality of Word-Star. They were cumbersome and difficult to use; however, they did point the way to a more integrated approach which eventually left its mark on the word processing programs currently available.

Besides mail merge capabilities, nearly all word processing programs now feature the ability to access remote databases (if the computer system includes a modem) and to do at least simple mathematical operations. Most current word processing programs not only create data files but also allow the direct usage of files generated by any of several standalone database management programs and spreadsheet programs. Those sorts of programs, conversely, now frequently offer fairly sophisticated word processing functions.

GENERAL CHARACTERISTICS

All word processing software can perform a number of similar functions. They do not all look alike, nor are the function commands issued in the same manner from the keyboard or menus, but they all share certain generic characteristics. First, all require original input from an alphanumeric keyboard. This may seem rather basic but not all applications require a keyboard. *Keyboarding* is the term usually used to distinguish the activity from typing. The motions are similar but the keystrokes are saved by the equipment to enable later reuse or manipulation.

Besides the alphanumeric keys, each keyboard contains the function keys that give word processing its unique character. Function keys do not usually cause characters to appear on the screen. Rather, they allow manipulation of characters and blocks of text as well as free movement throughout a document. Function keys, however they are implemented in a given program, perform similar basic word processing tasks in the general categories of formatting, editing, or locating.

Most formatting functions in word processing software are similar in effect to those of a typewriter, with the difference that the locations of such things as margins and tabs, as well as line spacing, are stored along with the document and need not be reset each time a document is called up. Often these instructions are embedded as special codes in the text and the operator can call them into view or not as desired.

Location keys on a standard typewriter include the carriage return, the space bar, and the backspace key. With a word processor, this is only the beginning. A marker, usually a flashing underline or rectangle called a cursor, shows the place where action is occurring. All systems have keys to control the position and motion of the cursor. Standard movements include LINE UP/DOWN, WORD RIGHT/LEFT, TOP/BOTTOM OF SCREEN, and NEXT PAGE. All word processors also include the ability to find particular groups, or "strings" of characters. Most allow special markers to be placed in text to allow rapid movement from marker to marker. The ability to "find" is happily coupled with the ability to "replace." For example, in a business letter, you might refer to the recipient as "Dick." You discover, in time, that he prefers to be called "Richard." Rather than hunting through the letter manually, you issue the command to find "Dick" and replace it with "Richard."

"Find and replace," as it is called, is a wonderful thing and well worth the price of admission but it can be dangerous, particularly for beginners. Unless you specify otherwise, the computer will discover every occurrence of a particular "string," whether inside a word or not. Suppose you wish to replace "Don" with "Donald." Your document emerges with such new words as "Donald't" or "Donaldkey." Most programs allow a search for "whole words only," which would avoid such troubles, but in many cases the user must remember to tell the program to use the option.

The true value of a word processor can be found in the editing functions. This is where a document is revised to fit changing circumstances or a rough draft is polished. No longer must the whole document be retyped; indeed, often only very small bits need be changed. DELETE is probably the most heavily used editing function. When the key is depressed, one character disappears.

Usually, a rough draft contains several organizational errors—paragraphs in the wrong places. In olden times it was necessary literally to "cut and paste" pieces of the rough draft to rearrange things into proper order. The process was both messy and frustrating. With a word processor, the problem very nearly solves itself. A paragraph is marked, the cursor is moved to the proper location, a couple of keys are tapped, and a miracle occurs. The text is inserted right where it is needed with no muss, no spilled glue, and nothing lost, and the entire job is finished in much less time.

EASE OF USE

After several weeks of practice, most word processors become very easy to use. The most common functions become automatic, the less common but still frequent functions are easily recalled, and even the obscure commands are at least available with some thought. But learning is a difficult task and requires the investment of time and practice. The investment will be well rewarded but, to some, it is daunting.

LEARNING THE PROGRAM

A full-featured word processing program is a very complex tool and no one can simply "sit down at the keyboard" and make it dance. In WordStar, for example, every alphabetical key has at least two purposes; most have three. The obvious one is to type in the appropriate character. The second purpose comes about when the "control" key is pressed along with an alpha key. A function is performed, often only after pressing one further key. The arrangement is fairly logical and, once practiced, is easily memorized.

Many people have made the mistake of thinking, "I'll pick it up as I go along." Although it is possible to do just that, it is also very inefficient. Most experts will advise you to follow the tutorial exercises supplied with the program. The exercises will at least expose you to every feature and ability of your word processor. You'll know what it can do. Then, and only then, is the time to play with the program. You will discover many things that were merely hinted at in the tutorial. Also, though it may be a thick and heavy book, the "reference" manual is vital. If possible, read it cover to cover. Although you may learn your program quite well, you will never outgrow the need to "look it up." Modern word processing programs are very complex and often offer more than one way to solve a particular problem.

Advertising has made many people believe that these programs are "easy to learn." As with most advertising, that statement is true and it is not. One 8-hour day given entirely to learning your program will usually be sufficient to get a good start. You may have also heard that the "documentation" is often hard to understand. If you follow the tutorial as advised, you will find that the rest of the documentation becomes remarkably more pleasant to read. And, as many of these programs cost $350 or more, it really makes good sense to invest some time in learning the full capabilities of the one you choose.

CHOOSING A PROGRAM

In selection of a word processing program, most experts advise that the purpose for which it will be used be taken into consideration. Each program began as the solution to a particular problem. Some programs are better for generating business letters. Some are superb for legal papers and contracts. Others do a remarkable job of aiding the creative writer. Unfortunately, the advertising for them is often a poor guide, as all programs try to present themselves as being all things to all people. Your best guides are the reviews in computer magazines, other people who have the programs you are considering, and your dealer's training classes. The last may seem to be a rather expensive way to find out but it has these advantages: It is the only way to use the program without buying it; it is the only way to learn enough to truly compare the various programs. Also, you will be spending a lot of time with your word processor after you buy it. It makes sense to find out whether you can live with it ahead of time.

For several years, the trend was toward making word processors more and more complex and the "high-end" packages are still very much that way. Recently some software publishers have begun offering "stripped-down" versions of their big packages. Many people do not have a need for industrial-strength features and, recognizing this, the publishers have met the market with lower prices while still offering a high-quality product.

The very first word processors were dedicated machines; they did nothing else. Then, with the personal computer revolution, nearly all word processors became just one of several programs on a general-purpose machine. Now, as electronic prices continue to fall, the dedicated word processor has reemerged, often in the size of a conventional portable typewriter. These new machines are actually computers but programmed only for one purpose. They generally have small screens, fairly sophisticated programming, built-in printers, and the ability to store text on removable disks. Some can connect to full-fledged computers or telephone lines for file transfer.

DESIRABLE FEATURES

One of the great attractions of a word processor is its ability to spell. It really cannot spell, of course, but it certainly gives a good imitation. All the "spellchecker" programs work on the same principle: that of comparing the words keyed in with a list of words held in memory. Because the "dictionary" or list of words is finite, it is inevitable that some perfectly fine words will not be in it. When the spellchecker finds a word it does not recognize, the user has the option of correcting the spelling—most programs give suggested alternatives—or telling the program to allow the word to stand as typed. A spellchecker should allow the user to enter words not found in the main dictionary into a "personal" or "update" dictionary.

Everybody makes mistakes and the opportunity to undo those mistakes is one of the major attractions of word processing software. But what if you make a mistake while correcting a mistake, for example, the mistake of deleting the entire contents of a file? Most programs keep backup copies of all work files on disk. If you should make such a mistake—and nearly everyone has or will—the backup copy should be there. Some packages allow the user to turn off the backup feature. That is almost always a bad idea.

Some programs will allow you to exit without saving your file! If you do so, your work will have been wasted. Look for some kind of "fail-safe" feature. Even the worst-designed programs usually ask you whether you really want to lose all the work you have just done. Your program should allow you the option of "dumping out" without saving anything. The best designs seem to be those programs that save the most recent work unless explicitly told not to do so.

KINDS OF PROGRAMS

The design of a word processing program is a function of what it is expected to do, what problems it is expected to solve. Some programs were envisioned as being primarily for the writing of letters and memos. These tend to be "page oriented," requiring the operator to, metaphorically, insert a new sheet of paper when the previous one is full. In some of the older versions, the text does not automatically flow from one page to another when parts are added or deleted. These programs tend to resemble a typewriter in nearly all respects. Tabs and margins are set at the beginning of the document and can be difficult to change later in the file.

A program intended for general business use, including letters but also proposals and agreements, will be oriented toward the use of "boilerplate." It will be relatively easy to copy text from other files into the current document. Often, these programs are also page oriented but not as rigidly as the previous class. Text is easier to format; margins and tabs are more flexible. "Find and replace" is usually very well implemented in this class of programs.

The creative writer has differing needs from the business user. Boilerplate is seldom used but the ability to link several files, such as book chapters, together while printing can be quite important. Some writers like to have a "clean screen," with nothing but the words they type on it. Most of the programs favored by writers allow at least the ruler and status lines to be turned off. A few have none to begin with. The creative writer needs a program that formats a manuscript properly, double-spaced, while allowing single spacing on the screen. The program should also allow very easy, almost unnoticeable transitions from page to page.

A few programs, most notably Word-Star, allow the user to make extensive modifications to the default or factory settings. Others are extremely rigid, allowing few, if any, changes. The rigid ones have the advantage of consistency; the customizable ones, the advantage of comfort.

With the advent of a usable WINDOWS operating environment, a new sort of word processor has appeared. Known as "frame-oriented" systems, these take advantage of the graphical capabilities of Windows. The look and feel, at least, are derived from desktop publishing programs. A "frame" or box is shown on the page and the text is typed within it. Reformatting is a simple matter of changing the size of the frame, and often quite complex page layouts can be achieved. Because they are so graphically oriented, this kind of program often requires a laser printer for the best output results.

COMPANION PROGRAMS

As word processors become omnipresent in the workplace and at home, several sorts of companion programs have evolved to make life a little easier. Among them are "Style Checkers," the advertising for which promises to clean up bad grammar and to point out cliched writing. There appears to be a good market for this sort of program but its usefulness seems to lie mainly in checking for mechanical faults, mismatched parentheses, for example.

Each word processing program uses its own file format for storing text. WordPerfect will not read MultiMate or WordStar or Microsoft Word files. The others will not read each other's files either. Microsoft Word will read some Macintosh files, as can XyWrite (but not the same files). All of these programs save files in ASCII but the page formatting is lost in that case. As information is passed electronically more and more often, the need for adequate file format conversion utility programs becomes evident. The need has been at least partially, if imperfectly, filled. Some word processors have file conversion utilities included, and standalone packages are available.

An outliner program, particularly one that runs "in the background" to be keyed into and out of while the word processor is running, is a fine thing to have on a computer. Most high-end word processing packages come with an outliner. The degree of integration varies. WordPerfect, for example, has a very well integrated outlining system. With an outliner, thoughts can be jotted down in no particular order; then order is drawn from what seems to be chaos. This is particularly effective for the writing of proposals or technical papers, the type of document that generally has rigid organizations. The thoughts can be easily placed in the proper sequence in the outliner before the first draft is attempted.

As hard disks of mammoth capacity become more common, so will the various "finder" programs, which search the entire disk drive for occurrences of a character string and allow the user to peek inside each file in which the string occurs.

For Further Reading

Banks, M. A., and A. Dibell. 1989. *Word processing secrets for writers.* Cincinnati: Writer's Digest Books. Covers the subject well, from selection of software and equipment to submitting manuscripts.

Bergerud, M., and J. Gonzalez. 1984. *Word/information processing: Concepts of office automation.* 2nd ed. New York: Wiley. Exhaustive textbook with case studies.

Cole, B. C. 1985. *Beyond word processing.* New York: McGraw-Hill. Good advice on using outline processors. Some information obsolete.

Gadney, A. 1984. *Selecting the right word processor.* Glendale, Calif.: Festival Publications. Covers all important and most secondary considerations for both business and personal applications.

Hurwood, B. J., ed. 1986. *Writing becomes electronic.* New York: Congdon & Weed. Three dozen writers discuss many facets of computers. Contributors range from William F. Buckley to Eric Van Lustbader.

McWilliams, P. A. 1984. *The word processing book: A short course in computer literacy.* Rev. ed. New York: Quantum Press/Doubleday. The quintessential book for the beginner. Buying guide outdated but advice still excellent. Amusing and thorough.

Munday, M. F. 1985. *Opportunities in word processing.* Lincolnwood, Ill.: VGM Career Horizons. An overview of what it takes to be a professional word processing clerk.

Price, J. and L. P. Urban. 1984. *The definitive word processing book.* New York: Penguin.

Outdated information but a good look at word processing as it was. List of products is fascinating.

Zinsser, W. 1983. *Writing with a word processor.* New York: Harper & Row. Amusing and serious by turns. Covers nearly all the mistakes a beginner can make.

Walter Hawn

WORKSTATIONS

A *workstation* is a high-powered single-user multitasking computer designed for graphics-intensive and/or computationally intensive applications.

The definition is operational and relative to the state of the art of commercially available single-user computer platforms. The workstation is characterized by an intermediate level of cost and performance between "host"-based computing (minicomputer and mainframe) and the personal computer.

HISTORY

The workstation in the modern sense began with Sun Microsystems and Apollo Computer in 1982. The initial machines used Motorola 68000 family central processing units (CPUs) and provided performance in the range of 1–2 million instructions per second (MIPS). The systems ran under the UNIX operating system, were capable of multitasking operation, and could provide high-performance graphics by the then current standards.

Within five years the migration from complex instruction set computer (CISC) processors to reduced instruction set computer (RISC) processors was well under way. In 1987 standard-level workstations were based on the 4-MIPS 25-MHz 68020 processor. In that year, Sun Microsystems released the Sun 4/260 workstation, which provided 10-MIPS performance on a Sun SPARC RISC processor. Hewlett-Packard released the 9000 series (model 8255RX) RISC-based workstation, which performed at 8 MIPS.

In 1987 workstation computing cost $5,000 per MIPS. Common projections were that workstations would cost $1,000 per MIPS by 1990. Performance was expected to double every 18 months to 2 years. In actuality, by 1991, market-leading workstations were delivered at $300 per MIPS. IBM provided versions of the RS/6000 workstation at 50 MIPS and Hewlett-Packard released a 70-MIPS version of the HP 9000. Performance was doubling every 12–18 months.

In comparison, early personal computers such as the IBM PC AT performed at rates in the range of 0.4 MIPS. In 1991, the fastest personal computers were based on the 32-bit Intel 80486, which is rated at 16.5 MIPS.

The effective level of performance for a workstation or any other computer is dependent upon other factors in addition to raw CPU performance. Because of this fact, other units of computing performance, such as megaflops or MFLOPS (million floating-point operations per second), have joined the MIPS measure.

The current leading vendor to the work-

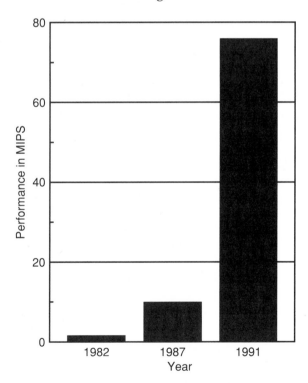

FIGURE 1. Evolution of workstation performance as measured in millions of instructions per second (MIPS).

TABLE 1. Workstation Vendors, 1990

	Percent
SUN Microsystems	39
Hewlett-Packard[2]	20
Digital Equipment	17
IBM	5
Intergraph	4
Other	15

[2]Includes Apollo.

Source: International Data Corp.

station market is Sun Microsystems. Sun's original major competitor, Apollo, was acquired by Hewlett-Packard in April 1989. In 1990, worldwide shipment of workstations totaled 370,800 units. The 1990 ranking of vendors is given in Table 1, and the comparative performance of entry-level machines from the major vendors, in Table 2. (This ranking of introductory level workstation products was current at the time of writing. Given the rate of development and commercialization of the underlying technology and the resultant equipment, the performance ranking among major vendors is certain to change constantly.)

Groupings of vendors have developed on the basis of common processors and versions of UNIX. Three major groupings are Sun Microsystems and value-added resellers of Sun equipment; the Advanced Computing Environment (ACE) consortium; and the IBM/Apple effort.

Sun has aggressively marketed its SPARC processor, its version of UNIX, and its graphic user interface (GUI) to value-added resellers. As of 1991, twenty-four Sun clone workstations had been announced.

The ACE consortium is developing a common workstation architecture incorporating the MIPS R3000 processor, an operating system based on Microsoft's New Technology (NT) executive, and the SCO Open

TABLE 2. Performance of Selected Workstations

	MIPS	MFLOPS
HP 720	57	17
IBM RS/6000 320	29.5	8.5
SUN Sparcstation 2	28.5	4.2
DECstation 5000	24	3.7

Desktop GUI. Member computer companies include Compaq and Digital Equipment.

The joint effort between IBM and Apple is the most recent consortium effort. The intent is to produce a common architecture based on the IBM RISC processor and AIX, an IBM version of UNIX, combined with the Apple GUI technology.

WORKSTATION CHARACTERISTICS

The workstation is characterized by four properties:

- high-performance CPU;
- high-speed, high-resolution graphics (typically involving use of separate graphics processors);
- multitasking operating system (typically a dialec of UNIX);
- capability for network operation.

The high-performance CPU—in other words, raw computing power—is the most heavily emphasized factor in the discussion of technical workstations. Given the tasks for which these workstations are designed, this emphasis is reasonable. Technical numeric computation and high-performance graphics applications consume enormous amounts of computing power. It appears that there is no hard upper limit to the demand for computing power.

Since current personal computers are providing performance comparable to or exceeding that of earlier generations of workstations, it is not unexpected that many tasks identified with workstations are in fact done on high-performance personal computers. The general pattern in organizations is to use multiple personal computers in ratio to higher-performance workstations.

USES FOR WORKSTATIONS

The original applications of workstations are in graphics- and computing-intensive professional applications. A second and growing application area is as a replacement for minicomputers in group computing database applications.

Since humans are visual creatures, the

ability to produce and manipulate graphics images is important to many categories of tasks. The availability and accessibility of workstations have made computer support for entire categories of work feasible. Examples of such applications include:

- Design and production engineering, including COMPUTER-AIDED DESIGN AND MANUFACTURING (CAD/CAM).
- Visual communications, including PRESENTATION GRAPHICS, MULTIMEDIA, training, and video production.
- Graphic arts, including electronic publishing, illustration, graphic design, and fine art.
- Scientific and medical visualization, imaging, and graphics-based analysis.
- Mapping and GEOGRAPHIC INFORMATION SYSTEMS, including geophysics, cartography, and remote sensing.

IMPLICATIONS

Workstation technology is a significant part of the trend to downsize and distribute computing resources. Applications, such as CAD/CAM or finite element analysis, that previously required access to a large minicomputer or a mainframe can now be made available to more staff economically and without extensive scheduling. Many tasks are made more feasible because of increased timeliness and therefore will tend to get done more readily.

The use of workstations as departmental database engines reduces the cost of entry and support for such systems. Application areas that currently exhibit this trend include manufacturing data and quality management and laboratory information management.

References

Curran, L. 1991. HP speeds up the workstation race. *Electronics*, April, pp. 43–48.

Gantz, J. 1991. Graphics industry, the market at large. *Computer Graphics World*, April, pp. 27–33.

Goering, R. 1987. Engineering tools move to the desktop. *Computer Design*, July, pp. 37–48.

Heller, M. 1987. The PC/workstation convergence: An explosion of opportunity. *Engineering & Scientific Computing*, August, pp. 7–10.

Runyan, L. 1991. A retrospective, 40 years on the frontier. *Datamation*, March 15, pp. 34–57.

Jeffery L. Cawley

WOZNIAK, STEPHEN G.

Stephen G. Wozniak was born in 1950. He was the son of an engineer; his father, Francis, helped design satellite guidance systems at the Lockheed Missiles & Space Company plant in Sunnyvale, California, not far from Intel and Fairchild Semiconductor. Francis taught his son the fundamentals of electronics and encouraged him to experiment on his own. Woz, as Stephen was known to his friends, became an avid electronics hobbyist. He had a talent for electronics, and he built all sorts of gadgets, including a transistor radio. By the time he was in the sixth grade, he had decided to become an electronics engineer.

Woz was bored by school. He shone in the few classes that interested him, mathematics and science, and did poorly in the rest. Electronics and computers were his greatest interests, and neither his junior high school nor his high school had much to offer him in either subject. He took to reading computer manuals and programming textbooks on his own, and he soon pulled ahead of his fellow students and even his teachers. When he was 13, he built a transistorized calculator that won first prize in a Bay Area science fair. He was drawn to minicomputers most of all, admiring their compactness, accessibility, and inexpensiveness. By the end of high school, Woz knew that he wanted to become a computer engineer. Woz graduated from Homestead High School in Cupertino, California.

Woz attended the University of Colorado for 1 year and later transferred to De Anza College, a junior college in Cupertino. He later left school altogether and worked for a year as a programmer for a small computer company. In 1971, he tried college again at the University of California at Berkeley. That did not last long and he dropped out and went to work as an engineer in the calculator division of Hewlett-Packard Company in Palo Alto, California.

In the summer of 1971, a friend introduced him to a quiet, intense, long-haired teenager by the name of Steven JOBS. Jobs, who was 16 years old at the time, was an electronic hobbyist as well as a student at Homestead High School, Woz's alma mater.

The introduction of the Altair microcomputer had led to the formation of computer clubs all over the country, including one in Silicon Valley known as the Homebrew Computer Club. Woz was a founding member of this club and was one of the most active members. Steve Jobs also attended meetings at the Homebrew Computer Club.

In 1975, Jobs and Woz bought a $25 microprocessor and built a computer in the living room of Jobs's parents' house in Palo Alto. Although it was not as powerful as other available computers, it was cheaper and less complicated, and it included circuits that enabled it to be connected directly to a display monitor. Woz did most of the work, but Jobs, who was trying to persuade Woz to go into business with him, chipped in with many suggestions. The computer was called the Apple I. Jobs and Woz set up a partnership, Apple Computer Inc., to market the computer.

In 1977, Jobs and Woz went on to develop a more sophisticated computer, the elegant-looking Apple II. By late 1980, more than 130,000 Apple II computers had been sold. By the end of 1983 Apple Computer had almost 4,700 employees and $983 million in sales. Today Apple Computer is a multibillion-dollar business.

Wozniak, who was always more interested in engineering than management, took leave from Apple Computer to pursue other things, such as earning a computer science degree under an alias from the University of California in the early 1980s. In 1985, he left Apple Computer to start a company called CL9 (as in "cloud nine"). Here he designed an infrared remote control device that can operate any component of a home entertainment system, from television to VCR, regardless of the manufacturers.

For Further Reading

Augarten, S. 1984. *Bit by bit,* pp. 276–81. New York: Ticknor & Fields.

Donald D. Spencer

APPENDIX

COMPUTING ASSOCIATIONS

There are many different types of groups in the computing field; they are made up of individual computing professionals, computing organizations, and individual or company users of computer hardware or software. These groups vary in structure, qualifications for membership, size, purpose, and governance. Many groups are made up of individual members primarily involved in some aspect of computing. These groups are generally professional, educational, or technical societies. Another somewhat overlapping classification is user groups; they are made up of individuals or representatives of groups that use a particular type of computer hardware or software. Other groups serve functions in the area of standards, representation of the United States in international organizations, accreditation, etc. In this article the associations will be divided into three categories: (1) scientific, professional, technical, and educational societies comprised chiefly of individual members; (2) user groups; and (3) other groups.

SCIENTIFIC, PROFESSIONAL, TECHNICAL, AND EDUCATIONAL SOCIETIES

Hundreds of organizations might be named in this section. As computing permeates every facet of life, more and more specialized organizations are formed of professionals with interests in computing or some specialized applications area. Below a few of the larger and established societies are listed, with some information about the group; then a few additional societies are listed with their major publication, to give a sense of the breadth of interests covered by these organizations.

Association for Computing Machinery (ACM); 94,000 members

This largest scientific, educational, and technical association in the computing sciences field was founded in 1947. Its purpose, as stated in its membership application form, is "to advance the sciences and arts of information processing; to promote the free interchange of information about the sciences and arts of information processing both among specialists and among the public; and to develop and maintain the integrity and competence of individuals engaged in the practice of information processing." ACM publishes fourteen archival journals (published quarterly unless otherwise indicated): *Communications of the ACM* (monthly), *Journal of the ACM*, *Computing Surveys*, *Computing Reviews*, *Collected Algorithms* (five volumes plus quarterly updates), *ACM Guide to Computing Literature* (annual), *Transactions on Mathematical Software*, *Transactions on Database Systems*, *Transactions on Programming Languages and Systems*, *Transactions on Graphics*, *Transactions on Information Systems*, *Transactions on Computer Systems*, *Transactions on Software Engineering Methodology*, and *Transactions on Modeling & Computer Simulation*.

ACM sponsors thirty-four special-interest groups (SIGs), each of which has some form of publication for its members, sponsors some form of technical activity ranging from very large conferences to small workshops, and supports technical excellence in its particular area of specialization. These SIGs are:

SIGACT (automata and computability theory)
SIGADA (Ada)
SIGAPL (APL)
SIGAPP (applied computing)
SIGARCH (computer architecture)

SIGART (artificial intelligence)

SIGBDP (business data processing and management)

SIGBIO (biomedical computing)

SIGCAPH (computers and the physically handicapped)

SIGCAS (computers and society)

SIGCHI (computers and human interaction)

SIGCOMM (data communication)

SIGCPR (computer personnel research)

SIGCSE (computer science education)

SIGCUE (computer uses in education)

SIGDA (design automation)

SIGDOC (documentation)

SIGFORTH (Forth)

SIGGRAPH (computer graphics)

SIGIR (information retrieval)

SIGLINK (hypertext/hypermedia)

SIGMETRICS (measurement and evaluation)

SIGMICRO (microprogramming)

SIGMOD (management of data)

SIGNUM (numerical mathematics)

SIGOIS (office information systems)

SIGOPS (operating systems)

SIGPLAN (programming languages)

SIGSAC (security, audit, and control)

SIGSAM (symbolic and algebraic manipulation)

SIGSIM (simulation)

SIGSMALL/PC (small and personal computing systems and applications)

SIGSOFT (software engineering)

SIGUCCS (university and college computing services)

ACM also sponsors many prestigious awards, the most notable being the Turing Award, presented annually to the person selected for his or her technical contributions to the computing community. A $25,000 prize accompanies this award.

Computer Professionals for Social Responsibility (CPSR); over 2,000 members

CPSR was founded in 1981 to educate policymakers, computer professionals, and the public about the social impacts of computers. It promotes the discussion and critical evaluation of social and technical issues within the community of computer professionals, sponsors local chapters, and holds at least one annual conference. Publications include a quarterly newsletter, articles, books, and educational materials.

Data Processing Management Association (DPMA); over 40,000 members

DPMA, originally the National Machine Accountants Association, was founded in 1951 and adopted its present name in 1962. DPMA introduced the first certification program in the computing field, for certified data processor (CDP), in 1962. This certification program is now operated by the Institute for Certification of Computer Professionals (ICCP) and includes, in addition to the CDP, the certified computer programmer (CCP) program, with specialties in business programming, scientific programming, or systems programming. DPMA traditionally had strong local chapters, and it sponsors student chapters, self-study courses, a management development series on videotape, and on-site seminars. DPMA developed guidelines for business information systems curricula in undergraduate institutions and encourages members to become counselors for the Scout computer merit badge. The major publication of DPMA is the *Journal of Data Management*.

Institute of Electrical and Electronic Engineers—Computer Society (IEEE-CS); over 100,000 members

IEEE-CS is a special interest group of the IEEE and is the largest professional society in the computing science community. Its name dates from 1972, although the group originated as the Computer Group of the Institute of Radio Engineers in 1951. The Computer Society supports thirty-three technical committees, groups of professionals with common interests in various specialized aspects of software, hardware, and applications. The archival publications of the Computer Society include *Computer, IEEE Computer Graphics and Applications, IEEE Design and Test, IEEE Expert, IEEE Micro, IEEE Software, Transactions on Computers, Transactions on Knowledge and Data Engineering, Transactions on Parallel and Distributed Systems, Transactions on Pattern Analysis and Machine Intelligence,* and *Transactions on Software Engineering.*

The Computer Society sponsors over 100 conferences, workshops, and tutorials every year. In addition, it publishes a large number of the tutorials and conference proceedings, produces or distributes videotapes, and supports over 100 standards projects.

With ACM, the Computer Society established the Computing Sciences Accreditation Board (CSAB), which has been recognized by the Council on Postsecondary Accreditation (COPA). Recently these two associations published guidelines for undergraduate education in computing science and engineering, *Computing Curricula 1991: Report of the ACM/IEEE-CS Joint Curriculum Task Force.*

International Society for Technology in Education (ISTE); over 6,000 individual members and 60 organizational affiliates

In 1989 the International Association of Computer Educators (IACE) (previously called the Association of Educational Data Systems, which was founded in 1962) and the International Council of Computer Educators (ICCE) (formerly the Oregon Council of Computer Educators, which was founded in the late 1960s) joined to become ISTE.

The ISTE mission is:

- To improve education through the appropriate use of technology.
- To provide a prominent information center and source of leadership for educational professionals, policymakers, and educational organizations worldwide.
- To support a strong regional affiliate membership committed to a grass-roots effort to improve the educational use of technology.
- To foster an active partnership between leaders in business and education who seek to realize the potential of educational technology.

ISTE publishes *The Computing Teacher* and *ISTE Update: People, Events, and News in Education Technology* eight times each year in addition to the quarterly *Journal of Research on Computing in Education.* In addition, ISTE publishes books and courseware, sponsors workshops and symposia, offers independent study courses, and supports SIGs. Each of these SIGs has a quarterly publication, and most have annual meetings. The SIGs and their publications are:

HyperSIG (hypermedia/multimedia): *HyperNEXUS: Journal of Hypermedia and Multimedia Studies*

SIGLogo (Logo): *Logo Exchange*

SIGCS (computer science): *SIGCS Journal*

SIGTC (technology coordinator): *SIGTC Connections*

SIGTE (teacher educators): *Journal of Computing in Teacher Education*

SIG/Tel (telecommunications): *Telecommunications in Education (T.I.E.) News*

Following are examples of specialized professional, scientific, and educational societies with their major publication, unless it is a newsletter for members; for these publications (a) indicates annually, (b) bimonthly, (m) monthly, (q) quarterly, and (s) semiannually:

Agricultural Computer Association (ACA)

American Association for Artificial Intelligence (AAAI); *AI Magazine* (q)

American Association for Medical Systems and Informatics (AAMSI)

American Association of Microcomputer Investors (AAMI); *AAMI Journal* (b)

American Association of Public Welfare Information Systems Management (AAPWISM)

American Society for Information Science (ASIS)

Association for Computational Linguistics (ACL); *Computational Linguistics* (q)

Association for Computer Aided Design in Architecture (ACADIA)

Association for Computers and the Humanities (ACH); *Computers and the Humanities* (q)

Association for Development of Computer-Based Instructional Systems (ADCIS); *Journal of Computer-Based Instruction* (q)

Association for Educational Communications and Technology (AECT) (b)

Association for Federal Information Resources Management (AFFIRM); *The Affirmation*

Association of the Institute for Certification of Computer Professionals (AICCP)

Association for Systems Management (ASM); *Journal of Systems Management* (m)

Association for Women in Computing (AWC)

Cognitive Science Society (CSS); *Cognitive Science* (q)

College and University Machine Records Conference (CUMREC)

Communications Security Association (COMSEC); *COMSEC Letter* (m)

Computer-Assisted Language Learning and Instruction Consortium (CALICO); *CALICO Journal* (q)

Computer Law Association (CLA)

Computer Press Association (CPA)

Computer Use in Social Services Network (CUSSN)

Computerized Radiology Society (CRS); *Computerized Radiology* (b)

EDP Auditors Association (EDPAA); *EDP Auditor Journal* (q)

Educational Products Information Exchange Institute (EPIE); *EPIEgram* (m)

Federation of Government Information Processing Councils, Inc. (FGIPCI)

Independent Computer Consultants Association (ICCA) *The Independent* (b)

International Association for Mathematics and Computers in Simulation (IAMCS); *Applied Numerical Mathematics* (b), *Mathematics and Computers in Simulation* (b)

Law School Computer Group (LSCG)

Library and Information Technology Association (LITA); *Information Technology and Libraries* (q)

Machine Vision Association (MVA)

Mailing List User and Supplier Association

Microcomputer Education Application Network (MEAN)

Microcomputer Investors Association (MCIA) *MicroComputer Investor* (s)

National Center for Computer Crime Data (NCCCD); *Computers and Security* (q), *Conscience in Computing* (q), plus annual statistical reports

National Computer Graphics Association (NCGA); *Computer Graphics Today* (m)

National Society of Computer/Genealogists (NSA); *The Computer/Genealogist* (q)

9 to 5, National Association of Working Women

Office Automation Society International (OASI); *Office Automation News* (m)

Office Technology Management Association (OTMA); *The Word* (b)

Operations Research Society of America (ORSA); *Operations Research* (b), *Interfaces* (b)

Society for Applied Learning Technology (SALT); *Journal of Educational Technology Systems* (q)

Society for Computer Simulation (SCS); *Simulation* (m), *Transactions* (q)

Society of Data Educators (SDE); *Journal of Computer Information Systems* (q)

Society for Industrial and Applied Mathematics (SIAM); *Journal of Computing* (q), *Journal of Scientific and Statistical Computing* (q), plus several other journals

Society for Information Management (SIM); *MIS Quarterly* (q)

Special Libraries Association (SLA); *SpeciaList* (m), *Special Libraries* (q)

Telecommunications Research and Action Center (TRAC); *Access, Journal of Telecommunications Reform* (m), *Teletips* (q)

Travel Agents Computer Society (TACOS); *Update* (b)

USER GROUPS

Groups of this type were formed as early as the mid-1950s. These groups have very diverse structures, histories, and longevity. The organizations may be international, national, regional, or local in nature. Some of the organizations are formed to influence the product being used; other organizations are more in the nature of a mutual support group to develop individual expertise and to share ideas and software. The groups are frequently formed by a few people and often are very informal. As the groups grow and mature they frequently become formal organizations with elected officers, constitutions, bylaws, or charters. As the product matures and develops an installed base, the users' group generally has less influence than when the product is first introduced. As products are discontinued, the corresponding users' group generally disbands.

The first large user group was SHARE, which was formed in about 1955 by users and potential users of the IBM 704. This activist group was formed to provide support for users and to influence the hardware manufacturer to provide better support for users of its hardware. One of the most important early functions of the group was to share software. SHARE accomplished this by supporting a library of software routines for its members. National SHARE meetings provided a forum for lobbying IBM to develop software, such as operating systems, to meet the specifications developed by the users. Though the IBM 704 is seen only in museums today, SHARE is an active organization of users of large IBM systems.

There has been a users' group for nearly every major computer that has been manufactured and for some software applications. Examples of the early groups are: CUBE (Cooperating Users of Burroughs Computers), formed in 1962 by the merger of CUE (Burroughs B220 users' group) and DUO (Datatron, B205, users); USE (UNIVAC Scientific Exchange) was formed in 1956. As new computer hardware is marketed, new users' groups form. As computer companies go out of business, the associated users' group usually ceases to exist. In the early phase of a users' group it is frequently very active and dedicated to influencing the manufacturer to serve the user community better by providing better technical support, improved software and hardware, and by soliciting user input for improved systems. Users frequently assist each other in solving problems they encounter in using the product and exchange ideas and software. Information about currently active users' groups is usually available from the computer manufacturer or its local sales representative.

There are many varieties of user groups. The early groups were individuals or companies that used particular computers; later some groups formed that used a particular class of computers (e.g., minicomputers). In the 1980s many local groups of users of personal computers were formed. This type of user group varied widely from place to place, was frequently made up of hobbyists, had a high rate of turnover in membership, sometimes took on civic projects, published a newsletter, established shareware exchanges, and had meetings to demonstrate new

equipment and/or software. There were also personal computer groups that specialized in particular applications (e.g., educational software).

The Boston Computer Society (BCS); about 30,000 members in the late 1980s.

This is an example of a group of users of personal computers who formed a local group in 1977 that has grown into a worldwide group of microcomputer users. There are special subgroups of users of various microcomputers. This nonprofit group encourages the exchange of software and provides publications, workshops, and referrals. SIGs include: artificial intelligence (AI), consultants, databases, dentists, graphics, high-school students, investment, medical, networking, programming languages, publishing, real estate, robotics, and social impact. BCS is affiliated with the Boston Computer Museum. This is probably the largest microcomputer user group.

Digital Equipment Computer Users' Society (DECUS); over 120,000 members

This is an example of a user group that focuses on the equipment of one computer manufacturer. DECUS was founded in 1961. Its purpose is to (1) promote effective use of computer systems manufactured and distributed by DEC, (2) promote exchange of information and ideas among members, (3) provide feedback to DEC, and (4) establish standards. The group sponsors over twenty SIGs, maintains a library of programs for DEC computers, holds semiannual symposia for the exchange of technical and managerial information, and sponsors a nationwide electronic conferencing service, DECUServe, which is available 24 hours a day, 7 days a week. (*DEC Professional* 10[3]:10,154).

Guidance for Users of Integrated Data-Processing Equipment (GUIDE)

This is another example of a user group made up of companies that use one brand of computers for data processing applications. It is one of the earliest user groups, founded in 1956. Its purpose is to develop and share ideas about administration of large-scale computers, productivity, operation, programming, and systems development for large-scale IBM computers.

SHARE

This is thought to be the earliest user group. It was formed in 1955, and Jack Strong was elected its first president. The group was made up of representatives from seventeen installations that were using or anticipated using the IBM 704. During the first decade of its existence SHARE was interested almost exclusively in scientific computing. The early efforts of SHARE were largely concentrated on developing standards and conventions that allowed the sharing of programs among users. This interest remains as SHARE also concentrates on providing feedback on all vendor-supplied software, programming languages processors, and operating and database systems. SHARE was incorporated in 1969, became self-supporting, is no longer obligated to IBM, and has widened its purview.

The following list of user groups should give some idea of the types of such groups in existence today. Information about user groups can frequently be obtained from the product producer or from listings of meetings in computer-oriented magazines and journals. Many of the user groups publish newsletters for members. The larger—particularly national and international—user groups usually hold meetings, workshops, or conferences and generally publish proceedings of these meetings.

Amdahl Users' Group (AUG)

American Software Users' Group (ASUG); companies that use the products of American Software, Inc.

Association of Minicomputer Users (AMU); *Minicomputer Software* (q)

Capital PC Users' Group (CPCUG)

COMMON; users of the smaller IBM computer systems

Compucats' Computer Club (CCC); local personal computer club

Cooperating Users of Burroughs Equipment (CUBE)

Federation of NCR User Groups (FNUG)

Interchange; users of Perkin-Elmer computer equipment

International Society of Wang Users (ISWU); *Techknowledge* (data and word processing magazine) (m)

International Software A.G. Users' Group (ISAGUG)

International Tandem Users' Group (ITUG)

Loyal Ontario Group Interested in Computers (LOGIC); largest Canadian Apple user group; *Mapple Orchard* (m)

MUMPS Users' Group (MUG); users of MUMPS software, originally for health care applications but now widely used in business applications

National Epson Users' Group (NEUG)

National On-line Circuit (NOC); supports local/regional on-line user groups

NCA Users' Group; users of NCA software

Prime Users' Group (PUG)

Recognition Technologies Users' Association (RTUA)

SAS Users' Group International (SUGI)

Texas Instruments Mini/Microcomputer Information Exchange (TI-MIX)

XYVision Users' Group (XUG)

OTHER GROUPS

In addition to the associations discussed above, other groups perform unique functions within the computing and information sciences field. These groups may represent the United States in international organizations, establish standards in the field, evaluate and/or disseminate and/or produce artifacts for use in the field, or coordinate and/or advise constituent groups in the use of or furtherance of the field. Several examples of these organizations are given below. This is not comprehensive, since the list would be too long.

American National Standards Institute (ANSI)

Founded in 1918 to promote voluntary national standards in both the public and private sectors. Currently ANSI forms committees of computer users and companies to develop and disseminate industry standards —for example, ANSI COBOL. ANSI has committees that work on programming languages, electronic data interchange, and physical devices such as magnetic tapes and disks. ANSI is the U.S. member of the International Standards Organization (ISO).

Association of Data Processing Service Organizations (ADAPSO)

Founded in 1960 as a group of companies that provide data processing services for a fee. The purpose of ADAPSO is to improve management methods and establish standards for performance.

Computer and Business Equipment Manufacturers' Association (CBEMA)

An organization of manufacturers and developers of information processing and communication products, software, and services for business. The purpose of CBEMA is to cooperate in the development of information processing standards in the United States.

Computer and Communications Industry Association (CCIA)

Works with NIST to keep its members informed of regulatory policy that affects computer, peripheral, and data communication manufacturers; software developers; and leasing, service, and equipment repair companies.

Computing Sciences Accreditation Board (CSAB)

CSAB was formed by the ACM and the IEEE-Computer Society in 1985. The Computer Science Accreditation Commission (CSAC) is the first and only commission under CSAB and was recognized in 1990 by COPA as the only group that may accredit undergraduate programs in the computing sciences. As of 1991, 107 programs had been accredited.

CONDUIT

Formed in 1971 by five regional computer centers to share computer-based instructional (CBI) ideas. CONDUIT develops, identifies, evaluates, and distributes computer-based instructional materials, primarily for use at the undergraduate level. It conducts research on methods for the development and design of CBI.

EDUCOM

As stated in its quarterly publication *EDUCOM Review*, "EDUCOM, founded in 1964, is a non profit consortium of higher education institutions which facilitates the introduction, use, access to, and management of information resources in teaching, learning, scholarship and research. EDUCOM's work is done in cooperation and partnership with the broader education and library communities, professional societies, government at all levels, and information industries." EDUCOM coordinates BITNET, the largest computer network in higher education; sponsors conferences and seminars; publishes monographs; maintains a consulting group; and through "EDUCOM Educational Uses of Information Technology (EUIT) Program undertakes activities that improve faculty and student access to information technology; promote its integration into teaching and learning; influence national development of information technology as a resource for education; and support professional growth for [a] broad range of information technology professionals."

International Federation of Information Processing Societies (IFIPS)

IFIPS was established in 1960 and is an international organization made up of professional/technical societies. Each country may have only one full member. That member must represent the information processing activities of its nation. Until the American Federation of Information Processing Societies (AFIPS) was disbanded in 1990, it was the U.S. member of IFIPS. Currently the United States is not represented at IFIPS; however, some associations are trying to work out representation.

The goals of IFIPS are to advance information technology; to promote international cooperation in information processing; to encourage research, development, and application of information processing for the advancement of science and humanity; to foster the exchange of ideas in the field of information processing; and to promote education in the information processing field.

IFIPS has an international congress every three years. Most of the actual work of IFIPS is carried out by its Technical Committees (TCs) and Working Groups (WGs) under each TC. Each TC is made up of a representative from IFIP representative societies and supervises the WGs under its area. WGs are made up of specialists in their particular area. In addition to the international congress, TCs sponsor conferences and publish proceedings and papers. The current TCs are:

TC 2	Programming
TC 3	Education
TC 4	Health Care and Biomedical Research
TC 5	Computer Applications in Technology
TC 6	Data Communication
TC 7	System Modeling and Optimization
TC 8	Information Systems
TC 9	Relationship Between Computers and Society
TC 10	Digital Systems Design

International Standards Organization (ISO)

ISO was founded in 1946 to set international standards. This is accomplished through more than 150 committees and 2,000 subcommittees. Membership is by country; more than 75 countries are members. ANSI is the U.S. member of ISO.

National Institute of Standards and Technology (NIST) (formerly the National Bureau of Standards)

This is the agency of the U.S. government that defines standards.

Doris K. Lidtke

COMPUTER COMPONENT MANUFACTURERS

One megabyte of memory, if it had been available in 1959, would have required a room 7 ft square and 8 ft high; that same amount of memory is now available in about one-half cubic inch. The cost for this amount of memory has dropped from $600,000 to $200 in the last 10 years! Computers are constructed of a variety of components, including the central processing unit and additional peripherals and devices. All of these are composed primarily of one or more chips, which are miniaturized electronic circuits.

A new revolution in computer hardware has been underway as manufacturers miniaturize the computer logic circuitry, and as more and faster circuits are integrated. Manufacturers of computer components have evolved their products as the demands of the computer industry changed. The purpose of this article is to provide a history of the development of these components and to identify and describe the major component manufacturers.

HISTORICAL DEVELOPMENT

When computers were first developed in the 1940s, electromechanical relays served as the on–off switching devices. These worked like a simple light switch, clicking on and off regularly as electricity passed through them. These required enormous space and created a great deal of noise as they performed their jobs. We can look back to the first MARK I, which was 51 feet across and 8 feet high, to gain a sense of the size of the earliest computers. Although this first computer could in 1 day solve calculations that had previously taken 6 months, researchers dreamed of better ways to accomplish the same tasks.

Vacuum tubes soon replaced these relays. Vacuum tubes have no moving parts and they control the flow of current by electrical forces alone. Although the tubes were a considerable improvement over the electromechanical relays, they had problems, too. The tubes were made of fragile glass, and the filament had to warm up; also, the tubes had a propensity toward overheating and consumed large amounts of power. The first computers to use tubes had thousands of them, and as they frequently failed, a continual effort was required to keep things operational.

In 1947 John Bardeen, Walter Brattain, and William Shockley of Bell Laboratories invented the transistor and the computer industry began to change rapidly. Transistors, electronic devices that control current flow without the use of a vacuum, serve as the nerve cells of today's computers because they are long-lasting, compact, and low in power requirements. Transistors began as discrete components, each packaged as a single unit made up of a pinhead-sized piece of germanium encased in a metal cylinder, and then soldered onto a printed circuit board to interconnect with other transistors and components. But these first transistors had to be hand-wired and -soldered; the circuits proved to be very expensive and were still relatively large.

In the late 1950s Jack Kilby, an engineer with Texas Instruments, made a major discovery that ushered in the age of microcomputers as we know them. He found a way to produce an integrated circuit. An integrated circuit is simply an entire electronic circuit and its interconnections constructed at one time on a single silicon chip with tiny circuits etched on it. Each chip can do the work of thousands of transistors.

Soon after Kilby's discovery was announced, however, more sophisticated developments began to replace it. A planar process, which produced a flat transistor, was the first improvement. That led to a more fully integrated circuit developed by Robert Noyce that eliminated the need for hand wiring. Soon after that, a new company, Intel, produced the first processor that performed the arithmetic and logic functions of several chips. This microprocessor, named the 4004, was called a "computer on a chip." Now, through a process of photoprinting, or combining photographic and engraving methods to etch fine circuits, the process has become even more highly developed.

COMPONENT MANUFACTURING IN THE 1990s

Through the 1970s and 1980s manufacturers continued to design computer components that were smaller, faster, and less expensive than previous models. Computers now have increased memory and speed but their uses do not stop there. To help recover the cost of research and development, manufacturers seek new uses for these microprocessors. We recognize the use of microprocessors in calculators, video games, and home appliances, but they are also found in other everyday consumer products, such as automobiles, fire alarms, cameras, and heating and cooling systems. Manufacturers continue to develop even faster and more powerful superchips.

By the 1980s very large scale integration (VLSI), in which hundreds of thousands of transistors are placed on a single microchip, became commonplace. In fact, the technologies and processes used to make these microscopic integrated circuits are themselves made possible by computers. The components include a variety of microprocessors that provide extended capabilities, such as DRAM (dynamic random-access memory), SRAM (static random-access memory), virtual (or simulated) storage, VHSIC (very high speed integrated circuit), and chips for multitasking and parallel processing that allow computers to perform several tasks at one time.

An example of a future use can be found in the Intelligent Vehicle and Highway Systems (IVHS), which have been targeted as a crucial facet of the National Advisory Committee on Semiconductors' national strategy. These systems are designed to employ microprocessors, low-cost satellite receivers, radar-based collision avoidance systems, and other sensors to improve safety by helping drivers maintain control, providing drivers with on-board mapping ability, and alerting drivers to maintenance problems. The potential sales have begun attracting the attention of some of the largest corporations involved in computer component manufacturing, with a goal for initial systems to be available in 1994 model cars.

The component manufacturing industry has been highly profitable; however, it is also susceptible to the effects of economic swings. An industrywide organization, the Semiconductor Industry Association (SIA), considers the industry to be truly heterogeneous, consisting of a variety of product families. Some of these are growing rapidly and some are in decline. In addition, according to the U.S. Commerce Department, by "1988 the U.S. semiconductor chip companies' share of the world market was 36 percent, down from 63 percent in 1980. For the same period, Japan's share of the world market rose from 25 percent to 53 percent" (Lyons 1990). This shift in the world's purchasing of computer components has had a major influence on U.S. companies.

COMPONENT MANUFACTURING COMPANIES

Some component companies exist only to produce specific computer components; other manufacturers produce components as only one of many product lines. Of the hundreds of companies that produce computer components, four stand out as leaders in the field.

Intel

Intel Corporation is one of the best-known manufacturers of computer components. Besides semiconductors, Intel produces computer peripheral equipment and devices, which can be used with computers to increase their efficiency and range of activities. Dr. Robert Noyce founded the Intel Corporation in 1968 when he left Fairchild Electronics. As a public standalone company, Intel now has 29,000 employees and yearly revenues of $3,126.8 million.

Intel introduced the chips that powered the first IBM personal computers (PCs) and PC clones in 1978. They were known as 8086 or 8088 chips. Next they began to produce some of the industry's most successful microprocessor chips with their 286, 386, and 486. In 1991 came the 486SX, which was designed to bring mainframe power to everyone. Intel also pioneered a marketing approach aimed directly at consumers in an effort to encourage computer manufacturers to buy and use their proprietary, or patented, chips. Other companies, particularly Advanced Micro Devices, have tried to overcome Intel's initiative and garner some of the market by developing a clone of these chips.

Motorola, Inc.

Located in Schaumburg, Illinois, this public standalone company has been in the elec-

tronics business since 1928. It has moved from the production of broadcasting and radio equipment into the production of semiconductors and defense and aerospace electronics. Motorola is ranked number two in the semiconductor and related devices industry.

With 104,000 employees, Motorola produces and sells components worth about $9,620 million per year. The company is particularly known for its 680X0 chip family, which is used in Apple, NeXT Computer, Inc., and Hewlett-Packard computers. In 1991 the company began to ship their newly developed 68040 chip, which had been anxiously awaited by the aforementioned companies. This chip was touted as the cheapest, fastest, and smallest of its type.

Texas Instruments

Texas Instruments, located in Dallas, Texas, was founded in 1938 as a public company. At first, Texas Instruments produced test equipment and military electronics but moved quickly to the manufacture of home electronics and semiconductors. Texas Instruments also produces its own computers. With a gross income of $6,521.9 million per year and 73,854 employees, it is one of the largest manufacturers of semiconductors and related computer components.

When Jack Kilby discovered the basic semiconductor technology in the 1950s, Texas Instruments filed a patent for the process. The company continues to negotiate agreements with companies that use this technology or that develop new chips from the basic work. These agreements, which license other companies, provide a large income for Texas Instruments.

Advanced Micro Devices, Inc.

Founded in 1969, Advanced Micro Devices, Inc., is located in Sunnyvale, California, and is considered to be a growing power in the industry. The company employs 13,000 people and has annual revenues of more than $1,104 million per year. It specializes in complex monolithic integrated circuits.

In March 1991, Advanced Micro Devices began shipping clones of the Intel 386 chip to computer manufacturers. Intel's 5-year monopoly on the most popular PC chip was challenged and the resulting competition within the computer component industry could result in reduced prices and development of new components for consumers.

OTHER COMPONENT MANUFACTURERS

The following four manufacturers are smaller, but represent major growth and innovation in the field. Although they are not yet leaders in the production of computer components, the industry changes rapidly and this information constantly needs to be updated.

Apollo Systems

Apollo Systems Division is a private division of the Hewlett-Packard Company. Located in Chelmsford, Massachusetts, Apollo employs 2,000 and has an annual income of $220 million. Its general mission is the manufacture of computer components and computers. The primary products include electronic computers and components, wide-area networks (WAN), local-area networks (LAN), and airline reservation equipment. Apollo Systems also makes computer graphics workstations.

Beall Technologies

Beall Technologies, located in New Jersey, is a private company founded in 1971. It produces computer peripheral switching, fiber-optic channel extenders, cables, and metering panels. Although relatively small by other computer component manufacturing standards, Beall Technologies has a specific line of products and consistently maintains 50 employees with a gross income of $22 million.

National Semiconductor Corporation

A leading manufacturer of semiconductors, computer peripherals, and other related devices, National Semiconductor Corporation has been in this field since 1959. Located in the Silicon Valley, Santa Clara, California, this company has annual revenues of $1,647.9 million. It employs more than 32,000 people in the production of linear and digital integrated circuits.

Nippon Electric Company

Founded in 1963, Nippon Electric Company America is owned by the Japanese Nippon Electric Corporation. Nippon Electric Company America is one of a growing number of foreign-owned companies that produce computer components. With more than 2,800 employees and yearly revenues of $910 million, it is considered one of the leading producers of computer components. It also produces facsimile, mobile telephones, digital microwaves, and other radio and television broadcasting and communication equipment.

CONCLUSION

One begins to see that in the 1990s, unlike the early years of computers, component manufacturers are highly specialized and industrialized, and constitute a significant part of the production of computers. For the manufacturers of computer components, the future certainly will bring discoveries that allow these manufacturers to produce microchips for faster processing and larger memory capabilities for less money. The results will be significant for society.

Reference
Lyons, D. J. 1990. Failing semiconductor industry bodes poorly for U.S. PC makers. *PC Week* 7(1):127.

For Further Reading
Adams, R. B., and D. Davison. 1989. *Computer basics.* Richmond, Va.: Time-Life Books Inc.

Brandt, R. 1991. Intel: Way out in front, but the footsteps are getting louder. *Business Week*, April 29, pp. 88–89.

Dordick, H. S. 1986. *Understanding modern telecommunications.* New York: McGraw-Hill.

Scharf, P., and J. Chattin-McNichols. 1986. *Understanding the computer age.* Hasbrouck Heights, N.J.: Hayden Book Co.

Schneiderman, R. 1986. *Computers: From Babbage to the fifth generation.* New York: Franklin Watts.

Wedemeyer, D. J. 1986. The new age of telecommunication: Setting the stage for education. *Educational Technology* 26(October):7–13.

Zipper, S. 1991. Automotive electronics. *Electronic News*, April 15, pp. 18, 22.

Lynne Schrum

COMPUTER PERIPHERAL MANUFACTURERS

The companies represented here have been selected from all sizes of firms. Each was chosen primarily on the basis of innovative products or industry leadership. The list is neither exhaustive nor definitive. The products manufactured by these companies include, but are not limited to, the peripheral product groups listed.

The reference number assigned to each product group is used to reference particular manufacturing emphasis given to these products by a particular manufacturer. The appropriate reference number(s) is indicated in the product specialization section for each company. If no specific numbers are given, then the company manufactures a comprehensive line of products that includes most of the product groups.

If the company chosen for this appendix is a subsidiary, then the parent company name is also given, after the slash. In addition to the product information, the listing for each company contains the main office address and phone number, the date of incorporation, the number of employees, and a brief description of the company's business.

PRODUCT GROUPS

Input Devices
1. Digitizers
2. Joysticks
3. Light pens
4. Mice
5. Touch-sensitive entry devices
6. Track balls
7. Other

Output Devices
8. Camera systems
9. Computer output microfilm
10. Cathode-ray tube (CRT) copiers
11. Film recorders
12. Large screen projectors
13. Monitors/displays
14. Plotters
15. Printers
16. Terminals

PERIPHERAL COMPANIES

AST Research
2121 Alton Avenue, Irvine, CA 92714
(714) 863–1333
Incorporated: 1980   Employees: 1,350

AST designs, manufactures, and markets personal computer systems and a broad range of board-level enhancement and connectivity products for business and professional users. They also manufacture board-level enhancement products including expansion, data communications, local area networks, and graphics products.

Product Specialization: 13

Aydin Controls/Aydin Corporation
4545 West Brown Deer Road, Milwaukee, WI 53223
(414) 355–0400
Incorporated: 1967   Employees: 874

Aydin develops and manufactures communications equipment and systems including avionics and data links; computer

equipment and command, control, and communications systems; radars, radar simulation, and electronic warfare equipment. Aydin also designs and installs turnkey communications systems for satellite and troposcatter applications.
Product Specialization: 2, 6, 16

Brother International Corporation-Information Systems Division

35, 9-chome, Horita-dori, Mizuhoku, Nagoya 467, Japan
(052) 824–2511
Incorporated: 1934   Employees: 5,463
This company is engaged in the manufacture and sale of sewing machines, home electric appliances, knitting machines, business machines, machine tools, and electronic organs.
Product Specialization: 15

Calcomp, Inc./Division of Lockheed Corporation

4500 Park Granada Boulevard, Calabasas, CA 91399
(818) 712–2000
Incorporated: 1932   Employees: 82,500
Calcomp's primary businesses embrace research, development, and production of aerospace and defense products and systems. The information systems segment comprises development and marketing of specialized computer software and services and production of computer graphics equipment.
Product Specialization: 1, 4, 13, 14, 15

Commodore Business Machines, USA/Commodore Business Machines, Ltd.

1200 Wilson Drive, West Chester, PA 19380
(215) 431–9100
Incorporated: 1976   Employees: N/A
Commodore is engaged in the manufacture of advanced microcomputer systems, semiconductor components, and consumer electronic products. Research is devoted primarily to the development of new products using solid-state integrated circuitry, computer technology, and consumer electronics.
Product Specialization: 1, 4

Compaq Computer Corporation

20555 SH 249, Houston, TX 77070
(713) 370–0670
Incorporated: 1982   Employees: 9,700
Compaq designs, develops, manufactures, and markets high-performance personal computers, personal computer systems, and related products for business and professional users.
Product Specialization: Comprehensive

Dataproducts Corporation

6200 Canoga Avenue, Woodland Hills, CA 91365
(818) 887–8000
Incorporated: 1962   Employees: 3,550
Dataproducts and its subsidiaries design, develop, manufacture, and market a broad range of data handling and output equipment consisting of printers and associated products, digital communications equipment, and airborne sensors and controllers.
Product Specialization: 15

Digital Equipment Corporation

146 Main Street, Maynard, MA 01754
(508) 493–5111
Incorporated: 1957   Employees: 125,800
Digital Equipment Corporation is a supplier of networked computer systems. It designs, manufactures, sells, and services computers and associated peripheral equipment and related software and supplies. The company's products are used worldwide in a variety of applications and programs.
Product Specialization: Comprehensive

Dotronics, Inc.

160 First Street SE, New Brighton, MN 55112–7894
(612) 633–7025
Incorporated: 1980   Employees: N/A
Dotronics is engaged in the development, manufacture, and marketing of monochrome and cathode-ray tube displays for computer terminals and medical and graphic display applications.
Product Specialization: 13

E. I. Du Pont de Nemours & Company
1007 Market Square, Wilmington, DE 19898
(302) 774–1000
Incorporated: 1915   Employees: 145,787
Du Pont has six principal business segments: industrial products, fibers, polymers, petroleum, coal, and diversified businesses. In its diversified businesses it sells imaging systems, which include chemical and electronic imaging consumable products, equipment and systems for printing, nondestructive testing, engineering reproduction, and specialty imaging.
Product Specialization: 1, 15

EKTRON Applied Imaging/A Kodak Company
343 State Street, Rochester, NY 14650
(716) 724–4000
Incorporated: 1901   Employees: 82,850
EKTRON is engaged primarily in developing, manufacturing, and marketing imaging, information systems, chemicals, and health products. The information systems segment consists of businesses that serve the imaging and information needs of business, industry, and government.
Product Specialization: 1, 11, 14, 15

Electrohome Ltd.
809 Wellington Street, North, Kitchener, Ontario, Canada N2G 4J6
(519) 744–7111
Incorporated: 1933   Employees: 1,666
Electrohome operates in two business segments: All aspects of Canadian radio and TV broadcasting in related fields and equipment, and the international marketing of its commercial electronics group.
Product Specialization: 12

Everex Systems, Inc.
48431 Milmont Drive, Fremont, CA 94538
(415) 498–1111
Incorporated: 1983   Employees: 1,585
Everex develops, manufactures, and markets personal computer systems and related peripheral products.
Product Specialization: 6, 13, 15

General Electric Company
3135 Easton Turnpike, Fairfield, CT 06431
(203) 373–2431
Incorporated: 1892   Employees: 292,200
General Electric is one of the largest and most diversified industrial corporations in the world. Its operations are highly decentralized. The industry segments consist of aerospace, aircraft engines, broadcasting, industrial automation, major appliances, materials power systems, and technical products and services.
Product Specialization: 16

General Parametrics Corporation
7 Morgan Street, Irvine, CA 92718
Incorporated: 1978   Employees: 1,714
This company designs, develops, contracts to produce, and markets microprocessor-controlled paper handling devices for office copiers and computer-controlled printers.
Product Specialization: 11, 13

Gerber Systems Technology, Inc./Gerber Scientific, Inc.
4944 Belmont Avenue, Youngstown, OH 44501
(216) 759–8888
Incorporated: 1948   Employees: 1,365
Gerber is a holding company and through its subsidiaries it designs, develops, manufactures, markets, and services technologically advanced computer-aided design and manufacturing systems to meet the needs of users in a broad range of industries. The company turnkeys interactive graphic production systems and photoplotting equipment that automate the production of artwork.
Product Specialization: 1, 4, 10, 14, 15, 16

Gretag Systems, Inc./CIBA-GEIGY AG
Basel, Switzerland
Incorporated: 1884   Employees: 92,553
Gretag is engaged in the manufacture and sale of pharmaceuticals, dyes and pigments, industrial chemicals, agrochemicals,

photo products, resins, adhesives, and plastic consumer and electronic equipment products.

Product Specialization: 12

Hewlett-Packard Company

3000 Hanover Street, Palo Alto, CA 94304
(415) 857–1501
Incorporated: 1947   Employees: 95,000

Hewlett-Packard designs, manufactures, and services electronic products and systems for measurements and computation. The company's computer systems can be grouped into two major categories: (1) single-user systems such as workstations and personal computers, and (2) associated peripherals and multiple-user systems such as minicomputers.

Product Specialization: Comprehensive

Honeywell, Inc.

Honeywell Plaza, Minneapolis, MN 55408
(612) 870–5200
Incorporated: 1927   Employees: 65,312

Honeywell is an international electronic controls corporation that supplies automation and control systems for homes and buildings, industry, and space and aviation. The company develops and applies advanced technology products and services to conserve energy, improve productivity, provide safe controls for space and aircraft, and meet defense needs.

Product Specialization: 10, 15

Houston Instrument N.V./AMETEK, Inc.

470 Friendship Road, Harrisburg, PA 17105–3608
(717) 564–0100
Incorporated: 1930   Employees: 24,400

The company produces electrical connection, switching, and programming devices, including solderless terminals, splices, multiple connectors, coaxial connectors, packaging and interconnection devices, and programming systems. It also produces other electrical and electronic equipment.

Product Specialization: 1, 14, 15

Howtek, Inc.

21 Park Avenue, Hudson, NH 03051
(603) 882–5200
Incorporated: 1984   Employees: 90

Howtek designs, engineers, develops, and markets color input and output peripherals and systems for the microcomputer market and the graphic arts market.

Product Specialization: 1, 15

International Business Machines Corporation

Armonk, NY 10504
(914) 765–1900
Incorporated: 1911   Employees: 383,220

IBM's operations are primarily in the field of advanced information technology systems, equipment, and services to solve the increasingly complex problems of business, government, science, space exploration, defense, education, medicine, and many other areas of human activity. IBM's products include information processing products and systems, program products, communications systems, and related supplies and services.

Product Specialization: Comprehensive

Kensington Microware Ltd./American Brands, Inc.

32 Loockerman Square, Suite 1–100, Dover, DE 19901–6727
Incorporated: 1986   Employees: 44,900

The company is a small subsidiary of American Brands. The parent company is a holding company whose principal businesses are the sale of insurance, alcohol, and tobacco products.

Product Specialization: 6

Koala Technologies Corporation

1560 Montague Expressway, San Jose, CA 95131
(408) 432–7500
Incorporated: 1986   Employees: 105

Koala operates through two core business groups: product distribution and rotational molding. The product distribution group manufactures, distributes, and markets electrical power conditioning products and peripheral information input products along with the associated software in the microcomputer peripheral market.

Product Specialization: 1

Management Graphics, Inc.
USA/Management Graphics, Inc. (Canada)

1450 Lodestar Road, Downsview, Ontario, Canada M3J 3C1
(416) 638–8877
Incorporated: 1979   Employees: N/A

This company designs, develops, and markets proprietary computer software used for the creation of computer graphic images that are reproduced on 35-mm slides as well as a variety of other output formats. It also operates a service bureau that allows customers to create computer-generated graphics and have such graphics reproduced in other output formats.

Product Specialization: 9, 11

Mitsubishi Electric Sales America,
Inc./Mitsubishi Electric Corporation (Japan)

2040 Ardmore Boulevard, Pittsburgh, PA 15221
(412) 636-3432
Incorporated: 1921   Employees: 89,113

Mitsubishi manufactures electronics and electrical appliances, information processing equipment, and new communications systems incorporating teleconferencing technology, satellite relay, and optical fiber communications. Among the company's main products are space development, communication and information processing, electronic devices, energy, transportation, building equipment and systems, industrial equipment, audiovisual equipment, and home electronics.

Product Specialization: 12, 13, 15

Moniterm Corporation

5740 Green Circle Drive, Minnetonka, MN 55343–9074
(612) 935–4151
Incorporated: 1978   Employees: N/A

Moniterm designs, manufactures, and markets high-performance, high-resolution video display monitors that are used in various computer applications. This includes computer-aided design, manufacturing, and engineering; engineering workstations, office automation systems, computer typesetting, medical scanning systems, and other applications that require precise visual representation.

Product Specialization: 13, 16

National Semiconductor Corporation

2900 Semiconductor Drive, Santa Clara, CA 95052
Incorporated: 1959   Employees: 32,200

This company is engaged in the development, manufacture, and marketing of a broad range of semiconductor products including microprocessors, linear integrated circuits, digital integrated circuits, hybrid circuits and subsystems, electronic packaging, and miscellaneous services and supplies for the semiconductor industry.

Product Specialization: 4

NEC America Inc./NEC Corporation

8 Old Sod Farm Road, Melville, NY 11747
(516) 753–7000
Incorporated: 1899   Employees: 114,600

NEC is a leading global supplier of a broad range of communications systems and equipment; computers and industrial electronic systems; electron devices, including semiconductor devices; and home electronics products.

Product Specialization: 12, 13, 15

Nissei Sangyo America, Ltd./Hitachi Ltd.

6, Kanda-Surugadai 4-chome, Chiyoda-ku, Tokyo 101, Japan
Incorporated: 1910   Employees: 290,811

Nissei Sangyo America is engaged in the production and distribution of consumer products; power systems and equipment; information and communication systems and electronic devices; industrial machinery and plants; and wire, cable, metals, chemicals, and other products.

Product Specialization: 13, 15

Panasonic Technologies, Inc./Matsushita Electric Industrial Company Ltd.

One Panasonic Way, Secaucus, NJ 07094
(201) 348-7000
Incorporated: 1935   Employees: 198,300

Matsushita Electric is Japan's largest manufacturer of consumer electric and electronic products and one of the world's largest in these fields. It is also an expanding presence in nonconsumer product fields such as information/communication equipment and electronic components.

Product Specialization: 7, 8, 11, 12, 13, 15

Peripheral Products Division/Ricoh Company, Ltd.

15-5 Minami-Aoyama 1-chome, Minato-ku, Tokyo 107, Japan
(003) 479-3111
Incorporated: 1936   Employees: N/A

This company manufactures and markets office equipment such as copiers and related supplies, telephone facsimile equipment, data processing systems, printers, duplicators, information storage and retrieval systems, and supplies for all of these types of equipment and other products. It is heavily involved in research and development of, for example, new microchips and other technological products.

Product Specialization: 15

Princeton Graphics Systems/World Wide Technology, Inc.

Suite 120, Fidelity Court, 259 Radnor-Chester Road, Radnor, PA 19087
(215) 964-0652
Incorporated: 1987   Employees: 345

This company's businesses operate in the field of computer communications. Activities include the manufacture and sale of intelligent computer add-on printed circuit boards, computer monitors, application soft-

ware, and the development of multiuser operating software.

Product Specialization: 13

Scan-Graphics, Inc.

700 Abbott Drive, Broomall, PA 19008-4373
(215) 328-1040
Incorporated: 1985   Employees: 33

Scan-Graphics designs, manufactures, and markets a full line of front-end imaging equipment and software products that are used in the scanning and conversion of hard copy document and microfilm images to a computer database. The product line includes large format document scanners with a wide range of scan-serve products that operate and control scanners.

Product Specialization: 1

Science Accessories Corporation

200 Watson Boulevard, Stratford, CT 06497
(203) 386-9978
Incorporated: 1971   Employees: 35

This company develops, manufactures, and markets sonic digitizers, which use the speed of sound to measure distance and determine coordinates; these measurements are then fed to a host computer.

Product Specialization: 1

Sharp Electronics Corporation/Sharp Corporation

Sharp Plaza, Mahwah, NJ 07430-2135
(201) 529-8200
Incorporated: 1935   Employees: 32,298

Sharp manufactures and sells a wide variety of electronic products including television sets and equipment, audio and video equipment, home appliances and apparatus, office and industrial equipment, and electronic components.

Product Specialization: 1, 12, 13, 15

Sony Corporation of America/Sony Corporation

9 West 57th Street, New York, NY 10019
(212) 371-5800
Incorporated: 1946   Employees: 95,600

Sony is engaged in the development, manufacture, and sale of various kinds of electronic equipment, instruments, and devices. Sony emphasizes research and development activities and the manufacture of innovative products. Sony's principal manufacturing facilities are located in Japan, the United States, Europe, and Asia, and its products are marketed by sales subsidiaries and unaffiliated local distributors throughout the world.

Product Specialization: 8, 13

Summagraphics Corporation
60 Silvermine Road, Seymour, CT 06483
(203) 881–5400
Incorporated: 1972   Employees: N/A
Summagraphics is engaged in the design, manufacture, and marketing of computer graphic digitizing tablets.

Product Specialization: 1

Sun Microsystems, Inc.
2550 Garcia Avenue, Mountain View, CA 94043
(415) 960–1300
Incorporated: 1982   Employees: 7,090
Sun is a supplier of network-based distributed computing systems, including workstations, servers, the UNIX operating system, and productivity software, all using industry standards and an open systems strategy.

Product Specialization: Comprehensive

Systonetics, Inc.
1561 East Orangethorpe Avenue, Suite 200, Fullerton, CA 92631
(714) 680–0910
Incorporated: 1969   Employees: 22
Systonetics's principal business is the sale of interactive project management computer software and services for use on large projects.

Product Specialization: 14, 15

Tektronix, Inc.
14150 SW Karl Braun Drive, Beaverton, OR 97077
(503) 627–7111
Incorporated: 1946   Employees: 15,708
Tektronix's products cover a wide range of electronic instrumentation. They include test and measurement instruments, graphic display and design devices and systems, and communications instruments and equipment. The design automation and information display products cover a broad range of output devices and associated software, some of which use artificial intelligence.

Product Specialization: 1, 15, 16

Toshiba Corporation
1-1 shibaura 1-chome, Minato-Ku, Tokyo 105, Japan
Incorporated: 1875   Employees: 125,000
Toshiba is a broad-based producer of commercial and consumer electronics that it distributes and sells in a worldwide market. Major business lines and products include information systems, telecommunication systems, medical systems, semiconductors, electron tubes and other electronic devices, nuclear power plants, industrial electrical devices, elevators, escalators, consumer electronics, and household appliances.

Product Specialization: 8

Versatec, Inc./Xerox Corporation
800 Long Ridge Road, Stamford, CT 06904
(203) 968–3000
Incorporated: 1906   Employees: 111,400
Xerox is a multinational company in the document processing and insurance and other financial services businesses. The document processing activities encompass developing, manufacturing, marketing, servicing, and financing of a broad range of document products designed to improve office productivity. These include copiers, electronic printers, workstations, networks, and other related products.

Product Specialization: 14, 15

Wang Laboratories, Inc.
One Industrial Avenue, Lowell, MA 01851
(508) 459–5000
Incorporated: 1955   Employees: 26,800

Wang designs and markets computer systems and provides related products and services. These products are used primarily for data and text processing functions. The company's products and services are designed to permit the effective management of operations and to facilitate communication.

Product Specialization: 16

W. L. Lomerson

INTERACTIVE VIDEO MANUFACTURERS

Following are some of the major companies presently producing interactive video components. Because of the volatile nature of the technology market, this listing can by no means be considered comprehensive.

NEC CORPORATION

NEC Corporation was incorporated in Japan in 1899 under the name Nippon Electric Company, Limited, and changed to the current name in 1983. Originally concentrating on radio communications and home electronics, the company entered the computer market in 1954.

NEC established its first overseas manufacturing subsidiary in 1968 in Mexico, followed in subsequent years by subsidiaries in Australia, Brazil, Iran, Ireland, Korea, Malaysia, Singapore, Taiwan, the United Kingdom, and the United States. The company presently has a total of seventy-three consolidated subsidiaries, with fifty-six in Japan and seventeen in other countries. NEC operates eight major plants in the Tokyo vicinity, plus subsidiary plants and affiliates throughout the rest of Japan and in other parts of the world. The company has approximately 115,000 employees nationwide.

Primary products of NEC Corporation are mainframe and small business computers, digital and electronic switching systems, industrial transmission systems, semiconductor devices, and home electronics products. With total instructional systems revenues in 1990 of approximately $8,230,500, NEC ranks number five among global computer marketers. Its major competitor is International Business Machines Corporation (IBM), whose aggressive marketing and compatibility options with Hitachi and Fujitsu systems have moved that company into first place among instructional systems suppliers.

The NEC Japan home office is at the NEC Building, 7–1 Shiba 5-chome, Minato-ku, Tokyo 108–01, Japan. Telephone: (03) 454–1111. Telex: NECTOK J22686. Fax: (03) 798–1510/1519. NEC maintains fifty-nine offices in the United States, with headquarters at NEC America, Inc., 8 Old Sod Farm Road, Melville, NY 11747. Telephone: (516) 753–7000.

HITACHI, LTD.

Hitachi, Ltd., founded in Japan in 1910, was incorporated in 1920. In recent ventures the company has joined with Electronic Data Systems Corporation to form Hitachi Data Systems Corporation, and plans to distribute mainframe and peripheral equipment through National Advanced Systems.

The company has a total of fifty-nine consolidated subsidiaries. This includes eighteen overseas offices located in Los Angeles, Washington D.C., Buenos Aires, Caracas, Mexico City, Sao Paulo, Brussels, Moscow, Johannesburg, Kuwait, Tehran, Bangkok, Beijing, Dalian, Guangzhou, Jakarta, Kuala Lumpur, New Delhi, Seoul, Shanghai, and Taipei. Hitachi has approximately 290,811 employees nationwide.

Hitachi produces and distributes mainframe computers, microcomputers, minicomputers, consumer products, power systems and equipment, information and communications systems, electronic devices, industrial machinery, plus wire, cable, metals, software, and other peripherals. Total instructional systems revenues in 1990 totaled approximately $6,273,700, placing the company in sixth place among instructional systems computing vendors. Hitachi's major rival for the global market is Fujitsu Ltd.

Hitachi's principal office is located at

6, Kanda-Surugadai 4-chome, Chiyoda-ku, Tokyo 101, Japan. Telephone: (81-3) 253-2186.

FUJITSU LTD.

Fujitsu was established in Japan on June 10, 1935, when it took over the manufacture of telephone sets, telephone exchange equipment, and related equipment from Fuji Electric Company, Ltd. In 1972 the company acquired a 30 percent interest in Amdahl Corporation, then increased the interest to 49.5 percent in March of 1984.

The company has a total of ninety-eight consolidated subsidiaries, of which sixty-seven are domestic and thirty-one are overseas operations. Manufacturing plants are located in eleven cities in Japan, and there is one systems laboratory in Tokyo. Overseas offices are in Algiers, Amman, Bangkok, Beijing, Bogota, Hawaii, Jakarta, Kuala Lumpur, London, Munich, New Delhi, New York, Paris, Shanghai, and Taipei. The total number of employees nationwide is approximately 104,503.

Fujitsu's major strength is in the manufacture of mainframe computers, but the company also produces data processing systems, telecommunications systems and equipment, semiconductors, and other advanced electronic components. Among instructional systems dealers, Fujitsu ranks fourth, with total instructional systems revenues of $8,740,000 in 1990. Fujitsu's major competitor for the international market is IBM.

The company's main office is located at 6-1, Marunouchi, 1-chome, Chiyoda-ku, Tokyo, 100, Japan. Telephone: 03–216–3211. Telex: J22833. The office in the United States is located at 680 Fifth Avenue, New York, NY 10019. Telephone: (212) 265–5360. Telex: 234969. Fax: (212) 541-9071.

PHILIPS INDUSTRIES

N. V. Philips Gloellampenfabrieken was incorporated in The Netherlands on August 29, 1912, as successor to Philips & Company, which was founded in 1891 as an incandescent lamp factory. Through acquisitions and mergers, Philips has grown to a widely diversified multinational group of companies engaged primarily in manufacture and distribution of electrical and electronic products, systems, and equipment.

Five product sectors constitute the major product activities of the company: (1) lighting, (2) consumer products, (3) professional products and systems, (4) components, and (5) miscellaneous products, which includes a variety of activities not closely related to any of the other product sectors, most of which are produced in the United States and France.

Philips in 1989 made a major breakthrough in the field of compact-disk interactive with a system combining sound, images, data, and text on a compact disk and information in a dialog with the user. A leading market for this product is being found in automobile service centers to assist with repairs.

The company has subsidiaries in eighteen countries of Europe, twelve countries of Latin America, eleven countries of Africa, fifteen countries of Asia, and in the United States, Canada, Australia, and New Zealand. The total number of employees in all of these subsidiaries is approximately 304,800.

With total revenues of $2,601,600 in 1990, Philips ranks eighteenth among instructional systems producers.

The main office is located at Groenewoudseweg 1, 5621 BA Eindhoven, The Netherlands. Telephone: (31-40) 791111.

SONY CORPORATION

Incorporated in Japan in May 1946 as Tokyo Telecommunications Engineering Corporation (Tokyo Tsushin Kogyo Kabushiki Kaisha), the name Sony Corporation was adopted in January 1958.

Sony is engaged in the development, manufacture, and sale of audio and video equipment and other products used in consumer electronics. The company classifies its products in five groups: (1) video equipment, (2) audio equipment, (3) televisions, (4) other products (which include semiconductors), and (5) record business and movie business. Sony has been marketing optical videodisc players to customers since 1981, and began in 1987 to market the multidisc player, which plays compact disks (CDs), CD-videos, and laser disks.

Sony has forty-three principal subsidiaries and affiliates in Japan, seven in the United States, and thirty-four distributed among Canada, Panama, Brazil, Germany, United Kingdom, France, Switzerland, The Netherlands, Belgium, Denmark, Austria, Italy, Spain, Saudi Arabia, Hong Kong, Singapore, Malaysia, Thailand, Korea, Taiwan, and Australia.

Sony employs approximately 95,600 workers nationwide. Its main office is located at 7-35 Kitashinagawa 6-chome Shinagawa-ku, Tokyo 141, Japan. Telephone: (03) 448–2111. Telex: 22262 (SONYCORP J22262). Fax: (03) 448–2244. Other offices are located at 9 West 57th Street, New York, NY 10019, telephone: (212) 371-5800, and at Sony House, South Street, Staines, Middlesex, TW18 4PF, United Kingdom, telephone: 0784-467000.

PIONEER ELECTRONIC CORPORATION (PIONEER KABUSHIKI KAISHA)

Established in 1938 and incorporated in 1947 as the Fukuin Electric Works Ltd., Pioneer Electronic Corporation adopted its current name in 1961.

Pioneer manufactures and markets electronic products classified into four groups: (1) audio products such as stereo component systems; (2) video products comprising laser vision (LV) players, CD/LV compatible players, disks, personal computers; (3) car electronics products; and (4) other products consisting of cable television equipment, telephone answering devices, and so on.

The company maintains seventeen plants in Japan, three in the United States, and one each in Belgium, Spain, and France. In addition, eight principal subsidiaries are located in Japan, eleven in North America, and fifteen in other parts of the world.

Pioneer has 3,260 employees and maintains a head office at 2-5 Kasumigaseki 3-chome, Chiyoda-ku, Tokyo 100, Japan. Telephone: (03) 593-6710. Telex: 222-2457 PRIMA J.

TOSHIBA

Originated as The Group in 1875 in Tokyo, the company was incorporated in 1904 under the name Shibaura Engineering Works. Through merger with Hakunetsu-sha (established 1890), Tokyo Shibaura Electric Company, Ltd., evolved in 1939. The original focus of the company was on incandescent lamps.

Toshiba's four major product areas are (1) information/communication systems, (2) electronic devices, (3) heavy electrical apparatus, and (4) consumer products, which include audio and video products.

The company has thirty-four principal subsidiaries and affiliates in Japan, five in North America, seven in Latin America, eighteen in Europe, eleven in Asia, two in Australia, and ten overseas affiliates.

Toshiba employs approximately 125,000 workers nationwide. With total instructional system revenues of $3,441,300, the company ranks eleventh among other instructional systems producers.

Headquarters for Toshiba are located at 1-1 Shibaura 1-Chome, Minato-Ku, Tokyo 105, Japan. Telex: J22587 TOSHIBA.

MATSUSHITA ELECTRIC INDUSTRIAL COMPANY, LTD.

Matsushita was incorporated in 1935 as the successor to an unincorporated enterprise founded in 1918 by Mr. Konosuke Matsushita, whose philosophy was to provide consumer goods at reasonable price. Growth in recent years is attributed to increased production of electronics and precision technology, notably video cassette recorder (VCR) products. Matsushita's goal is to become the world's leader in electronics manufacturing.

Seven major products areas are identified: (1) information/communication, such as facsimile machines, telephones, and word processors; (2) factory automation consisting of robot machinery; (3) semiconductors; (4) new audiovisual products, including television monitors, VCRs, and optical fiber transmissions; (5) automotive electronics; (6) housing-related products; and (7) integrated air-conditioning systems.

Matsushita maintains 343 separate factories, located mainly in Japan, Asia, North America, South America, and Europe. The company employs approximately 198,299 workers nationwide.

The company's executive office is located at 1006 Oaza Kadoma, Kadoma City, Osaka, Japan. Its U.S. subsidiary office is at One Panasonic Way, Secaucus, NJ 07094. Telephone: (201) 348-7000.

Joanne Lambert

MAINFRAME COMPUTER MANUFACTURERS

INTERNATIONAL BUSINESS MACHINES CORPORATION (IBM)

History
In 1911, three companies, the Computing Scale Company, the International Time Recording Company, and Bundy Manufacturing, consolidated to incorporate as the Computing-Tabulating-Recording Company. In 1924, this company merged with the International Business Machines Corporation and assumed its name.

IBM helped pioneer the information processing industry as it evolved from the electromechanical punched-card machines and vacuum tube calculators of the early days to today's powerful electronic computers that execute instructions in billionths of a second. In 1952, IBM introduced its first production computer designed for scientific calculations.

Throughout the years, IBM has often joined with other companies whose strengths complement and extend its own. To date, IBM has relationships with more than 10,000 joint marketers, system integrators, and business partners to support their System/400 and PS/2 customers. Through 1989, IBM had established more than 75 equity alliances with partners ranging from companies such as Sears and Siemens to small entrepreneurial software ventures.

Recent announcements include a Direct Access Storage Device; a 4-million-bit memory chip; a joint agreement with Siemens AG to develop 64-million-bit dynamic random-access memory (DRAM) chips; a partnership with Supercomputer Systems for the accelerated development of parallel supercomputers; and the formation of ARDIS, a new company launched to provide the first commercially available nationwide advanced radio data information service.

Current Status
Size. IBM's manufacturing and development facilities in the United States had a combined floor space of 68.2 million square feet in 1989. Similar facilities in 16 other countries totaled 27.1 million square feet. An additional 1 million square feet are scheduled for completion in 1990. Plants and laboratories are located in Arizona, California, Colorado, Florida, Kentucky, Maryland, Minnesota, New Jersey, New York (seven), North Carolina (two), Texas, Vermont, and Virginia.

Location. Corporate headquarters are located in Armonk, New York 10504. Telephone: (914) 765-1900.

Gross income. Total sales for 1989 were $62.710 billion.

Number of employees. As of December 31, 1989, there were 383,220 employees.

General Mission and Primary Products
IBM's operations are mainly in the field of advanced information technology systems, equipment, and services. Products include information processing products and systems, software, communications systems, workstations, typewriters, and related supplies and services.

CONTROL DATA CORPORATION

History
Control Data was organized in 1957 in Minnesota. In 1968 it combined with Commer-

cial Credit Company, originally incorporated in 1912, to form a Delaware corporation. Credit Commercial Company changed its name to Control Data Corporation. However, Commercial Credit still operates as a wholly owned unconsolidated subsidiary of Control Data.

Prior to 1968, significant acquisitions included Bendix Computer, Cedar Engineering, and Autocon Industries. Since 1968, Control Data has acquired full or part ownership in such companies as American Business Systems, Marshall Communications, Precision Data Card, Ticketron Inc., Great Western Loan and Trust Company, International Finance Corp., Electronic Realty Associates Inc., United School Services of America, and Radio/TV Reports, Inc.

In 1972, a joint venture agreement with National Cash Register Co. formed Computer Peripherals. In 1975, an agreement with Honeywell Inc. formed Magnetic Peripherals.

Current Status

Size. As of March 1990, principal production and office facilities were located in Minnesota, California, Ohio, Maryland, New York, Illinois, Canada, Germany, France, and England. Worldwide, the companies' facilities had a combined floor space of over 11 million square feet, of which 3.3 million represented manufacturing and warehousing.

Location. Corporate offices are located at 8100 34th Avenue South, Minneapolis, Minnesota 55440. Telephone: (612) 853-8100.

Gross income. Total sales for 1989 were $2.934 billion.

Number of employees. As of December 31, 1989, there were 18,000 employees.

General Mission and Primary Products

Control Data Corporation serves specialized computer and information markets in four major product service areas: computer systems and services, data storage products, government systems, and information services.

DATA GENERAL CORPORATION

History

Data General incorporated in Delaware in 1968. Since 1976, acquisitions include WSA Systems and Services, Digital Computer Controls, Nippon Mine-Computer Corp., General Risk Insurance Company, and Dama Technologies Corp.

In 1989, Data General formed a joint venture with three international partners to market computers in the Soviet Union. This represented the first venture that combined a Soviet software firm, a major U.S. computer supplier, and a European industrial firm to bring computer and industrial automation technology to commerce and industry in the Soviet Union.

Current Status

Size. Data General has more than 300 sales and service locations in 60 countries. Administrative, research and development, and manufacturing facilities are housed in approximately 1.3 million square feet.

Location. Corporate offices are located at 4400 Computer Drive, Westboro, Massachusetts 01580. Telephone: (503) 366-8911.

Gross income. Total sales for 1989 were $1.313 billion.

Number of employees. As of September 30, 1989, there were 13,740 employees.

General Mission and Primary Products

Data General Corporation is engaged in the design, manufacture, and sale of general-purpose computer and communication systems. It also provides peripheral equipment, software, and related products and services, including training and maintenance.

HONEYWELL INCORPORATED

History

The Minneapolis Heat Regulator Company and the Honeywell Heating Specialties Company incorporated in 1927 in Delaware as Minneapolis-Honeywell Regulator Company. The present name was adopted in 1964.

Its most recent acquisitions include Megadyne Corp., Action Communications, Disc Instruments, Sharecom Houston, Krayden Electronics, Sperry Aerospace Group, and companies in France, Switzerland, Germany, and the United Kingdom.

In 1983, the company entered into a joint venture agreement with a Swedish telecommunications firm, L.M. Ericsson, to design, develop, and market voice and data communications products. In 1986, Honeywell and NEC Corporation established a joint venture to market the NEC Super Computer in the United States and Canada.

Current Status

Size. Honeywell and its subsidiaries operate facilities of approximately 25.6 million square feet for use as production, office, and warehouse space. Facilities are maintained in eighteen states and twenty-nine countries.

Location. Corporate offices are located at Honeywell Plaza, Minneapolis, Minnesota 55408. Telephone: (612) 870-5200.

Gross income. Total sales for 1989 were $6.058 billion.

Number of employees. As of December 31, 1989, there were 65,312 employees.

General Mission and Primary Products

Honeywell is an international electronic controls corporation that supplies automation and controls systems for homes and buildings, industry, and space and aviation.

UNISYS CORPORATION

History

Unisys incorporated in 1984 in Delaware as a successor to Burroughs Corporation. Burroughs incorporated in 1905 as Burroughs Adding Machine Company, a successor to American Arithometer Company, which had incorporated in Missouri in 1886. The present name was adopted in 1986.

Major acquisitions since 1970 include Graphic Sciences, Redactron, Systems Research Inc., Memorex, and Sperry Corporation.

In 1987, Unisys and the Australian government reached an agreement for a partnership to perform research and development in advanced networking and fourth-generation-language technologies.

In 1988, Unisys announced it was working with American Telephone and Telegraph to assist in enhancing the functionality of the open Applications Operating Environment for UNIX System V. The company also signed a technology agreement with Sun Microsystems to license Sun's SPARC microprocessor design as a basis for future high-performance UNIX systems.

Current Status

Size. As of December 31, 1989, Unisys had 112 major facilities in the United States with a combined floor space of approximately 19.2 million square feet. About 90 percent of this space is located in California, Illinois, Michigan, Minnesota, New Jersey, Pennsylvania, Utah, and Virginia.

Outside of the United States, there were forty-eight major facilities with a combined total of approximately 5.2 million square feet. Most of this space was located in Australia, Brazil, Canada, France, Germany, Italy, Mexico, the Netherlands, Sweden, Switzerland, and the United Kingdom.

Location. General offices: P.O. Box 500, Blue Bell, Pennsylvania 19424-0001. Telephone: (215) 986-5777.

Gross income. Total sales for 1989 were $10.096 billion.

Number of employees. As of December 31, 1989, there were 82,300 employees.

General Mission and Primary Products

Unisys designs, manufactures, markets, and supports commercial, defense, and other information processing equipment and related software. Principal information systems products and services include mainframes and peripherals, workstations, software and related services, equipment maintenance, and custom products and services.

Beverly Abbey

MICROCOMPUTER AND MINICOMPUTER MANUFACTURERS

Ten years ago, it was reasonably possible to observe the distinctions among the various sizes of computers and the companies that designed and manufactured them. Now, however, there are numerous companies (nine of which will be discussed) that manufacture and produce computers of various types. The focus of the companies in this section is on microcomputers and minicomputers. A microcomputer (also called personal computer or PC) is a computer whose central processing unit is a microprocessor or microchip. The microcomputer is generally considered to be a low-cost machine intended for personal and office use. The microcomputer has grown bigger in power and smaller in size at the same time. Generally computers sold over the counter in computer stores and department stores are microcomputers. The minicomputer is not built around a microprocessor and is considered to be the computer intermediate between microcomputers and mainframes in cost and computing power.

APPLE COMPUTER, INC.

Apple Computer, Inc. was founded in 1976 in a Santa Clara Valley garage and has since expanded to become a multibillion-dollar company. It is a Fortune 200 company that does business in more than 120 countries. At the end of the 1990 fiscal year, Apple reported eight elected officers and thirty-six appointed officers. These officers represent Apple Corporate, Manufacturing and Research and Development, Apple USA, Apple Pacific, Apple Europe, and Claris Corporation. Net sales for the 1990 fiscal year were $5,284,013,000.

The general mission of Apple Computer, Inc. is to develop, manufacture, and market personal computer systems for business, education, government, and the home. Apple offers an extensive line of products that include personal computers, communications products, peripherals, and system software.

For more information, contact Apple Computer, Inc., 20525 Mariani Avenue, Cupertino, CA 95014. Telephone: (408) 996-1010.

COMMODORE INTERNATIONAL LIMITED

Commodore International Limited was founded in 1958 in Toronto, Canada, by Jack Tramiel. At the end of the 1990 fiscal year, Commodore reported net sales of $1.5 million. The general mission of Commodore International Limited is the independent manufacturing and marketing of personal computers. Commodore offers an extensive line of MS-DOS PC compatibles, the classic C64 computer, and the Amiga multimedia computer.

For more information, contact Commodore International Limited, 1200 Wilson Drive, West Chester, PA 19280. Telephone: (215) 431-9100.

COMPAQ COMPUTER CORPORATION

Compaq Computer Corporation was founded in 1981 in Houston, Texas. At the end of the 1989 fiscal year, Compaq reported net sales of $2.9 billion and a net income of $333 million. The general mission of Compaq is to make transportable IBM PC clones. It has 9,500 employees worldwide. Compaq offers an extensive line of desktop, portable, and laptop personal computers.

For more information, contact Compaq Computer Corporation, 20555 State Hwy 249, Houston, TX 77070. Telephone: (800) 231-0900, (713) 370-0670.

DELL COMPUTER CORPORATION

Dell Computer Corporation was founded as PC's Limited in May 1984. The company uses a direct-to-the-customer marketing approach. Dell has more than 1,900 employees worldwide, with 1,400 located in Austin, Texas. At the end of the 1990 fiscal year Dell reported a net income of $27.2 million and $546.2 million in sales.

The general mission of Dell Computer Corporation is to manufacture and market personal computer products. The primary competitors of Dell Computer are AST, Compaq, and IBM.

For more information, contact Dell Computer Corporation, 9505 Arboretum Blvd., Austin, TX 78759-7299. Telephone: (800) 426-5150.

DIGITAL EQUIPMENT CORPORATION

Digital Equipment Corporation (DEC) was founded in 1957 in Maynard, Massachusetts, and has since expanded to become a multi-billion-dollar company. At the end of the 1990 fiscal year, DEC reported a net income of $74,393,000.

The general mission of DEC is to develop, manufacture, and market personal computer systems. DEC offers an extensive line of products, which include network computer systems, networking products, minicomputer systems, software and services, high-end personal computers, communications products, peripherals, system software, and mainframe computers. The primary competitor of DEC is IBM.

For more information, contact Digital

Equipment Corporation, 146 Main Street, Maynard, MA 01754-2571. Telephone: (508) 493-5111.

KAYPRO

Kaypro was founded in 1953 as Non-Linear Systems Inc., and manufactured and sold electronic instruments for aerospace, defense, and industrial applications. In 1981, the company began engineering and manufacturing portable microcomputer systems for business and professional use and became Kaypro. In June 1982, Kaypro shipped their first microcomputer. In 1988 Kaypro headquarters was located near San Diego, California, with 277 full-time employees and an $8.1-million gross profit. In 1990, Kaypro declared bankruptcy.

The general mission of Kaypro was to market general-purpose microcomputers and peripherals to retail dealers and value-added resellers. The primary products for Kaypro included general-purpose microcomputers (IBM XT and AT compatibles). The primary competitors for Kaypro were Apple, Dell Corporation, Epson, Tandy, and IBM.

For more information, contact Kaypro, 533 Stevens Avenue, Solana Beach, CA 92075. Telephone: (619) 481-4300.

SUN MICROSYSTEMS INC.

Sun Microsystems was founded in 1982 in Mountain View, California. At the end of the 1990 fiscal year, Sun reported a net income of $111,179,000.

Sun designs, manufactures, markets, and services general-purpose computing systems based on networked workstations and servers.

For more information, contact Sun Microsystems Inc., 2550 Garcia Av., PAL1-510, Mountain View, CA 94043. Telephone: (415) 960-1300.

TANDY CORPORATION

Tandy Corporation was founded in the early 1900s as a family leather business. Tandy purchased Radio Shack in 1963 and has since expanded to become a multibillion-dollar company. It is a Fortune 500 company that does business worldwide. At the end of the 1990 fiscal year, Tandy reported net sales of $4.5 billion. Tandy Corporation has more than 7,000 electronics retailer stores and twenty-nine manufacturing operations in the United States and overseas. Net sales for the 1990 fiscal year were $4.5 billion and net income was $290,347,000.

The general mission of Tandy Corporation is to develop, manufacture, and retail a wide range of consumer electronics, including audio, video, telephony, personal computer, and magnetic media technologies.

For more information, contact Tandy Corporation, 700 One Tandy Center, Fort Worth, TX 76102. Telephone: (817) 390-3011.

ZENITH DATA SYSTEMS

Zenith Data Systems was founded in 1979 by Zenith Electronics Corporation and is a multibillion-dollar company. Net sales for the 1990 fiscal year were $1.2 billion.

The general mission of Zenith Data Systems is to manufacture and market portable laptop and desktop file-server personal computers for single and multiuser applications. Zenith offers an extensive line of products, which include personal computers, communications products, peripherals, and system software.

For more information, contact Zenith Data Systems, 1000 Milwaukee Avenue, Glenview, IL 60025. Telephone: (708) 808-5000.

Kathlyn Y. Canaday

SUPERCOMPUTER MANUFACTURERS

Mainframe computers were the most readily available computer system throughout the 1960s and provided business and industry with the necessary power for much of their data processing and scientific applications needs. During this time there was very little difference in computer system configuration and design. The mainframe was built around a chassis, or "main frame," and cost from a few hundred thousand to one or two million dollars. The mainframe was, and still is today, the primary "large" computer system and is classified as a general-purpose computer, that is, one that serves multiple users at the same time for a variety of tasks.

In the mid-1970s, the need for computing power on the extreme ends of the computing system spectrum became more acute, and luckily, with this need came the necessary new hardware developments. Circuit miniaturization and creation of the microprocessor led to the development of the microcomputer system of the late 1970s and 1980s. The microcomputer system, some costing less than one thousand dollars, is unique in that its central processing unit is a single computer on a chip. The push toward large-scale integration, implementation of multiprocessors, and availability of high-capacity storage devices also allowed for the development of another class of computers —the supercomputer.

Supercomputers are generally characterized as being the fastest, most powerful, and most expensive computers today. The supercomputer, like the mainframe, is a general-purpose computer, but one designed to solve problems that require very high speed computation and often referred to as a "number cruncher." Supercomputers are utilized to solve a variety of complex problems in government, business, and industry. The federal government is one of the largest owners of supercomputers where they assist in such tasks as defense operations, internal revenue data processing, and space exploration. Because of the supercomputer's importance for use in weapons design, the U.S. government has forbidden their sale to Communist countries. Although the number of supercomputers is measured only in the hundreds, their importance in the computing industry cannot be overlooked.

Supercomputers often build up so

much internal heat that special cooling facilities are required. Some supercomputers are air cooled, while many require circulating fluid to cool the circuitry. A supercomputer may use primary memory measured in gigabytes, or billions of bytes of data, whereas the standard large mainframe system often has millions of bytes of storage. Mainframe computers most often have a word length of 32 bits, whereas supercomputers use word lengths of 64 bits or more. Speed of execution is measured in either megaflops or gigaflops. A megaflop is one million instructions per second; a gigaflop is one billion instructions per second. Projections of performance of one trillion operations per second, or teraflop, by 1995 have been made.

Supercomputers attain high performance by distributing tasks among specialized system units for speed and economic functioning. This is usually achieved by assigning tasks such as input/output and numerical operations to input/output ports and vector processors. Having multiple operations occurring at the same time is a key to supercomputer functionality.

Supercomputers generally cost in the multimillion dollar range. A smaller class of supercomputers, the minisupercomputer, provides high-speed processing at a lower cost. Although minisupercomputers will handle the same word sizes as the supercomputers and will run many of the supercomputer applications, their speed is not as great. These minisupercomputers are considered to be somewhere between the supercomputer and mainframe computer systems. Just as the minicomputer had significant impact on the mainframe industry in the 1960s, today the minisupercomputer is providing high-performance computing power to a much broader range of customers.

The following sections provide further information on supercomputers and minisupercomputers and the companies that manufacture them. Cray Research, ETA Systems, Fujitsu, Hitachi, IBM, and NEC are companies supplying supercomputers. Alliant Computer Systems, Convex Computer Corporation, and Scientific Computer Systems offer minisupercomputers.

CRAY RESEARCH, INCORPORATED

Seymour CRAY is considered by most to be the innovator most responsible for the supercomputer industry. Cray first worked for Control Data Corporation, where he helped invent computers that were at that time called supercomputers. In 1972 he left Control Data to form Cray Research in Minneapolis, Minnesota. By 1976, Cray Research delivered the first in a series of Cray supercomputers, the CRAY-1. This system computed at 160 megaflops and cost approximately $7 million. A total of 63 CRAY-1 systems were installed following its introduction. Although it is no longer being manufactured, and in fact Seymour Cray is no longer with the company he founded, it still is widely used and is active in the resale market.

The CRAY-2 (Figure 1) was introduced in 1985 with a 4.2-nanosecond clock time, compared with 12.5 nanoseconds for the CRAY-1, and with 256 times the memory capacity. The CRAY-2 requires immersion cooling in inert fluorocarbon liquid. Although providing significantly more power, the CRAY-2 price was typically in the $15 million range.

The CRAY X-MP was introduced in 1982 as a significantly different option to the CRAY-1 and CRAY-2. This system was the first supercomputer that offered multiprocessing. Now, the newest addition to the CRAY line, the CRAY Y-MP (Figure 2) provides for a faster clock than the X-MP and features a larger number of processors.

FIGURE 1. The CRAY-2 supercomputer system.

FIGURE 2. The CRAY Y-MP supercomputer system. *Photo: Paul Shambroom.*

ETA SYSTEMS, INCORPORATED

ETA Systems was created by Control Data Corporation and is responsible for the development and production of the ETA-10 supercomputer. It also supports the existing installations of the Cyber 205 once sold by Control Data. ETA Systems is headquartered in St. Paul, Minnesota, and is owned largely by Control Data Corporation.

The ETA-10 is a multiprocessor machine with memory expansion to 256 million words. A potential performance level of 10 gigaflops is claimed. Although operation at normal room temperature is possible, maximum performance requires immersion in liquid nitrogen at a temperature about −175°C.

The Cyber 205 was one of the first supercomputers utilizing LSI MOS technology. The Cyber was a refitting of the Control Data STAR-100.

FUJITSU

Fujitsu leads in market share in computer sales in Japan where it uses the brand name Facom. In the United States and Europe, supercomputers manufactured by Fujitsu are marketed by Amdahl. Amdahl Corporation is based in Sunnyvale, California, and is known for its production and sales of IBM-compatible mainframes. Supercomputers available include the Amdahl 500, 1100, 1200, and 1400. The Amdahl is a vector

processing machine cooled by chilled air with peak processing speeds over 1 gigaflop for the top-of-the-line machine.

HITACHI, LIMITED

National Advanced Systems (NAS) of San Jose, California, is the U.S. distributor of Hitachi's supercomputer system. Hitachi S-810 and S-810 model systems have a peak performance of 630 megaflops. Chilled air cools the machine, which is described as an array processing system.

INTERNATIONAL BUSINESS MACHINES CORPORATION

The IBM 3090 supercomputer (Figure 3), first shipped in 1985, was built by taking a basic mainframe computer system and adding vector processors. The 3090 system uses multiple processors to increase speed and performance. One, two, four, or six processors may be added to the system configuration.

The new IBM ES/9000 family (Figure 4) includes an extremely wide range of air-cooled and water-cooled models. Prices range from less than one hundred thousand to over twenty million dollars. The water-cooled models are the more expensive. The 9000 series system can outperform the earlier 3090 series by an order of 2.7 times. Improvements include the use of fiberoptic

FIGURE 3. The IBM 3090, model 600S. *Photo courtesy IBM.*

FIGURE 4. The IBM ES/9000, model 900. *Photo courtesy IBM.*

channels. It has twice the memory capacity of the 3090 series.

NEC CORPORATION

NEC Corporation of Tokyo, Japan, first announced its SX series of supercomputers in 1983. Since that time several models have been added; the SX-X was announced in 1990. HNSX Supercomputers, Inc. markets the NEC computers in the United States. The SX-X is touted to be the first supercomputer from a non-American manufacturer that has been designed for the American market. Multiple processors for the SX-X provide a range of performance from 1.4 to 22 gigaflops.

MINISUPERCOMPUTER COMPANIES

Several companies now provide a wide selection of minisupercomputers. Most of these systems utilize a UNIX-based operating system and provide for multiple high-level languages (FORTRAN is the most common). Alliant Computer Systems of Acton, Massachusetts, offers a line of minisupercomputers ranging in price from approximately $100,000 to $1,000,000. Convex Computer Corporation offers a minisupercomputer with integrated vector processing with a computer architecture similar to that of Cray. Convex is based in Richardson, Texas. Scientific Computer Systems of San Diego, California, offers the SCS-40, a 64-bit machine that utilizes the CRAY X-MP instruction set.

For Further Reading

Karin, S., and N. P. Smith. 1987. *The supercomputer era.* New York: Harcourt Brace Jovanovich.

Lazou, C. 1988. *Supercomputers and their use.* Oxford: Clarendon Press.

Smith, N. P. 1990. *Supercomputing review.* San Diego, Calif.: Harcourt Brace Jovanovich.

Szymanski, R., D. Szymanski, N. Morris, and D. Pulschen. 1988. *Introduction to computers and information systems.* Columbus, Ohio: Merrill.

James L. Poirot

TELECOMMUNICATIONS COMPANIES

The era of modern telecommunications (from Greek and Latin words signifying "far speaking") dates from the 1830s, with the invention of the telegraph by Samuel F. B. Morse. In 1844, Morse sent the first public telegraph message, "What hath God wrought," over an experimental line from the Supreme Court building in Washington, D.C., to his assistant in Baltimore. Within a few years, several regional telegraph companies had been formed. In 1856, those were merged to form the Western Union Company, which was to dominate the telecommunications industry for half a century. A transcontinental telegraph line was completed in 1861, enabling for the first time instantaneous communication from coast to coast.

Of course, the telegraph could not transmit different tones, but only a series of dots and dashes, sounds distinguished from one another by their duration. Later developments in telecommunications technology would enable the transmission of the human voice, video images, and high-speed computer data. Also, the development of microwave transmission and space satellites would free electronic telecommunications from the constraints of wires.

AMERICAN TELEPHONE & TELEGRAPH (AT&T)

In 1876, in his Boston workshop, Alexander Graham Bell uttered the first words spoken over a telephone. Public demonstrations of his invention were given that summer at the Centennial Exposition held in Philadelphia. In 1877, the first rudimentary telephone exchange was established in Boston. A pattern was established of creating a separate company to provide service in each community that wanted telephones. Until 1894, the original Bell patent ensured that the only legitimate phone companies were those affiliated with or licensed by the Bell interests. Outside the United States, telephone operations were slower to develop and were generally taken over and conducted by governmental units, often the post office.

In 1885, the Bell companies established a subsidiary that was named the American Telephone & Telegraph Company. The purpose of the new company was to establish and coordinate a nationwide system of long-distance telephone lines connecting the local exchanges. In 1899, the local Bell companies were merged into AT&T, which now became the parent company. AT&T was to be the dominant factor in the telecommunications industry for the next century. Its Western Electric subsidiary manufactured most of the telephone equipment used in the world. Its Bell Laboratories became renowned for technological innovations, averaging one patent per day for the first 50 years of its existence. Stereophonic sound, the transistor, the laser, and the communications satellite are representative of the items invented or developed primarily by Bell Laboratories.

In 1974, the Department of Justice filed an antitrust suit against AT&T, claiming that it illegally monopolized telecommunications service and equipment. In 1982, a consent decree was signed that provided for the breakup of AT&T. Effective January 1, 1984, the twenty-two wholly owned Bell operating companies were spun off into seven regional holding companies (RHCs). The shareholders of AT&T were issued one share of each new holding company for each 10 shares of AT&T held on that date.

The seven RHCs and their headquarter cities are as follows: NYNEX (New York); Bell Atlantic (Philadelphia); Bell South (Atlanta); American Information Technologies, also known as Ameritech (Chicago); Southwestern Bell (St. Louis); US West (Denver); and Pacific Telesis (San Francisco). Each RHC had between 70,000 and 100,000 employees and operating revenues of between $7.2 billion and $9.6 billion during 1984, their first year of operation.

Prior to divestiture, AT&T was the largest company in the world, with almost one million employees and total operating revenues of about $65 billion. After divestiture, it had 373,000 employees and operating revenues of $33 billion. As of December 31, 1990, AT&T had 273,700 employees and annual operating revenues of $37.3 billion.

Since divestiture of the operating companies, AT&T has provided no local phone service; however, it has continued to provide both national and international long-distance service. It also continues to manufacture electrical components and chips, telephones, and switching systems.

AT&T describes itself as being in the business of providing for the movement and management of information. By the terms of the consent decree, AT&T is no longer limited to regulated telecommunications businesses. It has expanded the scope of its activities far beyond merely providing phone equipment and service. It has developed a line of computers featuring the UNIX operating system and C programming language, both of which were developed at Bell Laboratories during the late 1960s and early 1970s. AT&T has also become one of the leading companies in the new field of systems integration. As such, acting on its own and through various joint ventures, it provides its clients with the ability to coordinate and network voice, video, and text data.

GENERAL TELEPHONE & ELECTRONICS (GTE)

Organized in 1935, the General Telephone & Electronics Corporation provides local telephone service to over twelve million households and businesses in thirty-one states. According to *Fortune Magazine,* it is now the single largest utility in the United States, as measured by assets, operating revenues, and number of employees (approximately 155,000 people), GTE's consolidated earnings for calendar 1990 were $18.4 billion. Telephone operations account for approximately 70 percent of annual operating income.

GTE is a leader in mobile telecommunications. Its Mobilnet provides cellular mobile telephone service to almost 600,000 subscribers in 34 metropolitan markets. Its Follow-Me-Roaming service enables customers in over 100 markets to more easily receive calls while traveling in different service areas. Its Airfone provides air-to-ground service to passengers on 1,400 commercial aircraft.

GTE Spacenet operates a multisatellite communications system that provides national and international network services. GTE Directories sells Yellow Pages advertising space and publishes more than 1,000 telephone books worldwide. Other divisions provide voice mail, electronic funds transfer, and various forms of consulting and systems integration services.

Besides manufacturing various pieces of telephone equipment, GTE produces a variety of lighting fixtures, chemicals, and electronic components. It is one of the top three makers of fluorescent and incandescent lamps in the world.

MICROWAVE COMMUNICATIONS, INC. (MCI)

In 1963, a new company called Microwave Communications, Inc. (MCI) petitioned the Federal Communications Commission for permission to provide telecommunications service between Chicago and St. Louis. Finally granted in 1969, this link was the first wedge into AT&T's regulated monopoly of long-distance service. Incorporated in its present form in 1968, MCI now operates the world's second largest long-distance telecommunications network.

MCI subscribers may make long-distance phone calls to any location in the United States and to 165 other countries. Transmission can be made by voice, telex, cablegram, facsimile, and other data formats. MCI Mail is a leader in the transmission of time-sensitive, electronic mail.

At the end of 1990, MCI had 24,500 employees. Revenues for that year were $7.7 billion.

NYNEX

NYNEX is representative of the seven regional holding companies that were established in 1984 in connection with the AT&T divestiture. NYNEX provides local phone service in New York and New England. In 1984, it had operating revenues of $9.6 billion and employed 94,900 individuals. By the end of 1990, revenues had grown to $13.6 billion and the number of employees had grown to 94,000.

Besides providing local telephone services, the seven RHCs have each expanded the range of their business interests and services. NYNEX offers credit services, software, and systems integration. It is one of the nation's largest network integrators, assisting clients to facilitate communication between nodes of local-area networks (LANs) and wide-area networks (WANs). Nonphone income constitutes approximately 14 percent of NYNEX's total revenues.

For Further Reading

Brooks, J. 1975. *Telephone: The first hundred years.* New York: Harper & Row.
Stone, A. 1989. *Wrong number: The breakup of AT&T.* New York: Basic Books.

S. Willard Elieson

Index

Page numbers in boldface indicate a major discussion.

Artificial intelligence (*cont.*)
  natural language processing, 699, 700–701
  problem solving and state space search, 65–67
  production systems, 67–68
  robotics, 847
  Turing, Alan, 945
  videodisc system, 958
Artificial intelligence in the automotive industry, **73–75**
Artificial Intelligence Corporation, 701
Artificial intelligence in engineering design, **75–79**
Artificial neurons. *See* Neuron, artificial
Artificial reality. *See* Virtual reality
Arts, computers in the, **79–83**
  graphic artist career, 143
  hypermedia, 506–508
  literary analysis, 608–611
  music, 80, 691–697, 948, 959
  see also Graphics, computer
ASCII (American Standard Code for Information Interchange)
  bar code, 109
  bit-string data representation and conversion, 223, 708
  character code description, 116
  comma-delimited text, 584
  control codes for handshaking, 454
  and FORTRAN programming, 404
  and word processor compatability, 989
Ashby, W. R., 219
ASOS. *See* Automated Surface Observation System
Assembler program, 487
Assembly language, 452, 484, 486, 548, 550, 586, 589, 896
Asset management, 129
Assignment statement, Modula-2, 679
Associated Merchandising Corporation (AMC), 841
Associated Press (AP), 561
Association for Computing Machinery (ACM), 489, 649, 945, 967, 995–996
  curriculum guidelines, 1, 4–5, 6
  ethical guidelines, 376
Association of Data Processing Service Organizations (ADAPSO), 1001

Associations, computing. *See* Computing associations
Associative networks. *See* Semantic networks
Asteroids (video game), 407
AST Research, 1006
Astronomy, computers in, **83–87**
  modeling, 86–87
  navigation, 703–706
  planetary geology, 416
  visible light and electromagnetic spectrum, 84–85
Asymetrix, 506
Asynchronous communications port, 167
AT&T. *See* American Telephone & Telegraph
AT&T Unix, 729
Atanasoff, John, 549
Atari, 407
Athletics. *See* Sports, computer applications in
Atkinson, Bill, 506
Atkinson, Richard, 333, 343
Atlas*Graphics, 882
ATMs. *See* Automated teller machines
Atom (LISP symbol), 604, 802
Atomic bomb. *See* Kemeny, John G.; Von Neumann, John
Atomic data, 275
Atrex (AI system), 74
Attack (sound), 895
Attendance tracking, 833
Attorneys. *See* Legal applications of computers
Attractor, in chaos theory, 159–161
Attributes
  data, 225, 266
  database, 231
  knowledge bases and expert systems, 576
  pattern recognition, 759
Attribute time stamping, database, 713
Audio
  laser disk technology, 955, 958, 959
  see also Compact disks; Videotape players
Audio Visual Connection (AVC), 687
Audit function, in information systems, 535
Auditing in computer environments, **87–94**
  careers in, 151

financial statements, 88
  internal controls, 88–90
  verification, 90–94
  see also Accounting use of computers
Audit trails
  and access control, 14
  and document image processing, 352
Auten, J., 592
Authology (authoring language), 98
Authoring languages, systems, and environments, **95–100**
  and educational computing, 335, 366
  examples of, 97–98
  features, 96–97
  future developments, 99–100
  issues, 98–99
  law enforcement, 595
  see also Languages, computer
Authorization list, 14
Auto attendants, voice mail, 971
AutoCAD, 182
AUTOCITE (legal database), 600
AutoDesk, 182
Autodialing, 211, 642
Automated Facial Composite Systems, 592
Automated Fingerprint Identification System (AFIS), 591–592
Automated guided vehicle (AGV), 634
Automated Integrated Reservation System. *See* AIRS
Automated Mathematician (AM), 625–626
Automated Surface Observation System (ASOS), 663–664
Automated teller machines (ATMs), 106–107, 391, 393–394, 488
Automatic Computing Engine (ACE), 945
Automatic parallelizer, 922
Automatic star tracker, 705
Automatic theorem-proving, 71, 576
Automation
  home systems (intelligent houses), 494, 495–496, 498
  prototyping in, 809–810
  see also Computer applications; Robotics; specific fields
Automotive industry
  artificial intelligence, 73–75
  bar code use, 110

voice mail, 971
see also specific industries, e.g.
    Aerospace, computer
    applications in
Bus structure, 436, 437, 441, 462,
    466
    data transfer, 451, 455, 456, 460
    in mainframe/minicomputer
      systems, 462–463
    slots, 227
Bus/tree topology, 613, 614
Byron, Augusta Ada, 106, **133–134,**
    483
Byron, Lord (George Gordon
    Byron), 133, 134
Bytes
    and character code storage, 116
    and data transfer, 450–451, 452
    and memory capacity, 439
    see also Bits

C

C, 41, 487, 589
    for biomechanical research, 124
    components, 801–802, 804
    and database management, 241
    and database programming, 247
    manipulation of memory
      addresses, 896
    and supercomputer
      programming, 922
    syntax, 588
C++, 805
    as object-oriented paradigm,
      724, 805
    for parallel computing, 751
Cable
    computer network, 708–709
    fax transmission, 386–388
Cable News Network (CNN), 561
CAC. *See* Climate Analysis Center
Cache memory, 440, 441, 467
CADAM, 180
CAD/CAM. *See* Computer-aided
    design and manufacturing
CAI. *See* Computer-assisted
    instruction
Calcomp, Inc./Division of
    Lockheed Corporation, 1007
Calculation. *See* History of
    computing
Calculators
    Babbage design, 105
    as computer mathematical
      software, 646

desk-top and hand-held, 483
first-generation computers as,
    549
Leibniz design, 483, 603
Pascal design, 483, 755
Calculus. *See* Predicate calculus
Calendaring, electronic, 132,
    728–729
Caley (program), 926
Calibration standards, 166, 582
California, University of (Berkeley),
    426
California, University of (Los
    Angeles)
    distributed computing, 319
    virus research, 964–965
California, University of (San
    Diego),
    UCSD Pascal, 756
California State University
    (Fresno), 481
CAM. *See* Computer-aided
    manufacturing; Content
    addressable memory
Camal (program), 926
Camcorder, 495
Camera-ready copy, 947
Cameras, digital electronic, 690
Campaigns, political. *See* Political
    uses of computers
Campbell Soup Corporation, 473
"Can a Machine Think?" (Turing),
    945
Candidate keys, 231, 242
CanDo (multimedia authoring), 687
Cannon, Annie Jump, 86
Canonical form, 322
Capability lists, 14
Capacitance electronic disk. *See*
    CED
Capacitive screens, 304
Capacitive system, 956
Capacity requirements planning
    (CRP), 639, 735
Capek, Karel, 847
Cap'n Crunch (John Draper), 429
Cardiopulmonary resuscitation
    (CPR), videodisc training
    program, 958
Cardiovascular disease, 472
Card-oriented languages, 403
Cards, Jacquard and Hollerith,
    135–139, 587, 838–839
Careers in computing, **139–147**
    academic degree programs, 6–8,
      141
    education and training, 141

job potential, 142
licensing and certification, 147
opportunities, 142–147
Careers in information systems,
    147–157
    academic degree programs, 1–5
    job possibilities, 149–151
    management, 153
    potential paths, 154–156
    suggestions for management of,
      156
Carnegie Institute of Technology,
    574
Carried load, 818
Carry look-ahead adders (CSAs),
    436
Cartesian configuration (robotics),
    848
Cartesian coordinate system
    (architecture), 56–57
CASE. *See* Computer-aided
    software engineering
Case-based reasoning (CBR),
    78–79
CASE command, in Algol, 40, 45
Case constructs
    in C, 802
    Modula-2, 679
Cash flow, 844–845
Cash machines. *See* Automated
    teller machines (ATMs)
CAST (authoring language), 98
Casualty Reporting, Information
    Sorting, and Identification
    System (CRISIS), 594
CATA. *See* Computer-Assisted
    Target Analysis
Cataloging, library material, 530
Cathode ray tube (CRT), 31, 38,
    111
    and data acquisition boards, 226
    and data entry, 263
    screen design, 442, 444–445
    see also Monitors
CATI. *See* Computer-assisted
    telephone interviewing
CAT-scan. *See* Computer-axial
    tomography (CAT) scan
CAV. *See* Constant angular velocity
CBEMA. *See* Computer and
    Business Equipment
    Manufacturers' Association
CBMSs. *See* Computer-based
    messaging systems
CBR. *See* Case-based reasoning
CB Simulator (information service
    conferencing), 528